THE AMERICAN
COMMONWEALTH

James Bryce

JAMES BRYCE

THE AMERICAN COMMONWEALTH

With an Introduction by Gary L. McDowell

VOLUME I

Liberty Fund
Indianapolis

This book is published by Liberty Fund, Inc., a foundation established to encourage study of the ideal of a society of free and responsible individuals.

The cuneiform inscription that serves as our logo and as the design motif for our endpapers is the earliest-known written appearance of the word "freedom" (*amagi*), or "liberty." It is taken from a clay document written about 2300 B.C. in the Sumerian city-state of Lagash.

Frontispiece: James Bryce, Regius Professor of Civil Law, Oxford University, 1870–93. From H. A. L. Fisher, *James Bryce: Viscount Bryce of Dechmont, O.M.,* vol. 1 (London: Macmillan, 1927).
Front cover: *Declaration of Independence in Congress, at the Independence Hall, Philadelphia, July 4th, 1776* (detail) by John Trumbull, 1786–1819. United States Capitol Art Collection. Photograph courtesy Architect of the Capitol.

Liberty Fund, Inc.
8335 Allison Pointe Trail, Suite 300
Indianapolis, Indiana 46250-1684

Library of Congress Cataloging-in-Publication Data

Bryce, James Bryce, Viscount, 1838–1922.
    The American commonwealth / James Bryce.
       p.   cm.
    Includes bibliographical references and index.
    ISBN 0-86597-116-1 (set : hardcover : alk. paper).—ISBN
0-86597-117-X (set : pbk. : alk. paper).—ISBN 0-86597-118-8 (vol.
1 : hardcover : acid-free paper).—ISBN 0-86597-119-6 (vol. 1 :
paperback : acid-free paper).—ISBN 0-86597-120-X (vol. 2 :
hardcover : acid-free paper).—ISBN 0-86597-121-8 (vol. 2 :
paperback : acid-free paper).
    1. United States—Politics and government.   2. State governments—
United States.   3. United States—Social conditions.   I. Title.
JK246.B9 1995
320.473—dc20

                                    95-11187

15 14 13 12 11 10 09 08 07 06 C 7 6 5 4 3
14 13 12 11 10 09 08 07 06 00 P 6 5 4 3 2

To my friends and colleagues

Albert Venn Dicey

Thomas Erskine Holland

Contents

───── V O L U M E I ─────

PART I

The National Government

P A R T   I I

The State Governments

Appendix

───── V O L U M E   I I ─────

Introduction

He knew us better than we know ourselves, and he went about and among us and gave us the boon of his illuminating wisdom derived from the lessons of the past.

Chief Justice William Howard Taft
October 12, 1922

James Bryce's *The American Commonwealth* is a classic work, not only of American politics but of political science. Eschewing the theoretical depths of democracy that Alexis de Tocqueville had plumbed, and lacking the partisan purposes for which Alexander Hamilton and his colleagues had penned *The Federalist*, Bryce sought to capture the America of his time, to present "within reasonable compass, a full and clear view of the facts of today."[1] As Bryce's biographer would later put it, *The American Commonwealth* "was a photograph taken and exhibited by a political philosopher, not a history, not a picture of what was, not an account of how it had come to be."[2] But, as with photographs that aspire to art, the more one studies Bryce's snapshot of a long-vanished America, the more one sees.

Bryce's fascination with America began in earnest on his first visit to the United States in 1870. It is worth remembering that the country he first saw was only five years past the assassination of Abraham Lincoln and but a year after the first transcontinental railway had been completed; it would be another seven years before the last of the federal troops of Reconstruction

---

[1] James Bryce, *The American Commonwealth*, I:4.

[2] H. A. L. Fisher, *James Bryce: Viscount Bryce of Dechmont, O.M.*, 2 vols. (London: Macmillan, 1927), I:234–35. In addition to Fisher's biographical narrative, this work contains a selection of letters to and from Bryce.

Two excellent critical accounts of Bryce are Edmund Ions, *James Bryce and American Democracy, 1870–1922* (London: Macmillan, 1968), and Hugh Tulloch, *James Bryce's "American Commonwealth": The Anglo-American Background* (London: Royal Historical Society, 1988).

were finally withdrawn from the South in 1877. The America of which Bryce first took note was a geographically sprawling society kept only loosely in touch by telegraph and newspapers—telephones and radios being still decades away.

When *The American Commonwealth* appeared in 1888, America was the youngest nation in a world still defined by ancient orders. The British Empire bustled beneath Victoria's scepter and Russia creaked beneath the feudal splendor of Tsar Alexander III. The devastation of the Great War and the loss of innocence it would bring was more than a quarter of a century away; Lenin was but a schoolboy of eighteen, and Hitler would not be born until 1889.

The America of Bryce's observations has long since passed; indeed, it was already gone by the time of his death in 1922. When he first published *The American Commonwealth*, the population of the entire country, then only thirty-eight states strong, was a mere sixty million; New York took the lead with 5,082,871, while California boasted a meager 864,694 spread across its 155,980 square miles. Nevada peaked at 62,266 isolated souls. Dakota (which would be divided the next year into North Dakota and South Dakota), Wyoming, Montana, Idaho, Washington, Utah, New Mexico, and Arizona were all still territories; and Oklahoma was Indian Territory, not to become a state until 1907.

By the end of Bryce's life, the 1920 census had sketched a nation with a population of 105,710,620 (not including the territories of Alaska and Hawaii) divided among forty-eight states. New York's population had nearly doubled to 10,385,000; California's had quadrupled to 3,427,000. Even Nevada had grown to 77,000. By 1920, America was an increasingly urban nation with problems Bryce could not have envisioned when he began writing *The American Commonwealth* in 1884.[3]

Demographic changes were not all; nor were they the most important changes. Constitutionally and politically, the American commonwealth of 1922 was much changed from that of the 1880s. Between the publication of the first edition of *The American Commonwealth* and Bryce's death there had been four constitutional amendments, three serious and one frivolous. In addition to the ill-fated 18th Amendment prohibiting intoxicating liquors (repealed by the 21st Amendment in 1933), the fundamental structure of the Constitution was altered by allowing the income tax (16th Amendment

---

[3] By way of comparison, in 1992 the population of the United States had reached 255,082,000; New York, 18,119,000; California had far outstripped the Empire State, reaching 30,867,000. Nevada had exploded to 1,327,000.

in 1913), by providing for the direct election of Senators (17th Amendment, also in 1913), and by giving women the right to vote (19th Amendment in 1920). The politics of the Gilded Age that Bryce first chronicled had passed into the Progressive Era, and with that passage had come a plethora of social reform legislation. The creation of the Interstate Commerce Commission in 1887 had been but a foreshadowing of the coming age of national regulation: the Sherman Anti-Trust Act (1890); the Pure Food and Drug Act (1906); and the Child Labor Act (1916), among many others, quickly followed.

The America that Bryce first saw was also a nation of buoyant optimism, a country fairly bursting with the democratic zeal and commercial impatience Tocqueville had celebrated half a century earlier. Like Tocqueville before him, but for different reasons, Bryce saw in America more than America. "The institutions of the United States," he wrote, "are something more than an experiment, for they are believed to disclose and display the type of institutions towards which, as if by a law of fate, the rest of civilized mankind are forced to move, some with swifter, others with slower, but all with unresting feet." The United States was a nation of "enormous and daily increasing influence."[4] It was essential, Bryce believed, that the world be given a clear account of what made up this robust and rambunctious republic. For good or ill, America was simply the most exceptional nation in the history of the world. And James Bryce was just the man to capture that exceptionalism in all its glory.

I

James Bryce was a Scotsman of sturdy Presbyterian stock, born on May 10, 1838, in Belfast, Ireland. In 1846 the family moved from its beloved Ulster when Bryce's father took up duties back in Scotland at the High School in Glasgow. From his earliest days, young James was consumed by his curiosity about natural history, geography, and politics. When he turned sixteen, after his high school studies in Glasgow and, for a period, back in Belfast, Bryce matriculated at Glasgow University, where he spent three years steeped in the study of the classics, logic, and mathematics. Glasgow was "deficient" when it came to offering the atmosphere of intellectual camaraderie students would enjoy in Oxford or Cambridge; yet Bryce would later recall "not a few long arguments over the freedom of the will and other metaphysical topics to which the Scottish mind was prone." Moreover,

---

[4] Bryce, *The American Commonwealth*, I:1.

there were occasions aplenty for "an incessant sharpening of wits upon one another's whetstones."[5] When he left Glasgow in 1857, Bryce was more than ready for the illustrious academic career that awaited him at Oxford.

When Bryce went up to Oxford to stand for a scholarship at Trinity College in May 1857, he found himself confronted by the demands of the Church of England. The young Scots Presbyterian could not bring himself to sign the Thirty-nine Articles of the Established Church, as was required of all Trinity scholars. Better to forego an Oxford education and all the advantages it would bring, Bryce believed, than to turn his back on the faith of his fathers and submit to the Anglican sacrament; to have done so would have been "dishonourable." Bryce persevered "in the cause of liberty and dissent" with an eye toward breaking up the "obnoxious statute altogether." When he finally succeeded in winning the scholarship without agreeing to the Thirty-nine Articles, Bryce's stance won praise as nothing less than "the triumph of liberalism in Oxford." Even so, Bryce was never awarded his M.A. because of his refusal; he did, however, earn his B.A. and a D.C.L.[6]

At Oxford, Bryce distinguished himself as an extraordinary student, sweeping up first-class degrees and an assortment of scholarly honors in his academic wake. Having taken his degree from Trinity in 1862, Bryce won a fellowship in Oriel College, a position that would allow him the flexibility of pursuing an Oxford academic career or being called to the bar in London. Soon after beginning to teach in Oxford, Bryce despaired that the place was "dolorous," lacking any semblance of "motion and progress." In time, Oxford would prove too stultifying a place for the young scholar, once described by his friend and colleague Albert V. Dicey as "the life of our party."[7]

London beckoned. By 1864, Bryce would insist that the capital was "the best place in the world for anyone to learn his own insignificance."[8] With its sheer drudgery, the legal training to which he had turned in Lincoln's Inn bored Bryce.

> Streaming down Oxford Street, about 11 every morning to the Inn; then books, very dreary books it must be said, most of them interminable records of minute facts through which it is not easy to trace the course of a consistent and clarifying principle till 1:30; then lunch often in some man's company and dropping about a little, then more books till 5:30; then dinner in the hall of Lincoln's Inn,

[5] Fisher, *James Bryce*, I:22; 25.
[6] Ibid., 42; 40; 43; 38.
[7] Ibid., 55; 58; 59.
[8] Ibid., 63.

disagreeable in this that one rises from table to walk two miles through narrow dirty streets homeward.[9]

It did not take long, however, for Bryce to look up from his legal studies and discover the great and vibrant intellectual universe that was London. His key to this world came with the publication of his first book, the revision of his essay for which he had been awarded the Arnold Prize at Oxford in 1862. When it appeared in 1864 as *The Holy Roman Empire*, it was quickly praised as having placed Bryce—then but twenty-six years old—"on a level with men who have given their lives to historical study."[10] James Bryce, the public scholar, had begun his ascent.

In 1870 Bryce's labors in Roman history, as well as the law, paid a substantial dividend. On April 11, William Gladstone wrote to him offering him the Regius Chair of Civil Law in the University of Oxford. Founded by King Henry VIII, the Regius Professorship had once been filled by the great civilian Alberic Gentile.[11] Bryce would serve as Regius Professor of Civil Law until 1893, and from that illustrious post he contributed greatly to the revival of scholarly interest in Roman law and the civilian tradition in the British universities. The same year that Bryce assumed his professorship was the year that he and Dicey set off for the United States.

Bryce's introduction to the nation he would come to know so well was enhanced through the efforts of Leslie Stephen, who kindly opened the very best doors for the two young Englishmen. Through Stephen, Bryce and Dicey met Charles Eliot, Ralph Waldo Emerson, Henry Wadsworth Longfellow, James Russell Lowell, and both the senior and the junior Oliver Wendell Holmes. The young English legal scholars were especially interested in conversations they had with the leading lights of the Harvard Law School, Christopher Columbus Langdell, James Barr Ames, and James Bradley Thayer.[12] America was an intellectually vibrant place, and Bryce was smitten: "It was almost a case of love at first sight."[13] Upon his return to England, Bryce committed his enthusiasm to print, publishing several articles on American society in English periodicals.[14]

Neither the practice of law nor the scholarly pursuits of Oxford was

---

[9] Ibid.

[10] Ibid., 65.

[11] Ibid., 130.

[12] Tulloch, *James Bryce's "American Commonwealth,"* 125.

[13] Fisher, *James Bryce*, I:137.

[14] For a superb bibliography of works by and about Bryce, see Tulloch, *James Bryce's "American Commonwealth,"* 244–65.

sufficient to satisfy Bryce's restless and robust nature. In 1880 he stood for Parliament and was elected as a member of the Liberal Party to represent Tower Hamlets in London's East End. It was a poor and working-class constituency and gave Bryce the opportunity to learn a great deal about the social structures of Britain.[15] But for all his gifts, he was not at the start a very distinguished legislator.

> A certain lack of pliability, an insistent voice, a temperament somewhat deficient in the good-humoured composure which is one of the most valuable of Parliamentary gifts, a turn of phrase incisive rather than humorous, a prevailingly serious outlook coupled with the defect . . . of excessive indulgence in historical disquisitions and analogies, these little blemishes of manner and method concealed from his fellow Members of Parliament the remarkable qualities which belonged to him.[16]

Years of public service would wear away those rough edges until, in the end, Bryce was deemed "one of the best and more graceful public speakers in the country."[17] Yet in his early political career, he was often seen, as his more radical parliamentary critic Joseph Chamberlain disparagingly dubbed him, as the "professor."

It was during these busy years as lawyer, scholar, and Member of Parliament that Bryce began to focus in a serious way on what would become his greatest legacy. He returned to the United States for his second visit in 1881, during which he crossed the continent and swept through the South. In the decade since his first visit, James Bryce had become a man of some renown in both the scholarly and the political worlds.[18] In 1883 he returned for his third tour, and it was at that point that he began assiduously to collect material for *The American Commonwealth*, to sort through the mass of details he assembled, and to draw conclusions worth reporting. The more he learned, the more selective he became. "When I first visited America eighteen years ago," he warned his readers in the introduction to *The American Commonwealth*, "I brought home a swarm of bold generalizations. Half of them were thrown overboard after a second visit in 1881. Of the half that remained, some were dropped into the Atlantic when I returned across it after a third visit in 1883–84: and although the two later journeys gave birth to some new views, these views are fewer and more

---

[15] Fisher, *James Bryce*, I:173–74.
[16] Ibid., 176.
[17] Ibid., 178.
[18] Ions, *James Bryce and American Democracy*, 90.

discreetly cautious than their departed sisters of 1870." That caution manifested itself in an approach that was coolly analytical. "I have striven," Bryce insisted, "to avoid the temptations of the deductive method, and to present simply the facts of the case, arranging and connecting them as best I can, but letting them speak for themselves rather than pressing upon the reader my own conclusions." Bryce saw himself as a chronicler, a reporter, not as a political philosopher; it would be far better if his readers created grand theories from the facts he presented than if he presented them with "theories ready made."[19] It was precisely such "elevated thinking" and grand "speculative views of democracy" which, in Bryce's view, had rendered Tocqueville's *Democracy in America* something less than a practical treatise for men of the real world. It was for this reason that Bryce endeavored to shun the abstract in favor of the concrete.[20]

The differences between *Democracy in America* and *The American Commonwealth* are immediately seen. Whereas Tocqueville saw fit to spend but a single chapter on state and municipal governments, a mere 38 pages, Bryce devoted seventeen chapters, 255 densely packed pages, to the same topic. Similarly, on political parties, Tocqueville provided yet another single chapter, and this no more than 6 pages. Bryce, on the other hand, offered twenty-three chapters totalling 243 pages. And when it came to the structure and functions of the national government, Bryce produced a staggering 392 pages in thirty-four chapters; Tocqueville mustered only 75 pages in four chapters.

II

One cannot fully appreciate either Bryce's scholarly objective or his literary achievement without first understanding his rejection of Tocqueville. The greatest weakness of *Democracy in America*, in Bryce's judgment, was that it was decidedly unscientific, filled as it was with the Frenchman's moral musings about democracy generally. Tocqueville himself had confessed as

---

[19] Bryce, *The American Commonwealth*, I:4.

[20] Bryce's judgment about *Democracy in America* is "far more important for what it discloses about Bryce and his time than for what it says about Tocqueville. It enunciated two basic points about *The American Commonwealth* and its author. Bryce's model of social science prescribed his method. His Anglo-American outlook prescribed his substance. Each was of course a function of the other. Together . . . they gave Bryce the grounds for his case against Tocqueville." Abraham S. Eisenstadt, "Bryce's America and Tocqueville's," in Abraham S. Eisenstadt, ed., *Reconsidering Tocqueville's "Democracy in America"* (New Brunswick: Rutgers University Press, 1988), 269.

much: "I admit that I saw in America more than America; it was the shape of democracy itself which I sought, its inclinations, character, prejudices, and passions; I wanted to understand it so as at least to know what we have to fear or hope therefrom."[21] Such a venture as that undertaken by Tocqueville led inevitably to "fanciful" pictures being drawn, "plausible in the abstract . . . [but] unlike the facts which contemporary America sets before us." Bryce's alternative was to "bid farewell to fancy" and endeavor to see things as they actually were in nineteenth-century America.[22] Specificity, not generalization, was what was demanded; empiricism was the essence of Bryce's science of politics.[23]

When and where Bryce first came across the works of Tocqueville is not clear. However, by the time of his third trip to the United States in 1883, he was sufficiently familiar with *Democracy in America* to conduct a seminar at Johns Hopkins University under the direction of Professor Herbert Baxter Adams. Adams's graduate history seminar was a preeminent academic gathering, and among the students in Bryce's class were John Dewey, John Franklin Jameson, and Woodrow Wilson.[24] The seminar focused on *Democracy in America*; the concern was Tocqueville's interpretation of America and his predictions about democratic government. Bryce pushed his students to question the assumptions that lay at the foundation of Tocqueville's monumental and influential work.[25] The fruit of the seminar was the publication in 1887 of "The Predictions of Hamilton and de Tocqueville" in the *Johns Hopkins Studies in Historical and Political Science*.[26]

In this important study, Bryce praised Tocqueville and his work. The author was "a singularly fair and penetrating European philosopher" whose work was one of "rare literary merit." *Democracy in America*, observed Bryce, is "one of the few treatises on the philosophy of politics which has risen to the rank of a classic." The great work was nothing less than "a model of art and a storehouse of ethical maxims."[27]

---

[21] Alexis de Tocqueville, *Democracy in America*, J. P. Mayer and Max Lerner, eds., trans. George Lawrence (New York: Harper & Row, 1966), 12. For a thorough treatment of Bryce's reaction to Tocqueville, see Tulloch, *James Bryce's "American Commonwealth,"* 62–70.

[22] Bryce, *The American Commonwealth*, II:1426.

[23] "In emphasizing the particularity and distinctiveness of the United States he not only provided a more authentic picture of America, but also suggested that 'democratic' evils were neither inevitable nor ineradicable; specific American evils could be remedied by applying specifically American antidotes." Tulloch, *James Bryce's "American Commonwealth,"* 63–64.

[24] For a detailed account of the seminar, see Ions, *James Bryce and American Democracy*, 118.

[25] Ibid., 118–19.

[26] The article is in Volume II of this Liberty Fund edition, pp. 1530–70.

[27] Ibid., 1531; 1543; 1543.

Niceties aside, Bryce plunged his critical dagger: "The first observation [about *Democracy in America*] is that not only are its descriptions of democracy as displayed in America no longer true in many points, but that in certain points they were never true. That is to say, some were true of America, but not of democracy in general, while others were true of democracy in general but not true of America." The weaknesses of Tocqueville were three. First, he had opted for the deductive method Bryce deplored: Tocqueville's "power of observation, quick and active as it was, did not lead but followed the march of his reasonings . . . [so that] the facts he cites are rather illustrations than the sources of his conclusions."[28]

The second defect of Tocqueville's study is that while he wrote about America "his heart was in France, and the thought of France, never absent from him, unconsciously colored every picture that he drew." The result of this narrow view is that he "failed to grasp the substantial identity of the American people with the English." Bryce was blunt: "he has not grasped, as perhaps no one but an Englishman or an American can grasp, the truth that the American people is an English people, modified in some directions by the circumstances of its colonial life and its more popular government, but in essentials the same." Coupled with his deductive bent, this focus on France led Tocqueville into simple errors: "Much that he remarks in the mental habits of the ordinary American, his latent conservatism, for instance, his indifference to amusement as compared with material comfort, his commercial eagerness and tendency to take a commercial view of all things, might have been just as well remarked of the ordinary middle-class Englishman, and has nothing to do with a Democratic government."[29]

The third problem with Tocqueville's work is the result of the first two: "*Democracy in America* is not so much a political study as a work of edification." As such, it is simply not an accurate "picture and criticism of the government and people of the United States." In Bryce's steely scientific view, *Democracy in America* failed the test of objectivity. "Let it be remembered that in spite of its scientific form, it is really a work of art rather than a work of science, and a work suffused with strong, though carefully repressed emotion." The most damning deficiency, Bryce argued, is that Tocqueville "soars far from the ground and is often lost in the clouds of his own sombre

[28] Ibid., 1544; 1544.
[29] Ibid., 1544; 1546; 1546. Bryce went so far as to refer to the Americans as "the English of America." *The American Commonwealth*, I:317.

meditations."[30] As a result, his treatise offered more a colorful "landscape" than an accurate "map" of America. And whatever its great artistic and philosophic achievement, there was still the need for a map. It was precisely Bryce's desire "to try and give [his] countrymen some juster views than they have had about the United States" that led him to craft *The American Commonwealth* as a grand atlas of American politics and society.[31]

The deficiencies Bryce found in *Democracy in America* spawned in him a sense of caution and modesty. Lest he fall into the same trap as Tocqueville, he was determined never to mistake "transitory for permanent causes." While there was nothing in Tocqueville's account that was "simply erroneous," there was much distortion. Tocqueville tended to build too great a "superstructure of inference, speculation and prediction" on too slight a foundation: "The fact is there, but it is perhaps a smaller fact than he thinks, or a transient fact, or a fact whose importance is, or shortly will be, diminished by other facts which he has not adequately recognized."[32] In Bryce's estimation, the real world was far too untidy for such lofty generalizations as those Tocqueville offered. This was especially true when it came to his understanding of democracy itself.

For Bryce, the issue was simple: "Democracy really means nothing more or less than the rule of the whole people expressing their sovereign will by their votes."[33] In his view, Tocqueville had painted with too broad a brush. Rather than speak of democracy as a form of government, he was wont to speak of democracy as a spirit of the age, something as irresistible as it was intangible. This Bryce rejected:

> Democratic government seems to me, with all deference to his high authority, a cause not so potent in the moral and social sphere as he deemed it; and my object has been less to discuss its merits than to paint the institutions and the people of America as they are, tracing what is peculiar to them not merely to the sovereignty of the masses, but also to the history and traditions of the race, to its fundamental ideas, to its material environment.[34]

Bryce was only incidentally concerned with what Tocqueville had called the *mores* of the people; the Englishman cared more about institutions than ideology, more about the mechanics of politics than the manners of society.

---

[30] Bryce, "The Predictions of Hamilton and de Tocqueville," Volume II of this edition, 1547; 1543; 1547; 1548.

[31] As quoted in Ions, *James Bryce and American Democracy*, 121.

[32] Ibid., 447; 447; 447.

[33] James Bryce, *Modern Democracies*, 2 vols. (London: Macmillan, 1921), I:viii.

[34] Bryce, *The American Commonwealth*, I:3–4.

Bryce conceded that part of Tocqueville's problem—but only a part—was the time in which he wrote. The sober republicanism of Founders such as Alexander Hamilton had given way to the democratic intoxication of the Jacksonians. "The anarchic teachings of Jefferson had borne fruit," Bryce explained. "Administration and legislation, hitherto left to the educated classes, had been seized by the rude hands of men of low social position and scanty knowledge."[35] Thus, what Tocqueville took to be the inherent characteristics of the democratic spirit of the modern age were, in fact, merely the manifestations of a peculiarly perverted exercise of democratic governance during a particularly vulgar and raucous period of American history. The "brutality and violence" of those days had skewed Tocqueville's account of his grand theory of the tyranny of the majority.[36]

Tocqueville's study was influential and generated in his followers the belief that "democracy is the child of ignorance, the parent of dullness and conceit. The opinion of the greatest number being the universal standard, everything is reduced to the level of vulgar minds. Originality is stunted, variety disappears, no man thinks for himself, or, if he does, fears to express what he thinks." This unhealthy view had been spawned by Tocqueville's exaggeration of the effect forms of government actually have on society; such an exaggeration ignored the complexity of the relationship between "the political and the intellectual life of a country." All this Bryce denied: "It is not democracy that had paid off a gigantic debt and raised Chicago out of a swamp. Neither is it democracy that had hitherto denied the United States philosophers like Burke and poets like Wordsworth."[37]

The "narcotic power of democracy" of which Tocqueville warned was, in fact, the result not merely of the form of government in the United States, but of "a mixed and curiously intertwined variety of other causes which have moulded the American mind during the past two centuries." Many of the attributes of the Americans "must be mainly ascribed to the vast size of the country, the vast numbers and intellectual homogeneity of its native white population, the prevalence of social equality, a busy industrialism, a restless changefulness of occupation, and the absence of a leisured class dominant in matters of taste—conditions that have little or nothing to do with political institutions."[38]

Tocqueville's *Democracy in America* had to be taken with great caution

[35] Ibid., II:992.
[36] Ibid.
[37] Ibid., 1423; 1424; 1425.
[38] Ibid., 1428; 1429; 1427.

by those other nations who might seek prescriptions for their own political ills in its pages. By focusing on what he considered to be the general truths of democracy, Tocqueville seemed to be suggesting that his "new political science . . . for a world itself quite new"[39] was indeed a political manual for the rest of the world. By ignoring the mundane particulars of America for his more dazzling generalizations, Tocqueville had glossed over the deep and abiding significance of the differences between nations.

In Bryce's view, "although the character of democratic government in the United States is full of instruction for Europeans, it supplies few conclusions directly bearing on the present politics of any European country, because both the strong and the weak points of the American people are not exactly repeated anywhere in the Old World."[40] To Bryce, the most important thing about similarities was the difference they implied; history could not be as prescriptive as Tocqueville implied: "A thinker duly exercised in historical research will carry his stores of the world's political experience about with him, not as a book of prescriptions or recipes from which he can select one to apply to a given case, but rather as a physician carries a treatise of pathology which instructs him in the general principles to be followed in observing the symptoms and investigating the causes of the maladies that come before him."[41] It long remained an article of faith for Bryce that while "prediction in physics may be certain, in politics it can be no more than probable."[42]

III

Bryce "proposed to himself the aim of portraying the whole political system of the country, in its practice as well as its theory, of explaining not only the national government but the state governments, not only the Constitution but the party system, not only the party system but the ideas, temper, habits of the sovereign people."[43] By striving to go behind the formal legal and institutional structures to the "ideas, temper, habits" of the people, Bryce was, of course, edging closer to Tocqueville than he was willing to acknowledge. Moreover, he was not without his own ulterior motives. As Tocqueville sought to instruct France about lessons to be gleaned from

---

[39] Tocqueville, *Democracy in America*, 6.
[40] Bryce, *The American Commonwealth*, II:1274.
[41] Ibid., 1273–74.
[42] Bryce, *Modern Democracies*, II:16.
[43] Bryce, *The American Commonwealth*, I:2.

America, so did Bryce seek to teach his countrymen—and in ways not dissimilar. If Tocqueville wrote with France in mind, Bryce most assuredly wrote with England in mind. For Tocqueville, the great virtue of American federalism and the "incomplete" national government created by the Constitution of 1787 was to teach the importance of decentralized institutions in fending off the bureaucratic tyranny of centralized power, albeit democratic power. For Bryce, the lessons of American federalism were also useful; they tended to support the idea of home rule for Ireland as against the pressures of unionism in resolving the problems posed by Irish independence.[44]

Bryce had an overarching pedagogic political purpose that went beyond particular British policy battles of the day, however. He was concerned about the ignorance of the United States displayed by his countrymen; even in those most attentive to the great international issues of the day Bryce detected a worrying condescension born of misunderstanding. Assuming America still to be merely a rustic and vulgar outpost of uncultured country folk, Bryce's colleagues failed to grasp the increasing industrialization and urbanization that were coming to characterize the United States. It was these factors that were rendering America of "enormous and daily increasing influence," an influence Britain could ill afford to ignore.[45] It is this concern to encourage a proper understanding of America in England, above all others, that reveals *The American Commonwealth* as the intellectual threshold of the "special relationship" between Britain and America that has been of such importance throughout the twentieth century.

Bryce's study of America ultimately fell short of the scientific standard he had set for himself. He was as much a prisoner of his methodology as Tocqueville had been of his. While Bryce visited on three separate occasions between 1870 and 1883, his time in America amounted only to nine months, the same length of time Tocqueville had roamed the nation half a century earlier. As a result, Bryce was as dependent on anecdotal information about the United States as Tocqueville was; in some ways, Bryce's dependence is even more obvious. Bryce's network of friendships and acquaintances, though arguably larger than Tocqueville's, was better defined, which meant that the lens through which he observed American society and politics had been ground to a certain curve. Indeed, "the America he entered did not

---

[44] "Bryce . . . no less than his reader, moved in a political atmosphere obsessed with the Irish Question, and . . . the example of the United States held peculiar relevance to this debate." Tulloch, *James Bryce's "American Commonwealth,"* 78–79.

[45] Ions, *James Bryce and American Democracy,* 126–28; Bryce, *The American Commonwealth,* I:1.

centre on the ward districts or working man's clubs, or immigrant aid societies, but rather on civil service commissions, universities, reform clubs and the editorial offices of genteel journals."[46] As one critic put it at the time: "Mr. Bryce sees America through the rim of a champagne glass, to the strains of soft music, and in the smiles of fair women."[47]

For all his pretensions of objectivity, Bryce was very much the prisoner of his class. His view was colored by his basic liberalism, whether of the Gladstone variety at home or the establishment liberals with whom he associated in the United States. Nearly to a man, these were East Coast activists of progressive instincts; nary a one of them was close to being a Southerner or a defender of the rights of states against the increasing presence of the national government. The liberal nationalism they displayed, their confidence in the power of government to reform the inconveniences of the human condition, fit in well with Bryce's own prejudices about the purposes of government. The circle of American friends in whom he put so much confidence ensured that Bryce's work, in the end, would inevitably suffer from the subjectivity he sought so strenuously to avoid.

The biases one perceives in *The American Commonwealth* are largely the result of Bryce's method of actively involving these acquaintances in the creation of the book. The list of those who served him as *de facto* research assistants is nothing less than an intellectual and political honor roll of the age. Among those who contributed to *The American Commonwealth* were Thomas Cooley (on constitutional issues), Oliver Wendell Holmes (on legal education), Senator Carl Schurz (on the Senate), Theodore Roosevelt (on municipal government and civil service reform), Woodrow Wilson (on Congress), Arthur Sedgwick (on the Erie Ring), and Frank Goodnow (on municipal government and the Tweed Ring.)[48] The assistance they gave Bryce was not limited to culling facts for his use or to reading and commenting on early drafts and later revisions. Goodnow, for example, actually wrote in his own name the chapter in the first edition entitled "The Tweed Ring in New York City," as did Seth Low the chapter entitled "An American View of Municipal Government in the United States." In part, these farmed-out chapters were given over to Goodnow and Low "to prevent

---

[46] Tulloch, *James Bryce's "American Commonwealth,"* 90.

[47] As quoted in Francis W. Coker, "How Bryce Gathered His Materials and What Contemporary Reviewers Thought of the Work," in Robert C. Brooks, ed., *Bryce's "American Commonwealth": Fiftieth Anniversary* (New York: The Macmillan Company, 1939), 167.

[48] For biographical sketches of those who assisted Bryce, see Tulloch, *James Bryce's "American Commonwealth,"* 234–42.

the pirating of the work by American publishers, who at that time were not constrained by copyright laws except where the author was an American citizen."[49] But whatever the legal reasons, the contributions of Low and Goodnow are only the most visible of debts Bryce incurred in writing *The American Commonwealth*.

In a speech before the Pilgrims' Society in 1907, Bryce, by then Ambassador to the United States, recollected the sources for his great book.

> I am a good listener . . . and I wrote [*The American Commonwealth*] out of conversations to which I listened. I talked to everybody I could find in the United States, not only to statesmen in the halls of Congress, not only at dinner parties, but on the decks of steamers, in smoking cars, to drivers of wagons upon the Western prairies, to ward politicians and city bosses.[50]

The itineraries of Bryce's first three journeys through America suggest he was not exaggerating.[51] While his closest friends, and those who ultimately exerted the greatest influence on the work as a whole, may have been one or two steps removed from the political fray, Bryce was never inclined to sidestep the nitty and the gritty of American life; he rubbed shoulders with all kinds, from the gun-toting prospectors of Leadville, Colorado, and waitresses in a hotel in the White Mountains to the cigar-chomping pols he met at the New York State Democratic Party Convention, complete with Boss Tweed himself, "a fat, largish man, with an air of self-satisfied good humour and a great deal of shrewd knavery in eye and mouth."[52] At every turn, Bryce's methods for getting his original and impressionistic information were "unorthodox."

> He read all parts of newspapers: noting the rates of interest on mortgage loans; counting eighteen advertisements of clairvoyants and soothsayers in a San Francisco newspaper and concluding that they were a sign of a "tendency of this shrewd and educated people to relapse into the oldest and most childish forms of superstition." He smelt dollar bills in Wisconsin and detected that they had the odor of skins and furs used by the newly arrived Swedes and Norwegians. In a town of the Far West he borrowed a locomotive engine from the stationmaster, in order to run out a few miles to see "a piece of scenery." He heard or read all sorts of speeches—in legislatures, political party meetings, court trials, Fourth of

---

[49] Ibid., 136. The Goodnow chapter was dropped from the second edition because one of the Tweed Ring, Oakey Hall, had sued for libel. See pp. 91–94.

[50] As quoted in Tulloch, *James Bryce's "American Commonwealth,"* 58.

[51] A superb account of Bryce's trips and meetings is to be found in Ions, *James Bryce and American Democracy*, 39–132.

[52] As quoted in Ions, *James Bryce and American Democracy*, 71.

July celebrations, and at funerals and dinners—and concludes that American oratory was as bad as that of the rest of the world, except that the toasts at public dinners seemed slightly fewer and better than in England.[53]

Such methods, however unorthodox in a scholarly sense, were essential if Bryce, like Tocqueville before him, were to peek behind the institutional facade of the American commonwealth and capture the great and motive force of the American people. While Bryce relied for his facts on everything from the great works of the American political order, such as *The Federalist*, to more practical publications, such as the *Ohio Voters' Manual*, in rounding out his picture of America he simply had to move beyond mere "books and documents."[54] For the deeper, less tangible aspects of American life, Bryce had to "trust to a variety of flying and floating sources, to newspaper paragraphs, to the conversation of American acquaintances, to impressions formed on the spot from seeing incidents and hearing stories and anecdotes, the authority of which, though it seemed sufficient at the time, cannot always be remembered."[55] Bryce himself estimated that "five-sixths of [*The American Commonwealth*] was derived from conversations with Americans in London and the United States and only one-sixth from books."[56] His broad purpose was to make America come alive for his readers; words could not always be trusted: "[T]he United States and their people . . . make on the visitor an impression so strong, so deep, so fascinating, so interwoven with a hundred threads of imagination and emotion, that he cannot hope to reproduce it in words, and to pass it on undiluted to their minds."[57] While it might be, strictly speaking, impossible to capture such feelings, Bryce was determined to come as close as possible. Through his sprawling collection of hard facts and figures joined with colorful anecdotal recollections, he sought to convey to his readers the basic belief to which he would always cling: "America excites an admiration which must be felt upon the spot to be understood." It was this emotion, this excitement that Bryce wanted to transport to the common rooms of Oxford, the ministerial cubicles of Whitehall, and the drawing rooms of Mayfair. The immediate success of *The American Commonwealth* suggests that he did just that.

Bryce's study was greeted with high praise, both in England and the

---

[53] Coker, "How Bryce Gathered His Materials and What Contemporary Reviewers Thought of the Work," 157–58.

[54] Bryce, *The American Commonwealth*, II:683.

[55] Ibid., 683–84.

[56] Fisher, *James Bryce*, I:238.

[57] Ibid., 10.

United States. Woodrow Wilson in the *Political Science Quarterly* hailed it as "a great work . . . a noble work."[58] Lord Acton in the *English Historical Review* (which Bryce had helped to found) thought that Bryce's "three stout volumes" were indeed "a far deeper study of real life" than Tocqueville had achieved.[59] It was, Acton wrote to Bryce, "resolutely actual" in its account of America.[60] Gladstone viewed it as nothing less than "an event in the history of the United States."[61]

For all the praise *The American Commonwealth* enjoyed, there were criticisms. Both Acton and Wilson, for instance, complained that the book was oddly ahistorical. Acton voiced his regret that Bryce had chosen "to address the unhistoric mind," while Wilson concluded that the primary weakness of the work—its failure to move beyond facts toward any "guiding principles of government"—was the result of Bryce's "sparing use of history."[62] Other critics were harsher. The seemingly ever-curmudgeonly *Spectator* scoffed that "human nature revolts at two thousand large-octavo pages about anything, even though it be the American republic."[63] There were other problems that, once alerted to the concerns of his critics, Bryce endeavored to correct in later editions, including his treatment of blacks, the American South, immigration, and foreign policy. He also turned to new developments (in the third edition, the most complete revision), such as tendencies in current legislation and the increasing importance of universities in American life.

The greatest weakness of *The American Commonwealth*, however, turned out to be a feature that its author reckoned was its greatest strength. Bryce's determination to get his facts straight and present them clearly rendered the book more time-bound than he may have imagined when he undertook the project; as a concrete account of America, it had no shelf life.[64] The facts and figures which he had so carefully gathered quickly faded into inaccuracy

---

[58] See pp. 1571 and 1584 in Volume II of this edition.

[59] Ibid., 1587 and 1586.

[60] As quoted in Tulloch, *James Bryce's "American Commonwealth,"* 6.

[61] As quoted in Tulloch, *James Bryce's "American Commonwealth,"* 79.

[62] Volume II of this edition, pp. 1587; 1579.

[63] As quoted in Coker, "How Bryce Gathered His Materials and What Contemporary Reviewers Thought of the Work," 162.

[64] At one level, however, it seems Bryce appreciated the futility of any factual profile of America from the moment he set pen to paper: "America changes so fast that every few years a new crop of books is needed to describe the new face which things have put on, the new problems that have appeared, the new ideas germinating among her people, the new and unexpected developments for evil as well as for good of which her established institutions have been found capable." *The American Commonwealth*, I:2.

and irrelevance. It was simply impossible to keep up. Moreover, Bryce "resolutely declined" to undertake a complete revision of the work. While new editions appeared in 1889, 1893, and 1910 (and additional revisions in 1913, 1914, and 1920), *The American Commonwealth* was doomed to be seen primarily as a tract for its time.[65] All or most of the revisions were at best marginal, seeking merely to keep the book up-to-date with statistical changes and new laws and major policies. Bryce never reconsidered the fundamental assumptions which underlay the work as a whole. The result was that the gulf widened between its facts and its teachings about democracy in America.[66] This led Harold Laski to indict Bryce for his "insatiable appetite for facts and his grotesque inability to weigh them."[67] This was the result, as Woodrow Wilson had pointed out, of Bryce having taken as his task "rather exposition than judgment."[68] By 1920, the scholarly consensus among Bryce's friends was that *The American Commonwealth* was "altogether out of focus." Rather than revise it, it was thought best to leave it "undisturbed," an artifact of a bygone era. All that remained of value, Charles Beard concluded, were its "philosophic views."[69]

It is when Bryce moves away from the details of government to his reflections on American society that the lasting virtues of *The American Commonwealth* shine most clearly, unobscured by the mists of time. Even though many of his more abstract observations are rooted in the concrete circumstances of the world around him—in such chapters as "Why the Best Men Do Not Go Into Politics," "Corruption," and "Laissez Faire"—Bryce cuts through the particular facts of his day to expose something more timeless about the nature of the American people. Surely there has never been a more perennial subject in American politics than the one Bryce described simply as "Why Great Men Are Not Chosen Presidents." Beneath the structures of government, behind the mechanics of checks and balances and federalism, Bryce captured essential truths about what the American Founders frequently called the genius of the American people.

But that is not all. There is yet greater depth to Bryce's study than simply the permanent characteristics of democracy in America. Not unlike

---

[65] Tulloch, *James Bryce's "American Commonwealth,"* 189–90.

[66] "Things change very fast in America and a picture which was true in 1888 was no longer a likeness twenty-five years later, so that the more verisimilar the original portrait the more injury it was likely to suffer from the superimposition of certain features of a likeness taken at a later date." Fisher, *James Bryce,* I:239.

[67] As quoted in Tulloch, *James Bryce's "American Commonwealth,"* 190.

[68] Volume II of this edition, p. 1572.

[69] As quoted in Tulloch, *James Bryce's "American Commonwealth,"* 194.

Tocqueville, Bryce also drew out the lessons of democracy for the modern age on whose threshold he stood. His reflections on such problems as "The Fatalism of the Multitude" and "The Influence of Religion" reveal his deepest teachings to be much closer to Tocqueville than he would have cared to admit. But the reason is clear: America herself refuses to be reduced to the sterile formalism of value-free discourse; scientific explanation cannot capture the political whole that lies beyond the sum of the institutional parts. If America is not an ideal democracy, it is at least one that has always aspired to idealism. From the very beginning, it has been a nation that demands moral reflection to be truly understood. Ultimately, Bryce, like Tocqueville, did indeed see more in America than America herself; he, too, saw democracy *writ* large, in spite of himself, he, too, understood there were surely lessons to be drawn for the benefit of the world, both in his day and in the unforeseeable future. In the end, his most abiding teachings, those still-relevant "philosophic views," echo Tocqueville's warnings about the problems and the prospects of the democratic age. "The more democratic republics become," Bryce wrote, "the more the masses grow conscious of their own power, the more do they need to live, not only by patriotism, but by reverence and self-control, and the more essential to their well being are those sources whence reverence and self-control flow."[70]

IV

The American Commonwealth was not the totality of James Bryce's life. He published ten other books and dozens of articles and reviews, and contributed numerous chapters to edited volumes on topics that ranged from the Ottoman Empire to the League of Nations. All the while he continued to travel the world and maintain a vigorous correspondence with the great and the good of his day.

Although he relinquished his chair of law at Oxford in 1893, Bryce's political career continued unabated. In 1885 he stood again for Parliament, this time to represent South Aberdeen; he went on to represent that constituency for twenty-one uninterrupted years, standing down only when he became the British ambassador to the United States in 1906. He held that post until 1913. Upon his retirement from Washington, James Bryce became Viscount Bryce of Dechmont and entered the House of Lords, where he remained an active participant in the great debates of the day.

[70] Bryce, *The American Commonwealth*, II:1398.

Of all Lord Bryce's public accomplishments, none was perhaps as important as his service as ambassador to the nation he so loved. During his seven diplomatic years, Bryce built upon his great reputation and his legions of friends to pull the United States and the United Kingdom ever closer together.[71] He never faltered in his belief that the Americans were, at heart and in their history, Englishmen. As such, the two nations had a natural attachment that set them apart from the rest of the world. The unity of their interests went beyond the expediency of the moment; they were linked at the deepest, most moral level of politics. They shared too much in common—law, literature, and religion—to be too long separated by the wedge of disagreement. By both his pen and his politics, James Bryce shored up the foundation of the "special relationship" between Britain and America that would see them through the calamitous twentieth century as the bastions of freedom.

James Bryce died quietly and unexpectedly in his sleep on January 22, 1922, in Sidmouth, Devon, where he and Marion, his wife of thirty-three years, had gone for a holiday. He was mourned in both London and Washington as a man unsurpassed in his devotion to democracy and liberty, ever guided by "the deep moral purpose which directed every thought and action of his life."[72] He was buried next to his parents in the Grange Cemetery in Edinburgh. On October 12, 1922, a bronze bust of James Bryce was placed in the Capitol of the United States with an inscription that no doubt would have pleased him: "James, Viscount Bryce, Friend and Ambassador to the American People and Interpreter of their Institutions."

Gary L. McDowell
Institute of United States Studies
University of London

---

[71] Bryce spoke throughout the country during his tenure as Ambassador to the United States. See James Bryce, *University and Historical Addresses* (London: Macmillan, 1913).

[72] As quoted in Ions, *James Bryce and American Democracy*, 293.

Publisher's Note

The first edition of James Bryce's *The American Commonwealth* appeared in 1888. It was published in London by Macmillan & Co. as a three-volume set and is the only edition of the book to be released in England. A two-volume edition of the work, using smaller type, was published at the same time in New York, and all subsequent editions have been limited to two volumes.

Two chapters in this first edition were written by Americans so that Bryce could obtain an American copyright (at that time the United States had not joined the International Copyright Union). Seth Low, a leader of the municipal reform movement and later president of Columbia University and mayor of New York, wrote chapter 52, "An American View of Municipal Government in the United States"; and Professor Frank J. Goodnow of Columbia University, a prominent political scientist and author of pioneer studies in the field of public administration, wrote chapter 88, "The Tweed Ring in New York City."

In 1889, Macmillan reprinted the first edition but omitted the Goodnow chapter on the Tweed Ring because it had become the object of a libel suit. This chapter was also suppressed in the second edition of the work, which was published in 1893 with many revisions and additions. Bryce later rewrote the Goodnow chapter, however, and changed the title to "The Tammany Ring in New York City." It was introduced in the extensively revised third edition published in 1910. But Bryce did not significantly alter the substance of this controversial chapter. He used every name that Goodnow had used and simply moderated the tone and updated the story.

The publisher heralded the 1910 edition as a "new edition completely revised throughout with additional chapters." The changes were not as extensive as this suggests, but Bryce had added a great deal of new material since the first edition, including supplementary materials on political parties and amendments to the Constitution, and new chapters on American universities and colleges, immigration, the South since the Civil War, and what was then called "the Negro problem." Seth Low also made modest revisions of his chapter on municipal government for the third edition.

In all of its essential attributes, the third edition published in 1910 represents Bryce's final and most mature reflections on American institutions. In 1914, Bryce brought some statistics and the appendix up to date, and he apparently made a few additional minor corrections and additions before his death in 1922; but these changes did not significantly alter the work. Macmillan continued to publish the updated third edition in New York as late as 1941. The 1941 edition of *The American Commonwealth*, which encompasses all of the changes, corrections, and additions to the first three editions entered by Bryce, was used in the preparation of this new Liberty Fund edition.

In this new edition of Bryce's classic, the reader will also note that the appendix has been expanded to include an essay by Bryce entitled "The Predictions of Hamilton and De Tocqueville" (originally published in 1887 by Johns Hopkins University) and two contemporaneous book reviews of *The American Commonwealth*, published in 1889, by Woodrow Wilson and Lord Acton, respectively.

Although capitalization and punctuation have been modernized for the convenience of the reader, Bryce's style, including spelling and grammar, has been preserved intact. Footnotes and bracketed material are those of Bryce, except as otherwise noted.

Preface to the First Edition

As the introductory chapter of this work contains such explanations as seem needed of its scope and plan, the Author has little to do in this place except express his thanks to the numerous friends who have helped him with facts, opinions, and criticisms, or by the gift of books or pamphlets. Among these he is especially indebted to the Hon. Thomas M. Cooley, now Chairman of the Inter-State Commerce Commission in Washington; Mr. James B. Thayer of the Harvard Law School, Cambridge, Mass.; Hon. Seth Low, formerly Mayor of Brooklyn; Mr. Theodore Roosevelt of New York; Mr. G. Bradford of Cambridge, Mass.; and Mr. Theodore Bacon of Rochester, N.Y.; by one or other of whom the greater part of the proofs of these volumes have been read. He has also received valuable aid from Mr. Justice Holmes of the Supreme Court of Massachusetts; Mr. Theodore Dwight, late Librarian of the State Department at Washington; Mr. H. Villard of New York; Dr. Albert Shaw of Minneapolis; Mr. Jesse Macy of Grinnell, Ia.; Mr. Simeon Baldwin and Dr. George P. Fisher of Newhaven, Conn.; Mr. Henry C. Lea of Philadelphia; Col. T. W. Higginson of Cambridge, Mass.; Mr. Bernard Moses of Berkeley, Cal.; Mr. A. B. Houghton of Corning, N.Y.; Mr. John Hay of Washington; Mr. Henry Hitchcock of St. Louis, Mo.; President James B. Angell of Ann Arbor, Mich.; Hon. Andrew D. White of Syracuse, N.Y.; Mr. Frank J. Goodnow of New York; Dr. Atherton of the State College, Pennsylvania; and the U.S. Bureau of Education. No one of these gentlemen is, however, responsible for any of the facts stated or views expressed in the book.

The Author is further indebted to Mr. Low and Mr. Goodnow for two chapters which they have written, and which contain, as he believes, matter of much interest relating to municipal government and politics.

He gladly takes this opportunity of thanking for their aid and counsel four English friends: Mr. Henry Sidgwick, who has read most of the proofs with great care and made valuable suggestions upon them; the Rev. Stopford A. Brooke, whose literary criticisms have been very helpful; Mr. Albert V. Dicey, and Mr. W. Robertson Smith.

He is aware that, notwithstanding the assistance rendered by friends in America, he must have fallen into not a few errors, and without asking to be excused for these, he desires to plead in extenuation that the book has been written under the constant pressure of public duties as well as of other private work, and that the difficulty of obtaining in Europe correct information regarding the constitutions and laws of American States and the rules of party organizations is very great.

When the book was begun, it was intended to contain a study of the more salient social and intellectual phenomena of contemporary America, together with descriptions of the scenery and the aspects of nature and human nature in the West, all of whose States and Territories the Author has visited. But as the work advanced, he found that to carry out this plan it would be necessary either unduly to curtail the account of the government and politics of the United States, or else to extend the book to a still greater length than that which, much to his regret, it has now reached. He therefore reluctantly abandoned the hope of describing in these volumes the scenery and life of the West. As regards the non-political topics which were to have been dealt with, he has selected for discussion in the concluding chapters those of them which either were comparatively unfamiliar to European readers, or seemed specially calculated to throw light on the political life of the country, and to complete the picture which he has sought to draw of the American Commonwealth as a whole.

October 22, 1888.

Preface to the Edition of 1910

As the introductory chapter of this book contains such explanations as seem needed of its scope and plan, I have little to do here except advert to the alterations made in it since it was first published in 1888. Some years afterwards, in 1893–95, a revised and much enlarged edition appeared; and since that date various minor corrections and additions have from time to time been made. Now in 1910 I find that so many changes have taken place in the United States that a further complete revision has become necessary, and that some note ought to be taken of certain new phenomena in American politics and society. In this edition, accordingly, there have been introduced, sometimes in the text, sometimes in supplementary notes, concise descriptions of such phenomena.

Besides these corrections and additions, which do not affect the general plan, four new chapters have been added. One deals with the transmarine dominions of the United States acquired since 1888, a second with the huge influx of immigrants who have been arriving from Central and Southern Europe, a third with the more recent phases of the Negro problem in the South, and a fourth with the remarkable development in late years of the American universities.

My friend, Mr. Seth Low, formerly mayor of New York, has been kind enough to rewrite the chapter on municipal government which he contributed to the first edition, and which contains matter of much interest relating to city government and city politics.

I am indebted to Professor Beard of Columbia University for information on several topics which I could not personally investigate. Besides the difficulties of selection and compression which attend any attempt to deal in two volumes with so vast a subject as that of this treatise, I have found in revising it a further difficulty in the fact that many political institutions in the United States, such as forms of city government, the party nominating machinery, and the methods of direct popular legislation, are at present in a transitory or experimental condition; the variations between one state and another growing more numerous with the emergence of new ideas and new schemes of reform. It would have been impossible to find space to describe these otherwise than in outline, even could I, under the heavy pressure of other duties, have found time to study all these things minutely. But an effort has been made to call attention to the more important among these new political arrangements, and to give in each case the most recent facts, though I am for obvious reasons precluded from adding comments on many of the facts which it is proper to state.

It was with some anxiety that I entered on this revision, fearing lest the hopeful spirit with which my observation of American institutions from 1870 to 1894 had inspired me might be damped by a close examination of their more recent phases. But all I have seen and heard during the last few years makes me more hopeful for the future of popular government. The forces working for good seem stronger today than they have been for the last three generations.

In the prefaces to the first and third editions I expressed my thanks to a large number of friends, American and English, who had helped me. Many of those to whom I was most indebted have now passed away. To those who happily remain I renew the expression of my gratitude, and am glad to thank also many others, too numerous to be all mentioned by name, in the United States, who have within the last few years helped me in a thousand ways towards acquiring a more thorough knowledge of their country.

I venture to take this opportunity of saying how deeply I appreciate the extraordinary kindness with which this attempt, made by one who was then, comparatively speaking, a stranger, to describe American institutions, has been received in the United States, and of which I have received so many proofs in travelling to and fro throughout the country.

James Bryce

October 22, 1910.

Note to Edition of 1914

This new edition has been carefully revised in order to introduce into the text the changes made by recent amendments to the Constitution, and otherwise to bring the book up to date.

February 26, 1914.

List of Presidents

1789–1793	GEORGE WASHINGTON
1793–1797	Re-elected
1797–1801	JOHN ADAMS
1801–1805	THOMAS JEFFERSON
1805–1809	Re-elected
1809–1813	JAMES MADISON
1813–1817	Re-elected
1817–1821	JAMES MONROE
1821–1825	Re-elected
1825–1829	JOHN QUINCY ADAMS
1829–1833	ANDREW JACKSON
1833–1837	Re-elected
1837–1841	MARTIN VAN BUREN
1841–1845	WILLIAM HENRY HARRISON (died 1841)
	JOHN TYLER
1845–1849	JAMES KNOX POLK
1849–1853	ZACHARY TAYLOR (died 1850)
	MILLARD FILLMORE
1853–1857	FRANKLIN PIERCE
1857–1861	JAMES BUCHANAN
1861–1865	ABRAHAM LINCOLN
1865–1869	Re-elected (died 1865)
	ANDREW JOHNSON
1869–1873	ULYSSES S. GRANT
1873–1877	Re-elected
1877–1881	RUTHERFORD B. HAYES
1881–1885	JAMES ABRAM GARFIELD (died 1881)
	CHESTER A. ARTHUR
1885–1889	STEPHEN GROVER CLEVELAND
1889–1893	BENJAMIN HARRISON
1893–1897	GROVER CLEVELAND
1897–1901	WILLIAM McKINLEY
1901–1905	Re-elected (died 1901)
	THEODORE ROOSEVELT
1905–1909	THEODORE ROOSEVELT
1909–1913	WILLIAM HOWARD TAFT
1913–	WOODROW WILSON

Dates of Some Remarkable Events in the History of the North American Colonies and United States

1606	First charter of Virginia.
1607	First settlement in Virginia.
1620	First settlement in Massachusetts.
1664	Taking of New Amsterdam (New York).
1759	Battle of Heights of Abraham and taking of Quebec.
1775	Beginning of the Revolutionary War.
1776	Declaration of Independence.
1781	Formation of the Confederation.
1783	Independence of United States recognized.
1787	Constitutional Convention at Philadelphia.
1788	The Constitution ratified by nine states.
1789	Beginning of the federal government.
1793	Invention of the cotton gin.
1803	Purchase of Louisiana from France.
1812–14	War with England.
1812–15	Disappearance of the Federalist Party.
1819	Purchase of Florida from Spain.
1819	Steamers begin to cross the Atlantic.
1820	The Missouri Compromise.
1828–32	Formation of the Whig Party.
1830	First passenger railway opened.
1840	National nominating conventions regularly established.
1844	First electric telegraph in operation.
1845	Admission of Texas to the Union.
1846–48	Mexican War and cession of California.
1852–56	Fall of the Whig Party.
1854–56	Formation of the Republican Party.
1857	Dred Scott decision delivered.
1861–65	War of Secession.
1869	First transcontinental railway completed.
1877	Final withdrawal of Federal troops from the South.
1879	Specie payments resumed.
1898	War with Spain: annexation of Hawaii.
1899	Cession by Spain of Puerto Rico and the Philippine Islands.
1904	Acquisition of the Canal Zone at the Isthmus of Panama.

Area, Population, and Date of Admission of the States

The thirteen original states, in the order
in which they ratified the Constitution

	Foreign Policy and Territorial Extension Ratified the Constitution	Area in square miles	Population (1910)
Delaware	1787	2,050	202,322
Pennsylvania	1787	45,215	7,665,111
New Jersey	1787	7,815	2,537,167
Georgia	1788	59,475	2,609,121
Connecticut	1788	4,990	1,114,756
Massachusetts	1788	8,315	3,366,416
Maryland	1788	12,210	1,295,346
South Carolina	1788	30,570	1,515,400
New Hampshire	1788	9,305	430,572
Virginia	1788	42,450	2,061,612
New York	1788	49,170	9,113,614
North Carolina	1789	52,250	2,206,287
Rhode Island	1790	1,250	542,610

States subsequently admitted, in the order of their admission

Vermont	1791	9,565	355,956
Kentucky	1792	40,400	2,289,905
Tennessee	1796	42,050	2,184,789
Ohio	1802	41,060	4,767,121
Louisiana	1812	48,720	1,656,388
Indiana	1816	36,350	2,700,876
Mississippi	1817	46,810	1,797,114
Illinois	1818	56,650	5,638,591
Alabama	1819	52,250	2,138,093
Maine	1820	33,040	742,371
Missouri	1821	69,415	3,293,335
Arkansas	1836	53,850	1,574,449
Michigan	1837	58,915	2,810,173
Florida	1845	58,680	752,619
Texas	1845	265,780	3,896,514

	Ratified the Constitution	Area in square miles	Population (1910)
Iowa	1846	56,025	2,224,771
Wisconsin	1848	56,040	2,333,860
California	1850	158,360	2,377,549
Minnesota	1858	83,365	2,075,708
Oregon	1859	96,030	672,765
Kansas	1861	82,080	1,690,949
W. Virginia	1863	24,780	1,221,119
Nevada	1864	110,700	81,875
Nebraska	1867	77,510	1,192,214
Colorado	1876	103,925	799,024
N. Dakota	1889	70,795	577,056
S. Dakota	1889	77,650	583,888
Montana	1889	146,080	376,053
Washington	1889	69,180	1,141,990
Wyoming	1890	97,890	145,965
Idaho	1890	84,800	325,954
Utah	1895–96	84,970	373,351
Oklahoma	1907	70,057	1,657,155
Arizona	1911	113,020	204,354
New Mexico	1911	122,580	327,301

Territories, Etc.

	Area	Population (1910)
Hawaiian Islands	6,449	191,909
Alaska	590,884	64,356
District of Columbia	70	331,069
Philippine Islands[1]	127,853	7,635,426
Porto Rico	3,435	1,118,012

[1] According to the census taken in 1903 under the direction of the War Department.

C H A P T E R   1

Introductory

What do you think of our institutions?" is the question addressed to the European traveller in the United States by every chance acquaintance. The traveller finds the question natural, for if he be an observant man his own mind is full of these institutions. But he asks himself why it should be in America only that he is so interrogated. In England one does not inquire from foreigners, nor even from Americans, their views on the English laws and government; nor does the Englishman on the Continent find Frenchmen or Germans or Italians anxious to have his judgment on their politics. Presently the reason of the difference appears. The institutions of the United States are deemed by inhabitants and admitted by strangers to be a matter of more general interest than those of the not less famous nations of the Old World. They are, or are supposed to be, institutions of a new type. They form, or are supposed to form, a symmetrical whole, capable of being studied and judged all together more profitably than the less perfectly harmonized institutions of older countries. They represent an experiment in the rule of the multitude, tried on a scale unprecedentedly vast, and the results of which everyone is concerned to watch. And yet they are something more than an experiment, for they are believed to disclose and display the type of institutions towards which, as by a law of fate, the rest of civilized mankind are forced to move, some with swifter, others with slower, but all with unresting feet.

When our traveller returns home he is again interrogated by the more intelligently curious of his friends. But what now strikes him is the inaptness of their questions. Thoughtful Europeans have begun to realize, whether with satisfaction or regret, the enormous and daily increasing influence of the United States, and the splendour of the part reserved for them in the development of civilization. But such men, unless they have themselves

1

crossed the Atlantic, have seldom either exact or correct ideas regarding the phenomena of the New World. The social and political experiments of America constantly cited in Europe both as patterns and as warnings are hardly ever cited with due knowledge of the facts, much less with comprehension of what they teach; and where premises are misunderstood inferences must be unsound.

It is such a feeling as this, a sense of the immense curiosity of Europe regarding the social and political life of America, and of the incomparable significance of American experience, that has led and will lead so many travellers to record their impressions of the Land of the Future. Yet the very abundance of descriptions in existence seems to require the author of another to justify himself for adding it to the list.

I might plead that America changes so fast that every few years a new crop of books is needed to describe the new face which things have put on, the new problems that have appeared, the new ideas germinating among her people, the new and unexpected developments for evil as well as for good of which her established institutions have been found capable. I might observe that a new generation grows up every few years in Europe, which does not read the older books, because they are old, but may desire to read a new one. And if a further reason is asked for, let it be found in this, that during the last fifty years no author has proposed to himself the aim of portraying the whole political system of the country in its practice as well as its theory, of explaining not only the national government but the state governments, not only the Constitution but the party system, not only the party system but the ideas, temper, habits of the sovereign people. Much that is valuable has been written on particular parts or aspects of the subject, but no one seems to have tried to deal with it as a whole; not to add that some of the ablest writers have been either advocates, often professed advocates, or detractors of democracy.

To present such a general view of the United States both as a government and as a nation is the aim of the present book. But in seeking to be comprehensive it does not attempt to be exhaustive. The effort to cover the whole ground with equal minuteness, which a penetrating critic—the late Karl Hillebrand—remarked upon as a characteristic fault of English writers, is to be avoided not merely because it wearies a reader, but because it leads the writer to descant as fully upon matters he knows imperfectly as upon those which his own tastes and knowledge qualify him to deal with. I shall endeavour to omit nothing which seems necessary to make the political life and the national character and tendencies of the Americans intelligible to

Europeans, and with this view shall touch upon some topics only distantly connected with government or politics. But there are also many topics, perhaps no more remote from the main subject, which I shall pass lightly over, either because they have been sufficiently handled by previous writers, or because I have no such minute acquaintance with them as would make my observations profitable. For instance, the common-school system of the United States has been so frequently and fully described in many easily accessible books that an account of it will not be expected from me. But American universities have been generally neglected by European observers, and may therefore properly claim some pages. The statistics of manufactures, agriculture, and commerce, the systems of railway finance and railway management, are full of interest, but they would need so much space to be properly set forth and commented on that it would be impossible to bring them within the present volumes, even had I the special skill and knowledge needed to distil from rows of figures the refined spirit of instruction. Moreover, although an account of these facts might be made to illustrate the features of American civilization, it is not necessary to a comprehension of American character. Observations on the state of literature and religion are necessary, and I have therefore endeavoured to convey some idea of the literary tastes and the religious habits of the people, and of the part which these play in forming and colouring the whole life of the country.

The book which it might seem natural for me to take as a model is the *Democracy in America* of Alexis de Tocqueville. It would indeed, apart from the danger of provoking a comparison with such an admirable master of style, have been an interesting and useful task to tread in his steps, and seek to do for the United States of 1888, with their sixty millions of people, what he did for the fifteen millions of 1832. But what I have actually tried to accomplish is something different, for I have conceived the subject upon quite other lines. To Tocqueville America was primarily a democracy, the ideal democracy, fraught with lessons for Europe, and above all for his own France. What he has given us is not so much a description of the country and people as a treatise, full of fine observation and elevated thinking, upon democracy, a treatise whose conclusions are illustrated from America, but are founded, not so much on an analysis of American phenomena, as on general views of democracy which the circumstances of France had suggested. Democratic government seems to me, with all deference to his high authority, a cause not so potent in the moral and social sphere as he deemed it; and my object has been less to discuss its merits than to paint the institutions and people of America as they are, tracing what is peculiar in them not merely to the sovereignty of the masses, but also to the history and traditions of the race, to its fundamental ideas, to its material environment. I have striven to avoid the temptations of the deductive method, and to present simply the facts of the case, arranging and connecting them as best I can, but letting them speak for themselves rather than pressing upon the reader my own conclusions. The longer anyone studies a vast subject, the more cautious in inference does he become. When I first visited America in the year 1870, I brought home a swarm of bold generalizations. Half of them were thrown overboard after a second visit in 1881. Of the half that remained, some were dropped into the Atlantic when I returned across it after a third visit in 1883-84; and although the two later journeys gave birth to some new views, these views are fewer and more discreetly cautious than their departed sisters of 1870. I can honestly say that I shall be far better pleased if readers of a philosophic turn find in the book matter on which they feel they can safely build theories for themselves, than if they take from it theories ready made.

To have dealt with the subject historically would have been profitable as well as pleasant, for the nature of institutions is best understood when their growth has been traced and illustrations adduced of their actual working. If I have made only a sparing use of this method, it has been from no want of love for it, but because a historical treatment would have seldom been compatible with my chief aim, that of presenting, within reasonable compass, a full and clear view of the facts of today. American history, of which Europeans know scarcely anything, may be wanting in colour and romance when compared with the annals of the great states of the Old World; but it is eminently rich in political instruction. I hope that my American readers, who, if I am not mistaken, know the history of their country better than the English know that of England, will not suppose that I have ignored this instruction, but will allow for the omissions rendered necessary by the magnitude of the subject which I am trying to compress into two volumes. Similar reasons compel me to deal succinctly with the legal aspects of the Constitution; but the lay reader may possibly deem this brevity a merit.

Even when limited by the exclusion of history and law, the subject remains so vast and complex as to make necessary an explanation of the conception I have formed of it, and of the plan upon which the book has been constructed.

There are three main things that one wishes to know about a national commonwealth, viz., its framework and constitutional machinery, the methods by which it is worked, the forces which move it and direct its course. It is natural to begin with the first of these. Accordingly, I begin with the government; and as the powers of government are twofold, being vested partly in the national or federal authorities and partly in the states, I begin with the national government, whose structure presents less difficulty to European minds, because it resembles the national government in each of their own countries. Part I therefore contains an account of the several federal authorities, the president, Congress, the courts of law. It describes the relations of the national or central power to the several states. It discusses the nature of the Constitution as a fundamental supreme law, and shows how this stable and rigid instrument has been in a few points expressly, in many others tacitly and half-unconsciously modified.

Part II deals similarly with the state governments, examining the constitutions that have established them, the authorities which administer them, the practical working of their legislative bodies. And as local government is a matter of state regulation, there is also given some account of the systems of rural and city government which have been created in the various states, and which have, rural government for its merits and city government for its faults, become the theme of copious discussion among foreign students of American institutions.

(Part III) The whole machinery, both of national and of state governments, is worked by the political parties. Parties have been organized far more elaborately in the United States than anywhere else in the world, and have passed more completely under the control of a professional class. The party organizations in fact form a second body of political machinery, existing side by side with that of the legally constituted government, and scarcely less complicated. Politics, considered not as the science of government, but as the art of winning elections and securing office, has reached in the United States a development surpassing in elaborateness that of England or France as much as the methods of those countries surpass the methods of Servia or Roumania. Part III contains a sketch of this party system, and of the men who "run" it, topics which deserve and would repay a fuller examination than they have yet received even in America, or than my limits permit me to bestow.

(Part IV) The parties, however, are not the ultimate force in the conduct of affairs. Behind and above them stands the people. Public opinion, that is, the mind and conscience of the whole nation, is the opinion of persons who are included in the parties, for the parties taken together are the nation; and the parties, each claiming to be its true exponent, seek to use it for their purposes. Yet it stands above the parties, being cooler and larger minded than they are; it awes party leaders and holds in check party organizations. No one openly ventures to resist it. It determines the direction and the character of national policy. It is the product of a greater number of minds than in any other country, and it is more indisputably sovereign. It is the central point of the whole American polity. To describe it, that is, to sketch the leading political ideas, habits, and tendencies of the American people, and show how they express themselves in action, is the most difficult and also the most vital part of my task; and to this task the twelve chapters of Part IV are devoted.

(Part V) As the descriptions given and propositions advanced in treating of the party system and of public opinion are necessarily general, they seem to need illustration by instances drawn from recent American history. I collect three such instances in Part V, and place there a discussion of several political questions which lie outside party politics, together with some chapters in which the attempt is made to estimate the strength and weakness of democratic government as it exists in the United States, and to compare the phenomena which it actually shows with those which European speculation has attributed to democracy in general.

(Part VI) At this point the properly political sections of the book end. But there are certain nonpolitical institutions, certain aspects of society, certain intellectual or spiritual forces, which count for so much in the total life of the country, in the total impression which it makes and the hopes for the future which it raises, that they cannot be left unnoticed. These, or rather such of them as are of most general interest, and have been least understood in Europe, will be found briefly treated in Part VI. In the view which I take of them, they are all germane, though not all equally germane, to the main subject of the book, which is the character, temper, and tendencies of the American nation, as they are expressed primarily in political and social institutions, secondarily in literature and manners.

This plan involves some repetition. But an author who finds himself obliged to choose between repetition and obscurity ought not to doubt as to his choice. Whenever it has been necessary to trace a phenomenon to its source, or to explain a connection between several phenomena, I have not hesitated, knowing that one must not expect a reader to carry in his mind all that has been told already, to restate a material fact, or reenforce a view which gives to the facts what I conceive to be their true significance.

It may be thought that a subject of this great compass ought, if undertaken at all, to be undertaken by a native American. No native American has, however, undertaken it. Such a writer would doubtless have great advantages over a stranger. Yet there are two advantages which a stranger, or at least a stranger who is also an Englishman, with some practical knowledge of English politics and English law, may hope to secure. He is struck by certain things which a native does not think of explaining, because they are too obvious; and whose influence on politics or society, one to whom they seem part of the order of nature forgets to estimate. And the stranger finds it easier to maintain a position of detachment, detachment not only from party prejudice, but from those prepossessions in favour of persons, groups, constitutional dogmas, national pretensions, which a citizen can scarcely escape except by falling into that attitude of impartial cynicism which sours and perverts the historical mind as much as prejudice itself. He who regards a wide landscape from a distant height sees its details imperfectly, and must unfold his map in order to make out where each village lies, and how the roads run from point to point. But he catches the true perspective of things better than if he were standing among them. The great features of the landscape, the valleys, slopes, and mountains, appear in their relative proportion: he can estimate the height of the peaks and the breadth of the plains. So one who writes of a country not his own may turn his want of familiarity with details to good account if he fixes his mind strenuously on the main characteristics of the people and their institutions, while not forgetting to fill up gaps in his knowledge by frequent reference to native authorities. My own plan has been first to write down what struck me as the salient and dominant facts and then to test, by consulting American friends and by a further study of American books, the views which I had reached.

To be nonpartisan, as I trust to have been, in describing the politics of the United States, is not difficult for a European, especially if he has the good fortune to have intimate friends in both the great American parties. To feel and show no bias in those graver and more sharply accentuated issues which divide men in Europe, the issues between absolutism, oligarchy, and democracy; between strongly unified governments and the policy of decentralization, this is a harder task, yet a not less imperative duty. This much I can say, that no fact has been either stated or suppressed, and no opinion put forward, with the purpose of serving any English party doctrine or party policy, or in any way furnishing arguments for use in any English controversy. The admirers and the censors of popular government are equally likely to find in the present treatise materials suited to their wishes; and in many cases, if I may judge from what has befallen some of my predecessors, they will draw from these materials conclusions never intended by the author.

Few things are more difficult than to use aright arguments founded on the political experience of other countries. As the chief practical use of history is to deliver us from plausible historical analogies, so a comprehension of the institutions of other nations enables us to expose sometimes the ill-grounded hopes, sometimes the idle fears, which loose reports about those nations generate. Direct inferences from the success or failure of a particular constitutional arrangement or political usage in another country are rarely sound, because the conditions differ in so many respects that there can be no certainty that what flourishes or languishes under other skies and in another soil will likewise flourish or languish in our own. Many an American institution would bear a different fruit if transplanted to England, as there is hardly an English institution which has not undergone, like the plants and animals of the Old World, some change in America. The examination and appraisement of the institutions of the United States is no doubt full of instruction for Europe, full of encouragement, full of warning; but its chief value lies in what may be called the laws of political biology which it reveals, in the new illustrations and enforcements it supplies of general truths in social and political science, truths some of which were perceived long ago by Plato and Aristotle, but might have been forgotten had not America poured a stream of new light upon them. Now and then we may directly claim transatlantic experience as accrediting or discrediting some specific constitutional device or the policy of some enactment. But even in these cases he who desires to rely on the results shown in America must first satisfy himself that there is such a parity of conditions and surroundings in respect to the particular matter as justifies him in reasoning directly from ascertained results there to probable results in his own country.

It is possible that these pages, or at least those of them which describe the party system, may produce on European readers an impression which I neither intend nor desire. They may set before him a picture with fewer lights and deeper shadows than I have wished it to contain. Many years ago I travelled in Iceland with two friends. We crossed the great desert by a seldom trodden track, encountering, during two months of late autumn, rains, tempests, snowstorms, and other hardships too numerous to recount. But the scenery was so grand and solemn, the life so novel, the character of the people so attractive, the historic and poetic traditions so inspiring, that we returned full of delight with the marvellous isle. When we expressed this enchantment to our English friends, we were questioned about the conditions of travel, and forced to admit that we had been frozen and starved, that we had sought sleep in swamps or on rocks, that the Icelanders lived in huts scattered through a wilderness, with none of the luxuries and few even of the comforts of life. Our friends passed over the record of impressions to dwell on the record of physical experiences, and conceived a notion of the island totally different from that which we had meant to convey. We perceived too late how much easier it is to state tangible facts than to communicate impressions. If I may attempt to apply the analogy to the United States and their people, I will say that they make on the visitor an impression so strong, so deep, so fascinating, so inwoven with a hundred threads of imagination and emotion, that he cannot hope to reproduce it in words, and to pass it on undiluted to other minds. With the broad facts of politics it is otherwise. These a traveller can easily set forth, and is bound in honesty to set forth, knowing that in doing so he must state much that is sordid, much that will provoke unfavourable comment. The European reader grasps these tangible facts, and, judging them as though they existed under European conditions, draws from them conclusions disparaging to the country and the people. What he probably fails to do, because this is what the writer is most likely to fail in enabling him to do, is to realize the existence in the American people of a reserve of force and patriotism more than sufficient to sweep away all the evils which are now tolerated, and to make the politics of the country worthy of its material grandeur and of the private virtues of its inhabitants. America excites an admiration which must be felt upon the spot to be understood. The hopefulness of her people communicates itself to one who moves among them, and makes him perceive that the graver faults of politics may be far less dangerous there than they would be in Europe. A hundred times in writing this book have I been disheartened by the facts I was stating; a hundred times has the recollection of the abounding strength and vitality of the nation chased away these tremors.

There are other risks to which such a book as this is necessarily exposed. There is the risk of supposing that to be generally true which the writer has himself seen or been told, and the risk of assuming that what is now generally true is likely to continue so. Against the former of these dangers he who is forewarned is forearmed; as to the latter I can but say that whenever I have sought to trace a phenomenon to its causes I have also sought to inquire whether these causes are likely to be permanent, a question which it is well to ask even when no answer can be given. I have attributed less to the influence of democracy than most of my predecessors have done, believing that explanations drawn from a form of government, being easy and obvious, ought to be cautiously employed. Someone has said that the end of philosophy is to diminish the number of causes, as the aim of chemistry is to reduce that of the elemental substances. But it is an end not to be hastily pursued. A close analysis of social and political phenomena often shows us that causes are more complex than had at first appeared, and that that which had been deemed the main cause is active only because some inconspicuous, but not less important, condition is also present. The inquisition of the forces which move society is a high matter; and even where certainty is unattainable it is some service to science to have determined the facts, and correctly stated the problems, as Aristotle remarked long ago that the first step in investigation is to ask the right questions.

I have, however, dwelt long enough upon the perils of the voyage: it is now time to put to sea. We shall begin with a survey of the national government, examining its nature and describing the authorities which compose it.

PART I

THE NATIONAL GOVERNMENT

C H A P T E R   2

The Nation and the States

Some years ago the American Protestant Episcopal Church was occupied at its triennial convention in revising its liturgy. It was thought desirable to introduce among the short sentence prayers a prayer for the whole people; and an eminent New England divine proposed the words "O Lord, bless our nation." Accepted one afternoon on the spur of the moment, the sentence was brought up next day for reconsideration, when so many objections were raised by the laity to the word "nation," as importing too definite a recognition of national unity, that it was dropped, and instead there were adopted the words "O Lord, bless these United States."

To Europeans who are struck by the patriotism and demonstrative national pride of their transatlantic visitors, this fear of admitting that the American people constitute a nation seems extraordinary. But it is only the expression on its sentimental side of the most striking and pervading characteristic of the political system of the country, the existence of a double government, a double allegiance, a double patriotism. America—I call it America (leaving out of sight South America, Canada, and Mexico), in order to avoid using at this stage the term United States—America is a commonwealth of commonwealths, a republic of republics, a state which, while one, is nevertheless composed of other states even more essential to its existence than it is to theirs.

This is a point of so much consequence, and so apt to be misapprehended by Europeans, that a few sentences may be given to it.

When within a large political community smaller communities are found existing, the relation of the smaller to the larger usually appears in one or other of the two following forms. One form is that of a league, in which a number of political bodies, be they monarchies or republics, are bound together so as to constitute for certain purposes, and especially for the

13

purpose of common defence, a single body. The members of such a composite body or league are not individual men but communities. It exists only as an aggregate of communities, and will therefore vanish so soon as the communities which compose it separate themselves from one another. Moreover it deals with and acts upon these communities only. With the individual citizen it has nothing to do, no right of taxing him, or judging him, or making laws for him, for in all these matters it is to his own community that the allegiance of the citizen is due. A familiar instance of this form is to be found in the Germanic Confederation as it existed from 1815 till 1866. The Hanseatic League in mediæval Germany, the Swiss Confederation down till the present century, are other examples.

In the second form, the smaller communities are mere subdivisions of that greater one which we call the nation. They have been created, or at any rate they exist, for administrative purposes only. Such powers as they possess are powers delegated by the nation, and can be overridden by its will. The nation acts directly by its own officers, not merely on the communities, but upon every single citizen; and the nation, because it is independent of these communities, would continue to exist were they all to disappear. Examples of such minor communities may be found in the departments of modern France and the counties of modern England. Some of the English counties were at one time, like Kent or Dorset, independent kingdoms or tribal districts; some, like Bedfordshire, were artificial divisions from the first. All are now merely local administrative areas, the powers of whose local authorities have been delegated from the national government of England. The national government does not stand by virtue of them, does not need them. They might all be abolished or turned into wholly different communities without seriously affecting its structure.

The American federal republic corresponds to neither of these two forms, but may be said to stand between them. Its central or national government is not a mere league, for it does not wholly depend on the component communities which we call the states. It is itself a commonwealth as well as a union of commonwealths, because it claims directly the obedience of every citizen, and acts immediately upon him through its courts and executive officers. Still less are the minor communities, the states, mere subdivisions of the Union, mere creatures of the national government, like the counties of England or the departments of France. They have over their citizens an authority which is their own, and not delegated by the central government. They have not been called into being by that government. They—that is, the older ones among them—existed before it. They could exist without it.

The central or national government and the state governments may be compared to a large building and a set of smaller buildings standing on the same ground, yet distinct from each other. It is a combination sometimes seen where a great church has been erected over more ancient homes of worship. First the soil is covered by a number of small shrines and chapels, built at different times and in different styles of architecture, each complete in itself. Then over them and including them all in its spacious fabric there is reared a new pile with its own loftier roof, its own walls, which may perhaps rest on and incorporate the walls of the older shrines, its own internal plan.[1] The identity of the earlier buildings has however not been obliterated; and if the later and larger structure were to disappear, a little repair would enable them to keep out wind and weather, and be again what they once were, distinct and separate edifices. So the American states are now all inside the Union, and have all become subordinate to it. Yet the Union is more than an aggregate of states, and the states are more than parts of the Union. It might be destroyed, and they, adding a few further attributes of power to those they now possess, might survive as independent self-governing communities.

This is the cause of that immense complexity which startles and at first bewilders the student of American institutions, a complexity which makes American history and current American politics so difficult to the European who finds in them phenomena to which his own experience supplies no parallel. There are two loyalties, two patriotisms; and the lesser patriotism, as the incident in the Episcopal convention shows, is jealous of the greater. There are two governments, covering the same ground, commanding, with equally direct authority, the obedience of the same citizen.

The casual reader of American political intelligence in European newspapers is not struck by this phenomenon, because state politics and state affairs generally are seldom noticed in Europe. Even the traveller who visits America does not realize its importance, because the things that meet his eye are superficially similar all over the continent, and that which Europeans call the machinery of government is in America conspicuous chiefly by its absence. But a due comprehension of this double organization is the first and indispensable step to the comprehension of American institutions: as the elaborate devices whereby the two systems of government are kept from clashing are the most curious subject of study which those institutions present.

How did so complex a system arise, and what influences have moulded

---

[1] I do not profess to indicate any one building which exactly corresponds to what I have attempted to describe, but there are (besides the Church of the Holy Sepulchre at Jerusalem) several both in Italy and in Egypt that seem to justify the simile.

it into its present form? This is a question which cannot be answered without a few words of historical retrospect. I am anxious not to stray far into history, because the task of describing American institutions as they now exist is more than sufficiently heavy for one writer and one book. But a brief and plain outline of the events which gave birth to the federal system in America, and which have nurtured national feeling without extinguishing state feeling, seems the most natural introduction to an account of the present Constitution, and may dispense with the need for subsequent explanations and digressions.

CHAPTER 3

The Origin of the Constitution

W hen in the reign of George III troubles arose between England and her North American colonists, there existed along the eastern coast of the Atlantic thirteen little communities, the largest of which (Virginia) had not much more than half a million of free people, and the total population of which did not reach three millions. All owed allegiance to the British Crown; all, except Connecticut and Rhode Island, received their governors from the Crown;[1] in all, causes were carried by appeal from the colonial courts to the English Privy Council. Acts of the British Parliament ran there, as they now run in the British colonies, whenever expressed to have that effect, and could overrule such laws as the colonies might make. But practically each colony was a self-governing commonwealth, left to manage its own affairs with scarcely any interference from home. Each had its legislature, its own statutes adding to or modifying the English common law, its local corporate life and traditions, with no small local pride in its own history and institutions, superadded to the pride of forming part of the English race and the great free British realm. Between the various colonies there was no other political connection than that which arose from their all belonging to this race and realm, so that the inhabitants of each enjoyed in every one of the others the rights and privileges of British subjects.

When the oppressive measures of the home government roused the colonies, they naturally sought to organize their resistance in common.[2] Singly they would have been an easy prey, for it was long doubtful whether

---

[1] In Maryland, Pennsylvania, and Delaware, however, the governor was, during the larger part of the colonial period, appointed by the "Proprietor."

[2] There had been a congress of delegates from seven colonies at Albany in 1754 to deliberate on measures relative to the impending war with France, but this, of course, took place with the sanction of the mother country, and was a purely temporary measure.

even in combination they could make head against regular armies. A congress of delegates from nine colonies held at New York in 1765 was followed by another at Philadelphia in 1774, at which twelve were represented, which called itself Continental (for the name American had not yet become established),[3] and spoke in the name of "the good people of these colonies," the first assertion of a sort of national unity among the English of America. The second congress, and the third which met in 1775 and in which thereafter all the colonies were represented, was a merely revolutionary body, called into existence by the war with the mother country. But in 1776 it declared the independence of the colonies, and in 1777 it gave itself a new legal character by framing the "Articles of Confederation and Perpetual Union,"[4] whereby the thirteen states (as they then called themselves) entered into a "firm league of friendship" with each other, offensive and defensive, while declaring that "each State retains its sovereignty, freedom, and independence, and every power, jurisdiction, and right which is not by this Confederation expressly delegated to the United States in Congress assembled."

This Confederation, which was not ratified by all the states till 1781, was rather a league than a national government, for it possessed no central authority except an assembly in which every state, the largest and the smallest alike, had one vote, and this assembly had no jurisdiction over the individual citizens. There was no federal executive, no federal judiciary, no means of raising money except by the contributions of the states, contributions which they were slow to render, no power of compelling the obedience to Congress either of states or of individuals. The plan corresponded to the wishes of the colonists, who did not yet deem themselves a nation, and who in their struggle against the power of the British Crown were resolved to set over themselves no other power, not even one of their own choosing. But it worked badly even while the struggle lasted, and after the immediate danger from England had been removed by the peace of 1783, it worked still worse, and was in fact, as Washington said, no better than anarchy. The states were indifferent to Congress and their common concerns, so indifferent that it was found difficult to procure a quorum of states for weeks

[3] Till the middle of last century the name "American" seems to have denoted the native Indians, as it does in Wesley's hymn "The dark Americans convert." So Sir Thomas Browne writes, "As for sopition of reason and the diviner particle from drink, tho' American religion approve, and Pagan piety of old hath practised it, etc." The War of Independence gave it its present meaning.

[4] See these Articles in the Appendix at the end of this volume.

or even months after the day fixed for meeting. Congress was impotent, and commanded respect as little as obedience. Much distress prevailed in the trading states, and the crude attempts which some legislatures made to remedy the depression by emitting inconvertible paper, by constituting other articles than the precious metals legal tender, and by impeding the recovery of debts, aggravated the evil, and in several instances led to seditious outbreaks.[5] The fortunes of the country seemed at a lower ebb than even during the war with England.

Sad experience of their internal difficulties, and of the contempt with which foreign governments treated them, at last produced a feeling that some firmer and closer union was needed. A convention of delegates from five states met at Annapolis in Maryland in 1786 to discuss methods of enabling Congress to regulate commerce, which suffered grievously from the varying and often burdensome regulations imposed by the several states. It drew up a report which condemned the existing state of things, declared that reforms were necessary, and suggested a further general convention in the following year to consider the condition of the Union and the needed amendments in its Constitution. Congress, to which the report had been presented, approved it, and recommended the states to send delegates to a convention, which should "revise the Articles of Confederation, and report to Congress and the several legislatures such alterations and provisions therein as shall, when agreed to in Congress and confirmed by the States, render the Federal Constitution adequate to the exigencies of government and the preservation of the Union."

The Convention thus summoned met at Philadelphia on the 14th May 1787, became competent to proceed to business on May 25th, when seven states were represented, and chose George Washington to preside. Delegates attended from every state but Rhode Island, and among these delegates was to be found nearly all the best intellect and the ripest political experience the United States then contained. The instructions they had received limited their authority to the revision of the Articles of Confederation and the proposing to Congress and the state legislatures such improvements as were

---

[5] Rhode Island was the most conspicuous offender. This singular little commonwealth, whose area is 1,085 square miles (less than that of Ayrshire or Antrim), is of all the American states that which has furnished the most abundant analogies to the republics of antiquity, and which best deserves to have its annals treated of by a philosophic historian. The example of her disorders did much to bring the other states to adopt that federal Constitution which she was herself the last to accept.

required therein.[6] But with admirable boldness, boldness doubly admirable in Englishmen and lawyers, the majority ultimately resolved to disregard these restrictions, and to prepare a wholly new Constitution, to be considered and ratified neither by Congress nor by the state legislatures, but by the peoples of the several states.

This famous assembly, which consisted of fifty-five delegates, thirty-nine of whom signed the Constitution which it drafted, sat nearly five months, and expended upon its work an amount of labour and thought commensurate with the magnitude of the task and the splendour of the result. The debates were secret, and fortunately so, for criticism from without might have imperilled a work which seemed repeatedly on the point of breaking down, so great were the difficulties encountered from the divergent sentiments and interests of different parts of the country, as well as of the larger and smaller states.[7] The records of the Convention were left in the hands of Washington, who in 1796 deposited them in the State Department. In 1819 they were published by J. Q. Adams. In 1840 there appeared the very full and valuable notes of the discussions kept by James Madison (afterwards twice president), who had been one of the most useful members of the body. From these records and notes[8] the history of the Convention has been written.

[6] It was strongly urged when the draft Constitution came up for ratification in the state conventions that the Philadelphia Convention had no power to do more than amend the Articles of Confederation. To these objections Mr. Wilson, speaking in the Pennsylvania Convention, made answer as follows: "The business, we are told, which was intrusted to the late Convention was merely to amend the present Articles of Confederation. This observation has been frequently made, and has often brought to my mind a story that is related of Mr. Pope, who it is well known was not a little deformed. It was customary for him to use this phrase, 'God mend me,' when any little accident happened. One evening a link boy was lighting him along, and coming to a gutter the boy jumped nimbly over it. Mr. Pope called to him to turn, adding 'God mend me!' The arch rogue, turning to light him, looked at him and repeated 'God mend you! He would sooner make half a dozen new ones.' This would apply to the present Confederation, for it would be easier to make another than to amend this."—Elliot's *Debates*, vol. ii, p. 472.

[7] Benjamin Franklin, who was one of the delegates from Pennsylvania (being then eighty-one years of age), was so much distressed at the difficulties which arose and the prospect of failure that he proposed that the Convention, as all human means of obtaining agreement seemed to be useless, should open its meetings with prayer. The suggestion, remarkable as coming from one so well known for his sceptical opinions, might have been adopted but for the fear that the outside public might thus learn how grave the position of affairs was. The original of Franklin's proposition, written in his own still clear and firm hand, with his note stating that only three or four agreed with him, is preserved in the State Department at Washington, where may be also seen the draft of the Constitution with the signatures of the thirty-nine delegates.

[8] They are printed in the work called Elliot's *Debates*, which also contains the extremely interesting debates in some of the state conventions which ratified the Constitution. The most complete account is now to be found in *Records of the Federal Convention of 1787*, published in 1911 by

It is hard today, even for Americans, to realize how enormous those difficulties were. The Convention had not only to create *de novo*, on the most slender basis of preexisting national institutions, a national government for a widely scattered people, but they had in doing so to respect the fears and jealousies and apparently irreconcilable interests of thirteen separate commonwealths, to all of whose governments it was necessary to leave a sphere of action wide enough to satisfy a deep-rooted local sentiment, yet not so wide as to imperil national unity.[9] Well might Hamilton say: "The establishment of a Constitution, in time of profound peace, by the voluntary consent of a whole people, is a prodigy to the completion of which I look forward with trembling anxiety."[10] And well he might quote the words of David Hume (*Essays*, "The Rise of Arts and Sciences"): "To balance a large State or society, whether monarchical or republican, on general laws, is a work of so great difficulty that no human genius, however comprehensive, is able by the mere dint of reason and reflection to effect it. The judgments of many must unite in the work; experience must guide their labour; time must bring it to perfection; and the feeling of inconveniences must correct the mistakes which they inevitably fall into in their first trials and experiments."

It was even a disputable point whether the colonists were already a nation or only the raw material out of which a nation might be formed.[11] There were elements of unity, there were also elements of diversity. All spoke the same language. All, except a few descendants of Dutchmen and Swedes in New York and Delaware, some Germans in Pennsylvania, some children of French Huguenots in New England and the Middle states, belonged to

---

the Yale University Press. For some remarks on constitutional conventions in general, see the note to this chapter at the end of this volume.

[9] The nearest parallels to such a federal Union as that formed in 1789 were then to be found in the Achæan and Lycian Leagues, which, however, were not mere leagues, but federated nations. Both are referred to by the authors of the *Federalist* (see *post*), but their knowledge was evidently scanty. The acuteness of James Wilson had perceived that the two famous confederations of modern Europe did not supply a model for America. He observed in the Pennsylvania Convention of 1787: "The Swiss cantons are connected only by alliances. The United Netherlands are indeed an assemblage of societies; but this assemblage constitutes no new one, and therefore it does not correspond with the full definition of a Confederate Republic."—Elliot's *Debates*, vol. ii, p. 422. The Swiss Confederation has now become a republic at once federal and national, coming in most respects very near to its American model.

[10] *Federalist*, No. 85.

[11] Mr. Wilson said in the Pennsylvania Convention of 1787: "By adopting this Constitution we shall become a nation; we are not now one. We shall form a national character; we are now too dependent on others." He proceeds with a remarkable prediction of the influence which American freedom would exert upon the Old World.—Elliot's *Debates*, vol. ii, p. 526.

the same race.[12] All, except some Roman Catholics in Maryland, professed the Protestant religion. All were governed by the same English common law, and prized it not only as the bulwark which had sheltered their forefathers from the oppression of the Stuart kings, but as the basis of their more recent claims of right against the encroachments of George III and his colonial officers. In ideas and habits of life there was less similarity, but all were republicans, managing their affairs by elective legislatures, attached to local self-government, and animated by a common pride in their successful resistance to England, which they then hated with a true family hatred, a hatred to which her contemptuous treatment of them added a sting.

On the other hand their geographical position made communication very difficult. The sea was stormy in winter; the roads were bad; it took as long to travel by land from Charleston to Boston as to cross the ocean to Europe, nor was the journey less dangerous. The wealth of some states consisted in slaves, of others in shipping; while in others there was a population of small farmers, characteristically attached to old habits. Manufactures had hardly begun to exist. The sentiment of local independence showed itself in intense suspicion of any external authority; and most parts of the country were so thinly peopled that the inhabitants had lived practically without any government, and thought that in creating one they would be forging fetters for themselves. But while these diversities and jealousies made union difficult, two dangers were absent which have beset the framers of constitutions for other nations. There were no reactionary conspirators to be feared, for everyone prized liberty and equality. There were no questions between classes, no animosities against rank and wealth, for rank and wealth did not exist.

It was inevitable under such circumstances that the Constitution, while aiming at the establishment of a durable central power, should pay great regard to the existing centrifugal forces. It was and remains what its authors styled it, eminently an instrument of compromises; it is perhaps the most successful instance in history of what a judicious spirit of compromise may effect.[13] Yet out of the points which it was for this reason obliged to leave

[12] The Irish, a noticeable element in North Carolina and parts of Pennsylvania, Virginia, and New Hampshire, were not Catholic Celts but Scoto-Irish Presbyterians from Ulster, who, animated by resentment at the wrongs and religious persecution they had suffered at home, had been among the foremost combatants in the Revolutionary War.

[13] Hamilton observed of it in 1788: "The result of the deliberations of all collective bodies must necessarily be a compound as well of the errors and prejudices as of the good sense and wisdom of the individuals of whom they are composed. The compacts which are to embrace thirteen distinct States in a common bond of amity and union must as necessarily be a compromise of as

unsettled there arose fierce controversies, which after two generations, when accumulated irritation and incurable misunderstanding had been added to the force of material interests, burst into flame in the War of Secession.

The draft Constitution was submitted, as its last article provided, to conventions of the several states (i.e., bodies specially chosen by the people[14] for the purpose) for ratification. It was to come into effect as soon as nine states had ratified, the effect of which would have been, in case the remaining states, or any of them, had rejected it, to leave such states standing alone in the world, since the old Confederation was of course superseded and annihilated. Fortunately all the states did eventually ratify the new Constitution, but two of the most important, Virginia and New York,[15] did not do so till the middle of 1788, after nine others had already accepted it; and two, North Carolina and Rhode Island, at first refused, and only consented to enter the new Union more than a year later, when the government it had created had already come into operation.

There was a struggle everywhere over the adoption of the Constitution, a struggle which gave birth to the two great parties that for many years divided the American people. The chief source of hostility was the belief that a strong central government endangered both the rights of the states and the liberties of the individual citizen. Freedom, it was declared, would perish, freedom rescued from George III would perish at the hands of her own children.[16] Consolidation (for the word centralization had not yet been invented) would extinguish the state governments and the local institutions they protected. The feeling was very bitter, and in some states, notably in Massachusetts and New York, the majorities were dangerously narrow. Had the decision been left to what is now called "the voice of the people," that is, to the mass of the citizens all over the country, voting at the polls, the voice of the people would probably have pronounced against the Constitution, and this would have been still more likely if the question had been voted

---

many dissimilar interests and inclinations. How can perfection spring from such materials?" —*Federalist*, No. 85.

[14] The suffrage was then a limited one, based on property.

[15] Virginia was then much the largest state (population in 1790, 747,610). New York was reckoned among the smaller states (population 340,120) but her central geographical position made her adhesion extremely important.

[16] In the Massachusetts Convention of 1788 Mr. Nason delivered himself of the following pathetic appeal: "And here, sir, I beg the indulgence of this honourable body to permit me to make a short apostrophe to Liberty. O Liberty, thou greatest good! thou fairest property! with thee I wish to live—with thee I wish to die! Pardon me if I drop a tear on the peril to which she is exposed. I cannot, sir, see this highest of jewels tarnished—a jewel worth ten thousand worlds; and shall we part with it so soon? On no."—Elliot's *Debates*, vol. ii, p. 133.

on everywhere upon the same day, seeing that several doubtful states were influenced by the approval which other states had already given. But the modern "plebiscital" method of taking the popular judgment had not been invented. The question was referred to conventions in the several states. The conventions were composed of able men, who listened to thoughtful arguments, and were themselves influenced by the authority of their leaders. The counsels of the wise prevailed over the prepossessions of the multitude. Yet these counsels would hardly have prevailed but for a cause which is apt to be now overlooked. This was the dread of foreign powers.[17] The United States had at that time two European monarchies, Spain and England, as its neighbours on the American continent. France had lately held territories to the north of them in Canada, and to the south of them in Louisiana.[18] She had been their ally against England, she became in a few years again the owner of territories west of the Mississippi. The fear of foreign interference, the sense of weakness, both at sea and on land, against the military monarchies of Europe, was constantly before the mind of American statesmen, and made them anxious to secure at all hazards a national government capable of raising an army and navy, and of speaking with authority on behalf of the new republic. It is remarkable that the danger of European aggression or complications was far more felt in the United States from 1783 down till about 1820, than it has been during the last half century when steam has brought Europe five times nearer than it then was.

Several of the conventions which ratified the Constitution accompanied their acceptance with an earnest recommendation of various amendments to it, amendments designed to meet the fears of those who thought that it encroached too far upon the liberties of the people. Some of these were adopted, immediately after the original instrument had come into force, by the method it prescribes, viz., a two-thirds majority in Congress and a majority in three-fourths of the states. They are the amendments of 1791, ten in number, and they constitute what the Americans, following a venerable English precedent, call a Bill or Declaration of Rights.

---

[17] Other chief causes were the financial straits of the Confederation and the economic distress and injury to trade consequent on the disorganized condition of several states. See the observations of Mr. Wilson in the Pennsylvania Convention (Elliot's *Debates*, vol. ii, p. 524). He shows that the case was one of necessity, and winds up with the remark, "The argument of necessity is the patriot's defence as well as the tyrant's plea."

[18] The vast territory then called Louisiana was transferred by France to Spain in 1762, but Spanish government was not established there till 1789. It was ceded by Spain to France in 1800, and purchased by the United States from Napoleon in 1803. Spain had originally held Florida, ceded it to Britain in 1763, received it back in 1783, and in 1819 sold it to the United States.

The Constitution of 1789[19] deserves the veneration with which the Americans have been accustomed to regard it. It is true that many criticisms have been passed upon its arrangement, upon its omissions, upon the artificial character of some of the institutions it creates. Recognizing slavery as an institution existing in some states, and not expressly negativing the right of a state to withdraw from the Union, it has been charged with having contained the germ of civil war, though that germ took seventy years to come to maturity. And whatever success it has attained must be in large measure ascribed to the political genius, ripened by long experience, of the Anglo-American race, by whom it has been worked, and who might have managed to work even a worse drawn instrument. Yet, after all deductions, it ranks above every other written constitution for the intrinsic excellence of its scheme, its adaptation to the circumstances of the people, the simplicity, brevity, and precision of its language, its judicious mixture of definiteness in principle with elasticity in details.[20] One is therefore induced to ask, before proceeding to examine it, to what causes, over and above the capacity of its authors, and the patient toil they bestowed upon it, these merits are due, or in other words, what were the materials at the command of the Philadelphia Convention for the achievement of so great an enterprise as the creation of a nation by means of an instrument of government. The American Constitution is no exception to the rule that everything which has power to win the obedience and respect of men must have its roots deep in the past, and that the more slowly every institution has grown, so much the more enduring is it likely to prove. There is little in that Constitution that is absolutely new. There is much that is as old as Magna Charta.

The men of the Convention had the experience of the English Constitution. That Constitution, very different then from what it is now, was even then not quite what they thought it. Their view was tinged not only by recollections of the influence exercised by King George III, an influence due to transitory

---

[19] One may call the Constitution after either the year 1787, when it was drafted, or the year 1788, when it was accepted by the requisite number of states, or the year 1789, when it took full effect, the Congress of the Confederation having fixed the first Wednesday in March in that year as the day when it should come into force. The year 1789 has the advantage of being easily remembered, because it coincides with the beginning of the great revolutionary movements of modern Europe. The Confederation may be taken to have expired with the expiry of its Congress, and its Congress died for want of a quorum.

[20] The literary Bostonians laid hold at once of its style as proper for admiration. Mr. Ames said in the Massachusetts Convention of 1788, "Considered merely as a literary performance, the Constitution is an honour to our country. Legislators have at length condescended to speak the language of philosophy."—Elliot's *Debates*, vol. ii, p. 55.

causes, but which made them overrate its monarchical element,[21] but also by the presentation of it which they found in the work of Mr. Justice Blackstone. He, as was natural in a lawyer and a man of letters, described rather its theory than its practice, and its theory was many years behind its practice. The powers and functions of the cabinet, the overmastering force of the House of Commons, the intimate connection between legislation and administration, these which are to us now the main characteristics of the English Constitution were still far from fully developed. But in other points of fundamental importance they appreciated and turned to excellent account its spirit and methods.

They had for their oracle of political philosophy the treatise of Montesquieu on the spirit of laws, which, published anonymously at Geneva forty years before, had won its way to an immense authority on both sides of the ocean. Montesquieu, contrasting the private as well as public liberties of Englishmen with the despotism of continental Europe, had taken the Constitution of England as his model system, and had ascribed its merits to the division of legislative, executive, and judicial functions which he discovered in it, and to the system of checks and balances whereby its equilibrium seemed to be preserved. No general principle of politics laid such hold on the constitution-makers and statesmen of America as the dogma that the separation of these three functions is essential to freedom. It had already been made the groundwork of several state constitutions. It is always reappearing in their writings; it was never absent from their thoughts. Of the supposed influence of other continental authors, such as Rousseau, or even of English thinkers such as Burke, there are few direct traces in the federal Constitution or in the classical contemporaneous commentary on and defence of it[22] which we owe to the genius of Hamilton and his hardly less famous coadjutors, Madison and Jay. But we need only turn to the Declaration of Independence and the original constitutions of the states, particularly the Massachusetts Constitution of 1780, to perceive that abstract theories regarding human rights had laid firm hold on the national mind. Such theories naturally expanded with the practice of republican government, and have at various times been extremely potent factors in American history. But the influence

---

[21] There is a tendency in colonists to overestimate the importance of the Crown, whose conspicuous position as the authority common to the whole empire makes it an object of special interest and respect to persons living at a distance. It touches their imagination, whereas assemblies excite their criticism.

[22] *The Federalist*, a series of papers published in the New York newspapers in advocacy of the federal Constitution when the question of accepting it was coming before the New York State Convention.

of France and her philosophers belongs chiefly to the years succeeding 1789, when Jefferson, who was fortunately absent in Paris during the Constitutional Convention, headed the democratic propaganda.

Further, they had the experience of their colonial and state governments, and especially, for this was freshest and most in point, the experience of the working of the state constitutions, framed at or since the date when the colonies threw off their English allegiance. Many of the Philadelphia delegates had joined in preparing these instruments: all had been able to watch and test their operation. They compared notes as to the merits, tested by practice, of the devices which their states had respectively adopted. They had the inestimable advantage of knowing written or rigid constitutions in the concrete; that is to say, of comprehending how a system of government actually moves and plays under the control of a mass of statutory provisions defining and limiting the powers of its several organs. The so-called Constitution of England consists largely of customs, precedents, traditions, understandings, often vague and always flexible. It was quite a different thing, and for the purpose of making a constitution for the American nation an even more important thing, to have lived under and learnt to work systems determined by the hard and fast lines of a single document having the full force of law, for this experience taught them how much might safely be included in such a document and how far room must be left under it for unpredictable emergencies and unavoidable development.

Lastly, they had in the principle of the English common law that an act done by any official person or lawmaking body beyond his or its legal competence is simply void, a key to the difficulties which the establishment of a variety of authorities not subordinate to one another, but each supreme in its own defined sphere, necessarily involved. The application of this principle made it possible not only to create a national government which should leave free scope for the working of the state governments, but also so to divide the powers of the national government among various persons and bodies as that none should absorb or overbear the others. By what machinery these objects were attained will appear when we come to consider the effect of a written or rigid constitution embodying a fundamental law, and the functions of the judiciary in expounding and applying such a law.[23]

---

[23] See *post* Chapters 23 and 33.

C H A P T E R   4

Nature of the Federal Government

The acceptance of the Constitution of 1789 made the American people a nation. It turned what had been a league of states into a federal state, by giving it a national government with a direct authority over all citizens. But as this national government was not to supersede the governments of the states, the problem which the Constitution-makers had to solve was twofold. They had to create a central government. They had also to determine the relations of this central government to the states as well as to the individual citizen. An exposition of the Constitution and criticism of its working must therefore deal with it in these two aspects, as a system of national government built up of executive powers and legislative bodies, like the monarchy of England or the republic of France, and as a federal system linking together and regulating the relations of a number of commonwealths which are for certain purposes, but for certain purposes only, subordinated to it. It will conduce to clearness if these two aspects are kept distinct; and the most convenient course will be to begin with the former, and first to describe the American system as a national system, leaving its federal character for the moment on one side.

It must, however, be remembered that the Constitution does not profess to be a complete scheme of government, creating organs for the discharge of all the functions and duties which a civilized community undertakes. It presupposes the state governments. It assumes their existence, their wide and constant activity. It is a scheme designed to provide for the discharge of such and so many functions of government as the states did not, and indeed could not, or at any rate could not adequately, possess and discharge. It is therefore, so to speak, the complement and crown of the state constitutions, which must be read along with it and into it in order to make it cover the whole field of civil government, as do the constitutions of such countries as France, Belgium, Italy.

The administrative, legislative, and judicial functions for which the federal Constitution provides are those relating to matters which must be deemed common to the whole nation, either because all the parts of the nation are alike interested in them, or because it is only by the nation as a whole that they can be satisfactorily undertaken. The chief of these common or national matters are:[1]

War and peace: treaties and foreign relations generally
Army and navy
Federal courts of justice
Commerce, foreign and between the several states
Currency
Copyright and patents
The post office and post roads
Taxation for the foregoing purposes, and for the general support of the government
The protection of citizens against unjust or discriminating legislation by any state[2]

This list includes the subjects upon which the national legislature has the right to legislate, the national executive to enforce the federal laws and generally to act in defence of national interests, the national judiciary to adjudicate. All other legislation and administration is left to the several states, without power of interference by the federal legislature or federal executive.

Such then being the sphere of the national government, let us see in what manner it is constituted, of what departments it consists.

The framers of this government set before themselves four objects as essential to its excellence, viz.:

---

[1] The full list will be found in the Constitution, art. I, § 8 (printed in the Appendix), with which may be compared the British North America Act 1867 (30 and 31 Vict. cap. 8), and the Federal Council of Australasia Act 1885 (48 and 49 Vict. cap. 60), and the Swiss Constitution of 1874 (arts. 8, 22, 30, 42, 54, 64, 67-70), the Constitution of the Commonwealth of Australia, drafted by an Australian convention and enacted in 1900 by the Imperial Parliament in the Commonwealth of Australia Act of that year and the (much more unitary) Constitution of the South African Union, passed as an act of the Imperial Parliament in 1910.
[2] Amendments XIV and XV.

Its vigour and efficiency

The independence of each of its departments (as being essential to the permanency of its form)

Its dependence on the people

The security under it of the freedom of the individual

The first of these objects they sought by creating a strong executive, the second by separating the legislative, executive, and judicial powers from one another, and by the contrivance of various checks and balances, the third by making all authorities elective and elections frequent, the fourth both by the checks and balances aforesaid, so arranged as to restrain any one department from tyranny, and by placing certain rights of the citizen under the protection of the written Constitution.

They had neither the rashness nor the capacity necessary for constructing a constitution a priori. There is wonderfully little genuine inventiveness in the world, and perhaps least of all has been shown in the sphere of political institutions. These men, practical politicians who knew how infinitely difficult a business government is, desired no bold experiments. They preferred, so far as circumstances permitted, to walk in the old paths, to follow methods which experience had tested.[3] Accordingly they started from the system on which their own colonial governments, and afterwards their state governments, had been conducted. This system bore a general resemblance to the British Constitution; and in so far it may with truth be said that the British Constitution became a model for the new national government. They held England to be the freest and best-governed country in the world, but were resolved to avoid the weak points which had enabled King George III to play the tyrant, and which rendered English liberty, as they thought, far inferior to that which the constitutions of their own states secured. With this venerable mother, and these children, better in their judgment than the mother, before their eyes, they created an executive magistrate, the president, on the model of the state governor, and of the British Crown. They created a legislature of two houses, Congress, on the model of the two houses of their state legislatures, and of the British Parliament. And following the precedent of the British judges, irremovable

[3] J.R. Lowell has said with equal point and truth of the men of the Convention: "They had a profound disbelief in theory and knew better than to commit the folly of breaking with the past. They were not seduced by the French fallacy that a new system of government could be ordered like a new suit of clothes. They would as soon have thought of ordering a suit of flesh and skin. It is only on the roaring loom of time that the stuff is woven for such a vesture of their thought and experience as they were meditating."—Address on Democracy, delivered Oct. 6, 1884.

except by the Crown and Parliament combined, they created a judiciary appointed for life, and irremovable save by impeachment.[4]

In these great matters, however, as well as in many lesser matters, they copied not so much the Constitution of England as the constitutions of their several states, in which, as was natural, many features of the English Constitution had been embodied. It has been truly said that nearly every provision of the federal Constitution that has worked well is one borrowed from or suggested by some state constitution; nearly every provision that has worked badly is one which the Convention, for want of a precedent, was obliged to devise for itself. To insist on this is not to detract from the glory of that illustrious body, for if we are to credit them with less inventiveness than has sometimes been claimed for them, we must also credit them with a double portion of the wisdom which prefers experience to a priori theory, and the sagacity which selects the best materials from a mass placed before it, aptly combining them to form a new structure.[5]

Of minor divergences between their work and the British Constitution I shall speak subsequently. But one profound difference must be noted here. The British Parliament had always been, was then, and remains now, a sovereign and constituent assembly. It can make and unmake any and every law, change the form of government or the succession to the Crown, interfere with the course of justice, extinguish the most sacred private rights of the citizen. Between it and the people at large there is no legal distinction, because the whole plenitude of the people's rights and powers resides in it, just as if the whole nation were present within the chamber where it sits. In point of legal theory it is the nation, being the historical successor of the Folk Moot of our Teutonic forefathers. Both practically and legally, it is today the only and the sufficient depository of the authority of the nation; and is therefore, within the sphere of law, irresponsible and omnipotent.

In the American system there exists no such body. Not merely Congress alone, but also Congress and the president conjoined, are subject to the Constitution, and cannot move a step outside the circle which the Constitution has drawn around them. If they do, they transgress the law and exceed their powers. Such acts as they may do in excess of their powers are void, and

---

[4] Minor differences between the English and American systems are that the American federal judge is appointed by the president, "with the advice and consent of the Senate," an English judge by the Crown alone: an American judge is impeachable by the House of Representatives, and tried by the Senate, an English judge is removable by the Crown on an address by both houses.

[5] See note to this chapter in the Appendix for further remarks on the influence of the state constitutions.

may be, indeed ought to be, treated as void by the meanest citizen. The only power which is ultimately sovereign, as the British Parliament is always and directly sovereign, is the people of the states, acting in the manner prescribed by the Constitution, and capable in that manner of passing any law whatever in the form of a constitutional amendment.

This fundamental divergence from the British system is commonly said to have been forced upon the men of 1787 by the necessity, in order to safeguard the rights of the several states, of limiting the competence of the national government.[6] But even supposing there had been no states to be protected, the jealousy which the American people felt of those whom they chose to govern them, their fear lest one power in the government should absorb the rest, their anxiety to secure the primordial rights of the citizens from attack, either by magistrate or by legislature, would doubtless have led, as happened with the earlier constitutions of revolutionary France, to the creation of a supreme constitution or fundamental instrument of government, placed above and controlling the national legislature itself. They had already such fundamental instrument in the charters of the colonies, which had passed into the constitutions of the several states; and they would certainly have followed, in creating their national constitution, a precedent which they deemed so precious.

The subjection of all the ordinary authorities and organs of government to a supreme instrument expressing the will of the sovereign people, and capable of being altered by them only, has been usually deemed the most remarkable novelty of the American system. But it is merely an application to the wider sphere of the nation, of a plan approved by the experience of the several states. And the plan had, in these states, been the outcome rather of a slow course of historical development than of conscious determination taken at any one point of their progress from petty settlements to powerful republics. Nevertheless, it may well be that the minds of the leaders who guided this development were to some extent influenced and inspired by recollections of the English Commonwealth of the seventeenth century, which had seen the establishment, though for a brief space only, of a genuine supreme or rigid constitution, in the form of the famous Instrument of Government of 1653, and some of whose sages had listened to the discourses in which James Harrington, one of the most prescient minds of

---

[6] It is often assumed by writers on constitutional subjects that a federal government presupposes a written or rigid constitution. This is not necessarily so. There may be, and have been, federations with no fundamental law unalterable by the usual legislative authority. The Achæan League had apparently none.

that great age, showed the necessity for such a constitution, and laid down its principles, suggesting that, in order to give it the higher authority, it should be subscribed by the people themselves.

We may now proceed to consider the several departments of the national government. It will be simplest to treat of each separately, and then to examine the relations of each to the others, reserving for subsequent chapters an account of the relations of the national government as a whole to the several states.

C H A P T E R   5

The President

Everyone who undertakes to describe the American system of government is obliged to follow the American division of it into the three departments—executive, legislative, judicial. I begin with the executive, as the simplest of the three.

The president is the creation of the Constitution of 1789. Under the Confederation there was only a presiding officer of Congress, but no head of the nation.

Why was it thought necessary to have a president at all? The fear of monarchy, of a strong government, of a centralized government, prevailed widely in 1787. George III was an object of bitter hatred: he remained a bogey to succeeding generations of American children. The Convention found it extremely hard to devise a satisfactory method of choosing the president, nor has the method they adopted proved satisfactory. That a single head is not necessary to a republic might have been suggested to the Americans by those ancient examples to which they loved to recur. The experience of modern Switzerland has made it still more obvious to us now. Yet it was settled very early in the debates of 1787 that the central executive authority must be vested in one person; and the opponents of the draft Constitution, while quarrelling with his powers, did not accuse his existence.

The explanation is to be found not so much in the wish to reproduce the British Constitution as in the familiarity of the Americans, as citizens of the several states, with the office of state governor (in some states then called president) and in their disgust with the feebleness which Congress had shown under the Confederation in its conduct of the war, and, after peace was concluded, of the general business of the country. Opinion called for a man, because an assembly had been found to lack promptitude and vigour. And it may be conjectured that the alarms felt as to the danger from one man's predominance were largely allayed by the presence of George Washington. Even while the debates were proceeding, everyone must have thought of him as the proper person to preside over the Union as he was then presiding over the Convention. The creation of the office would seem justified by the existence of a person exactly fitted to fill it, one whose established influence and ripe judgment would repair the faults then supposed to be characteristic of democracy, its impulsiveness, its want of respect for authority, its incapacity for pursuing a consistent line of action.

Hamilton felt so strongly the need for having a vigorous executive who could maintain a continuous policy, as to propose that the head of the state should be appointed for good behaviour, i.e., for life, subject to removal by impeachment. The proposal was disapproved, though it received the support of persons so democratically minded as Madison and Edmund Randolph; but nearly all sensible men, including many who thought better of democracy than Hamilton himself did, admitted that the risks of foreign war, risks infinitely more serious in the infancy of the Republic than they have subsequently proved, required the concentration of executive powers into a single hand. And the fact that in every one of their commonwealths there existed an officer in whom the state constitution vested executive authority, balancing him against the state legislature, made the establishment of a federal chief magistrate seem the obvious course.

Assuming that there was to be such a magistrate, the statesmen of the Convention, like the solid practical men they were, did not try to construct him out of their own brains, but looked to some existing models. They therefore made an enlarged copy of the state governor, or to put the same thing differently, a reduced and improved copy of the English king. He is George III shorn of a part of his prerogative by the intervention of the Senate in treaties and appointments, of another part by the restriction of his action to federal affairs, while his dignity as well as his influence are diminished by his holding office for four years instead of for life.[1] His salary is too small to permit him either to maintain a court or to corrupt the legislature; nor can he seduce the virtue of the citizens by the gift of titles of nobility, for such titles are altogether forbidden. Subject to these

---

[1] When the Romans got rid of their king, they did not really extinguish the office, but set up in their consul a sort of annual king, limited not only by the short duration of his power, but also by the existence of another consul with equal powers. So the Americans hoped to restrain their president not merely by the shortness of his term, but also by diminishing the power which they left to him; and this they did by setting up another authority to which they entrusted certain executive functions, making its consent necessary to the validity of certain classes of the president's executive acts. This is the Senate, whereof more anon.

precautions, he was meant by the Constitution-framers to resemble the state governor and the British king, not only in being the head of the executive, but in standing apart from and above political parties. He was to represent the nation as a whole, as the governor represented the state commonwealth. The independence of his position, with nothing either to gain or to fear from Congress, would, it was hoped, leave him free to think only of the welfare of the people.

This idea appears in the method provided for the election of a president. To have left the choice of the chief magistrate to a direct popular vote over the whole country would have raised a dangerous excitement, and would have given too much encouragement to candidates of merely popular gifts. To have entrusted it to Congress would have not only subjected the executive to the legislature in violation of the principle which requires these departments to be kept distinct, but have tended to make him the creature of one particular faction instead of the choice of the nation. Hence the device of a double election was adopted, perhaps with a faint reminiscence of the methods by which the doge was then still chosen at Venice and the emperor in Germany. The Constitution directs each state to choose a number of presidential electors equal to the number of its representatives in both houses of Congress. Some weeks later, these electors meet in each state on a day fixed by law, and give their votes in writing for the president and vice-president.[2] The votes are transmitted, sealed up, to the capital and there opened by the president of the Senate in the presence of both houses and counted. To preserve the electors from the influence of faction, it is provided that they shall not be members of Congress, nor holders of any federal office. This plan was expected to secure the choice by the best citizens of each state, in a tranquil and deliberate way, of the man whom they in their unfettered discretion should deem fittest to be chief magistrate of the Union. Being themselves chosen electors on account of their personal merits, they would be better qualified than the masses to select an able and honourable man for president. Moreover, as the votes are counted promiscuously, and not by states, each elector's voice would have its weight. He might be in a minority in his own state, but his vote would nevertheless tell because it would be added to those given by electors in other states for the same candidate.

No part of their scheme seems to have been regarded by the Constitution-

---

[2] Originally the person who received most votes was deemed to have been chosen president, and the person who stood second, vice-president. This led to confusion, and was accordingly altered by the twelfth constitutional amendment, adopted in 1804, which provides that the president and vice-president shall be voted for separately.

makers of 1787 with more complacency than this,[3] although no part had caused them so much perplexity. No part has so utterly belied their expectations. The presidential electors have become a mere cog-wheel in the machine; a mere contrivance for giving effect to the decision of the people. Their personal qualifications are a matter of indifference. They have no discretion, but are chosen under a pledge—a pledge of honour merely, but a pledge which has never (since 1796) been violated—to vote for a particular candidate. In choosing them the people virtually choose the president, and thus the very thing which the men of 1787 sought to prevent has happened—the president is chosen by a popular vote. Let us see how this has come to pass.

In the first two presidential elections (in 1789 and 1792) the independence of the electors did not come into question, because everybody was for Washington, and parties had not yet been fully developed. Yet in the election of 1792 it was generally understood that electors of one way of thinking were to vote for Clinton as their second candidate (i.e, for vice-president) and those of the other side for John Adams. In the third election (1796) no pledges were exacted from electors, but the election contest in which they were chosen was conducted on party lines, and although, when the voting by the electors arrived, some few votes were scattered among other persons, there were practically only two presidential candidates before the country, John Adams and Thomas Jefferson, for the former of whom the electors of the Federalist party, for the latter those of the Republican (Democratic)[4] party were expected to vote. The fourth election was a regular party struggle, carried on in obedience to party arrangements. Both Federalists and Republicans put the names of their candidates for president and vice-president before the country, and round these names the battle raged. The notion of leaving any freedom or discretion to the electors had vanished, for it was felt that an issue so great must and could be decided by the nation alone. From that day till now there has never been any question of reviving the true and original intent of the plan of double election. Even in 1876 the suggestion that the disputed election might be settled by leaving the electors free to choose, found no favor. Hence nothing has ever turned on the

---

[3] "The mode of appointment of the chief magistrate of the United States is almost the only part of the system which has escaped without some censure, or which has received the slightest mark of approbation from its opponents." *Federalist*, No. 68, cf. No. 1. And see the observations of Mr. Wilson in the Convention of Pennsylvania, Elliot's *Debates*, vol. ii.

[4] The party then called Republican has, since about 1830–40, been called Democratic. The party now called Republican did not arise till 1854.

personality of the electors. They are now so little significant that to enable the voter to know for which set of electors his party desires him to vote, it is often thought well to put the name of the presidential candidate whose interest they represent at the top of the voting ticket on which their own names are printed. Nor need this extinction of the discretion of the electors be regretted, because what has happened in somewhat similar cases makes it certain that the electors would have so completely fallen under the control of the party organizations as to vote simply at the bidding of the party managers. Popular election is therefore, whatever may be its defects, a healthier method, for it enables the people to reject candidates whom the low morality of party managers would approve.

The completeness and permanence of this change has been assured by the method which now prevails of choosing the electors. The Constitution leaves the method to each state, and in the earlier days many states entrusted the choice to their legislatures. But as democratic principles became developed, the practice of choosing the electors by direct popular vote, originally adopted by Virginia, Pennsylvania, and Maryland, spread by degrees through the other states, till by 1832 South Carolina was the only state which retained the method of appointment by the legislature. She dropped it in 1868, and popular election now rules everywhere, though any state may go back to the old plan if it pleases.[5] In some states the electors were for a time chosen by districts, like members of the House of Representatives. But the plan of choice by a single popular vote over the whole of the state found increasing favour, seeing that it was in the interest of the party for the time being dominant in the state. In 1828 Maryland was the only state which clung to district voting. She, too, adopted the "general ticket" system in 1832, since which year it was universal until 1891, when Michigan reverted to the district system, the party then dominant in her legislature conceiving that they would thereby secure some districts, and therefore some electors of their own colour, although they could not carry the state as a whole.[6] (This in fact happened in 1892). Thus the issue comes directly before the people. The parties nominate their respective candidates, as hereafter described (Chapters 69 and 70), a tremendous "campaign" of stump speaking, newspaper writing, street parades, and torchlight processions sets in and rages for about four months: the polling for electors takes place

---

[5] Colorado, not having time, after her admission to the Union in 1876, to provide by law for a popular choice of electors to vote in the election of a president in the November of that year, left the choice to the legislature, but now elects its presidential electors by popular vote like the other states.

[6] In 1893 this law was repealed and the "general ticket" system restored.

early in November, on the same day over the whole Union, and when the result is known the contest is over, because the subsequent meeting and voting of the electors in their several states is mere matter of form.

So far the method of choice by electors may seem to be merely a roundabout way of getting the judgment of the people. It is more than this. It has several singular consequences, unforeseen by the framers of the Constitution. It has made the election virtually an election by states, for the system of choosing electors by "general ticket" over the whole state causes the whole weight of a state to be thrown into the scale of one candidate, that candidate whose list of electors is carried in the given state.[7] In the election of 1884, New York State had thirty-six electoral votes. Each party ran its list or "ticket" of thirty-six presidential electors for the state, who were bound to vote for the party's candidate, Mr. Blaine or Mr. Cleveland. The Democratic list (i.e., that which included the thirty-six Cleveland electors) was carried by a majority of 1,100 out of a total poll exceeding 1,100,000. Thus, all the thirty-six electoral votes of New York were secured for Mr. Cleveland, and these thirty-six determined the issue of the struggle over the whole Union, in which nearly 10,000,000 popular votes were cast. The hundreds of thousands of votes given in New York for the Blaine or Republican list did not go to swell the support which Mr. Blaine obtained in other states, but were utterly lost. Hence in a presidential election, the struggle concentrates itself in the doubtful states, where the great parties are pretty equally divided, and is languid in states where a distinct majority either way may be anticipated, because, since it makes no difference whether a minority be large or small, it is not worth while to struggle hard to increase a minority which cannot be turned into a majority. And hence also a man may be, and has been,[8] elected president by a minority of popular votes.

---

[7] A list is usually carried entire if carried at all, because it would be foolish for the partisans of a candidate to vote for some only and not for all of the electors whose only function is to vote for him. However, the electors on a ticket seldom receive exactly the same number of popular votes; and thus it sometimes happens that when the election is close, one or two electors of the beaten party find their way in. In California in 1880 one out of the six electors in the Democratic ticket, being personally unpopular, failed to be carried, though the other five were. Similarly in California, Ohio, and Oregon in 1892 one elector belonging to the defeated list was chosen, and in North Dakota, was presented the surprising spectacle of the Republican, Democratic, and "Populist" parties each winning one elector. In the election of 1908 Maryland chose six Democratic and two Republican electors.

[8] This happened in 1876, when Mr. Hayes received, on the showing of his own partisans, 252,000 popular votes less than those given for Mr. Tilden; and in 1888, when Mr. Harrison was 95,534 popular votes behind Mr. Cleveland.

It is an odd result of the system that the bestowal of the suffrage on the Negroes has operated against the Republican party which bestowed it. The Southern states received in respect of this

When such has been the fate of the plan of 1787, it need hardly be said that the ideal president, the great and good man above and outside party, whom the judicious and impartial electors were to choose, has not been secured. The ideal was realized once and once only in the person of George Washington. His successor in the chair (John Adams) was a leader of one of the two great parties then formed, the other of which has, with some changes, lasted down to our own time. Jefferson, who came next, was the chief of that other party, and his election marked its triumph. Nearly every subsequent president has been elected as a party leader by a party vote, and has felt bound to carry out the policy of the men who put him in power.[9] Thus instead of getting an Olympian president raised above faction, America has, despite herself, reproduced the English system of executive government by a party majority, reproduced it in a more extreme form, because in England the titular head of the state, in whose name administrative acts are done, stands in isolated dignity outside party politics. The disadvantages of the American plan are patent; but in practice they are less serious than might be expected, for the responsibility of a great office and the feeling that he represents the whole nation have tended to sober and control the president. Except as regards patronage, he has seldom acted as a mere tool of faction, or sought to abuse his administrative powers to the injury of his political adversaries.

The Constitution prescribes no limit for the reeligibility of the president. He may go on being chosen for one four year period after another for the term of his natural life. But tradition has supplied the place of law. Elected in 1789, Washington submitted to be reelected in 1792. But when he had served his second term he absolutely refused to serve a third, urging the risk to republican institutions of suffering the same man to continue constantly in office. Jefferson, Madison, Monroe, and Jackson obeyed the precedent, and did not seek, nor their friends for them, reelection after two terms. After them no president was reelected, except Lincoln, down to General Grant. Grant was president from 1869 to 1873, and again from 1873 to 1877, then came Mr. Hayes; and in 1880 an attempt was made to break the unwritten rule in Grant's favour. Each party, as will be more fully explained

---

increase in their free population 37 additional presidential votes, and these were in the elections of 1880, 1884, 1888, and 1892, all thrown for the Democratic candidate.

[9] James Monroe was chosen president in 1820 with practical unanimity; but this was because one of the two parties had for the time been crushed out and started no candidate. So also J.Q. Adams, Monroe's successor, can hardly be called a party leader. After him the party-chosen presidents go on without interruption.

hereafter, nominates its candidates in a gigantic party assembly called the national convention. In the Republican party convention of 1880 a powerful group for the delegates put forward Grant for nomination as the party candidate, alleging his special services as a ground for giving him the honour of a third term. Had there not been among the Republicans themselves a section personally hostile to Grant, or rather to those who surrounded him, the attempt might have succeeded, though it would probably have involved defeat at the polls. But this hostile section found the prepossession of the people against a third term so strong that, by appealing to the established tradition, they defeated Grant in the convention, and nominated Mr. Garfield, who was victorious at the ensuing election. This precedent was at that time taken as practically decisive for the future, because General Grant, though his administration had been marked by grave faults, was an exceptionally popular figure. A principle affirmed against him seemed not likely to be departed from in favour of any aspirant for many elections to come. And in 1912 a large body of seceders from the National Republican Convention held a convention of their own which nominated Mr. Roosevelt who had served two terms all but a few months.

The Constitution (amend. XII, which in this point repeats the original art. XI, § 1) requires for the choice of a president "a majority of the whole number of electors appointed." If no such majority is obtained by any candidate, i.e, if the votes of the electors are so scattered among different candidates, that out of the total number (which in 1912 was 529, and will increase as new members are added to the Senate and the House) no one receives an absolute majority (i.e, at least 265 votes), the choice goes over to the House of Representatives, who are empowered to choose a president from among the three candidates who have received the largest number of electoral votes. In the House the vote is taken by states, a majority of all the states (i.e, at present of twenty-five states out of forty-eight) being necessary for a choice. As all the members of the House from a state have but one collective vote, it follows that if they are equally divided among themselves, the vote of that state is lost. Supposing this to be the case in half the total number of states, or supposing the states so to scatter their votes that no candidate receives an absolute majority, then no president is chosen, and the vice-president (supposing one to have been chosen) becomes president.

Only twice has the election gone to the House. In 1800, when the rule still prevailed that the candidate with the largest number of votes became president, and the candidate who came second vice-president, Jefferson and

Aaron Burr received the same number. The Jeffersonian electors meant to make him president, but as they had also all voted for Burr, there was a tie. After a long struggle the House chose Jefferson. Feeling ran high, and had Jefferson been kept out by the votes of the Federalist party, who hated him more than Burr, his partisans might possibly have taken up arms.[10] In 1824 Andrew Jackson had 99 electoral votes, and his three competitors (J. Q. Adams, Crawford, and Clay) 162 votes between them. The House chose J. Q. Adams by a vote of thirteen states against seven for Jackson and four for Crawford.[11] In this mode of choice, the popular will may be still less recognized than it is by the method of voting through presidential electors, for if the twenty-five smaller states were through their representatives in the House to vote for candidate A, and the twenty-three larger states for candidate B, A would be seated, though the population of the former set of states is, of course, very much below that of the latter.

The Constitution seems, though its language is not explicit, to have intended to leave the counting of the votes to the president of the Senate (the vice-president of the United States); and in early days this officer superintended the count, and decided questions as to the admissibility of doubtful votes. However, Congress has in virtue of its right to be present at the counting assumed the further right of determining all questions which arise regarding the validity of electoral votes, and has, it need hardly be said, determined them on each occasion from party motives. This would be all very well were a decision by Congress always certain of attainment. But it often happens that one party has a majority in the Senate, another party in the House, and then, as the two houses vote separately and each differently from the other, a deadlock results. I must pass by the minute and often tedious controversies which have arisen on these matters. But one case deserves special mention, for it illustrates an ingrained and formidable weakness of the present electoral system.

In 1876, Mr. Hayes was the Republican candidate for the presidency, Mr. Tilden the Democratic. The former carried his list of electors in seventeen states, whose aggregate electors numbered 163, and the latter carried his list also in 17 states, whose aggregate electors numbered 184. (As the total number of electors was then 369, 184 was within one of being

---

[10] The votes of two states were for a long time divided; but Hamilton's influence at last induced the Federalist members to abstain from voting against Jefferson, whom he thought less dangerous than Burr. His action—highly patriotic, for Jefferson was his bitter enemy—cost him his life at Burr's hands.

[11] Clay, unlucky throughout in his ambitions for the presidency, had stood fourth in the electoral vote, and so could not be chosen by the House. Jackson had received the largest popular vote in those states where electors were chosen by the people.

a half of that number.) Four states remained out of the total thirty-eight, and in each of these four two sets of persons had been chosen by popular vote, each set claiming, on grounds too complicated to be here explained, to be the duly chosen electors from those states respectively.[12] The electoral votes of these four states amounted to twenty-two, so that if in any one of them the Democratic set of electors had been found to have been duly chosen, the Democrats would have secured a majority of electoral votes, whereas even if in all of them Republican electors had been chosen, the Republican electors would have had a majority of one only. In such circumstances the only course for the Republican leaders, as good party men, was to claim all these doubtful states. This they promptly did—party loyalty is the last virtue that deserts politicians—and the Democrats did the like.

Meanwhile the electors met and voted in their respective states. In the four disputed states the two sets of electors met, voted, and sent up to Washington, from each of these four, double returns of the electoral votes. The result of the election evidently depended on the question which set of returns should be admitted as being the true and legal returns from the four states respectively. The excitement over the whole Union was intense, and the prospect of a peaceful settlement remote, for the Constitution appeared to provide no means of determining the legal questions involved. Congress, as remarked above, had in some previous instances assumed jurisdiction, but seeing that the Republicans had a majority in the Senate, and the Democrats in the House of Representatives, it was clear that the majority in one House would vote for admitting the Republican returns, the majority in the other for admitting the Democratic. Negotiations between the leaders at last arranged a method of escape. A statute was passed creating an electoral commission of five senators, five members of the House of Representatives, and five justices of the Supreme Court, who were to determine all questions as to the admissibility of electoral votes from states sending up double returns.[13] Everything now turned on the composition of the electoral commission, a body such as had never before been created.

---

[12] In Oregon the question was whether one of the chosen electors was disqualified because he was a postmaster. In Florida there were complaints of fraud, in South Carolina of intimidation, in Louisiana two rival state governments existed, each claiming the right to certify electoral returns. There had doubtless been a good deal of fraud and some violence in several of the Southern states.

[13] Power was reserved to Congress to set aside by a vote of both houses the decisions of the commission, but as the two houses differed in every case, the Democrats of the House always voting against each determination of the commission, and the Republicans of the Senate supporting it, this provision made no difference.

The Senate appointed three Republicans and two Democrats. The House of Representatives appointed three Democrats and two Republicans. So far there was an exact balance. The statute had indicated four of the justices who were to sit, two Republicans and two Democrats, and had left these four to choose a fifth. This fifth was the odd man whose casting vote would turn the scale. The four justices chose a Republican justice, and this choice practically settled the result, for every vote given by the members of the commission was a strict party vote.[14] They were nearly all lawyers, and had all taken an oath of impartiality. The legal questions were so difficult, and for the most part so novel, that it was possible for a sound lawyer and honest man to take in each case either the view for which the Republicans or that for which the Democrats contended. Still it is interesting to observe that the legal judgment of every commissioner happened to coincide with his party proclivities.[15] All the points in dispute were settled by a vote of eight to seven in favour of the returns transmitted by the Republican electors in the four disputed states, and Mr. Hayes was accordingly declared duly elected by a majority of 185 electoral votes against 184. The decision may have been right as matter of law—it is still debated by lawyers—and there had been so much force and fraud on both sides in Florida, Louisiana, and South Carolina, that no one can say on which side substantial justice lay. Mr. Tilden deserves the credit of having induced his friends both to agree to a compromise slightly to his own disadvantage, and to accept peaceably, though with long and loud complaints, a result which baffled their hopes. I tell the story here because it points to a grave danger in the presidential system. The stake played for is so high that the temptation to fraud is immense; and as the ballots given for the electors by the people are received and counted by state authorities under state laws, an unscrupulous state faction has opportunities for fraud at its command. In 1887 Congress, having had the subject pressed on its attention by successive presidents, took steps to provide against a recurrence of the danger described. It passed a statute enacting that tribunals appointed in and by each state shall determine what electoral votes from the state are legal votes; and that if the state has appointed no such tribunal, the two houses of Congress shall determine which votes (in case of double returns) are legal. If the houses differ the

[14] The commission decided unanimously that the Democratic set of electors from South Carolina were not duly chosen, but they divided eight to seven as usual on the question of recognizing the Republican electors of that state.

[15] The same phenomenon has been observed in committees of the English House of Commons appointed to deal with purely legal questions, or to sit in a virtually judicial capacity.

vote of the state is lost. It is, of course, possible under this plan that the state tribunal may decide unfairly; but the main thing is to secure some decision. Unfairness is better than uncertainty.

A president is removable during his term of office only by means of impeachment, a procedure familiar on both sides of the Atlantic in 1787, when the famous trial of Warren Hastings was still lingering on at Westminster. Impeachment, which had played no small part in the development of English liberties, was deemed by the Americans of those days a valuable element in their new Constitution, for it enabled Congress to depose, and the fear of it might be expected to restrain, a treasonably ambitious president. In obedience to state precedents,[16] it is by the House of Representatives that the president is impeached, and by the Senate, sitting as a law court, with the chief justice of the Supreme Court, the highest legal official of the country, as presiding officer, that he is tried. A two-thirds vote is necessary to conviction, the effect of which is simply to remove him from and disqualify him for office, leaving him "liable to indictment, trial, judgment, and punishment, according to law" (Constitution, art. I, § 3, art. II, § 4). The impeachable offences are "treason, bribery, or other high crimes and misdemeanours," an expression which some have held to cover only indictable offences, while others extend it to include acts done in violation of official duty and against the interests of the nation, such acts, in fact, as were often grounds for the English impeachments of the seventeenth century. As yet, Andrew Johnson is the only president who has been impeached. His headstrong conduct made his removal desirable, but as it was doubtful whether any single offence justified a conviction, several senators politically opposed to him voted for acquittal.[17] A two-thirds majority not having been secured upon any one article (the numbers being thirty-five for conviction, nineteen for acquittal) he was declared acquitted, a result now generally approved.

In case of the removal of a president by his impeachment, or of his death, resignation, or inability to discharge his duties, the vice-president steps into his place. The vice-president is chosen at the same time, by the same electors, and in the same manner as the president. His only functions are to

---

[16] Impeachment was taken, not directly from English usage, but rather from the constitutions of Virginia (1776), and Massachusetts (1780), which had, no doubt following the example of England, established this remedy against culpable officials.

[17] They may have doubted the expediency of displacing him at that moment; or their political prepossessions against him may have been restrained by a doubt whether the evidence was quite sufficient to support a quasi-criminal charge.

preside in the Senate and to succeed the president. Failing both president and vice-president it was formerly provided by statute, not by the Constitution, that the presiding officer for the time being of the Senate should succeed to the presidency, and, failing him, the Speaker of the House of Representatives. To this plan there was the obvious objection that it might throw power into the hands of the party opposed to that to which the lately deceased president belonged; and it has therefore been now (by an act of 1886) enacted that on the death of a president (including a vice-president who has succeeded to the presidency) the secretary of state shall succeed, and after him other officers of the administration, in the order of their rank. Five presidents (Harrison, Taylor, Lincoln, Garfield, McKinley) have died in office, the three latter killed by assassins, and been succeeded by vice-presidents, and in the first and third of these instances the succeeding vice-president has reversed the policy of his predecessor, and become involved in a quarrel with the party which elected him, such as has never yet broken out between a man elected to be president and his party. In practice very little pains are bestowed on the election of a vice-president. The convention which selects the party candidates usually gives the nomination to this post to a man in the second rank, sometimes as a consolation to a disappointed candidate for the presidential nomination, sometimes to a friend of such a disappointed candidate in order to "placate" his faction, sometimes to a person from whom large contributions to the campaign fund may be expected, sometimes as a compliment to an elderly leader who is personally popular, sometimes perhaps even to a man whom it is sought to shelve for the time being. If the party carries its candidate for president, it also as a matter of course carries its candidate for vice-president, and thus if the president happens to die, a man who may, like Tyler or Johnson, be of no great personal account, steps into the chief magistracy of the nation.

CHAPTER 6

Presidential Powers and Duties

The powers and duties of the president as head of the federal executive are the following:

Command of federal army and navy and of militia of several states when called into service of the United States

Power to make treaties, but with advice and consent of the Senate, i.e., consent of two-thirds of senators present;

to appoint ambassadors and consuls, judges of Supreme Court, and all other higher federal officers, but with advice and consent of Senate;

to grant reprieves and pardons for offences against the United States, except in cases of impeachment;

to convene both houses on extraordinary occasions;

to disagree with (i.e., to send back for reconsideration) any bill or resolution passed by Congress, but subject to the power of Congress to finally pass the same, after reconsideration, by a two-thirds majority in each house

Duty to inform Congress of the state of the Union, and to recommend measures to Congress;

to commission all the officers of the United States;

to receive foreign ambassadors;

to "take care that the laws be faithfully executed"

These functions group themselves into four classes:

Those which relate to foreign affairs
Those which relate to domestic administration
Those which concern legislation
The power of appointment

The conduct of foreign policy would have been a function of the utmost importance had not America, happy America, stood apart[1] down till 1898 in a world of her own, unassailable by European powers, easily superior to the other republics of her continent, but with no present motive for aggression upon them. The president, however, has rarely been allowed a free hand in foreign policy. He cannot declare war, for that belongs to Congress, though to be sure he may, as President Polk did in 1845-46, bring affairs to a point at which it is hard for Congress to refrain from the declaration. Treaties require the approval of two-thirds of the Senate; and in order to secure this, it is usually necessary for the executive to be in constant communication with the Foreign Affairs Committee of that body. The House of Representatives has no legal right to interfere, but it often passes resolutions enjoining or disapproving a particular line of policy; and sometimes invites the Senate to coincide in these expressions of opinion, which then become weightier. The president is nowise bound by such resolutions, and has more than once declared that he does not regard them. But as some treaties, especially commercial treaties, cannot be carried out except by the aid of statutes, and as no war can be entered on without votes of money, the House of Representatives can sometimes indirectly make good its claim to influence. Many delicate questions, some of them not yet decided, have arisen upon these points, which the Constitution has, perhaps unavoidably, left in half light. In all free countries it is most difficult to define the respective spheres of the legislature and executive in foreign affairs, for while publicity and parliamentary control are needed to protect the people, promptitude and secrecy are the conditions of diplomatic success. Practically, however, and for the purposes of ordinary business, the president is independent of the House, while the Senate, though it can prevent his settling anything, cannot keep him from unsettling everything. He, or possibly his secretary of state, if the president should not have leisure to give close or continuous attention to foreign policy, retains an unfettered initiative, by means of which he may embroil the country abroad or excite passion at home.

The direct domestic authority of the president is in time of peace very small, because by far the larger part of law and administration belongs to the state governments, and because federal administration is regulated by statutes which leave little discretion to the executive. In war time, however, and especially in a civil war, it expands with portentous speed. Both as commander in chief of the army and navy, and as charged with the "faithful

---

[1] As to the changed position since 1898, see Chap. 96, Vol. II.

execution of the laws," the president is likely to be led to assume all the powers which the emergency requires. How much he can legally do without the aid of statutes is disputed, for the acts of President Lincoln during the earlier part of the War of Secession, including his proclamation suspending the writ of habeas corpus, were subsequently legalized by Congress; but it is at least clear that Congress can make him, as it did make Lincoln, almost a dictator. And how much the war power may include appears in this, that by virtue of it and without any previous legislative sanction President Lincoln issued his emancipation proclamations of 1862 and 1863, declaring all slaves in the insurgent states to be thenceforth free, although these states were deemed to be in point of law still members of the Union.[2]

It devolves on the executive as well as on Congress to give effect to the provisions of the Constitution whereby a republican form of government is guaranteed to every state; and a state may, on the application of its legislature, or executive (when the legislature cannot be convened), obtain protection against domestic violence. Where, as in Louisiana in 1873, there are two governments disputing by force the control of a state, or where an insurrection breaks out, as in Rhode Island in 1840-42, or where riots stop the movement of mail trains on a railroad, as happened in Illinois in 1894, this power becomes an important one, for it involves the employment of troops, and may enable the president (since it is usually on him that the duty falls) to establish the government he prefers to recognize.[3] Fortunately the case has been one of rare occurrence.

The president has the right of speaking to the nation by addresses or proclamations, a right not expressly conferred by the Constitution, but

---

[2] The proclamation was expressed not to apply to states which had not seceded, nor to such parts of seceding states as had then already been reconquered by the Northern armies. Slavery was finally legally extinguished everywhere by the thirteenth constitutional amendment of 1865.

[3] In the Louisiana case federal troops were employed: in the Rhode Island case the president authorized the sending in of the militia of Massachusetts and Connecticut, but the Rhode Island troops succeeded in suppressing the rebellion, whose leader was ultimately convicted of high treason against the state and imprisoned. See as to the guarantee of order and republican government in the states, the case of *Luther* v. *Borden* (7 How. 42) and the instructive article of Judge T. M. Cooley in the *International Review* for January 1875. He observes: "The obligation to guarantee a republican form of government to the States, and to protect them against invasion and domestic violence, is one imposed upon 'the United States.' The implication is that the duty was not to depend for its fulfilment on the legislative department exclusively, but that all departments of the government, or at least more than one, were or might be charged with some duty in this regard. It has been Congress which hitherto has assumed to act upon the guarantee, while application for protection against domestic violence has, on the other hand, been made to the president. From the nature of the case the judiciary can have little or nothing to do with questions arising under this provision of the Constitution."

inherent in his position. Occasions requiring its exercise are uncommon. On entering office, it is usual for the new magistrate to issue an inaugural address, stating his views on current public questions. Washington also put forth a farewell address, but Jackson's imitation of that famous document was condemned as a piece of vainglory. It is thought bad taste for the president to go round on a political stumping tour, and Andrew Johnson injured himself by the practice. But he retains the right of making political speeches with all the other rights of the ordinary citizen, including that of voting at federal as well as state elections in his own state. He is constantly invited to speak on nonpartisan occasions, and he is free to confer with and advise the leaders of his own party.

The position of the president as respects legislation is a peculiar one. The king of England is a member of the English legislature, because Parliament is in theory his Great Council which he summons and in which he presides, hearing the complaints of the people, and devising legislative remedies.[4] It is as a member of the legislature that he assents to the bills it presents to him, and the term "veto power," since it seems to suggest an authority standing outside to approve or reject, does not happily describe his right of dealing with a measure which has been passed by the council over which he is deemed to preside, though he now no longer appears in it except at the beginning and ending of a session. The American president is not a member of either house of Congress. He is a separate authority whom the people, for the sake of protecting themselves against abuses of legislative power, have associated with the legislature for the special purpose of arresting its action by his disapproval.[5] So again the king of England can initiate legislation. According to the older Constitution, statutes purported to be made, and were till the middle of the fifteenth century actually made, by him, but "with the advice and consent of the Lords Spiritual and Temporal and of the Commons."[6] According to the modern practice, nearly all

---

[4] It need hardly be said that the actual separation of Parliament into two branches, each of which deliberates apart under the presidency of its own chairman (the chairman of one house named by the sovereign, whom he represents, that of the other chosen by the House, but approved by the sovereign), does not exclude the theory that the King, Lords, and Commons constitute the common council of the nation.

[5] The term "veto" was not used in the Convention of 1787: men talked of the president's "qualified negative."

[6] In the fourteenth century English statutes are expressed to be made by the king, "par conseil et par assentement" of the lords and the commonalty. The words "by the authority" of the Lords and Commons first appear in the eleventh year of Henry VI (1433), and from the first of Henry VII (1485) downwards a form substantially the same as the present is followed, viz.: "Be it

important measures are brought into Parliament by his ministers, and nominally under his instructions. The American president cannot introduce bills, either directly or through his ministers, for they do not sit in Congress.[7] All that the Constitution permits him to do in this direction is to inform Congress of the state of the nation, and to recommend the measures which his experience in administration shows to be necessary. This latter function is discharged by the messages which the president addresses to Congress. The most important is that sent by the hands of his private secretary at the beginning of each session.

George Washington used to deliver his addresses orally, like an English king, and drove in a coach and six to open Congress with something of an English king's state. But Jefferson, when his turn came in 1801, whether from republican simplicity, as he said himself, or because he was a poor speaker, as his critics said, began the practice of sending communications in writing; and this has been followed ever since. The message usually— for besides the long one at the opening of a congressional session, others are sent as occasion requires—discusses the leading questions of the moment, indicates mischiefs needing a remedy, and suggests the requisite legislation. There are however persons in Congress who view with jealousy the action of the executive, though justified by precedent, when a bill drafted by a member of the administration is laid before either house, and as no minister sits there to explain and defend bills and there may be no majority to pass them, the message may be a shot in the air without practical result. It is rather a manifesto, or declaration of opinion and policy, than a step towards legislation. Congress need not take action; members go their own ways and bring in their own bills.

Far more effective is the president's part in the last stage of legislation, for here he finds means provided for carrying out his will. When a bill is presented to him, he may sign it, and his signature makes it law. If,

---

enacted by the King's most excellent Majesty, by and with the advice and consent of the Lords Spiritual and Temporal, and Commons, and by the authority of the same."

[7] Nevertheless, the Congressional Globe for July 14, 1862, records that "The President (*pro tempore*) of the Senate presented the following message from the President of the United States: 'Fellow Citizens of the Senate and the House of Representatives: Herewith is the draft of a bill to compensate any State which may abolish slavery within its limits, the passage of which, substantially as presented, I respectfully and earnestly recommend. Abraham Lincoln.' " The bill was thereupon read a second time, and a debate arose as to whether the president had a right to submit bills. In the House the message as a whole was referred to the Special Committee on Emancipation.

however, he disapproves of it, he returns it within ten days to the house in which it originated, with a statement of his grounds of disapproval. If both houses take up the bill again and pass it by a two-thirds majority in each house, it becomes law forthwith without requiring the president's signature.[8] If it fails to obtain this majority it drops.

Considering that the arbitrary use, by George III and his colonial governors, of the power of refusing bills passed by a colonial legislature had been a chief cause of the Revolution of 1776, it is to the credit of the Americans that they inserted this apparently undemocratic provision (which, however, existed in the Constitution of Massachusetts of 1780) in the Constitution of 1789.[9] It has worked wonderfully well. Most presidents have employed it sparingly, and only where they felt either that there was a case for delay, or that the country would support them against the majority in Congress. Perverse or headstrong presidents have been generally defeated by the use of the two-thirds vote to pass the bill over their objections. Washington "returned" or vetoed two bills only; his successors down till 1830, seven. Jackson made a bolder use of his power—a use which his opponents denounced as opposed to the spirit of the Constitution; yet until the accession of President Cleveland in 1885 the total number vetoed was only 132 (including the so-called pocket vetoes) in ninety-six years.[10] From 1892 to the end of Mr. Roosevelt's second administration in 1909 there were 108 vetoes, making in all 541. In his first term Mr. Cleveland vetoed 301, the great majority being bills for granting pensions to persons who served in the Northern armies during the War of Secession. Though many of these bills had been passed with little or no opposition, two only were repassed over his veto. The only president who acted recklessly was Andrew

---

[8] If Congress adjourns within the ten days allowed the president for returning the bill, it is lost. His retaining it under these circumstances at the end of a session is popularly called a "pocket veto."

[9] The New York State Constitution of 1777 gave a veto to the governor and judges of the highest court acting together.

[10] Of these 132 (some reckon 128), 21 emanated from Johnson and 43 from Grant, while John Adams, Jefferson, J. Q. Adams, Van Buren, Taylor, and Fillmore sent no veto messages at all. (W. H. Harrison and Garfield died before they had any opportunity.) President McKinley vetoed 14 bills, President Roosevelt, 34. Among the most important vetoes were those of several Reconstruction bills by Johnson (these were repassed by two-thirds votes), that of a paper currency measure, the so-called Inflation Bill, by Grant, and that of the Dependent Pension Bill by Cleveland. No bill was passed "over a veto" until 1845. Until 1885 only 27 had been passed over a veto, 15 of these in the time of Johnson. Presidents have occasionally (e.g., Lincoln more than once) in signing a bill stated objections to it which Congress has thereupon obviated by supplementary legislation.

Johnson. In the course of his three years' struggle with Congress, he returned the chief bills passed for carrying out their Reconstruction policy, but as the majority opposed to him was large in both houses, these bills were promptly passed over his veto.

So far from exciting the displeasure of the people by resisting the will of their representatives, a president generally gains popularity by the bold use of his veto power. It conveys the impression of firmness; it shows that he has a view and does not fear to give effect to it. The nation, which has often good grounds for distrusting Congress, a body liable to be moved by sinister private influences, or to defer to the clamour of some noisy section outside, looks to the man of its choice to keep Congress in order, and has approved the extension which practice has given to the power. The president's "qualified negative" was proposed by the Convention of 1787 for the sake of protecting the Constitution, and in particular, the executive, from congressional encroachments. It has now come to be used on grounds of general expediency, to defeat any measure which the executive deems pernicious either in principle or in its probable results.

The reasons why the veto provisions of the Constitution have succeeded appear to be two. One is that the president, being an elective and not a hereditary magistrate, is responsible to the people, and has the weight of the people behind him. The people regard him as an indispensable check, not only upon the haste and heedlessness of their representatives, the faults which the framers of the Constitution chiefly feared, but upon their tendency, a tendency whose mischievous force experience has revealed, to yield either to pressure from any section of their constituents, or to temptations of a private nature. The other reason is that a veto need never take effect unless there is a substantial minority exceeding one-third in one or other house of Congress, which agrees with the president. Such a minority shares his responsibility and encourages him to resist the threats of a majority, while if he has no substantial support in public opinion, his opposition is easily overborne. Hence this arrangement is preferable to a plan, such as that of the French Constitution of 1791[11] (under which the king's veto could be overriden by passing a bill in three successive years), for enabling the executive simply to delay the passing of a measure which may be urgent, or which a vast majority of the legislature may desire. In its practical working the presidential veto power furnishes an interesting illustration of

---

[11] As the majority in France was unable to attain its will by constitutional means without waiting three years, it was the more disposed to overthrow the constitution.

the tendency of unwritten or flexible constitutions to depart from, of written or rigid constitutions to cleave to, the letter of the law. The strict legal theory of the rights of the head of the state is in this point exactly the same in England and in America. But whereas it is now the undoubted duty of an English king to assent to every bill passed by both houses of Parliament, however strongly he may personally disapprove its provisions,[12] it is the no less undoubted duty of an American president to exercise his independent judgment on every bill, not sheltering himself under the representatives of the people, or foregoing his own opinion at their bidding.[13]

As the president is charged with the whole federal administration, and responsible for its due conduct, he must of course be allowed to choose his executive subordinates. But as he may abuse this tremendous power the Constitution associates the Senate with him, requiring the "advice and consent" of that body to the appointments he makes.[14] This confirming power has become a political factor of the highest moment. The framers of the Constitution probably meant nothing more than that the Senate should check the president by rejecting nominees who were personally unfit for the post to which he proposed to appoint them. The Senate has always, except in its struggle with President Johnson, left the president free to

---

[12] Queen Elizabeth, in 1597, assented to forty-three bills passed in that session, and "advised herself upon" forty-eight. William III refused to assent to five bills. The last instance of the use of the "veto power" in England was by Queen Anne in 1707 on a Scotch militia bill. Mr. Todd (*Parliamentary Government in the English Colonies*, vol. ii, p. 319) mentions that in 1858 changes in a private railway bill were compelled by an intimation to its promoters that, if they were not made, the royal power of rejection would be exercised.

[13] The practical disuse of the "veto power" in England is due not merely to the decline in the authority of the Crown, but to the fact that, since the Revolution, the Crown acts only on the advice of responsible ministers, who necessarily command a majority in the House of Commons. A bill therefore cannot be passed against the wishes of the ministry unless in the rare case of their being ministers on sufferance, and even in that event they would be able to prevent its passing by advising the Crown to prorogue or dissolve Parliament before it had gone through all its stages. In 1868 a bill (the Irish Church Suspension Bill) was carried through the House of Commons by Mr. Gladstone against the opposition of the then Tory ministry which was holding office on sufferance; but it was rejected on second reading by a large majority in the House of Lords. Had that House seemed likely to accept it the case would have arisen which I have referred to, and the only course for the ministry would have been to dissolve Parliament.

It was urged against the provision in the Constitution of 1789 for the president's veto that the power would be useless, because in England the Crown did not venture to use it. Wilson replied by observing that the English Crown had not only practically an antecedent negative, but also a means of defeating a bill in the House of Lords by creating new peers.—Elliot's *Debates*, vol. ii, p. 472.

[14] Congress is however permitted to vest in the president alone the appointment to such "inferior offices" as it thinks fit.

choose his cabinet ministers. But it early assumed the right of rejecting a nominee to any other office on any ground which it pleased, as for instance, if it disapproved his political affiliations, or wished to spite the president. Presently the senators from the state wherein a federal office to which the president had made a nomination lay, being the persons chiefly interested in the appointment, and most entitled to be listened to by the rest of the Senate when considering it, claimed to have a paramount voice in deciding whether the nomination should be confirmed. Their colleagues approving, they then proceeded to put pressure on the president. They insisted that before making a nomination to an office in any state he should consult the senators from that state who belonged to his own party, and be guided by their wishes. Such an arrangement benefited all senators alike, because each obtained the right of practically dictating the appointments to those federal offices which he most cared for, viz., those within the limits of his own state; and each was therefore willing to support his colleagues in securing the same right for themselves as regarded their states respectively. Of course when a senator belonged to the party opposed to the president, he had no claim to interfere, because places are as a matter of course given to party adherents only. When both senators belonged to the president's party they agreed among themselves as to the person whom they should require the president to nominate. By this system, which obtained the name of the "courtesy of the Senate", the president was practically enslaved as regards appointments, because his refusal to be guided by the senator or senators within whose state the office lay exposed him to have his nomination rejected. The senators, on the other hand, obtained a mass of patronage by means of which they could reward their partisans, control the federal civil servants of their state, and build up a faction devoted to their interests.[15] Successive presidents chafed under the yoke, and sometimes carried their nominees either by making a bargain or by fighting hard with the senators who sought to dictate to them. But it was generally more prudent to yield, for an offended senator could avenge a defeat by playing the president a shrewd trick in some other matter; and as the business of confirmation is transacted in secret session, intriguers have little fear of the public before their eyes. The senators might, moreover, argue that they knew best what would strengthen the party in their state, and that the men of their choice

[15] As the House of Representatives could not allow the Senate to engross all the federal patronage, there has been a tendency towards a sort of arrangement, according to which the greater state offices belong to the senators, while as regards the lesser ones, lying within their respective Congressional districts, members of the House are recognized as entitled to recommend candidates.

were just as likely to be good as those whom some private friend suggested to the president. Thus the system throve and still thrives, though it received a blow from the conflict in 1881 between President Garfield and one of the New York senators, Mr. Roscoe Conkling. This gentleman, finding that Mr. Garfield would not nominate to a federal office in that state the person he proposed, resigned his seat in the Senate, inducing his co-senator Mr. Platt to do the same. Both then offered themselves for reelection by the state legislature of New York, expecting to obtain from it an approval of their action, and thereby to cow the president. The state legislature, however, in which a faction hostile to the two senators had become powerful, rejected Mr. Conkling and Mr. Platt in favour of other candidates. So the victory remained with Mr. Garfield, while the nation, which had watched the contest eagerly, rubbed its hands in glee at the unexpected denouement.

It need hardly be added that the "courtesy of the Senate" would never have attained its present strength but for the growth, in and since the time of President Jackson, of the so-called Spoils System, whereby holders of federal offices have been turned out at the accession of a new president to make way for the aspirants whose services, past or future, he is expected to requite or secure by the gift of places.[16]

The right of the president to remove from office has given rise to long controversies on which I can only touch. In the Constitution there is not a word about removals; and very soon after it had come into force the question arose whether, as regards those offices for which the confirmation of the Senate is required, the president could remove without its consent. Hamilton had argued in the *Federalist* (though there is reason to believe that he afterwards changed his opinion) that the president could not so remove, because it was not to be supposed that the Constitution meant to give him so immense and dangerous a reach of power. Madison argued soon after the adoption of the Constitution that it did permit him so to remove, because the head of the executive must have subordinates whom he can trust, and may discover in those whom he has appointed defects fatal to their usefulness. This was also the view of John Marshall. When the question came to be settled in the Senate during the presidency of Washington, Congress, influenced perhaps by respect for his perfect uprightness, took the Madisonian view and recognized the power of removal as vested in the president alone. So matters stood till a conflict arose in 1866 between President Johnson and the Republican majority in both houses of Congress. In 1867, Congress

---

[16] See next page, and see also Chap. 65, Vol. II.

fearing that the president would dismiss a great number of officials who sided with it against him, passed an act, known as the Tenure of Office Act, which made the consent of the Senate necessary to the removal of officeholders, even of the president's (so-called) cabinet ministers, permitting him only to suspend them from office during the time when Congress was not sitting. The constitutionality of this act has been much doubted, and its policy is now generally condemned. It was a blow struck in the heat of passion. When President Grant became president in 1869, the act was greatly modified, and in 1887 it was repealed.

How dangerous it is to leave all offices tenable at the mere pleasure of a partisan executive using them for party purposes, has been shown by the fruits of the Spoils System. On the other hand a president ought to be free to choose his chief advisers and ministers, and even in the lower ranks of the civil service it is hard to secure efficiency if a specific cause, such as could be proved to a jury, must be assigned for dismissal.

The Constitution permits Congress to vest in the courts of law or in "the heads of departments" the right of appointing to "inferior offices." This provision has been used to remove many posts from the nomination of the president, and by the Civil Service Reform Act of 1883 competitive examinations were instituted for about thirty-four thousand. Of the now enormous number of posts—there were, in 1909, 367,794 officers and employees of the executive civil service—nearly two-thirds were in that year subject to such examinations. A greater number, however, including many postmasterships and many places under the Treasury, remain in the gift of the president;[17] while even as regards those which lie with his ministers, he may be invoked if disputes arise between the minister and politicians pressing the claims of their respective friends. The business of nominating is in ordinary times so engrossing as to leave the chief magistrate of the nation little time for his other functions.

Artemus Ward's description of Abraham Lincoln swept along from room to room in the White House by a rising tide of office-seekers is hardly an exaggeration. From the 4th of March, when Mr. Garfield came into power, till he was shot in the July following, he was engaged almost incessantly in questions of patronage.[18] Yet the president's individual judgment has little

---

[17] Recently presidents have under the power given them by statute placed large groups of offices under the competitive system.

[18] It is related that a friend, meeting Mr. Lincoln one day during the war, observed, "You look anxious, Mr. President; is there bad news from the front?" "No," answered the president, "it isn't the war: it's that postmastership at Brownsville, Ohio."

scope. He must reckon with the Senate; he must requite the supporters of the men to whom he owes his election: he must so distribute places all over the country as to keep the local wire-pullers in good humour, and generally strengthen the party by "doing something" for those who have worked or will work for it. Although the minor posts are practically left to the nomination of the senators or congressmen from the state or district, conflicting claims give infinite trouble, and the more lucrative offices are numerous enough to make the task of selection laborious as well as thankless and disagreeable. In every country statesmen find the dispensing of patronage the most disagreeable part of their work; and the more conscientious they are, the more does it worry them. No one has more to gain from a thorough scheme of civil service reform than the president. The present system throws work on him unworthy of a fine intellect, and for which a man of fine intellect may be ill qualified. On the other hand the president's patronage is, in the hands of a skilful intriguer, an engine of far-spreading potency. By it he can oblige a vast number of persons, can bind their interests to his own, can fill important places with the men of his choice. Such authority as he has over the party in Congress, and therefore over the course of legislation, such influence as he exerts on his party in the several states, and therefore over the selection of candidates for Congress, is due to his patronage. Unhappily, the more his patronage is used for these purposes, the more it is apt to be diverted from the aim of providing the country with the best officials.

In quiet times the direct legal power of the president is not great, but his influence may be great if he combines tact with courage. He is hampered at every turn by the necessity of humouring his party. The trivial and mechanical parts of his work leave him too little leisure for framing large schemes of policy, while in carrying them out he needs the cooperation of Congress, which may be jealous, or indifferent, or hostile. His power to affect legislation largely depends on his personal capacity for leadership, and of course also on the strength of his party in Congress. In troublous times it is otherwise, for immense responsibility is then thrown on one who is both the commander in chief and the head of the civil executive. Abraham Lincoln wielded more authority than any single Englishman has done since Oliver Cromwell. It is true that the ordinary law was for some purposes practically suspended during the War of Secession. But it might again have to be similarly suspended, and the suspension makes the president a sort of dictator.

Setting aside these exceptional moments, the dignity and power of the presidential office, as distinguished from the personal influence which a particularly able or energetic president may exert, did not greatly grow between the time of Andrew Jackson, the last president who, not so much through his office as by his personal ascendency and the vehemence of his character, led and guided his party from the chair, and the death of President McKinley in 1901. Here, too, one sees how a rigid or supreme Constitution serves to keep things as they were. But for its iron hand, the office would surely, in a country where great events have been crowded on one another and opinion changes rapidly under the teaching of events, have either risen or fallen, have gained strength or lost it.

In no European country is there any personage to whom the president can be said to correspond. If we look at parliamentary countries like England, Italy, Belgium, he resembles neither the sovereign nor the prime minister, for·the former is not a party chief at all, and the latter is palpably and confessedly nothing else. The president enjoys more authority, if less dignity, than a European king. He has powers for the moment narrower than a European prime minister, but these powers are more secure, for they do not depend on the pleasure of a parliamentary majority, but run on to the end of his term. One naturally compares him with the French president, but the latter has a prime minister and cabinet, dependent on the chamber, at once to relieve and to eclipse him: in America the president's cabinet is a part of himself and has nothing to do with Congress. The president of the Swiss Confederation is merely the chairman for a year of the Administrative Federal Council (*Bundesrath*), and can hardly be called the executive chief of the nation.

The difficulty in forming a just estimate of the president's power arises from the fact that it differs so much under ordinary and under extraordinary circumstances. This is a result which republics might seem specially concerned to prevent, and yet it is specially frequent under republics, as witness the cases of Rome and of the Italian cities in the Middle Ages. In ordinary times the president may be compared to the senior or managing clerk in a large business establishment, whose chief function is to select his subordinates, the policy of the concern being in the hands of the board of directors. But when foreign affairs become critical, or when disorders within the Union require his intervention—when, for instance, it rests with him to put down an insurrection or to decide which of two rival state governments he will recognize and support by arms—everything may depend on his judgment, his courage, and his hearty loyalty to the principles of the Constitution.

It used to be thought that hereditary monarchs were strong because they reigned by a right of their own, not derived from the people. A president is strong for the exactly opposite reason, because his rights come straight from the people. We shall have frequent occasion to observe that nowhere is the rule of public opinion so complete as in America, or so direct; that is to say, so independent of the ordinary machinery of government. Now the president is deemed to represent the people no less than do the members of the legislature. Public opinion governs by and through him no less than them, and makes him powerful even against a popularly elected Congress. This is a fact to be remembered by those Europeans who seek in the strengthening of the hereditary principle a cure for the faults of government by assemblies. And it also suggests the risk that attaches to power vested in the hands of a leader directly chosen by the people. A high authority observes:[19]

> "Our holiday orators delight with patriotic fervour to draw distinctions between our own and other countries, and to declare that here the law is master and the highest officer but the servant of the law, while even in free England the monarch is irresponsible and enjoys the most complete personal immunity. But such comparisons are misleading, and may prove mischievous. In how many directions is not the executive authority in America practically superior to what it is in England! And can we say that the President is really in any substantial sense any more the servant of the law than is the Queen? Perhaps if we were candid we should confess that the danger that the executive may be tempted to a disregard of the law may justly be believed greater in America than in countries where the chief magistrate comes to his office without the selection of the people; and where consequently their vigilance is quickened by a natural distrust."

Although few presidents have shown any disposition to strain their authority, it has often been the fashion in America to be jealous of the president's action, and to warn citizens against what is called "the one man power." General Ulysses S. Grant was hardly the man to make himself a tyrant, yet the hostility to a third term of office which moved many people who had not been alienated by the faults of his administration, rested not

---

[19] Judge T. M. Cooley, in the *International Review* for Jan. 1875. He quotes the words of Edward Livingston: "The gloss of zeal for the public service is always spread over acts of oppression, and the people are sometimes made to consider that as a brilliant exertion of energy in their favour which, when viewed in its true light, would be found a fatal blow to their rights. In no government is this effect so easily produced as in a free republic; party spirit, inseparable from its existence, aids the illusion, and a popular leader is allowed in many instances impunity, and sometimes rewarded with applause, for acts which would make a tyrant tremble on his throne."

merely on reverence for the example set by Washington, but also on the fear that a president repeatedly chosen would become dangerous to republican institutions. This particular alarm seems to a European groundless. I do not deny that a really great man might exert ampler authority from the presidential chair than its recent occupants have done. The same observation applies to the popedom and even to the English throne. The president has a position of immense dignity, an unrivalled platform from which to impress his ideas (if he has any) upon the people. But it is hard to imagine a president overthrowing the existing Constitution. He has no standing army, and he cannot create one. Congress can checkmate him by stopping supplies. There is no aristocracy to rally round him. Every state furnishes an independent centre of resistance. If he were to attempt a coup d'état, it could only be by appealing to the people against Congress, and Congress could hardly, considering that it is reelected every two years, attempt to oppose the people. One must suppose a condition bordering on civil war, and the president putting the resources of the executive at the service of one of the intending belligerents, already strong and organized, in order to conceive a case in which he will be formidable to freedom. If there be any danger, it would seem to lie in another direction. The larger a community becomes the less does it seem to respect an assembly, the more is it attracted by an individual man. A bold president who knew himself to be supported by a majority in the country, might be tempted to override the law, and deprive the minority of the protection which the law affords it. He might be a tyrant, not against the masses, but with the masses. But nothing in the present state of American politics gives weight to such apprehensions.

Observations on the Presidency

Although the president has been, not that independent good citizen whom the framers of the Constitution contemplated, but, at least since 1829, a party man, seldom much above the average in character or abilities, the office has attained the main objects for which it was created. Such mistakes as have been made in foreign policy, or in the conduct of the administrative departments, have been rarely owing to the constitution of the office or to the errors of its holder. This is more than one who should review the history of Europe during the last hundred years could say of any European monarchy. Nevertheless, the faults chargeable on hereditary kingship, faults more serious than Englishmen, who have watched with admiration the wisdom of the Crown ever since the accession of Queen Victoria in 1837, usually realize, must not make us overlook certain defects incidental to the American presidency, perhaps to any plan of vesting the headship of the state in a person elected for a limited period.

In a country where there is no hereditary throne nor hereditary aristocracy, an office raised far above all other offices offers too great a stimulus to ambition. This glittering prize, always dangling before the eyes of prominent statesmen, has a power stronger than any dignity under a European crown to lure them (as it lured Clay and Webster) from the path of straightforward consistency. One who aims at the presidency—and all prominent politicians do aim at it—has the strongest possible motives to avoid making enemies. Now a great statesman ought to be prepared to make enemies. It is one thing to try to be popular—an unpopular man will be uninfluential—it is another to seek popularity by pleasing every section of your party. This is the temptation of presidential aspirants.

A second defect is that the presidential election, occurring once in four years, throws the country for several months into a state of turmoil, for which there may be no occasion. Perhaps there are no serious party issues to be decided, perhaps the best thing would be that the existing administration should pursue the even tenor of its way. The Constitution, however, requires an election to be held, so the whole costly and complicated machinery of agitation is put in motion; and if issues do not exist, they have to be created.[1] Professional politicians who have a personal interest in the result, because it involves the gain or loss of office to themselves, conduct what is called a "campaign," and the country is forced into a factitious excitement from midsummer, when each party selects the candidate whom it will nominate, to the first week of November, when the contest is decided. There is some political education in the process, but it is bought dearly, not to add that business, and especially finance, is disturbed, and much money spent unproductively.

Again, these regularly recurring elections produce a discontinuity of policy. Even when the new president belongs to the same party as his predecessor, he usually nominates a new cabinet, having to reward his especial supporters. Many of the inferior offices are changed; men who have learned their work make way for others who have everything to learn. If the new president belongs to the opposite party, the change of officials is far more sweeping, and involves larger changes of policy. The evil would be more serious were it not that in foreign policy, where the need for continuity is greatest, the United States have little to do, and that the cooperation of the Senate in this department qualifies the divergence of the ideas of one president from those of another.

Fourthly. The fact that he has been deemed reeligible once, but (practically) only once (at least in continuation of his existing term[2]), has operated unfavourably on the president. He is tempted to play for a renomination by pandering to sections of his own party, or using his patronage to conciliate influential politicians. On the other hand, if he is in his second term of office, he has no longer much motive to regard the interests of the nation at large, because he sees that his own political death is near. It may be answered that these two evils will correct one another, that the president will in his first term be anxious to win the respect of the nation, in his

---

[1] In England, also, there is necessarily a campaign once at least in every five years, when a general election takes place, and sometimes oftener. But note that in England: (1) this is the only season of disturbance, whereas in America the Congressional elections furnish a second; (2) the period is usually shorter (three to six weeks, not four months); (3) there are usually real and momentous issues, dividing the great parties, which the nation had to settle.

[2] See p. 40 *supra*. There was however some talk of nominating Mr. Cleveland after an interval from his second term, and no precedent, except the failure in Grant's case, exists to dissuade this.

second he will have no motive for yielding to the pressure of party wire-pullers; while in reply to the suggestion that if he were held ineligible for the next term, but eligible for any future term, both sets of evils might be avoided, and both sets of benefits secured, it can be argued that such a provision would make that breach in policy which may now happen only once in eight years, necessarily happen once in four years. It would, for instance, have prevented the reelection of Abraham Lincoln in 1864.

The founders of the Southern Confederacy of 1861-65 were so much impressed by the objections to the present system that they provided that their president should hold office for six years, but not be reeligible. It has recently been suggested that the Constitution might be amended in this sense.

Fifthly. An outgoing president is a weak president. During the four months of his stay in office after his successor has been chosen, he declines, except in cases of extreme necessity, to take any new departure, to embark on any executive policy which cannot be completed before he quits office. This is, of course, even more decidedly the case if his successor belongs to the opposite party.[3]

Lastly. The result of an election may be doubtful, not from equality of votes, for this is provided against, but from a dispute as to the validity of votes given in or reported from the states. The difficulty which arose in 1876 cannot, owing to the legislation of 1887, recur in quite the same form. But cases may arise in which the returns from a state of its electoral votes will, because notoriously obtained by fraud or force, fail to be recognized as valid by the party whose candidate they prejudice. Few presidential elections have passed without charges of this kind, and these charges are not always unfounded. Should manifest unfairness coincide with popular excitement over a really important issue, the self-control of the people, which in 1877, when no such issue was involved, held in check the party passions of their leaders, might prove unequal to the strain of such a crisis.

Further observations on the president, as a part of the machinery of

---

[3] Freeman (*History of Federal Government*, 302) adduces from Polybius (iv, 6, 7) a curious instance showing that the same mischief arose in the Achaian League: "The Ætolians chose for an inroad the time when the official year (of the Achaian General) was drawing to its close, as a time when the Achaian counsels were sure to be weak. Aratos, the General elect, was not yet in office; Timoxenos, the outgoing General, shrunk from energetic action so late in his year, and at last yielded up his office to Aratos before the legal time." This effort of Timoxenos to escape from the consequences of the system could not have occurred in governments like those of Rome, England, or the United States, where "the reign of law" is far stricter than it was in the Greek republics.

government, will be better reserved for the discussion of the relations of the executive and legislative departments. I will therefore only observe here that, even when we allow for the defects last enumerated, the presidential office, if not one of the conspicuous successes of the American Constitution, is nowise to be deemed a failure. The problem of constructing a stable executive in a democratic country is so immensely difficult that anything short of a failure deserves to be called a success. Now the president has, for more than a century, carried on the internal administrative business of the nation with due efficiency. As he has the ear of the country, he can force upon its attention questions which Congress may be neglecting, and if he be a man of constructive ideas and definite aims, he may guide and inspire its political thought. Once or twice, as when Jefferson purchased Louisiana, and Lincoln emancipated the slaves in the revolted states, he has courageously ventured on stretches of authority, held at the time to be doubtfully constitutional, yet necessary, and approved by the judgment of posterity. He has kept the machinery working quietly and steadily when Congress has been distracted by party strife, or paralyzed by the dissensions of the two houses, or enfeebled by the want of first-rate leaders. The executive has been able, at moments of peril, to rise into a dictatorship, as during the War of Secession, and when peace returned, to sink back into its proper constitutional position. It has shown no tendency so far to rise above and override other authorities as to pave the way for a monarchy.

Europeans are struck by the faults of a plan which plunges the nation into a whirlpool of excitement once every four years, and commits the headship of the state to a party leader chosen for a short period.[4] But there is another aspect in which the presidential election may be regarded, and one whose importance is better appreciated in America than in Europe. The election is a solemn periodical appeal to the nation to review its condition, the way in which its business has been carried on, the conduct of the two great parties. It stirs and rouses the nation as nothing else does, forces everyone not merely to think about public affairs but to decide how he judges the parties. It is a direct expression of the will of twelve millions of voters, a force before which everything must bow. It refreshes the sense of national duty; and at great crises it intensifies national patriotism. A presidential election is sometimes, as in 1800, and as again most notably in 1860 and 1864, a

---

[4] Such faults as belong to the plan of popular election are not necessarily incident to the existence of a president; for in France the chief magistrate is chosen by the chambers, and the interposition between him and the legislature of a responsible ministry serves to render his position less distinctly partisan.

turning-point in history. In form it is nothing more than the choice of an administrator who cannot influence policy otherwise than by refusing his assent to bills. In reality it is the deliverance of the mind of the people upon all such questions as they feel able to decide. A curious parallel may in this respect be drawn between it and a general election of the House of Commons in England. A general election is in form a choice of representatives, with reference primarily to their views upon various current questions. In substance it may be a national vote, committing executive power to some one prominent statesman. Thus the elections of 1868, 1874, 1880, were practically votes of the nation to place Mr. Gladstone or Mr. Disraeli at the head of the government. So conversely in America, a presidential election, which purports to be merely the selection of a man, is often in reality a decision upon issues of policy, a condemnation of the course taken by one party, a mandate to the other to follow some different course.

The choice of party leaders as presidents has in America caused far less mischief than might have been expected. Nevertheless, those who have studied the scheme of constitutional monarchy as it works in England, or Belgium, or Italy, or the reproductions of that scheme in British colonies, where the Crown-appointed governor stands outside the strife of factions as a permanent official, will, when they compare the institutions of these countries with the American presidency, be impressed by the merits of a plan which does not unite all the dignity of office with all the power of office, and which, by placing the titular chief of the executive above and apart from party, makes the execution of the law appear to proceed from a nonpartisan source, and tells the civil and military services that they are the servants rather of the nation than of any section of the nation, suggesting to them that their labours ought to be rendered with equal heartiness to whatever party may hold the reins of government. Party government may be necessary. So far as we can see, it is necessary. But it is an unfortunate necessity; and whatever tends to diminish its mischievous influence upon the machinery of administration, and to prevent it from obtruding itself upon foreign states; whatever holds up a high ideal of devotion to the nation as a majestic whole, living on from century to century while parties form and dissolve and form again, strengthens and ennobles the commonwealth and all its citizens.

Such an observation of course applies only to monarchy as a political institution. Socially regarded, the American presidency deserves nothing but admiration. The president is simply the first citizen of a free nation, depending for his dignity on no title, no official dress, no insignia of state. It was originally proposed, doubtless in recollection of the English Commonwealth of the seventeenth century, to give him the style of "Highness," and "Protector of the Liberties of the United States." Others suggested "Excellency";[5] and Washington is said to have had leanings to the Dutch style of "High Mightiness." The head of the ruling president does not appear on coins, nor even on postage stamps.[6] His residence at Washington, formerly called officially "the Executive Mansion," but now "the White House," a handsome building with two low wings and a portico supported by Corinthian pillars, said to have been modelled upon the Duke of Leinster's house at Carton in Kildare, stands in a shrubbery, and has the air of a large suburban villa rather than of a palace. The rooms, though spacious, are not spacious enough for the crowds that attend the public receptions. The president's salary, which is only $75,000 (£15,000) a year, does not permit display, nor indeed is display expected from him.

Washington, which even so lately as the days of the war, was a wilderness of mud and Negroes, with a few big houses scattered here and there, has now become one of the handsomest capitals in the world, and cultivates the graces and pleasures of life with eminent success. Besides its political society and its diplomatic society, it has grown to be a winter resort for men of wealth and leisure from all over the continent. It is a place where a court might be created, did anyone wish to create it. No president has made the attempt; and as the earlier career of the chief magistrate and his wife has seldom qualified them to lead the world of fashion, none is likely to make it. However, the action of the wife of President Hayes, an estimable lady, whose ardent advocacy of temperance caused the formation of many total abstinence societies, called by her name, showed that there may be fields in which a president's consort can turn her exalted position to good account, while of course such gifts or charms as she possesses will tend to increase his popularity.

To a European observer, weary of the slavish obsequiousness and lip-deep adulation with which the members of reigning families are treated on the eastern side of the Atlantic, fawned on in public and carped at in private, the social relations of an American president to his people are eminently

---

[5] In ridicule of this the more democratic members of Congress proposed to call that more ornamental than useful officer the vice-president "His Superfluous Excellency."

[6] The portraits on postage stamps are those of eminent past presidents—Washington, Jefferson, Jackson, Taylor, Lincoln, Grant, Garfield, McKinley, and of a few eminent statesmen, such as Franklin, Hamilton, Clay, Webster, Scott, Perry, Stanton. Sometimes a historical event is depicted, such as the founding of Jamestown in Virginia when the tercentenary of that event arrived in 1907.

refreshing. There is a great respect for the office, and a corresponding respect for the man as the holder of the office, if he has done nothing to degrade it. There is no servility, no fictitious self-abasement on the part of the citizens, but a simple and hearty deference to one who represents the majesty of the nation, the sort of respect which the proudest Roman paid to the consulship, even if the particular consul was, like Cicero, a "new man." The curiosity of the visitors who throng the White House on reception days is sometimes too familiar; but this fault tends to disappear, and presidents have now more reason to complain of the persecutions they endure from an incessantly observant journalism. After oscillating between the ceremonious state of George Washington, who drove to open Congress in his coach and six, with outriders and footmen in livery, and the ostentatious plainness of Citizen Jefferson, who would ride up alone and hitch his horse to the post at the gate,[7] the president has settled down into an attitude between that of the mayor of a great English town on a public occasion, and that of a European cabinet minister on a political tour. He is followed about and fêted, and in every way treated as the first man in the company; but the spirit of equality which rules the country has sunk too deep into every American nature for him to expect to be addressed with bated breath and whispering reverence. He has no military guard, no chamberlains or grooms-in-waiting; his everyday life is simple; his wife enjoys precedence over all other ladies, but is visited and received just like other ladies; he is surrounded by no such pomp and enforces no such etiquette as that which belongs to the governors even of second-class English colonies, not to speak of the viceroys of India and Ireland.

It begins to be remarked in Europe that monarchy, which used to be deemed politically dangerous but socially useful, has now, since its claws have been cut, become politically valuable, but of more doubtful social utility. In the United States the most suspicious democrat—and there are democrats who complain that the office of president is too monarchical—cannot accuse the chief magistracy of having tended to form a court, much less to create those evils which thrive in the atmosphere of European courts. No president dare violate social decorum as European sovereigns have so often done. If he did, he would be the first to suffer.

---

[7] Mr. H. Adams (*First Administration of Jefferson*, vol. i, p. 197) has, however, shown that at his inauguration Jefferson walked.

Why Great Men Are Not Chosen Presidents

Europeans often ask, and Americans do not always explain, how it happens that this great office, the greatest in the world, unless we except the papacy, to which anyone can rise by his own merits, is not more frequently filled by great and striking men. In America, which is beyond all other countries the country of a "career open to talents," a country, moreover, in which political life is unusually keen and political ambition widely diffused, it might be expected that the highest place would always be won by a man of brilliant gifts. But from the time when the heroes of the Revolution died out with Jefferson and Adams and Madison, no person except General Grant, had, down till the end of last century, reached the chair whose name would have been remembered had he not been president, and no president except Abraham Lincoln had displayed rare or striking qualities in the chair. Who now knows or cares to know anything about the personality of James K. Polk or Franklin Pierce? The only thing remarkable about them is that being so commonplace they should have climbed so high.

Several reasons may be suggested for the fact, which Americans are themselves the first to admit.

One is that the proportion of first-rate ability drawn into politics is smaller in America than in most European countries. This is a phenomenon whose causes must be elucidated later: in the meantime it is enough to say that in France, where the half-revolutionary conditions that lasted for some time after 1870, made public life exciting and accessible; in Germany, where an admirably organized civil service cultivates and develops statecraft with unusual success; in England, where many persons of wealth and leisure seek to enter the political arena, while burning questions touch the interests of all classes and make men eager observers of the combatants, the total quantity of talent devoted to parliamentary or administrative work has been larger, relatively to the population, than in America, where much of the best ability, both for thought and for action, for planning and for executing, rushes into a field which is comparatively narrow in Europe, the business of developing the material resources of the country.

Another is that the methods and habits of Congress, and indeed of political life generally, seem to give fewer opportunities for personal distinction, fewer modes in which a man may commend himself to his countrymen by eminent capacity in thought, in speech, or in administration, than is the case in the free countries of Europe. This is a point to be explained in later chapters. I merely note here in passing what will there be dwelt on.

A third reason is that eminent men make more enemies, and give those enemies more assailable points, than obscure men do. They are therefore in so far less desirable candidates. It is true that the eminent man has also made more friends, that his name is more widely known, and may be greeted with louder cheers. Other things being equal, the famous man is preferable. But other things never are equal. The famous man has probably attacked some leaders in his own party, has supplanted others, has expressed his dislike to the crotchet of some active section, has perhaps committed errors which are capable of being magnified into offences. No man stands long before the public and bears a part in great affairs without giving openings to censorious criticism. Fiercer far than the light which beats upon a throne is the light which beats upon a presidential candidate, searching out all the recesses of his past life. Hence, when the choice lies between a brilliant man and a safe man, the safe man is preferred. Party feeling, strong enough to carry in on its back a man without conspicuous positive merits, is not always strong enough to procure forgiveness for a man with positive faults.

A European finds that this phenomenon needs in its turn to be explained, for in the free countries of Europe brilliancy, be it eloquence in speech, or some striking achievement in war or administration, or the power through whatever means of somehow impressing the popular imagination, is what makes a leader triumphant. Why should it be otherwise in America? Because in America party loyalty and party organization have been hitherto so perfect that anyone put forward by the party will get the full party vote if his character is good and his "record," as they call it, unstained. The safe candidate may not draw in quite so many votes from the moderate men of the other side as the brilliant one would, but he will not lose nearly so many from his own ranks. Even those who admit his mediocrity will vote straight when the moment for voting comes. Besides, the ordinary American voter does not object to mediocrity. He has a lower conception of the qualities requisite to make a statesman than those who direct public opinion in Europe have. He likes his candidate to be sensible, vigorous, and, above all, what he calls "magnetic," and does not value, because he sees no need for, originality or profundity, a fine culture or a wide knowledge. Candidates are selected to be run for nomination by knots of persons who, however expert as party tacticians, are usually commonplace men; and the choice between those selected for nomination is made by a very large body, an assembly of nearly a thousand delegates from the local party organizations over the country, who are certainly no better than ordinary citizens. How this process works will be seen more fully when I come to speak of those nominating conventions which are so notable a feature in American politics.

It must also be remembered that the merits of a president are one thing and those of a candidate another thing. An eminent American is reported to have said to friends who wished to put him forward, "Gentlemen, let there be no mistake. I should make a good president, but a very bad candidate." Now to a party it is more important that its nominee should be a good candidate than that he should turn out a good president. A nearer danger is a greater danger. As Saladin says in *The Talisman*, "A wild cat in a chamber is more dangerous than a lion in a distant desert." It will be a misfortune to the party, as well as to the country, if the candidate elected should prove a bad president. But it is a greater misfortune to the party that it should be beaten in the impending election, for the evil of losing national patronage will have come four years sooner. "B" (so reason the leaders), "who is one of our possible candidates, may be an abler man than A, who is the other. But we have a better chance of winning with A than with B, while X, the candidate of our opponents, is anyhow no better than A. We must therefore run A." This reasoning is all the more forcible because the previous career of the possible candidates has generally made it easier to say who will succeed as a candidate than who will succeed as a president; and because the wire-pullers with whom the choice rests are better judges of the former question than of the latter.

After all, too, a president need not be a man of brilliant intellectual gifts. His main duties are to be prompt and firm in securing the due execution of the laws and maintaining the public peace, careful and upright in the choice of the executive officials of the country. Eloquence, whose value is apt to be overrated in all free countries, imagination, profundity of thought or extent of knowledge, are all in so far a gain to him that they make him "a bigger man," and help him to gain a greater influence over the nation, an influence which, if he be a true patriot, he may use for its good. But they are not necessary for the due discharge in ordinary times of the duties of his post. Four-fifths of his work is the same in kind as that which devolves on the chairman of a commercial company or the manager of a railway, the work of choosing good subordinates, seeing that they attend to their business, and taking a sound practical view of such administrative questions as require his decision. Firmness, common sense, and most of all, honesty, an honesty above all suspicion of personal interest, are the qualities which the country chiefly needs in its chief magistrate.

So far we have been considering personal merits. But in the selection of a candidate many considerations have to be regarded besides personal merits, whether of a candidate, or of a possible president. The chief of these considerations is the amount of support which can be secured from different states or from different "sections" of the Union, a term by which the Americans denote groups of states with a broad community of interest. State feeling and sectional feeling are powerful factors in a presidential election. The Middle West and Northwest, including the states from Ohio to Montana, is now the most populous section of the Union, and therefore counts for most in an election. It naturally conceives that its interests will be best protected by one who knows them from birth and residence. Hence prima facie a man from that section makes the best candidate. A large state casts a heavier vote in the election; and every state is of course more likely to be carried by one of its own children than by a stranger, because his fellow citizens, while they feel honoured by the choice, gain also a substantial advantage, having a better prospect of such favours as the administration can bestow. Hence, *cæteris paribus*, a man from a large state is preferable as a candidate. The problem is further complicated by the fact that some states are already safe for one or other party, while others are doubtful. The Northwestern and New England states have usually tended to go Republican; while nearly all of the Southern states have, since 1877, been pretty certain to go Democratic. *Cæteris paribus*, a candidate from a doubtful state, such as New York or Indiana have usually been, is to be preferred.

Other minor disqualifying circumstances require less explanation. A Roman Catholic, or an avowed disbeliever in Christianity, would be an undesirable candidate. For many years after the Civil War, anyone who had fought, especially if he fought with distinction, in the Northern army, enjoyed great advantages, for the soldiers of that army rallied to his name.

The two elections of General Grant, who knew nothing of politics, and the fact that his influence survived the faults of his long administration, are evidence of the weight of this consideration.

Long ago on a railway journey in the Far West I fell in with two newspapermen from the state of Indiana, who were taking their holiday. The conversation turned on the next presidential election. They spoke hopefully of the chances for nomination by their party of an Indiana man, a comparatively obscure person, whose name I had never heard. I expressed some surprise that he should be thought of. They observed that he had done well in state politics, that there was nothing against him, that Indiana would work for him. "But," I rejoined, "ought you not to have a man of more commanding character? There is Senator A. Everybody tells me that he is the shrewdest and most experienced man in your party, and that he has a perfectly clean record. Why not run him?" "Why, yes," they answered, "that is all true. But you see he comes from a small state, and we have got that state already. Besides, he wasn't in the war. Our man was. Indiana's vote is worth having, and if our man is run, we can carry Indiana."

"Surely the race is not to the swift, nor the battle to the strong, neither yet bread to the wise, nor yet riches to men of understanding, nor yet favour to men of skill, but time and chance happeneth to them all."

These secondary considerations do not always prevail. Intellectual ability and strength of character must influence the choice of a candidate. When a man has once impressed himself on the nation by force, courage, and rectitude, the influence of those qualities may be decisive. They naturally count for more when times are critical. Reformers declare that their weight will go on increasing as the disgust of good citizens with the methods of professional politicians increases. But for many generations past it is not the greatest men in the Roman Church that have been chosen popes, nor the most brilliant men in the Anglican Church that have been appointed archbishops of Canterbury.

Although several presidents have survived their departure from office by many years, only two, John Quincy Adams and recently Mr. Roosevelt, have played a part in politics after quitting the White House.[1] It may be that the ex-president has not been a great leader before his accession to office; it may be that he does not care to exert himself after he has held and dropped the great prize, and found (as most have found) how little of a

[1] J. Q. Adams was elected to the House of Representatives within three years from his presidency, and there became for seventeen years the fearless and formidable advocate of what may be called the national theory of the Constitution against the slaveholders.

prize it is. Something, however, must also be ascribed to other features of the political system of the country. It is often hard to find a vacancy in the representation of a given state through which to reenter Congress; it is disagreeable to recur to the arts by which seats are secured. Past greatness is rather an encumbrance than a help to resuming a political career. Exalted power, on which the unsleeping eye of hostile critics was fixed, has probably disclosed all a president's weaknesses, and has either forced him to make enemies by disobliging adherents, or exposed him to censure for subservience to party interests. He is regarded as having had his day; he belongs already to the past, and unless, like Grant, he is endeared to the people by the memory of some splendid service, or is available to his party as a possible candidate for a further term of office, he may sink into the crowd or avoid neglect by retirement. Possibly he may deserve to be forgotten; but more frequently he is a man of sufficient ability and character to make the experience he has gained valuable to the country, could it be retained in a place where he might turn it to account. They managed things better at Rome, gathering into their Senate all the fame and experience, all the wisdom and skill, of those who had ruled and fought as consuls and prætors at home and abroad.

We may now answer the question from which we started. Great men have not often been chosen presidents, first because great men are rare in politics; secondly, because the method of choice does not bring them to the top; thirdly, because they are not, in quiet times, absolutely needed. Let us close by observing that the presidents, regarded historically, fall into three periods, the second inferior to the first, the third rather better than the second.

Down till the election of Andrew Jackson in 1828, all the presidents had been statesmen in the European sense of the word, men of education, of administrative experience, of a certain largeness of view and dignity of character. All except the first two had served in the great office of secretary of state; all were known to the nation from the part they had played. In the second period, from Jackson till the outbreak of the Civil War in 1861, the presidents were either mere politicians, such as Van Buren, Polk, or Buchanan, or else successful soldiers,[2] such as Harrison or Taylor, whom their party found useful as figureheads. They were intellectual pygmies beside the real leaders of that generation—Clay, Calhoun, and Webster. A

---

[2] Jackson himself was something of both politician and soldier, a strong character, but a narrow and uncultivated intellect.

new series begins with Lincoln in 1861. He and General Grant, his successor, who cover sixteen years between them, belong to the history of the world. The other less distinguished presidents of this period contrast favourably with the Polks and Pierces of the days before the war, if they are not, like the early presidents, the first men of the country. If we compare the twenty presidents who were elected to office between 1789 and 1900 with the twenty English prime ministers of the same period, there are but six of the latter, and at least eight of the former whom history calls personally insignificant, while only Washington, Jefferson, Lincoln, and Grant can claim to belong to a front rank represented in the English list by seven or possibly eight names.[3] It would seem that the natural selection of the English parliamentary system, even as modified by the aristocratic habits of that country, had more tendency to bring the highest gifts to the highest place than the more artificial selection of America.

---

[3] The American average would be further lowered were we to reckon in the four vice-presidents who, down to 1900, succeeded on the death of the president. Yet the English system does not always secure men personally eminent. Addington, Perceval, and Lord Goderich are no better than Tyler or Fillmore, which is saying little enough.

Of presidents since 1900 it is not yet time to speak.

The Cabinet

There is in the government of the United States no such thing as a cabinet in the English sense of the term. But I use the term, not only because it is current in America to describe the chief ministers of the president, but also because it calls attention to the remarkable difference which exists between the great officers of state in America and the similar officers in the free countries of Europe.

Almost the only reference in the Constitution to the ministers of the president is that contained in the power given him to "require the opinion in writing of the principal officer in each of the executive departments upon any subject relating to the duties of their respective offices." All these departments have been created by acts of Congress. Washington began in 1789 with four only, at the head of whom were the following four officials:

secretary of state
secretary of the treasury
secretary of war
attorney general

In 1798 there was added a secretary of the navy, in 1829 a postmaster general,[1] in 1849 a secretary of the interior, in 1888 a secretary of agriculture, in 1903 a secretary of commerce and labour, and in 1913 a secretary of labour.

These ten now make up what is called the cabinet.[2] Each receives a salary

---

[1] The postmaster general had been previously deemed a subordinate in the Treasury Department, although the office was organized by act of Congress in 1794; he has been held to belong to the cabinet since Jackson in 1829 invited him to cabinet meetings.

[2] There is also an Interstate Commerce Commission, with large powers over railways, created in February 1887 by act of Congress; and a Civil Service Commission created in 1883. The Fisheries

of $12000 (£2400). All are appointed by the president, subject to the consent of the Senate (which is practically never refused), and may be removed by the president alone. Nothing marks them off from any other officials who might be placed in charge of a department, except that they are summoned by the president to his private council.

None of them can vote in Congress, art. XI, § 6 of the Constitution providing that "no person holding any office under the United States shall be a member of either House during his continuance in office."

This restriction was intended to prevent the president not merely from winning over individual members of Congress by the allurements of office, but also from making his ministers agents in corrupting or unduly influencing the representatives of the people, as George III and his ministers corrupted the English Parliament. There is a passage in the *Federalist* (Letter 40) which speaks of "Great Britain, where so great a proportion of the members are elected by so small a proportion of the people, where the electors are so corrupted by the representatives, and the representatives so corrupted by the Crown." The Fathers of the Constitution were so resolved to avert this latter form of corruption that they included in the Constitution the provision just mentioned. Its wisdom has sometimes been questioned. But it deserves to be noticed that the Constitution contains nothing to prevent ministers from being present in either house of Congress and addressing it,[3] as the ministers of the king of Italy or of the French president may do in either chamber of Italy or France.[4] It is absolutely silent on the subject of communications between officials (other than the president) and the representatives of the people.

The president has the amplest range of choice for his ministers. He usually forms an entirely new cabinet when he enters office, even if he belongs to the same party as his predecessor. He can and sometimes does take men

---

Commission, the Census, and the Coast Survey belong to the Department of Commerce, Education to the Department of the Interior, Immigration to the Department of Labor.

[3] In February 1881 a committee of eight senators unanimously reported in favour of a plan to give seats (of course without the right to vote) in both houses of Congress to cabinet ministers, they to attend on alternate days in the Senate and in the House. The committee recommended that the necessary modification in the rules should be made, adding that they had no doubt of the constitutionality of the proposal. Nothing has so far been done to carry out this report. Congress does not like the idea, yet the advantages to Congress itself are obvious, for it would secure opportunities of questioning ministers. In Switzerland the Federal Councillors habitually appear and speak in both houses, although members of neither.

[4] The Italian ministers usually are members of one or other house. Of course they cannot vote except in the house to which they have been chosen.

who not only have never sat in Congress, but have not figured in politics at all, who may never have sat in a state legislature nor held the humblest office.[5] Generally, of course, the persons chosen have already made for themselves a position of at least local importance. Often they are those to whom the new president owes his election, or to whose influence with the party he looks for support in his policy. Sometimes they have been his most prominent competitors for the party nominations. Thus Mr. Lincoln in 1860 appointed Mr. Seward and Mr. Chase to be his secretary of state and secretary of the treasury respectively, they being the two men who had come next after him in the selection by the Republican party of a presidential candidate.

The most dignified place in the cabinet is that of the secretary of state. It is the great prize often bestowed on the man to whom the president is chiefly indebted for his election, or at any rate on one of the leaders of the party. In early days, it was regarded as the stepping-stone to the presidency. Jefferson, Madison, Monroe, J. Q. Adams, and Van Buren, had all served as secretaries to preceding presidents. The conduct of foreign affairs is the chief duty of the State Department: its head has therefore a larger stage to play on than any other minister, and more chances of fame. His personal importance is all the greater because the president is usually so much absorbed by questions of patronage as to be forced to leave the secretary to his own devices. Hence the foreign policy of the administration is practically that of the secretary, except so far as the latter is controlled by the Senate. The State Department has also the charge of the great seal of the United States, keeps the archives, publishes the statutes, and of course instructs and controls the diplomatic and consular services. It is often said of the president that he is ruled, or as the Americans express it, "run," by his secretary; but this happens only when the secretary is the stronger man, and in the same way it has been said of presidents before now that they were, like sultans, ruled by their wives, or by their boon companions.

The secretary of the treasury is minister of finance. His function was of the utmost importance at the beginning of the government, when a national system of finance had to be built up and the federal government rescued from its grave embarrassments. Hamilton, who then held the office, effected both; and the work of Gallatin, who served under Jefferson, was scarcely

---

[5] Only two members of Mr. Harrison's cabinet, formed in 1889, and only two of Mr. Taft's cabinet, formed in 1909, had ever sat in Congress.

less important. During the War of Secession, it became again powerful, owing to the enormous loans contracted and the quantities of paper money issued, and it remains so now, because it has the management (so far as Congress permits) of the currency and the national debt. The secretary has, however, by no means the same range of action as a finance minister in European countries, for as he is excluded from Congress, although he regularly reports to it, he has nothing directly to do with the imposition of taxes, and very little with the appropriation of revenue to the various burdens of the state.[6]

The secretary of the interior is far from being the omnipresent power which a minister of the interior is in France or Italy, or even a home secretary in England, since nearly all the functions which these officials discharge belong in America to the state governments or to the organs of local government. He is chiefly occupied in the management of the public lands, still of immense value, despite the lavish grants made to railway companies, and with the conduct of Indian affairs, a troublesome and unsatisfactory department, which was long a reproach to the United States, and may from time to time become so, till the Indians themselves disappear or have been civilized. Patents and pensions, the latter a source of great expense and abuse, also belong to his province, as do the meteorological office, the geological survey, and the reclamation office.

The duties of the secretaries of war, of the navy, of agriculture, of commerce, of labour, and of the postmaster general may be gathered from their names. But the attorney general is sufficiently different from his English prototype to need a word of explanation. He is not only public prosecutor and standing counsel for the United States, but also to some extent what is called on the European continent a minister of justice. He has a general oversight—it can hardly be described as a control—of the federal judicial departments, and especially of the prosecuting officers called district attorneys, and executive court officers, called United States marshals. He is the legal adviser of the president in those delicate questions, necessarily frequent under the Constitution of the United States, which arise as to the limits of the executive power and the relations of federal to state authority, and generally in all legal matters. His opinions are frequently published officially, as a justification of the president's conduct, and an indication of

[6] See *post*, Chapter 17 (Congressional Finance), where it will be shown that the chairmen of the Committees on Ways and Means and of Appropriations are practically additional ministers of finance.

the view which the executive takes of its legal position and duties in a pending matter.[7] Some of them have indeed a quasi-judicial authority, for when a department requests his opinion on a question of law, as for instance, regarding the interpretation of a statute, that opinion is deemed authoritative for the officials, although, of course, a judgment of a federal court would upset it. His power to institute or abstain from instituting prosecutions under federal acts is also a function of much moment. The attorney general is always a lawyer of eminence, though not necessarily in the front rank of the profession, for political considerations have much to do with determining the president's choice.[8]

The creation of the departments of commerce and of labour was an evidence of that extension of the functions of government into new fields which is no less remarkable in the United States than it is in Europe. Among the duties of the former are the supervision of corporations (other than railroads) doing interstate business, lighthouses, the coast and geodetic survey, merchant shipping, the census, and trade statistics. The latter has within its sphere the administration of the immigration laws.

It will be observed that from this list of ministerial offices several are wanting which exist in Europe. Thus there is no minister of education, because that department of business belongs to the several states;[9] no minister of public worship, because the United States government has nothing to do with any particular form of religion; no minister of public works, because grants made for this purpose come direct from Congress without the intervention of the executive, and are applied as Congress directs.[10] Neither was there, till the Philippine Isles and Puerto Rico were acquired, any colonial office. Since that date (1899) a Bureau of Insular Affairs has been established and placed under the War Department, to take charge of these dependencies. Much of the work which in Europe would devolve on members of the administration falls in America to committees of Congress,

---

[7] Another variance from the practice of England, where the opinions of the law officers of the Crown are always treated as confidential.

[8] The solicitor general is a sort of assistant to the attorney, and not (as in England) a colleague.

[9] There was established by acts of 1867 and 1869 a Bureau of Education, attached to the Department of the Interior, but its function is only to collect and diffuse information on educational subjects. This it does with assiduity and success.

[10] Money voted for river and harbour improvements is voted in sums appropriated to each particular piece of work. The work is supervised by officers of the Engineer Corps of the United States Army, under the general direction of the War Department. Public buildings are erected under the direction of an official called the supervising architect, who is attached to the Treasury Department. The Weather Bureau belongs to the Department of Agriculture, as do the Bureau of Chemistry and the administration of the Pure Food laws.

especially to committees of the House of Representatives. This happens particularly as regards taxation, public works, and the management of the Territories, for each of which matters there exists a committee in both houses. Some controversy has arisen in Washington regarding the respective precedence of cabinet ministers and of senators. The point is naturally of more importance as regards the wives of the claimants than as regards the claimants themselves.

The respective positions of the president and his ministers are, as has been already explained, the reverse of those which exist in the constitutional monarchies of Europe. There the sovereign is irresponsible and the minister responsible for the acts which he does in the sovereign's name. In America the president is responsible because the minister is nothing more than his servant, bound to obey him, and independent of Congress. The minister's acts are therefore legally the acts of the president. Nevertheless the minister is also responsible and liable to impeachment for offences committed in the discharge of his duties. The question whether he is, as in England, impeachable for giving bad advice to the head of the state has never arisen, but upon the general theory of the Constitution it would rather seem that he is not, unless of course his bad counsel should amount to a conspiracy with the president to commit an impeachable offence. In France the responsibility of the president's ministers does not in theory exclude the responsibility of the president himself, although practically it makes a great difference, because he, like the English Crown, acts through ministers supported by a majority in the Chamber.

So much for the ministers taken separately. It remains to consider how an American administration works as a whole, this being in Europe the most peculiar and significant feature of the parliamentary or so-called "cabinet" system.

In America the administration does not work as a whole. It is not a whole. It is a group of persons, each individually dependent on and answerable to the president, but with no joint policy, no collective responsibility.[11]

When the Constitution was established, and George Washington chosen first president under it, it was intended that the president should be outside and above party, and the method of choosing him by electors was contrived

---

[11] In America people usually speak of the president and his ministers as the "administration," not as the "government," apparently because he and they are not deemed to govern in the European sense. The latter expression is not very old in England. Fifty years ago people usually said "the ministry" when they now say "the government." In France and Germany ministry is the term used, while *Gouvernement* and *Regierung* denote the executive *qua* executive.

with this very view. Washington belonged to no party, nor indeed, though diverging tendencies were already manifest, had parties yet begun to exist. There was therefore no reason why he should not select his ministers from all sections of opinion. As he was responsible to the nation and not to a majority in Congress, he was not bound to choose persons who agreed with the majority in Congress. As he, and not the ministry, was responsible for executive acts done, he had to consider, not the opinions or affiliations of his servants, but their capacity and integrity only. Washington chose as secretary of state Thomas Jefferson, already famous as the chief draftsman of the Declaration of Independence, and as attorney general another Virginian, Edmund Randolph, both men of extreme democratic leanings, disposed to restrict the action of the federal government within narrow limits. For secretary of the treasury he selected Alexander Hamilton of New York, and for secretary of war Henry Knox of Massachusetts. Hamilton was by far the ablest man among those who soon came to form the Federalist party, the party which called for a strong executive, and desired to subordinate the states to the central authority. He soon became recognized as its leader. Knox was of the same way of thinking. Dissensions presently arose between Jefferson and Hamilton, ending in open hostility, but Washington retained them both as ministers till Jefferson retired in 1794 and Hamilton in 1795. The second president, John Adams, kept on the ministers of his predecessor, being in accord with their opinions, for they and he belonged to the now full-grown Federalist party. But before he quitted office he had quarrelled with most of them, having taken important steps without their knowledge and against their wishes. Jefferson, the third president, was a thorough-going party leader, who naturally chose his ministers from his own political adherents. As all subsequent presidents have been seated by one or other party, all have felt bound to appoint a party cabinet though not necessarily one of strong party men. Their party expects it; and they prefer to be advised by people of their own way of thinking.

So far, an American cabinet resembles a British one. It is composed of members of one party, if not of prominent party leaders. But now mark the differences. The parliamentary system of England and of those countries which like Belgium, Italy, and the self-governing British colonies, have more or less modelled themselves upon England, rests on four principles.

The head of the executive is irresponsible. Responsibility attaches to the cabinet, i.e., to the body of ministers who advise him, so that if he errs, it is through their fault; they suffer and he escapes. The ministers cannot allege, as a defence for any act of theirs, the command of the Crown. If the Crown gives them an order of which they disapprove, they ought to resign.

The ministers sit in the legislature, practically forming in England, as has been observed by Bagehot, the most acute of English constitutional writers, a committee of the legislature, chosen by the majority for the time being.

The ministers are accountable to the legislature, and must resign office[12] as soon as they lose its confidence.

The ministers are jointly as well as severally liable for their acts: i.e., the blame of an act done by any of them falls on the whole cabinet, unless one of them chooses to take it entirely on himself and retire from office. Their responsibility is collective.

None of these principles holds true in America. The president is personally responsible for his acts, not indeed to Congress, but to the people, by whom he is chosen. No means exist of enforcing this responsibility, except by impeachment, but as his power lasts for four years only, and is much restricted, this is no serious evil. He cannot avoid responsibility by alleging the advice of his ministers, for he is not bound to follow it, and they are bound to obey him or retire. The ministers do not sit in Congress. They are not accountable to it, but to the president, their master. It may request their attendance before a committee, as it may require the attendance of any other witness, but they have no opportunity of expounding and justifying to Congress as a whole their own, or rather their master's, policy. Hence an adverse vote of Congress does not affect their or his position. If they propose to take a step which requires money, and Congress refuses the requisite appropriation, the step cannot be taken. But a dozen votes of censure will neither compel them to resign nor oblige the president to pause in any line of conduct which is within his constitutional rights. This, however strange it may seem to a European, is a necessary consequence of the fact that the president, and by consequence his cabinet, do not derive their authority from Congress. Suppose (as befell in 1878-79) a Republican president, with a Democratic majority in both houses of Congress. The president, unless of course he is convinced that the nation has changed its mind since it elected him, is morally bound to follow out the policy which he professed as a candidate, and which the majority of the nation must be held in electing him to have approved. That policy is, however, opposed to the views of the present majority of Congress. They are right to check him as far as they

---

[12] In England and some other countries (e.g., the self-governing British colonies) they have the alternative of dissolving Parliament, subject to a somewhat undefined, but not wholly extinct, right of the Crown or the Governor to refuse a dissolution in certain cases.

can. He is right to follow out his own views and principles in spite of them so far as the Constitution and the funds at his disposal permit. A deadlock may follow. But deadlocks may happen under any system, except that of an omnipotent sovereign, be he a man or an assembly, the risk of deadlocks being indeed the price which a nation pays for the safeguard of constitutional checks.

In this state of things one cannot properly talk of the cabinet apart from the president. An American administration resembles not so much the cabinets of England and France as the group of ministers who surround the czar or the sultan, or who executed the bidding of a Roman emperor like Constantine or Justinian. Such ministers are severally responsible to their master, and are severally called in to counsel him, but they have not necessarily any relations with one another, nor any duty of collective action. So while the president commits each department to the minister whom the law provides, and may if he chooses leave it altogether to that minister, the executive acts done are his own acts, by which the country will judge him; and still more is his policy as a whole his own policy, and not the policy of his ministers taken together.[13] The ministers meet in council (often twice every week while Congress is sitting), but may not have much to settle when they meet, since they have no parliamentary tactics to contrive, few bills to prepare, few problems of foreign policy to discuss. They are not a government, as Europeans understand the term; they are a group of heads of departments, whom the chief, though he usually consults them separately, often finds it useful to bring together in one room for a talk about politics, including appointments, or to settle some administrative question which lies on the borderland between the provinces of two ministers. A significant illustration of the contrast between the English and American systems may be found in the fact that whereas an English monarch has never (since Queen Anne's time) sat in his own cabinet, because if he did he would be deemed accountable for its decisions, an American president always does, because he is accountable, and really needs advice to help him, not to shield him.[14]

The so-called cabinet is unknown to the statutes as well as to the Constitution of the United States. So is the English cabinet unknown to the

---

[13] Lincoln decided on his emancipation proclamation without consulting his cabinet, although he read the draft of it to them for criticism.

[14] Another illustration of the contrast may be found in the fact that when the head of a department is absent from Washington the undersecretary of the department is often asked to replace him in the cabinet council.

law of England. But then the English cabinet is a part, is, in fact, a committee, though no doubt an informal committee, of a body as old as Parliament itself, the Privy Council, or Curia Regis. Of the ancient institutions of England which reappear in the Constitution of the United States, the Privy Council is not one.[15] It may have seemed to the Convention of 1787 to be already obsolete. Even in England it was then already a belated survival from an earlier order of things, and now it lives on only in its committees, three of which, the Board of Trade, the Board of Education, and the Agricultural Department, serve as branches of the administration, one, the Judicial Committee, is a law court, and one, the Cabinet, is the virtual executive of the nation.[16] The framers of the American Constitution saw its unsuitability to their conditions. It was nominated, while with them a council must have been elective. Its only effect would have been to control the president, but for domestic administration control is scarcely needed, because the president has only to execute the laws, while in foreign affairs and appointments the Senate controls him already. A third body, over and above the two houses of Congress, was in fact superfluous. The Senate may appear in some points to resemble the English Privy Council of the seventeenth century, because it advises the executive in certain matters; but there is all the difference in the world between being advised by those whom you have yourself chosen and those whom election by others forces upon you. So it happens that the relations of the Senate and the president are seldom cordial, much less confidential, even when he and the majority of the Senate belong to the same party, because the Senate and the president are rival powers jealous of one another.

Note on Army and Navy

The army and navy of the United States have greatly increased in recent years.

---

[15] A privy council, however, appears in the original Constitution of Delaware; and there were in many states councils for advising the governor. When James Wilson was proposing that the executive should consist of a single person, he was asked whether this person was to have a council, and answered that he desired "to have no council which oftener serves to cover than to prevent malpractices."—Elliot's *Debates*, vol. v, 151. So Randolph argued that councillors would impair the president's responsibility. (See *post* Chapter 41.)

[16] The first three of these are formal, the functions being discharged by a single minister, while the Cabinet, though composed of members of the Privy Council, is not formally constituted as a committee.

Number of officers and men in the army was in 1889   26,235
    In 1912 it was   Officers   4,947
                                             Men   87,279
The cost of the army was in 1889 $42,381,671
    In 1913 the army appropriations reached $103,747,441

In the navy the number of officers and men was:

    In 1889   9,831
    In 1913   57,178

In 1889 there were six fighting ships in the navy.
In 1912 there were 208 fighting ships classified as follows:

Battleships (Besides nine old battleships)	29
Cruisers, First class	15
Second class	3
Third class	14
Gunboats	21
Monitors	10
Destroyers	49
Torpedo boats	32
Submarines	35

In 1889 the cost of the navy was $25,767,348.19; in 1913, it was $123,220,707

The Senate

Ｔhe national legislature of the United States, called Congress, consists of two bodies, sufficiently dissimilar in composition, powers, and character to require a separate description.

The Senate consists of two persons from each state, who must be inhabitants of that state, and at least thirty years of age. They were until 1913 elected by the legislature of their state for six years, but are now under the Seventeenth Amendment to the Constitution elected by the registered voters of the state. They are reeligible. One-third retire every two years, so that the whole body is renewed in a period of six years, the old members being thus at any given moment twice as numerous as the new members elected within the last two years. As there are now forty-eight states, the number of senators, originally twenty-six, is now ninety-six. This great and unforeseen augmentation must be borne in mind when considering the purposes for which the Senate was created, for some of which a small body is fitter than a large one. As there remain no Territories which can be formed into states,[1] the number of senators will not (unless, indeed, existing states are divided) rise beyond ninety-six. This is of course much below the present nominal strength of the English House of Lords[2] (above six hundred), and below that of the French Senate (three hundred), and the Prussian Herrenhaus. No senator can hold any office under the United States. The vice-president of the Union is ex officio president of the Senate, but has no vote, except a casting vote when the numbers are equally divided. Failing him (if, for instance, he dies, or falls sick, or succeeds to the presidency), the Senate

---

[1] I reckon in neither the Hawaiian Islands nor Alaska, because the former is hardly likely, within the near future, nor the latter for a long time to come, to contain a civilized white population such as would entitle either of them to be formed into states. See Chap. 96, Vol. II.

[2] At the accession of George III the House of Lords numbered only 174 members.

chooses one of its number to be president pro tempore. His authority in questions of order is very limited, the decision of such questions being held to belong to the Senate itself.[3]

The functions of the Senate fall into three classes—legislative, executive, and judicial.[4] Its legislative function is to pass, along with the House of Representatives, bills which become acts of Congress on the assent of the president, or even without his consent if passed a second time by a two-thirds majority of each house, after he has returned them for reconsideration. Its executive functions are: (*a*) To approve or disapprove the president's nominations of federal officers, including judges, ministers of state, and ambassadors; (*b*) to approve, by a majority of two-thirds of those present, of treaties made by the president—i.e., if less than two-thirds approve, the treaty falls to the ground. Its judicial function is to sit as a court for the trial of impeachments preferred by the House of Representatives.

The most conspicuous, and what was at one time deemed the most important feature of the Senate, is that it represents the several states of the Union as separate commonwealths, and is thus an essential part of the federal scheme. Every state, be it as great as New York or as small as Delaware, sends two senators, no more and no less.[5] This arrangement was long resisted by the delegates of the larger states in the Convention of 1787, and ultimately adopted because nothing less would reassure the smaller states, who feared to be overborne by the larger. It is now the provision of the Constitution most difficult to change, for "no State can be deprived of its equal suffrage in the Senate without its consent," a consent most unlikely to be given. There has never, in point of fact, been any division of interests

[3] The powers of the Lord Chancellor as Speaker of the English House of Lords are much narrower than those of the Speaker in the House of Commons. It is worth notice that as the vice-president is not chosen by the Senate, but by the people, and is not strictly speaking a member of the Senate, so the Lord Chancellor is not chosen to preside by the House of Lords, but by the sovereign, and is not necessarily a peer. This, however, seems to be merely a coincidence, and not the result of a wish to imitate England.

[4] To avoid prolixity, I do not give in the text all the details of the constitutional powers and duties of the houses of Congress: these will be found in the text of the Constitution printed in the Appendix.

[5] New York is twice as large as Scotland, and more populous than Scotland and Wales taken together. Delaware is a little smaller than Norfolk, with about the population of Dorsetshire. It is therefore as if Dorsetshire had in one House of a British legislature as much weight as Scotland and Wales put together, a state of things not very conformable to democratic theory. Nevada has now a population estimated at a little over eighty thousand, but is as powerful in the Senate as New York. This state, which largely consists of burnt-out mining camps, has been really a sort of rotten borough for, and is controlled by, the great "silver men."

or consequent contest between the great states and the small ones.[6] But the provision for the equal representation of all states had the important result of making the slaveholding party, during the thirty years which preceded the Civil War, eager to extend the area of slavery in order that by creating new slave states they might maintain at least an equality in the Senate, and thereby prevent any legislation hostile to slavery.

The plan of giving representatives to the states as commonwealths has had several useful results. It has provided a basis for the Senate unlike that on which the other house of Congress is chosen. Every nation which has formed a legislature with two houses has experienced the difficulty of devising methods of choice sufficiently different to give a distinct character to each house. Italy has a Senate composed of persons nominated by the Crown. The Prussian House of Lords is partly nominated, partly hereditary, partly elective. The Spanish senators are partly hereditary, partly official, partly elective. In the Germanic Empire, the Federal Council consists of delegates of the several kingdoms and principalities. France appoints her senators by indirect election. In England the nonspiritual members of the House of Lords now sit by hereditary right; and those who propose to reconstruct that ancient body are at their wits' end to discover some plan by which it may be strengthened, and made practically useful, without such a direct election as that by which members are chosen to the House of Commons.[7] The American plan, which is older than any of those in use on the European continent, is also better, because it is not only simple, but natural, i.e., grounded on and consonant with the political conditions of America. It produces a body which is both strong in itself and different in its collective character from the more popular House.

Till 1913, it also constituted, as Hamilton anticipated, a link between the state governments and the national government. It is a part of the latter, but its members derive their title to sit in it from their choice by state legislatures. In one respect this connection is no unmixed benefit, for it has helped to make the national parties powerful, and their strife intense, in these last-named bodies. Every vote in the Senate was so important to the great parties

---

[6] Hamilton perceived that this would be so; see his remarks in the Constitutional Convention of New York in 1788.—Elliot's *Debates*, vol. ii, p. 213.

[7] Under a statute of 1876, two persons (now four persons) may be appointed by the Crown to sit as Lords of Appeal, with the dignity of baron for life. The Scotch and Irish peers enjoy hereditary peerages, but are elected by their fellow peers to sit in the House of Lords, the latter for life, the former for each parliament.

that they are forced to struggle for ascendency in each of the state legislatures by whom the senators were elected. The method of choice in these bodies was formerly left to be fixed by the laws of each state, but as this gave rise to much uncertainty and intrigue, a federal statute was passed in 1866 providing that each house of a state legislature shall first vote separately for the election of a federal senator, and that if the choice of both houses shall not fall on the same person, both houses in joint meeting shall proceed to a joint vote, a majority of all the members elected to both houses being present and voting. Even under this arrangement, a senatorial election often leads to long and bitter struggles; the minority endeavouring to prevent a choice, and so keep the seat vacant. Moreover such struggles gave occasion for efforts to influence the doubtful members of a legislature out of which charges of improper methods often arose.

The method of choosing the Senate by indirect election used to excite the admiration of foreign critics, who have found in it a sole and sufficient cause of the excellence of the Senate as a legislative and executive authority. I shall presently inquire whether the critics were right. Be that as it may, the method was before the close of last century becoming increasingly unpopular. Choice by a legislature had come to mean choice by a party majority in a legislative caucus, and the determination of that caucus had often been prearranged by a small group of party managers; or if that did not happen secretly, it had been settled in a party convention which directed the members of the party in the legislature how to cast their votes. There was anyhow little room left for free selection by the legislature. The people, or rather those wire-pullers who manage the people and act in their name, had usually settled the matter beforehand. So hard is it to make any scheme of indirect election work according to its original design; so hard is it to keep even a written and rigid constitution from bending and warping under the actual forces of politics.

Cases moreover occurred in which a rich man practically bought his election. One such led, in 1912, to the expulsion of a newly elected senator for bribery.

While public sentiment was growing more and more hostile to the method of election by state legislatures, and resolutions calling for a change were being passed by these legislatures themselves at the bidding of that sentiment, a plan was discovered by which what amounted to a direct popular election was secured in an indirect way. In 1904 Oregon provided, by a law passed by the people under the initiative method of legislation contained in the constitution of that state, that the political parties might in the party primaries nominate persons for election as United States senators, and that the people might at the ensuing election of the state legislature select by their votes one of these nominees as their choice for senator. Along with this it was also enacted that a candidate for the state legislature might on his nomination either: (1) declare that he would, if elected, vote for that person as United States senator who had received the largest popular vote and thus become "the people's choice"; or, (2) declare that he would consider the popular vote as merely "a recommendation." Or he might make no declaration at all. In 1908 a majority of the members elected to the legislature, having made the former declaration, felt bound to carry it out, and the person who had received the highest popular vote was accordingly elected by that majority, although he was a Democrat and they were Republicans. Thus the people got their way and the federal Constitution was not formally transgressed. In 1909 Nebraska adopted a similar law.

The flank of the Constitution having been thus, so to speak, turned, the battle was virtually over, and the Senate, hitherto hostile to popular election, presently gave way. An amendment transferring the election to the peoples of the states was passed in Congress and accepted by the legislatures of all the states in 1913.[8]

How the new plan will work remains to be seen. It has some obvious merits, and it need not tend to make the Senate a less independent body, for it has in recent years been quite as prone to "play to the gallery" as the House or any other directly elected chamber. But it may add immensely to the expense falling on candidates, as well as to the labour thrown on them in stumping the state; and if it causes senators to be less frequently reelected at the end of their term, it will reduce the element of long political experience heretofore present in it more largely than in the House.

As to the element of expense involved in direct elections, it may be said that the sum which can be spent by candidates for the Senate is fixed by the law of 1911 at $10,000 and that this amount cannot be exceeded under the new arrangement. The obvious reply to this is that under the old system many senators paid nothing at all for their campaign expenses and that the law just referred to does not limit the amount which may be spent by the friends of a candidate in his campaign. It is money from outside sources that is to be feared more than heavy expenditures by the candidates themselves. On the other hand, it is notorious that large sums of money

---

[8] As is provided in the Constitution of the Australian Commonwealth, where each state elects its senators by direct popular vote.

were often paid by candidates seeking their election from state legislatures; and many champions of the new order say that it is better for the money to be spent in a statewide campaign of publicity than in the secret confines of the legislative caucus.

Members of the Senate vote as individuals, that is to say, the vote a senator gives is his own and not that of his state. It was otherwise in the Congress of the old Confederation before 1789; it is otherwise in the present Federal Council of the German Empire, in which each state votes as a whole, though the number of her votes is proportioned to her population. Accordingly, in the American Senate, the two senators from a state may belong to opposite parties; and this often happens in the case of senators from states in which the two great parties are pretty equally balanced, and the majority oscillates between them.[9] As the state legislatures sit for short terms (the larger of the two houses usually for two years only), a senator has during the greater part of his six years' term to look for reelection not to the present but to a future state legislature,[10] and this circumstance tends to give him somewhat more independence.

The length of the senatorial term was one of the provisions of the Constitution which were most warmly attacked and defended in 1788. A six years' tenure, it was urged, would turn the senators into dangerous aristocrats, forgetful of the legislature which had appointed them; and some went so far as to demand that the legislature of a state should have the right to recall its senators.[11] Experience has shown that the term is by no means too long; and its length is one among the causes which have made it easier for senators than for members of the House to procure reelection, a result which, though it offends the doctrinaires of democracy, worked well for the country. Senators from the smaller states were more frequently reelected than those from the larger, because in the small states the competition of ambitious men is less keen, politics less changeful, the people perhaps more steadily attached to a man whom they have once honoured with their

---

[9] It was arranged from the beginning of the federal government that the two senatorships from the same state should never be vacant at the same time except in case of a death or "deadlock."

[10] If a vacancy occurs in a senatorship at a time when the state legislature is not sitting, the executive of the state is empowered to fill it up until the next meeting of the state legislature. This power is specially important if the vacancy occurs at a time when parties are equally divided in the Senate.

[11] This was recommended by a Pennsylvanian convention, which met after the adoption of the Constitution to suggest amendments. See Elliot's *Debates*, vol. ii, p. 545. A state legislature sometimes passes resolutions instructing its senators to vote in a particular way, but the senators are of course in no way bound to regard such instructions.

confidence. The senator from such a state generally found it more easy to maintain his influence over his own legislature; not to add that if the state should be amenable to the power of wealth, his wealth will tell for more than it could in a large state. Yet no small state was ever more controlled by one man than the great state of Pennsylvania by its "bosses" ever since the Civil War years. The average age of the Senate is less than might be expected. Three-fourths of its members are under sixty. The importance of the state he represents makes no great difference to the influence which a senator enjoys; this depends on his talents, experience, and character; and as the small state senators have often the advantage of long service and a safe seat, they are often among the most influential.

The Senate resembles the upper houses of Europe, and differs from those of the British colonies, and of most of the states of the Union, in being a permanent chamber. It is an undying body, with an existence continuous since its first creation; and though it changes, it does not change all at once, as do assemblies created by a singular popular election, but undergoes an unceasing process of gradual renewal, like a lake into which streams bring fresh water to replace that which the issuing river carries out. As Harrington said of the Venetian Senate, "being always changing, it is forever the same." This provision was designed to give the Senate that permanency of composition which might qualify it to conduct or control the foreign policy of the nation. An incidental and more valuable result has been the creation of a set of traditions and a corporate spirit which have tended to form habits of dignity and self-respect. The new senators, being only one-third, or less, are readily assimilated; and though the balance of power shifts from one party to another according to the predominance of one or other party, it shifts more slowly than in bodies directly chosen all at once, and a policy is therefore less apt to be suddenly reversed.

The legislative powers of the Senate being, except in one point, the same as those of the House of Representatives, will be described later. That one point is a restriction as regards money bills. On the ground that it is only by the direct representatives of the people that taxes ought to be levied, and in obvious imitation of the venerable English doctrine, which had already found a place in several state constitutions, the Constitution (art. I, §7) provides that "All bills for raising revenue shall originate in the House of Representatives, but the Senate may propose or concur with amendments, as on other bills." In practice, while the House strictly guards its right of origination, the Senate largely exerts its power of amendment, and wrangles with the House over taxes, and still more keenly over appropriations. Almost every session ends with a dispute, a conference, a compromise. Among the rules (a few extracts from which, touching some noteworthy points, will be found in the Appendix) there is none providing for a closure of debate (although an attempt to introduce such a rule was made by Henry Clay, and renewed in 1890), nor any limiting the length either of a debate or of a speech. The Senate is proud of having conducted its business without the aid of such regulations, and this has been due, not merely to the small size of the assembly, but to the sense of its dignity which has usually pervaded its members, and to the power which the opinion of the whole body has exercised on each. Where every man knows his colleagues intimately, each, if he has a character to lose, stands in awe of the others, and has so strong a sense of his own interest in maintaining the moral authority of the chamber, that he is slow to resort to extreme methods which might lower it in public estimation. Till recently, systematic obstruction, or, as it is called in America, "filibustering," familiar to the House, was almost unknown in the calmer air of the Senate. When it was applied some years ago by the Democratic senators to stop a bill to which they strongly objected, their conduct was not disapproved by the country, because the whole party, a minority very little smaller than the Republican majority, supported it, and people believed that nothing but some strong reason would have induced the whole party so to act. Accordingly the majority yielded.

The absence of a closure rule is a fact of great political moment. In 1890 it prevented the passage of a bill, already accepted by the House, for placing federal elections under the control of federal authorities, a measure which would have powerfully affected the Southern states, and might possibly have raised civil commotions.

Divisions are taken, not by separating the senators into lobbies and counting them, as in the British Parliament, but by calling the names of senators alphabetically. The Constitution provides that one-fifth of those present may demand that the yeas and nays be entered in the journal. Every senator answers to his name with aye or no. He may, however, ask the leave of the Senate to abstain from voting; and if he is paired, he states, when his name is called, that he has paired with such and such another senator, and is thereupon excused.

When the Senate goes into executive session, the galleries are cleared and the doors closed; and the obligation of secrecy is supposed to be enforced by the penalty of expulsion to which a senator, disclosing confidential proceedings, makes himself liable. Practically, however, newspaper men find little difficulty in ascertaining what passes in secret session.[12] The threatened punishment has never been inflicted, and occasions often arise when senators feel it to be desirable that the public should know what their colleagues have been doing. There have been movements within the Senate against maintaining secrecy, particularly with regard to the confirming of nominations to office; and there is also a belief in the country that publicity would make for purity. But while some of the black sheep of the Senate love darkness because their works are evil, other members of undoubted respectability defend the present system because they think it supports the power and dignity of their body.

[12] It used to be said that secrecy was better observed in the case of discussions on treaties than where appointments are in question. Once a Western newspaper published an account of what took place in a secret session. A committee appointed to inquire into the matter questioned every senator. Each swore that he had not divulged the proceedings, and the newspaper people also swore that their information did not come from any senator. Nothing could be ascertained, and nobody was punished.

The Senate as an Executive
and Judicial Body

The Senate is not only a legislative but also an executive chamber; in fact in its early days the executive functions seem to have been thought the more important; and Hamilton went so far as to speak of the national executive authority as divided between two branches, the president and the Senate. These executive functions are two, the power of approving treaties, and that of confirming nominations to office submitted by the president.

To what has already been said regarding the functions of the president and Senate as regards treaties (see above, Chapter 6) I need only add that the Senate through its right of confirming or rejecting engagements with foreign powers, secures a general control over foreign policy; though it must be remembered that many of the most important acts done in this sphere (as for instance the movement of troops or ships) are purely executive acts, not falling under this control. It is in the discretion of the president whether he will communicate current negotiations to it and take its advice upon them, or will say nothing till he lays a completed treaty before it. One or other course is from time to time followed, according to the nature of the case, or the degree of friendliness existing between the president and the majority of the Senate. But in general, the president's best policy is to keep the leaders of the senatorial majority, and in particular the Committee on Foreign Relations, informed of the progress of any pending negotiation. He thus feels the pulse of the Senate, which, like other assemblies, has a collective self-esteem leading it to strive for all the information and power it can secure, and while keeping it in good humour, can foresee what kind of arrangement it may be induced to sanction. Much depends upon the confidence which the Senate feels in the judgment of the secretary of state and on the tact which he shows in his dealings with senators. The right of going into secret session enables the whole Senate to consider despatches communicated by the president; and though treaties are sometimes considered in open session, important matters having first been submitted to the Foreign Relations Committee, can thus be discussed without the disadvantage of publicity. Of course no momentous secret can be long kept,[1] even by the committee, according to the proverb in the Elder Edda—"Tell one man thy secret, but not two; if three know, the world knows."

This control of foreign policy by the Senate goes far to meet the difficulties which popular governments find in dealing with foreign powers. If each step to be taken must be previously submitted to the ruling assembly, the nation is forced to show its whole hand, and precious opportunities of winning an ally or striking a bargain may be lost. If on the other hand the executive is permitted to conduct negotiations in secret, there is always the risk, either that the governing assembly may disavow what has been done, a risk which makes foreign states legitimately suspicious and unwilling to negotiate, or that the nation may have to ratify, because it feels bound in honour by the act of its executive agents, arrangements which its judgment condemns. Participation by the Senate in negotiations diminishes these difficulties, because it apprises the executive of what the judgment of the ratifying body is likely to be, and it commits that body by advance. The necessity of ratification by the Senate in order to give effect to a treaty, enables the country to retire from a doubtful bargain, though in a way which other powers find disagreeable, as England did when the Senate rejected the Reverdy-Johnson Treaty of 1869. European statesmen may ask what becomes under such a system of the boldness and promptitude so often needed to effect a successful coup in foreign policy, or how a consistent attitude can be maintained if there is in the chairman of the Foreign Relations Committee a sort of second foreign secretary. The answer is that America is not Europe. The problems which the State Department of the United States has to deal with have been far fewer and usually far simpler than those of the Old World. The Republic, though her power has now crossed the Pacific, keeps consistently to her own side of the Atlantic; and it is a merit of the system of senatorial control that it has tended, by discouraging the executive from schemes which may prove resultless, to diminish the taste for foreign enterprises, and to save the country from being entangled with alliances, protectorates, responsibilities of all sorts beyond its own frontiers. It is the

---

[1] Cæsar Borgia complained that the Florentine Republic could not keep a secret.

easier for the Americans to practise this reserve because they need no alliances, standing unassailable in their own hemisphere. The circumstances of England, with her powerful European neighbours, her Indian Empire, and her colonies scattered over the world, are widely different. Yet different as the circumstances of England are, the day may come when in England the question of limiting the at present wide discretion of the executive in foreign affairs will have to be dealt with.[2] The example of the American Senate may then be cited, but there is of course this important difference between the two countries, that in England Parliament can dismiss ministers who have concluded a treaty which it disapproves, whereas in the United States a president, not being similarly removable by Congress, would be exempt from any control were the Senate not associated with him in the making of a treaty.

The Senate may and occasionally does amend a treaty, and return it amended to the president. There is nothing to prevent it from proposing a draft treaty to him, or asking him to prepare one, but this is not the practice. For ratification a vote of two-thirds of the senators present is required. This gives great power to a vexatious minority, and increases the danger, evidenced by several incidents in the history of the Union, that the Senate or a faction in it may deal with foreign policy in a narrow, sectional, electioneering spirit. When the interest of any group of states is, or is supposed to be, against the making of a given treaty, that treaty may be defeated by the senators from those states. They tell the other senators of their own party that the prospects of the party in the district of the country whence they come will be improved if the treaty is rejected and a bold aggressive line is taken in further negotiations. Some of these senators, who care more for the party than for justice or the common interests of the country, rally to the cry, and all the more gladly if their party is opposed to the president in power, because in defeating the treaty they humiliate his administration. Thus the treaty may be rejected, and the settlement of the question at issue indefinitely postponed. It may be thought that a party acting in this vexatious way will suffer in public esteem. This happens in extreme cases; but the public are usually so indifferent to foreign affairs, and so little skilled in judging of them, that offences of the kind described

[2] Parliament of course may and sometimes does interfere; but the majority which supports the ministry of the day usually forbears to press the Foreign Office for information which it is declared to be undesirable to furnish.

   In 1886 a resolution was all but carried in the House of Commons, desiring all treaties to be laid before Parliament for its approval before being finally concluded.

may be committed with practical impunity. It is harder to fix responsibility on a body of senators than on the executive; and whereas the executive has usually an interest in settling diplomatic troubles, whose continuance it finds annoying, the Senate has no such interest, but is willing to keep them open so long as some political advantage can be sucked out of them. The habit of using foreign policy for electioneering purposes is not confined to America. It has been seen in England, and in France, and even in monarchical Germany. But in America the treaty-confirming power of the Senate opens a particularly easy and tempting door to such practices.

The other executive function of the Senate, that of confirming nominations submitted by the president, has been discussed in the chapter on the powers of that officer. It is there explained how senators have used their right of confirmation to secure for themselves a huge mass of federal patronage, and how by means of this right, a majority hostile to the president can thwart and annoy him. Sometimes he ought to be thwarted; yet the protection which the Senate provides against abuses of his nominating power is far from complete.

Does the control of the Senate operate to prevent abuses of patronage by the president? To some extent it does, yet less completely than could be wished. When the majority belongs to the same party as the president, appointments are usually arranged, or to use a familiar expression, "squared," between them, with a view primarily to party interests. When the majority is opposed to the president, they are tempted to agree to his worst appointments, because such appointments discredit him and his party with the country, and become a theme of hostile comment in the next electioneering campaign. As the initiative is his, it may be the nominating president, and not the confirming Senate, whom public opinion will condemn. These things being so, it may be doubted whether this executive function of the Senate is now a valuable part of the Constitution. It was designed to prevent the president from making himself a tyrant by filling the great offices with his accomplices or tools. That danger has passed away, if it ever existed; and Congress has other means of muzzling an ambitious chief magistrate. The more fully responsibility for appointments can be concentrated upon him, and the fewer the secret influences to which he is exposed, the better will his appointments be. On the other hand, it must be admitted that the participation of the Senate causes in practice less friction and delay than might have been expected from a dual control. The appointments to the cabinet offices are confirmed as a matter of course. Those of diplomatic officers are seldom rejected. "Little tiffs" are frequent when the senatorial majority is in opposition to the executive, but the machinery, if it does not work smoothly, works well enough to carry on the ordinary business of the country, though a European observer, surprised that a democratic country allows such important business to be transacted with closed doors, is inclined to agree with the view lately advanced in the Senate that nominations ought to be discussed publicly rather than in secret executive session.

The judicial function of the Senate is to sit as a high court for the trial of persons impeached by the House of Representatives. The senators "are on oath or affirmation," and a vote of two-thirds of those present is needed for a conviction. Of the process, as affecting the president, I have spoken in Chapter 5. It is applicable to other officials. Besides President Johnson, eight persons in all have been impeached, viz.:

> Six federal judges, of whom three were acquitted, and three convicted, one for violence and drunkenness, another for having joined the Secessionists of 1861, a third (a judge of the Commerce Court) for conduct in pending suits which tended to his own profit. Impeachment is the only means by which a federal judge can be got rid of.
>
> One senator, who was acquitted for want of jurisdiction, the Senate deciding that a senatorship is not a "civil office" within the meaning of art. III, § 4 of the Constitution.
>
> One minister, a secretary of war, who resigned before the impeachment was actually preferred, and escaped on the ground that being a private person he was not impeachable.

Rarely as this method of proceeding has been employed, it could not be dispensed with; and it is better that the Senate should try cases in which a political element is usually present, than that the impartiality of the Supreme Court should be exposed to the criticism it would have to bear, did such political questions come before it. Most senators are or have been lawyers of eminence, so that so far as legal knowledge goes they are competent members of a court.

The Senate: Its Working and Influence

Most Americans consider the Senate one of the successes of their Constitution, a worthy monument of the wisdom and foresight of its founders. Foreign observers have repeated this praise, and have perhaps, in their less perfect knowledge, sounded it even more loudly.

The aims with which the Senate was created, the purposes it was to fulfil, are set forth, under the form of answers to objections, in five letters (61–65), all by Alexander Hamilton, in the *Federalist*.[1] These aims were the five following:

To conciliate the spirit of independence in the several states, by giving each, however small, equal representation with every other, however large, in one branch of the national government;

To create a council qualified, by its moderate size and the experience of its members, to advise and check the president in the exercise of his powers of appointing to office and concluding treaties;

To restrain the impetuosity and fickleness of the popular House, and so guard against the effects of gusts of passion or sudden changes of opinion in the people;

To provide a body of men whose greater experience, longer term of membership, and comparative independence of popular election, would make them an element of stability in the government of the nation, enabling it to maintain its character in the eyes of foreign states, and to preserve a continuity of policy at home and abroad;

---

[1] See also Hamilton's speeches in the New York Convention.—Elliot's *Debates*, vol. ii, p. 301 *sqq*.

To establish a court proper for the trial of impeachments, a remedy
deemed necessary to prevent abuse of power by the executive.

All of these five objects have been more or less perfectly attained; and
the Senate has acquired a position in the government which Hamilton
scarcely ventured to hope for. In 1788 he wrote: "Against the force of the
immediate representatives of the people, nothing will be able to maintain
even the constitutional authority of the Senate, but such a display of
enlightened policy, and attachment to the public good, as will divide with
the House of Representatives the affections and support of the entire body
of the people themselves."

It may be doubted whether the Senate has excelled the House in attachment
to the public good; but it has certainly shown greater capacity for managing
the public business, and has won the respect, if not the affections, of the
people, by its sustained intellectual power.

The *Federalist* did not think it necessary to state, nor have Americans
generally realized, that this masterpiece of the Constitution-makers was in
fact a happy accident. No one in the Convention of 1787 set out with the
idea of such a Senate as ultimately emerged from their deliberations. It grew
up under the hands of the Convention, as the result of the necessity for
reconciling the conflicting demands of the large and the small states. The
concession of equal representation in the Senate induced the small states to
accept the principle of representation according to population in the House
of Representatives; and a series of compromises between the advocates of
popular power, as embodied in the House, and those of monarchical power,
as embodied in the president, led to the allotment of attributes and functions
which have made the Senate what it is. When the work which they had
almost unconsciously perfected was finished, the leaders of the Convention
perceived its excellence, and defended it by arguments in which we feel the
note of sincere conviction. Yet the conception they formed of it differed
from the reality which has been evolved. Although they had created it as a
branch of the legislature, they thought of it as being first and foremost a
body with executive functions. And this, at first, it was. The traditions of
the old Congress of the Confederation, in which the delegates of the states
voted by states, the still earlier traditions of the executive councils, which
advised the governors of the colonies while still subject to the British Crown,
clung about the Senate and affected the minds of the senators. It was a
small body, originally of twenty-six, even in 1810 of thirty-four members
only, a body not ill fitted for executive work. Its members, regarding

themselves as a sort of congress of ambassadors from their respective states, were accustomed to refer for advice and instructions each to his state legislature. So late as 1828, a Senator after arguing strongly against a measure declared that he would nevertheless vote for it, because he believed his state to be in its favour.[2] For the first five years of its existence, the Senate sat with closed doors, occupying itself chiefly with the confidential business of appointments and treaties, and conferring in private with the ministers of the president. Not till 1816 did it create, in imitation of the House, those standing committees which the experience of the House had shown to be, in bodies where the executive ministers do not sit, the necessary organs for dealing with legislative business. Its present character as a legislative body, not less active and powerful than the other branch of Congress, is the result of a long process of evolution, a process possible (as will be more fully explained hereafter) even under the rigid Constitution of the United States, because the language of the sections which define the competence of the Senate is wide and general. But in gaining legislative authority, it has not lost its executive functions, although those which relate to treaties are largely exercised on the advice of the standing Committee on Foreign Relations. And as respects these executive functions it stands alone in the world. No European state, no British colony, entrusts to an elective assembly that direct participation in executive business which the Senate enjoys.

What is meant by saying that the Senate has proved a success?

It has succeeded by effecting that chief object of the Fathers of the Constitution, the creation of a centre of gravity in the government, an authority able to correct and check on the one hand the "democratic recklessness" of the House, on the other the "monarchical ambition" of the president. Placed between the two, it is necessarily the rival and generally the opponent of both. The House can accomplish nothing without its concurrence. The president can be checkmated by its resistance. These are, so to speak, negative or prohibitive successes. It has achieved less in the way of positive work, whether of initiating good legislation or of improving the measures which the House sends it. But the whole scheme of the American Constitution tends to put stability above activity, to sacrifice the productive energies of the bodies it creates to their power of resisting

---

[2] A similar statement was made in 1883 by a senator from Arkansas in justifying his vote for a bill he disapproved. But the fact that from early days downwards the two senators from a state might (and did) vote against one another shows that the true view of the senator is that he represents the people and not the government of his state.

changes in the general fabric of the government. The Senate has succeeded in making itself eminent and powerful. It has drawn the best talent of the nation, so far as that talent flows to politics, into its body, has established an intellectual supremacy, has furnished a vantage ground from which men of ability may speak with authority to their fellow citizens.

To what causes are these successes to be ascribed? Hamilton assumed that the Senate would be weaker than the House of Representatives, because it would not so directly spring from, speak for, be looked to by, the people. This was a natural view, especially as the analogy between the position of the Senate towards the House of Representatives in America, and that of the House of Lords towards the House of Commons in Great Britain, an analogy constantly present to the men of 1787, seemed to suggest that the larger and more popular chamber must dwarf and overpower the smaller one. But the Senate has proved no less strong, and morally more influential, than its sister House of Congress. The analogy was unsound, because the British House of Lords is hereditary and the Senate representative. In these days no hereditary assembly, be its members ever so able, ever so wealthy, ever so socially powerful, can speak with the authority which belongs to those who speak for the people. Mirabeau's famous words in the Salle des Menus at Versailles, "We are here by the will of the people, and nothing but bayonets shall send us hence," express the whole current of modern feeling. Now the Senate, albeit not chosen by direct popular election, does represent the people; and what it may lose through not standing in immediate contact with the masses, it gains in representing such ancient and powerful commonwealths as the states. A senator from New York or Pennsylvania speaks for, and is responsible to, millions of men. No wonder he has an authority beyond that of the long-descended nobles of Prussia, or the peers of Britain whose possessions stretch over whole counties.

This is the first reason for the strength of the Senate, as compared with the upper chambers of other countries. It is built on a solid foundation of ultimate choice by the people and consequent responsibility to them. A second cause is to be found in its small size. A small body educates its members better than a large one, because each member has more to do, sooner masters the business not only of his committee but of the whole body, feels a livelier sense of the significance of his own action in bringing about collective action. There is less disposition to abuse the freedom of debate. Party spirit may be as intense as in great assemblies, yet it is mitigated by the disposition to keep on friendly terms with those whom, however much you may dislike them, you have constantly to meet, and by the feeling of a common interest in sustaining the authority of the body. A senator soon gets to know each of his colleagues—they were originally only twenty-five—and what each of them thinks of him; he becomes sensitive to their opinion; he is less inclined to pose before them, however he may pose before the public. Thus the Senate formed, in its childhood, better habits in discussing and transacting its business than would have been formed by a large assembly; and these habits its maturer age retains. Its comparative permanence has also worked for good. Six years, which seem a short term in Europe, are in America a long term when compared with the two years for which the House of Representatives and the assemblies of nearly all the states are elected, long also when compared with the swiftness of change in American politics. A senator has the opportunity of thoroughly learning his duties, and of proving that he has learnt them. He becomes slightly more independent of his constituency, which in America, where politicians catch at every passing breeze of opinion, is a clear gain. Nevertheless he must be frequently at work in his state, and struggle to maintain his influence among local politicians there.

The smallness and the permanence of the Senate have however another important influence on its character. They contribute to one main cause of its success, the superior intellectual quality of its members. Every European who has described it, has dwelt upon the capacity of those who compose it, and most have followed Tocqueville in attributing this capacity to the method of double election. In supposing that the choice of senators by the state legislature had proved a better means than direct choice by the people of discovering and selecting the fittest men they missed the real cause. I have already remarked that since the Civil War the legislatures did little more than register and formally complete a choice already made by the party managers, and perhaps ratified in the party convention. But apart from this recent development, and reviewing the whole hundred years' history of the Senate, the true explanation of its capacity is to be found in the superior attraction which it has for the ablest and most ambitious men. A senator has more power than a member of the House, more dignity, a longer term of service, a more independent position. Hence every federal politician aims at a senatorship, and looks on the place of representative as a stepping-stone to what is in this sense an upper house, that it is the house to which representatives seek to mount. It is no more surprising that the average capacity of the Senate should surpass that of the House, than that the average cabinet minister of Europe should be abler than the average member of the legislature.

What is more, the Senate so trains its members as to improve their political efficiency. Several years of service in a small body, with important and delicate executive work, are worth twice as many years of jostling in the crowd of representatives at the other end of the Capitol. If the Senate does not find the man who enters it already superior to the average of federal politicians, it makes him superior. But natural selection, as has been said, usually seats upon its benches the best ability of the country that has flowed into political life, and would do so no less were the election in form a direct one by the people at the polls.

Most of the leading men of the last century have sat in the Senate, and in it were delivered most of the famous speeches which illumine, though too rarely, the wearisome debates over states' rights and slavery from 1825 till 1860. One of these debates, that in the beginning of 1830, which called forth Daniel Webster's majestic defence of the Constitution, was long called par excellence "the great debate in the Senate."[3]

Of the ninety-two senators who sat in the Sixty-first Congress (1909–11) thirty-six had sat in the other house of Congress, and thirty-nine had served in state legislatures.[4] In the Sixty-second Congress (1911–13) out of ninety-six senators, twenty-eight had sat in the House of Representatives, and thirty-nine in state legislatures. Many had been judges or state governors; many had sat in state conventions. Nearly all had held some public function. A man must have had considerable experience of affairs, and of human nature in its less engaging aspects, before he enters this august conclave. But experience is not all gain. Practice makes perfect in evildoing no less than in well-doing. The habits of local politics and of work in the House of Representatives by which the senators have been trained, while they develop shrewdness and quickness in all characters, tell injuriously on characters of the meaner sort, leaving men's views narrow, and giving them a taste as well as a talent for intrigue.

The chamber in which the Senate meets is rectangular, but the part occupied by the seats is semicircular in form, the vice-president of the United States, who acts as presiding officer, having his chair on a marble dais, slightly raised, in the centre of the chord, with the senators all turned

---

[3] In those days the Senate sat in that smaller chamber which is now occupied by the Supreme Federal Court.

[4] I cannot be sure of the absolute actual accuracy of these figures, which I have compiled from the *Congressional Directory*, because some Senators do not set forth the whole of their political career. The proportion of senators who have previously been members of the House of Representatives is larger among the senators from the older states than it is in the West.

towards him as they sit in curving rows, each in an armchair, with a desk in front of it. The floor is about as large as the whole superficial area of the British House of Commons, but as there are great galleries on all four sides, running back over the lobbies, the upper part of the chamber and its total air space much exceeds that of the English house. One of these galleries is appropriated to the president of the United States; the others to ladies, diplomatic representatives, the press, and the public. Behind the senatorial chairs and desks there is an open space into which strangers can be brought by the senators, who sit and talk on the sofas there placed. Members of foreign legislatures are allowed access to this outer "floor of the Senate." There is, especially when the galleries are empty, a slight echo in the room, which obliges most speakers to strain their voices. Two or three pictures on the walls somewhat relieve the cold tone of the chamber, with its marble platform and sides unpierced by windows, for the light enters through glass compartments in the ceiling.

A senator always addresses the chair "Mr. President," and refers to other senators by their states, "The senator from Ohio," "The senator from Tennessee." When two senators rise at the same moment, the chair calls on one, indicating him by his state, "The senator from Minnesota has the floor."[5] Senators of the Democratic party sit, and apparently always have sat, on the right of the chair, Republican senators on the left; but, as already explained, the parties do not face one another. The impression which the place makes on a visitor is one of businesslike gravity, a gravity which though plain is dignified. It has the air not so much of a popular assembly as of a diplomatic congress. The English House of Lords, with its fretted roof and windows rich with the figures of departed kings, its majestic throne, its Lord Chancellor in his wig on the woolsack, its benches of lawn-sleeved bishops, its bar where the Commons throng at a great debate, is not only more gorgeous and picturesque in externals, but appeals far more powerfully to the historical imagination, for it seems to carry the Middle Ages down into the modern world. The Senate is modern, severe, and practical. So, too, few debates in the Senate rise to the level of the better debates in the English chamber. But the Senate seldom wears that air of listless vacuity

[5] A late president of the Senate was in the habit of distinguishing the two senators from the state of Arkansas, by calling on one as the senator for "Arkansas" (pronounced as written, with accent on the penult), and the other as the senator for "Arkansaw," with the second syllable short. As Europeans often ask which is the correct pronunciation, I may say that in 1904 the legislature of Arkansas by a "joint resolution" declared that the accent ought to be on the first and last syllables, and that the final *s* ought not to be sounded.

and superannuated indolence which the House of Lords presents on all but a few nights of every session. The faces are keen and forcible, as of men who have learned to know the world, and have much to do in it; the place seems consecrated to great affairs.

As might be expected from the small number of the audience, as well as from its character, discussions in the Senate are apt to be sensible and practical. Speeches are shorter and less fervid than those made in the House of Representatives, for the larger an assembly the more prone is it to declamation. The least useful debates are those on show days, when a series of set discourses are delivered on some prominent question. Each senator brings down and fires off in the air a carefully prepared oration which may have little bearing on what has gone before. In fact the speeches are made not to convince the assembly—no one dreams of that—but to keep a man's opinions before the public and sustain his fame. The question at issue has usually been already settled, either in a committee or in a "caucus" of the party which commands the majority, so that these long and sonorous harangues are mere rhetorical thunder addressed to the nation outside.

The Senate now contains many men of great wealth. Some, an increasing number, are senators because they are rich; a few are rich because they are senators; while in the remaining cases the same talents which have won success in law or commerce have brought their possessor to the top in politics also. The commercial element is stronger now than formerly; but the majority are or have been lawyers. Some senators used to practice before the Supreme Court, but that is now rare. Complaints are occasionally levelled against the aristocratic tendencies which wealth is supposed to have bred, and sarcastic references are made to the sumptuous residences which senators have built on the new avenues of Washington. While admitting that there is more sympathy for the capitalist class among these rich men than there would be in a Senate of poor men, I must add that the Senate is far from being a class body like the upper houses of England or Prussia or Spain or Denmark. It is substantially representative, by its composition as well as by legal delegation, of all parts of American society; it is far too dependent, and far too sensible that it is dependent, upon public opinion, to undertake the championship of the rich, although doubtless more in sympathy with them than is the House. The senators, however, indulge some social pretensions. They are the nearest approach to an official aristocracy that has yet been seen in America. They and their wives are allowed precedence at private entertainments, as well as on public occasions, over members of the House, and of course over private citizens. Jefferson might turn in his grave if he knew of such an attempt to introduce European distinctions of rank into his democracy; yet as the office is temporary, and the rank vanishes with the office, these pretensions are harmless; it is only the universal social equality of the country that makes them noteworthy. Apart from such petty advantages, the position of a senator, who can count on reelection, is the most desirable in the political world of America. It gives as much power and influence as a man need desire. It secures for him the ear of the public. It is more permanent than the presidency or a cabinet office, requires less labour, involves less vexation, though still great vexation, by importunate office-seekers.

European writers on America used to be too much inclined to idealize the Senate. Admiring its structure and function, they have assumed that the actors must be worthy of their parts. They were encouraged in this tendency by the language of many Americans. As the Romans were never tired of repeating that the ambassador of Pyrrhus had called the Roman senate an assembly of kings, so Americans of refinement, who are ashamed of the turbulent House of Representatives, were at one time wont to talk of the Senate as an Olympian dwelling place of statesmen and sages. That it never was; and still less would anybody now so describe it. It is a company of shrewd and vigorous men who have fought their way to the front by the ordinary methods of American politics, and on many of whom the battle has left its stains. There are abundant opportunities for intrigue in the Senate, because its most important business is done in the secrecy of committee rooms or of executive session; and many senators are intriguers. There are opportunities for misusing senatorial powers. Scandals have sometimes arisen from the practice of employing as counsel before the Supreme Court, senators whose influence has contributed to the appointment or confirmation of the judges.[6] There are opportunities for corruption and blackmailing, of which unscrupulous men are well known to take advantage. Such men are fortunately few; but considering how demoralized are the legislatures of a few states, their presence must be looked for; and the rest of the Senate, however it may blush for them, is obliged to work with them and to treat them as equals. The contagion of political vice is nowhere so swiftly potent as in legislative bodies, because you cannot taboo a man who has got a vote. You may loathe him personally, but he is the people's choice. He has a right to share in the government of the country; you are grateful to him

---

[6] In 1886, a bill was brought in forbidding members of either house of Congress to appear in the federal courts as counsel for any railroad company or other corporation which might, in respect of its having received land grants, be affected by federal legislation.

when he saves you on a critical division; you discover that "he is not such a bad fellow when one knows him"; people remark that he gives good dinners, or has an agreeable wife; and so it goes on till falsehood and knavery are covered under the cloak of party loyalty.

As respects ability, the Senate cannot be profitably compared with the English House of Lords, because that assembly consists of some thirty eminent and as many ordinary men attending regularly, with a multitude of undistinguished persons who rarely appear, and take no real share in the deliberations. Setting the Senate beside the House of Commons, the average natural capacity of its ninety-six members is not above that of the ninety-six best men in the English house. There is more variety of talent in the latter, and a greater breadth of culture. On the other hand, the Senate excels in legal knowledge as well as in practical shrewdness. The House of Commons contains more men who could give a good address on a literary or historical subject; the Senate together with a very few eminent lawyers, has more who could either deliver a rousing popular harangue or manage the business of a great trading company, these being the forms of capacity commonest among congressional politicians. An acute American observer said (writing in 1885) and the description is still true:

> "The Senate is just what the mode of its election and the conditions of public life in this country make it. Its members are chosen from the ranks of active politicians, in accordance with a law of natural selection to which the State legislatures are commonly obedient; and it is probable that it contains, consequently, the best men that our system calls into politics. If these best men are not good, it is because our system of government fails to attract better men by its prizes, not because the country affords or could afford no finer material. The Senate is in fact, of course, nothing more than a part, though a considerable part, of the public service; and if the general conditions of that service be such as to starve statesmen and foster demagogues, the Senate itself will be full of the latter kind, simply because there are no others available."[7]

This judgment is severe, but not unjust. Whether the senators of today are inferior in ability and integrity to those of seventy, forty, twenty years ago, is not easy to determine. But it must be admitted, however regretfully, that they are less independent, less respected by the people, less influential with the people, than were their predecessors; and their wealth, which has made them fear the reproach of wanting popular sympathies, may count for something in this decline.

[7] Woodrow Wilson, *Congressional Government*, p. 194.

The place which the Senate holds in the constitutional system of America cannot be fully appreciated till the remaining parts of the system have been described. This much, however, may be claimed for it, that it has been and is still, though perhaps less than formerly, a steadying and moderating power. One cannot say, in the language of European politics, that it has represented aristocratic principles, or antipopular principles, or even conservative principles. Each of the great historic parties has in turn commanded a majority in it, and the difference between their strength has seldom been marked for any great while. On none of the great issues that have divided the nation has the Senate been, for any long period, decidedly opposed to the other house of Congress. It showed no more capacity than the House for grappling with the problems of slavery extension. It was scarcely less ready than the House to strain the Constitution by supporting Lincoln in the exercise of the so-called war powers, or subsequently by cutting down presidential authority in the struggle between Congress and Andrew Johnson, though it refused to convict him when impeached by the House. All the fluctuations of public opinion tell upon it, nor does it venture, any more than the House, to confront a popular impulse, because it is, equally with the House, subject to the control of the great parties, which seek to use while they obey the dominant sentiment of the hour.

But the fluctuations of opinion tell on it less energetically than on the House of Representatives. They reach it more slowly and gradually, owing to the system which renews it by one-third every second year, so that it sometimes happens that before the tide has risen to the top of the flood in the Senate it has already begun to ebb in the country. The Senate has been a stouter bulwark against agitation, not merely because a majority of the senators have always four years of membership before them, within which period public feeling may change, but also because the senators have been individually stronger men than the representatives. They are less democratic, not in opinion, but in temper, because they are more self-confident, because they have more to lose, because experience has taught them how fleeting a thing popular sentiment is, and how useful a thing continuity in policy is. The Senate has therefore usually kept its head better than the House of Representatives. It has expressed more adequately the judgment, as contrasted with the emotion, of the nation; and at least since 1896 it has been the body to which property and the financial powers chiefly look for support. In this sense it does constitute a "check and balance" in the federal government. Of the three great functions which the Fathers of the Constitution meant it to perform, the first, that of securing the rights of the smaller states, is no longer important; while the second, that of advising or controlling the executive in appointments as well as in treaties, has given rise to evils possibly commensurate with its benefits. But the third duty is still well discharged, for "the propensity of a single and numerous assembly to yield to the impulse of sudden and violent passions" is frequently, though not invariably, restrained.

The House of Representatives

The House of Representatives, usually called for shortness, the House, represents the nation on the basis of population, as the Senate represents the states.

But even in the composition of the House the states play an important part. The Constitution provides[1] that "representatives and direct taxes shall be apportioned among the several states according to their respective numbers," and under this provision Congress allots so many members of the House to each state in proportion to its population at the last preceding decennial census, leaving the state to determine the districts within its own area for and by which the members shall be chosen. These districts are now equal or nearly equal in size; but in laying them out there is ample scope for the process called "gerrymandering,"[2] which the dominant party in a state rarely fails to apply for its own advantage. Where a state legislature

---

[1] Constitution, art. I, § 2, par. 3; cf. amendment XIV, § 2.

[2] So called from Elbridge Gerry, a leading Democratic politician in Massachusetts (a member of the Constitutional Convention of 1787, and in 1812 elected vice-president of the United States), who when Massachusetts was being redistricted contrived a scheme which gave one of the districts a shape like that of a lizard. Stuart, the well-known artist, entering the room of an editor who had a map of the new districts hanging on the wall over his desk observed, "Why, this district looks like a salamander," and put in the claws and eyes of the creature with his pencil. "Say rather a Gerrymander," replied the editor; and the name stuck. The aim of gerrymandering, of course, is so to lay out the one-membered districts as to secure in the greatest possible number of them a majority for the party which conducts the operation. This is done sometimes by throwing the greatest possible number of hostile voters into a district which is anyhow certain to be hostile, sometimes by adding to a district where parties are equally divided some place in which the majority of friendly voters is sufficient to turn the scale. There is a district in Mississippi (the so-called Shoe String district) 500 miles long by 40 broad, and another in Pennsylvania resembling a dumbbell. South Carolina furnishes some beautiful recent examples. And in Missouri a district has been contrived longer, if measured along its windings, than the state itself, into which as large a number as possible of the Negro voters were thrown.

has failed to redistribute the state into congressional districts, after the state has received an increase of representatives, the additional member or members are elected by the voters of the whole state on a general ticket, and are called "representatives at large." Recently one state (Maine) elected all its representatives on this plan, while another (Kansas) elected three by districts and four by general ticket. Each district, of course, lies wholly within the limits of one state. When a seat becomes vacant the governor of the state issues a writ for a new election, and when a member desires to resign his seat he does so by letter to the governor.

The original House which met in 1789 contained only 65 members, the idea being that there should be one member for every 30,000 persons. As population grew and new states were added, the number of members was increased. Originally Congress fixed the ratio of members to population, and the House accordingly grew; but latterly, fearing a too rapid increase, it has fixed the number of members with no regard for any precise ratio of members to population. Under a statute of 1891, the number was fixed at 356, being, according to the census of 1890, one member to about 174,000 souls. In 1909, the number had reached 391. In 1911, under the census of 1910, it was increased to 435. Five states, Delaware, Nevada, Wyoming, Arizona, New Mexico, have one representative each; five have two each; while New York has 43, and Pennsylvania 36. Besides these full members there are also Territorial delegates, one from each of the Territories, regions enjoying a species of self-government, but not yet formed into states.[3] These delegates sit and speak, but have no right to vote, being unrecognized by the Constitution. They are, in fact, merely persons whom the House, under a statute, admits to its floor and permits to address it.

The quorum of the House, as of the Senate, is a majority of the whole number. Till the Fifty-first Congress the custom had been to treat as absent all members who did not answer to their names on a roll call, but in 1890, one party persistently refusing to answer in order to prevent the transaction of business, Speaker Reed asserted the right of counting for the purposes of a quorum all he saw present. A rule was then passed directing him so to count. This was dropped in the next Congress but in 1894 restored, substituting two tellers for the Speaker.

The electoral franchise on which the House is elected is for each state the same as that by which the members of the more numerous branch of the state legislature are chosen. Originally franchises varied much in different

[3] As to the Territories, see Chapter 47 *post*.

states; and this was a principal reason why the Convention of 1787 left the matter to the states to settle: now what is practically manhood (which in five states includes womanhood) suffrage prevails in the Northern and Western states. A state, however, has a right of limiting the suffrage as it pleases, and many states do exclude persons convicted of crime, paupers, illiterates, etc. By the Fifteenth Amendment to the Constitution (passed in 1870) "the right of citizens of the United States to vote shall not be denied or abridged by any State on account of race, colour, or previous condition of servitude," while by the Fourteenth Amendment (passed in 1868) "the basis of representation in any State is reduced in respect of any male citizens excluded from the suffrage, save for participation in rebellion or other crimes." This was designed to give the former slave states a motive for keeping their suffrage wide, but the fact remains that the franchise by which the federal legislature is chosen may differ, and does in some points actually differ in different parts of the Union.[4]

Members are elected for two years, and the election always takes place in the even years, 1912, 1914, and so forth. Thus the election of every second Congress coincides with that of a president; and admirers of the Constitution find in this arrangement another of their favourite "checks," because while it gives the incoming president a Congress presumably, though by no means necessarily, of the same political complexion as his own, it enables the people within two years to express their approval or disapproval of his conduct by sending up another House of Representatives which may support or oppose the policy he has followed. The House does not in the regular course of things meet until a year has elapsed from the time when it has been elected, though the president may convoke it sooner, i.e, a House elected in November 1914 will not meet till December 1915, unless the president summons it in "extraordinary session" some time after March 4, 1915, when the previous House expires. This summons has been issued fifteen times since 1789. It so often brought ill luck to the summoning president that a sort of superstition against it grew.[5] The question is often mooted whether a new Congress ought not by law to meet within six months

---

[4] Rhode Island retained till 1888 a small property qualification for electors, and in some states payment of a poll tax is made a condition to the exercise of electoral rights. See Chapter 40 on state legislatures.

    As to the recent restrictions of the suffrage in the states where slavery existed down till the War of Secession, see Vol. II, Chaps. 93–95.

[5] This ill luck is supposed (says Mr. Blaine in his *Twenty Years in Congress*) to attach especially to May sessions, which reminds one of the superstition against May marriages mentioned by John Knox apropos of the marriage of Mary Queen of Scots and Darnley.

after its election, for there are inconveniences in keeping an elected House unorganized and Speakerless for a twelvemonth. But the country is not so fond of Congress as to desire more of it. It is a singular result of the present arrangement that the old House continues to sit for nearly four months after the members of the new House have been elected, and that a measure may still be passed in the expiring Congress, against which the country has virtually pronounced at the general elections already held for its successor. In the Fifty-first Congress the House voted more than five-hundred millions of dollars in its appropriation bills after a new Congress had been elected, and when therefore it had in strictness no longer any constituents.

The expense of an election varies greatly from district to district. Sometimes, especially in great cities where illegitimate expenditure is more frequent and less detectible than in rural districts, it rises to a sum of $10,000 or more; sometimes it is trifling.[6] No estimate of the average can be formed, because no returns of congressional election expenses are required by law; but as a rule a seat costs less than one for a county division does in England.[7] A candidate, unless very wealthy, is not expected to pay the whole expense out of his own pocket, but is aided often by the local contributions of his friends, sometimes by a subvention from the election funds of the party in the state. All the official expenses, such as for clerks, polling booths, etc., are paid by the public. Although bribery is not rare, comparatively few elections are impeached, for the difficulty of proof is increased by the circumstance that the House, which is the investigating and deciding authority, does not meet till a year after the election. As a member is elected for two years only, and the investigation would probably drag on during the whole of the first session, it is scarcely worth while to dispute the return for the sake of turning him out for the second session.[8] In many states, drinking places are closed on the election day.

Among the members of the House there are few young men, and still

---

[6] As to bribery, see Chap. 67, Vol. II.

[7] A statute of 1910 requires national committees and national congressional campaign committees, and all organizations which in two or more states influence or attempt to influence the result of an election of representatives in Congress, to file with the Clerk of the House an account of all contributions received by or promised to it stating the persons contributing and the amounts.

In England the fixing a maximum, proportioned to the number of electors, has greatly reduced the cost of elections. The average expenditure, all kinds of lawful expense included, seems, in county constituencies, to be from £1,200 to £1,500, and in boroughs from £500 to £600.

[8] It was once proposed to transfer to a judicial tribunal the trial of election cases, which are now usually decided on party lines.

fewer old men. The immense majority are between forty and sixty. Lawyers abound, including in that term both those who in Great Britain are called barristers or advocates, and those who are called attorneys, there being in America no distinction between these two branches of the profession. An analysis of the House in the Fiftieth Congress showed that 203 members, or nearly two-thirds of the whole number, had been trained or had practiced as lawyers, and in subsequent Congresses the proportions have varied but little. In the Sixty-first the proportion of lawyers was slightly larger, especially among Southern members. Of course many of these had practically dropped law as a business and given themselves wholly to politics. Next in number come the men engaged in manufactures or commerce, in agriculture, or banking, or journalism, but no one of these occupations counted one-third so many members.[9] Ministers of religion are very rare; there were, however, two in the Fifty-second Congress. No military or naval officer, and no person in the civil service of the United States, can sit. Scarcely any of the great railway men go into Congress, a fact of much significance when one considers that they are really the most powerful people in the country; and of the numerous lawyer members very few are leaders of the bar in their respective states. The reason is the same in both cases. Residence in Washington makes practice at the bar of a great city difficult or impossible, and men in lucrative practice would not generally sacrifice their profession in order to sit in the House, while railway managers or financiers are too much engrossed by their business to be able to undertake the duties of a member. The absence of railway men by no means implies the absence of railway influence, for it is as easy for a company to influence legislation from without Congress as from within.

Most members, including nearly all Western men, have received their early education in the common schools, but rather more than one-half of the whole number have also graduated in a university or college. This does not necessarily mean what it would mean in Europe, for some of the smaller colleges are no better than English grammar schools and not as good as German gymnasia. It is noticeable that in the accounts of their career which members prepare for the pages of the *Congressional Directory*, they usually dwell upon the fact of their graduation, or state that they have "received an

---

[9] In the Sixty-first there would appear from the *Congressional Directory* to have been 201 lawyers, 63 persons engaged in manufactures, commerce, or finance, 23 agriculturists, 13 journalists, and 2 physicians. As some members do not state their occupations, no complete analysis can be given.

academic education."[10] Less than half have served in the legislature of their own state. In the Sixty-second Congress (1911–13) 128 out of 394 had sat in a state legislature. Not many are wealthy, and few are very poor, while hardly any were at the time of their election working men. Of course no one could be a working man while he sits, for he would have no time to spare for his trade, and the salary would more than meet his wants. Nothing prevents an artisan from being returned to Congress, but there seems little disposition among the working classes to send one of themselves;[11] and the nomination system interposes obstacles to their standing as candidates of either of the great parties, though they sometimes stand as Labour men or Socialists.

A member of the House enjoys the title of Honourable, which is given to him not merely within the House (as in England), but in the world at large, as for instance in the addresses of his letters. As he shares it with members of state senates, all the higher officials, both federal and state, and judges, the distinction is not deemed a high one.

The House has no share in the executive functions of the Senate, nothing to do with confirming appointments or approving treaties. On the other hand, it has the exclusive right of initiating revenue bills and of impeaching officials, features borrowed, through the state constitutions, from the English House of Commons, and of choosing a president in case there should be no absolute majority of presidential electors for any one candidate. This very important power it exercised in 1801 and 1825.[12]

Setting extraordinary sessions aside, every Congress has two sessions, distinguished as the first or long and the second or short. The long session begins in the fall of the year after the election of a Congress, and continues, with a recess at Christmas, till the July or August following. The short session begins in the December after the July adjournment, and lasts till the 4th of March following. The whole working life of a House is thus from ten to twelve months. Bills do not, as in the English Parliament, expire at the end of each session; they run on from the long session to the short one. All however that have not been passed when the fatal 4th March arrives perish forthwith, for the session being fixed by statute cannot be extended

[10] In the Sixty-first Congress 197 had received a "collegiate," 78 an "academic," and 73 a "common-school" education.

[11] In the Fifty-eighth Congress (1903–1905) there were two union labour members, described as Independents.

[12] See above, Chapter 5.

at pleasure.[13] There is consequently a terrible scramble to get business pushed through in the last week or two of a Congress. Sometimes the clock of the House is put back in order to enable the Speaker who faces it to allow business to be taken after the true noon has been passed on the last day. I have seen this done openly amid the merriment of the House and the galleries.

The House usually meets at noon, and sits till four or six o'clock, though towards the close of a session these hours are lengthened. Occasionally when obstruction occurs, or when at the very end of a session messages are going backwards and forwards between the House, the Senate, and the president, it sits all night long.

The usages and rules of procedure of the House, which differ in many respects from those of the Senate, are too numerous to be described here. I will advert only to a few points of special interest, choosing those which illustrate American political ideas or bring out the points of likeness and unlikeness between Congress and the English Parliament.

An oath or affirmation of fidelity to the Constitution of the United States is (as prescribed by the Constitution) taken by all members;[14] also by the clerk, the sergeant-at-arms, the doorkeeper, and the postmaster.

The sergeant-at-arms is the treasurer of the House, and pays to each member his salary and mileage. He has the custody of the mace, and the duty of keeping order, which in extreme cases he performs by carrying the mace into a throng of disorderly members. This symbol of authority, which (as in the House of Commons) is moved from its place when the House goes into committee, consists of the Roman *fasces*, in ebony, bound with silver bands in the middle and at the ends, each rod ending in a spear head, at the other end a globe of silver, and on the globe a silver eagle ready for flight. English precedent suggests the mace, but as it could not be surmounted by a crown, Rome has prescribed its design.

---

[13] Senate bills also expire at the end of a Congress.

   The snowstorms that frequently occur at Washington in the beginning of March have led to proposals to extend the session till April or May and have the president inaugurated then.

[14] The oath is administered by the Speaker, and in the form following: "I do solemnly swear (or affirm) that I will support the Constitution of the United States against all enemies, foreign and domestic; that I will bear true faith and allegiance to the same; that I take this obligation freely without any mental reservation or purpose of evasion, and that I will well and faithfully discharge the duties of the office on which I am about to enter, so help me God. "Allegiance" to a legal instrument would have seemed an odd expression to those ages in which the notion of allegiance arose; yet it fairly conveys the idea that obedience is due to the will of the people, which has taken tangible and permanent shape in the document they have enacted.

The proceedings each day begin with prayers, which are conducted by a chaplain who is appointed by the House, not (as in England) by the Speaker, and who may, of course, be selected from any religious denomination. Lots are drawn for seats at the beginning of the session, each member selecting the place he pleases according as his turn arrives. Although the Democrats are mostly to the Speaker's right hand, members cannot, owing to the arrangement of the chairs, sit in masses palpably divided according to party, a circumstance which deprives invective of much of its dramatic effect. One cannot, as in England, point the finger of scorn at "hon. gentlemen opposite." Every member is required to remain uncovered in the House.

A member addresses the Speaker and the Speaker only, and refers to another member not by name but as the "gentleman from Pennsylvania," or as the case may be, without any particular indication of the district which the person referred to represents. As there are thirty-six gentlemen from Pennsylvania, and the descriptives used in the English House of Commons (learned, gallant, right honourable) are not in use, facilities for distinguishing the member intended are not perfect. A member usually speaks from his seat, but many speak from the clerk's desk or from a spot close to the Speaker's chair. A rule (often disregarded) forbids anyone to pass between the Speaker and the member speaking, a curious bit of adherence to English usage.

Divisions were originally (rule of 17th April 1789) taken by going to the right and left of the chair, according to the old practice of the English House of Commons.[15] This having been found inconvenient, a resolution of 9th June 1789 established the present practice, whereby members rise in their seats and are counted in the first instance by the Speaker, but if he is in doubt, or if a count be required by one-fifth of those present (which cannot be less than one-tenth of the whole House), then by two tellers named by the Speaker, between whom, as they stand in the middle gangway, members pass. When a call of yeas and nays is so demanded, the clerk calls the full roll of the House and each member answers aye or no to his name or says "*no vote.*" When the whole roll has been called, it is called over a second time to let those vote who have not voted in the first call. Members may now change their votes. Those who have entered the House after their names

---

[15] It was not until 1836 that the present system of recording the names of members who vote by making them pass through lobbies was introduced at Westminster—a significant result of the Reform Act of 1832. Till then one party remained in the House while the other retired into the lobby, and only the numbers were recorded.

were passed on the second call cannot vote, but often take the opportunity of rising to say that they would, if then present in the House, have voted for (or against) the motion. All this is set forth in the *Congressional Record*, which also contains a list of the members not voting and of the pairs.

A process which consumes so much time, for it may take more than an hour to call through the names, is an obvious and effective engine of obstruction. It is frequently so used, for it can be demanded not only on questions of substance, but on motions to adjourn. This is a rule which the House cannot alter, for it rests on an express provision of the Constitution, art. I, § 5.

No one may speak more than once to the same question, unless he be the mover of the motion pending, in which case he is permitted to reply after every member choosing to speak has spoken. This rule is however frequently broken.

Speeches are limited to one hour, subject to a power to extend this time by unanimous consent, and may, in Committee of the Whole House, be limited to five minutes. So far as I could learn, this hour rule works very well, and does not tend to bring speeches up to that length as a regular thing. A member is at liberty to give part of his time to other members, and this is in practice constantly done. The member speaking will say: "I yield the floor to the gentleman from Ohio for five minutes," and so on. Thus a member who has once secured the floor has a large control of the debate.

The great remedy against prolix or obstructive debate is the so-called previous question, which is moved in the form, "Shall the main question be now put?" and when ordered closes forthwith all debate, and brings the House to a direct vote on that main question.[16] On the motion for the putting of the main question no debate is allowed; but it does not destroy the right of the member "reporting the measure under consideration" from a committee, to wind up the discussion by his reply. This closure of the debate may be moved by any member without the need of leave from the Speaker, and requires only a bare majority of those present. When directed by the House to be applied in committee, for it cannot be moved after the House has gone into committee, it has the effect of securing five minutes to the mover of any amendment, and five minutes to the member who first "obtains the floor" (gets the chance of speaking) in opposition to it, permitting no one

[16] See Rule XVII.

else to speak. A member in proposing a resolution or motion usually asks at the same time for the previous question upon it, so as to prevent it from being talked out.

Closure by previous question, first established in 1811, is in almost daily use, and is considered so essential to the progress of business that I never found any member or official who thought it could be dispensed with. Even the senators, who object to its introduction into their own much smaller chamber, agree that it must exist in a large body like the House. That it is not much abused is attributed to the fear of displeasing the people, and to the sentiment within the House itself in favour of full and fair discussion, which sometimes induces the majority to refuse the previous question when demanded by one of their own party, or on behalf of a motion which they are as a whole supporting. "No one," I was assured, "who is *bonâ fide* discussing a subject in a sensible way would be stopped by the application of the previous question. On the other hand we should never get appropriation bills through without it."

Notwithstanding this powerful engine for expediting business, obstruction, or, as it is called in America, filibustering, is by no means unknown. It is usually practised by making repeated motions for the adjournment of a debate, or for "taking a recess" (suspending the sitting), or for calling the yeas and nays. Between one such motion and another some business must intervene, but as the making of a speech is "business," there is no difficulty in complying with this requirement. No speaking is permitted on these obstructive motions, yet by them time may be wasted for many continuous hours, and if the obstructing minority is a strong one, it generally succeeds, if not in defeating a measure, yet in extorting a compromise. It must be remembered that owing to the provision of the Constitution above mentioned, the House is in this matter not sovereign even over its own procedure. That rules are not adopted, as they might be, which would do more than the present system does to extinguish filibustering, is due partly to this provision, partly to the notion that it is prudent to leave some means open by which a minority can make itself disagreeable, and to the belief that adequate checks exist on any gross abuse of such means.[17] These checks are two. One is the fact that filibustering will soon fail unless conducted by nearly the whole of the party which happens to be in a minority, and that so large a section of the House will not be at the trouble of joining in it unless upon some really

---

[17] In 1890 a rule was passed declaring that "no dilatory motion shall be entertained by the Speaker." This of course leaves it to him to decide what is dilatory (Rule XVI, par. 10).

serious question. Some few years ago, seventeen or eighteen members tried to obstruct systematically a measure they objected to, but their number proved insufficient, and the attempt failed. But at an earlier date, during the Reconstruction troubles which followed the war, the opposition of the solid Democratic party, then in a minority, succeeded in defeating a bill for placing five of the Southern states under military government. The other check is found in the fear of popular disapproval. If the nation sees public business stopped and necessary legislation delayed by factious obstruction, it will visit its displeasure both upon the filibustering leaders individually, and on the whole of the party compromised. However hot party spirit may be, there is always a margin of moderate men in both parties whom the unjustifiable use of legally permissible modes of opposition will alienate. Since such men can make themselves felt at the polls when the next election arrives, respect for their opinion cools the passion of congressional politicians. Thus the general feeling is that as the power of filibustering is in extreme cases a safeguard against abuses of the system of closure by "previous question," so the good sense of the community is in its turn a safeguard against abuses of the opportunities which the rules still leave open. One ex-Speaker, who had had large experience in leading both a majority and a minority of the House, observed to me that he thought the rules, taken all in all, as near perfection as any rules could be. This savours of official optimism. We all know the attachment which those who have grown old in working a system show to its faults as well as to its merits. Still, true is it that congressmen generally complain less of the procedure under which they live, and which seems to an English observer tyrannical, than do members of the English House of Commons of the less rigid methods of their own ancient and famous body. I know no better instance of the self-control and good humour of Americans than the way in which the minority in the House generally submit to the despotism of the majority, consoling themselves with the reflection that it is all according to the rules of the game, and that their turn will come in due course. To use the power of closing debate as stringently at Westminster as it is used at Washington would revolutionize the life of the House of Commons.[18] But the House of Representatives is an assembly of a very different nature. Like the House of Commons it is a legislating, if hardly to be deemed a governing, body. But it is not a debating body. It rules through and by its committees, in which discussion is

---

[18] The Rules of Procedure in the House of Commons have become much stricter now (1914) than they were in 1888 when the above was first written.

unchecked by any closing power; and the whole House does little more than register by its votes the conclusions which the committees submit. One subject alone, the subject of revenue, that is to say, taxation and appropriation, receives genuine discussion by the House at large. And although the power of limiting debate is often applied to expedite such business, it is seldom applied till opportunity has been given for the expression of all relevant views.

The rules regarding the procedure in Committee of the Whole House are in the main similar to those of the British House of Commons; but the chairman of such a committee is not (as usually in England) a permanent chairman of Ways and Means, but a person nominated by the Speaker on each occasion. A rule, not duly observed, forbids any member to speak twice to any question, until every member desiring to speak shall have spoken.[19]

The House has a power of going into secret session whenever confidential communications are received from the president, or a member informs it that he has communications of a secret nature to make. But this power, though employed in early days, is now in disuse. Every word spoken is reported by official stenographers and published in the *Congressional Record*, and the huge galleries are never cleared.

The number of bills brought into the House every year is very large, and has steadily increased. In the Thirty-seventh Congress (1861–63) the total number of bills introduced was 1,026, viz., 613 House bills, and 433 Senate bills. In the Fifty-first Congress (1889–91) the number had risen further, to 19,646 (including joint resolutions), of which 14,328 were introduced in the House, 5,318 in the Senate.[20] In the Sixty-second there had been a further rise, for the bills and joint resolutions introduced in the House reached about 29,000, and those in the Senate approached 9,000. In the British House of Commons the number of public bills introduced was, in the session of 1892, 335 (20 of which had come from the Lords), besides 80 provisional order bills. In 1908 the total number of bills of all kinds introduced was 482, of which 297 were public bills, 56 provisional order bills, and 127 private bills. America is, of course, a far larger country, and more than twice as populous, but the legislative competence of Congress is incomparably smaller than that of the British Parliament, seeing that the chief part of the field both of public bill and private bill legislation belongs

---

[19] Proceedings in Committee of the Whole may be expedited by limiting (by a vote of the House) discussion in committee to a certain fixed period.

[20] Of these, 2,201 passed both houses, and 2,171 were approved by the president.

in America to the several states. By far the larger number of bills in Congress are what would be called in England "private" or "local and personal" bills, i.e., they establish no general rule of law but are directed to particular cases. Such are the numerous bills for satisfying persons with claims against the federal government, and for giving or restoring pensions to individuals alleged to have served in the Northern armies during the War of Secession. It is only to a very small extent that bills can attempt to deal with ordinary private law, since most of that topic belongs to state legislation. The proportion of bills that pass to bills that fail is a very small one, not one-thirtieth.[21] As in England so even more in America, bills are lost less by direct rejection than by failing to reach their third reading, a mode of extinction which the good nature of the House, or the unwillingness of its members to administer snubs to one another, would prefer to direct rejection, even were not the want of time a sufficient excuse to the committees for failing to report them. One is told in Washington that few bills are brought in with a view to being passed. They are presented in order to gratify some particular persons or places, and it is well understood in the House that they must not be taken seriously. Sometimes a less pardonable motive exists. The great commercial corporations, and especially the railroad companies, are often through their land grants and otherwise brought into relations with the federal government. Bills are presented in Congress which purport to withdraw some of the privileges of these companies, or to establish or favour rival enterprises, but whose real object is to levy blackmail on these wealthy bodies, since it is often cheaper for a company to buy off its enemy than to defeat him either by the illegitimate influence of the lobby, or by the strength of its case in open combat. Several great corporations have thus to maintain a permanent staff at Washington for the sake of resisting legislative attacks upon them, some merely extortionate, some intended to win local popularity.

The title and attributions of the Speaker of the House are taken from his famous English original. But the character of the office has greatly altered from that original. The note of the Speaker of the British House of Commons is his impartiality. He has indeed been chosen by a party, because a majority means in England a party. But on his way from his place on the benches to

---

[21] In the British Parliamentary Session of 1908, 74 public bills (out of 297 introduced) became law, of which 21 were private members bills; 55 provisional order bills were also passed. The number of public bills introduced has increased in England since 1867, though not so rapidly as in America, but private (i.e., unofficial) members have great difficulty in passing their bills, recent changes in parliamentary procedure having reduced their chances.

the chair he is expected to shake off and leave behind all party ties and sympathies. Once invested with the wig and gown of office he has no longer any political opinions, and must administer exactly the same treatment to his political friends and to those who have been hitherto his opponents, to the oldest or most powerful minister and to the youngest or least popular member. His duties are limited to the enforcement of the rules and generally to the maintenance of order and decorum in debate, including the selection, when several members rise at the same moment, of the one who is to carry on the discussion. These are duties of great importance, and his position one of great dignity, but neither the duties nor the position imply political power. It makes little difference to any English party in Parliament whether the occupant of the chair has come from their own or from the hostile ranks. The Speaker can lower or raise the tone and efficiency of the House as a whole by the way he presides over it; but a custom as strong as law forbids him to render help to his own side even by private advice. Whatever information as to parliamentary law he may feel free to give must be equally at the disposal of every member.

In America the Speaker has immense political power, and is permitted, nay expected, to use it in the interests of his party. At one time he ruled and led almost as Rouher led and ruled the French Chamber under Louis Napoleon. In calling upon members to speak he prefers those of his own side. He decides in their favour such points of order as are not distinctly covered by the rules. His authority over the arrangement of business is so large that he can frequently advance or postpone particular bills or motions in a way which determines their fate. One much respected Speaker once went the length of intimating that he would not allow a certain bill, to which he strongly objected, to be so much as presented to the House; and this he could do by refusing to recognize the member desiring to present it. Although the Speaker seldom delivers a speech in the House, he may and does advise the other leaders of his party privately; and when they "go into caucus" (i.e., hold a party meeting to determine their action on some pending question) he is present and gives counsel. He is usually the most eminent member of the party who has a seat in the House, and is really, so far as the confidential direction of its policy goes, almost its leader. His most important privilege is, however, the nomination of the numerous standing committees already referred to. In the first Congress (April 1789) the House tried the plan of appointing its committees by ballot; but this worked so ill that in January 1790 the following rule was passed: "All committees shall be appointed by the Speaker unless otherwise specially directed by the

House." This rule has been readopted by each successive Congress since then.[22] Not only does he, at the beginning of each Congress, select all the members of each of these committees, he even chooses the chairman of each, and thereby vests the direction of its business in hands approved by himself.[23] The chairman is of course always selected from the party which commands the House, and the committee is so composed as to give that party a majority. Since legislation, and so much of the control of current administration as the House has been able to bring within its grasp, belong to these committees, their composition practically determines the action of the House on all questions of moment, and as the chairmanships of the more important committees are the posts of most influence, the disposal of them is a tremendous piece of patronage by which a Speaker can attract support to himself and his own section of the party, reward his friends, give politicians the opportunity of rising to distinction or practically extinguish their congressional career. The Speaker is, of course, far from free in disposing of these places. He has been obliged to secure his own election to the chair by promises to leading members and their friends; and while redeeming such promises, he must also regard the wishes of important groups of men or types of opinion, must compliment particular states by giving a place on good committees to their prominent representatives, must avoid nominations which could alarm particular interests. These conditions surround the exercise of his power with trouble and anxiety. Yet after all it is power, power which in the hands of a capable and ambitious man was from 1890 to 1910 so far-reaching that it was then no exaggeration to call him the second political figure in the United States, with an influence upon the fortunes of men and the course of domestic events superior, in ordinary times and in capable hands, to the president's, although shorter in its duration and less patent to the world.[24] His authority has now been reduced, but it is still great, and may regain its former extension.

---

[22] In England select committees on public matters are appointed by the House, i.e., practically by the "whips" of the several parties, though sometimes a discussion in the House leads to the addition of other members. Hybrid committees are appointed partly by the House and partly by the Committee of Selection. Private bill committees are appointed by the Committee of Selection. This committee is a small body of the older and more experienced members, intended to represent fairly all parties and sections of opinion.

[23] In 1910 an alteration in the rules was made which reduced the power of the Speaker, vesting some of it in a committee.

[24] "The appointment of the committees implies the distribution of work to every member. It means the determination of the cast business shall take. It decides for or against all large matters of policy, or may so decide; for while Speakers will differ from each other greatly in force of character and in the wish to give positive direction to affairs, the weakest man cannot escape

The choice of a Speaker is therefore a political event of much significance; and the whole policy of a Congress sometimes turns upon whether the man selected represents one or another of two divergent tendencies in the majority. The distribution of members among the committees, which used to be left to him, but is now in the hands of a committee of the majority, is a critical point in the history of a Congress, and one which is watched with keen interest. As the chairmanships of the chief committees are posts of great significance forming a sort of second set of ministerial office, and as they may be compared to the cabinet offices of Europe, so the Speaker is himself a great party leader as well as the president of a deliberative assembly.

Although expected to serve his party in all possible directions, he must not resort to all possible means. Both in the conduct of debate and in the formation of committees a certain measure of fairness to opponents is required from him. He must not palpably wrest the rules of the House to their disadvantage, though he may decide all doubtful points against them. He must give them a reasonable share of "the floor" (i.e., of debate). He must concede to them proper representation on committees.

The dignity of the Speaker's office is high. He receives $12,000 a year. In rank he stands next after the vice-president and on a level with the justices of the Supreme Court. Washington society was once agitated by a claim of his wife to take precedence over the wives of these judges, a claim so ominous in a democratic country that efforts were made to have it adjusted without a formal decision.

---

from the necessity of arranging the appointments with a view to the probable character of measures which will be agitated. This, however, is far from the measure of the Speaker's power. All rules are more or less flexible. The current of precedents is never consistent or uniform. The bias of the Speaker at a critical moment will turn the scale. Mr. Randall as Speaker determined the assent of the House to the action of the Electoral Commission [of 1877]. Had he wished for a revolutionary attempt to prevent the announcement of Hayes's election, no one who has had experience in Congress, at least, will doubt that he could have forced the collision."—From an article in the New York *Nation* of April 4, 1878, by an experienced member of Congress.

CHAPTER 14

The House at Work

An Englishman expects to find his House of Commons reproduced in the House of Representatives. He has the more reason for this notion because he knows that the latter was modelled on the former, has borrowed many of its rules and technical expressions, and regards the procedure of the English chamber as a storehouse of precedents for its own guidance.[1] The notion is delusive. Resemblances of course there are. But an English parliamentarian who observes the American House at work is more impressed by the points of contrast than by those of similarity. The life and spirit of the two bodies are wholly different.

The room in which the House meets is in the south wing of the Capitol, the Senate and the Supreme Court being lodged in the north wing. It is more than thrice as large as the English House of Commons, with a floor about equal in area to that of Westminster Hall, 139 feet long by 93 feet wide and 36 feet high. Light is admitted through the ceiling. There are on all sides deep galleries running backwards over the lobbies, and capable of holding two thousand five hundred persons. The proportions are so good that it is not till you observe how small a man looks at the farther end, and how faint ordinary voices sound, that you realize its vast size. The seats are arranged in curved concentric rows looking towards the Speaker, whose

---

[1] Both the Senate and the House of Representatives have recognized Jefferson's *Manual of Parliamentary Practice* as governing the House when none of its own rules (or of the joint rules of Congress) are applicable. This manual, prepared by President Jefferson, is based on English precedents.

A recent (1909) edition of this manual with the Rules of the House appended has been enriched by the valuable notes of Mr. Asher C. Hinds, then clerk at the Speaker's table. For a favourable view of the Rules of the House as they appear to those who are conversant with that body, reference may be made to articles on the subject in the *American Review of Reviews* for April, 1909, and in the *American Political Science Review* for May, 1909.

handsome marble chair is placed on a raised marble platform projecting slightly forward into the room, the clerks and the mace below in front of him, in front of the clerks the official stenographers, to the right the seat of the sergeant-at-arms. Each member has a revolving armchair, and had till 1913 a roomy desk in front of it, where he wrote and kept his papers. Behind these chairs runs a railing, and behind the railing is an open space into which some classes of strangers may be brought, where sofas stand against the wall, and where smoking is occasionally practiced, even by strangers, though the rules forbid it.

When you enter, your first impression is of noise and turmoil, a noise like that of short sharp waves in a Highland loch, fretting under a squall against a rocky shore. The scratching of pens, the clapping of hands to call the pages, keen little boys who race along the gangways, the pattering of many feet, the hum of talking on the floor and in the galleries, make up a din over which the Speaker with the sharp taps of his hammer, or the orators straining shrill throats, find it hard to make themselves audible. Nor is it only the noise that gives the impression of disorder. Often three or four members are on their feet at once, each shouting to catch the Speaker's attention. Others, tired of sitting still, rise to stretch themselves, while the Western visitor, long, lank, and imperturbable, leans his arms on the railing, chewing his cigar, and surveys the scene with little reverence. Less favourable conditions for oratory cannot be imagined, and one is not surprised to be told that debate was more animated and practical in the much smaller room which the House formerly occupied.

Not only is the present room so big that only a powerful and well-trained voice can fill it, but the desks and chairs make a speaker feel as if he were addressing furniture rather than men, while of the members few seem to listen to the speeches. It is true that they sit in the House instead of running out into the lobbies as people do in the British House of Commons, but they are more occupied in talking or writing, or reading newspapers, than in attending to the debate. To attend is not easy, for only a shrill voice can overcome the murmurous roar; and one sometimes finds the newspapers in describing an unusually effective speech, observe that "Mr. So-and-So's speech drew listeners about him from all parts of the House." They could not hear him where they sat, so they left their places to crowd in the gangways near him. "Speaking in the House," said an American writer, "is like trying to address the people in the Broadway omnibuses from the kerbstone in front of the Astor House. . . . Men of fine intellect and of good ordinary elocution have exclaimed in despair that in the House of Representatives the mere physical effort to be heard uses up all the powers, so that intellectual action becomes impossible. The natural refuge is in written speeches or in habitual silence, which one dreads more and more to break."

It is hard to talk calm good sense at the top of your voice, hard to unfold a complicated measure. A speaker's vocal organs react upon his manner, and his manner on the substance of his speech. It is also hard to thunder at an unscrupulous majority or a factious minority when they do not sit opposite to you, but beside you, and perhaps too much occupied with their papers to turn round and listen to you. The Americans think this an advantage, because it prevents scenes of disorder. They may be right; but what order gains oratory loses. The desks encouraged inattention by enabling men to write their letters; but though nearly everybody agreed that they would be better away, it was not till 1913 that they were removed. At the same time benches were substituted for the comfortable swinging chairs which invited members to loll at ease or doze comfortably during dull debates. The members are thus brought closer together, but the size of the hall was not reduced. So too the huge galleries add to the area the voice has to fill; but the public like them, and might resent a removal to a smaller room. It is surprising to see how well filled the galleries sometimes remain through a succession of dull speeches. The smoking shocks an Englishman, but not more than the English practice of wearing hats in both houses of Parliament shocks an American. Interruptions, and interjected remarks, are not more frequent—when I have been present they seemed to be much less frequent— than in the House of Commons. Applause is given more charily, as is usually the case in America. Instead of "Hear, hear," there is a clapping of hands and hitting of desks. Applause is sometimes given from the galleries; and occasionally at the end of a session both the members below and the strangers in the galleries above have been known to join in singing some popular ditty. I have heard a whistling solo extremely well given.

There is little good speaking. I do not mean merely that fine oratory, oratory which presents valuable thoughts in eloquent words, is rare, for it is rare in all assemblies. But in the House of Representatives a set speech upon any subject of importance tends to become not an exposition or an argument but a piece of elaborate and high-flown declamation. Its author is often wise enough to send direct to the reporters what he has written out, having read aloud a small part of it in the House. When it has been printed *in extenso* in the *Congressional Record* (leave to get this done being readily obtained) he has copies struck off and distributes them among his constituents. Thus everybody is pleased and time is saved.[2]

That there is not much good business debating, by which I mean a succession of comparatively short speeches addressed to a practical question, and hammering it out by the collision of mind with mind, arises not from any want of ability among the members, but from the unfavourable conditions under which the House acts. Most of the practical work is done in the standing committees, while much of the House's time is consumed in pointless discussions, where member after member delivers himself upon large questions, not likely to be brought to a definite issue. Many of the speeches thus called forth have a value as repertories of facts, but the debate as a whole is unprofitable and languid. On the other hand the five-minute debates which take place, when the House imposes that limit of time, in Committee of the Whole on the consideration of a bill reported from a standing committee, are often lively, pointed, and effective. The topics which excite most interest and are best discussed are those of taxation and the appropriation of money, more particularly to public works, the improvement of rivers and harbours, erection of federal buildings, and so forth. This kind of business is indeed to most of its members the chief interest of Congress, the business which evokes the finest skill of a tactician and offers the severest temptations to a frail conscience. As a theatre or school either of political eloquence or political wisdom, the House has been inferior not only to the Senate but to most European assemblies. Nor does it enjoy much consideration at home. Its debates are very shortly reported in the Washington papers as well as in those in Philadelphia and New York. They are not widely read except in very exciting times, and do little to instruct or influence public opinion.

This is of course only one part of a legislature's functions. An assembly may despatch its business successfully and yet shine with few lights of genius. But the legislation on public matters which the House turns out is scanty in quantity and generally mediocre in quality. What is more, the House tends to avoid all really grave and pressing questions, skirmishing round them, but seldom meeting them in the face or reaching a decision which marks an advance. If one makes this observation to an American, he replies that at this moment there are few such questions lying within the

---

[2] I was told that formerly speeches might be printed in the *Record* as a matter of course, but that, a member having used this privilege to print and circulate a poem, the right was restrained.

competence of Congress, and that in his country representatives must not attempt to move faster than their constituents. This latter remark is eminently true; it expresses a feeling which has gone so far that Congress conceives its duty to be to follow and not to seek to lead public opinion. The harm actually suffered so far is not grave. But the European observer cannot escape the impression that Congress might fail to grapple with a serious public danger, and is at present hardly equal to the duty of guiding and instructing the political intelligence of the nation.

In all assemblies one must expect abundance of unreality and pretence, many speeches obviously addressed to the gallery, many bills meant to be circulated but not to be seriously proceeded with. However, the House seems to indulge itself more freely in this direction than any other chamber of equal rank. Its galleries are large, holding two thousand five hundred persons. But it talks and votes, I will not say to the galleries, for the galleries cannot hear it, but as if every section of American opinion was present in the room. It adopts unanimously resolutions which perhaps no single member in his heart approves of, but which no one cares to object to, because it seems not worth while to do so. This habit sometimes exposes it to a snub, such as that administered by Bismarck in the matter of the resolution of condolence with the German Parliament on the death of Lasker, a resolution harmless indeed, but so superfluous as to be almost obtrusive. A practice unknown to Europeans is of course misunderstood by them, and sometimes provokes resentment. Bills are frequently brought into the House proposing to effect impossible objects by absurd means, which astonish a visitor, and may even cause disquiet in other countries, while few people in America notice them, and no one thinks it worth while to expose their emptiness. American statesmen keep their pockets full of the loose cash of empty compliments and pompous phrases, and become so accustomed to scatter it among the crowd that they are surprised when a complimentary resolution or electioneering bill, intended to humour some section of opinion at home, is taken seriously abroad. The House is particularly apt to err in this way, because having no responsibility in foreign policy, and little sense of its own dignity, it applies to international affairs the habits of election meetings.

Watching the House at work, and talking to the members in the lobbies, an Englishman naturally asks himself how the intellectual quality of the body compares with that of the House of Commons. His American friends have prepared him to expect a marked inferiority. They are fond of running down congressmen. The cultivated New Englanders and New Yorkers do this out of intellectual fastidiousness, and in order to support the role which they unconsciously fall into when talking to Europeans. The rougher Western men do it because they would not have congressmen either seem or be better in any way than themselves, since that would be opposed to republican equality. A stranger who has taken literally all he hears is therefore surprised to find so much character, shrewdness, and keen though limited intelligence among the representatives. Their average business capacity did not seem to me below that of members of the House of Commons. True it is that great lights, such as usually adorn the British Chamber, are absent; true also that there are fewer men who have received a high education which has developed their tastes and enlarged their horizons. The want of such men seriously depresses the average. It is raised, however, by the almost total absence of two classes hitherto well represented in the British Parliament, the rich, dull parvenu, who has bought himself into public life, and the perhaps equally unlettered young sporting or fashionable man who, neither knowing nor caring anything about politics, has come in for a county or (before 1885) a small borough, on the strength of his family estates. Few congressmen sink to so low an intellectual level as these two sets of persons, for congressmen have almost certainly made their way by energy and smartness, picking up a knowledge of men and things "all the time." In respect of width of view, of capacity for penetrating thought on political problems, representatives are scarcely above the class from which they came, that of second-rate lawyers or farmers, less often merchants or petty manufacturers. They do not pretend to be statesmen in the European sense of the word, for their careers, which have made them smart and active, have given them little opportunity for acquiring such capacities. As regards manners they are not polished, because they have not lived among polished people; yet neither are they rude, for to get on in American politics one must be civil and pleasant. The standard of parliamentary language, and of courtesy generally, has been steadily rising during the last few decades; and scenes of violence and confusion such as occasionally convulse the French Chamber, and were common in Washington before the War of Secession, are now rare.

On the whole, the most striking difference between the House of Representatives and European popular assemblies is its greater homogeneity. The type is marked; the individuals vary little from the type. In Europe all sorts of persons are sucked into the vortex of the legislature—nobles and landowners, lawyers, physicians, businessmen, artisans, journalists, men of learning, men of science. In America five representatives out of six are politicians pure and simple, members of a class as well defined as anyone of the above-mentioned European classes. The American people, though it is composed of immigrants from every country and occupies a whole continent, tends to become more uniform than most of the great European peoples; and this characteristic is palpable in its legislature.

Uneasy lies the head of an ambitious congressman,[3] for the chances are almost even that he will lose his seat at the next election. It was observed in 1788 that half of the members of each successive state legislature were new members, and this average was long maintained in the federal legislature, rather less than half keeping their seats from one Congress to the next. In recent years reelection has grown more frequent, and in the Sixty-first Congress (1909–11), only 74 members out of 391 had not served before. Sixteen members had served during nine or more previous terms, i.e., for eighteen years or more. In England the proportion of members reelected from Parliament to Parliament has been higher. Anyone can see how much influence this constant change in the composition of the American House must have upon its legislative efficiency.

I have kept to the last the feature of the House which an Englishman finds the strangest.

It has parties, but they are headless. There is neither government nor opposition. There can hardly be said to be leaders, and till 1900 there were no whips.[4] No person holding any federal office or receiving any federal salary can be a member of it. That the majority may be and often is opposed to the president and his cabinet, does not strike Americans as odd, because they proceed on the theory that the legislative ought to be distinct from the executive authority. Since no minister sits, there is no official representative of the administration. Neither is there any permanent unofficial representative. And as there are no members whose opinions expressed in debate are followed, so there are none whose duty it is to be always on the spot to look after members to vote, secure a quorum, and tell their friends which way the bulk of the party is going.

So far as the majority has a chief, that chief is the Speaker, often chosen by them as their ablest and most influential man; but as the Speaker seldom joins in debate (though he may do so by leaving the chair, having put someone else in it), the chairman of the most important committee, that of

---

[3] The term "congressman" is commonly used to describe a member of the House of Representatives, though of course it ought to include senators also. So in England "Member of Parliament" means member of the House of Commons, though it covers all persons who have seats in the House of Lords.

[4] See as to whips, Chapter 19 *post*.

Ways and Means, enjoys a sort of eminence, and comes nearer than anyone else to the position of leader of the House.[5] But his authority does not always enable him to secure cooperation for debate among the best speakers of his party, putting up now one now another, after the fashion of an English prime minister, and thereby guiding the general course of the discussion.

The minority need not formally choose a chief, nor is there usually anyone among them whose career marks him out as practically the first man, but there is generally someone who is regarded as leading, and the person whom they have put forward as their party candidate for the Speakership, giving him what is called "the complimentary nomination," has a sort of vague claim to be so regarded. This honour carries little real authority. On one occasion the Speaker of the last preceding Congress, who had received such a complimentary nomination from his party against the candidate whom the majority elected, found immediately afterwards that so far from treating him as leader, they left him, on some motion which he made, in a ridiculously small minority. Of course when an exciting question comes up, some man of marked capacity and special knowledge will often become virtually leader, in either party, for the purposes of the debates upon it. But he will not necessarily command the votes of his own side.

How then does the House work?

If it were a chamber, like those of France or Germany, divided into four or five sections of opinion, none of which commands a steady majority, it would not work at all. But parties are few in the United States, and their cohesion tight. There are usually two only, so nearly equal in strength that the majority cannot afford to dissolve into groups like those of France. Hence upon all large national issues, whereon the general sentiment of the party has been declared, both the majority and the minority know how to vote, and vote solid, though upon minor issues much latitude is allowed.

If the House were, like the English House of Commons, to some extent an executive as well as a legislative body—one by whose cooperation and support the daily business of government had to be carried on—it could not work without leaders and whips. This it is not. It neither creates, nor controls, nor destroys, the administration, which depends on the president, himself the offspring of a direct popular mandate.

"Still," it may be replied, "the House has important functions to discharge. Legislation comes from it. Supply depends on it. It settles the tariff, and votes money for the civil and military services, besides passing measures

---

[5] The chairman of the Committee on Appropriations has perhaps as much real power.

to cure the defects which experience must disclose in the working of every government, every system of jurisprudence. How can it satisfy these calls upon it without leaders and organization?"

To a European eye, it does not seem to satisfy them. It votes the necessary supplies, but not wisely, giving sometimes too much, sometimes too little money, and taking no adequate securities for the due application of the sums voted. For many years it fumbled over both the tariff problem and the currency problem. It produces few useful laws, and leaves on one side many grave practical questions. An Englishman is disposed to ascribe these failures to the fact that as there are no leaders, there is no one responsible for the neglect of business, the miscarriage of bills, the unwise appropriation of public funds. "In England," he says, "the ministry of the day bears the blame of whatever goes wrong in the House of Commons. Having a majority, it ought to be able to do what it desires. If it pleads that its measures have been obstructed, and that it cannot under the faulty procedure of the House of Commons accomplish what it seeks, it is met, and crushed, by the retort that in such case it ought to have the procedure changed. What else is its majority good for but to secure the efficiency of Parliament? In America there is no person against whom similar charges can be brought. Although conspicuous folly or perversity on the part of the majority tends to discredit them collectively with the public, and may damage them at the next presidential or congressional election, still, responsibility, to be effective, ought to be fixed on a few conspicuous leaders. Is not the want of such men, men to whom the country can look, and whom the ordinary members will follow, the cause of some of the faults which are charged on Congress, of its hesitations, its inconsistencies and changes, its ignoble surrenders to some petty clique, its deficient sense of dignity, its shrinking from troublesome questions, its proclivity to jobs?"

Two American statesmen to whom such a criticism was submitted, replied as follows: "It is not for want of leaders that Congress has forborne to settle the questions mentioned, but because the division of opinion in the country regarding them has been faithfully reflected in Congress. The majority has not been strong enough to get its way; and this has happened, not only because abundant opportunities for resistance arise from the methods of doing business, but still more because no distinct impulse or mandate towards any particular settlement of these questions has been received from the country. It is not for Congress to go faster than the people. When the country knows and speaks its mind, Congress will not fail to act." The significance of this reply lies in its pointing to a fundamental difference between the conception of the respective positions and duties of a representative body and of the nation at large entertained by Americans, and the conception which has hitherto prevailed in Europe. Europeans have thought of a legislature as belonging to the governing class. In America there is no such class. Europeans think that the legislature ought to consist of the best men in the country, Americans that it should be a fair average sample of the country. Europeans think that it ought to lead the nation, Americans that it ought to follow the nation.

Without some sort of organization, an assembly of three hundred and thirty men would be a mob, so necessity has provided in the system of committees a substitute for the European party organization. This system of committees will be explained in the next chapter; for the present it is enough to observe that when a matter which has been (as all bills are) referred to a committee, comes up in the House to be dealt with there, the chairman of the particular committee is treated as a leader *pro hac vice*, and members who knew nothing of the matter are apt to be guided by his speech or his advice given privately. If his advice is not available, or is suspected because he belongs to the opposite party, they seek direction from the member in charge of the bill, if he belongs to their own party, or from some other member of the committee, or from some friend whom they trust. When a debate arises unexpectedly on a question of importance, members are often puzzled how to vote. The division being taken, they get someone to move a call of yeas and nays, and while this slow process goes on, they scurry about asking advice as to their action, and give their votes on the second calling over if not ready on first. If the issue is one of serious consequence to the party, a recess is demanded by the majority, say for two hours. The House then adjourns, each party "goes into caucus" (the Speaker possibly announcing the fact), and debates the matter with closed doors. Then the House resumes, and each party votes solid according to the determination arrived at in caucus. In spite of these expedients, surprises and scratch votes are not uncommon.

I have spoken of the din of the House of Representatives, of its air of restlessness and confusion, contrasting with the staid gravity of the Senate, of the absence of dignity both in its proceedings and in the bearing and aspect of individual members. All these things notwithstanding, there is something impressive about it, something not unworthy of the continent for which it legislates.

This huge gray hall, filled with perpetual clamour, this multitude of keen and eager faces, this ceaseless coming and going of many feet, this irreverent public, watching from the galleries and forcing its way on to the floor, all speak to the beholder's mind of the mighty democracy, destined in another century to form one half of civilized mankind, whose affairs are here debated. If the men are not great, the interests and the issues are vast and fateful. Here, as so often in America, one thinks rather of the future than of the present. Of what tremendous struggles may not this hall become the theatre in ages yet far distant, when the parliaments of Europe have shrunk to insignificance?

The Committees of Congress

The most abiding difficulty of free government is to get large assemblies to work promptly and smoothly either for legislative or executive purposes. We perceive this difficulty in primary assemblies of thousands of citizens, like those of ancient Athens or Syracuse; we see it again in the smaller representative assemblies of modern countries. Three methods of overcoming it have been tried. One is to leave very few and comparatively simple questions to the assembly, reserving all others for a smaller and more permanent body, or for executive officers. This was the plan of the Romans, where the *comitia* (primary assemblies) were convoked only to elect magistrates and pass laws, which were short, clear, and submitted *en bloc*, without possibility of amendment, for a simple yes or no. Another method is to organize the assemblies into well-defined parties, each recognizing and guided by one or more leaders, so that on most occasions and for most purposes the rank and file of members exert no volition of their own, but move like battalions at the word of command. This has been the English system since about the time of Queen Anne. It was originally worked by means of extensive corruption; and not till this phase was passing away did it become an object of admiration to the world. Latterly it has been reproduced in the parliaments of most modern European states and of the British colonies. The third method, which admits of being more or less combined with the second, is to divide the assembly into a number of smaller bodies to which legislative and administrative questions may be referred, either for final determination or to be examined and reported on to the whole body. This is the system of committees, applied to some small extent in England, to a larger extent in France under the name of *bureaux* and *commissions*, and most of all in the United States. Some account of its rules and working there is essential to a comprehension of the character of Congress and of the relations of the legislative to the executive branch of the federal government.

When Congress first met in 1789, both houses found themselves, as the state legislatures had theretofore been and still are, without official members and without leaders.[1] The Senate occupied itself chiefly with executive business, and appointed no standing committees until 1816. The House however had bills to discuss, plans of taxation to frame, difficult questions of expenditure, and particularly of the national debt, to consider. For want of persons whose official duty required them, like English ministers, to run the machine by drafting schemes and bringing the raw material of its work into shape, it was forced to appoint committees. At first there were few; even in 1802 we find only five. As the numbers of the House increased and more business flowed in, additional committees were appointed; and as the House became more and more occupied by large political questions, minor matters were more and more left to be settled by these select bodies. Like all legislatures, the House constantly sought to extend its vision and its grasp, and the easiest way to do this was to provide itself with new eyes and new hands in the shape of further committees. The members were not, like their contemporaries in the English House of Commons, well-to-do men, mostly idle; they were workers and desired to be occupied. It was impossible for them all to speak in the House; but all could talk in a committee. Every permanent body cannot help evolving some kind of organization. Here the choice was between creating one ruling committee which should control all business, like an English ministry, and distributing business among a number of committees, each of which should undertake a special class of subjects. The latter alternative was recommended, not only by its promising a useful division of labour, but by its recognition of republican equality. It therefore prevailed, and the present elaborate system grew slowly to maturity.

To avoid the tedious repetition of details, I have taken the House of Representatives and its committees for description, because the system is more fully developed there than in the Senate. But a very few words on the Senate may serve to prevent misconceptions.

There were in the Sixty-first Congress (1909) seventy-two Senate commit-

---

[1] The Congress of the Confederation (1781-88) had been a sort of diplomatic congress of envoys from states, and furnished few precedents available for the Congress under the new constitution.

tees, appointed for two years, being the period of a Congress.[2] They and their chairmen are chosen not by the presiding officer but by the Senate itself, voting by ballot. Practically they are selected by a caucus of the majority and minority meeting in secret conclave, and then carried wholesale by vote in the Senate. Each consists of from three to seventeen members, few having less than five or more than fourteen, and all senators sit on more than one committee, some upon four or more. The chairman is appointed by the Senate and not by the committees themselves. There are also select committees appointed for a special purpose and lasting for one session only. (Senate committees sometimes sit during the recess.) Every bill introduced goes after its first and second reading (which are granted as of course) to a standing committee, which examines and amends it, and reports it back to the Senate.

There were in the Sixty-second Congress fifty-four standing committees of the House, i.e., committees appointed under standing regulations, and therefore regularly formed at the beginning of every Congress. Each committee consists of from three to twenty-one members, seven and nineteen being the commonest numbers. Every member of the House is placed on some one committee, not many on more than one. Besides these, select committees, seldom exceeding ten, on particular subjects of current interest are appointed from time to time. A complete list of the committees will be found at the end of this chapter. The most important standing committees are the following: Ways and means; appropriations; elections; banking and currency; accounts; rivers and harbours; judiciary (including changes in private law as well as in courts of justice); railways and canals; foreign affairs; naval affairs; military affairs; insular affairs; public lands; agriculture; claims; and the several committees on the expenditures of the various departments of the administration (war, navy, etc.)

The members of every standing committee are nominated at the beginning of each Congress, and sit through its two sessions. They are selected nominally by the House but practically by the Committee on Ways and Means, whose selections the House approves. The majority members of that committee are chosen by the caucus of the majority party in the House, the House as a whole approving the choice made by the caucus. The member first named is its chairman.

---

[2] Although the Senate is a permanent body, its proceedings are for some purposes regulated with reference to the reelection every two years of the House; just as in England the peers are summoned afresh at the beginning of each Parliament.

To some one of these standing committees each and every bill is referred. Its second as well as its first reading is granted as of course, and without debate, since there would be no time to discuss the immense number of bills presented. When read a second time it is referred under the general rules to a committee; but doubts often arise as to which is the appropriate committee, because a bill may deal with a subject common to two or more jurisdictions, or include topics some of which belong to one jurisdiction, others to another. The disputes which may in such cases arise between several committees lead to keen debates and divisions, because the fate of the measure may depend on which of two possible paths it is made to take, since the one may bring it before a tribunal of friends, the other before a tribunal of enemies. Such disputes are determined by the vote of the House itself.

Not having been discussed, much less affirmed in principle, by the House, a bill comes before its committee with no presumption in its favour, but rather as a shivering ghost stands before Minos in the nether world. It is one of many, and for the most a sad fate is reserved. The committee may take evidence regarding it, may hear its friends and its opponents. They usually do hear the member who has introduced it, since it seldom happens that he has himself a seat on the committee. Members who are interested approach the committee and state their case there, not in the House, because they know that the House will have neither time nor inclination to listen. The committee can amend the bill as they please, and although they cannot formally extinguish it, they can practically do so by reporting adversely, or by delaying to report it till late in the session, or by not reporting it at all.

In one or other of these ways nineteen-twentieths of the bills introduced meet their death, a death which the majority doubtless deserve, and the prospect of which tends to make members reckless as regards both the form and the substance of their proposals. A motion may be made in the House that the committee do report forthwith, and the House can of course restore the bill, when reported, to its original form. But these expedients rarely succeed, for few are the measures which excite sufficient interest to induce an impatient and overburdened assembly to take additional work upon its own shoulders or to overrule the decision of a committee.

The deliberations of committees are usually secret. Evidence is frequently taken with open doors, but the newspapers do not report it, unless the matter excite public interest; and even the decisions arrived at are often noticed in the briefest way. It is out of order to canvass the proceedings of a committee in the House until they have been formally reported to it; and the report submitted does not usually state how the members have voted, or contain more than a very curt outline of what has passed. No member speaking in the House is entitled to reveal anything further.

A committee have technically no right to initiate a bill but as they can either transform one referred to them, or, if none has been referred which touches the subject they seek to deal with, can procure one to be brought in and referred to them, their command of their own province is unbounded. Hence the character of all the measures that may be passed or even considered by the House upon a particular branch of legislation depends on the composition of the committee concerned with that branch. Some committees, such as those on naval and military affairs, and those on the expenditure of the several departments, deal with administration rather than legislation. They may summon the officials of the departments before them, and interrogate them as to their methods and conduct. Authority they have none, for officials are responsible only to their chief, the president, who may refuse to allow the official to appear; but the power of questioning is sufficient to check if not to guide the action of a department, since imperative statutes may follow, and the department, sometimes desiring legislation and always desiring money, has strong motives for keeping on good terms with those who control legislation and the purse. It is through these committees chiefly that the executive and legislative branches of government touch one another. Yet the contact, although the most important thing in a government, is the thing which the nation least notices, and has the scantiest means of watching.

The scrutiny to which the administrative committees subject the departments is so close and constant as to occupy much of the time of the officials and seriously interfere with their duties. Not only are they often summoned to give evidence; they are required to furnish minute reports on matters which a member of Congress could ascertain for himself. Nevertheless the House committees are not certain to detect abuses or peculation, for special committees of the Senate have repeatedly unearthed dark doings which had passed unsuspected the ordeal of a House investigation. After a bill has been debated and amended by the committee it is reported back to the House, and is taken up when that committee is called in its order. One hour is allowed to the member whom his fellow committeemen have appointed to report. He seldom uses the whole of this hour, but allots part of it to other members, opponents as well as friends, and usually concludes by moving the previous question. This precludes subsequent amendments and leaves only an hour before the vote is taken. As on an average each committee (excluding the two or three great ones) has only two hours out of the whole ten months of Congress allotted to it to present and have discussed all its bills, it is plain that few measures can be considered, and each but shortly, in the House. The best chance of pressing one through is under the rule which permits the suspension of standing orders by a two-thirds majority during the last six days of the session.

What are the results of this system?

It destroys the unity of the House as a legislative body. Since the practical work of shaping legislation is done in the committees, the interest of members centres there, and they care less about the proceedings of the whole body. It is as a committeeman that a member does his real work. In fact the House has become not so much a legislative assembly as a huge panel from which committees are selected.

It prevents the capacity of the best members from being brought to bear upon any one piece of legislation, however important. The men of most ability and experience are chosen to be chairmen of the committees, or to sit on the two or three greatest. For other committees there remains only the rank and file of the House, a rank and file nearly half of which is new at the beginning of each Congress. Hence every committee (except the aforesaid two or three) is composed of ordinary persons, and it is impossible, save by creating a special select committee, to get together what would be called in England "a strong committee," i.e., one where half or more of the members are exceptionally capable. The defect is not supplied by discussion in the House, for there is no time for such discussion.

It cramps debate. Every foreign observer has remarked how little real debate, in the European sense, takes place in the House of Representatives. The very habit of debate, the expectation of debate, the idea that debate is needed, have vanished, except as regards questions of revenue and expenditure, because the centre of gravity has shifted from the House to the committees.

It lessens the cohesion and harmony of legislation. Each committee goes on its own way with its own bills just as though it were legislating for one planet and the other committees for others. Hence a want of policy and method in Congressional action. The advance is haphazard; the parts have little relation to one another or to the whole.

It gives facilities for the exercise of underhand and even corrupt influence. In a small committee the voice of each member is well worth securing, and may be secured with little danger of a public scandal. The press cannot, even when the doors of committee rooms stand open, report the proceedings of sixty bodies; the eye of the nation cannot follow and mark what goes on within them; while the subsequent proceedings in the House are too hurried to permit a ripping up there of suspicious bargains struck in the purlieus of the Capitol, and fulfilled by votes given in a committee. I do not think that corruption, in its grosser forms, is rife at Washington. It appears chiefly in the milder form of reciprocal jobbing or (as it is called) "logrolling." But the arrangements of the committee system have produced and sustain the class of professional "lobbyists," persons who make it their business to "see" members and procure, by persuasion, importunity, or the use of inducements, the passing of bills, public as well as private, which involve gain to their promoters.

It reduces responsibility. In England, if a bad act is passed or a good bill rejected, the blame falls primarily upon the ministry in power whose command of the majority would have enabled them to defeat it, next upon the party which supported the ministry, then upon the individual members who are officially recorded to have "backed" it and voted for it in the House. The fact that a select committee recommended it—and comparatively few bills pass through a select committee—would not be held to excuse the default of the ministry and the majority. But in the United States the ministry cannot be blamed, for the cabinet officers do not sit in Congress; the House cannot be blamed because it has only followed the decision of its committee; the committee may be an obscure body, whose members are too insignificant to be worth blaming. The chairman is possibly a man of note, but the people have no leisure to watch sixty chairmen: they know Congress and Congress only; they cannot follow the acts of those to whom Congress chooses to delegate its functions. No discredit attaches to the dominant party, because they could not control the acts of the eleven men in the committee room. Thus public displeasure rarely finds a victim, and everybody concerned is relieved from the wholesome dread of damaging himself and his party by negligence, perversity, or dishonesty. Only when a scandal has arisen so serious as to demand investigation is the responsibility of the member to his constituents and the country brought duly home.

It lowers the interests of the nation in the proceedings of Congress.[3]

---

[3] "The doubt and confusion of thought which must necessarily exist in the minds of the vast majority of voters as to the best way of exerting their will in influencing the action of an assembly whose organization is so complex, whose acts are apparently so haphazard, and in which responsibility is spread so thin, throws constituencies into the hands of local politicians who are more visible and tangible than are the leaders of Congress, and generates the while a profound distrust of Congress as a body whose actions cannot be reckoned beforehand by any standard of promises made at elections or any programmes announced by conventions."—Woodrow Wilson, *Congressional*

Except in exciting times, when large questions have to be settled, the bulk of real business is done not in the great hall of the House but in this labyrinth of committee rooms and the lobbies that surround them. What takes place in view of the audience is little more than a sanction, formal indeed but hurried and often heedless, of decisions procured behind the scenes, whose mode and motives remain undisclosed. Hence people cease to watch Congress with that sharp eye which every principal ought to keep fixed on his agent. Acts pass unnoticed whose results are in a few months discovered to be so grave that the newspapers ask how it happened that they were allowed to pass.

The country of course suffers from the want of the light and leading on public affairs which debates in Congress ought to supply. But this is more fairly chargeable to defects of the House which the committees are designed to mitigate than to the committees themselves. The time which the committee work leaves for the sittings of the House is long enough to permit due discussion did better arrangements exist for conducting it.

It throws power into the hands of the chairmen of committees, especially, of course, of those which deal with finance and with great material interests. They become practically a second set of ministers, before whom the departments tremble, and who, though they can neither appoint nor dismiss a postmaster or a tide-waiter, can by legislation determine the policy of the branch of administration which they oversee. This power is not necessarily accompanied by responsibility, because it is largely exercised in secret.

It enables the House to deal with a far greater number of measures and subjects than could otherwise be overtaken; and has the advantage of enabling evidence to be taken by those whose duty it is to reshape or amend a bill. It replaces the system of interrogating ministers in the House which prevails in most European chambers; and enables the working of the administrative departments to be minutely scrutinized.

It sets the members of the House to work for which their previous training has fitted them much better than for either legislating or debating "in the grand style." They are shrewd, keen men of business, apt for talk in committee, less apt for wide views of policy and elevated discourse in an assembly. The committees are therefore good working bodies, but bodies which confirm congressmen in the intellectual habits they bring with them instead of raising them to the higher platform of national questions and interests.

Government, a thoughtful book most of the remarks in which remain true today, though it was published more than a quarter of a century ago.

Summing up, we may say that under this system the House despatches a vast amount of work and does the negative part of it, the killing off of worthless bills, in a thorough way. Were the committees abolished and no other organization substituted, the work could not be done. But much of it, including most of the private bills, ought not to come before Congress at all; and the more important part of what remains, viz., public legislation, is dealt with by methods securing neither the pressing forward of the measures most needed, nor the due debate of those that are pressed forward.

Why, if these mischiefs exist, is the system of committee legislation maintained?

It is maintained because none better has been, or, as most people think, can be devised. "We have," say the Americans, "four hundred members in the House, most of them eager to speak, nearly all of them giving constant attendance. The bills brought in are so numerous that in our two sessions, one of seven or eight months, the other of three months, not one-twentieth could be fairly discussed on second reading or in Committee of the Whole. If even this twentieth were discussed, no time would remain for supervision of the departments of state. That supervision itself must, since it involves the taking of evidence, be conducted by committees. In England one large and strong committee, viz., the ministry of the day, undertakes all the more important business, and watches even the bills of private members. Your House of Commons could not work for a single sitting without such a committee, as is proved by the fact that when you are left for a little without a ministry, the House adjourns. We cannot have such a committee, because no officeholder sits in Congress. Neither can we organize the House under leaders, because prominent men have among us little authority, since they are unconnected with the executive, and derive from the people no title to leadership.[4] Neither can we create a ruling committee of the majority, because this would be disliked as an undemocratic institution. Hence our only course is to divide the unwieldy multitude into small bodies capable of dealing with particular subjects. Each of them is no doubt powerful in its own sphere, but that sphere is so small that no grave harm can result.

[4] In England the prime minister and the leader of the opposition (often an ex-prime minister) have been recognized as leaders not only by the candidates who at the last preceding general election have declared their willingness to support one or other, but also by the rank and file of their respective parties. These leaders have thus a sort of right to the allegiance of their followers, though a right which they may forfeit. In America no candidate pledges himself to support a particular congressional leader. It would be thought unbecoming in him to do so. His allegiance is to the party, and his constituents do not expect him to support any given person, however eminent.

The acts passed may not be the best possible; the legislation of the year may resemble a patchwork quilt, where each piece is different in colour and texture from the rest. But as we do not need much legislation, and as nearly the whole field of ordinary private law lies outside the province of Congress, the mischief is slighter than you Europeans expect. If we made legislation easier, we might have too much of it; and in trying to give it the more definite character you suggest, we might make it too bold and sweeping. Be our present system bad or good, it is the only system possible under our Constitution, and the fact that it was not directly created by that instrument, but has been evolved by the experience of four or five generations, shows how strong must be the tendencies whose natural working has produced it."

Note to Chapter 15

LIST OF STANDING COMMITTEES of the House in the Sixty-first Congress, Second Session. (Corrected to April, 1910.)

On Ways and Means; Appropriations; Judiciary; Banking and Currency; Coinage, Weights and Measures; Interstate and Foreign Commerce; Rivers and Harbours; Merchant Marine and Fisheries; Agriculture; Elections (three Committees); Foreign Affairs; Military Affairs; Naval Affairs; Post Office and Post Roads; Public Lands; Indian Affairs; Territories; Railways and Canals; Manufactures; Mines and Mining; Public Buildings and Grounds; Pacific Railroads; Levees and Improvements of the Mississippi River; Education; Labour; Militia; Patents; Invalid Pensions; Pensions; Claims; War Claims; Private Land Claims; District of Columbia; Revision of the Laws; nine committees on expenditures—in the State Department, Treasury Department, War Department, Navy Department, Post Office Department, Interior Department, Department of Justice, Agriculture, Department of Commerce and Labour, and Public Buildings; Rules; Accounts; Mileage; Library; Printing; Enrolled Bills; Select Committees—Reform in the Civil Service; Election of President and Vice-President; Census; Ventilation and Acoustics; Alcoholic Liquor Traffic; Irrigation of Arid Lands; Immigration and Naturalization; Industrial Arts and Expositions; Disposition of Useless Papers in the Executive Departments (joint).

The committees in the Sixty-second Congress differed very little from this list.

Congressional Legislation

Legislation is more specifically and exclusively the business of Congress than it is the business of governing parliaments such as those of England, France, and Italy. We must therefore, in order to judge of the excellence of Congress as a working machine, examine the quality of the legislation which it turns out.

Acts of Congress are of two kinds, public and private. Passing by private acts for the present, though they occupy a large part of Congressional time,[1] let us consider public acts. These are of two kinds, those which deal with the law or its administration, and those which deal with finance, that is to say, provide for the raising and application of revenue. I devote this chapter to the former class, and the next to the latter.

There are many points of view from which one may regard the work of legislation. I suggest a few only, in respect of which the excellence of the work may be tested; and propose to ask: What security do the legislative methods and habits of Congress offer for the attainment of the following desirable objects? viz.:

1. The excellence of the substance of a bill, i.e., its tendency to improve the law and promote the public welfare
2. The excellence of the form of a bill, i.e., its arrangement and the scientific precision of its language
3. The harmony and consistency of an act with the other acts of the same session
4. The due examination and sifting in debate of a bill
5. The publicity of a bill, i.e., the bringing it to the knowledge of the

---

[1] Some remarks on private bills will be found in Note A to this chapter at the end of this volume.

country at large, so that public opinion may be fully expressed regarding it

6. The honesty and courage of the legislative assembly in rejecting a bill, however likely to be popular, which their judgment disapproves

7. The responsibility of some person or body of persons for the enactment of a measure, i.e., the fixing on the right shoulders of the praise for passing a good, the blame for passing a bad, act

The criticisms that may be passed on American practice under the preceding heads will be made clearer by a comparison of English practice. Let us therefore first see how English bills and acts stand the tests we are to apply to the work of Congress.

In England public bills fall into two classes: those brought in by the ministry of the day as responsible advisers of the sovereign, and those brought in by private members. In point of law and in point of form there is no difference between these classes. Practically there is all the difference in the world, because a government bill has behind it the responsibility of the ministry, and presumably the weight of the majority which keeps the ministry in office. The ministry dispose of a half or more of the working time of the House, and have therefore much greater facilities for pushing forward their bills. Nearly all the most important bills, which involve large political issues, are government bills, so that the hostile critic of a private member's bill will sometimes argue that the House ought not to permit the member to proceed with it, because it is too large for any unofficial hands. This premised, we may proceed to the seven points above mentioned.

1. In England, as the more important bills are government bills, their policy is sure to have been carefully weighed. The ministry have every motive for care, because the fortunes of a first-class bill are their own fortunes. If it is rejected, they fall. A specially difficult bill is usually framed by a committee of the cabinet, and then debated by the cabinet as a whole before it appears in Parliament. Minor bills are settled in the departments by the parliamentary head with his staff of permanent officials.

2. In England, government bills are prepared by the official government draftsmen, two eminent lawyers with several assistants, who constitute an office for this purpose. Private members who are lawyers often draft their own bills; those who are not generally employ a barrister. The drafting of government bills has much improved of late years, and the faults of form observable in British acts are chiefly due to amendments made in Committee of the Whole House.

3. The harmony of one government bill with others of the same session is secured by the care of the official draftsmen, as well as by the fact that all emanate from one and the same ministry. No such safeguards exist in the case of private members' bills, but it is of course the duty of the ministry to watch these legislative essays, and get Parliament to strike out of any one of them whatever is inconsistent with another measure passed or intended to be passed in the same session.

4. Difficult and complicated bills which raise no political controversy are sometimes referred to a select committee, which goes through them and reports them as amended to the House. They are afterwards considered, and often fully debated, first in Committee of the Whole, and then by the House on the stage of report from Committee of the Whole to the House. Such bills are now often referred to what are called grand committees, i.e., committees of at least fifty appointed in each session for the consideration of particular kinds of business, discussion in which replaces the discussion in Committee of the Whole. Many bills, however, never go before select or grand committees. While measures which excite political feeling or touch any powerful interest (such as that of landowners or railroads or liquor dealers) are exhaustively debated, others may slip through unobserved. The enormous pressure of work and the prolixity with which some kinds of business are discussed, involve the hurrying other business through with scant consideration.

5. Except in the case of discussions at unseasonable hours, the proceedings of Parliament are so far reported in the leading newspapers and commented on by them that bills, even those of private members, generally become known to those whom they may concern. There is usually a debate on the second reading, and this debate attracts notice.

6. A government bill is, by the law of its being, exposed to the hostile criticism of the opposition, who have an interest in discrediting the ministry by disparaging their work. As respects private members' bills, it is the undoubted duty of some minister to watch them, and to procure their amendment or rejection if he finds them faulty. This duty is discharged less faithfully than might be wished, but perhaps as well as can be expected from weak human nature, often tempted to conciliate a supporter or an "interest" by allowing a measure to go through which ought to have been stopped.

7. Responsibility for everything done in the House rests upon the ministry of the day, because they are the leaders of the majority. If they allow a private member to pass a bad bill, if they stop him when trying to pass a

good bill, they are in theory no less culpable than if they pass a bad bill of their own. Accordingly, when the second reading of a measure of any consequence is moved, it is the duty of some member of the ministry to rise, with as little delay as possible, and state whether the ministry support it, or oppose it, or stand neutral. Standing neutral is, so far as responsibility to the country goes, practically the same thing as supporting. The opposition, as an organized body, are not expected to express their opinion on any bills except those of high political import. Needless to say, private members are also held strictly responsible for the votes they give, these votes being all recorded and published next morning. Of course both parties claim praise or receive blame from the country in respect of their attitude towards bills of moment, and when a session has produced few or feeble acts the opposition charge the ministry with sloth or incompetence.

The rules and usages I have described constitute valuable aids to legislation, and the quality of English and Scottish legislation, take it all and all, is good; that is to say, the statutes are such as public opinion (whether rightly or wrongly) demands, and are well drawn for the purposes they aim at.

Let us now apply the same tests to the legislation of Congress. What follows refers primarily to the House, but is largely true of the Senate, because in the Senate also the committees play an important part.

In neither house of Congress are there any government bills. All measures are brought in by private members because all members are private. The nearest approach to the government bill of England is one brought in by a leading member of the majority in pursuance of a resolution taken in the congressional caucus of that majority. This seldom happens. One must therefore compare the ordinary congressional bill with the English private member's bill rather than with a government measure, and expect to find it marked by the faults that mark the former class. The second difference is that whereas in England the criticism and amendment of a bill takes place in Committee of the Whole, and of other public bills in one of the large standing committees introduced since 1883, in the House of Representatives it takes place in a small committee of twenty members or less, often of seven. In the Senate also the committees do most of the work, but the Committee of the Whole occasionally debates a bill pretty fully.

Premising these dissimilarities, I go to the seven points before mentioned.

1. The excellence of the substance of a bill introduced in Congress depends entirely on the wisdom and care of its introducer. He may, if self-distrustful, take counsel with his political allies respecting it. But there is no security for its representing any opinion or knowledge but his own. It

may affect the management of an executive department, but the introducing member does not command departmental information, and will, if the bill passes, have nothing to do with the carrying out of its provisions. On the other hand, the officials of the government cannot submit bills; and if they find a congressman willing to bring them in, must leave the advocacy and conduct of the measure largely in his hands.

2. The drafting of a measure depends on the pains taken and skill exerted by its author. Senate bills are usually well drafted because many senators are experienced lawyers; House bills are often crude and obscure. There does not exist either among the executive departments or in connection with Congress, any legal office charged with the duty of preparing bills, or of seeing that the form in which they pass is technically satisfactory.

3. The only security for the consistency of the various measures of the same session is to be found in the fact that those which affect the same matter ought to be referred to the same committee. However, it often happens that there are two or more committees whose spheres of jurisdiction overlap, so that of two bills handling cognate matters, one may go to Committee A and the other to Committee B. Should different views of policy prevail in these two bodies, they may report to the House bills containing mutually repugnant provisions. There is nothing except unusual vigilance on the part of some member interested, to prevent both bills from passing. That mischief from this cause is not serious arises from the fact that out of the multitude of bills introduced, few are reported and still fewer become law.

4. The function of a committee of either house of Congress extends not merely to the sifting and amending of the bills referred to it, but to practically redrawing them, if the committee desires any legislation, or rejecting them by omitting to report them till near the end of the session if it thinks no legislation needed. Every committee is in fact a small bureau of legislation for the matters lying within its jurisdiction. It has for this purpose the advantage of time, of the right to take evidence, and of the fact that some of its members have been selected from their knowledge of or interest in the topics it has to deal with. On the other hand, it suffers from the nonpublication of its debates, and from the tendency of all small and secret bodies to intrigues and compromises, compromises in which general principles of policy are sacrificed to personal feeling or selfish interest. Bills which go in black or white come out gray. They may lose all their distinctive colour; or they may be turned into a medley of scarcely consistent provisions.

The member who has introduced a bill may not have a seat on the committee, and may therefore be unable to protect his offspring. Other members of the House, masters of the subject but not members of the committee, can only be heard as witnesses. Although therefore there are full opportunities for the discussion of the bill by the committee, it often emerges in an unsatisfactory form, or is quietly suppressed, because there is no impetus of the general opinion of the House or the public to push it through. When the bill comes back to the House the chairman or other reporting member of the committee generally moves the previous question, after which no amendment can be offered. Debate ceases and the bill is promptly passed or lost. In the Senate there is a better chance of discussion, for the Senate, having more time and fewer speakers, can review to some real purpose the findings of its committees.

5. As there is no debate on the introduction or on the second reading of a bill, the public is not necessarily apprised of the measures which are before Congress. An important measure is of course watched by the newspapers and so becomes known; minor measures go unnoticed.

6. The general good nature of Americans, and the tendency of members of their legislatures to oblige one another by doing reciprocal good turns, dispose people to let any bill go through which does not injure the interest of a party or of a person. Such good nature counts for less in a committee, because a committee has its own views and gives effect to them. But in the House there are few views, though much impatience. The House has no time to weigh the merits of a bill reported back to it. Members have never heard it debated. They know no more of what passed in the committee than the report tells them. If the measure is palpably opposed to their party tenets, the majority will reject it; if no party question arises they usually adopt the view of the committee.

7. What has been said already will have shown that except as regards bills of great importance, or directly involving party issues, there can be little effective responsibility for legislation. The member who brings in a bill is not responsible, because the committee generally alters his bill. The committee is little observed and the details of what passed within the four walls of its room are not published. The great parties in the House are but faintly responsible, because their leaders are not bound to express an opinion, and a vote taken on a nonpartisan bill is seldom a strict party vote. Individual members are no doubt responsible, and a member who votes against a popular measure, one for instance favoured by the working men, will suffer

for it.[2] But the responsibility of individuals, most of them insignificant, half of them destined to vanish, like snowflakes in a river, at the next election, gives little security to the people.

The best defence that can be advanced for this system is that it has been naturally evolved as a means of avoiding worse mischiefs. It is really a plan for legislating by a number of commissions. Each commission, receiving suggestions in the shape of bills, taking evidence upon them, and sifting them in debate, frames its measures and lays them before the House in a shape which seems designed to make amendment in details needless, while leaving the general policy to be accepted or rejected by a simple vote of the whole body. In this last respect the plan may be compared with that of the Romans during the Republic, whose general assembly of the people approved or disapproved of a bill as a whole, without power of amendment, a plan which had the advantage of making laws clear and simple. At Rome, however, bills could be proposed only by a magistrate upon his official responsibility; they were therefore comparatively few and sure to be carefully drawn. The members of American legislative commissions have no special training, no official experience, little praise or blame to look for, and no means of securing that the overburdened House will ever come to a vote on their proposals. There is no more agreement between the views of one commission and another than what may result from the fact that the majority in both belongs to the same party.

Add to the conditions above described the fact that the House in its few months of life has not time to deal with one-twentieth of the many thousand bills which are thrown upon it, that it therefore drops the enormous majority unconsidered, though some of the best may be in this majority, and passes many of those which it does pass by a suspension of the rules which leaves everything to a single vote,[3] and the marvel comes to be, not that legislation is faulty, but that an intensely practical people tolerates such defective machinery. Some reasons may be suggested tending to explain this phenomenon.

Legislation is a difficult business in all free countries, and perhaps more difficult the more free the country is, because the discordant voices are more

---

[2] The member who has taken this course is the worse off, because he rarely has an opportunity of explaining by a speech in the House his reason for his vote, and is therefore liable to the imputation of having been "got at" by capitalists.

[3] This can be done by a two-thirds vote during the last six days of a session and on the first and third Mondays of each month.

numerous and less under control. America has sometimes sacrificed practical convenience to her dislike to authority.

The Americans surpass all other nations in their power of making the best of bad conditions, getting the largest results out of scanty materials or rough methods. Many things in that country work better than they ought to work, so to speak, or could work in any other country, because the people are shrewdly alert in minimizing such mischiefs as arise from their own haste or heedlessness, and have a great capacity for self-help.

Aware that they possess this gift, the Americans have been content to leave their political machinery unreformed. Persons who propose comprehensive reforms are suspected as theorists and faddists. The national inventiveness, active in the spheres of mechanics and moneymaking, spends little of its force on the details of governmental methods, and the interest in material development tends to diminish the interest felt in politics. Nevertheless a certain change of attitude is evidenced by the much greater attention now given in the universities to the teaching of the principles and practice of government and administration.

The want of legislation on topics where legislation is needed breeds fewer evils than would follow in countries like England or France where Parliament is the only lawmaking body. The powers of Congress are limited to comparatively few subjects: its failures are supposed seldom to touch the general well-being of the people, or the healthy administration of the ordinary law.

The faults of bills passed by the House are often cured by the Senate, where discussion, if not conducted with a purer public spirit, is at least more leisurely and thorough. The committee system produces in that body also some of the same flabbiness and colourlessness in bills passed. But the blunders, whether in substance or of form, of the one chamber are frequently corrected by the other, and many bad bills fail owing to a division of opinion between the houses.

The Speaker had and the managing committee now has, through their control of business in the House, what practically amounts to a veto upon bills; and not a few thus perish.

The president's veto kills off some vicious measures. He does not trouble himself about defects of form; but where a bill seems to him opposed to sound policy, it is his constitutional duty to disapprove it, and to throw on Congress the responsibility of passing it "over his veto" by a two-thirds vote. A good president accepts this responsibility.

Congressional Finance

Finance is a sufficiently distinct and important department of legislation to need a chapter to itself; nor does any legislature devote so large a proportion of its time than does Congress to the consideration of financial bills. These are of two kinds: those which raise revenue by taxation, and those which direct the application of the public funds to the various expenses of the government. At present Congress raises all the revenue it requires by indirect taxation,[1] and chiefly by duties of customs and excise; so taxing bills are practically tariff bills, the excise duties being comparatively little varied from year to year.

The method of passing both kinds of bills is unlike that of most European countries. In England, with which, of course, America can be most easily compared, although both the levying and the spending of money are absolutely under the control of the House of Commons, the House of Commons originates no proposal for either. It never either grants money or orders the raising of money except at the request of the Crown. Once a year the Chancellor of the Exchequer lays before it, together with a full statement of the revenue and expenditure of the past twelve months, estimates of the expenditure for the coming twelve months, and suggestions for the means of meeting that expenditure by taxation or by borrowing. He embodies these suggestions in resolutions on which, when the House has accepted them, bills are grounded imposing certain taxes or authorizing the raising of a loan. The House may of course amend the bills in details, but no private member ever proposes a taxing bill, for it is no concern of anyone's except the

---

[1] During the Civil War, direct taxes were levied (the proceeds of which have, however, been since returned to the states); and many other kinds of taxes besides those mentioned in the text have been imposed at different times.

ministry to fill the public treasury.[2] The estimates prepared by the several administrative departments (Army, Navy, Office of Works, Foreign Office, etc.), and revised by the Treasury, specify the items of proposed expenditure with much particularity, and fill three or more bulky volumes, which are delivered to every member of the House. These estimates are debated in Committee of the Whole House, explanations being required from the ministers who represent the Treasury and the several departments and are passed in a long succession of separate votes. Members may propose to reduce any particular grants, but not to increase them; no money is ever voted for the public service except that which the Crown has asked for through its ministers. The Crown must never ask for more than it actually needs, and hence the ministerial proposals for taxation are carefully calculated to raise just so much money as will easily cover the estimated expenses for the coming year. It is reckoned almost as great a fault in the finance minister if he has needlessly overtaxed the people, as if he has so undertaxed them as to be left with a deficit. If at the end of a year a substantial surplus appears, the taxation for next year is reduced in proportion, supposing that the expenditure remains the same. Every credit granted by Parliament expires of itself at the end of the financial year.

In the United States the secretary of the treasury sends annually to Congress a report containing a statement of the national income and expenditure and of the condition of the public debt, together with remarks on the system of taxation and suggestions for its improvement. He also sends what is called his annual letter, enclosing the estimates, framed by the various departments, of the sums needed for the public services of the United States during the coming year.[3] So far the secretary is like a European finance minister, except that he communicates with the chamber on paper instead of making his statement and proposals orally. But here the resemblance stops. Everything that remains in the way of financial legislation is done by Congress and its committees, the president having no further hand in the

---

[2] Of course a private member may carry a resolution involving additional expenditure; but even this is at variance with the stricter constitutional doctrine and practice; a doctrine regarded by the statesmen of the last generation as extremely valuable, because it restrains the propensity of a legislature to yield to demands emanating from sections or classes, which may entail heavy and perhaps unprofitable charges on the country. See the observations of Mr. Gladstone in the House of Commons, March 22, 1886.

[3] This has now become a bulky volume. In it he neither endorses nor criticizes the estimates.

matter,[4] although he may send messages pressing Congress to vote for money for some purpose which he deems important.

The business of raising money belongs to one committee only, the standing Committee on Ways and Means, consisting of nineteen members. Its chairman is always a leading man in the party which commands a majority in the House. This committee prepares and reports to the House the bills needed for imposing or continuing the various customs duties, excise duties, etc. The report of the secretary has been referred by the House to this committee, but the latter does not necessarily base its bills upon or in any way regard that report. Neither does it in preparing them start from an estimate of the sums needed to support the public service. It does not, because it cannot; for it does not know what grants for the public service will be proposed by the spending committees, since the estimates submitted in the secretary's letter furnish no trustworthy basis for a guess. It does not, for the further reason that the primary object of customs duties has for many years past been not the raising of revenue, but the protection of American industries by subjecting foreign products to a very high tariff. This tariff (further raised in 1890 and 1897, altered in 1909, and reduced in 1913) brought in an income far exceeding the current needs of the government. Two-thirds of the war debt having been paid off, the fixed charges shrank to one-third of what they were when the war ended, yet this tariff remains with few modifications, surpluses constantly accumulating in the national treasury, until in 1890 a pension act was passed which increased expenditures so largely as almost to absorb even the growing surplus. The Committee on Ways and Means has therefore no motive for adapting taxation to expenditure. The former seemed likely to be always in excess while the protective tariff stood, and the protective tariff stood for commercial or political reasons unconnected with national finance.[5] Of recent finance it would be difficult to speak without entering on controversial ground.

---

[4] Now however the president has received by statute the power of examining the estimates and making recommendations regarding them.

[5] For a long time surpluses were got rid of by paying off debt; but when financiers began to hold that a certain portion of the debt ought to be kept on foot for banking and currency purposes, much discussion arose as to how the accumulating balance should be disposed of. The Pension Act, although primarily intended to gratify the survivors of the Northern armies in the Civil War, seems to have been also designed to so deplete the Treasury as to remove one reason for reducing the protective tariff. Since then pension expenditure has increased, military and naval expenditure has increased, and though the tariff has been raised and revenue from customs has grown, expenditure has sometimes (as for instance in 1909) been in excess of revenue.

When the revenue bills come to be debated in Committee of the Whole House similar causes prevent them from being scrutinized from the purely financial point of view. Debate turns on those items of the tariff which involve gain or loss to influential groups. Little inquiry is made as to the amount needed and the adaptation of the bills to produce that amount and no more. It is the same with ways and means bills in the Senate. Communications need not pass between the committees of either house and the Treasury. The person most responsible, the person who most nearly corresponds to an English Chancellor of the Exchequer, or a French Minister of Finance, is the chairman of the House Committee on Ways and Means. But he stands in no official relation to the Treasury, and is not required to exchange a word or a letter with its staff. Neither, of course, can he count on a majority in the House. Though he is a leading man he is not a leader, i.e., he has no claim on the votes of his own party, many of whom may disapprove of and cause the defeat of his proposals. This befell in 1886, when the chairman of this committee, an able man, and perhaps, after the Speaker, the most considerable person in the Democratic majority, was beaten in his attempted reform of the tariff.

The business of spending money used to belong to the Committee on Appropriations, but in 1883 a new committee, that on Rivers and Harbours, received a large field of expenditure; and in 1886 sundry other supply bills were referred to sundry standing committees. The Committee on Appropriations starts from, but does not adopt, the estimates sent in by the secretary of the treasury, for the appropriation bills it prepares usually make large and often reckless reductions in these estimates. The Rivers and Harbours Committee proposes grants of money for what are called "internal improvements," nominally in aid of navigation, but practically in order to turn a stream of public money into the state or states where each "improvement" is to be executed. More money is wasted in this way than what the parsimony of the Appropriations Committee can save. Each of the other standing committees, including the Committee on Pensions, a source of infinite waste,[6] proposes grants of money, not knowing nor heeding what is being proposed by other committees, and guided by the executive no further than

[6] The annual expenditure on pensions was in 1887, $75,000,000 (£15,000,000). Under the statute of 1890, it had risen in 1894 to $142,092,818, with 994,762 pensioners on the roll, 39 years after the end of the War of Secession. In 1912, 43 years after the war, it stood at $152,986,433. The total amount expended in pensions for service in the Northern armies during the War of Secession alone had, in 1908, reached $3,533,593,025 (about £707,000,000).

the members choose. All the expenditures recommended must be met by appropriation bills, but into their propriety the Appropriations Committee cannot inquire.

Every revenue bill must, of course, come before the House; and the House, whatever else it may neglect, never neglects the discussion of taxation and money grants. These are discussed as fully as the pressure of work permits, and are often added to by the insertion of fresh items, which members interested in getting money voted for a particular purpose or locality suggest. These bills then go to the Senate, which forthwith refers them to its committees. The Senate Committee on Finance deals with revenue-raising bills; the Committee on Appropriations with supply bills. Both sets then come before the whole Senate. Although it cannot initiate appropriation bills, the Senate has long ago made good its claim to amend appropriations bills, and does so freely, adding items and often raising the total of the grants. When the bills go back to the House, the House usually rejects the amendments; the Senate adheres to them, and a conference committee is appointed, consisting of three senators and three members of the House, by which a compromise is settled, hastily and in secret, and accepted, generally in the last days of the session, by a hard-pressed but reluctant House. Even as enlarged by this committee, the supply voted is usually found inadequate, so a deficiency bill is introduced in the following session, including a second series of grants to the departments.

The European reader will ask how all this is or can be done by Congress without frequent communication from or to the executive government. There are such communications, for the ministers, anxious to secure appropriations adequate for their respective departments, talk to the chairmen and appear before the committees to give evidence as to departmental needs. But Congress does not look to them for guidance as in the early days it looked to Hamilton and Gallatin. If the House cuts down their estimates they turn to the Senate and beg it to restore the omitted items; if the Senate fail them, the only resource left is a deficiency bill in the next session. If one department is so starved as to be unable to do its work, while another obtains lavish grants which invite jobbery or waste, it is the committees, not the executive, whom the people ought to blame. If, by a system of logrolling, vast sums are wasted upon useless public works, no minister has any opportunity to interfere, any right to protest. A minister cannot, as in England, bring Congress to reason by a threat of resignation, for it would make no difference to Congress if the whole cabinet were to resign, unless of course the congressmen most conspicuously concerned should be so palpably in fault that the people could be roused to vigorous disapproval.

What has been here stated may be summarized as follows:

There is practically no connection between the policy of revenue raising and the policy of revenue spending, for these are left to different committees whose views may be opposed, and the majority in the House has no recognized leaders to remark the discrepancies or make one or other view prevail. In the Forty-ninth Congress a strong free trader was chairman of the tax-proposing Committee on Ways and Means, while a strong protectionist was chairman of the spending Committee on Appropriations.

There is no relation between the amount proposed to be spent in any one year, and the amount proposed to be raised. But for the fact that the high tariff produces a large annual surplus, a financial breakdown would speedily ensue.

The knowledge and experience of the permanent officials either as regards the productivity of taxes, and the incidental benefits or losses attending their collection, or as regards the nature of various kinds of expenditure and their comparative utility, can be turned to account only by interrogating these officials before the committees. Their views are not stated in the House by a parliamentary chief, nor tested in debate by arguments addressed to him which he must there and then answer.

Little check exists on the tendency of members to deplete the public treasury by securing grants for their friends or constituents, or by putting through financial jobs for which they are to receive some private consideration. If either the majority of the Committee on Appropriations or the House itself suspects a job, the grant proposed may be rejected. But it is the duty of no one in particular to scent out a job, and to defeat it by public exposure.

The nation is sometimes puzzled by a financial policy varying from year to year, and controlled by no responsible leaders, and it feels less interest than it ought in congressional discussions, nor has it confidence in Congress.[7]

---

[7] "The noteworthy fact that even the most thorough debates in Congress fail to awaken any genuine or active interest in the minds of the people has had its most striking illustrations in the course of our financial legislation, for though the discussions which have taken place in Congress upon financial questions have been so frequent, so protracted, and so thorough, engrossing a large part of the time of the House on their every recurrence, they seem in almost every instance to have made scarcely any impression upon the public mind. The Coinage Act of 1873, by which silver was demonetized, had been before the country many years ere it reached adoption, having been time and again considered by committees of Congress, time and again printed and discussed in one shape or another, and having finally gained acceptance apparently by sheer persistence and

The result on the national finance is unfortunate. A thoughtful American publicist remarks, "So long as the debit side of the national account is managed by one set of men, and the credit side by another set, both sets working separately and in secret without public responsibility, and without intervention on the part of the executive official who is nominally responsible; so long as these sets, being composed largely of new men every two years, give no attention to business except when Congress is in session, and thus spend in preparing plans the whole time which ought to be spent in public discussion of plans already matured, so that an immense budget is rushed through without discussion in a week or ten days—just so long the finances will go from bad to worse, no matter by what name you call the party in power. No other nation on earth attempts such a thing, or could attempt it without soon coming to grief, our salvation thus far consisting in an enormous income."

It may be replied to this criticism that the enormous income, added to the fact that the tariff is imposed for protection rather than for revenue, is not only the salvation of the United States government under the present system, but also the cause of that system. Were the tariff framed with a view to revenue only, no higher taxes would be imposed than the public service required, and a better method of balancing the public accounts would follow. America is the only country in the world whose difficulty is not to raise money but to spend it.[8] But it is equally true that Congress is contracting lax habits, and ought to change them.

How comes it, if all this be true, that the finances of America have been so flourishing, and in particular that the Civil War debt was paid off with such regularity and speed that the total public debt of $3,000,000,000

---

importunity. The Resumption Act of 1875, too, had had a like career of repeated considerations by committees, repeated printings and a full discussion by Congress, and yet when the Bland Silver Bill of 1878 was on its way through the mills of legislation, some of the most prominent newspapers of the country declared with confidence that the Resumption Act had been passed inconsiderately and in haste; and several members of Congress had previously complained that the demonetization scheme of 1873 had been pushed surreptitiously through the courses of its passage, Congress having been tricked into accepting it, doing it scarcely knew what."—Woodrow Wilson, *Congressional Government*, p. 148. This remark, however, would not apply to the tariff debates of 1890, 1909, and 1913.

[8] For twenty-eight years up to 1892, there had been surpluses, the smallest of $2,344,000 in 1874, the largest of $145,543,000 in 1882. The surplus for the year ending 30th June, 1890, was about $44,000,000. The receipts from customs alone were greater by about $48,000,000 in 1890 than in 1885. The total revenue of the year ending June 30, 1892, was $425,000,000, and the total expenditure $415,000,000, the receipts from customs duties having declined, and the expenditure, especially on pensions, having increased. In 1899, and in several other years since, there were deficits.

(£600,000,000) in 1865 had sunk in 1890 to $1,000,000,000 (£200,000,000)? Does not so brilliant a result speak of a continuously wise and skilful management of the national revenue?

The swift reduction of the debt seems to be due to the following causes:

To the prosperity of the country which, with one interval of trade depression, has for twenty-five years been developing its amazing natural resources so fast as to produce an amount of wealth which is not only greater, but more widely diffused through the population, than in any other part of the world.[9]

To the spending habits of the people, who allow themselves luxuries such as the masses enjoy in no other country, and therefore pay more than any other people in the way of indirect taxation. The fact that federal revenue is raised by duties of customs and excise makes the people far less sensible of the pressure of taxation than they would be did they pay directly.

To the absence, down till 1899, of the military and naval charges which press so heavily on European states.

To the maintenance of an exceedingly high tariff at the instance of interested persons who have obtained the public ear and can influence Congress. It was the acceptance of the policy of protection, rather than any deliberate conviction that the debt ought to be paid off, that caused the continuance of a tariff whose huge and constant surpluses have enabled the debt to be reduced.

Europeans, admiring and envying the rapidity with which the Civil War debt was reduced were in those years disposed to credit the Americans with brilliant financial skill. That, however, which was really admirable in the conduct of the American people was not their judgment in selecting particular methods for raising money, but their readiness to submit during and immediately after the war to unprecedentedly heavy taxation. The interests (real or supposed) of the manufacturing classes have caused the maintenance of the tariff then imposed; nature, by giving the people a spending power which rendered the tariff marvellously productive, did the rest.

Under the system of congressional finance here described America wastes millions annually. But her wealth is so great, her revenue so elastic, that she is not sensible of the loss. She has the glorious privilege of youth, the privilege of committing errors without suffering from their consequences.

---

[9] In 1907 the total revenue of the national government from all sources was $846,725,340, and in 1912, $992,249,230. The total expenditure was in 1907, $762,488,753, and in 1912, $965,273,678. The total public interest bearing debt stood in 1908 at $963,776,770.

The Relations of the Two Houses

The creation by the Constitution of 1789 of two chambers in the United States, in place of the one chamber which existed under the Confederation has been usually ascribed by Europeans to mere imitation of England; and one learned writer goes so far as to suggest that if England had possessed three chambers, like the States General of France, or four, like the Diet of Sweden, a crop of three-chambered or four-chambered legislatures would, in obedience to the example of happy and successful England, have sprung up over the world. There were, however, better reasons than deference to English precedents to justify the division of Congress into two houses and no more; and so many indubitable instances of such a deference may be quoted that there is no need to hunt for others. Not to dwell upon the fact that there were two chambers in all but two[1] of the thirteen original states, the Convention of 1787 had two solid motives for fixing on this number, a motive of principle and theory, a motive of immediate expediency.

The chief advantage of dividing a legislature into two branches is that the one may check the haste and correct the mistakes of the other. This advantage is purchased at the price of some delay, and of the weakness which results from a splitting up of authority. If a legislature be constituted of three or more branches, the advantage is scarcely increased, the delay and weakness are immensely aggravated. Two chambers can be made to work together in a way almost impossible to more than two. As the proverb says, "Two's company, three's none." If there be three chambers, two are sure to intrigue and likely to combine against the third. The difficulties of carrying a measure without sacrificing its unity of principle, of fixing responsibility, of securing

---

[1] Pennsylvania and Georgia; the former of which added a Senate in 1789, the latter in 1790. See *post*, Chapter 40 on state legislatures.

the watchful attention of the public, serious with two chambers, become enormous with three or more.

To these considerations there was added the practical ground that the division of Congress into two houses supplied a means of settling the dispute which raged between the small and the large states. The latter contended for a representation of the states in Congress proportioned to their respective populations, the former for their equal representation as sovereign commonwealths. Both were satisfied by the plan which created two chambers in one of which the former principle, in the other of which the latter principle was recognized. The country remained a federation in respect of the Senate, it became a nation in respect of the House: there was no occasion for a third chamber.

The respective characters of the two bodies are wholly unlike those of the so-called upper and lower chambers of Europe. In Europe there is always a difference of political complexion generally resting on a difference in personal composition. There the upper chamber represents the aristocracy of the country, or the men of wealth, or the high officials, or the influence of the Crown and court; while the lower chamber represents the multitude. Between the Senate and the House there is no such difference. Both equally represent the people, the whole people, and nothing but the people. The individual members come from the same classes of the community; though in the Senate, as it has more rich men (in proportion to numbers) than has the House, the influence of capital has latterly been more marked. Both have been formed by the same social influences; and the social pretensions of a senator expire with his term of office. Both are possessed by the same ideas, governed by the same sentiments, equally conscious of their dependence on public opinion. The one has never been, like the English House of Commons, a popular pet, the other never, like the English House of Lords, a popular bugbear.

What is perhaps stranger, the two branches of Congress have not exhibited that contrast of feeling and policy which might be expected from the different methods by which they are chosen. In the House the large states are predominant: ten out of forty-eight (less than one-fourth) return an absolute majority of the 443 representatives. In the Senate these same ten states have only twenty members out of ninety-six, less than a fourth of the whole. In other words, these ten states are more than sixteen times as powerful in the House as they are in the Senate. But as the House has never been the organ of the large states, nor prone to act in their interest, so neither has the Senate been the stronghold of the small states, for American politics have never turned upon an antagonism between these two sets of commonwealths. Questions relating to states' rights and the greater or less extension of the powers of the national government have played a leading part in the history of the Union. But although small states might be supposed to be specially zealous for states' rights, the tendency to uphold them has been no stronger in the Senate than in the House. In one phase of the slavery struggle the Senate happened to be under the control of the slaveholders while the House was not; and then of course the Senate championed the sovereignty of the states. But this attitude was purely accidental, and disappeared with its transitory cause.

The real differences between the two bodies have been indicated in speaking of the Senate, and the consequent greater facilities for debate, to the somewhat superior capacity of its members, to the habits which its executive functions form in individual senators, and have formed in the whole body.

In Europe, where the question as to the utility of second chambers is actively canvassed, two objections are made to them, one that they deplete the first or popular chamber of able men, the other that they induce deadlocks and consequent stoppage of the wheels of government. On both arguments light may be expected from American experience.

Although the Senate does draw off from the House many of its ablest men, it is not clear, paradoxical as the observation may appear, that the House would be much the better for retaining those men. The faults of the House are mainly due, not to want of talent among individuals, but to its defective methods, and especially to the absence of leadership. These are faults which the addition of twenty or thirty able men would not cure. Some of the committees would be stronger, and so far the work would be better done. But the House as a whole would not (assuming its rules and usages to remain what they are now) be distinctly a greater power in the country. On the other hand, the merits of the Senate are largely due to the fact that it trains to higher efficiency the ability which it has drawn from the House, and gives that ability a sphere in which it can develop with better results. Were the Senate and the House thrown into one, the country might suffer more by losing the Senate than it would gain by improving the House, for the united body would have the qualities of the House and not those of the Senate.

Collisions between the two houses are frequent. Each is jealous and combative. Each is prone to alter the bills that come from the other; and the Senate in particular knocks about remorselessly those favourite children of the House, the appropriation bills. The fact that one house has passed a bill goes but a little way in inducing the other to pass it; the Senate would reject twenty House bills as readily as one. Deadlocks, however, disagreements over serious issues which stop the machinery of administration, are not common. They rarely cause excitement or alarm outside Washington, because the country, remembering previous instances, feels sure they will be adjusted, and knows that either house would yield were it unmistakably condemned by public opinion. The executive government goes on undisturbed, and the worst that can happen is the loss of a bill which may be passed some months later. Even as between the two bodies there is no great bitterness in these conflicts, because the causes of quarrel do not lie deep. Sometimes it is self-esteem that is involved, the sensitive self-esteem of an assembly. Sometimes one or other house is playing for a party advantage. That intensity which in the similar contests of Europe arises from class feeling is absent, because there is no class distinction between the two American chambers. Thus the country seems to be watching a fencing match rather than a *combat à outrance*.

I dwell upon this substantial identity of character in the Senate and the House because it explains the fact, surprising to a European, that two perfectly coordinate authorities, neither of which has any more right than its rival to claim to speak for the whole nation, manage to get along together. Their quarrels are professional and personal rather than conflicts of adverse principles. The two bodies are not hostile elements in the nation, striving for supremacy, but servants of the same master, whose word of rebuke will quiet them.

It must, however, be also remembered that in such countries as England, France, and Italy, the popular chamber stands in very close relation with the executive government, which it has virtually installed and which it supports. A conflict between the two chambers in such countries is therefore a conflict to which the executive is a party, involving issues which may be of the extremest urgency; and this naturally intensifies the struggle. For the House of Lords in England or the Senate in Italy to resist a demand for legislation made by the ministry, who are responsible for the defence and peace of the country, and backed by the representative House, is a more serious matter than almost any collision between the Senate and the House can be in America.[2]

---

[2] Of course a case may be imagined in which the president should ask for legislation, as Lincoln did during the war, and one house of Congress should grant, the other refuse, the acts demanded. But such cases are less likely to occur in America than in Europe under the cabinet system.

The United States is the only great country in the world (for the Australian Commonwealth is scarcely an exception) in which the two houses are really equal and coordinate. Such a system could hardly work, and therefore could not last, if the executive were the creature of either or of both, nor unless both were in touch with the sovereign people, although that touch is, owing to the system of nominations (see Part III *post*), not so close as it appears to be.

When each chamber persists in its own view, the regular proceeding is to appoint a committee of conference, consisting of three members of the Senate and three of the House, sometimes however of a larger number. These six meet in secret, and generally settle matters by a compromise, which enables each side to retire with honour. When appropriations are involved, a sum intermediate between the smaller one which the House proposes to grant and the larger one desired by the Senate is adopted. If no compromise can be arranged, and if the action of the president, who may conceivably give his moral support (backed by the possibility of a veto) to one or another chamber, does not intervene, the conflict continues till one side yields or it ends by an adjournment, which of course involves the failure of the measure disagreed upon. The House at one time tried to coerce the Senate into submission by adding "riders," as they are called, to appropriation bills, i.e., annexing or "tacking" (to use the English expression) pieces of general legislation to bills granting sums of money. This puts the Senate in the dilemma of either accepting the unwelcome rider, or rejecting the whole bill, and thereby withholding from the executive the funds it needs. This happened in 1855 and 1856. However, the Senate stood firm, and the House gave way. The device had previously been attempted (in 1849) by the Senate in tacking a proslavery provision to an appropriation bill which it was returning to the House, and it was revived by both houses against President Andrew Johnson in 1867.

In a contest the Senate usually, though not invariably, gets the better of the House. It is smaller, and can therefore more easily keep its majority together; its members are more experienced; and it has the great advantage of being permanent, whereas the House is a transient body. The Senate can hold out, because if it does not get its way at once against the House, it may do so when a new House comes up to Washington. The House cannot afford to wait, because the hour of its own dissolution is at hand. Besides, while the House does not know the Senate from inside, the Senate, many of whose members have sat in the House, knows all the "ins and outs" of its rival, can gauge its strength and play upon its weakness.

General Observations on Congress

After this inquiry into the composition and working of each branch of Congress, it remains for me to make some observations which apply to both houses, and which may tend to indicate the features that distinguish them from the representative assemblies of the Old World. The English reader must bear in mind three points which, in following the details of the last few chapters, he may have forgotten. The first is that Congress is not, like the parliaments of England, France, and Italy, a sovereign assembly, but is subject to the Constitution, which only the people can change. The second is, that it neither appoints nor dismisses the executive government, which springs directly from popular election. The third is, that its sphere of legislative action is limited by the existence of nearly fifty governments in the several states, whose authority is just as well based as its own, and cannot be curtailed by it.

I. The choice of members of Congress is locally limited by law and by custom. Under the Constitution every representative and every senator must when elected be an inhabitant of the state whence he is elected. Moreover, state law has in many and custom practically in all states, established that a representative must be resident in the congressional district which elects him.[1] The only exceptions to this practice occur in large cities where occasionally a man is chosen who lives in a different district of the city from that which returns him; but such exceptions are extremely rare.[2] This

---

[1] The best legal authorities hold that a provision of this kind is invalid, because state law has no power to narrow the qualifications for a federal representative prescribed by the Constitution of the United States. And Congress would probably so hold if the question arose in a case brought before it as to a disputed election. So far as I have been able to ascertain, the point has never arisen for determination.

[2] I have however known of one or two cases in New England and in the city of New York in which persons not resident in the district have been elected. In New York on one occasion it was strongly

restriction, inconvenient as it is both to candidates, whose field of choice in seeking a constituency it narrows, and to constituencies, whom it debars from choosing persons, however eminent, who do not reside in their midst, seems to Americans so obviously reasonable that few persons, even in the best educated classes, will admit its policy to be disputable. In what are we to seek the causes of this opinion?

Firstly. In the existence of states, originally separate political communities, still for many purposes independent, and accustomed to consider the inhabitant of another state as almost a foreigner. A New Yorker, Pennsylvanians would say, owes allegiance to New York; he cannot feel and think as a citizen of Pennsylvania, and cannot therefore properly represent Pennsylvanian interests. This sentiment has spread by a sort of sympathy, this reasoning has been applied by a sort of analogy, to the counties, the cities, the electoral districts of the state itself. State feeling has fostered local feeling; the locality deems no man a fit representative who has not by residence in its limits, and by making it his political home, the place where he exercises his civic rights, become soaked with its own local sentiment.

Secondly. Much of the interest felt in the proceedings of Congress relates to the raising and spending of money. Changes in the tariff may affect the industries of a locality; or a locality may petition for an appropriation of public funds to some local public work, the making of a harbour, or the improvement of the navigation of a river. In both cases it is thought that no one but an inhabitant can duly comprehend the needs or zealously advocate the demands of a neighbourhood.

Thirdly. Inasmuch as no high qualities of statesmanship are expected from a congressman, a district would think it a slur to be told that it ought to look beyond its own borders for a representative; and as the post is a paid one, the people feel that a good thing ought to be kept for one of themselves rather than thrown away on a stranger. It is by local political work, organizing, canvassing, and haranguing, that a party is kept going: and this work must be rewarded.

A perusal of the chapter of the *Federalist*, which argues that one representative for thirty thousand inhabitants will sufficiently satisfy republican needs, suggests another reflection. The writer refers to some who held a numerous representation to be a democratic institution, because it enabled every small district to make its voice heard in the national Congress. Such

---

urged against a candidate that the side of the street in which he lived was not within the ward he was standing for. Sometimes a man moves into a district in order to be chosen there.

representation then existed in the state legislatures. Evidently the habits of the people were formed by these state legislatures, in which it was a matter of course that the people of each township or city sent one of themselves to the assembly of the state. When they came to return members to Congress, they followed the same practice. A stranger had no means of making himself known to them and would not think of offering himself. That the habits of England are different may be due, so far as the eighteenth century is concerned, to the practice of borough-mongering, under which candidates unconnected with the place were sent down by some influential person, or bought the seat from the corrupt corporation or the limited body of freemen. Thus the notion that a stranger might do well enough for a borough grew up, while in counties it remained, till 1885, a maxim that a candidate ought to own land in the county—the old law required a freehold qualification somewhere[3]—or ought to live in, or ought at the very least (as I once heard a candidate, whose house lay just outside the county for which he was standing, allege on his own behalf) to look into the county from his window while shaving in the morning.[4] The English practice might thus seem to be an exception due to special causes, and the American practice that which is natural to a free country, where local self-government is fully developed and rooted in the habits of the people. It is from their local government that

---

[3] The old law (9 Anne, c. 5) required all members to possess a freehold qualification somewhere. All property qualifications were abolished by statue in 1858. Of the last five prime ministers who have sat in the House of Commons none has represented his place of residence.

[4] The English habit of allowing a man to stand for a place with which he is personally unconnected would doubtless be favoured by the fact that many ministers are necessarily members of the House of Commons. The inconvenience of excluding a man from the service of the nation because he could not secure his return in the place of his residence would be unendurable. No such reason exists in America, because ministers cannot be members of Congress. In France, Germany, Italy, and in Canada the practice resembles that of England, i.e., many members sit for places where they do not reside, though a candidate residing in the place he stands for has a certain advantage.

It is remarkable that the original English practice required the member to be a resident of the county or borough which returned him to Parliament. This is said to be a requirement at common law (witness the words "de comitatu tuo" in the writ for the election addressed to the sheriff); and was expressly enacted by the statute 1 Henry V. cap. 1. But already in the time of Elizabeth the requirement was not enforced; and in 1681 Lord Chief Justice Pemberton ruled that "little regard was to be had to that ancient statute 1 Henry V. forasmuch as common practice hath been ever since to the contrary." The statute was repealed by 14 Geo. III cap. 50.—See Anson, *Law and Custom of the Constitution*, vol. i, p. 83; Stubbs, *Constit. Hist.*, vol. iii, p. 424. Dr. Stubbs observes that the object of requiring residence in early times was to secure "that the House of Commons should be a really representative body." Mr. Hearn (*Government of England*) suggests that the requirement had to be dropped because it was hard to find country gentlemen (or indeed burgesses) possessing the legal knowledge and statesmanship which the constitutional struggles of the sixteenth and seventeenth centuries demanded.

the political ideas of the American people have been formed; and they have applied to their state assemblies and their national assembly the customs which grew up in the smaller area.[5]

These are the best explanations I can give of a phenomenon which strikes Europeans all the more because it exists among a population more unsettled and migratory than any in the Old World. But they leave me still surprised at this strength of local feeling, a feeling not less marked in the new regions of the Far West than in the venerable commonwealths of Massachusetts and Virginia. Fierce as is the light of criticism which beats upon every part of that system, this point remains uncensured, because assumed to be part of the order of nature.

So far as the restriction to residents in a state is concerned it is intelligible. The senator was originally a sort of ambassador from his state. He is chosen by the legislature or collective authority of his state. He cannot well be a citizen of one state and represent another. Even a representative in the House from one state who lived in another might be perplexed by a divided allegiance, though there are groups of states, such as those of the Northwest, whose great industrial interests are substantially the same. But what reason can there be for preventing a man resident in one part of a state from representing another part, a Philadelphian, for instance, from being returned for Pittsburgh, or a Bostonian for Pittsfield in the west of Massachusetts? In Europe it is not found that a member is less active or successful in urging the local interests of his constituency because he does not live there. He is often more successful, because more personally influential or persuasive than any resident whom the constituency could supply; and in case of a conflict of interests he always feels his efforts to be owing first to his constituents, and not to the place in which he happens to reside.

The mischief is twofold. Inferior men are returned, because there are many parts of the country which do not grow statesmen, where nobody, or at any rate nobody desiring to enter Congress, is to be found above a moderate level of political capacity. And men of marked ability and zeal are prevented from forcing their way in. Such men are produced chiefly in

[5] When President Garfield was one of the leaders of the House of Representatives it happened that his return for the district in which he resided became doubtful, owing to the strength of the Democratic party there. His friend Mr. John Hay (to whom I owe the anecdote), anxious to make sure that he should somehow be returned to the House, went into the adjoining district to sound the Republican voters there as to the propriety of running Mr. Garfield for their constituency. They laughed at the notion, "Why, he don't live in our deestrict." I have heard of a case in which a member of Congress having after his election gone to live in a neighbouring district, was thereupon compelled by the pressure of public opinion to resign his seat.

the great cities of the older states. There is not room enough there for nearly all of them, but no other doors to Congress are open. Boston, Chicago, New York, Philadelphia, could furnish six or eight times as many good members as there are seats in these cities. As such men cannot enter from their place of residence, they do not enter at all, and the nation is deprived of the benefit of their services. Careers are moreover interrupted. A promising politician may lose his seat in his own district through some fluctuation of opinion, or perhaps because he has offended the local wire-pullers by too much independence. Since he cannot find a seat elsewhere he is stranded; his political life is closed, while other young men inclined to independence take warning from his fate. Changes in the state laws would not remove the evil, for the habit of choosing none but local men is rooted so deeply that it might probably long survive the abolition of a restrictive law, and it is just as strong in states where no such law exists.[6]

II. Every senator and representative receives a salary at present fixed at $7,500 per annum, besides an allowance (called mileage) of 20 cents (10d.) per mile for travelling expenses for one journey to and from Washington, $1,500 for clerk hire, and a sum for stationery. The salary is looked upon as a matter of course. It was not introduced for the sake of enabling working men to be returned as members, but on the general theory that all public work ought to be paid for.[7] The reasons for it are stronger than in England or France, because the distance to Washington from most parts of the United States is so great, and the attendance required there so continuous, that a man cannot attend to his profession or business while sitting in Congress. If he loses his livelihood in serving the community, the community ought to compensate him, not to add that the class of persons whose private means put them above the need of a lucrative calling, or of compensation for interrupting it, is comparatively small even now, and hardly existed when the Constitution was framed. Cynics defend the payment of congressmen on another ground, viz., that "they would steal worse if they didn't get it," and would make politics, as Napoleon made war, support itself. Be the thing bad or good, it is at any rate necessary, so that no one talks of abolishing it. For that reason its existence furnishes no argument for its introduction into a small country with a large leisured and wealthy class. In

---

[6] In Maryland, a state almost divided into two parts by Chesapeake Bay, it has been the practice that one of the two senators should be chosen from the residents east of the bay, the other from those of the western shore.

[7] Benjamin Franklin argued strongly in the Convention of 1787 against this theory, but found little support. See his remarkable speech in Mr. John Bigelow's *Life of Franklin*, vol. iii, p. 389.

fact, the conditions of European countries are so different from those of America that one must not cite American experience either for or against the remuneration of legislative work. I do not believe that the practice works ill by preventing good men from entering politics, for they feel no more delicacy in accepting their $7,500 than an English duke does in drawing his salary as a secretary of state. It may strengthen the tendency of members to regard themselves as mere delegates, but that tendency has other and deeper roots. It contributes to keep up a class of professional politicians, for the salary, though small in comparison with the incomes earned by successful merchants or lawyers, is a prize to men of the class whence professional politicians mostly come. But those European writers who describe it as the formative cause of that class are mistaken. That class would have existed had members not been paid, would continue to exist if payment were withdrawn. On the other hand, the benefit which Europeans look for from the payment of legislators, viz., the introduction of a large number of representative working men, has hitherto been little desired and even less secured. Few such persons appear as candidates in America; and until recently the working class did not deem itself, nor think of acting as, a distinct body with special interest.[8]

III. A congressman's tenure of his place, though tending to grow longer, is still usually short. Senators are sometimes returned for two, four, or (in a few of the older states) even for five successive terms by the legislatures of their states, although it may befall even the best of them to be thrown out by a change in the balance of parties, or by the intrigues of an opponent. But a member of the House can seldom feel safe in the saddle. If he is so eminent as to be necessary to his party, or if he maintains intimate relations with the leading local wire-pullers of his district, he may in the Eastern and Middle, and still more in the Southern states, hold his ground for four or five Congresses, i.e., for eight or ten years. Few do more than this. In the West a member is fortunate if he does even this. Out there a seat is regarded as a good thing which ought to go round. It has a salary. It sends a man, free of expense, for two winters and springs to Washington and lets him and his wife and daughters see something of the fine world there. Local leaders cast sheep's eyes at the seat, and make more or less open bargains between themselves as to the order in which they shall enjoy it. So far from its being a reason for reelecting a man that he has been a member already, it was, and is still in parts of the West, a reason for passing him by, and

---

[8] Payment is the rule in the British self-governing colonies. In France and some at least of the German states (though not in the Reichstag) representatives are paid. In Italy they receive no salary, but a free pass over the railroads.

giving somebody else a turn. Rotation in office, dear to the Democrats of Jefferson's school a century ago, still charms the less educated, who see in it a recognition of equality, and have no sense of the value of special knowledge or training. They like it for the same reason that the democrats of Athens liked the choice of magistrates by lot. It is a recognition and application of equality. An ambitious congressman is therefore forced to think day and night of his renomination, and to secure it not only by procuring, if he can, grants from the federal treasury for local purposes, and places for the relatives and friends of the local wire-pullers who control the nominating conventions, but also by sedulously "nursing" the constituency during the vacations. No habit could more effectually discourage noble ambition or check the growth of a class of accomplished statesmen. There are few walks of life in which experience counts for more than it does in parliamentary politics. It is an education in itself, an education in which the quick-witted Western American would make rapid progress were he suffered to remain long enough at Washington. At present he is not suffered, for nearly one-half of each successive House has usually consisted of new men, while the old members are too much harassed by the trouble of procuring their reelection to have time or motive for the serious study of political problems. This is what comes of the notion that politics is neither a science, nor an art, nor even an occupation, like farming or storekeeping, in which one learns by experience, but a thing that comes by nature, and for which one man of common sense is as fit as another.[9]

IV. The last-mentioned evil is aggravated by the short duration of a Congress. Short as it seems, the two years' term was warmly opposed, when the Constitution was framed, as being too long.[10] The constitutions of the several states, framed when they shook off the supremacy of the British Crown, all fixed one year, except the ultrademocratic Connecticut and Rhode Island, where under the colonial charters a legislature met every six months, and South Carolina, which had fixed two years. So essential to republicanism was this principle deemed, that the maxim "where annual elections end tyranny begins" had passed into a proverb; and the authors of the *Federalist* were obliged to argue that the limited authority of Congress, watched by the executive on one side, and the state legislatures on the other, would prevent so long a period as two years from proving dangerous to

---

[9] In recent years, a tendency to reelect members seems to be growing.

[10] In the Massachusetts Convention of 1788, when this question was being discussed, "General Thomson then broke out into the following pathetic apostrophe, 'O my country, never give up your annual elections: young men, never give up your jewel.' He apologized for his zeal." —Elliot's *Debates*, vol. ii, p. 16.

liberty, while it was needed in order to enable the members to master the laws and understand the conditions of different parts of the Union. At present the two years' term is justified on the ground that it furnishes a proper check on the president by interposing an election in the middle of his term. One is also told that these frequent elections are necessary to keep up popular interest in current politics, nor do some fail to hint that the temptations to jobbing would overcome the virtue of members who had a longer term before them. Where American opinion is unanimous, it would be presumptuous for a stranger to dissent. Yet the remark may be permitted that the dangers originally feared have proved chimerical. There is no country whose representatives are more dependent on popular opinion, more ready to trim their sails to the least breath of it. The public acts, the votes, and speeches of a member from Oregon or Texas can be more closely watched by his constituents than those of a Virginian member could be watched in 1789.[11] And as the frequency of elections involves inexperienced members, the efficiency of Congress suffers.

V. The numbers of the two American houses seem small to a European when compared on the one hand with the population of the country, on the other with the practice of European states. The Senate has 96 members against the British House of Lords with over 600, and the French Senate with 300. The House has 443 against the British House of Commons with 670, and the French and Italian chambers with 584 and 508 respectively.

The Americans, however, doubt whether both their houses have not already become too large. They began with 26 in the Senate, 65 in the House, numbers then censured as too small, but which worked well, and gave less encouragement to idle talk and vain display than the crowded halls of today. The inclination of wise men is to try to diminish further increase when the number of 400 has been reached, for they perceive that the House already suffers from disorganization, and fear that a much larger one would prove unmanageable.[12]

---

[11] Of course his conduct in committee is rarely known, but I doubt whether the shortness of the term makes him more scrupulous.

[12] There is force in the following observations which I copy from the 54th and 57th numbers of the *Federalist*: "A certain number at least seems necessary to secure the benefits of free consultation and discussion, and to guard against too easy a combination for improper purposes; as on the other hand, the number ought to be kept within a certain limit in order to avoid the confusion and intemperance of a multitude. In all very numerous assemblies, of whatever characters composed, passion never fails to wrest the sceptre from reason. Had every Athenian citizen been a Socrates, every Athenian assembly would still have been a mob. . . . In all legislative assemblies, the greater the number comprising them may be, the fewer will be the men who will in fact direct their proceedings. The larger the number, the greater will be the proportion of members of limited information and of weak capacities. Now it is precisely on characters of this description

VI. American congressmen are more assiduous in their attendance than the members of most European legislatures. The great majority not only remain steadily at Washington through the session, but are usually to be found in the Capitol, often in their chamber itself, while a sitting lasts. There is therefore comparatively little trouble in making the quorum of one-half,[13] except when the minority endeavours to prevent its being made, whereas in England the House of Lords, whose quorum is three, has seldom thirty peers present, and the House of Commons often finds a difficulty, especially during the dinner hour, in securing its modest quorum of forty.[14] This requirement of a high quorum, which is prescribed in the Constitution, has doubtless helped to secure a good attendance. Other causes are the distance from Washington of the residences of most members, so that it is not worth while to take the journey home for a short sojourn, and the fact that very few attempt to carry on any regular business or profession while the session lasts. Those who are lawyers, or merchants, or manufacturers, leave their work to partners; but many are politicians and nothing else. In Washington, a city without commerce or manufactures, political or semi-political intrigue is the only gainful occupation possible; for the Supreme Court practice is conducted almost entirely by lawyers coming from a distance. The more democratic a county is, so much the more regular is the attendance, so much closer the attention to the requests of constituents which a member is expected to render.[15] Apart from that painful duty of finding

---

that the eloquence and address of the few are known to act with all their force. In the ancient republics where the whole body of the people assembled in person, a single orator, or an artful statesman, was generally seen to rule with as complete a sway as if a sceptre had been placed in his single hand. On the same principle the more multitudinous a representative assembly may be rendered, the more it will partake of the infirmities incident to collective meetings of the people. Ignorance will be the dupe of cunning, and passion the slave of sophistry and declamation. The people can never err more than in supposing that by multiplying their representatives beyond a certain limit they strengthen the barrier against the government of a few. Experience will forever admonish them that, on the contrary, *after securing a certain number for the purposes of safety, of local information, and of diffusing sympathy with the whole society*, they will counteract their own views by every addition to their representatives."

It is true that the House of Commons with 670 members has not been found unmanageable. The number present, however, rarely exceeds 450; and there is sitting accommodation on the floor for only 360.

[13] Though sometimes the sergeant-at-arms is sent round Washington with a carriage to fetch members down from their residences to the Capitol.

[14] Oliver Cromwell's House of 360 members, including 30 from Scotland and 30 from Ireland, had a quorum of 60.

[15] Before the Reform Bill of 1832 there were rarely more than 200 members present in the House of Commons, and it usually sat for two or three hours only in each day. One of the members for Hampshire, about 1820, sat for thirteen years, being in perfect health, and was only thrice in the House. Nor was this deemed a very singular case.

places for constituents which consumes so much of a congressman's time, his duties are not heavier than those of a member of the English Parliament who desires to keep abreast of current questions. The sittings are neither so long nor so late as those of the House of Commons; the questions that come up not so multifarious, the blue books to be read less numerous, the correspondence (except about places) not more troublesome. The position of senator is more onerous than that of a member of the House, not only because his whole state, and not merely a district, has a direct claim upon him, but also because, as one of a small body, he incurs a larger individual responsibility, and sits upon two or more committees instead of on one only.

VII. The want of opportunities for distinction in Congress is one of the causes which make a political career unattractive to most Americans.[16] It takes a new member at least a session to learn the procedure of the House. Full dress debates are rare, newspaper reports of speeches delivered are curt and little read. The most serious work is done in committees; it is not known to the world, and much of it results in nothing, because many bills which a committee has considered are perhaps never even voted on by the House. A place on a good House committee is to be obtained by favour, and a high-spirited man might find it hard to secure it. Ability, tact, and industry make their way in the long run in Congress, as they do everywhere else. But in Congress there is, for most men, no long run. Only very strong local influence, or some remarkable party service rendered, will enable a member to keep his seat through two or three successive Congresses. Nowhere therefore does the zeal of a young politician sooner wax cold than in the House of Representatives. Unfruitful toil, the toil of turning a crank which does nothing but register its own turnings, or of writing contributions which an editor steadily rejects, is of all things the most disheartening. It is more disheartening than the nonrequital of merit; for that at least spares the self-respect of the sufferer. Now toil for the public is usually unfruitful in the House of Representatives, indeed in all houses. But toil for the pecuniary interests of one's constituents and friends is fruitful, for it obliges people, it wins the reputation of energy and smartness, it has the promise not only of a renomination, but of that possible seat in the Senate which is the highest ambition of the congressman. Power, fame, perhaps even riches, sit upon that pinnacle. But the thin spun life is usually slit before the fair guerdon has been found. Few young men of high gifts and fine tastes look forward

---

[16] See also Chap. 58 *post*, Vol. II.

to entering public life, for the probable disappointments and vexations of a life in Congress so far outweigh its attractions that nothing but exceptional ambition or a strong sense of public duty suffices to draw such men into it. Law, education, literature, the higher walks of commerce, finance, or railway work, offer a better prospect of enjoyment or distinction.

Inside Washington, the representative is dwarfed by the senator and the federal judges. Outside Washington he enjoys no great social consideration,[17] especially in the Northern states, for in the South his position retains some of its old credit. His opinion is not quoted with respect. He seems to move about under a prima facie suspicion of being a jobber, and to feel that the burden of proof lies on him to show that the current jests on this topic do not apply to him. Rich men therefore do not seek, as in England, to enter the legislature in order that they may enter society. They will get no entrée which they could not have secured otherwise. Nor is there any opportunity for the exercise of those social influences which tell upon members, and still more upon members' wives and daughters, in European legislatures. It may of course be worth while to "capture" a particular senator, and for that purpose to begin by capturing his wife. But the salon plays no sensible part in American public life.

The country does not go to Congress to look for its presidential candidates as England looks to Parliament for its prime ministers. The opportunities by which a man can win distinction there are few. He does not make himself familiar to the eye and ear of the world. Congress, in short, is not a focus of political life as are the legislatures of France, Italy, and England. Though it has become more powerful against the several states than it was formerly, though it has extended its arms in every direction, and sometimes encroached upon the executive, it has not become more interesting to the people, nor strengthened its hold on their respect and affection.

VIII. Neither in the Senate nor in the House are there any recognized leaders. There is no ministry, no ex-ministry leading an opposition, no chieftains at the head of definite groups who follow their lead, as the Irish Nationalist members in the British Parliament follow Mr. Parnell, and a large section of the Left in the French and German chambers followed M. Clemenceau and Dr. Windthorst. So too, there did not exist, until 1900, a

---

[17] A few years ago an eminent Englishman, visiting one of the colleges for women in New England, and wishing to know something of the social standing of the students, remarked, "I suppose you have a good many young ladies here belonging to the best families, daughters of members of Congress and so forth?" The question excited so much amusement that it was repeated to me months afterwards not only as an instance of English ignorance but as a merry jest.

regularly working agency for securing either that members shall be apprised of the divisions to be expected, or that they should vote in those divisions in a particular way.

To anyone familiar with the methods of the English Parliament this seems incomprehensible. How, he asks, can business go on at all, how can each party make itself felt as a party with neither leader nor whips?

I have mentioned the whips. Let me say a word on this vital, yet even in England little appreciated, part of the machinery of constitutional government. Each party in the House of Commons has, besides its leaders, a member of the House nominated by the chief leader as his aide-de-camp, and called the whipper-in, or, for shortness, the whip. The whip's duties are (1) to inform every member belonging to the party when an important division may be expected, and if he sees the member in or about the House, to keep him there until the division is called; (2) to direct the members of his own party how to vote; (3) to obtain pairs for them if they cannot be present to vote; (4) to "tell," i.e., count the members in every party division; (5) to "keep touch" of opinion within the party, and convey to the leader a faithful impression of that opinion, from which the latter can judge how far he may count on the support of his whole party in any course he proposes to take. A member in doubt how he shall vote on a question with regard to which he has no opinion of his own, goes to the whip for counsel. A member who without grave cause stays away unpaired from an important division to which the whip has duly summoned him is guilty of a misdemeanour only less flagrant than that of voting against his party. A ministerial whip is further bound to "keep a house," i.e., to secure that when government business is being considered there shall always be a quorum of members present, and of course also to keep a majority, i.e., to have within reach a number of supporters sufficient to give the ministry a majority on any ministerial division.[18] Without the constant presence and activity of the ministerial whip the wheels of government could not go on for a day, because the ministry would be exposed to the risk of casual defeats which would destroy their credit and might involve their resignation. Similarly the opposition, and any third or fourth party, find it necessary to have their

---

[18] That which was at one time the chief function of the ministerial whip, viz., to pay members for the votes they gave in support of the government, has been extinct for a century and a half. He is still, however, the recognized organ for handling questions of political patronage, and is therefore called the Patronage Secretary to the Treasury. People who want places for their friends—there are now extremely few—or titles for themselves—these are more numerous and eagerly desired—still address their requests to him, which he communicates to the prime minister with his opinion as to whether the applicant's public or party services justify the request.

whip, because it is only thus that they can act as a party, guide their supporters, and bring their full strength to bear on a division. Hence when a new party is formed, its first act, that by which it realizes and proclaims its existence, is to name whips, to whom its adherents may go for counsel, and who may in turn receive their suggestions as to the proper strategy for the party to adopt.[19] So essential are these officers to the discipline of English parliamentary armies that an English politician's first question when he sees Congress is, "Where are the whips?" his next, "How in the world do you get on without them?"

The answer to this question is threefold. Whips are not so necessary at Washington as at Westminster. A sort of substitute for them has been devised. Congress does to some extent suffer from the inadequacy of the substituted device.[20]

A division in Congress has not the importance it has in the House of Commons. There it may throw out the ministry. In Congress it never does more than affirm or negative some particular bill or resolution. Even a division in the Senate which involves the rejection of a treaty or of an appointment to some great office, does not disturb the tenure of the executive. Hence it is not essential to the majority that its full strength should be always at hand, nor has a minority party any great prize set before it as the result of a successful vote.

Questions, however, arise in which some large party interest is involved. There may be a bill by which the party means to carry out its main views of policy or perhaps to curry favour with the people, or a resolution whereby it hopes to damage a hostile executive. In such cases it is important to bring up every vote. Accordingly at the beginning of every Congress a caucus committee is elected by the majority, and it becomes the duty of the chairman and secretary of this committee (to whom, in the case of a party bill supported by the majority, there is added the chairman of the committee to which that bill has been referred, necessarily a member of the majority) to

[19] Even parties formed with a view to particular, and probably transitory issues, appoint one or more of their members as whips, because they could not otherwise act with that effect which only habitual concert gives. Each party has its whips in the House of Lords also, but as divisions there have less political significance their functions are less important.

[20] I allow the passage which follows to stand unaltered, because it describes the state of things which existed when this book was first written and for some time afterwards. In 1900, however, whips were introduced, the congressional caucus of each party in the House choosing one. The duty of the whip is to canvass his party on all doubtful issues and inform the leaders how many votes can be depended on. The gifts of tact, persuasion, and force are required to fit him for the delicate work of handling the hesitating or the disaffected. [Note to Edition of 1910.]

act as whips, i.e., to give notice of important divisions by sending out a "call" to members of the party, and to take all requisite steps to have a quorum and a majority present to push through the bill or resolution to which the party stands committed. *Mutatis mutandis* (for of course it is seldom an object with the minority to secure a quorum), the minority take the same course to bring up their men on important divisions. In cases of gravity or doubt, where it is thought prudent to consult or to restimulate the party, the caucus committee convokes a caucus, i.e., a meeting of the whole party, at which the attitude to be assumed by the party is debated with closed doors, and a vote taken as to the course to be adopted.[21] By this vote every member of the party is deemed bound, just as he would be in England by the request of the leader conveyed through the whip. Disobedience cannot be punished in Congress itself, except of course by social penalties; but it endangers the seat of the too independent member, for the party managers at Washington will communicate with the party managers in his district, and the latter will probably refuse to renominate him at the next election. The most important caucus of a Congress is that held at the opening to select the party candidate for the speakership, selection by the majority being of course equivalent to election. As the views and tendencies of the Speaker determine the composition of the committees, and thereby the course of legislation, his selection is a matter of supreme importance, and is preceded by weeks of intrigue and canvassing.

This process of "going into caucus" is the regular American substitute for recognized leadership, and has the advantage of seeming more consistent with democratic equality, because every member of the party has in theory equal weight in the party meeting. It is used whenever a line of policy has to be settled, or the whole party to be rallied for a particular party division. But of course it cannot be employed every day or for every bill. Hence when no party meeting has issued its orders, a member is free to vote as he pleases, or rather as he thinks his constituents please. If he knows nothing of the matter, he may take a friend's advice, or vote as he hears some prominent man on his own side vote. Anyhow, his vote is doubtful, unpredictable; and consequently divisions on minor questions are uncertain. This is a further reason, added to the power of the standing committees,

---

[21] An experienced senator told me that the Senate caucus of his party used to meet on an average twice a month, the House caucus less frequently. A leading member of the House said that a "call" would be sent out, on an average, for about six measures in a session, i.e., from ten to twenty times altogether, according to the resistance offered to the measures of the majority. Sometimes a "call" of the majority is signed by the Speaker. General meetings of a party in Parliament are much less common in England.

why there is a want of consistent policy in the action of Congress. As its leading men have comparatively little authority, and there are no means whereby a leader could keep his party together on ordinary questions, so no definite ideas run through its conduct and express themselves in its votes. It moves in zigzags.

The freedom thus enjoyed by members on minor questions has the interesting result of preventing dissensions and splits in the parties. There are substances which cohere best when their contact is loose. Fresh fallen snow keeps a smooth surface even on a steep slope, but when by melting and regelation it has become ice, cracks and rifts begin to appear. A loose hung carriage will hold together over a road whose roughness would strain and break a more solid one. Hence serious differences of opinion may exist in a congressional party without breaking its party unity, for nothing more is needed than that a solid front should be presented on the occasions, few in each session, when a momentous division arrives. The appearance of agreement is all the more readily preserved because there is little serious debating, so that the advocates of one view seldom provoke the other section of their party to rise and contradict them; while a member who dissents from the bulk of his party on an important issue is slow to vote against it, because he has little chance of defining and defending his position by an explanatory speech.

The congressional caucus has in troublous times to be supplemented by something like obedience to regular leaders. Mr. Thaddeus Stevens, for instance, led with recognized authority the majority of the House in its struggle with President Andrew Johnson. The Senate is rather more jealous of the equality of all its members. No senator can be said to have any authority beyond that of exceptional talent and experience; and of course a senatorial caucus, since it rarely consists of more than forty persons, is a better working body than a House caucus, which may exceed two hundred.[22]

The European reader may be perplexed by the apparent contradictions in what has been said regarding the party organization of Congress. "Is the American House after all," he will ask, "more or less a party body than the British House of Commons? Is the spirit of party more or less strong in Congress than in the American people generally?"

For the purpose of serious party issues the House of Representatives is

---

[22] At one time the congressional caucus played in American history a great part which it has now renounced. From 1800 till 1824 party meetings of senators and representatives were held which nominated the party candidates for the presidency, who were then accepted by each party as its regular candidates. In 1828 the state legislatures made these nominations, and in 1832 the present system of national conventions (see *post*, in Vol. II) was introduced.

nearly as much a party body as the House of Commons. A member voting against his party on such an issue is more certain to forfeit his party reputation and his seat than is an English member. But for the purpose of ordinary questions, of issues not involving party fortunes, a representative is less bound by party ties than an English member, because he has neither leaders to guide him by their speeches nor whips by their private instructions.[23] The apparent gain is that a wider field is left for independent judgment on nonpartisan questions. The real loss is that legislation becomes weak and inconsistent. This conclusion is not encouraging to those who expect us to get rid of party in our legislatures. A deliberative assembly is, after all, only a crowd of men; and the more intelligent a crowd is, so much the more numerous are its volitions; so much greater the difficulty of agreement. Like other crowds, a legislature must be led and ruled. Its merit lies not in the independence of its members, but in the reflex action of its opinion upon the leaders, in its willingness to defer to them in minor matters, reserving disobedience for the issues in which some great principle overrides both the obligation of deference to established authority and the respect due to special knowledge.

The above remarks answer the second question also. The spirit of party may seem to be weaker in Congress than in the people at large. But this is only because the questions which the people decide at the polls are always questions of choice between candidates for office. These are definite questions, questions eminently of a party character, because candidates represent in the America of today not principles but parties. When a vote upon persons occurs in Congress, Congress gives a strict party vote. Were the people to vote at the polls on matters not explicitly comprised within a party platform (as they do now in states which have adopted the initiative and referendum), there would be much greater uncertainty than Congress displays. The habit of joint action which makes the life of a party is equally intense in every part of the American system. But in England the existence of a ministry and opposition in Parliament sweeps within the circle of party action many topics which in America are left outside, and therefore Congress seems, but is not, less permeated than Parliament by party spirit.

---

[23] For an interesting comparison of party voting in Congress and in the British House of Commons, see Mr. A. Lawrence Lowell's *Government of England*.

The Relations of Congress to the President[1]

So far as they are legislative bodies, the House and the Senate have similar powers and stand in the same relation to the executive.[2] We may therefore discuss them together, or rather the reader may assume that whatever is said of the House as a legislature is also true of the Senate.[3]

Although the Constitution forbids any federal official to be chosen a member of either the House or the Senate, there is nothing in it to prevent officials from speaking there; as indeed there is nothing to prevent either house from assigning places and the right to speak to anyone whom it chooses. In the early days Washington came down and delivered his opening speech. Occasionally he remained in the Senate during a debate, and even expressed his opinion there. When Hamilton, the first secretary of the treasury, prepared his famous report on the national finances, he asked the House whether they would hear him speak it, or would receive it in writing. They chose the latter course, and the precedent then set has been followed by subsequent ministers,[4] while that set in 1801 by President Jefferson when he transmitted his message in writing instead of delivering a speech, has

---

[1] The relations of the various organs of government to one another in the United States are so interesting and so unlike those which exist in most European countries, that I have found it necessary to describe them with some minuteness, and from several points of view. In this chapter an account is given of the actual working relations of the president and Congress; in the next chapter the general theory of the respective functions of the executive and legislative departments is examined, and the American view of the nature of these functions explained; while in Chapter 25, the American system as a whole is compared with the so-called "cabinet system" of England and her colonies.

[2] The House has the exclusive initiative in revenue bills; but this privilege does not affect what follows.

[3] The executive functions of the Senate have been discussed in Chapter 11.

[4] A committee of the Senate reported in favour of giving the right of speech to ministers (see note 3 to Chapter 9 *ante*); and this was provided in the Constitution of the Southern Confederacy (see

been similarly respected by all his successors. Thus neither house now hears a member of the executive; and when a minister appears before a committee, he appears primarily as a witness to answer questions, rather than to state and argue his own case. There is therefore little direct intercourse between Congress and the administration, and no sense of interdependence and community of action such as exists in other parliamentary countries.[5] Be it remembered also that a minister may never have sat in Congress, and may therefore be ignorant of its temper and habits. Six members of Mr. Cleveland's cabinet, in 1888, and seven of Mr. Taft's in 1909, had never had a seat in either house. The president himself, although he has been voted into office by his party, is not necessarily its leader, nor even one among its most prominent leaders. Hence he does not sway the councils and guide the policy of those members of Congress who belong to his own side. No duty lies on Congress to take up a subject to which he has called attention as needing legislation; and, in fact, the suggestions which he makes, year after year, are usually neglected, even when his party has a majority in both houses, or when the subject lies outside party lines. Members have sometimes complained of his submitting draft bills, although there are plenty of precedents for his doing so.

The president and his cabinet have no recognized spokesman in either house. A particular senator or representative may be in confidential communication with them, and be the instrument through whom they seek to act; but he would probably disavow rather than claim the position of an exponent of ministerial wishes. The president can of course influence members of Congress through patronage. He may give places to them or their friends; he may approve or veto bills in which they are interested; his ministers may allot lucrative contracts to their nominees. This power is considerable, but covert, for the knowledge that it was being used might damage the member in public estimation and expose the executive to imputations. The consequence of cutting off open relations has been to encourage secret

---

note to Chapter 30 at the end of this volume). The president may of course come into the Senate. None had, however, entered the House of Representatives until in 1913 President Wilson went there and instead of sending a written message delivered a speech to the Senate and the House together. No English king has entered the House of Commons, except Charles I in 1642, on the occasion of his attempt to seize the five members, when, says the *Journal*, "His Majesty came into the House and took Mr. Speaker's chair: 'Gentlemen, I am sorry to have this occasion to come unto you.'" The results did not encourage his successors to repeat the visit. But Charles II was sometimes present during debates in the House of Lords, and even exhorted the Lords to be more orderly; Anne sometimes appeared; and there would not, it is conceived, be anything to prevent the sovereign from being present now while debate is proceeding.

[5] The House once passed a bill for transferring Indian affairs from the secretary of the interior to the secretary of war without consulting either official.

influence, which may of course be used for legitimate purposes, but which, being exerted in darkness, is seldom above suspicion. When the president or a minister is attacked in Congress, it is not the duty of anyone there to justify his conduct. The accused official may send a written defence or may induce a member to state his case; but this method lacks the advantages of the European parliamentary system, under which the person assailed repels in debate the various charges, showing himself not afraid to answer fresh questions and grapple with new points. Thus by its exclusion from Congress the executive is deprived of the power of leading and guiding the legislature and of justifying in debate its administrative acts.

Next as to the power of Congress over the executive. Either house of Congress, or both houses jointly, can pass resolutions calling on the president or his ministers to take certain steps, or censuring steps they have already taken. The president need not obey such resolutions, need not even notice them. They do not shorten his term or limit his discretion.[6] If the resolution be one censuring the act of a minister, the president does not escape responsibility by throwing over the minister, because the law makes him, and not his servant or adviser, responsible.

Either house of Congress can direct a committee to summon and examine a minister, who, though he may legally refuse to attend, very rarely refuses. The committee, when it has got him, can do nothing more than question him. He may evade their questions, may put them off the scent by dexterous concealments. He may with impunity tell them that he means to take his own course. To his own master, the president, he standeth or falleth.

Congress may refuse to the president the legislation he requests, and thus, by mortifying and embarrassing him, may seek to compel his compliance with its wishes. It is only a timid president, or a president greatly bent on accomplishing some end for which legislation is needed, who will be moved by such tactics.

Congress can pass bills requiring the president or any minister to do or abstain from doing certain acts of a kind hitherto left to his free will and judgment, may, in fact, endeavour to tie down the officials by prescribing certain conduct for them in great detail. The president will presumably veto such bills, as contrary to sound administrative policy. If, however, he signs them, or if Congress passes them over his veto, the further question may

---

[6] In England a resolution of the House of Commons alone is treated as imperative in matters lying within the discretion of the executive, but then the House of Commons has the power of dismissing the government if its wishes are disregarded. There have even been instances of late years in which the executive has ceased to put in force the provisions of an unrepealed statute, because the House of Commons has expressed its disapproval of that statute.

arise whether they are within the constitutional powers of Congress, or are invalid as unduly trenching on the discretion which the Constitution leaves to the executive chief magistrate. If he (or a minister), alleging them to be unconstitutional, disobeys them, the only means of deciding whether he is right is by getting the point before the Supreme Court as an issue of law in some legal proceeding. This cannot always be done. If it is done, and the court decide against the president, then if he still refuses to obey, nothing remains but to impeach him.

Impeachment, of which an account has already been given, is the heaviest piece of artillery in the congressional arsenal, but because it is so heavy it is unfit for ordinary use. It is like a hundred-ton gun which needs complex machinery to bring it into position, an enormous charge of powder to fire it, and a large mark to aim at. Or to vary the simile, impeachment is what physicians call a heroic medicine, an extreme remedy, proper to be applied against an official guilty of political crimes, but ill adapted for the punishment of small transgressions. Although the one president (Andrew Johnson) against whom it has been used had for two years constantly, and with great intemperance of language, so defied and resisted Congress that the whole machinery of government had been severely strained, yet the Senate did not convict him, because no single offence had been clearly made out. Thus impeachment does not tend to secure, and indeed was never meant to secure, the cooperation of the executive with Congress.

It accordingly appears that Congress cannot compel the dismissal of any official. It may investigate his conduct by a committee and so try to drive him to resign. It may request the president to dismiss him, but if his master stands by him and he sticks to his place, nothing more can be done. He may of course be impeached, but one does not impeach for mere incompetence or laxity, as one does not use steam hammers to crack nuts. Thus we arrive at the result that while Congress may examine the servants of the public to any extent, may censure them, may lay down rules for their guidance, it cannot get rid of them. It is as if the directors of a company were forced to go on employing a manager whom they had ceased to trust, because it was not they but the stockholders who had appointed him.

There remains the power which in free countries has been long regarded as the citadel of parliamentary supremacy, the power of the purse. The Constitution keeps the president far from this citadel, granting to Congress the sole right of raising money and appropriating it to the service of the state. Its management of national finance is significantly illustrative of the plan which separates the legislative from the executive. In this supremely important matter, the administration, instead of proposing and supervising, instead of securing that each department gets the money that it needs, that no money goes where it is not needed, that revenue is procured in the least troublesome and expensive way, that an exact yearly balance is struck, that the policy of expenditure is self-consistent and reasonably permanent from year to year, is by its exclusion from Congress deprived of influence on the one hand, of responsibility on the other. The office of Finance Minister is put into commission, and divided between the chairmen of several unconnected committees of both houses. A mass of business which specially needs the knowledge, skill, and economical conscience of a responsible ministry, is left to committees which are powerful but not responsible, and to houses whose nominal responsibility is in practice sadly weakened by their want of appropriate methods and organization.

How far, then, does the power of the purse enable Congress to control the president? Much less than in European countries. Congress may check any particular scheme which the president favours by refusing supplies for it. If he were to engage in military operations—he cannot under the Constitution "declare war" for that belongs to Congress—the House might paralyse him by declining to vote the requisite army appropriations. If he were to repeat the splendid audacity of Jefferson by purchasing a new territory, they could withhold the purchase money. But if, keeping within the limits of his constitutional functions, he takes a different course from that they recommend, if for instance he should refuse, at their repeated requests, to demand the liberation of American citizens pining in foreign dungeons, or to suppress disorders in a state whose government had requested federal intervention, they would have to look on. To withhold the ordinary supplies, and thereby stop the machine of government, would injure the country and themselves far more than the president. They would, to use a common expression, be cutting off their nose to spite their face. They could not lawfully refuse to vote his salary, for that is guaranteed to him by the Constitution. They could not, except by a successful impeachment, turn him out of the White House or deprive him of his title to the obedience of all federal officials.

Accordingly, when Congress has endeavoured to coerce the president by the use of its money powers, the case being one in which it could not attack him by ordinary legislation (either because such legislation would be unconstitutional, or for want of a two-thirds majority), it has proceeded not by refusing appropriations altogether, as the British House of Commons would do in like circumstances, but by attaching what is called a "rider" to an appropriation bill. Many years ago the House formed, and soon began to indulge freely in, the habit of inserting in bills appropriating money to the purposes of the public service, provisions relating to quite different matters, which there was not time to push through in the ordinary way. In 1867 Congress used this device against President Johnson, with whom it was then at open war, by attaching to an army appropriation bill a clause which virtually deprived the president of the command of the army, entrusting its management to the general highest in command (General Grant). The president yielded, knowing that if he refused the bill would be carried over his veto by a two-thirds vote; and a usage already mischievous was confirmed. In 1879, the majority in Congress attempted to overcome, by the same weapon, the resistance of President Hayes to certain measures affecting the South which they desired to pass. They tacked these measures to three appropriation bills, army, legislative, and judiciary. The minority in both houses fought hard against the riders, but were beaten. The president vetoed all three bills, and Congress was obliged to pass them without the riders. Next session the struggle recommenced in the same form, and the president, by rejecting the money bills again compelled Congress to drop the tacked provisions. This victory, which was of course due to the fact that the dominant party in Congress could not command a two-thirds majority, was deemed to have settled the question as between the executive and the legislature, and may have permanently discouraged the latter from recurring to the same tactics.

President Hayes in his veto messages argued strongly against the whole practice of tacking other matters to money bills; and a rule of the House (not always strictly observed) now declares that an appropriation bill shall not carry any new legislation. It has certainly caused great abuses, and is forbidden by the constitutions of many states. A president once urged upon Congress the desirability of so amending the federal Constitution as to enable him, as a state governor is by some recent state constitutions allowed to do, to veto single items in an appropriation bill without rejecting the whole bill. Such an amendment is generally desired by enlightened men, because it would enable the executive to do its duty by the country in defeating many petty jobs which are now smuggled into these bills, without losing the supplies necessary for the public service which the bills provide. The change seems a small one, but its adoption would cure one of the defects due to the absence of ministers from Congress, and save the nation millions of dollars a year, by diminishing wasteful expenditure on local purposes. But the process of amending the Constitution is so troublesome that even a change which involves no party issues may remain unadopted long after the best opinion has become unanimous in its favour.

The Legislature and the Executive

The fundamental characteristic of the American national government is its separation of the legislative, executive, and judicial departments. This separation is the merit which the Philadelphia Convention chiefly sought to attain, and which the Americans have been wont to regard as most completely secured by their Constitution. In Europe, as well as in America, men are accustomed to talk of legislation and administration as distinct. But a consideration of their nature will show that it is not easy to separate these two departments in theory by analysis, and still less easy to keep them apart in practice. We may begin by examining their relations in the internal affairs of a nation, reserving foreign policy for a later part of the discussion.

People commonly think of the legislature as the body which lays down general rules of law, which prescribes, for instance, that at a man's death his children shall succeed equally to his property, or that a convicted thief shall be punished with imprisonment, or that a manufacturer may register his trade mark. They think of the executive as the person or persons who do certain acts under those rules, who lock up convicts, register trade marks, carry letters, raise and pay a police and an army. In finance the legislature imposes a tax, the executive gathers it, and places it in the treasury or in a bank, subject to legislative orders; the legislature votes money by a statute, appropriating it to a specific purpose; the executive draws it from the treasury or bank, and applies it to that purpose, perhaps in paying the army, perhaps in building a bridge.

The executive is, in civilized countries, itself the creature of the law, deriving therefrom its existence as well as its authority. Sometimes, as in France, it is so palpably and formally. The president of the Republic has been called into existence by the Constitution. Sometimes, as in England, it is so substantially, though not formally. The English Crown dates from a remote antiquity, when custom and belief had scarcely crystallized into law; and though Parliament has repeatedly determined its devolution upon particular persons or families—it is now held under the Act of Settlement— no statute has ever affected to confer upon it its rights to the obedience of the people. But practically it holds its powers at the pleasure of Parliament, which has in some cases expressly limited them, and in others given them a tacit recognition. We may accordingly say of England and of all constitutional monarchies as well as of republics that the executive in all its acts must obey the law, that is to say, if the law prescribes a particular course of action, the executive must take that course; if the law forbids a particular course, the executive must avoid it.

It is therefore clear that the extent of the power of the executive magistrate depends upon the particularity with which the law is drawn, that is, upon the amount of discretion which the law leaves to him. If the law is general in its terms, the executive has a wide discretion. If, for instance, the law prescribes simply that a duty of ten per cent *ad valorem* be levied on all manufactured goods imported, it rests with the executive to determine by whom and where that duty shall be collected, and on what principles it shall be calculated. If the law merely creates a post office, the executive may fix the rate of payment for letters and parcels, and the conditions on which they will be received and delivered. In these cases the executive has a large field within which to exert its free will and choice of means. Power means nothing more than the extent to which a man can make his individual will prevail against the wills of other men, so as to control them. Hence, when the law gives to a magistrate a wide discretion, he is powerful, because the law clothes his will with all the power of the state. On the other hand, if the law goes into very minute details, directing this to be done and that not to be done, it narrows the discretion of the executive magistrate. His personal will and choice are gone. He can no longer be thought of as a coordinate power in the state. He becomes a mere servant, a hand to carry out the bidding of the legislative brain, or, we may even say, a tool in the legislative hand.

As the legislature has been the body through which the people have chiefly asserted their authority, we find that lawmaking assemblies, whether primary or representative, have always sought to extend their province and to subject the executive to themselves. They have done this in several ways. In the democracies of ancient Greece the assembly of all citizens not only passed statutes of general application, but made peace or declared war; ordered an expedition to start for Sphacteria, and put Cleon at the head of it; commanded the execution of prisoners or reprieved them; conducted, in fact, most of the public business of the city by a series of direct decrees, all of which were laws, i.e., declarations of its sovereign will. It was virtually the government. The chief executive officers of Athens, called the generals, had little authority except over the military operations in the field. Even the Roman Constitution, a far more highly developed and scientific, though also a complicated and cumbrous system, while it wisely left great discretion to the chief magistrates (requiring them, however, to consult the Senate), yet permitted the passing *pro re nata* of important laws, which were really executive acts, such as the law by which Pompey received an extraordinary command against Mithridates. The Romans did not draw, any more than the Greek republics, a distinction between general and special legislation.[1]

This method, in which the people directly govern as a legislature, reducing the executive magistrates to mere instruments, is inapplicable in a large country, because the mass of citizens cannot come together as an assembly. It is highly inconvenient where the legislature, though a representative body, is very numerous. England, accordingly, and the nations which have imitated England,[2] have taken a different method. The people (that is, the qualified voters) have allowed an executive to subsist with apparently wide powers, but they virtually choose this executive, and keep it in so close and constant a dependence upon their pleasure, that it dare not act against what it believes their will to be. The struggle for popular liberties in England took at first the form of a struggle for the supremacy of law; that is to say, it was a struggle to restrain the prerogative of the king by compelling his ministers to respect the ancient customs of the land and the statutes passed in Parliament. As the customs were always maintained, and the range of the statutes constantly widened, the executive was by degrees hemmed in within narrow limits, its discretionary power restricted, and that characteristic

---

[1] *Cf.* Chapter 31 and notes thereto. The distinction is apt to be forgotten under a despotic monarch, who is at once the executive and the legislative authority. Nevertheless, even under an autocrat there are some general rules which his individual volition dares not change, because the universal opinion of the people approves them. The book of Daniel represents Darius as unable to revoke a general law he has once sanctioned, or to except a particular person from its operation; and the Turkish sultan cannot transgress, at least in points of importance, the Sheriat or Sacred Law.

[2] But during and immediately after the great Civil War the Long Parliament acted as both a legislative and an executive authority, as did the Convention through part of the French Revolution. And Parliament of course still retains its power of giving what are practically executive orders, e.g., it could pass a statute directing a particular island to be seized or another to be evacuated, as Heligoland was in 1890.

principle of the Constitution, which has been well called "the reign of law," was established. It was settled that the law, i.e., the ancient customs and the statutes, should always prevail against the discretion of the Crown and its ministers, and that acts done by the servants of the Crown should be justiciable, exactly like the acts of private persons. This once achieved, the executive fairly bridled, and the ministry made to hold office at the pleasure of the House of Commons, Parliament had no longer its former motive for seeking to restrict the discretion of the ministers of the Crown by minutely particular legislation, for ministers had become so accustomed to subjection that their discretion might be trusted. Parliament has, in fact, of late years begun to sail on the other tack, and allows ministers to do many things by regulations, schemes, orders in council, and so forth, which would previously have been done by statute, generally, however, reserving to itself a right of disapproval.

It may be asked how it comes, if this be so, that people nevertheless talk of the executive in England as being a separate and considerable authority. The answer is twofold. The English Crown has never been, so to speak, thrown into the melting pot and recast, but has continued, in external form and seeming, an independent and highly dignified part of the constitutional system.[3] Parliament has never asserted a direct control over certain parts of the royal prerogative, such as the bestowal of honours, the creation of peerages, the making of appointments to office. No one at this moment can say exactly what the royal prerogative does or does not include. And secondly, the actual executive, i.e., the ministry of the day, retains some advantages which are practically, though not legally, immense. It has an initiative in all legislation, a sole initiative in financial legislation. It is a

---

[3] An interesting illustration of the relations of the English executive to the legislature in the fourteenth and fifteenth centuries, when Parliament was little more than a pure legislature, is afforded by the present constitution of the tiny kingdom of the Isle of Man, the last survivor of those numerous kingdoms among which the British Isles were once divided. Its government is carried on by a governor (appointed by the English Crown), a council of eight (composed partly of persons nominated by the Crown and partly of ex-officio members holding posts to which they have been appointed by the Crown), and an elected representative assembly of twenty-four. The assembly is purely legislative, and cannot check the governor otherwise than by withholding the legislation he wishes for and such taxes as are annually voted. For the purposes of finance bills the assembly (House of Keys) and the council sit together but vote separately. The governor presides, as the English king did in his Great Council. The governor can stop any legislation he disapproves, and can retain his ministers against the will of the assembly. He is a true executive magistrate, commanding, moreover, like the earlier English kings, a considerable revenue which does not depend on the annual votes of the legislature. Here therefore is an Old World instance of the American system as contradistinguished from the cabinet system of England and her colonies.

small and well organized body placed in the midst of a much larger and less organized body (i.e., the two houses), on which therefore it can powerfully act. All patronage, ecclesiastical as well as civil, lies in its gift, and though it must not use this function so as to disgust the Commons, it has great latitude in the disposal of favours. While Parliament is sitting it disposes of a large part, sometimes of the whole, of the time of the House of Commons, and can therefore advance the measures it prefers, while retarding or evading motions it dislikes. During nearly half the year Parliament is not sitting, and the necessities of a great state placed in a restless world oblige a ministry to take momentous resolutions upon its own responsibility. Finally, it includes a few men who have obtained a hold on the imagination and confidence of the people, which emboldens them to resist or even to lecture Parliament, and often to prevail, not only against its first impulses, but possibly against its deliberate wishes. And an English ministry is strong not only because it so frankly acknowledges its dependence on the Commons as not to rouse the antagonism of that body, to which, be it remembered, most ministers belong, but also because it has another power outside to which it can, in extreme cases, appeal. It may dissolve Parliament, and ask the people to judge between its views and those of the majority of the House of Commons. Sometimes such an appeal succeeds. The power of making it is at all times a resource.

This delicate equipoise of the ministry, the House of Commons, and the nation acting at a general election, is the secret of the smooth working of the British Constitution. It reappears in two remarkable constitutions, which deserve fuller study than they have yet received from American or English publicists, those of Prussia and the new German Empire. There, however, the ministry is relatively stronger than in England, because the Crown retains not only a wider stretch of legal authority, but a greater moral influence over the people, who have had a shorter practice than the English in working free institutions, and who never forget that they are soldiers, and the king-emperor head of the army. A Prussian minister is so likely to have the nation on his side when he makes an appeal to it in the name of the king, and feels so confident that even if he defies the chambers without dissolving, the nation will not be greatly stirred, that he has sometimes refused to obey the legislature. This is one of those exceptions which illustrate the rule. The legislature is prevented from gaining ground on the executive, not so much by the constitution as by the occasional refusal of the executive to obey the constitution, a refusal made in reliance on the ascendency of the Crown.

So far we have been considering domestic policy. The case of foreign affairs differs chiefly in this, that they cannot be provided for beforehand by laws general in application, but minutely particular in wording. A governing assembly may take foreign affairs into its own hand. In the republics of antiquity the assembly did so, and was its own foreign office. The Athenian assembly received ambassadors, declared war, concluded treaties. It got on well enough while it had to deal with other republics like itself, but suffered when the contest came to be with an astute diplomatist like Philip of Macedon. The Roman Senate conducted the foreign policy of Rome, often with the skill to be expected from men of immense experience and ability, yet sometimes with a vacillation which a monarch would have been less likely to show. But the foreign relations of modern states are so numerous and complex, and so much entangled with commercial questions, that it has become necessary to create a staff of trained officials to deal with them. No large popular assembly could have either the time or the knowledge requisite for managing the ordinary business, much less could it conduct a delicate negotiation whose success would depend on promptitude and secrecy. Hence even democratic countries like France and England are forced to leave foreign affairs to a far greater degree than home affairs to the discretion of the ministry of the day. France reserves to the chambers the power of declaring war or concluding a treaty. England has so far adhered to the old traditions as to leave both to the Crown, though the first, and in most cases the second, must be exerted with the virtual approval of Parliament. The executive is as distinctly responsible to the legislature, as clearly bound to obey the directions of the legislature, as in matters of domestic concern. But the impossibility which the legislature in countries like France and England finds in either assuming executive functions in international intercourse, or laying down any rules by law for the guidance of the executive, necessarily gives the executive a wide discretion and a correspondingly large measure of influence and authority. The only way of restricting this authority would be to create a small foreign affairs committee of the legislature and to empower it to sit when the latter was not sitting. And this extreme course neither France nor England has yet taken, because the dependence of the ministry on the majority of the legislature has hitherto seemed to secure the conformity of the Foreign Office to the ideas and sentiments of that majority.

Before applying these observations to the United States, let us summarize the conclusions we have reached.

We have found that wherever the will of the people prevails, the legislature, since it either is or represents the people, can make itself omnipotent, unless checked by the action of the people themselves. It can do this in two ways. It may, like the republics of antiquity, issue decrees for particular cases as they arise, giving constant commands to all its agents, who thus become mere servants with no discretion left them. Or it may frame its laws with such particularity as to provide by anticipation for the greatest possible number of imaginable cases, in this way also so binding down its officials as to leave them no volition, no real authority.

We have also observed that every legislature tends so to enlarge its powers as to encroach on the executive; and that it has great advantages for so doing, because a succeeding legislature rarely consents to strike off any fetter its predecessor has imposed.

Thus the legitimate issue of the process would be the extinction or absorption of the executive as a power in the state. It would become a mere set of employees, obeying the legislature as the clerks in a bank obey the directors. If this does not happen, the cause is generally to be sought in some one or more of the following circumstances:

The legislature may allow the executive the power of appealing to the nation against itself (England).[4]

The people may from ancient reverence or the habit of military submission be so much disposed to support the executive as to embolden the latter to defy the legislature (Prussia).

The importance of foreign policy and the difficulty of taking it out of the hands of the executive may be so great that the executive will draw therefrom an influence reacting in favour of its general weight and dignity (Prussia, England, and, to some extent, France).

Let us now see how the founders of the American Constitution settled the relations of the departments. They were terribly afraid of a strong executive, and desired to reserve the final and decisive voice to the legislature, as representing the people. They could not adopt the Greek method of an assembly both executive and legislative, for Congress was to be a body with limited powers; continuous sittings would be inconvenient, and the division into two equally powerful houses would evidently unfit it to govern with vigour and promptitude. Neither did they adopt the English method of a legislature governing through an executive dependent upon it. It was urged in the Philadelphia Convention of 1787 that the executive ought to be appointed by and made accountable to the legislature, as being the supreme

---

[4] In France the president can dissolve the chambers, but only with the consent of the Senate.

power in the national government. This was overruled, because the majority of the Convention were fearful of "democratic haste and instability," fearful that the legislature would, in any event, become too powerful, and therefore anxious to build up some counter authority to check and balance it. By making the president independent, and keeping him and his ministers apart from the legislature, the Convention thought they were strengthening him, as well as protecting it from attempts on his part to corrupt it.[5] They were also weakening him. He lost the initiative in legislation which the English executive enjoys. He had not the English king's power of dissolving the legislature and throwing himself upon the country. Thus the executive magistrate seemed left at the mercy of the legislature. It could weave so close a network of statutes round him, like the net of iron links which Hephæstus throws over the lovers in the *Odyssey*, that his discretion, his individual volition, seemed to disappear, and he ceased to be a branch of the government, being nothing more than a servant working under the eye and at the nod of his master. This would have been an absorption of the executive into the legislature more complete than that which England now presents, for the English prime minister is at any rate a leader, perhaps as necessary to his parliamentary majority as it is to him, whereas the president would have become a sort of superior police commissioner, irremovable during four years, but debarred from acting either on Congress or on the people.

Although the Convention may not have realized how helpless such a so-called executive must be, they felt the danger of encroachments by an ambitious legislature, and resolved to strengthen him against it. This was done by giving the president a veto which it requires a two-thirds vote of Congress to override. In doing this they went back on their previous action. They had separated the president and his ministers from Congress. They now bestowed on him legislative functions, though in a different form. He became a distinct branch of the legislature, but for negative purposes only. He could not propose, but he could refuse. Thus the executive was strengthened, not as an executive, but by being connected with the legislature; and the legislature, already weakened by being divided into two coequal houses, was further weakened by finding itself liable to be arrested in any new departure on which two-thirds of both houses were not agreed.

When the two houses are of one mind, and the party hostile to the

---

[5] Their sense of the danger to a legislature from corruption by the executive was probably quickened by what they knew of the condition of the Irish Parliament, full, even after 1782, of placemen and pensioners. Much of the best blood of Ulster had emigrated to America in the preceding half century, and Irish politics must have excited a good deal of interest there.

president has a two-thirds majority in both, the executive is almost powerless. It may be right that he should be powerless, because such majorities in both houses presumably indicate a vast preponderance of popular opinion against him. The fact to be emphasized is, that in this case all "balance of powers" is gone. The legislature has swallowed up the executive, in virtue of the principle from which this discussion started, viz., that the executive is in free states only an agent who may be so limited by express and minute commands as to have no volition left him.

The strength of Congress consists in the right to pass statutes; the strength of the president in his right to veto them. But foreign affairs, as we have seen, cannot be brought within the scope of statutes. How then was the American legislature to deal with them? There were two courses open. One was to leave foreign affairs to the executive, as in England, giving Congress the same indirect control as the English Parliament enjoys over the Crown and ministry. This course could not be taken, because the president is independent of Congress and irremovable during his term. The other course would have been for Congress, like a Greek assembly, to be its own foreign office, or to create a foreign affairs committee of its members to handle these matters. As the objections to this course, which would have excluded the chief magistrate from functions naturally incidental to his position as official representative of the nation, were overwhelmingly strong, a compromise was made. The initiative in foreign policy and the conduct of negotiations were left to him, but the right of declaring war was reserved to Congress, and that of making treaties to one, the smaller and more experienced, branch of the legislature. A measure of authority was thus suffered to fall back to the executive which would have served to raise materially his position had foreign questions played as large a part in American politics as they have in French or English. They have, however, been comparatively unimportant, especially from 1815 till 1898, a time of external peace, except for the Mexican War of 1846.

It may be said that there was yet another source whence the executive might draw strength to support itself against the legislature, viz., those functions which the Constitution, deeming them necessarily incident to an executive, has reserved to the president and excluded from the competence of Congress. But examination shows that there is scarcely one of these which the long arm of legislation cannot reach. The president is commander in chief of the army, but the numbers and organization of the army are fixed by statute. The president makes appointments, but the Senate has the right of rejecting them, and Congress may pass acts specifying the qualifications of appointees, and reducing the salary of any official except the president himself and the judges. The real strength of the executive therefore, the rampart from behind which it can resist the aggressions of the legislature, is in ordinary times the veto power.[6] In other words, it survives as an executive in virtue not of any properly executive function, but of the share in legislative functions which it has received; it holds its ground by force, not of its separation from the legislature, but of its participation in a right properly belonging to the legislature.[7]

An authority which depends on a veto capable of being overruled by a two-thirds majority may seem frail. But the experience of a century has shown that, owing to the almost equal strength of the two great parties, the houses often differ, and there is rarely a two-thirds majority of the same colour in both. Hence the executive has enjoyed some independence. He is strong for defence, if not for attack. Congress can, except within that narrow sphere which the Constitution has absolutely reserved to him, baffle the president, can interrogate, check, and worry his ministers. But it can neither drive him the way it wishes him to go, nor dismiss them for disobedience or incompetence.

An individual man has some great advantages in combating an assembly. His counsels are less distracted. His secrets are better kept. He may sow discord among his antagonists. He can strike a more sudden blow. Julius Cæsar was more than a match for the Senate, Cromwell for the Long Parliament, even Louis Napoleon for the French Assembly of 1851. Hence, when the president happens to be a strong man, resolute, prudent, and popular, he may well hope to prevail against a body whom he may divide by the dexterous use of patronage, may weary out by inflexible patience, may overawe by winning the admiration of the masses, always disposed to rally round a striking personality. But in a struggle extending over a long course of years an assembly has advantages over a succession of officers, especially of elected officers. The Roman Senate encroached on the consuls,

---

[6] In moments of public danger, as during the War of Secession, the executive of course springs up into immense power, partly because the command of the army is then of the first importance; partly because the legislature, feeling its unfitness for swift and secret decisions, gives free rein to the executive, and practically puts its lawmaking powers at his disposal.

[7] What is said here of the national executive and national legislature is *a fortiori* true of the state executive and state legislatures. The state governor has little power of independent action whatever, being checked at every step by state statutes, and his discretion superseded by the minute directions which those statutes contain. He has not even ministers, because the other chief officials of the state are chosen, not by himself, but by popular vote. He has very little patronage; and he has no foreign policy at all. The state legislature would therefore prevail against him in everything, were it not for his veto and for the fact that the legislature is now generally restrained (by the provisions of the state constitution) from passing laws on many topics, and for that influence with the people which a strong and upright governor can exert. (See *post*, Chapters 37–45.)

though it was neither a legislature nor representative; the Carthaginian councils encroached on the suffetes; the Venetian councils encroached on the doge. Men come and go, but an assembly goes on forever; it is immortal, because while the members change, the policy, the passion for extending its authority, the tenacity in clinging to what has once been gained, remain persistent. A weak magistrate comes after a strong magistrate, and yields what his predecessor had fought for; but an assembly holds all it has ever won.[8] Its pressure is steady and continuous; it is always, by a sort of natural process, expanding its own powers and devising new methods for fettering its rival. Thus Congress, though it is no more respected or loved by the people now than it was in its earlier days, and has developed no higher capacity for promoting the best interests of the state, has succeeded in occupying most of the ground which the Constitution left debatable between the president and itself;[9] and would, did it possess a better internal organization, be more plainly than it now is the supreme power in the government.

In their effort to establish a balance of power, the framers of the Constitution so far succeeded that neither power has subjected the other. But they underrated the inconveniences which arise from the disjunction of the two chief organs of government. They relieved the administration from a duty which European ministers find exhausting and hard to reconcile with the conduct of administration—the duty of giving attendance in the legislature and taking the lead in its debates. They secured continuity of executive policy for four years at least, instead of leaving government at the mercy of fluctuating majorities in an excitable assembly. But they so narrowed the sphere of the executive as to prevent it from leading the country, or even its own party in the country, except indeed in a national crisis, or when the president happens to be exceptionally popular. They sought to make members of Congress independent, but in doing so they deprived them of some of the means which European legislators enjoy of learning how to administer, of learning even how to legislate in administrative topics. They condemned them to be architects without science, critics without experience, censors without responsibility.

---

[8] This is still more conspicuously the case when the members of the executive government do not sit in the assembly. When they do, and lead it, their influence tends to restrain legislative encroachments. Even the presence of persons who are likely to be soon called on to form the executive has its influence, for they are disposed to defend the constitutional position of an authority to which they hope in their turn to succeed. This has been frequently seen in England.

[9] The modification (in 1869) and repeal (in 1886) of the Tenure of Office Act (see above, p. 57) are scarcely instances to the contrary, because that act, even if constitutional, had proved difficult to work.

C H A P T E R   2 2

The Federal Courts

When in 1788 the loosely confederated states of North America united themselves into a nation, national tribunals were felt to be a necessary part of the national government. Under the Confederation there had existed no means of enforcing the treaties made or orders issued by the Congress, because the courts of the several states owed no duty to that feeble body, and had little will to aid it. Now that a federal legislature had been established, whose laws were to bind directly the individual citizen, a federal judicature was evidently needed to interpret and apply these laws, and to compel obedience to them. The alternative would have been to entrust the enforcement of the laws to state courts. But state courts were not fitted to deal with matters of a quasi-international character, such as admiralty jurisdiction and rights arising under treaties. They supplied no means for deciding questions between different states. They could not be trusted to do complete justice between their own citizens and those of another state. Being under the control of their own state governments, they might be forced to disregard any federal law which the state disapproved; or even if they admitted its authority, might fail in the zeal or the power to give due effect to it. And being authorities coordinate with and independent of one another, with no common court of appeal placed over them to correct their errors or harmonize their views, they would be likely to interpret the federal Constitution and statutes in different senses, and make the law uncertain by the variety of their decisions. These reasons pointed imperatively to the establishment of a new tribunal or set of tribunals, altogether detached from the states, as part of the machinery of the new government. Side by side of the thirteen different sets of state courts, whose jurisdiction under state laws and between their own citizens was left untouched, there arose a new and complex system of federal courts. The Constitution drew the outlines of the system. Congress perfected it by statutes; and as the details rest upon these statutes, Congress retains the power of altering them. Few American institutions are better worth studying than this intricate judicial machinery; few deserve more admiration for the smoothness of their working; few have more contributed to the peace and well-being of the country.

The federal courts fall into three classes:

The Supreme Court, which sits at Washington
The Circuit Courts of Appeals
The Circuit Courts
The District Courts

The Supreme Court is directly created by art. III, § 1 of the Constitution, but with no provision as to the number of its judges. Originally there were six; at present there are nine, a chief justice, with a salary of $13,000 and eight associate justices (salary $12,500). The justices are nominated by the president and confirmed by the Senate. They hold office during good behaviour, i.e., they are removable only by impeachment; and have thus a tenure even more secure than that of English judges, for the latter may be removed by the Crown on an address from both houses of Parliament.[1] Moreover, the English statutes secure the permanence only of the judges of the Supreme Court of judicature, not also of judges of county or other local courts, while the provisions of the American Constitution are held to apply to the inferior as well as the superior federal judges.[2] The Fathers of the Constitution were extremely anxious to secure the independence of their judiciary, regarding it as a bulwark both for the people and for the states against aggressions of either Congress or the president.[3] They affirmed the life tenure by an unanimous vote in the Convention of 1787, because they deemed the risk of the continuance in office of an incompetent judge a less evil than the subserviency of all judges to the legislature, which might flow from a tenure dependent on legislative will. The result has justified their expectations. The judges, although neither they nor anyone can wholly

---

[1] 12 and 13 William III, cap 2.; cf. 1 George III, cap. 23. The occasional resistance of the Parliament of Paris, whose members held office for life, to the French Crown may probably have confirmed the Convention of 1787 in its attachment to this English principle.

[2] As to United States judges in the Territories see Chapter 47.

[3] See Hamilton in *Federalist*, No. 78: "The standard of good behaviour for the continuance in office of the judicial magistracy is certainly one of the most valuable of the modern improvements in the practice of government. In a monarchy it is an excellent barrier to the despotism of the prince; in a republic it is a no less excellent barrier to the encroachments and oppressions of the legislative body."

escape the influence of party bias, have shown themselves independent of Congress and of party authority, yet the security of their position has rarely tempted them to breaches of judicial duty. Impeachment has been six times resorted to, once only against a justice of the Supreme Court, and then unsuccessfully.[4] Attempts have been made, beginning from Jefferson, who argued that judges should hold office for terms of four or six years only, to alter the tenure of the federal judges, as that of the state judges has been altered in most states; but Congress has always rejected the proposal.

The Supreme Court sits at Washington from October till July in every year. The presence of six judges is required to pronounce a decision, a rule which, by preventing the division of the court into two or more branches, retards the despatch of business, though it has the advantage of securing a thorough consideration of every case. The sittings are held in the Capitol, in the chamber formerly occupied by the Senate, and the justices wear black gowns, being not merely the only public officers, but the only nonecclesiastical persons of any kind whatever within the bounds of the United States who till recently used any official dress.[5] Every case is discussed by the whole body twice over, once to ascertain the opinion of the majority, which is then directed to be set forth in a written judgment; then again when that written judgment, which one of the judges has prepared, is submitted for criticism and adoption as the judgment of the court.

The Circuit Courts of Appeal have been created by Congress under a power in the Constitution to establish "inferior courts." There are at present nine judicial circuits, in which courts are held regularly. Each of these has two, three, or four Circuit judges (salary $7,000), and to each there is also allotted one of the justices of the Supreme Court. The Circuit Court of Appeal may be held either by a Circuit judge alone, or by the Supreme Court Circuit justice alone, or by both together, or by either sitting along with the District judge (hereafter mentioned) of the district wherein the particular Circuit Court is held, or by the District judge alone. To the Circuit Courts of Appeals are brought cases from District Courts, a further appeal lying, in some classes of cases, to the Supreme Court, to which moreover, in certain cases, a direct appeal from the District Courts may still be brought. There was formerly a Circuit Court, but that court was abolished in 1912 and its jurisdiction transferred to the District Courts.

The District Courts are the fourth and lowest class of federal tribunals.

---

[4] This was Samuel Chase of Maryland in 1804–1805. The other cases were of district federal judges and a judge of Commerce Court. (See p. 100 *supra*.)

[5] Now however in most universities the president and professors, and sometimes also the graduates, have begun to wear academic gowns and hoods on great occasions, such as the annual

They were in 1910 eighty-eight in number, and their judges receive salaries of $6,000 per annum. The Constitution does not expressly state whether they and the Circuit judges are to be appointed by the president and Senate like the members of the Supreme Court; but it has always been assumed that such was its intention, and the appointments are so made accordingly.

For the purpose of dealing with the claims of private persons against the federal government there has been established in Washington a special tribunal called the Court of Claims, with a chief justice (salary $6,500) and four other justices (salary $6,500), from which an appeal lies direct to the Supreme Court.

A Court of Customs Appeals was created under the Tariff Act of 1909 to decide questions relating to customs duties. It consists of a presiding judge and four associates (salary $10,000).

The jurisdiction of the federal courts extends to the following classes of cases, on each of which I say no more than what seems absolutely necessary to explain their nature.[6] All other cases have been left to the state courts, from which there does not lie (save as hereinafter specified) any appeal to the federal courts.

1. "Cases in law and equity arising under the constitution, the laws of the United States and treaties made under their authority."

In order to enforce the supremacy of the national Constitution and laws over all state laws, it was necessary to place the former under the guardianship of the national judiciary. This provision accordingly brings before a federal court every cause in which either party to a suit relies upon any federal enactment (including the Constitution and a treaty as well as a federal statute). It entitles a plaintiff who bases his case on a federal statute to bring his action in a federal court; it entitles a defendant who rests his defence on a federal enactment to have the action, if originally brought in a state court, removed to a federal court.[7] But, of course, if the action has originally been brought in a state court, there is no reason for removing it unless the

---

commencement. Gowns are worn by the judges in federal Circuit Courts and in the New York Court of Appeals.

[6] "All the enumerated cases of Federal cognizance are those which touch the safety, peace, and sovereignty of the nation, or which presume that State attachments, State prejudices, State jealousies, and State interests might sometimes obstruct or control the regular administration of justice. The appellate power in all these cases is founded on the clearest principles of policy and wisdom, and is necessary in order to preserve uniformity of decision upon all subjects within the purview of the Constitution."—Kent's *Commentaries* (Holmes' edition), vol. i, p. 320.

[7] The removal may be before or after judgment given, and in the latter event, by way of appeal or by writ of error.

authority of the federal enactment can be supposed to be questioned. Accordingly, the rule laid down by the Judiciary Act (1789) provides "for the removal to the Supreme Court of the United States of the final judgment or decree in any suit, rendered in the highest court of law or equity of a State in which a decision could be had, in which is drawn in question the validity of a treaty or statute of, or authority exercised under, the United States, and the decision is against their validity; or where is drawn in question the validity of a statute of, or an authority exercised under, any State, on the ground of their being repugnant to the Constitution, treaties, or laws of the United States, and the decision is in favour of their validity; or where any title, right, privilege, or immunity is claimed under the Constitution, or any treaty or statute of a commission held or authority exercised under the United States, and the decision is against the title, right, privilege, or immunity specially set up or claimed by either party under such Constitution, treaty, statute, commission, or authority. But to authorize the removal under that act, it must appear by the record, either expressly or by clear and necessary intendment, that some one of the enumerated questions did arise in the State court, and was there passed upon. It is not sufficient that it might have arisen or been applicable. And if the decision of the State court is in favour of the right, title, privilege, or exemption so claimed, the Judiciary Act does not authorize such removal, neither does it where the validity of the State law is drawn in question, and the decision of the State court is against its validity."[8]

The rule seems intricate, but the motive for it and the working of it are plain. Where in any legal proceeding a federal enactment has to be construed or applied by a state court, if the latter supports the federal enactment, i.e., considers it to govern the case, and applies it accordingly, the supremacy of federal law is thereby recognized and admitted. There is therefore no reason for removing the case to a federal tribunal. Such a tribunal could do no more to vindicate federal authority than the state court has already done. But if the decision of the state court has been against the applicability of the federal law, it is only fair that the party who suffers by the decision should be entitled to federal determination of the point, and he has accordingly an absolute right to carry it before the Supreme Court.[9]

The principle of this rule is applied even to executive acts of the federal

---

[8] Cooley, *Constitutional Limitations*, p. 16. For details regarding the removal of suits, and the restrictions when the amount in dispute is small, see Cooley, *Principles of Constitutional Law*, p. 122 *sqq.*; and see also the Act of March 3, 1887.

[9] Federal legislation may however be in a given case needed in order to confer upon federal courts jurisdiction over cases arising under a treaty. The question arose in the case of the lynching of

authorities. If, for instance, a person has been arrested by a federal officer, a state court has no jurisdiction to release him on a writ of habeas corpus, or otherwise to inquire into the lawfulness of his detention by federal authority, because, as was said by Chief Justice Taney, "The powers of the general government and of the State, although both exist and are exercised within the same territorial limits, are yet separate and distinct sovereignties, acting separately and independently of each other, within their respective spheres. And the sphere of action appropriated to the United States is as far beyond the reach of the judicial process issued by a State court as if the line of division was traced by landmarks and monuments visible to the eye."[10]

2. "Cases affecting ambassadors, other public ministers, and consuls."

As these persons have an international character, it would be improper to allow them to be dealt with by a state court which has nothing to do with the national government, and for whose learning and respectability there may exist no such securities as those that surround the federal courts.

3. "Cases of admiralty and maritime jurisdiction."

These are deemed to include not only prize cases but all maritime contracts, and all transactions relating to navigation, as well on the navigable lakes and rivers of the United States as on the high seas.

4. "Controversies to which the United States shall be a party."

This provision is obviously needed to protect the United States from being obliged to sue or be sued in a state court, to whose decision the national government could not be expected to submit. When a pecuniary claim is sought to be established against the federal government, the proper tribunal is the Court of Claims.

5. "Controversies between two or more States, between a State and citizens of another State, between citizens of different States, between citizens of the same State claiming lands under grants of different States, and between a State, or the citizens thereof, and foreign states, citizens, or subjects."

In all these cases a state court is likely to be, or at any rate to seem, a partial tribunal, and it is therefore desirable to vest the jurisdiction in judges equally unconnected with the plaintiff and the defendant. By securing

---

certain Italians at New Orleans in 1891. The Italian government in its complaints appealed to the treaty of 1871 between the United States and Italy, but it seems to have been held that Congress had not legislated so as to enable federal courts to deal with offences in breach of that treaty. In his inaugural address (March 1909), President Taft suggested that legislation was urgently needed for increasing the power of the executive to secure due protection in the states to foreign residents.

[10] *Ableman* v. *Booth*, 21 How. 516.

recourse to an unbiased and competent tribunal, the citizens of every state obtain better commercial facilities than they could otherwise count upon, for their credit will stand higher with persons belonging to other states if the latter know that their legal rights are under the protection, not of local and possibly prejudiced judges, but of magistrates named by the national government, and unamenable to local influences.[11]

One important part of the jurisdiction here conveyed has been subsequently withdrawn from the federal judicature. When the Constitution was submitted to the people, a principal objection urged against it was that it exposed a state, although a sovereign commonwealth, to be sued by the individual citizens of some other state. That one state should sue another was perhaps necessary, for what other way could be discovered of terminating disputes? But the power as well as the dignity of a state would be gone if it could be dragged into court by a private plaintiff. Hamilton (writing in the *Federalist*) met the objection by arguing that the jurisdiction-giving clause of the Constitution ought not to be so construed, but must be read as being subject to the general doctrine that a sovereign body cannot be sued by an individual without its own consent, a doctrine not to be excluded by mere implication but only by express words.[12] However, in 1793 the Supreme Court, in the famous case of *Chisholm* v. *The State of Georgia*,[13] construed the Constitution in the very sense which Hamilton had denied, holding that an action did lie against Georgia at the suit of a private plaintiff; and when Georgia protested and refused to appear, the Court proceeded (in 1794) to give judgment against her by default in case she should not appear and plead before a day fixed. Her cries of rage filled the Union, and brought other states to her help. An amendment (the eleventh) to the Constitution was passed through Congress and duly accepted by the requisite majority of the states, which declares that "the judicial power of the United States shall not be construed to extend to any suit commenced or prosecuted against one of the United States by citizens of another State or by citizens or subjects of any foreign states."[14] Under the protection of this amendment, not a few states have with impunity repudiated their debts.

[11] There are countries in Europe with which English merchants are unwilling to do business because they can seldom obtain justice from the courts against a native. Local feeling was, of course, much stronger in the America of 1787 than it is now. Englishmen who had claims against American citizens failed to obtain their enforcement from 1783 till the federal courts were established in 1789.

[12] *Federalist*, No. 81. The same view was contemporaneously maintained by John Marshall (afterwards chief justice) in the Virginia Convention of 1788.

[13] 2 Dall. 419.

[14] It has been held that the amendment applies only when a state is a party to the record, and therefore does not apply to the case of a state holding shares in a corporation. Neither does it

The jurisdiction of the Supreme Court is original in cases affecting ambassadors, and wherever a state is a party; in other cases it is appellate; that is, cases may be brought to it from the inferior federal courts and (under the circumstances before mentioned) from state courts. The jurisdiction is in some matters exclusive, in others concurrent with that of the state courts. Upon these subjects there have arisen many difficult and intricate questions, which I must pass by, because they would be unintelligible without long explanations.[15] One point, however, may be noted. The state courts cannot be invested by Congress with any jurisdiction, for Congress has no authority over them, and is not permitted by the Constitution to delegate any judicial powers to them. Hence the jurisdiction of a state court, wherever it is concurrent with that of federal judges, is a jurisdiction which the court possesses of its own right, independent of the Constitution. And in some instances where congressional statutes have purported to impose duties on state courts, the latter have refused to accept and discharge them.

The criminal jurisdiction of the federal courts, which extends to all offences against federal law, is purely statutory. "The United States as such can have no common law. It derives its powers from the grant of the people made by the Constitution, and they are all to be found in the written law, and not elsewhere."[16]

The procedure of the federal courts is prescribed by Congress, subject to some few rules contained in the Constitution, such as those which preserve the right of trial by jury in criminal cases[17] and suits at common law.[18] As "cases in law and equity" are mentioned, it is held that Congress could not accomplish such a fusion of law and equity as has been effected in several states of the Union, and was recently effected in England in 1873, but must maintain these methods of procedure as distinct, though administered by the same judges.

The law applied in the federal courts is of course first and foremost that enacted by the federal legislature, which, when it is applicable, prevails against any state law. But very often, as for instance in suits between

---

apply to appeals and writs of error. It is held to include suits against a state by one of its own citizens.

    In 1892 the Supreme Court decided (by a large majority) in the case of *United States* v. *Texas* that the United States can sue a state.

[15] The lawyer who is curious in such matters may be referred to Story's *Commentaries on the Constitution*, chapter xxxviii, and to the judgments of Chief Justice Marshall in the cases of *Martin* v. *Hunter* (1 Wheat. 304) and *Cohens* v. *Virginia* (6 Wheat. 406).

[16] Cooley, *Principles*, p. 131.

[17] Art. III, § 2.

[18] Amendment VII, § 1.

citizens of different states, federal law does not, or does only in a secondary way, come in question. In such instances the first thing is to determine what law it is that ought to govern the case, each state having a law of its own; and when this has been ascertained, it is applied to the facts, just as an English court would apply French or Scotch law in pronouncing on the validity of a marriage contracted in France or Scotland. In administering the law of any state (including its constitution, its statutes, and its common law, which in Louisiana is the civil law in its French form) the federal courts ought to follow the decisions of the state courts, treating those decisions as the highest authority on the law of the particular state. This doctrine is so fully applied that the Supreme Court has even overruled its own previous determinations on a point of state law in order to bring itself into agreement with the view of the highest court of the particular state. Needless to say, the state courts follow the decisions of the federal courts upon questions of federal law.[19]

For the execution of its powers each federal court has attached to it an officer called the United States marshal, corresponding to the sheriff in the state governments, whose duty it is to carry out its writs, judgments, and orders by arresting prisoners, levying execution, putting persons in possession, and so forth. He is entitled, if resisted, to call on all good citizens for help; if they will not or cannot render it, he must refer to Washington and obtain the aid of federal troops. There exists also in every judiciary district a federal public prosecutor, called the United States district attorney, who institutes proceedings against persons transgressing federal laws or evading the discharge of obligations to the federal treasury. Both sets of officials are under the direction of the attorney general, as head of the Department of Justice. They constitute a network of federal authorities covering the whole territory of the Union, and independent of the officers of the state courts and of the public prosecutors who represent the state governments. Where a state maintains a gaol for the reception of federal prisoners, the U.S. marshal delivers his prisoners to the state gaoler; where this provision is wanting, he must himself arrange for their custody.

The European reader may ask how it is possible to work a system so

---

[19] "The judicial department of every government is the appropriate organ for construing the legislative acts of that government. . . . On this principle the construction given by this (the supreme) court to the Constitution and laws of the United States is received by all as the true construction; and on the same principle the construction given by the courts of the various States to the legislative acts of those States is received as true, unless they come in conflict with the Constitution, laws, or treaties of the United States."—Marshall, C. J., in *Elmendorf* v. *Taylor*, 10 Wheat. 109.

extremely complex, under which every yard of ground in the Union is covered by two jurisdictions, with two sets of judges and two sets of officers, responsible to different superiors, their spheres of action divided only by an ideal line, and their action liable in practice to clash. The answer is that the system does work, and now, after an experience of four generations, works smoothly. It is more costly than the simpler systems of France, Prussia, or England, though, owing to the small salaries paid, the expense falls rather on litigants than on the public treasury. But it leads to few conflicts or heartburnings, because the key to all difficulties is found in the principle that wherever federal law is applicable federal law must prevail, and that every suitor who contends that federal law is applicable is entitled to have the point determined by a federal court. The acumen of the lawyers and judges, the wealth of accumulated precedents, make the solution of these questions of applicability and jurisdiction easier than a European practitioner can realize: while the law-respecting habits of the people and their sense that the supremacy of federal law and jurisdiction works to the common benefit of the whole people, secure general obedience to federal judgments. The enforcement of the law, especially the criminal law, in some parts of America leaves much to be desired; but the difficulties which arise are now due not to conflicts between state and federal pretensions but to other tendencies equally hostile to both authorities.

A word in conclusion as to the separation of the judicial from the other two departments, a point on which the framers of the Constitution laid great stress. The functions of the legislature are more easily distinguished from those of the judiciary than from those of the executive. The legislature makes the law, the judiciary applies it to particular cases by investigating the facts and, when these have been ascertained, by declaring what rule of law governs them. Nevertheless, there are certain points in which the functions of the two departments touch, certain ground debatable between the judiciary on the one hand and the legislature on the other. In most countries the courts have grown out of the legislature; or rather, the sovereign body, which, like Parliament, was originally both a law court and a legislature, has delivered over the bulk of its judicial duties to other persons, while retaining some few to be still exercised by itself.

America has in general followed the principles and practice of England. Like England, she creates no separate administrative tribunals such as exist in the states of the European continent, but allows officials to be sued in or indicted before the ordinary courts. Like England, she has given the judges (i.e., the federal judges) a position secured against the caprice of the legislature or executive. Like England, she recognizes judicial decisions as law until some statute has set them aside. In one respect she has improved on England—viz., in forbidding the legislature to exercise the powers of a criminal court, by passing acts of attainder or of pains and penalties, measures still legal, though virtually obsolete, in England.[20] In others, she diverges from England. England has practically ceased to use one branch of her Parliament as a court for the trial of impeachments. America still occasionally throws upon one house of Congress this function; which though it is ill suited to an ordinary court of justice, is scarcely better discharged by a political assembly. England has remitted to the courts of law the trial of disputed parliamentary elections; America still reserves these for Congress, and allows them to be disposed of by partisan votes, often with little regard to the merits. Special and local bills which vest in private hands certain rights of the state, such as public franchises, or the power of taking private property against the owner's will, are, though in form exercises of legislative power, really fitter to be examined and settled by judicial methods than by the loose opinion, the private motives, the lobbying, which determine legislative decisions where the control of public opinion is insufficiently provided for. England accordingly, though she refers such bills to committees of Parliament, directs these committees to apply a quasi-judicial procedure, and to decide according to the evidence tendered. America takes no such securities, but handles these bills like any others. Here therefore we see three pieces of ground debatable between the legislature and the judiciary. All of them originally belonged to the legislature. All in America still belong to it. England, however, has abandoned the first, has delivered over the second to the judges, and treats the third as matter to be dealt with by judicial rather than legislative methods. Such points of difference are worth noting, because the impression has prevailed in Europe that America is the country in which the province of the judiciary has been most widely extended.

---

[20] Neither house of Congress can punish a witness for contempt, after the fashion of the British Parliament (*Kilbourn* v. *Thompson*, 103 U.S. p. 168). See note 7 to Chapter 33 *post*.

The Courts and the Constitution

No feature in the government of the United States has awakened so much curiosity in the European mind, caused so much discussion, received so much admiration, and been more frequently misunderstood, than the duties assigned to the Supreme Court and the functions which it discharges in guarding the ark of the Constitution. Yet there is really no mystery about the matter. It is not a novel device. It is not a complicated device. It is the simplest thing in the world if approached from the right side.

In England and many other modern states there is no difference in authority between one statute and another. All are made by the legislature; all can be changed by the legislature. What are called in England constitutional statutes, such as Magna Charta, the Bill of Rights, the Act of Settlement, the Acts of Union with Scotland and Ireland, are merely ordinary laws, which could be repealed by Parliament at any moment in exactly the same way as it can repeal a highway act or lower the duty on tobacco.[1] The habit has grown up of talking of the British Constitution as if it were a fixed and definite thing. But there is in England no such thing as a constitution apart from the rest of the law: there is merely a mass of law, consisting partly of statutes and partly of decided cases and accepted usages, in conformity with which the government of the country is carried on from day to day, but which is being constantly modified by fresh statutes and cases. The same thing existed in ancient Rome, and everywhere in Europe a century ago. It is, so to speak, the "natural," and used to be the normal, condition of things in all countries, free or despotic.

[1] This doctrine, although long since well settled, would not have been generally accepted in the beginning of the seventeenth century. As Sir Thomas More had maintained that an act of Parliament could not make the king supreme head of the Church, so Coke held that the common law controlled acts of parliament and adjudged them void when against common right.

The condition of America is wholly different. There the name Constitution designates a particular instrument adopted in 1788, amended in some points since, which is the foundation of the national government. This Constitution was ratified and made binding, not by Congress, but by the people acting through conventions assembled in the thirteen states which then composed the Confederation. It created a legislature of two houses; but that legislature, which we call Congress, has no power to alter it in the smallest particular. That which the people have enacted, the people only can alter or repeal.

Here therefore we observe two capital differences between England and the United States. The former has left the outlines as well as the details of her system of government to be gathered from a multitude of statutes and cases. The latter has drawn them out in one comprehensive fundamental enactment. The former has placed these so-called constitutional laws at the mercy of her legislature, which can abolish when it pleases any institution of the country, the Crown, the House of Lords, the Established Church, the House of Commons, Parliament itself.[2] The latter has placed her Constitution altogether out of the reach of Congress, providing a method of amendment whose difficulty is shown by the fact that it has been very sparingly used.

In England Parliament is omnipotent. In America Congress is doubly restricted. It can make laws only for certain purposes specified in the Constitution, and in legislating for these purposes it must not transgress any provision of the Constitution itself. The stream cannot rise above its source.

Suppose, however, that Congress does so transgress, or does overpass the specified purposes. It may do so intentionally; it is likely to do so inadvertently. What happens? If the Constitution is to be respected, there must be some means of securing it against Congress. If a usurpation of power is attempted, how is it to be checked? If a mistake is committed, who sets it right?

The point may be elucidated by referring it to a wider category, familiar to lawyers and easily comprehensible by laymen, that of acts done by an agent for a principal. If a landowner directs his bailiff to collect rents for him, or to pay debts due to tradesmen, the bailiff has evidently no authority

---

[2] Parliament of course cannot restrict its own powers by any particular act, because that act might be repealed in a subsequent session, and indeed any subsequent act inconsistent with any of its provisions repeals *ipso facto* that provision. (For instance, the Act of Union with Scotland [6 Anne, c. 11] declared certain provisions of the Union, for the establishment of Presbyterian church government in Scotland, to be "essential and fundamental parts of the Union," but some of these provisions have been altered by subsequent statutes.) Parliament, could, however, extinguish itself by formally dissolving itself, leaving no legal means whereby a subsequent Parliament could be summoned.

to bind his employer by any act beyond the instructions given him, as, for instance, by contracting to buy a field. If a manufacturer directs his foreman to make rules for the hours of work and meals in the factory, and the foreman makes rules not only for those purposes, but also prescribing what clothes the workmen shall wear and what church they shall attend, the latter rules have not the force of the employer's will behind them, and the workmen are not to be blamed for neglecting them.

The same principle applies to public agents. In every country it happens that acts are directed to be done and rules to be made by bodies which are in the position of agents, i.e., which have received from some superior authority a limited power of acting and of rulemaking, a power to be used only for certain purposes or under certain conditions. Where this power is duly exercised, the act or rule of the subordinate body has all the force of an act done or rule made by the superior authority, and is deemed to be made by it. And if the latter be a lawmaking body, the rule of the subordinate body is therefore also a law. But if the subordinate body attempts to transcend the power committed to it, and makes rules for other purposes or under other conditions than those specified by the superior authority, these rules are not law, but are null and void. Their validity depends on their being within the scope of the lawmaking power conferred by the superior authority, and as they have passed outside that scope they are invalid. They do not justify any act done under them forbidden by the ordinary law. They ought not to be obeyed or in any way regarded by the citizens, because they are not law.

The same principle applies to acts done by an executive officer beyond the scope of his legal authority. In free countries an individual citizen is justified in disobeying the orders of a magistrate if he correctly thinks these orders to be in excess of the magistrate's legal power, because in that case they are not really the orders of a magistrate, but of a private person affecting to act as a magistrate. In England, for instance, if a secretary of state, or a police constable, does any act which the citizen affected by it rightly deems unwarranted, the citizen may resist, by force if necessary, relying on the ordinary courts of the land to sustain him. This is a consequence of the English doctrine that all executive power is strictly limited by the law, and is indeed a cornerstone of English liberty.[3] It is applied even as against the dominant branch of the legislature. If the House of Commons should act in

---

[3] See as to the different doctrine and practice of the European continent, and particularly as to the "administrative law" of France, the instructive remarks of Mr. Dicey in his *Law of the Constitution.*

excess of the power which the law and custom of Parliament has secured to it, a private individual may resist the officers of the House and the courts will protect him by directing him to be acquitted if he is prosecuted, or, if he is plaintiff in a civil action, by giving judgment in his favour.

An obvious instance of the way in which rules or laws made by subordinate bodies are treated is afforded by the bye-laws made by an English railway company or municipal corporation under powers conferred by an act of Parliament. So long as these bye-laws are within the scope of the authority which the act of Parliament has given, they are good, i.e., they are laws, just as much as if enacted in the act. If they go beyond it, they are bad, that is to say, they bind nobody and cannot be enforced. If a railway company which has received power to make bye-laws imposing fines up to the amount of forty shillings, makes a bye-law punishing any person who enters or quits a train in motion with a fine of fifty shillings or a week's imprisonment, that bye-law is invalid, that is to say, it is not law at all, and no magistrate can either imprison or impose a fine of fifty shillings on a person accused of contravening it. If a municipal corporation has been by statute empowered to enter into contracts for the letting of lands vested in it, and directed to make bye-laws, for the purpose of letting, which must provide, among other things, for the advertising of all lands intended to be let, and if it makes a bye-law in which no provision is made for advertising, and under that bye-law contracts for the letting of a piece of land, the letting made in pursuance of this bye-law is void, and conveys no title to the purchaser. All this is obvious to a lay as well as to a legal mind; and it is no less obvious that the question of the validity of the bye-law, and of what has been done under it, is one to be decided not by the municipal corporation or company, but by the courts of justice of the land.

Now, in the United States the position of Congress may for this purpose be compared to that of an English municipal corporation or railway company. The supreme lawmaking power is the people, that is, the qualified voters, acting in a prescribed way. The people have by their supreme law, the Constitution, given to Congress a delegated and limited power of legislation. Every statute passed under that power conformably to the Constitution has all the authority of the Constitution behind it. Any statute passed which goes beyond that power is invalid, and incapable of enforcement. It is in fact not a statute at all, because Congress in passing it was not really a lawmaking body, but a mere group of private persons.

Says Chief Justice Marshall, "The powers of the legislature are defined and limited; and that those limits may not be mistaken or forgotten, the

Constitution is written. To what purpose are powers limited and to what purpose is that limitation committed to writing, if those limits may at any time be passed by those intended to be restrained? The Constitution is either a superior paramount law, unchangeable by ordinary means, or it is on a level with ordinary legislative acts, and like any other acts, is alterable when the legislature shall please to alter it. If the former part of the alternative be true, then a legislative act contrary to the Constitution is not law. If the latter part be true, then written constitutions are absurd attempts on the part of the people to limit a power in its own nature illimitable." There is of course this enormous difference between Congress and any subordinate lawmaking authority in England, that Congress is supreme within its proper sphere, the people having no higher permanent organ to override or repeal such statutes as Congress may pass within that sphere; whereas in England there exists in Parliament a constantly present supervising authority, which may at any moment cancel or modify what any subordinate body may have enacted, whether within or without the scope of its delegated powers. This is a momentous distinction. But it does not affect the special point which I desire to illustrate, viz., that a statute passed by Congress beyond the scope of its powers is of no more effect than a bye-law made *ultra vires* by an English municipality. There is no mystery so far; there is merely an application of the ordinary principles of the law of agency. But the question remains, How and by whom, in case of dispute, is the validity or invalidity of a statute to be determined?

Such determination is to be effected by setting the statute side by side with the Constitution, and considering whether there is any discrepancy between them. Is the purpose of the statute one of the purposes mentioned or implied in the Constitution? Does it in pursuing that purpose contain anything which violates any clause of the Constitution? Sometimes this is a simple question, which an intelligent layman may answer. More frequently it is a difficult one, which needs not only the subtlety of the trained lawyer, but a knowledge of former cases which have thrown light on the same or a similar point. In any event it is an important question, whose solution ought to proceed from a weighty authority. It is a question of interpretation, that is, of determining the true meaning both of the superior law and of the inferior law, so as to discover whether they are inconsistent.

Now the interpretation of laws belongs to courts of justice. A law implies a tribunal, not only in order to direct its enforcement against individuals, but to adjust it to the facts, i.e., to determine its precise meaning and apply that meaning to the circumstances of the particular case. The legislature, which can only speak generally, makes every law in reliance on this power of interpretation. It is therefore obvious that the question, whether a congressional statute offends against the Constitution, must be determined by the courts, not merely because it is a question of legal construction, but because there is nobody else to determine it. Congress cannot do so, because Congress is a party interested. If such a body as Congress were permitted to decide whether the acts it had passed were constitutional, it would of course decide in its own favour, and to allow it to decide would be to put the Constitution at its mercy. The president cannot, because he is not a lawyer, and he also may be personally interested. There remain only the courts, and these must be the national or federal courts, because no other courts can be relied on in such cases. So far again there is no mystery about the matter.

Now, however, we arrive at a feature which complicates the facts, although it introduces no new principle. The United States is a federation of commonwealths, each of which has its own constitution and laws. The federal Constitution not only gives certain powers to Congress, as the national legislature, but recognizes certain powers in the states, in virtue whereof their respective peoples have enacted fundamental state laws (the state constitutions) and have enabled their respective legislatures to pass state statutes. However, as the nation takes precedence of the states, the federal Constitution, which is the supreme law of the land everywhere, and the statutes duly made by Congress under it, are preferred to all state constitutions and statutes; and if any conflict arise between them, the latter must give way. The same phenomenon therefore occurs as in the case of an inconsistency between the Constitution and a congressional statute. Where it is shown that a state constitution or statute infringes either the federal Constitution or a federal (i.e., congressional) statute, the state constitution or statute must be held and declared invalid. And this declaration must, of course, proceed from the courts, nor solely from the federal courts; because when a state court decides against its own statutes or constitution in favour of a federal law, its decision is final.

It will be observed that in all this there is no conflict between the law courts and any legislative body. The conflict is between different kinds of laws. The duty of the judges is as strictly confined to the interpretation of the laws cited to them as it is in England or France; and the only difference is that in America there are laws of four different degrees of authority, whereas in England all laws (excluding mere bye-laws, Privy Council ordinances, etc.) are equal because all proceed from Parliament. These four kinds of American laws are:

    I. The Federal Constitution
    II. Federal statutes
    III. State constitutions
    IV. State statutes[4]

The American law court therefore does not itself enter on any conflict with the legislature. It merely secures to each kind of law its due authority. It does not even preside over a conflict and decide it, for the relative strength of each kind of law has been settled already. All the court does is to point out that a conflict exists between two laws of different degrees of authority. Then the question is at an end, for the weaker law is extinct, or, to put the point more exactly, a flaw has been indicated which makes the world see that if the view of the court be correct, the law is in fact null. The court decides nothing but the case before it; and anyone may, if he thinks the court wrong, bring up a fresh case raising again the question whether the law is valid.[5]

This is the abstract statement of the matter; but there is also an historical one. Many of the American colonies received charters from the British Crown, which created or recognized colonial assemblies, and endowed these with certain powers of making laws for the colony. Such powers were of course limited, partly by the charter, partly by usage, and were subject to the superior authority of the Crown or of the British Parliament. Questions sometimes arose in colonial days whether the statutes made by these assemblies were in excess of the powers conferred by the charter; and if the statutes were found to be in excess, they were held invalid by the courts, that is to say, in the first instance, by the colonial courts, or, if the matter was carried to England, by the Privy Council.[6]

---

[4] Of these, the federal Constitution prevails against all other laws. Federal statutes, if made in pursuance of and conformably to the Constitution, prevail against III and IV. If in excess of the powers granted by the Constitution, they are wholly invalid. A state constitution yields to I and II, but prevails against the statutes of the state.

    Treaties have the same authority as federal statutes (they may be altered by statute). It need hardly be said that executive or departmental orders made under powers conferred by a statute have statutory force.

[5] This happened in the legal tender question (see next chapter). But in ninety-nine instances out of a hundred, the legal profession and the public admit the correctness, and therewith the authority, of the view which the court has taken. The court has itself declared that its declaration of the unconstitutionality of a statute must nowise be taken as amounting to a repeal of that statute. See *In re Rahrer*, 140 U.S. Rep. p. 545.

[6] The same thing happens even now as regards the British colonies. The question was lately argued before the Privy Council whether the legislature of the Dominion of Canada, created by the British North America Act of 1867 (an imperial statute), had power to extinguish the right of appeal from the supreme court of Canada to the British queen in council.

When the thirteen American colonies asserted their independence in 1776, they replaced these old charters by new constitutions,[7] and by these constitutions entrusted their respective legislative assemblies with certain specified and limited legislative powers. The same question was then liable to recur with regard to a statute passed by one of these assemblies. If such a statute was in excess of the power which the state constitution conferred on the state legislature, or in any way transgressed the provisions of that constitution, it was invalid, and acts done under it were void. The question, like any other question of law, came for decision before the courts of the state. Thus, in 1786, the supreme court of Rhode Island held that a statute of the legislature which purported to make a penalty collectible on summary conviction, without trial by jury, gave the court no jurisdiction, i.e., was invalid, the colonial charter, which was then still in force as the constitution of the state, having secured the right of trial by jury in all cases.[8] When the Constitution of the United States came into operation in 1789, and was declared to be paramount to all state constitutions and state statutes, no new principle was introduced; there was merely a new application, as between the nation and the states, of the old doctrine that a subordinate and limited legislature cannot pass beyond the limits fixed for it. It was clear, on general principles, that a state law incompatible with a federal law must give way; the only question was: What courts are to pronounce upon the question whether such incompatibility exists? Who is to decide whether or not the authority given to Congress has been exceeded, and whether or not the state law contravenes the federal Constitution or a federal statute?

In 1787 the only then-existing courts were the state courts. If a case coming before them raised the point whether a state constitution or statute was inconsistent with the federal Constitution or a statute of Congress, it was their duty to decide it, like any other point of law. But their decision could not safely be accepted as final, because, being themselves the offspring of, and amenable to, the state governments, they would naturally tend to uphold state laws against the federal Constitution or statutes. Hence it became necessary to set up courts created by the central federal authority and coextensive with it—that is to say, those federal courts which have

[7] Connecticut and Rhode Island, however, went on under the old charters, with which they were well content. See as to this whole subject, Chapter 37, on state constitutions.

[8] In the case of *Trevett* v. *Weedon*, the first case of importance in which a legislative act was held unconstitutional for incompatibility with a state constitution, although the doctrine seems to have been laid down by the supreme court of New Jersey in *Holmes* v. *Walton* (1780), as well as in Virginia in 1782, and in New York in 1784. See Judge Elliott's article in *Political Science Quarterly* for June 1890, p. 233.

been already described. The matter seems complicated, because we have to consider not only the superiority of the federal Constitution to the federal legislature, but also the superiority of both the federal Constitution and federal statutes to all state laws. But the principle is the same and equally simple in both sets of cases. Both are merely instances of the doctrine, that a lawmaking body must not exceed its powers, and that when it has attempted to exceed its powers, its so-called statutes are not laws at all, and cannot be enforced.

In America the supreme lawmaking power resides in the people. Whatever they enact is universally binding. All other lawmaking bodies are subordinate, and the enactments of such bodies must conform to the supreme law, else they will perish at its touch, as a fishing smack goes down before an ocean steamer. And these subordinate enactments, if at variance with the supreme law, are invalid from the first, although their invalidity may remain for years unnoticed or unproved. It can be proved only by the decision of a court in a case which raises the point for determination. The phenomenon cannot arise in a country whose legislature is omnipotent, but naturally[9] arises wherever we find a legislature limited by a superior authority, such as a constitution which the legislature cannot alter.

In England the judges interpret acts of Parliament exactly as American judges interpret statutes coming before them. If they find an act conflicting with a decided case, they prefer the act to the case, as being of higher authority. As between two apparently conflicting acts, they prefer the later, because it is the last expression of the mind of Parliament. If they misinterpret the mind of Parliament, i.e., if they construe an act in a sense which Parliament may not have intended, their decision is nevertheless valid, and will be followed by other courts of the same rank until Parliament speaks its mind again by another act. The only difference between their position and that of their American brethren is that they have never to distinguish between the authority of one enactment and of another, otherwise than by looking to the date, and that they therefore need never to inquire whether an act of Parliament was invalid when first passed. Invalid it could not have been, because Parliament is omnipotent, and Parliament is omnipotent

---

[9] I do not say "necessarily," because there are countries on the European continent where, although there exists a constitution superior to the legislature, the courts are not allowed to hold a legislative act invalid, because the legislature is deemed to have the right of taking its own view of the constitution. This seems to be the case both in France and in Switzerland. So in the German Empire the Reichskammergericht cannot question an act of the imperial legislature; and in Belgium, though it has been thought that the courts possess such a power, it is now held that they do not possess it.

because Parliament is deemed to be the people. Parliament is not a body with delegated or limited authority. The whole fulness of popular power dwells in it. The whole nation is supposed to be present within its walls.[10] Its will is law; or, as Dante says in a famous line, "its will is power."

There is a story told of an intelligent Englishman who, having heard that the Supreme Federal Court was created to protect the Constitution, and had authority given it to annul bad laws, spent two days in hunting up and down the federal Constitution for the provisions he had been told to admire. No wonder he did not find them, for there is not a word in the Constitution on the subject. The powers of the federal courts are the same as those of all other courts in civilized countries, or rather they differ from those of other courts by defect and not by excess, being limited to certain classes of cases. The so-called "power of annulling an unconstitutional statute" is a duty rather than a power, and a duty incumbent on the humblest state court when a case raising the point comes before it no less than on the Supreme Federal Court at Washington. When therefore people talk, as they sometimes do, even in the United States, of the Supreme Court as "the guardian of the Constitution," they mean nothing more than that it is the final court of appeal, before which suits involving constitutional questions may be brought up by the parties for decision. In so far the phrase is legitimate. But the functions of the Supreme Court are the same in kind as those of all other courts, state as well as federal. Its duty and theirs is simply to declare and apply the law; and where any court, be it a state court of first instance, or the federal court of last instance, finds a law of lower authority clashing with a law of higher authority, it must reject the former, as being really no law, and enforce the latter.

It is therefore no mere technicality to point out that the American judges do not, as Europeans are apt to say, "control the legislature," but simply interpret the law. The word "control" is misleading, because it implies that the person or body of whom it is used possesses and exerts discretionary personal will. Now the American judges have no discretionary will in the matter any more than has an English court when it interprets an act of

---

[10] The old writers say that the reason why an act of Parliament requires no public notification in the country is because it is deemed to be made by the whole nation, so that every person is present at the making of it. It is certainly true that the orthodox legal view of Parliament never regards it as exercising powers that can in any sense be called delegated. A remarkable example of the power which Parliament can exert as an ultimately and completely sovereign body is afforded by the Septennial Act (I Geo. I. st. 2, cap. 38). By this statute a Parliament in which the House of Commons had been elected for three years only, under the Triennial Act then in force, prolonged not only the possible duration of future Parliaments but its own term to seven years, taking to itself four years of power which the electors had not given it.

Parliament. The will that prevails is the will of the people, expressed in the Constitution which they have enacted. All that the judges have to do is to discover from the enactments before them what the will of the people is, and apply that will to the facts of a given case. The more general or ambiguous the language which the people have used, so much the more difficult is the task of interpretation, so much greater the need for ability and integrity in the judges. But the task is always the same in its nature. The judges have no concern with the motives or the results of an enactment, otherwise than as these may throw light on the sense in which the enacting authority intended it. It would be a breach of duty for them to express, I might almost say a breach of duty to entertain, an opinion on its policy except so far as its policy explains its meaning. They may think a statute excellent in purpose and working, but if they cannot find in the Constitution a power for Congress to pass it, they must brush it aside as invalid. They may deem another statute pernicious, but if it is within the powers of Congress, they must enforce it. To construe the law, that is, to elucidate the will of the people as supreme lawgiver, is the beginning and end of their duty. And if it be suggested that they may overstep their duty, and may, seeking to make themselves not the exponents but the masters of the Constitution, twist and pervert it to suit their own political views, the answer is that such an exercise of judicial will would rouse the distrust and displeasure of the nation, and might, if persisted in, provoke resistance to the law as laid down by the court, possibly an onslaught upon the court itself.

To insist upon the fact that the judiciary of the United States are not masters of the Constitution but merely its interpreters is not to minimize the importance of their functions, but to indicate their true nature. The importance of those functions can hardly be exaggerated. It arises from two facts. One is that as the Constitution cannot easily be changed, a bad decision on its meaning, i.e., a decision which the general opinion of the profession condemns, may go uncorrected. In England, if a court has construed a statute in a way unintended or unexpected, Parliament can set things right next session by amending the statute, and so prevent future decisions to the same effect. But American history shows only one instance in which an unwelcome decision on the meaning of the Constitution has been thus dealt with, viz., the decision, that a state could be sued by a private citizen,[11]

---

[11] See the last preceding chapter. The doctrine of the Dred Scott case (of which more anon) was set aside by the Fourteenth Amendment, but that amendment was intended to effect much more than merely to correct the court.

which led to the Eleventh Amendment, whereby it was declared that the Constitution should not cover a case which the court had held it did cover.

The other fact which makes the function of an American judge so momentous is the brevity, the laudable brevity, of the Constitution. The words of that instrument are general, laying down a few large principles. The cases which will arise as to the construction of these general words cannot be foreseen till they arise. When they do arise the generality of the words leaves open to the interpreting judges a far wider field than is afforded by ordinary statutes which, since they treat of one particular subject, contain enactments comparatively minute and precise. Hence, although the duty of a court is only to interpret, the considerations affecting interpretation are more numerous than in the case of ordinary statutes, more delicate, larger in their reach and scope. They sometimes need the exercise not merely of legal acumen and judicial fairness, but of a comprehension of the nature and methods of government which one does not demand from the European judge who walks in the narrow path traced for him by ordinary statutes. It is therefore hardly an exaggeration to say that the American Constitution as it now stands, with the mass of fringing decisions which explain it, is a far more complete and finished instrument than it was when it came fire-new from the hands of the Convention. It is not merely their work but the work of the judges, and most of all of one man, the great Chief Justice Marshall.

The march of democracy in England has disposed some English political writers of the very school which in the last generation pointed to America as a terrible example, now to discover that her republic possesses elements of stability wanting in the monarchy of the mother country. They lament that England should have no supreme court. Some have even suggested that England should create one. They do not seem to perceive that the dangers they discern arise not from the want of a court but from the omnipotence of the British Parliament. They ask for a court to guard the British Constitution, forgetting that Britain has no constitution, in the American sense, and never had one, except for a short space under Oliver Cromwell. The strongest court that might be set up in England could effect nothing so long as Parliament retains its power to change every part of the law, including all the rules and doctrines that are called constitutional. If Parliament were to lose that power there would be no need to create a supreme court, because the existing judges of the land would necessarily discharge the very functions which American judges now discharge. If Parliament were to be split up into four parliaments for England, Scotland, Ireland, and Wales, and a new federal assembly were to be established with limited legislative powers, powers defined by an instrument which neither the federal assembly nor any of the four parliaments could alter, questions would forthwith arise as to the compatibility both of acts passed by the assembly with the provisions of the instrument, and of acts passed by any of the four parliaments with those passed by the assembly. These questions would come before the courts and be determined by them like any other question of law. The same thing would happen if Britain were to enter into a federal pact with her colonies, creating an imperial council, and giving it powers which, though restricted by the pact to certain purposes, transcended those of the British Parliament. The interpretation of the pact would belong to the courts, and both Parliament and the supposed council would be bound by that interpretation.[12] If a new supreme court were created by Britain, it would be created not because there do not already exist courts capable of entertaining all the questions that could arise, but because the parties to the new constitution enacted for the United Kingdom, or the British Empire (as the case might be), might insist that a tribunal composed of persons chosen by some federal authority would be more certainly impartial. The preliminary therefore to any such "judicial safeguard" as has been suggested is the extinction of the present British Parliament and the erection of a wholly different body or bodies in its room.

These observations may suffice to show that there is nothing strange or mysterious about the relation of the federal courts to the Constitution. The plan which the Convention of 1787 adopted is simple, useful, and conformable to general legal principles. It is, in the original sense of the word, an elegant plan. But it is not novel, as was indeed observed by Hamilton in the *Federalist*. It was at work in the states before the Convention of 1787 met. It was at work in the thirteen colonies before they revolted from England. It is an application of old and familiar legal doctrines. Such novelty as there is belongs to the scheme of a supreme or rigid constitution, reserving the ultimate power to the people, and limiting in the same measure the power of the legislature.[13]

---

[12] Assuming of course that the power of altering the pact was reserved to some authority superior to either the council or Parliament.

[13] So Mr. Wilson observed (speaking of the state constitutions) in the Pennsylvania Convention of 1787: "Perhaps some politician who has not considered with sufficient accuracy our political systems would observe that in our governments the supreme power was vested in the constitutions. This opinion approaches the truth, but does not reach it. The truth is that in our governments the supreme, absolute, and uncontrollable power *remains* in the people. As our constitutions are superior to our legislatures, so the people are superior to our constitutions."—Elliot's *Debates*, vol. ii, 432.

It is nevertheless true that there is no part of the American system which reflects more credit on its authors or has worked better in practice. It has had the advantage of relegating questions not only intricate and delicate, but peculiarly liable to excite political passions, to the cool, dry atmosphere of judicial determination. The relations of the central federal power to the states, and the amount of authority which Congress and the president are respectively entitled to exercise, have been the most permanently grave questions in American history, with which nearly every other political problem has become entangled. If they had been left to be settled by Congress, itself an interested party, or by any dealings between Congress and the state legislatures, the dangers of a conflict would have been extreme, and instead of one civil war there might have been several. But the universal respect felt for the Constitution, a respect which grows the longer it stands, has disposed men to defer to any decision which seems honestly and logically to unfold the meaning of its terms. In obeying such a decision they are obeying, not the judges, but the people who enacted the Constitution. To have foreseen that the power of interpreting the federal Constitution and statutes, and of determining whether or not state constitutions and statutes transgress federal provisions, would be sufficient to prevent struggles between the national government and the state governments, required great insight and great faith in the soundness and power of a principle. While the Constitution was being framed the suggestion was made, and for a time seemed likely to be adopted, that a veto on the acts of state legislatures should be conferred upon the federal Congress. Discussion revealed the objections to such a plan. Its introduction would have offended the sentiment of the states, always jealous of their autonomy; its exercise would have provoked collisions with them. The disallowance of a state statute, even if it did really offend against the federal Constitution, would have seemed a political move, to be resented by a political countermove. And the veto would often have been pronounced before it could have been ascertained exactly how the state statute would work, sometimes, perhaps, pronounced in cases where the statute was neither pernicious in itself nor opposed to the federal Constitution. But by the action of the courts the self-love of the state is not wounded, and the decision declaring one of their laws invalid

---

Mr. M'Kean, speaking in the same convention, quoted Locke's *Civil Government* (c. 2, § 140, and c. 13, § 152) as an authority for the proposition that the powers of Congress could be no greater than the positive grant might convey.

As to rigid constitutions, see Chapter 31 *post*; and, for a fuller treatment, an essay in my *Studies in History and Jurisprudence*.

is nothing but a tribute to the higher authority of that supreme enactment to which they were themselves parties, and which they may themselves desire to see enforced against another state on some not remote occasion. However, the idea of a veto by Congress was most effectively demolished in the Convention by Roger Sherman, who acutely remarked that a veto would seem to recognize as valid the state statute objected to, whereas if inconsistent with the Constitution it was really invalid already and needed no veto.

By leaving constitutional questions to be settled by the courts of law another advantage was incidentally secured. The court does not go to meet the question; it waits for the question to come to it. When the court acts it acts at the instance of a party. Sometimes the plaintiff or the defendant may be the national government or a state government, but far more frequently both are private persons, seeking to enforce or defend their private rights. For instance, in the famous case[14] which established the doctrine that a statute passed by a state repealing a grant of land to an individual made on certain terms by a previous statute is a law "impairing the obligation of a contract," and therefore invalid, under art. I, § 10 of the federal Constitution; the question came before the court on an action by one Fletcher against one Peck on a covenant contained in a deed made by the latter; and to do justice between plaintiff and defendant it was necessary to examine the validity of a statute passed by the legislature of Georgia. This method has the merit of not hurrying a question on, but leaving it to arise of itself. Full legal argument on both sides is secured by the private interests which the parties have in setting forth their contentions; and the decision when pronounced, since it appears to be, as in fact it is, primarily a decision upon private rights, obtains that respect and moral support which a private plaintiff or defendant establishing his legal right is entitled to from law-abiding citizens. A state might be provoked to resistance if it saw, as soon as it had passed a statute, the federal government inviting the Supreme Court to declare that statute invalid. But when the federal authority stands silent, and a year after in an ordinary action between Smith and Jones the court decides in favour of Jones, who argued that the statute on which the plaintiff relied was invalid because it transgressed some provision of the Constitution, everybody feels that Jones was justified in so arguing, and that since judgment was given in his favour he must be allowed to retain the money which the court has found to be his, and the statute which violated his private right must fall to the ground.

[14] *Fletcher* v. *Peck*, 6 Cranch, p. 87.

This feature has particularly excited the admiration of Continental critics. To an Englishman it seems perfectly natural, because it is exactly in this way that much of English constitutional law has been built up. The English courts had indeed no rigid documentary constitution by which to test the ordinances or the executive acts of the Crown, and their decisions on constitutional points have often been pronounced in proceedings to which the Crown or its ministers were parties. But they have repeatedly established principles of the greatest moment by judgments delivered in cases where a private interest was involved, grounding themselves either on a statute which they interpreted or on some earlier decision.[15] Lord Mansfield's famous declaration that slavery was legally impossible in England was pronounced in such a private case. *Stockdale* v. *Hansard*, in which the law regarding the publishing of debates in Parliament was settled, was an action by a private person against printers. The American method of settling constitutional questions, like all other legal questions, in actions between private parties, is therefore no new device, but a part of that priceless heritage of the English common law which the colonists carried with them across the sea, and which they have preserved and developed in a manner worthy of its own free spirit and lofty traditions.

Those err who suppose that the functions above described as pertaining to the American courts are peculiar to and essential to a federal government. These functions are not peculiar to a federation, because the distinction of fundamental laws and inferior laws may exist equally well in a unified government, did exist in each of the thirteen colonies up till 1776, did exist in each of the thirteen states from 1776 till 1789, does exist in every one of the forty-eight states now. Nor are they essential, because a federation may be imagined in which the central or national legislature should be theoretically sovereign in the same sense and to the same full extent as is the British Parliament.[16] The component parts of any confederacy will no doubt be generally disposed to place their respective states' rights under the protection of a compact unchangeable by the national legislature. But they need not do so, for they may rely on the command which as electors they have over that legislature, and may prefer the greater energy which a

---

[15] The independence of the English judges (since the Revolution) and of the American federal judges has of course largely contributed to make them trusted, and to make them act worthily of the trust reposed in them.

[16] It would appear that in the Achæan League the Assembly (which voted by cities) was sovereign, and could by its vote vary the terms of the federal arrangements between the cities forming the federation; although the scantiness of our data and what may be called the want of legal-mindedness among the Greeks make this and similar questions not easy of determination.

sovereign legislature promises to the greater security for states' rights which a limited legislature implies. In the particular case of America it is abundantly clear that if there had been in 1787 no states jealous of their powers, but an united nation creating for itself an improved frame of government, the organs of that government would have been limited by a fundamental law just as they have in fact been, because the nation, fearing and distrusting the agents it was creating, was resolved to fetter them by reserving to itself the ultimate and overriding sovereignty.

The case of Switzerland shows that the American plan is not the only one possible to a federation. The Swiss Federal Court, while instituted in imitation of the American, is not the only authority competent to determine whether a cantonal law is void because inconsistent with the federal Constitution, for in some cases recourse must be had not to the Court but to the Federal Council, which is a sort of executive cabinet of the Confederation. And the Federal Court is bound to enforce every law passed by the federal legislature, even if it appear to conflict with the Constitution. In other words, the Swiss Constitution has reserved some points of cantonal law for an authority not judicial but political, and has made the federal legislature the sole judge of its own powers, the authorized interpreter of the Constitution, and an interpreter not likely to proceed on purely legal grounds.[17] To an English or American lawyer the Swiss copy seems neither so consistent with sound theory nor so safe in practice as the American original. But the statesmen of Switzerland felt that a method fit for America might be ill-fitted for their own country, where the latitude given to the executive is greater; and the Swiss habit of constantly recurring to popular vote makes it less necessary to restrain the legislature by a permanently enacted instrument. The political traditions of the European continent differ widely from those of England and America; and the federal judicature is not the only Anglo-American institution which might fail to thrive anywhere but in its native soil.

---

[17] See upon this fascinating subject, the provisions of the Swiss Federal Constitution of 1874, arts. 102, 110, and 114; also Dubs, *Das öffentliche Recht der Schweizerischen Eidgenossenschaft*, and a valuable pamphlet by M. Ch. Soldan, entitled *Du recours de Droit Public au Tribunal Fédéral*; Bâle, 1886. Dr. Dubs was himself the author of the plan whereby the federal legislature is made the arbiter of its own constitutional powers.

C H A P T E R   2 4

The Working of the Courts

Those readers who have followed thus far the account given of the federal courts have probably asked themselves how judicial authorities can sustain the functions which America requires them to discharge. It is plain that judges, when sucked into the vortex of politics, must lose dignity, impartiality, and influence. But how can judges keep out of politics, when political issues raising party passions come before them? Must not constitutional questions, questions as to the rights under the Constitution of the federal government against the states, and of the branches of the federal government against one another, frequently involve momentous political issues? In the troublous times during which the outlines of the English Constitution were settled, controversy often raged round the courts, because the decision of contested points lay in their hands. When Charles I could not induce Parliament to admit the right of levying contributions which he claimed, and Parliament relied on the power of the purse as its defence against Charles I, the question whether ship money could lawfully be levied was vital to both parties, and the judges held the balance of power in their hands. At that moment the law could not be changed, because the houses and the king stood opposed: hence everything turned on the interpretation of the existing law. In America the Constitution is at all times very hard to change; much more then must political issues turn on its interpretation. And if this be so, must not the interpreting court be led to assume a control over the executive and legislative branches of the government, since it has the power of declaring their acts illegal?

There is ground for these criticisms. The evil they point to has occurred and may recur. But it occurs very rarely, and may be averted by the same prudence which the courts have hitherto generally shown. The causes which have enabled the federal courts to avoid it, and to maintain their dignity and influence almost unshaken, are the following:

I. The Supreme Court—I speak of the Supreme Court because its conduct has governed that of inferior federal courts—has always declared that it is not concerned with purely political questions. Whenever it finds any discretion given to the president, any executive duty imposed on him, it considers the manner in which he exercises his discretion and discharges the duty to be beyond its province. Whenever the Constitution has conferred upon Congress a power of legislating, the court declines to inquire whether the use of the power was in the case of a particular statute passed by Congress either necessary or desirable, or whether it was exerted in a prudent manner, for it holds all such matters to be within the exclusive province of Congress.

> "In measures exclusively of a political, legislative, or executive character, it is plain that as the supreme authority as to these questions belongs to the legislative and executive departments, they cannot be re-examined elsewhere. Thus Congress, having the power to declare war, to levy taxes, to appropriate money, to regulate intercourse and commerce with foreign nations, their mode of executing these powers can never become the subject of re-examination in any other tribunal. So the power to make treaties being confided to the President and Senate, when a treaty is properly ratified, it becomes the law of the land, and no other tribunal can gainsay its stipulations. Yet cases may readily be imagined in which a tax may be laid, or a treaty made upon motives and grounds wholly beside the intention of the Constitution. The remedy, however, in such cases is solely by an appeal to the people at the elections, or by the salutary power of amendment provided by the Constitution itself."[1]

Adherence to this principle has enabled the court to avoid an immixture in political strife which must have destroyed its credit, has deterred it from entering the political arena, where it would have been weak, and enabled it to act without fear in the sphere of pure law, where it is strong. Occasionally, however, as I shall explain presently, the court has come into collision with the executive. Occasionally it has been required to give decisions which have worked with tremendous force on politics. The most famous of these was the Dred Scott case,[2] in which the Supreme Court, on an action by a Negro for assault and battery against the person claiming to be his master, declared that a slave taken temporarily to a free state and to a territory in which Congress had forbidden slavery, and afterwards returning into a slave

---

[1] Story, *Commentaries on the Constitution*, § 374.

[2] *Scott* v. *Sandford*, 19 How. 393. There is an immense literature about this case, the legal points involved in which are too numerous and technical to be here stated. It is noticeable that the sting of the decision lay rather in the *obiter dicta* than in the determination of the main question involved.

state and resuming residence there, was not a citizen capable of suing in the federal courts if by the law of the slave state he was still a slave. This was the point which actually called for decision; but the majority of the court, for there was a dissentient minority, went further, and delivered a variety of *dicta* on various other points touching the legal status of Negroes and the constitutional view of slavery. This judgment, since the language used in it seemed to cut off the hope of a settlement by the authority of Congress of the then (1857) pending disputes over slavery and its extension, did much to precipitate the Civil War.

Some questions, and among them many which involve political issues, can never come before the federal courts, because they are not such as are raisable in an action between parties. Of those which might be raised, some never happen to arise, while others do not present themselves in an action till some time after the statute has been passed or act done on which the court is called to pronounce. By that time it may happen that the warmth of feeling which expressed itself during debate in Congress or in the country has passed away, while the judgment of the nation at large has been practically pronounced upon the issue.

II. Looking upon itself as a pure organ of the law, commissioned to do justice between man and man, but to do nothing more, the Supreme Court has steadily refused to decide abstract questions, or to give opinions in advance by way of advice to the executive. When, in 1793, President Washington requested its opinion on the construction of the treaty of 1788 with France, the judges declined to comply.

This restriction of the Court's duty to the determination of concrete cases arising in suits has excited so much admiration from Tocqueville and other writers, that the corresponding disadvantages must be stated. They are these:

To settle at once and forever a disputed point of constitutional law would often be a gain both to private citizens and to the organs of the government. Under the present system there is no certainty when, if ever, such a point will be settled. Nobody may care to incur the trouble and expense of taking it before the court. A suit which raises it may be compromised or dropped.

When such a question, after perhaps the lapse of years, comes before the Supreme Court and is determined, the determination may be different from what the legal profession has expected, may alter that which has been believed to be the law, may shake or overthrow private interests based upon views now declared to be erroneous.[3] These are, no doubt, drawbacks

---

[3] The Dred Scott decision in 1857 declared the Missouri compromise, carried out by act of Congress in 1820, to have been beyond the powers of Congress, which, to be sure, had virtually repealed

incident to every system in which the decisions of courts play a great part. There are many points in the law of England which are uncertain even now, because they have never come before a court of high authority, or, having been decided in different ways by coordinate courts, have not been carried to the final court of appeal. But in England the inconvenience, should it be great, can be removed by an act of Parliament; and it can hardly be so great as it may be in America, where, since the doubtful point may be the true construction of the fundamental law of the Union, the president and Congress may be left in uncertainty as to how they shall shape their course. With the best wish in the world to act conformably to the Constitution, these authorities have no means of ascertaining before they act what, in the view of its authorized interpreters, the true meaning of the Constitution is. Moved by this consideration, seven states of the Union have by their constitutions empowered the governor or legislature to require the written opinions of the judges of the highest state court on points submitted to them.[4] But the president of the United States can only consult his attorney general,[5] and the houses of Congress have no legal adviser, though to be sure they are apt to receive a profusion of advice from their own legal members.[6]

III. Other causes which have sustained the authority of the court by saving it from immersion in the turbid pool of politics, are the strength of professional feeling among American lawyers, the relation of the bench to the bar, the power of the legal profession in the country. The keen interest which the profession takes in the law secures an unusually large number of acute and competent critics of the interpretation put upon the law by the judges. Such men form a tribunal to whose opinion the judges are sensitive, and all the more sensitive because the judges, like those of England, but unlike those of continental Europe, have been themselves practising counsel.

---

it in the year 1854 by the Kansas-Nebraska legislation. Decisions have been given on the Fourteenth and Fifteenth Amendments upsetting or qualifying congressional legislation passed years before.

[4] See Chapter 37 *post*. There exists a similar provision in the statute of 1875, creating the Supreme Court of Canada, and the Government of Ireland Bill, introduced into the House of Commons in 1886, but defeated there, contained (§ 25) a provision enabling the Lord-Lieutenant of Ireland or a secretary of state to refer a question for opinion to the judicial committee of the Privy Council. In the Home Rule Bill of 1893 this provision reappeared in the modified form of a power to obtain, in urgent cases, the opinion of the Judicial Committee on the constitutionality of an act passed by the Irish legislature.

[5] The president sometimes, for the benefit of the public, publishes the written opinion of the attorney general on an important and doubtful point; but such an opinion has authority only as a direction to executive officials, giving them guidance in the discharge of their duties.

[6] Each house has a Judiciary Committee which sometimes reports on the constitutional aspect of a bill.

The better lawyers of the United States do not sink their professional sentiment and opinion in their party sympathies. They know good law even when it goes against themselves, and privately condemn as bad law a decision none the less because it benefits their party or their client. The federal judge who has recently quitted the ranks of the bar remains in sympathy with it, respects its views, desires its approbation. Both his inbred professional habits, and his respect for those traditions which the bar prizes, restrain him from prostituting his office to party objects. Though he has usually been a politician, and owes his promotion to his party, his political trappings drop off him when he mounts the supreme bench. He has now nothing to fear from party displeasure, because he is irremovable (except by impeachment), nothing to hope from party favour, because he is at the top of the tree and can climb no higher. Virtue has all the external conditions in her favour. It is true that virtue is compatible with a certain bias of the mind, and compatible also with the desire to extend the power and jurisdiction of the court. But even allowing that this motive may occasionally sway the judicial mind, the circumstances which surround the action of a tribunal debarred from initiative, capable of dealing only with concrete cases that come before it at irregular intervals, unable to appropriate any of the sweets of power other than power itself, make a course of systematic usurpation more difficult and less seductive than it would be to a legislative assembly or an executive council. As the respect of the bench for the bar tends to keep the judges in the straight path, so the respect and regard of the bar for the bench, a regard grounded on the sense of professional brotherhood, ensure the moral influence of the court in the country. The bar has usually been very powerful in America, not only as being the only class of educated men who are at once men of affairs and skilled speakers, but also because there has been no nobility or territorial aristocracy to overshadow it.[7] Politics have been largely in its hands, and must remain so as long as political questions continue to be involved with the interpretation of constitutions. For the first sixty or seventy years of the Republic the leading statesmen were lawyers, and the lawyers as a whole moulded and led the public opinion of the country. Now to the better class of American lawyers law was a sacred science, and the highest court which dispensed it a sort of Mecca, towards which the faces of the faithful turned. Hence every constitutional case before the Supreme Court was closely watched, the reasonings of the Court studied, and its decisions appreciated as law apart

---

[7] See Chapter 104 *post*. Professional interest, stronger in the last generation than it is now, would seem to be still declining.

from their bearing on political doctrines. I have heard elderly men describe the interest with which, in their youth, a famous advocate who had gone to Washington to argue a case before the Supreme Court was welcomed by the bar of his own city on his return, how the rising men crowded round him to hear what he had to tell of the combat in that arena where the best intellects of the nation strove, how the respect which he never failed to express for the ability and impartiality of the Court communicated itself to them, how admiration bred acquiescence, and the whole profession accepted expositions of the law unexpected by many, perhaps unwelcome to most. When it was felt that the judges had honestly sought to expound the Constitution, and when the cogency of their reasoning was admitted, resentment, if any there had been, passed away, and the support which the bar gave to the Court ensured the obedience of the people.

That this factor in the maintenance of judicial influence proved so potent was largely due to the personal eminence of the judges. One must not call that a result of fortune which was the result of the wisdom of successive presidents in choosing capable men to sit on the supreme federal bench. Yet one man was so singularly fitted for the office of chief justice, and rendered such incomparable services in it, that the Americans have been wont to regard him as a special gift of favouring Providence. This was John Marshall, who presided over the Supreme Court from 1801 till his death in 1835 at the age of seventy-seven, and whose fame overtops that of all other American judges more than Papinian overtops the jurists of Rome or Lord Mansfield the jurists of England. No other man did half so much either to develop the Constitution by expounding it, or to secure for the judiciary its rightful place in the government as the living voice of the Constitution. No one vindicated more strenuously the duty of the Court to establish the authority of the fundamental law of the land, no one abstained more scrupulously from trespassing on the field of executive administration or political controversy. The admiration and respect which he and his colleagues won for the Court remain its bulwark. The traditions which were formed under him and them have continued in general to guide the action and elevate the sentiments of their successors.

Nevertheless, the Court has not always had smooth seas to navigate. It has more than once been shaken by blasts of unpopularity. It has not infrequently found itself in conflict with other authorities.

The first attacks arose out of its decision that it had jurisdiction to entertain suits by private persons against a state.[8] This point was set at rest by the

---

[8] *Chisholm* v. *Georgia*, see above, pp. 209–10.

Eleventh Amendment; but the states then first learnt to fear the Supreme Court as an antagonist. In 1801, in an application requiring the secretary of state to deliver a commission, it declared itself to have the power to compel an executive officer to fulfill a ministerial duty affecting the rights of individuals.[9] President Jefferson protested angrily against this claim, but it has been repeatedly reasserted, and is now undoubted law. It was in this same case that the Court first explicitly asserted its duty to treat as invalid an act of Congress inconsistent with the Constitution. In 1805 its independence was threatened by the impeachment of Justice Chase, the aim of the Republican (Democratic) party then dominant in Congress being to set a precedent for ejecting, by means of impeachment, judges (and especially Chief Justice Marshall), whose attitude on constitutional questions they condemned. The acquittal of Chase dispelled this danger; nor could John Randolph, who then led the House, secure the acceptance of an amendment to the Constitution which he thereupon proposed for enabling the president to remove federal judges on an address of both houses of Congress. In 1806 the Court for the first time pronounced a state statute void; in 1816 and 1821 it rendered decisions establishing its authority as a supreme court of appeal from state courts on "federal questions," and unfolding the full meaning of the doctrine that the Constitution and acts of Congress duly made in pursuance of the Constitution are the fundamental and supreme law of the land. This was a doctrine which had not been adequately apprehended even by lawyers, and its development, legitimate as we now deem it, roused opposition. The Democratic party which came into power under President Jackson in 1829, were specially hostile to a construction of the Constitution which seemed to trench upon states' rights,[10] and when in 1832 the Supreme Court ordered the state of Georgia to release persons imprisoned under a Georgian statute which the court declared to be invalid,[11] Jackson, whose duty it was to enforce the decision by the executive arm, remarked, "John Marshall has pronounced his judgment: let him enforce it if he can." The

---

[9] *Marbury* v. *Madison*, 1 Cranch, 137. In this case the court refused to issue the mandamus asked for, but upon the ground that the statute of Congress giving to the Supreme Court original jurisdiction to issue a mandamus was inconsistent with the Constitution. See also *Kendal* v. *United States*, 12 Peters, 616; *United States* v. *Schurz*, 102 U.S. 378.

[10] Martin van Buren (president 1837–41) expressed the feelings of the bulk of his party when he complained bitterly of the encroachments of the Supreme Court, and declared that it would never have been created had the people foreseen the powers it would acquire.

[11] This was only one act in the long struggle of the Cherokee Indians against the oppressive conduct of Georgia—conduct which the court emphatically condemned, though it proved powerless to help the unhappy Cherokees.

successful resistance of Georgia in the Cherokee dispute[12] gave a temporary, though only a temporary, blow to the authority of the Court, and marked the beginning of a new period in its history, during which, in the hands of judges mostly appointed by the Democratic party, it made no further advance in power.

In 1857 the Dred Scott judgment, pronounced by a majority of the judges, excited the strongest outbreak of displeasure yet witnessed. The Republican party, then rising into strength, denounced this decision in the resolutions of the convention which nominated Abraham Lincoln in 1860, and its doctrine as to citizenship was expressly negatived in the fourteenth constitutional amendment adopted after the War of Secession.

It was feared that the political leanings of the judges who formed the court at the outbreak of the war would induce them to throw legal difficulties in the prosecution of the measures needed for reestablishing the authority of the Union. These fears proved ungrounded, although some contests arose as to the right of officers in the Federal army to disregard writs of habeas corpus issued by the Court.[13] In 1868, having then become Republican in its sympathies by the appointment of new members as the older judges disappeared, it tended to sustain the congressional plan of reconstruction which President Johnson was endeavouring to defeat, and in subsequent cases it has given effect to most, though not to all, of the statutes passed by Congress under the three amendments which abolished slavery and secured the rights of the Negroes. In 1866 it refused to entertain proceedings instituted for the purpose of forbidding the president to execute the Reconstruction Acts.

Two of its later acts are thought by some to have affected public confidence. One of these was the reversal, first in 1871, and again, upon broader but not inconsistent grounds, in 1884, of the decision, given in 1870, which declared invalid the act of Congress making government paper a legal tender for debts. The original decision of 1870 was rendered by a majority of five to three. The Court was afterwards changed by the creation of an additional judgeship,[14] and by the appointment of a new member to

---

[12] The matter did not come to an absolute conflict, because before the time arrived for the court to direct the United States marshal of the district of Georgia to summon the *posse comitatus* and the president to render assistance in liberating the prisoners, the prisoners submitted to the state authorities, and were thereupon released. They probably believed that the imperious Jackson would persist in his hostility to the Supreme Court. No succeeding president has ever ventured to talk of defying the Court.

[13] See *Ex parte Milligan*, 4 Wall. 129.

[14] Appointed, however, under an act passed in April 1869.

fill a vacancy which occurred after the settlement, though before the delivery of the first decision. Then the question was brought up again in a new case between different parties, and decided in the opposite sense (i.e., in favour of the power of Congress to pass legal tender acts) by a majority of five to four. Finally, in 1884, another suit having brought up a point practically the same though under a later statute passed by Congress, the court determined with only one dissentient voice that the power existed.[15] This last decision excited some criticism, especially among the more conservative lawyers, because it seemed to remove restrictions hitherto supposed to exist on the authority of Congress, recognizing the right to establish a forced paper currency as an attribute of the sovereignty of the national government. But be the decision right or wrong, the reversal by the highest court in the land of its own previous decision may have tended to unsettle men's reliance on the stability of the law; while the manner of the earlier reversal, following as it did on the creation of a new judgeship and the appointment of two new justices, both known to be in favour of the view which the majority of the court had just disapproved, though apparently not appointed for that reason, disclosed a weak point in the constitution of the tribunal which may some day prove fatal to its usefulness.

The other misfortune was the interposition of the court in the presidential electoral dispute of 1877.[16] The five justices of the Supreme Court who were included in the electoral commission then appointed voted on party lines no less steadily than did the senators and representatives who sat on it. A function scarcely judicial, and certainly not contemplated by the Constitution, was then for the first time thrown upon the judiciary, and in discharging it the judiciary acted exactly like nonjudicial persons.

Notwithstanding this occurrence, which after all was quite exceptional, the credit and dignity of the Supreme Court stand very high. No one of its members has ever been suspected of corruption, and comparatively few have allowed their political sympathies to disturb their official judgment. Though for many years before 1909 every president has appointed only men of his own party, and frequently leading politicians of his own party,[17] each

[15] The earlier decision in favour of the power deduced it from war powers, the later from the general sovereignty of the national government. See *Hepburn* v. *Griswold*, 8 Wall. 603; *Legal Tender Cases*, 12 Wall. 457; *Juilliard* v. *Greenman*, 110 U.S. 421.

[16] See above, Chapter 5.

[17] President Taft (1909–13) appointed several persons to be judges who did not belong to his own party, the other party having at the time very few representatives on the supreme bench. Nonpolitical appointments are occasionally made in the several states by the governors, or even (as in the case of Chief Justice Redfield of Vermont) by the legislature.

new-made judge has left partisanship behind him, while no doubt usually retaining that bias or tendency of his mind which party training produces. When a large majority of judges belong to one party, the other party regret the fact, and welcome the prospect of putting in some of their own men as vacancies occur; yet the desire for an equal representation of both parties is based, not on a fear that suitors will suffer from the influence of party spirit, but on the feeling that when any new constitutional question arises it is right that the tendencies which have characterized the view of the Constitution taken by the Democrats on the one hand and the Republicans on the other, should each be duly represented.

Apart from these constitutional questions, the value of the federal courts to the country at large has been inestimable. They have done much to meet the evils which an elective and ill-paid state judiciary inflicts on some of the newer and a few even of the older states. The federal Circuit and District judges, small as are their salaries, are in most states individually superior men to the state judges, because the greater security of tenure induces abler men to accept the post. They exercise a wider power of changing the jury than most states allow to their judges. Being irremovable, they feel themselves independent of parties and politicians, whom the elected state judge, holding for a limited term, may be tempted to conciliate with a view to reelection. Plaintiffs, therefore, when they have a choice of suing in a state court or a federal court, frequently prefer the latter; and the litigant who belongs to a foreign country, or to a different state from that in which his opponent resides, may think his prospects of an unbiased decision better before it than before a state tribunal. Nor is it without interest to add that criminal justice is more strictly administered in the federal courts.

Federal judgeships of the second and third rank (Circuit and District) have been hitherto given to the members of the president's party, and by an equally well-established usage, to persons resident in the state or states where the Circuit or District Court is held. In 1891, however, a Republican president appointed two Democrats to be judges of the new Circuit Court of Appeals, and placed several Democrats on the (temporary) Private Land Claims Court. Cases of corruption are practically unknown, and partisanship, or subservience to powerful local interests, though sometimes charged, is infrequent. The chief defects have been the inadequacy of the salaries, and the insufficiency of the staff in the more populous commercial states to grapple with the vast and increasing business which flows in upon them. So too, in the Supreme Court, arrears have so accumulated that it is now more than three years from the time when a cause is entered till the day when it comes on for hearing. Some have proposed to meet this evil by limiting the right of appeal to cases involving a considerable sum of money; others would divide the Supreme Court into two divisional courts for the hearing of ordinary suits, reserving for the full court points affecting the construction of the Constitution.

One question remains to be put and answered.

The Supreme Court is the living voice of the Constitution,[18] that is, of the will of the people expressed in the fundamental law they have enacted. It is, therefore, as someone has said, the conscience of the people, who have resolved to restrain themselves from hasty or unjust action by placing their representatives under the restriction of a permanent law. It is the guarantee of the minority, who, when threatened by the impatient vehemence of a majority, can appeal to this permanent law, finding the interpreter and enforcer thereof in a court set high above the assaults of faction.

To discharge these momentous functions, the Court must be stable even as the Constitution is stable. Its spirit and tone must be that of the people at their best moments. It must resist transitory impulses, and resist them the more firmly the more vehement they are. Entrenched behind impregnable ramparts, it must be able to defy at once the open attacks of the other departments of the government, and the more dangerous, because impalpable, seductions of popular sentiment.

Does it possess, has it displayed, this strength and stability?

It has not always followed its own former decisions. This is natural in a court whose errors cannot be cured by the intervention of the legislature. The English final Court of Appeal always follows its previous decisions, though high authorities have declared that cases may be imagined in which it would refuse to do so. And that court (the House of Lords) can afford so to adhere, because, when an old decision begins to be condemned, Parliament can forthwith alter the law. But as nothing less than a constitutional amendment can alter the law contained in the federal Constitution, the Supreme Court must choose between the evil of unsettling the law by reversing, and the evil of perpetuating bad law by following, a former decision. It may reasonably, in extreme cases, deem the latter evil the greater.

The Supreme Court feels the touch of public opinion. Opinion is stronger

---

[18] The Romans called their chief judicial officer the prætor, "the living voice of the civil law"; but as this "civil law" consisted largely of custom, he naturally enjoyed a wider discretion in moulding and expanding as well as in expounding the law than do the American judges, who have a formally enacted constitution to guide and restrain them.

in America than anywhere else in the world, and judges are only men. To yield a little may be prudent, for the tree that cannot bend to the blast may be broken. There is, moreover, this ground at least for presuming public opinion to be right, that through it the progressive judgment of the world is expressed. Of course, whenever the law is clear, because the words of the Constitution are plain or the cases interpreting them decisive on the point raised, the court must look solely to those words and cases, and cannot permit any other consideration to affect its mind. But when the terms of the Constitution admit of more than one construction, and when previous decisions have left the true construction so far open that the point in question may be deemed new, is a court to be blamed if it prefers the construction which the bulk of the people deem suited to the needs of the time? A court is sometimes so swayed consciously, more often unconsciously, because the pervasive sympathy of numbers is irresistible even by elderly lawyers. A remarkable example is furnished by the decisions (in 1876) of the Supreme Court in the so-called Granger cases, suits involving the power of a state to subject railways and other corporations or persons exercising what are called "public trades" to restrictive legislation without making pecuniary compensation.[19] These decisions evidently represent a different view of the sacredness of private rights and of the powers of a legislature from that entertained by Chief Justice Marshall and his contemporaries. They reveal that current of opinion which now runs strongly in America against what are called monopolies and the powers of incorporated companies.

The Supreme Court has changed its colour, i.e., its temper and tendencies, from time to time, according to the political proclivities of the men who composed it. It changes very slowly, because the vacancies in a small body happen rarely, and its composition therefore often represents the predominance of a past and not of the presently ruling party. From 1789 down till the death of Chief Justice Marshall in 1835 its tendency was to the extension of the powers of the federal government and therewith of its own jurisdiction, because the ruling spirits in it were men who belonged to the old Federalist party, though that party fell in 1800, and disappeared

---

[19] See *Munn* v. *Illinois*, and the following cases in 94 U.S. Rep. 193 (with which compare *C. M. & St. P. R. R. Co.* v. *Minn.*, 134 U.S. 418; and *Budd* v. *N. Y.*, 12 S.C. Reporter, 648). This was one of those cases in which the Court felt bound to regard not only the view which it took itself of the meaning of the Constitution but that which a legislature might reasonably take.— See Chapter 34 *post*. As to the nonliability to make compensation where licences for the sale of intoxicants are forbidden, see *Mugler* v. *Kansas*, 123 U.S. Rep. 623.

I abstain from referring to more recent cases lest I should seem to be approaching a field at present highly controversial.

in 1814. From 1835 till the War of Secession its sympathies were with the doctrines of the Democratic party. Without actually abandoning the positions of the previous period, the Court, during these years when Chief Justice Taney presided over it, leant against any further extension of federal power or of its own jurisdiction. During and after the war, when the ascendency of the Republican party had begun to change the composition of the Court, a third period opened. Centralizing ideas were again powerful: the vast war powers asserted by Congress were in most instances supported by judicial decision; the rights of states while maintained (as in the Granger cases) as against private persons or bodies, were for a time regarded with less favour whenever they seemed to conflict with those of the federal government. In none of these three periods can the judges be charged with any prostitution of their functions to party purposes. Their action flowed naturally from the habits of thought they had formed before their accession to the bench, and from the sympathy they could not but feel with the doctrines on whose behalf they had contended. Even on the proverbially upright and impartial bench of England the same tendencies may be discerned. There are constitutional questions, and questions touching what may be called the policy of the law, which would be decided differently by one English judge or by another, not from any conscious wish to favour a party or a class, but because the views which a man holds as a citizen cannot fail to colour his judgment even on legal points.

The Fathers of the Constitution studied nothing more than to secure the complete independence of the judiciary. The president was not permitted to remove the judges, nor Congress to diminish their salaries. One thing only was either forgotten or deemed undesirable, because highly inconvenient, to determine, the number of judges in the Supreme Court. Here was a weak point, a joint in the Court's armour through which a weapon might some day penetrate. Congress having in 1801, pursuant to a power contained in the Constitution, established sixteen Circuit Courts, President Adams, immediately before he quit office, appointed members of his own party to the justiceships thus created. When President Jefferson came in, he refused to admit the validity of the appointments; and the newly elected Congress, which was in sympathy with him, abolished the Circuit Courts themselves, since it could find no other means of ousting the new justices. This method of attack, whose constitutionality has been much doubted, cannot be used against the Supreme Court, because that tribunal is directly created by the Constitution. But as the Constitution does not prescribe the number of justices, a statute may increase or diminish the number as Congress thinks fit. In 1866, when Congress was in fierce antagonism to President Johnson, and desired to prevent him from appointing any judges, it reduced the number, which was then ten, by a statute providing that no vacancy should be filled up till the number was reduced to seven. In 1869, when Johnson had been succeeded by Grant, the number was raised to nine, and presently the altered court allowed the question of the validity of the Legal Tender Act, just before determined, to be reopened. This method is plainly susceptible of further and possibly dangerous application. Suppose a Congress and president bent on doing something which the Supreme Court deems contrary to the Constitution. They pass a statute. A case arises under it. The Court on the hearing of the case unanimously declares the statute to be null, as being beyond the powers of Congress. Congress forthwith passes and the president signs another statute more than doubling the number of the justices. The president appoints to the new justiceships men who are pledged to hold the former statute constitutional. The Senate confirms his appointments. Another case raising the validity of the disputed statute is brought up to the court. The new justices outvote the old ones; the statute is held valid; the security provided for the protection of the Constitution is gone like a morning mist.

What prevents such assaults on the fundamental law—assaults which, however immoral in substance, would be perfectly legal in form? Not the mechanism of government, for all its checks have been evaded. Not the conscience of the legislature and the president, for heated combatants seldom shrink from justifying the means by the end. Nothing but the fear of the people, whose broad good sense and attachment to the great principles of the Constitution may generally be relied on to condemn such a perversion of its forms. Yet if excitement has risen high over the country, a majority of the people may acquiesce; and then it matters little whether what is really a revolution be accomplished by openly violating or by merely distorting the forms of law. To the people we come sooner or later: it is upon their wisdom and self-restraint that the stability of the most cunningly devised scheme of government will in the last resort depend.

Comparison of the American and European Systems

The relations to one another of the different branches of the government in the United States are so remarkable and so full of instruction for other countries, that it seems desirable, even at the risk of a little repetition, to show by a comparison with the cabinet or parliamentary system of European countries how this complex American machinery actually works.

The English system on which have been modelled, of course with many variations, the systems of France, Belgium, Holland, Italy, Germany, Hungary (where, however, the English scheme has been compounded with an ancient and very interesting native-born constitution), Sweden, Norway, Denmark, Spain, and Portugal, as well as the constitutions of the great self-governing English colonies in North America, the Cape, and Australasia— this English system places at the head of the state a person in whose name all executive acts are done, and who is (except in France) irresponsible and irremovable.[1] His acts are done by the advice and on the responsibility of ministers chosen nominally by him, but really by the representatives of the people, usually, but not necessarily, from among the members of the legislature. The representatives are, therefore, through the agents whom they select, the true government of the country. When the representative assembly ceases to trust these agents, the latter (unless they dissolve the legislature) resign, and a new set are appointed. Thus the executive as well as the legislative power really belongs to the majority of the representative chamber, though in appointing agents, an expedient which its size makes needful, it is forced to leave in the hands of these agents a measure of

---

[1] In the German Empire the ministers are comparatively independent of the Reichstag, i.e., it cannot displace them by a hostile vote as the British House of Commons practically can. In the British colonies the governor is irremovable by the colony, and irresponsible to its legislature, though responsible to and removable by the home government.

discretion sufficient to make them appear distinct from it, and sometimes to tempt them to acts which their masters disapprove. As the legislature is thus in a sense executive, so the executive government, the council of ministers or cabinet, is in so far legislative that the initiation of measures rests very largely with them, and the carrying of measures through the chamber demands their advocacy and counter pressure upon the majority of the representatives. They are not merely executive agents but also legislative leaders. One may say, indeed, that the legislative and executive functions are interwoven as closely under this system as under absolute monarchies, such as Imperial Rome or modern Russia; and the fact that taxation, while effected by means of legislation, is the indispensable engine of administration, shows how inseparable are these two apparently distinct powers.

Under this system the sovereignty of the legislature may be more or less complete. It is most complete in France; least complete in Germany and Prussia, where the power of the emperor and king has remained great. But in all these countries not only are the legislature and executive in close touch with one another, but they settle their disputes without reference to the judiciary. The courts of law cannot be invoked by the executive against the legislature, because questions involving the validity of a legislative act do not come before it, since the legislature is either completely sovereign, as in England, or the judge of its own competence, as in Belgium. The judiciary, in other words, does not enter into the consideration of the political part of the machinery of government.

This system of so-called cabinet government seems to Europeans now, who observe it at work over a large part of the world, an obvious and simple system. We are apt to forget that it was never seen anywhere till the English developed it by slow degrees, and that it is a very delicate system, depending on habits, traditions, and understandings which are not easily set forth in words, much less transplanted to a new soil.

We are also prone to forget how very recent it is. People commonly date it from the reign of King William III; but it worked very irregularly till the Hanoverian kings came to the throne, and even then it at first worked by means of a monstrous system of bribery and placemongering. In the days of George III the personal power of the Crown for a while revived and corruption declined.[2] The executive head of the state was, during the latter

---

[2] Corruption was possible, because the House of Commons did not look for support to the nation, its debates were scantily reported, it had little sense of responsibility. An active king was therefore able to assert himself against it, and to form a party in it, as well as outside of it, which regarded him as its head. This forced the Whigs to throw themselves upon the nation at large; the Tories

decades of the century, a factor apart from his ministers. They were not then, as now, a mere committee of Parliament dependent upon Parliament, but rather a compromise between the king's will and the will of the parliamentary majority. They deemed and declared themselves to owe a duty to the king conflicting with, sometimes overriding, their duty to Parliament. Those phrases of abasement before the Crown which when now employed by prime ministers amuse us by their remoteness from the realities of the case, then expressed realities. In 1787, when the Constitutional Convention met at Philadelphia, the cabinet system of government was in England still immature. It was so immature that its true nature had not been perceived.[3] And although we now can see that the tendency was really towards the depression of the Crown and the exaltation of Parliament, men might well, when they compared the influence of George III with that exercised by George I,[4] argue in the terms of Dunning's famous resolution, that "the power of the Crown has increased, is increasing, and ought to be diminished."[5]

did the same; corruption withered away; and as Parliament came more and more under the watchful eye of the people, and responsible to it, the influence of the king declined and vanished.

[3] Gouverneur Morris, however, one of the acutest minds in the Convention of 1787, remarked there, "Our President will be the British (Prime) Minister. If Mr. Fox had carried his India Bill, he would have made the Minister the King in form almost as well as in substance."—Elliot's *Debates*, vol. i, 361. Roger Sherman, though he saw the importance of the cabinet, looked on it as a mere engine in the Crown's hands. "The nation," he observed, in the Convention of 1787, "is in fact governed by the Cabinet council, who are the creatures of the Crown. The consent of Parliament is necessary to give sanction to their measures, and this they easily obtain by the influence of the Crown in appointing to all offices of honour and profit." It must be remembered that the House of Lords was far more powerful in 1787 than it now is, not only as a branch of the legislature, but in respect of the boroughs owned by the leading peers; and therefore the dependence of the ministry on the House of Commons was a less prominent feature of the Constitution than it is now.

[4] George III had the advantage of being a national king, whereas his two predecessors had been Germans by language and habits as well as by blood. His popularity contributed to his influence in politics. Mrs. Papendiek's Diary contains some amusing illustrations of the exuberant demonstrations of "loyalty" which he excited. When he went to Weymouth for sea bathing after his recovery from the first serious attack of lunacy, crowds gathered along the shore, and bands of music struck up "God Save the King" when he ducked his head beneath the brine.

[5] It is not easy to say when the principle of the absolute dependence of ministers on a parliamentary majority without regard to the wishes of the Crown passed into a settled doctrine. (Needless to say that it has received no formally legal recognition, but is merely usage.) The long coincidence during the dominance of Pitt and his Tory successors down till 1827 of the wishes and interests of the Crown with those of the parliamentary majority prevented the question from arising in a practical shape. Even in 1827 Mr. Canning writes to J. W. Croker:

"Am I to understand, then, that you consider the King [George IV] as completely in the hands of the Tory aristocracy as his father, or rather as George II was in the hands of the Whigs? If so, George III reigned and Mr. Pitt (both father and son) administered the Government in vain. I

The greatest problem that free peoples have to solve is how to enable the citizens at large to conduct or control the executive business of the state. England was in 1787 the only nation (the cantons of Switzerland were so small as scarcely to be thought of) that had solved this problem, first, by the development of a representative system, secondly, by giving to her representatives a large authority over the executive. The Constitutional Convention, therefore, turned its eyes to her when it sought to constitute a free government for the new nation which the "more perfect union" of the states was calling into conscious being.

Very few of the members of the Convention had been in England so as to know her Constitution, such as it then was, at first hand. Yet there were three sources whence light fell upon it, and for that light they were grateful. One was their experience in dealing with the mother country since the quarrel began. They saw in Britain an executive largely influenced by the personal volitions of the king, and in its conduct of colonial and foreign affairs largely detached from and independent of Parliament, since it was able to take tyrannical steps without the previous knowledge or consent of Parliament, and able afterwards to defend those steps by alleging a necessity whereof Parliament, wanting confidential information, could imperfectly judge. It was in these colonial and foreign affairs that the power of the Crown chiefly lay (as, indeed, to this day the authority of Parliament over the executive is smaller here than in any other department, because secrecy and promptitude are more essential), so they could not be expected to know for how much less the king counted in domestic affairs. Moreover, there was believed to be often a secret junto which really controlled the ministry, because acting in concert with the Crown; and the Crown had powerful engines at its disposal, bribes and honours, pensions and places, engines irresistible by the average virtue of representatives whose words and votes were not reported, and nearly half of whom were the nominees of some magnate.[6]

The second source was the legal presentation of the English Constitution in scientific textbooks, and particularly in Blackstone, whose famous *Commentaries*, first published in 1765 (their substance having been delivered as professional lectures at Oxford in 1758 and several succeeding years),

have a better opinion of the real vigour of the Crown when it chooses to put forth its own strength, and I am not without some reliance on the body of the people!"—*Croker Correspondence*, vol. i, p. 368.

[6] George III had pocket boroughs and a strong parliamentary following. Hamilton doubted whether the British Constitution could be worked without corruption.

had quickly become the standard authority on the subject. Now Blackstone, as is natural in a lawyer who looks rather to the strict letter of the law than to the practice which had grown up modifying it, describes the royal prerogative in terms more appropriate to the days of the Stuarts than to those in which he wrote, and dwells on the independence of the executive, while also declaring the withholding from it of legislative power to be essential to freedom.[7]

The third source was the view of the English Constitution given by the political philosophers of the eighteenth century, among whom, since he was by far the most important, we need look at Montesquieu alone.

When the famous treatise on *The Spirit of Laws* appeared in 1748, a treatise belonging to the small class of books which permanently turn the course of human thought, and which, unlike St. Augustine's *City of God*, turned it immediately instead of having to wait for centuries till the hour of its power arrived, it dwelt upon the separation of the executive, legislative, and judicial powers in the British Constitution as the most remarkable feature of that system. Accustomed to see the two former powers, and to some extent the third also, exercised by or under the direct control of the French monarch, Montesquieu attributed English freedom to their separation.[8] The king of Great Britain then possessed a larger prerogative than he has now, and as even then it seemed on paper much larger than it really was, it was natural that a foreign observer should underrate the executive character of the British Parliament and overrate the personal authority of the monarch. Now Montesquieu's treatise was taken by the thinkers of the next generation as a sort of Bible of political philosophy. Hamilton and Madison, the two

[7] See Blackstone, *Commentaries*, bk. i, chap. ii.—"Whenever the power of making and that of enforcing the laws are united together, there can be no public liberty. . . . Where the legislative and executive authority are in distinct hands, the former will take care not to entrust the latter with so large a power as may tend to the subversion of its own independence, and therewith of the liberty of the subject. . . . The Crown cannot of itself begin any alteration in the present established law; but it may approve or disapprove of the alterations suggested and consented to by the two Houses. The legislative, therefore, cannot abridge the executive power of any rights which it now has by law without its own consent." There is no hint here, or in chap. vii on the royal prerogative, that the royal power of disapproval had not been in fact exercised for some fifty years. Blackstone does not quote Montesquieu for the particular proposition that the powers must be separated, but has evidently been influenced by him. A little later he cites a famous dictum, "The President Montesquieu, though I trust too hastily, presages that as Rome, Sparta, and Carthage have lost their liberty and perished, so the Constitution of England will in time lose its liberty—will perish: it will perish whenever the legislative power shall become more corrupt than the executive."

[8] Locke had already remarked (*On Civil Government*, chap. xiv) that "the legislative and executive powers are in distinct hands in all moderated monarchies and well-framed governments."

earliest exponents of the American Constitution they had done so much to create, cite it in the *Federalist* much as the schoolmen cite Aristotle, that is, as an authority to which everybody will bow; and Madison in particular constantly refers to this separation of the legislative, executive, and judicial powers as the distinguishing note of a free government.

These views of the British Constitution tallied with and were strengthened by the ideas and habits formed in the Americans by their experience of representative government in the colonies, ideas and habits which were after all the dominant factor in the construction of their political system. In these colonies the executive power had been vested either in a governor sent from England by the Crown, or in certain Proprietors, to whom the English Crown had granted hereditary rights in a province. Each representative assembly, while it made laws and voted money for the purposes of its respective commonwealth, did not control the governor, because his commission issued from the British Crown, and he was responsible thereto. A governor had no parliamentary cabinet, but only officials responsible to himself and the Crown. His veto on acts of the colonial legislature was frequently used; and that body, with no means of controlling his conduct other than the refusal to vote money, was a legislature and nothing more. Thus the Americans found and admired in their colonial (or state) systems, a separation of the legislative from the executive branch, more complete than in England; and being already proud of their freedom, they attributed its amplitude chiefly to this cause.

From their colonial and state experience, coupled with these notions of the British Constitution, the men of 1787 drew three conclusions: First, that the vesting of the executive and the legislative powers in different hands was the normal and natural feature of a free government; secondly, that the power of the executive was dangerous to liberty, and must be kept within well-defined boundaries; thirdly, that in order to check the head of the state it was necessary not only to define his powers, and appoint him for a limited period, but also to destroy his opportunities of influencing the legislature. Conceiving that ministers, as named by and acting under the orders of the president, would be his instruments rather than faithful representatives of the people, they resolved to prevent them from holding this double character, and therefore forbade "any person holding office under the United States" to be a member of either house.[9] They deemed that in this way they had

[9] In 1700 the English Act of Settlement enacted that "no person who has an office or a place of profit under the King shall be capable of serving as a member of the House of Commons." This provision never took effect, having been repealed by the Act 4 Anne, c. 8. But the holding of the

rendered their legislature pure, independent, vigilant, the servant of the people, the foe of arbitrary power. Omnipotent, however, the framers of the Constitution did not mean to make it. They were sensible of the opposite dangers which might flow from a feeble and dependent executive. The proposal made in the first draft of the Constitution that Congress should elect the president, was abandoned, lest he should be merely its creature and unable to check it. To strengthen his position, and prevent intrigues among members of Congress for this supreme office, it was settled that the people should themselves, through certain electors appointed for the purpose, choose the president. By giving him the better status of a popular, though indirect, mandate, he became independent of Congress, and was encouraged to use his veto, which a mere nominee of Congress might have hesitated to do. Thus it was believed in 1787 that a due balance had been arrived at, the independence of Congress being secured on the one side and the independence of the president on the other. Each power holding the other in check, the people, jealous of their hardly won liberties, would be courted by each, and safe from the encroachments of either.

There was of course the risk that controversies as to their respective rights and powers would arise between these two departments. But the creation of a court entitled to place an authoritative interpretation upon the Constitution in which the supreme will of the people was expressed, provided a remedy available in many, if not in all, of such cases, and a security for the faithful observance of the Constitution which England did not, and under her system of an omnipotent Parliament could not, possess.

"They builded better than they knew." They divided the legislature from the executive so completely as to make each not only independent, but weak even in its own proper sphere. The president was debarred from carrying Congress along with him, as a popular prime minister may carry Parliament in England, to effect some sweeping change. He is fettered in foreign policy, and in appointments, by the concurrent rights of the Senate. He is forbidden to appeal at a crisis from Congress to the country. Nevertheless his office retains a measure of solid independence in the fact that the nation regards him as a direct representative and embodiment of its majesty, while the circumstance that he holds office for four years only makes it possible for him to do acts of power during those four years which would excite alarm from a permanent sovereign. Entrenched behind the ramparts of a rigid

---

great majority of offices under the Crown is now, by statute, a disqualification for sitting in the House of Commons. See Anson, *Law and Custom of the Constitution*, vol. i, p. 174.

Constitution, he has retained rights of which his prototype the English king has been gradually stripped. Congress on the other hand was weakened, as compared with the British Parliament in which one house has become dominant, by its division into two coequal houses, whose disagreement paralyzes legislative action. And it lost that direct control over the executive which the presence of ministers in the legislature, and their dependence upon a majority of the popular House, give to the Parliaments of Britain and her colonies. It has diverged widely from the English original which it seemed likely, with only a slight difference, to reproduce.

The British House of Commons has grown to the stature of a supreme executive as well as legislative council, acting not only by its properly legislative power, but through its right to displace ministers by a resolution of want of confidence, and to compel the sovereign to employ such servants as it approves. Congress remains a pure legislature, unable to displace a minister, unable to choose the agents by whom its laws are to be carried out, and having hitherto failed to develop that internal organization which a large assembly needs in order to frame and successfully pursue definite schemes of policy. Nevertheless, so far-reaching is the power of legislation, Congress has encroached, and may encroach still farther, upon the sphere of the executive. It encroaches not merely with a conscious purpose, but because the law of its being has forced it to create in its committees bodies whose expansion necessarily presses on the executive. It encroaches because it is restless, unwearied, always drawn by the progress of events into new fields of labour.

These observations may suffice to show why the Fathers of the Constitution did not adopt the English parliamentary or cabinet system. They could not adopt it because they did not know of its existence. They did not know of it because it was still immature, because Englishmen themselves had not understood it, because the recognized authorities did not mention it. There is not a word in Blackstone, much less in Montesquieu, as to the duty of ministers to resign at the bidding of the House of Commons, nor anything to indicate that the whole life of the House of Commons was destined to centre in the leadership of ministers. Whether the Fathers would have imitated the cabinet system had it been proposed to them as a model may be doubted. They would probably have thought that the creation of a frame of government so unified, so strong, so capable of swiftly and irresistibly accomplishing the purposes of a transitory majority as we now perceive it to be, might prove dangerous to those liberties of the several states, as well as of individual citizens, which filled the whole background of their landscape. But as the idea never presented itself, we cannot say that it was rejected, nor cite the course they took as an expression of their judgment against the system under which England and her colonies have so far prospered.

That system could not be deemed to have reached its maturity till the power of the people at large had been established by the Reform Act of 1832. For its essence resides in the delicate equipoise it creates between the three powers, the ministry, the House of Commons, and the people. The House is strong, because it can call the ministry to account for every act, and can, by refusing supplies, compel their resignation. The ministry are not defenceless, because they can dissolve Parliament, and ask the people to judge between it and them. Parliament, when it displaces a ministry, does not strike at executive authority; it merely changes its agents. The ministry, when they dissolve Parliament, do not attack Parliament as an institution; they recognize the supremacy of the body in asking the country to change the individuals who compose it. Both the House of Commons and the ministry act and move in the full view of the people, who sit as arbiters, prepared to judge in any controversy that may arise. The House is in touch with the people, because every member must watch the lights and shadows of sentiment which play over his own constituency. The ministry are in touch with the people, because they are not only themselves representatives, but are heads of a great party, sensitive to its feelings, forced to weigh the effect of every act they do upon the confidence which their party places in them. The only conjuncture which this system of "checks and balances" does not provide for is that of a ministry supported by a parliamentary majority pursuing a policy which was not presented to the people at the last general election, and of which the bulk of the people in fact disapprove.[10] This is a real danger, yet one which can seldom last long enough to work grave mischief, for the organs of public opinion are now so potent, and the opportunities for its expression so numerous, that the anger of a popular majority, perhaps even of a very strong minority, is likely to alarm both the ministry and the House, and to arrest them in their course.[11]

[10] A good example is furnished by Lord Beaconsfield's government from 1876 till 1880.

[11] "The dangers arising from a party spirit in Parliament exceeding that of the nation, and of a selfishness in Parliament contradicting the true interest of the nation, are not great dangers in a country where the mind of the nation is steadily political, and where its control over its representatives is constant. A steady opposition to a formed public opinion is hardly possible in our House of Commons, so incessant is the national attention to politics, and so keen the fear in the mind of each member that he may lose his valued seat."—Walter Bagehot, *English Constitution*, p. 241. These remarks of the most acute of English political writers written in 1872 are still true.

The drawback to this system of exquisite equipoise is the liability of its equilibrium to be frequently disturbed, each disturbance involving either a change of government, with immense temporary inconvenience to the departments, or a general election, with immense expenditure of money and trouble in the country. It is a system whose successful working presupposes the existence of two great parties and no more, parties each strong enough to restrain the violence of the other, yet one of them steadily preponderant in any given House of Commons. Where a third, perhaps a fourth, party appears, the conditions are changed. The scales of Parliament oscillate as the weight of this detached group is thrown on one side or the other; dissolutions become more frequent, and even dissolutions may fail to restore stability. The recent history of the Third French Republic has shown the difficulties of working a chamber composed of groups; and the same source of difficulty has more recently appeared in England.[12]

It is worth while to compare the form which a constitutional struggle takes under the cabinet system and under that of America.

In England, if the executive ministry displeases the House of Commons, the House passes an adverse vote. The ministry have their choice to resign or to dissolve Parliament. If they resign, a new ministry is appointed from the party which has proved itself strongest in the House of Commons; and cooperation being restored between the legislature and the executive, public business proceeds. If, on the other hand, the ministry dissolve Parliament, a new Parliament is sent up which, if favourable to the existing cabinet, keeps them in office, if unfavourable, dismisses them forthwith.[13] Accord is in either case restored. Should the difference arise between the House of Lords and a ministry supported by the House of Commons, and the former persist in rejecting a bill which the Commons send up, a dissolution is the constitutional remedy; and if the newly elected House of Commons reasserts the view of its predecessor, the Lords, according to the now recognized constitutional practice, yield at once. Should they, however, still stand out, there remains the extreme expedient, threatened in 1832, but never yet resorted to, of a creation by the sovereign (i.e., the ministry) of new peers sufficient to turn the balance of votes in the Upper House. Practically the

---

[12] An organized Third Party grew up in the House of Commons between 1874 and 1880, and an organized Fourth Party appeared in 1906.

[13] Recent instances, dating from Mr. Disraeli's resignation in December 1868, when the results of the election of that year were ascertained, have established the usage that a ministry quits office, without waiting to be turned out, when they know that the election has given a decisive majority to the opposition. The precedent was followed in 1874, 1880, and 1886, but not in 1885 and 1892, when the "regular" opposition had not an absolute majority, though the ministry was beaten. The usage, however, is not yet a rule of the Constitution.

ultimate decision always rests with the people, that is to say, with the party which for the moment commands a majority of electoral votes. This method of cutting knots applies to all differences that can arise between executive and legislature. It is a swift and effective method; in this swiftness and effectiveness lie its dangers as well as its merits.

In America a dispute between the president and Congress may arise over an executive act or over a bill. If over an executive act, an appointment or a treaty, one branch of Congress, the Senate, can check the president, that is, can prevent him from doing what he wishes, but cannot make him do what they wish. If over a bill which the president has returned to Congress unsigned, the two houses can, by a two-thirds majority, pass it over his veto, and so end the quarrel; though the carrying out of the bill in its details must be left to him and his ministers, whose dislike of it may render them unwilling and therefore unsuitable agents. Should there not be a two-thirds majority, the bill drops; and however important the question may be, however essential to the country some prompt dealing with it, either in the sense desired by the majority of Congress or in that preferred by the president, nothing can be done till the current term of Congress expires. The matter is then remitted to the people. If the president has still two more years in office, the people may signify their approval of his policy by electing a House in political agreement with him, or disapprove it by reelecting a hostile House. If the election of a new president coincides with that of the new House, the people have a second means provided of expressing their judgment. They may choose not only a House of the same or an opposite complexion to the last, but a president of the same or an opposite complexion. Anyhow they can now establish accord between one house of Congress and the executive.[14] The Senate, however, may still remain opposed to the president, and may not be brought into harmony with him until a sufficient time has elapsed for the majority in it to be changed by the choice of new senators by the state legislatures. This is a slower method than that of Britain. It may fail in a crisis needing immediate action; but it escapes the danger of a hurried and perhaps irrevocable decision.

Englishmen deem it a merit in their system that the practical executive

---

[14] It is of course possible that the people may elect at the same time a president belonging to one party and a House the majority whereof belongs to the other party. This happened in 1848, and again in 1876, when, however, the presidential election was disputed. It is rendered possible by the fact that the president is elected on a different plan from the House, the smaller states having relatively more weight in a presidential election, and the presidential electors being now chosen by "general ticket," not in districts.

of the country is directly responsible to the House of Commons. In the United States, however, not only in the national government, but in every one of the states, the opposite doctrine prevails—that the executive should be wholly independent of the legislative branch. Americans understand that this scheme involves a loss of power and efficiency, but they believe that it makes greatly for safety in a popular government. They expect the executive and the legislature to work together as well as they can, and public opinion does usually compel a degree of cooperation and efficiency which perhaps could not be expected theoretically. It is an interesting commentary on the tendencies of democratic government, that in America reliance is coming to be placed more and more, in the nation, in the state, and in the city, upon the veto of the executive as a protection to the community against the legislative branch. Weak executives frequently do harm, but a strong executive has rarely abused popular confidence. On the other hand, instances where the executive, by the use of his veto power, has arrested mischiefs due to the action of the legislature are by no means rare. This circumstance leads some Americans to believe that the day is not far distant when in England some sort of veto power, or other constitutional safeguard, must be interposed to protect the people against a hasty decision of their representatives.

While some bid England borrow from her daughter, other Americans (including two presidents), conceiving that the separation of the legislature from the executive has been carried too far in the United States, have suggested that the ministers of the president might be permitted to appear in both houses of Congress to answer questions, perhaps even to join in debate. It may be urged in support of this proposal that there is too much particularism in Congress and too strong a tendency to allow private moneyed "interests" to prevail against those general interests of the country as a whole which a British ministry is held bound to protect, and can by its command of the majority secure. But it might lead to changes more extensive than its advocates seem to contemplate. The more the president's ministers come into contact with Congress, the more difficult will it be to maintain the independence of Congress which he and they now possess. When, before the separation of Norway from Sweden, the Norwegian Stor Thing forced the king to consent to his ministers appearing in that legislature, the king, perceiving the import of the concession, resolved to choose in future ministers in accord with the party holding a majority in the Stor Thing. It is hard to say, when one begins to make alterations in an old house, how far one will be led on in rebuilding, and I doubt whether this change in the present American system, possibly in itself desirable, might not be found to involve a reconstruction large enough to put a new face upon several parts of that system.

In the history of the United States there have been four serious conflicts between the legislature and the executive. The first was that between President Jackson and Congress. It ended in Jackson's favour, for he got his way; but he prevailed because during the time when both houses were against him, his opponents had not a two-thirds majority. In the latter part of the struggle the (reelected) House was with him; and before he had quitted office his friends obtained a majority in the always-changing Senate. But his success was not so much the success of the executive office as of a particular president popular with the masses. The second contest, which was between President Tyler and both houses of Congress, was a drawn battle, because the majority in the houses fell short of two-thirds. In the third, between President Johnson and Congress, Congress prevailed; the enemies of the president having, owing to the disfranchisement of most Southern states, an overpowering majority in both houses, and by that majority carrying over his veto a series of acts so peremptory that even his reluctance to obey them could not destroy, though it sometimes marred, their efficiency. In the fourth case, referred to in a previous chapter, the victory remained with the president, because the congressional majority against him was slender. But a presidential victory is usually a negative victory. It consists not in his getting what he wants, but in his preventing Congress from getting what it wants.[15] The practical result of the American arrangements thus comes to be that when one party possesses a large majority in Congress it can overpower the president, taking from him all but a few strictly reserved functions, such as those of pardoning, of making promotions in the army and navy, and of negotiating (not of concluding treaties, for these require the assent of the Senate) with foreign states. Where parties are pretty equally divided, i.e., when the majority is one way in the Senate, the other way in the House, or when there is only a small majority against the president in both houses, the president is in so far free that new fetters cannot be laid upon him; but he must move under those which previous legislation has imposed, and can take no step for which new legislation is needed.

---

[15] In the famous case of President Jackson's removal of the government deposits of money from the United States Bank, the president did accomplish his object. But this was a very exceptional case, because one which had remained within the executive discretion of the president since no statute had happened to provide for it.

It is another and a remarkable consequence of the absence of cabinet government in America, that government does not mean the same thing there that it does in Europe. In France, Italy, and England the term means, that one set of men, united, or professing to be united, by holding one set of opinions, have obtained control of the whole machinery of government, and are working it in conformity with those opinions. Their majority in the country is represented by a majority in the legislature, and to this majority the ministry of necessity belongs. The ministry is the supreme committee of the party, and controls all the foreign as well as domestic affairs of the nation, because the majority is deemed to be the nation. It is otherwise in America. Men do, no doubt, talk of one party as being "in power," meaning thereby the party to which the then president belongs. But they do so because that party enjoys the spoils of office, in which to so many politicians the value of power consists. They do so also because in the early days the party which prevailed in the legislative usually prevailed also in the executive department, and because the presidential election was, and still is, the main struggle which proclaimed the predominance of one or other party.[16]

But the Americans, when they speak of the administration party as the party in power, have, in borrowing an English phrase, applied it to utterly different facts. Their "party in power" need have no "power" beyond that of securing places for its adherents. It may be in a minority in one house of Congress, in which event it accomplishes nothing, but can at most merely arrest adverse legislation, or in a small minority in both houses of Congress, in which event it must submit to see many things done which it dislikes. And if its enemies control the Senate, even its executive arm is paralyzed. Though party feeling has generally been stronger in America than in England, and even now covers a larger proportion of the voters, and enforces a stricter discipline, party government is distinctly weaker.

Those who lament the violence of European factions may fancy America an Elysium where legislation is just and reasonable, because free from bias, where pure and enlarged views of national interest override the selfish designs of politicians. It would be nearer the truth to say that the absence of party control operates chiefly to make laws less consistent, and to prevent extended schemes of policy from being framed, because the chance of

---

[16] The history of the Republic divides itself in the mind of most Americans into a succession of presidents and administrations, just as old-fashioned historians divided the history of England by the reigns of kings, a tolerable way of reckoning in the days of the Plantagenet monarchs, when the personal gifts of the sovereign were a chief factor in affairs, but absurd in the days of George IV and William IV.

giving continuous effect to them is small. The natural history of the party system, and of the methods whereby it is worked, belongs to a later part of this book. The system is complete, the methods are elaborate, but the Constitution opposes obstacles unknown in France or England to the complete control by a party of the whole government of the country.

We are now in a position to sum up the practical results of the system which purports to separate Congress from the executive, instead of uniting them as they are united under a cabinet government. I say "purports to separate," because the separation, significant as it is, is less complete than current language imports, or than the Fathers of the Constitution would seem to have intended. The necessary coherence of the two powers baffled them. These results are five:

The president and his ministers have no initiative in Congress, little influence over Congress, except what they can exert upon individual members through the bestowal of patronage, or upon their party in Congress by threatening it with popular displeasure.

Congress has, together with unlimited powers of inquiry, imperfect powers of control over the administrative departments.

The nation does not always know how or where to fix responsibility for misfeasance or neglect. The person and bodies concerned in making and executing the laws are so related to one another that each can generally shift the burden of blame on someone else, and no one acts under the full sense of direct accountability.

There is a loss of force by friction, i.e., part of the energy, force, and time of the men and bodies that make up the government is dissipated in struggles with one another. This belongs to all free governments, because all free governments rely upon checks. But the more checks, the more friction.

There is a risk that executive vigour and promptitude may be found wanting at critical moments.

We may include these defects in one general expression. There is in the American government, considered as a whole, a want of unity. Its branches are unconnected; their efforts are not directed to one aim, do not produce one harmonious result. The sailors, the helmsman, the engineer, do not seem to have one purpose or obey one will, so that instead of making steady way the vessel may pursue a devious or zigzag course, and sometimes merely turn round and round in the water. The more closely anyone watches from year to year the history of free governments, and himself swims in the deep-eddying time current, the more does he feel that current's force, so that human foresight and purpose seem to count for little, and ministers and parliaments to be swept along they know not whither by some overmastering fate or overruling providence. But this feeling is stronger in America than in Europe, because in America such powers as exist act with little concert and resign themselves to a conscious impotence. Clouds arise, blot out the sun overhead, and burst in a tempest; the tempest passes, and leaves the blue above bright as before, but at the same moment other clouds are already beginning to peer over the horizon. Parties are formed and dissolved, compromises are settled and assailed and violated, wars break out and are fought through and forgotten, new problems begin to show themselves, and the civil powers, presidents, and cabinets, and state governments, and houses of Congress, seem to have as little to do with all these changes, as little ability to foresee or avert or resist them, as the farmer, who sees approaching the tornado which will uproot his crop, has power to stay its devastating course.

A president can do little, for he does not lead either Congress or the nation. Congress cannot guide or stimulate the president, nor replace him by a man fitter for the emergency. The cabinet neither receive a policy from Congress nor give one to it. Each power in the state goes its own way, or wastes precious moments in discussing which way it shall go, and that which comes to pass seems to be a result not of the action of the legal organs of the state, but of some larger force which at one time uses their discord as its means, at another neglects them altogether. This at least is the impression which the history of the greatest problem and greatest struggle that America has seen, the struggle of the slaveholders against the Free Soil and Union party, culminating in the war of the rebellion, makes upon one who looking back on its events sees them all as parts of one drama. Inevitable the struggle may have been; and in its later stages passion had grown so hot, and the claims of the slaveholders so extravagant, that possibly under no scheme of government—so some high American authorities hold— could a peaceful solution have been looked for. Yet it must be remembered that the carefully devised machinery of the Constitution did little to solve that problem or avert that struggle, while the system of divided and balanced and limited powers, giving every advantage to those who stood by the existing law, and placing the rights of the states behind the bulwarks of an almost unalterable instrument, may have tended to aggravate the spirit of uncompromising resistance. The nation asserted itself at last, but not till the resources which the Constitution provided for the attainment of a peaceful solution had irretrievably failed.

Not wholly dissimilar was the course of events in the first years of the

French Revolution. The Constitution framed by the National Assembly in 1791 so limited the functions and authority of each power in the state that no one person, no one body, was capable of leading either the nation or the legislature, or of framing and maintaining a constructive policy. Things were left to take their own course. The boat drifted to the rapids, and the rapids hurried her over the precipice.[17]

This want of unity is painfully felt in a crisis. When a sudden crisis comes upon a free state, the executive needs two things, a large command of money and powers in excess of those allowed at ordinary times. Under the European system the duty of meeting such a crisis is felt to devolve as much on the representative chamber as on the ministers who are its agents. The chamber is therefore at once appealed to for supplies, and for such legislation as the occasion demands. When these have been given, the ministry moves on with the weight of the people behind it; and as it is accustomed to work at all times with the chamber, and the chamber with it, the piston plays smoothly and quickly in the cylinder. In America the president has at ordinary times little to do with Congress, while Congress is unaccustomed to deal with executive questions. Its machinery, and especially the absence of ministerial leaders and consequent want of organization, unfit it for promptly confronting practical troubles. It is apt to be sparing of supplies, and of that confidence which doubles the value of supplies. Jealousies of the executive, which are proper in quiet times and natural towards those with whom Congress has little direct intercourse, may now be perilous, yet how is Congress to trust persons not members of its own body nor directly amenable to its control? When dangers thicken the only device may be the Roman one of a temporary dictatorship. Something like this happened in the War of Seccession, for the powers then conferred upon President Lincoln, or exercised without congressional censure by him, were almost as much in excess of those enjoyed under the ordinary law as the authority of a Roman dictator exceeded that of a Roman consul.[18] Fortunately the habits of legality, which lie deep in the American as they did in the Roman people, reasserted themselves after the war was over, as they were wont to do at Rome in her earlier and better days. When the squall had passed the ship righted, and she has pursued her subsequent course on as even a keel as before.

---

[17] This Constitution of 1791 was framed under the same idea of the need for separating the executive and legislative departments which prevailed at Philadelphia in 1787. For want of a legitimate supreme power, power at last fell into the hands of the Committee of Public Safety, and afterwards of the Directory.

[18] For Lincoln's argument respecting his use of extraordinary powers, see note to Chapter 34 *post*.

The defects of the tools are the glory of the workman. The more completely self-acting is the machine, the smaller is the intelligence needed to work it; the more liable it is to derangement, so much greater must be the skill and care applied by one who tends it. The English Constitution, which we admire as a masterpiece of delicate equipoises and complicated mechanism, would anywhere but in England be full of difficulties and dangers. It stands and prospers in virtue of the traditions that still live among English statesmen and the reverence that has ruled English citizens. It works by a body of understandings which no writer can formulate, and of habits which centuries have been needed to instil. So the American people have a practical aptitude for politics, a clearness of vision and capacity for self-control never equalled by any other nation. In 1861 they brushed aside their darling legalities, allowed the executive to exert novel powers, passed lightly laws whose constitutionality remains doubtful, raised an enormous army, and contracted a prodigious debt. Romans could not have been more energetic in their sense of civic duty, nor more trustful to their magistrates. When the emergency had passed away the torrent which had overspread the plain fell back at once into its safe and well-worn channel. The reign of legality returned; and only four years after the power of the executive had reached its highest point in the hands of President Lincoln, it was reduced to its lowest point in those of President Johnson. Such a people can work any Constitution. The danger for them is that this reliance on their skill and their star may make them heedless of the faults of their political machinery, slow to devise improvements which are best applied in quiet times.

General Observations on the Frame of National Government

The account which has been so far given of the working of the American government has been necessarily an account rather of its mechanism than of its spirit. Its practical character, its temper and colour, so to speak, largely depend on the party system by which it is worked, and on what may be called the political habits of the people. These will be described in later chapters. Here, however, before quitting the study of the constitutional organs of government, it is well to sum up the criticisms we have been led to make, and to add a few remarks, for which no fitting place could be found in preceeding chapters, on the general features of the national government.

I. No part of the Constitution cost its framers so much time and trouble as the method of choosing the president. They saw the evils of a popular vote. They saw also the objections to placing in the hands of Congress the election of a person whose chief duty it was to hold Congress in check. The plan of having him selected by judicious persons, specially chosen by the people for that purpose, seemed to meet both difficulties, and was therefore recommended with confidence. The presidential electors have, however, turned out mere ciphers, and the president is practically chosen by the people at large. The only importance which the elaborate machinery provided in the Constitution retains, is that it prevents a simple popular vote in which the majority of the nation should prevail, and makes the issue of the election turn on the voting in certain "pivotal" states.

II. The choice of the president, by what is now practically a simultaneous popular vote, not only involves once in every four years a tremendous expenditure of energy, time, and money, but induces a sort of crisis which, if it happens to coincide with any passion powerfully agitating the people, may be dangerous to the commonwealth.

III. There is a risk that the result of a presidential election may be doubtful or disputed on the ground of error, fraud, or violence. When such a case arises, the difficulty of finding an authority competent to deal with it, and likely to be trusted, is extreme. Moreover, the question may not be settled until the preexisting executive has, by effluxion of time, ceased to have a right to the obedience of the citizens. The experience of the election of 1876 illustrates these dangers. Such a risk of interregna is incidental to all systems, monarchic or republican, which make the executive head elective, as witness the Romano-Germanic Empire of the Middle Ages, and the papacy. But it is more serious where he is elected by the people than where, as in France or Switzerland, he is chosen by the chambers.[1]

IV. The change of the higher executive officers, and of many of the lower executive officers also, which usually takes place once in four years, gives a jerk to the machinery, and causes a discontinuity of policy, unless, of course, the president has served only one term, and is reelected. Moreover, there is generally a loss either of responsibility or of efficiency in the executive chief magistrate during the last part of his term. An outgoing president may possibly be a reckless president, because he has little to lose by misconduct, little to hope from good conduct. He may therefore abuse his patronage, or gratify his whims with impunity. But more often he is a weak president.[2] He has little influence with Congress, because his patronage will soon come to an end, little hold on the people, who are already speculating on the policy of his successor. His secretary of state may be unable to treat boldly with foreign powers, who perceive that he has a diminished influence in the Senate, and know that the next secretary may have different views.

The question whether the United States, which no doubt needed a president in 1789 to typify the then created political unity of the nation, might not now dispense with one, has never been raised in America, where the people, though dissatisfied with the method of choice, value the office because it is independent of Congress and directly responsible to the people. Americans condemn any plan under which, as once befell in France, the

---

[1] In Switzerland the Federal Council of seven are elected by the two chambers, and then elect one of their own number to be their president, and therewith also president of the Confederation (Constit. of 1874, art. 98). In some British colonies it has been provided that, in case of the absence or death or incapacity of the Governor, the Chief Justice shall act as Governor. In India the senior member of Council acts in similar cases for the Viceroy.

[2] A British House of Commons in the last few months before its impending dissolution usually presents the same alternations of reckless electioneering and of a feebleness which recoils from any momentous decision.

legislature can drive a president from power and itself proceed to choose a new one.[3]

V. The vice-president's office is ill-conceived. His only ordinary function is to act as chairman of the Senate, but as he does not appoint the committees of that house, and has not even a vote (except a casting vote) in it, this function is of little moment. If, however, the president dies, or becomes incapable of acting, or is removed from office, the vice-president succeeds to the presidency. What is the result? The place being in itself unimportant, the choice of a candidate for it excites little interest, and is chiefly used by the party managers as a means of conciliating a section of their party. It becomes what is called "a complimentary nomination." The man elected vice-president is therefore rarely if ever, when selected, a man in the front rank. But when the president dies during his term of office, which has happened to five out of the twenty presidents, this possibly second-class man steps into a great place for which he was never intended. Sometimes, as in the case of Mr. Arthur, he fills the place respectably. Sometimes, as in that of Andrew Johnson, he throws the country into confusion.

He is *aut nullus aut Cæsar*.

VI. The defects in the structure and working of Congress, and in its relations to the executive, have been so fully dwelt on already that it is enough to refer summarily to them. They are:

The discontinuity of congressional policy
The want of adequate control over officials
The want of opportunities for the executive to influence the legislature
The want of any authority charged to secure the passing of such legislation as the country needs
The frequency of disputes between three coordinate powers, the president, the Senate, and the House

The maintenance of a continuous policy is a difficulty in all popular governments. In the United States it is specially so, because:

The executive head and his ministers are necessarily (unless when a president is reelected) changed once every four years
One house of Congress is changed every two years
Neither house recognizes permanent leaders
No accord need exist between Congress and the executive

---

[3] The question of replacing the president by a ministerial council is very rarely discussed in America. It has been mooted in France.

There may not be such a thing as a party in power, in the European sense, because the party to which the executive belongs may be in a minority in one or both houses of Congress, in which case it cannot do anything which requires fresh legislation; may be in a minority in the Senate, in which case it can take no administrative act of importance.

There is little true leadership in political action, because the most prominent man has no recognized party authority. Congress was not elected to support him. He cannot threaten disobedient followers with a dissolution of Parliament like an English prime minister. He has not even the French president's right of dissolving the House with the consent of the Senate.

There is often no general and continuous cabinet policy, because the cabinet has no authority over Congress, may perhaps have no influence with it.

There is no general or continuous legislative policy, because the legislature, having no recognized leaders, and no one guiding committee, acts through a large number of committees, independent of one another, and seldom able to bring their measures to maturity. What continuity exists is due to the general acceptance of a few broad maxims, such as that of nonintervention in the affairs of the Old World, and to the fact that a large nation does not frequently or lightly change its views upon leading principles. In minor matters of legislation there is little settled policy, for the houses trifle with questions, take them up in one session and drop them the next, seem insensible to the duty of completing work once begun, and are too apt to yield to the pressure which small sections, or even influential individuals in their constituencies, exert upon them to arrest some measure the public interest demands. Neither is there any security that Congress will attend to such defects in the administrative system of the country as may need a statute to correct them. In Europe the daily experience of the administrative departments discloses faults or omissions in the law which involve needless trouble to officials, needless cost to the treasury, needless injustice to classes of the people. Sometimes for their own sakes, sometimes from that desire to see things well done which is the life-breath of a good public servant, the permanent officials call the attention of their parliamentary chief, the minister, to the defective state of the law, and submit to him the draft of a bill to amend it. He brings in this bill, and if it involves no matter of political controversy (which it rarely does), he gets it passed. As an American minister has no means (except by the favour of a committee) of getting anything he proposes attended to by Congress, it is a mere chance if such amending statutes as these are introduced or pass into law. And it sometimes happens that when he sees the need for an improvement he cannot carry it, because selfish interests oppose it, and he has not that command of a majority by means of which a European minister is able to effect reforms.

These defects are all reducible to two. There is an excessive friction in the American system, a waste of force in the strife of various bodies and persons created to check and balance one another. There is a want of executive unity, and therefore a possible want of executive vigour. Power is so much subdivided that it is hard at a given moment to concentrate it for prompt and effective action. In fact, this happens only when a distinct majority of the people are so clearly of one mind that the several coordinate organs of government obey this majority, uniting their efforts to serve its will.

VII. The relations of the people to the legislature are in every free country so much the most refined and delicate, as well as so much the most important part of the whole scheme and doctrine of government, that we must not expect to find perfection anywhere. But comparing America with Great Britain since 1832, the working of the representative system in America seems somewhat inferior.

There are four essentials to the excellence of a representative system:

That the representatives shall be chosen from among the best men of the country, and, if possible, from its natural leaders;

That they shall be strictly and palpably responsible to their constituents for their speeches and votes;

That they shall have courage enough to resist a momentary impulse of their constituents which they think mischievous, i.e., shall be representatives rather than mere delegates;

That they individually, and the chamber they form, shall have a reflex action on the people, i.e., that while they derive authority from the people, they shall also give the people the benefit of the experience they acquire in the chamber, as well as of the superior knowledge and capacity they may be presumed to possess.

Americans declare, and no doubt correctly, that of these four requisites, the first, third, and fourth are not attained in their country. Congressmen are not chosen from among the best citizens. They mostly deem themselves mere delegates. They do not pretend to lead the people, being indeed seldom specially qualified to do so.

That the second requisite, responsibility, is not fully realized seems surprising in a democratic country, and indeed almost inconsistent with that conception of the representative as a delegate, which is supposed, perhaps erroneously, to be characteristic of democracies. Still the fact is there. One cause, already explained, is to be found in the committee system. Another is the want of organized leadership in Congress. In Europe, a member's responsibility usually takes the form of his being bound to support the leader of his party on all important divisions. In America, this obligation attaches only when the party has "gone into caucus," and there resolved upon its course. Not having the right to direct, the leader cannot be held responsible for the action of the rank and file. As a third cause we may note the fact that owing to the restricted competence of Congress many of the questions which chiefly interest the voter do not come before Congress at all, so that its proceedings are not followed with that close and keen attention which the debates and divisions of European chambers excite, and some may think that a fourth cause is found in the method by which candidates for membership of Congress are selected. That method is described in later chapters (see Chapters 59–66 *post*). Its effect has been to make congressmen (including senators) be, and feel themselves to be, the nominees of the party organizations rather than of the citizens, and thus it has interposed what may for some purposes be called a sort of nonconducting medium between the people and their representatives.

In general the reciprocal action and reaction between the electors and Congress, what is commonly called the "touch" of the people with their agents, is not sufficiently close, quick, and delicate. Representatives ought to give light and leading to the people, just as the people give stimulus and momentum to their representatives. This incidental merit of the parliamentary system is among its greatest merits. But in America the action of the voter fails to tell upon Congress. He votes for a candidate of his own party, but he does not convey to that candidate an impulse towards the carrying of particular measures, because the candidate when in Congress will be practically unable to promote those measures, unless he happens to be placed on the committee to which they are referred. Hence the citizen, when he casts his ballot, can seldom feel that he is advancing any measure or policy, except the vague and general policy indicated in his party platform. He is voting for a party, but he does not know what the party will do, and for a man, but a man whom chance may deprive of the opportunity of advocating the measures he cares most for.

Conversely, Congress does not guide and illuminate its constituents. It is amorphous, and has little initiative. It does not focus the light of the nation, does not warm its imagination, does not dramatize principles in the deeds and characters of men.[4] This happens because, in ordinary times, it lacks

---

[4] As an illustration of the want of the dramatic element in Congress, I may mention that some at least of the parliamentary debating societies in the American colleges (colleges for women included)

great leaders, and the most obvious cause why it lacks them, is its disconnection from the executive. As it is often devoid of such men, so neither does the country habitually come to it to look for them. In the old days, neither Hamilton, nor Jefferson, nor John Adams, in our own time, neither Stanton, nor Grant, nor Tilden, nor Cleveland, ever sat in Congress. Lincoln sat for two years only, and owed little of his subsequent eminence to his career there.

VIII. The independence of the judiciary, due to its holding for life, has been a conspicuous merit of the federal system, as compared with the popular election and short terms of judges in most of the states. Yet even the federal judiciary is not secure from the attacks of the two other powers, if combined. For the legislature may by statute increase the number of federal justices, increase it to any extent, since the Constitution leaves the number undetermined and the president may appoint persons whom he knows to be actuated by a particular political bias, perhaps even prepared to decide specific questions in a particular sense. Thus he and Congress together may obtain such a judicial determination of any constitutional question as they join in desiring, even although that question has been heretofore differently decided by the Supreme Court. The only safeguard is in the disapproval of the people.

It is worth remarking that the points in which the American frame of national government has proved least successful are those which are most distinctly artificial, i.e., those which are not the natural outgrowth of old institutions and well-formed habits, but devices consciously introduced to attain specific ends.[5] The election of the president and vice-president by electors appointed *ad hoc* is such a device. The functions of the judiciary do not belong to this category; they are the natural outgrowth of common

---

take for their model not either house of Congress but the British House of Commons, the students conducting their debates under the names of prominent members of that assembly. They say that they do this because Congress has no ministry and no leaders of the opposition.

[5] See Chapter 4 *ante*, and Note thereto in the Appendix.

This may seem to be another way of saying that nature, i.e., historical development, is wiser than the wisest men. Yet it must be remembered that what we call historical development is really the result of a great many small expedients invented by men during many generations for curing the particular evils in their government which from time to time had to be cured. The moral therefore is that a succession of small improvements, each made comformably to existing conditions and habits, is more likely to succeed than a large scheme, made all at once in what may be called the spirit of conscious experiment. The federal Constitution has been generally supposed in Europe to have been such a scheme, and its success has encouraged other countries to attempt similar bold and large experiments. This is an error. The Constitution of the United States is almost as truly the matured result of long and gradual historical development as the English Constitution itself.

law doctrines and of the previous history of the colonies and states; all that is novel in them, for it can hardly be called artificial, is the creation of courts coextensive with the sphere of the national government.

All the main features of American government may be deduced from two principles. One is the sovereignty of the people, which expresses itself in the fact that the supreme law—the Constitution—is the direct utterance of their will, that they alone can amend it, that it prevails against every other law, that whatever powers it does not delegate are deemed to be reserved to it, that every power in the state draws its authority, whether directly, like the House of Representatives, or in the second degree, like the president and the Senate, or in the third degree, like the federal judiciary, from the people, and is legally responsible to the people, and not to anyone of the other powers.

The second principle, itself a consequence of this first one, is the distrust of the various organs and agents of government. The states are carefully safeguarded against aggression by the central government. So are the individual citizens. Each organ of government, the executive, the legislature, the judiciary, is made a jealous observer and restrainer of the others. Since the people, being too numerous, cannot directly manage their affairs, but must commit them to agents, they have resolved to prevent abuses by trusting each agent as little as possible, and subjecting him to the oversight of other agents, who will harass and check him if he attempts to overstep his instructions.

Someone has said that the American government and Constitution are based on the theology of Calvin and the philosophy of Hobbes. This at least is true, that there is a hearty Puritanism in the view of human nature which pervades the instrument of 1787. It is the work of men who believed in original sin, and were resolved to leave open for transgressors no door which they could possibly shut.[6] Compare this spirit with the enthusiastic optimism of the Frenchmen of 1789. It is not merely a difference of race temperaments; it is a difference of fundamental ideas.

With the spirit of Puritanism there is blent a double portion of the spirit of legalism. Not only is there no reliance on ethical forces to help the government to work; there is an elaborate machinery of law to preserve the equilibrium of each of its organs. The aim of the Constitution seems to be not so much to attain great common ends by securing a good government as to avert the evils which will flow, not merely from a bad government,

---

[6] "That power might be abused," says Marshall in his *Life of Washington*, "was deemed a conclusive reason why it should not be conferred."

but from any government strong enough to threaten the preexisting communities or the individual citizen.

The spirit of 1776, as it speaks to us from the Declaration of Independence and the glowing periods of Patrick Henry, was largely a revolutionary spirit, revolutionary in its faith in abstract principles, revolutionary also in its determination to carry through a tremendous political change in respect of grievances which the calm judgment of history does not deem intolerable, and which might probably have been redressed by less trenchant methods. But the spirit of 1787 was an English spirit, and therefore a conservative spirit, tinged, no doubt, by the hatred to tyranny developed in the revolutionary struggle, tinged also by the nascent dislike to inequality, but in the main an English spirit, which desired to walk in the old paths of precedent, which thought of government as a means of maintaining order and securing to everyone his rights, rather than as a great ideal power, capable of guiding and developing a nation's life. And thus, though the Constitution of 1789 represented a great advance on the still oligarchic system of contemporary England, it was yet, if we regard simply its legal provisions, the least democratic of democracies. Had the points which it left undetermined, as for instance the qualifications of congressional electors, been dealt with in an aristocratic spirit, had the legislation of Congress and of the several states taken an aristocratic turn, it might have grown into an aristocratic system. The democratic character which it now possesses is largely the result of subsequent events, which have changed the conditions under which it had to work, and have delivered its development into the hands of that passion for equality which has become a powerful factor in the modern world everywhere.

He who should desire to draw an indictment against the American scheme of government might make it a long one, and might for every count in it cite high American authority and adduce evidence from American history. Yet a European reader would greatly err were he to conclude that this scheme of government is a failure, or is, indeed, for the purposes of the country, inferior to the political system of any of the great nations of the Old World.

All governments are faulty; and an equally minute analysis of the constitutions of England, or France, or Germany would disclose mischiefs as serious, relatively to the problems with which those states have to deal, as those we have noted in the American system. To anyone familiar with the practical working of free governments it is a standing wonder that they work at all. The first impulse of mankind is to follow and obey; servitude rather than freedom is their natural state. With freedom, when it emerges among the more progressive races, there come dissension and faction; and it takes many centuries to form those habits of compromise, that love of order, and that respect for public opinion which make democracy tolerable. What keeps a free government going is the good sense and patriotism of the people, or of the guiding class, embodied in usages and traditions which it is hard to describe, but which find, in moments of difficulty, remedies for the inevitable faults of the system. Now, this good sense and that power of subordinating sectional to national interests which we call patriotism, exist in higher measure in America than in any of the great states of Europe. And the United States, more than any other country, are governed by public opinion, that is to say, by the general sentiment of the mass of the nation, which all the organs of the national government and of the state governments look to and obey.[7]

A philosopher from Jupiter or Saturn who should examine the Constitution of England or that of America would probably pronounce that such a body of complicated devices, full of opportunities for conflict and deadlock, could not work at all. Many of those who examined the American Constitution when it was launched did point to a multitude of difficulties, and confidently predicted its failure. Still more confidently did the European enemies of free government declare in the crisis of the War of Secession that "the republican bubble had burst." Some of these censures were well grounded, though there were also defects which had escaped criticism, and were first disclosed by experience. But the Constitution has lived on in spite of all defects, and seems stronger now than at any previous epoch.

Every constitution, like every man, has "the defects of its good qualities." If a nation desires perfect stability it must put up with a certain slowness and cumbrousness; it must face the possibility of a want of action where action is called for. If, on the other hand, it seeks to obtain executive speed and vigour by a complete concentration of power, it must run the risk that power will be abused and irrevocable steps too hastily taken. "The liberty-loving people of every country," says Judge Cooley,[8] "take courage from American freedom, and find augury of better days for themselves from American prosperity. But America is not so much an example in her liberty as in the covenanted and enduring securities which are intended to prevent liberty degenerating into licence, and to establish a feeling of trust and repose under a beneficent government, whose excellence, so obvious in its freedom, is still more conspicuous in its careful provision for permanence

---

[7] The nature of public opinion and the way in which it governs are discussed in Part IV.
[8] Address to the South Carolina Bar Association, Dec. 1886.

and stability." Those faults on which I have laid stress, the waste of power by friction, the want of unity and vigour in the conduct of affairs by executive and legislature, are the price which the Americans pay for the autonomy of their states, and for the permanence of the equilibrium among the various branches of their government. They pay this price willingly, because these defects are far less dangerous to the body politic than they would be in a European country. Take for instance the shortcomings of Congress as a legislative authority. Every European country is surrounded by difficulties which legislation must deal with, and that promptly. But in America, where those relics of mediæval privilege and injustice that still cumber most parts of the Old World either never existed, or were long ago abolished, where all the conditions of material prosperity exist in ample measure, and the development of material resources occupies men's minds, where nearly all social reforms lie within the sphere of state action, in America there is less need and less desire than in Europe for a perennial stream of federal legislation. People have been contented if things go on fairly well as they are. Political philosophers, or philanthropists, perceive not a few improvements which federal statutes might effect, but the mass of the nation has not greatly complained, and the wise see Congress so often on the point of committing mischievous errors that they do not deplore the barrenness of session after session.

Every European state has to fear not only the rivalry but the aggression of its neighbours. Even Britain, so long safe in her insular home, has lost some of her security by the growth of steam navies, and has in her Indian and colonial possessions given pledges to Fortune all over the globe. She, like the powers of the European continent, must maintain her system of government in full efficiency for war as well as for peace, and cannot afford to let her armaments decline, her finances become disordered, the vigour of her executive authority be impaired, sources of internal discord continue to prey upon her vitals. But America lives in a world of her own, *ipsa suis pollens opibus, nihil indiga nostri.* Safe from attack, safe even from menace, she hears from afar the warring cries of European races and faiths, as the gods of Epicurus listened to the murmurs of the unhappy earth spread out beneath their golden dwellings,

> "Sejuncta a rebus nostris semotaque longe."

Had Canada or Mexico grown to be a great power, had France not sold Louisiana, or had England, rooted on the American continent, become a military despotism, the United States could not indulge the easy optimism which makes them tolerate the faults of their government. As it is, that which might prove to a European state a mortal disease is here nothing worse than a teasing ailment. Since the War of Secession ended, no serious danger has arisen either from within or from without to alarm transatlantic statesmen. Social convulsions from within, warlike assaults from without, seem now as unlikely to try the fabric of the American Constitution, as an earthquake to rend the walls of the Capitol. This is why the Americans submit, not merely patiently but hopefully, to the defects of their government. The vessel may not be any better built, or found, or rigged than are those which carry the fortunes of the great nations of Europe. She is certainly not better navigated. But for the present at least—it may not always be so— she sails upon a summer sea.

It must never be forgotten that the main object which the framers of the Constitution set before themselves has been achieved. When Siéyès was asked what he had done during the Reign of Terror, he answered, "I lived." The Constitution as a whole has stood and stands unshaken. The scales of power have continued to hang fairly even. The president has not corrupted and enslaved Congress; Congress has not paralyzed and cowed the president. The legislative may have sometimes appeared to be gaining on the executive department; but there are also times when the people support the president against the legislature, and when the legislature is obliged to recognize the fact. Were George Washington to return to earth, he might be as great and useful a president as he was more than a century ago. Neither the legislature nor the executive has for a moment threatened the liberties of the people. The states have not broken up the Union, and the Union has not absorbed the states. No wonder that the Americans are proud of an instrument under which this great result has been attained, which has passed unscathed through the furnace of civil war, which has been found capable of embracing a body of commonwealths more than three times as numerous, and with thirty-fold the population of the original states, which has cultivated the political intelligence of the masses to a point reached in no other country, which has fostered and been found compatible with a larger measure of local self-government than has existed elsewhere. Nor is it the least of its merits to have made itself beloved. Objections may be taken to particular features, and these objections point, as most American thinkers are agreed, to practicable improvements which would preserve the excellences and remove some of the inconveniences. But reverence for the Constitution has become so potent a conservative influence, that no proposal of fundamental change seems likely to be entertained. And this reverence is itself one of the most wholesome and hopeful elements in the character of the American people.

C H A P T E R   2 7

The Federal System

Having examined the several branches of the national government and the manner in which they work together, we may now proceed to examine the American commonwealth as a federation of states. The present chapter is intended to state concisely the main features which distinguish the federal system, and from which it derives its peculiar character. Three other chapters will describe its practical working, and summarize the criticisms that may be passed upon it.

The contests in the Convention of 1787 over the framing of the Constitution, and in the country over its adoption, turned upon two points: the extent to which the several states should be recognized as independent and separate factors in the construction of the national government, and the quantity and nature of the powers which should be withdrawn from the states to be vested in that government. It has been well remarked that "the first of these, the definition of the structural powers, gave more trouble at the time than the second, because the line of partition between the powers of the States and the Federal government had been already fixed by the whole experience of the country." But since 1791 there has been practically no dispute as to the former point, and little as to the propriety of the provisions which define the latter. On the interpretation of these provisions there has, of course, been endless debate, some deeming the Constitution to have taken more from the states, some less; while still warmer controversies have raged as to the matters which the instrument does not expressly deal with, and particularly whether the states retain their sovereignty, and with it the right of nullifying or refusing to be bound by certain acts of the national government, and in the last resort of withdrawing from the Union. As these latter questions (nullification and secession) have now been settled by the Civil War, we may say that in the America of today there exists a general agreement:

That every state on entering the Union finally renounced its sovereignty, and is now forever subject to the federal authority as defined by the Constitution;

That the functions of the states as factors of the national government are satisfactory, i.e., sufficiently secure its strength and the dignity of these communities;

That the delimitation of powers between the national government and the states, contained in the Constitution, is convenient, and needs no fundamental alteration.[1]

The ground which we have to tread during the remainder of this chapter is therefore no longer controversial ground, but that of well-established law and practice.

I. The distribution of powers between the national and the state governments is effected in two ways: positively, by conferring certain powers on the national government; negatively, by imposing certain restrictions on the states. It would have been superfluous to confer any powers on the states, because they retain all powers not actually taken from them. A lawyer may think that it was equally unnecessary and, so to speak, inartistic, to lay any prohibitions on the national government, because it could *ex hypothesi* exercise no powers not expressly granted. However, the anxiety of the states to fetter the master they were giving themselves caused the introduction of provisions qualifying the grant of express powers, and interdicting the national government from various kinds of action on which it might otherwise have been tempted to enter.[2] The matter is further complicated by the fact that the grant of power to the national government is not in all cases an exclusive grant; i.e., there are matters which both, or either, the states and the national government may deal with. "The mere grant of a power to Congress does not of itself, in most cases, imply a prohibition upon the States to exercise the like power. . . . It is not the mere existence of the

---

[1] The view that the power of Congress to legislate might usefully be so extended, by constitutional amendments, as to include such a subject as marriage and divorce, or to give it greater control over the agencies of transportation, is of course compatible with an acquiescence in the general scheme of delimitation of powers.

[2] Judge Cooley observes to me, "The prohibitions imposed by the Federal Constitution on the exercise of power by the general government were not, for the most part, to prevent its encroaching on the powers left with the States, but to preclude tyrannical exercise of powers which were unquestionably given to the Federal government. Thus Congress was forbidden to pass any bill of attainder; this was to prevent its dealing with Federal offences by legislative conviction and sentence. It was forbidden to pass *ex post facto* laws, and this undoubtedly is a limitation upon power granted; for with the same complete power in respect to offences against the general government which a sovereignty possesses, it might have passed such laws if not prohibited."

National power but its exercise which is incompatible with the exercise of the same power by the States."[3] Thus we may distinguish the following classes of governmental powers:

Powers vested in the national government alone
Powers vested in the states alone
Powers exercisable by either the national government or the states
Powers forbidden to the national government
Powers forbidden to the state governments

It might be thought that the two latter classes are superfluous, because whatever is forbidden to the national government is permitted to the states, and conversely, whatever is forbidden to the states is permitted to the national government. But this is not so. For instance, Congress can grant no title of nobility (art. I, § 9). But neither can a state do so (art. I, § 10). The national government cannot take private property for public use without just compensation (amendment V). Apparently neither can any state do so (amendment XIV, as interpreted in several cases). So no state can pass any law impairing the obligation of a contract (art. I, § 10). But the national government, although not subject to a similar direct prohibition, has received no general power to legislate as regards ordinary contracts, and might therefore in some cases find itself equally unable to pass a law which a state legislature, though for a different reason, could not pass.[4] So no state can pass any *ex post facto* law. Neither can Congress.

What the Constitution has done is not to cut in half the totality of governmental functions and powers, giving part to the national government and leaving all the rest to the states, but to divide up this totality of authority into a number of parts which do not exhaust the whole, but leave a residuum of powers neither granted to the Union nor continued to the states but reserved to the people, who, however, can put them in force only by the difficult process of amending the Constitution. In other words, there are things in America which there exists no organized and permanent authority capable of legally doing, not a state, because it is expressly forbidden, not the national government, because it either has not received the competence or has been expressly forbidden. Suppose, for instance, that there should arise a wish to pass for California such a measure as the Irish Land Act

---

[3] Cooley, *Principles*, p. 35; ef. *Sturges* v. *Crowninshield*, 4 Wheat. 122.
[4] Of course Congress can legislate regarding some contracts, and can impair their obligation. It has power to regulate commerce, it can pass bankrupt laws, it can make paper money legal tender.

passed by the British Parliament in 1881. Neither the state legislature of California, nor the people of California assembled in a constitutional convention, could pass such a measure, because it would violate the obligation of contracts, and thereby transgress art. I, § 10 of the federal Constitution. Whether the federal Congress could pass such a measure is at least extremely doubtful, because the Constitution, though it has imposed no prohibition such as that which restricts a state, does not seem to have conferred on Congress the right of legislating on such a matter at all.[5] If, therefore, an absolute and overwhelming necessity for the enactment of such a measure should arise, the safer if not the only course would be to amend the federal Constitution, either by striking out the prohibition on the states or by conferring the requisite power on Congress, a process which would probably occupy more than a year, and which requires the concurrence of two-thirds of both houses of Congress and of three-fourths of the states.

II. The powers vested in the national government alone are such as relate to the conduct of the foreign relations of the country and to such common national purposes as the army and navy, internal commerce, currency, weights and measures, and the post office, with provisions for the management of the machinery, legislative, executive, and judicial, charged with these purposes.[6]

The powers which remain vested in the states alone are all the other ordinary powers of internal government, such as legislation on private law, civil and criminal, the maintenance of law and order, the creation of local institutions, the provision for education and the relief of the poor, together with taxation for the above purposes.

III. The powers which are exercisable concurrently by the national government and by the states are:

> Powers of legislation on some specified subjects, such as bankruptcy and certain commercial matters (e.g., pilot laws and harbour regulations), but so that state legislation shall take effect only in the absence of federal legislation;
> Powers of taxation, direct or indirect, but so that neither Congress nor a state shall tax exports from any state, and so that neither any state

---

[5] It may of course be suggested that in case of urgent public necessity, such as the existence of war or insurrection, Congress might extinguish debts either generally or in a particular district. No such legislative power seems, however, to have been exerted or declared by the courts to exist, unless the principles of the last legal tender decision can be thought to reach so far.

[6] See art. I, § 8; art. II, § 2; art. III, § 2; art. IV, §§ 3 and 4; amendments XIII, XIV, XV, of the Constitution.

shall, except with the consent of Congress, tax any corporation or other agency created for federal purposes or any act done under federal authority, nor the national government tax any state or its agencies or property;[7]

Judicial powers in certain classes of cases where Congress might have legislated, but has not, or where a party to a suit has a choice to proceed either in a federal or a state court;

Powers of determining matters relating to the election of representatives and senators (but if Congress determines, the state law gives way).

IV. The prohibitions imposed on the national government are set forth in art. I, § 9, and in the first ten amendments. The most important are:

Writ of habeas corpus may not be suspended, nor bill of attainder or *ex post facto* law passed.[8]

No commercial preference shall be given to one state over another.

No title of nobility shall be granted.

No law shall be passed establishing or prohibiting any religion, or abridging the freedom of speech or of the press, or of public meeting, or of bearing arms.

No religious test shall be required as a qualification for any office under the United States.

No person shall be tried for a capital or otherwise infamous crime unless on the presentment of a grand jury, or be subjected to a second capital trial for the same offence, or be compelled to be a witness against himself, or be tried otherwise than by a jury of his state and district.

No common law action shall be decided except by a jury where the value in dispute exceeds $20, and no fact determined by a jury shall be re-examined otherwise than by the rules of the common law.[9]

V. The prohibitions imposed on the states are contained in Art. I, § 10, and in the three latest amendments. They are intended to secure the national government against attempts by the states to trespass on its domain, and to protect individuals against oppressive legislation.

No state shall—Make any treaty or alliance; coin money; make anything

---

[7] Federal direct taxes must be imposed according to the population of the states, and indirect taxes be made uniform throughout the United States. But see now amendment XVI to the Constitution.

[8] Similar limitations occur in some recent European constitutions. The term *ex post facto* law is deemed to refer to criminal laws only.

[9] Chiefly intended to prevent the methods of courts of equity from being applied in the federal courts as against the findings of a jury.

but gold and silver coin a legal tender; pass any bill of attainder, *ex post facto* law, or law impairing the obligation of contracts; grant any titles of nobility.

No state shall without the consent of Congress—Lay duties on exports or imports (the produce of such, if laid, going to the national treasury); keep troops or ships of war in peace time; enter into an agreement with another state or with any foreign power; engage in war, unless actually invaded or in imminent danger.

Every state must—Give credit to the records and judicial proceedings of every other state; extend the privileges and immunities of citizens to the citizens of other states; deliver up fugitives from justice to the state entitled to claim them.

No state shall have any but a republican form of government.

No state shall maintain slavery; abridge the privileges of any citizen of the United States, or deny to him the right of voting, in respect of race, colour, or previous servitude; deprive any person of life, liberty, or property without due process of law; deny to any person the equal protection of the laws.

Note that this list contains no prohibition to a state to do any of the following things: Establish a particular form of religion; endow a particular form of religion, or educational or charitable establishments connected therewith; abolish trial by jury in criminal or civil cases; suppress the freedom of speaking, writing, and meeting (provided that this be done equally as between different classes of citizens, and provided also that it be not done to such an extent as to amount to a deprivation of liberty without due process of law); limit the electoral franchise to any extent; extend the electoral franchise to women, minors, aliens.

These omissions are significant. They show that the framers of the Constitution had no wish to produce uniformity among the states in government or institutions, and little care to protect the citizens against abuses of state power.[10] They were content to trust for this to provisions of the state constitutions. Their chief aim was to secure the national government against encroachments on the part of the states, and to prevent causes of quarrel both between the central and state authorities and between the several states. The result has, on the whole, justified their action. So far from abusing their power of making themselves unlike one another, the states

---

[10] The Fourteenth and Fifteenth Amendments are in this respect a novelty. The only restrictions of this kind to be found in the instrument of 1789 are those relating to contracts and *ex post facto* laws.

have tended to be too uniform, and have made fewer experimental changes in their institutions.

VI. The powers vested in each state are all of them original and inherent powers, which belonged to the state before it entered the Union. Hence they are prima facie unlimited, and if a question arises as to any particular power, it is presumed to be enjoyed by the state, unless it can be shown to have been taken away by the federal Constitution; or, in other words, a state is not deemed to be subject to any restriction which the Constitution has not distinctly imposed.

The powers granted to the national government are delegated powers, enumerated in and defined by the instrument which has created the Union. Hence the rule that when a question arises whether the national government possesses a particular power, proof must be given that the power was positively granted. If not granted, it is not possessed, because the Union is an artificial creation, whose government can have nothing but what the people have by the Constitution conferred. The presumption is therefore against the national government in such a case, just as it is for the state in a like case.[11]

VII. The authority of the national government over the citizens of every state is direct and immediate, not exerted through the state organization, and not requiring the cooperation of the state government. For most purposes the national government ignores the states; and it treats the citizens of different states as being simply its own citizens, equally bound by its laws. The federal courts, revenue officers, and post office draw no help from any state officials, but depend directly on Washington. Hence, too, of course, there is no local self-government in federal matters. No federal official is elected by the people of any local area. Local government is purely a state affair.

On the other hand, the state in no wise depends on the national government for its organization or its effective working. It is the creation of its own inhabitants. They have given it its constitution. They administer its government. It goes on its own way, touching the national government at but few points. That the two should touch at the fewest possible points was the intent of those who framed the federal Constitution, for they saw that

---

[11] Congress must not attempt to interfere with the so-called "police power" of the states within their own limits. So when a statute of Congress had made it punishable to sell certain illuminating fluids inflammable at less than a certain specified temperature, it was held that this statute could not operate within a state, but only in the District of Columbia and the Territories, and a person convicted under it in Detroit was discharged (*United States* v. *De Witt*, 9 Wall. 41).

the less contact, the less danger of collision. Their aim was to keep the two mechanisms as distinct and independent of each other as was compatible with the still higher need of subordinating, for national purposes, the state to the central government.

VIII. It is a further consequence of this principle that the national government has but little to do with the states as states. Its relations are with their citizens, who are also its citizens, rather than with them as ruling commonwealths. In the following points, however, the Constitution does require certain services of the states:

It requires each state government to direct the choice of, and accredit to the seat of the national government, two senators and so many representatives as the state is entitled to send.

It requires similarly that presidential electors be chosen, meet, and vote in the states, and that their votes be transmitted to the national capital.

It requires each state to organize and arm its militia, which, when duly summoned for active service, are placed under the command of the president.

It requires each state to maintain a republican form of government. (Conversely, a state may require the national government to protect it against invasion or domestic violence.)

Note in particular that the national government does not, as in some other federations:

Call upon the states, as commonwealths, to contribute funds to its support;

Issue (save in so far as may be needed in order to secure a republican form of government) administrative orders to the states, directing their authorities to carry out its laws or commands;

Require the states to submit their laws to it, and veto such as it disapproves.

The first two things it is not necessary for the national government to do, because it levies its taxes directly by its own collectors, and enforces its laws, commands, and judicial decrees by the hands of its own servants. The last can be dispensed with because the state laws are *ipso jure* invalid, if they conflict with the Constitution or any treaty or law duly made under it (art. VI, § 2), while if they do not so conflict they are valid, any act of the national government notwithstanding.

Neither does the national government allow its structure to be dependent on the action of the states. "To make it impossible for a State or group of States to jeopardize by inaction or hostile action the existence of the central government," was a prime object with the men of 1787, and has greatly contributed to the solidity of the fabric they reared. The *de facto* secession of eleven states in 1860–61 interfered with the regular legal conduct neither of the presidential election of 1864 nor of the congressional elections from 1861 to 1865. Those states were not represented in Congress; but Congress itself went on diminished in numbers yet with its full legal powers, as the British Parliament would go on though all the peers and representatives from Scotland might be absent.

IX. A state is, within its proper sphere, just as legally supreme, just as well entitled to give effect to its own will, as is the national government within its sphere; and for the same reason. All authority flows from the people. The people have given part of their supreme authority to the national, part to the state governments. Both hold by a like title, and therefore the national government, although superior wherever there is a concurrence of powers, has no more right to trespass upon the domain of a state than a state has upon the domain of federal action. That the course which a state is following is pernicious, that its motives are bad and its sentiments disloyal to the Union, makes no difference until or unless it infringes on the sphere of federal authority. It may be thought that however distinctly this may have been laid down as a matter of theory, in practice the state will not obtain the same justice as the national government, because the court which decides points of law in dispute between the two is in the last resort a federal court, and therefore biased in favour of the federal government. In fact, however, little or no unfairness has arisen from this cause.[12] The Supreme Court may, as happened for twenty years before the War of Secession, be chiefly composed of states' rights men. In any case the court cannot stray far from the path which previous decisions have marked out.

X. There are several remarkable omissions in the Constitution of the American federation.

One is that there is no grant of power to the national government to coerce a recalcitrant or rebellious state. Another is that nothing is said as to the right of secession. Anyone can understand why this right should not have been granted. But neither is it mentioned to be negatived.

---

[12] "Whatever fluctuations may be seen in the history of public opinion during the period of our national existence, we think it will be found that the Supreme Court, so far as its functions required, has always held with a steady and even hand the balance between State and Federal power, and we trust that such may continue to be the history of its relation to that subject so long as it shall have duties to perform which demand of it a construction of the Constitution." —Judgment of the Supreme Court in *The Slaughter House Cases*, 16 Wall. 82.

There is no abstract or theoretic declaration regarding the nature of the federation and its government, nothing as to the ultimate supremacy of the central authority outside the particular sphere allotted to it, nothing as to the so-called sovereign rights of the states. As if with a prescience of the dangers to follow, the wise men of 1787 resolved to give no opening for abstract inquiry and metaphysical dialectic.[13] But in vain. The human mind is not to be so restrained. If the New Testament had consisted of no other writings than the Gospel of St. Matthew and the Epistle of St. James, there would have been scarcely the less a crop of speculative theology. The dryly legal and practical character of the Constitution did not prevent the growth of a mass of subtle and, so to speak, scholastic metaphysics regarding the nature of the government it created. The inextricable knots which American lawyers and publicists went on tying, down till 1861, were cut by the sword of the North in the Civil War, and need concern us no longer. It is now admitted that the Union is not a mere compact between commonwealths, dissoluble at pleasure, but an instrument of perpetual efficacy,[14] emanating

[13] The Declaration of Independence had already given them plenty of abstract propositions about human rights and human governments, so there was the less temptation to wander from the path of definite practical provisions.

[14] This view received judicial sanction in the famous case of *Texas* v. *White* (7 Wall. 700) decided by the Supreme Court after the war. It is there said by Chief Justice Chase, "The Union of the States never was a purely artificial and arbitrary relation. . . . It received definite form and character and sanction by the Articles of Confederation. By these the Union was solemnly declared to be 'perpetual.' And where these articles were found to be inadequate to the exigencies of the country, the Constitution was ordained 'to form a more perfect Union.' It is difficult to convey the idea of indissoluble unity more clearly than by these words. What can be indissoluble if a perpetual union, made more perfect, is not? But the perpetuity and indissolubility of the Union by no means implies the loss of distinct and individual existence, or of the right of self-government, by the States. . . . It may be not unreasonably said that the preservation of the States and the maintenance of their governments are as much within the design and care of the Constitution as the preservation of the Union and the maintenance of the national government. The Constitution, in all its provisions, looks to an indestructible Union composed of indestructible States. When, therefore, Texas became one of the United States she entered into an indissoluble relation. . . . There was no place for reconsideration or revocation except through revolution or through consent of the States. Considered therefore as transactions under the Constitution, the ordinance of secession adopted by the Convention, and ratified by a majority of the citizens of Texas, was absolutely null and utterly without operation in law. The obligations of the State as a member of the Union, and of every citizen of the State as a citizen of the United States, remained perfect and unimpaired." The state did not cease to be a state, nor her citizens to be citizens of the Union. See also the cases of *White* v. *Hart* (13 Wall. 646) and *Keith* v. *Clark* (97 U.S. 451).

  As respects the argument that the Union established by the Constitution of 1789 must be perpetual, because it is declared to have been designed to make a previous perpetual Union more perfect, it may be remarked, as matter of history, that this previous Union (that resting on the Articles of Confederation) had not proved perpetual, but was in fact put an end to by the

from the whole people, and alterable by them only in the manner which its own terms prescribe. It is "an indestructible Union of indestructible States."

It follows from the recognition of the indestructibility of the Union that there must somewhere exist a force capable of preserving it. The national government is now admitted to be such a force. It can exercise all powers essential to preserve and protect its own existence and that of the states, and the constitutional relation of the states to itself, and to one another.

"May it not," someone will ask, "abuse these powers, abuse them so as to extinguish the states themselves, and turn the federation into a unified government. What is there but the federal judiciary to prevent this catastrophe? And the federal judiciary has only moral and not also physical force at its command."

No doubt it may, but not until public opinion supports it in so doing—that is to say, not until the mass of the nation which now maintains, because it values, the federal system, is possessed by a desire to overthrow that system. Such a desire may express itself in proper legal form by carrying amendments to the Constitution which will entirely change the nature of the government. Or if the minority be numerous enough to prevent the passing of such amendments, and if the desire of the majority be sufficiently vehement, the majority which sways the national government may disregard legal sanctions and effect its object by a revolution. In either event—and both are improbable—the change which will have passed upon the sentiments of the American people will be a sign that federalism has done its work, and that the time has arrived for new forms of political life.

---

acceptance in 1788 of the new Constitution by the nine states who first ratified that instrument. After that ratification the Confederation was dead, and the states of North Carolina and Rhode Island, which for some months refused to come into the new Union, were clearly out of the old one, and stood alone in the world. May it not then be said that those who destroyed a Union purporting to be perpetual were thereafter stopped from holding it to have been perpetual, and from founding on the word "perpetual" an argument against those who tried to upset the new Union in 1861, as the old one had been upset in 1788. The answer to this way of putting the point seems to be to admit that the proceedings of 1788 were in fact revolutionary. In ratifying their new Constitution in that year, the nine states broke through and flung away their previous compact which purported to have been made forever. But they did so for the sake of forming a better and more enduring compact, and their extralegal action was amply justified by the necessities of the case.

Working Relations of the National and the State Governments

The characteristic feature and special interest of the American Union is that it shows us two governments covering the same ground yet distinct and separate in their action. It is like a great factory wherein two sets of machinery are at work, their revolving wheels apparently intermixed, their bands crossing one another, yet each set doing its own work without touching or hampering the other. To keep the national government and the state governments each in the allotted sphere, preventing collision and friction between them, was the primary aim of those who formed the Constitution, a task the more needful and the more delicate because the states had been until then almost independent and therefore jealous of their privileges, and because, if friction should arise, the national government could not remove it by correcting defects in the machinery. For the national government, being itself the creature of the Constitution, was not permitted to amend the Constitution, but could only refer it back for amendment to the people of the states or to their legislatures. Hence the men of 1787, feeling the cardinal importance of anticipating and avoiding occasions of collision, sought to accomplish their object by the concurrent application of two devices. One was to restrict the functions of the national government to the irreducible minimum of functions absolutely needed for the national welfare, so that everything else should be left to the states. The other was to give that government, so far as those functions extended, a direct and immediate relation to the citizens, so that it should act on them not through the states but of its own authority and by its own officers. These are fundamental principles whose soundness experience has approved, and which will deserve to be considered by those who in time to come may have in other countries to frame federal or quasi-federal constitutions. They were studied, and to a large extent, though in no slavish spirit, adopted by the founders of the present constitution of the Swiss Confederation, a constitution whose success bears further witness to the soundness of the American doctrines.

The working relations of the national government to the states may be considered under two heads, viz., its relations to the states as corporate bodies, and its relations to the citizens of the states as individuals, they being also citizens of the Union.

The national government touches the states as corporate commonwealths in three points. One is their function in helping to form the national government; another is the control exercised over them by the federal Constitution through the federal courts; the third is the control exercised over them by the federal legislature and executive in the discharge of the governing functions which these latter authorities possess.

I. The states serve to form the national government by choosing presidential electors, by choosing senators, and by fixing the franchise which qualifies citizens to vote for members of the House of Representatives.[1] No difficulty has ever arisen (except during the Civil War) from any unwillingness of the states to discharge these duties, for each state is eager to exercise as much influence as it can on the national executive and Congress. But note how much latitude has been left to the states. A state may appoint its presidential electors in any way it pleases. All states now do appoint them by popular vote. But during the first thirty years of the Union many states left the choice of electors to their respective legislatures. So a state may, by its power of prescribing the franchise for its state elections, prescribe whatever franchise it pleases for the election of its members of the federal House of Representatives, and may thus admit persons who would in other states be excluded from the suffrage, or exclude persons who would in other states be admitted. For instance, at least nine states now allow aliens (i.e., foreigners not yet naturalized) to vote; and nine[2] states admit women to vote at all state elections, thereby admitting them to vote also at congressional and presidential elections.[3] The only restriction imposed on state discretion in this respect is that of the Fifteenth Amendment, which forbids any person

[1] Congress may regulate by statute the times, places, and manner of holding elections for representatives, and has done so to some extent.

[2] In a tenth state, Illinois, women vote in local and presidential elections.

[3] So in some states tribal Indians are permitted to vote. It is odd that the votes of persons who are not citizens of the United States might, in a state where parties are nearly equal, turn the choice of presidential electors in that state, and thereby perhaps turn the presidential election in the Union.

to be deprived of suffrage, on "account of race, colour, or previous condition of servitude."[4]

II. The federal Constitution deprives the states of certain powers they would otherwise enjoy. Some of these, such as that of making treaties, are obviously unpermissible, and such as the state need not regret.[5] Others, however, seriously restrain their daily action. They are liable to be sued in the federal courts by another state or by a foreign power.[6] They cannot, except with the consent of Congress, tax exports or imports, or in any case pass a law impairing the obligation of a contract. They must surrender fugitives from the justice of any other state. Whether they have transgressed any of these restrictions is a question for the courts of law, and, if not in the first instance, yet always in the last resort a question for the federal Supreme Court. If it is decided that they have transgressed, their act, be it legislative or executive, is null and void.[7]

The president as national executive, and Congress as national legislature, have also received from the Constitution the right of interfering in certain specified matters with the governments of the states. Congress of course does this by way of legislation, and when an act of Congress, made within the powers conferred by the Constitution, conflicts with a state statute, the former prevails against the latter. It prevails by making the latter null and void, so that if a state statute has been duly passed upon a matter not forbidden to a state by the Constitution, and subsequently Congress passes an act on the same matter, being one whereon Congress has received the

---

[4] The constitutions of four states confine the suffrage to whites; and Idaho excludes Mongolians not born in the United States; but all such provisions are overridden by the fifteenth constitutional amendment.

[5] As the states had not been accustomed to act as sovereign commonwealths in international affairs, they yielded this right to the national government without demur; whereas Swiss history shows the larger cantons to have been unwilling to drop the practice of sending their own envoys to foreign powers and making bargains on their own behalf.

[6] No foreign state would however appear to have ever brought such a suit.

[7] Mr. Justice Miller observes (*Centennial Address at Philadelphia*) that "at no time since the formation of the Union has there been a period when there were not to be found on the statute books of some of the States acts passed in violation of the provisions of the Constitution regarding commerce, acts imposing taxes and other burdens upon the free interchange of commodities, discriminating against the productions of other States, and attempting to establish regulations of commerce, which the Constitution says shall only be done by Congress." All such acts are of course held invalid by the courts when questioned before them.

It has been held that a state cannot forbid a common carrier to bring into its jurisdiction intoxicating liquors from another state (*Bowman* v. *C. & N. W. Rly.* 125 U.S., p. 465); cf *Leisy* v. *Hardin*, 135 U.S., p. 100; *Minnesota* v. *Barber*, 136 U.S., p. 313. And see also *In re Rahrer*, 140 U.S., p. 564.

right to legislate, the state statute, which was previously valid, now becomes invalid to the extent to which it conflicts with the act of Congress. For instance, Congress has power to establish a uniform law of bankruptcy over the whole Union. Formerly, in the exercise of this power, it passed bankruptcy laws. When these were repealed, the subject was left to the state laws;[8] and still later, in 1898, Congress again legislated on the subject, depriving these state laws of their force.[9] If the law passed by Congress were again repealed, they would again spring into life. The field of this so-called concurrent legislation is large, for Congress has not yet exercised all the powers vested in it of superseding state action.

It was remarked in the last chapter that in determining the powers of Congress on the one hand and of a state government on the other, opposite methods have to be followed. The presumption is always in favour of the state; and in order to show that it cannot legislate on a subject, there must be pointed out within the four corners of the Constitution some express prohibition of the right which it prima facie possesses or some implied prohibition arising from the fact that legislation by it would conflict with legitimate federal authority.[10] On the other hand, the presumption is always against Congress, and to show that it can legislate, some positive grant of power to Congress in the Constitution must be pointed out.[11] When the grant is shown, then the act of Congress has, so long as it remains on the statute book, all the force of the Constitution itself. In some instances the grant of power to Congress to legislate is auxiliary to a prohibition imposed on the states. This is notably the case as regards the amendments to the Constitution, passed for the protection of the lately liberated Negroes. They interdict the states from either recognizing slavery, or discriminating in any way against any class of citizens; they go even beyond citizens in their care, and declare that "no State shall deny to any person within its jurisdiction the equal protection of the laws." Now, by each of these amendments, Congress is also empowered, which practically means enjoined, to "enforce by appropriate legislation" the prohibitions laid upon the states. Congress has done so, but some of its efforts have been held to go beyond the

[8] See the interesting case of *Sturges* v. *Crowninshield*, 4 Wheat. 196.

[9] They lost their force altogether, because the power of Congress being to establish a "uniform" law, the continued existence of statutes differing in the different states would prevent the law of bankruptcy from being uniform over the Union.

[10] Otherwise in the Federal Constitution of Canada. See in the Appendix Note (B) to Chapter 30.

[11] The grant need not, however, be express, for it has frequently been held that a power incidental or instrumental to a power expressly given may be conferred upon Congress by necessary implication. See *M'Culloch* v. *Maryland*, 4 Wheat. p. 316, and *post* Chapter 33.

directions of the amendments, and to be therefore void.[12] The grant of power has not covered them.

Where the president interferes with a state, he does so either under his duty to give effect to the legislation of Congress, or under the discretionary executive functions which the Constitution has entrusted to him. So if any state were to depart from a republican form of government, it would be his duty to bring the fact to the notice of Congress in order that the guarantee of that form contained in the Constitution might be made effective. If an insurrection broke out against the authority of the Union, he would (as in 1861) send federal troops to suppress it. If there should be rival state governments, each claiming to be legitimate, the president might, especially if Congress were not sitting, recognize and support the one which he deemed regular and constitutional.[13]

Are these, it may be asked, the only cases in which federal authority can interfere within the limits of a state to maintain order? Are law and order, i.e., the punishment of crimes and the enforcement of civil rights, left entirely to state authorities? The answer is:

Offences against federal statutes are justiciable in federal courts, and punishable under federal authority. There is no federal common law of crimes;

Resistance offered to the enforcement of a federal statute may be suppressed by federal authority;

Attacks on the property of the federal government may be repelled, and disturbances thence arising may be quelled by federal authority;

The judgments pronounced in civil causes by federal courts are executed by the officers of these courts;

All other offences and disorders whatsoever are left to be dealt with by the duly constituted authorities of the state, who are, however, entitled in one case to summon the power of the Union to their aid.

This case is that of the breaking out in a state of serious disturbances. The president is bound on the application of the state legislature or executive

---

[12] See the Appendix to the last edition of Story's *Commentaries*, and Desty's *Constitution of the United States Annotated*.

[13] In 1874–75 a contest having arisen in Louisiana between two governments each claiming to be the legal government of the state, federal military aid was supplied to one of them by the president and his action was afterwards approved by Congress. It has been doubted, however, whether the case could properly be deemed one of "domestic violence" within the meaning of art. IV, § 4 of the Constitution.

to quell such disturbances by the armed forces of the Union, or by directing the militia of another state to enter. Thus in 1794 Washington suppressed the so-called Whisky Insurrection in Pennsylvania by the militia of Pennsylvania, New Jersey, Virginia, and Maryland.[14] President Grant was obliged to use military force during the troubles which disturbed several of the Southern states after the Civil War; as was President Hayes, during the tumults in Pennsylvania caused by the great railway strikes of 1877. There have, however, been cases, such as the Dorr rebellion in Rhode Island in 1842,[15] in which a state has itself suppressed an insurrection against its legitimate government. It is the duty of a state to do so if it can, and to seek federal aid only in extreme cases, when resistance is formidable. The most remarkable recent instance of federal interposition occurred in 1894 when, during a railway strike in Illinois, mobs had stopped the passage of trains carrying the U. S. mails. President Cleveland, on the ground that federal property must be protected and the constitutional duty of carrying the mails discharged, sent federal troops to Chicago, though not asked to do so by the governor of Illinois, and secured the passage of the mail trains. His action was generally approved both by the legal profession and by the nation.

So far we have been considering the relations of the national government to the states as political communities. Let us now see what are its relations to the individual citizens of these states. They are citizens of the Union as well as of the states, and owe allegiance to both powers. Each power has a right to command their obedience. To which then, in case of conflict, is obedience due?

The right of the state to obedience is wider in the area of matters which it covers. Prima facie, every state law, every order of a competent state authority, binds the citizen, whereas the national government has but a limited power: it can legislate or command only for certain purposes or on certain subjects. But within the limits of its power, its authority is higher than that of the state, and must be obeyed even at the risk of disobeying the state. An instance in which a state official suffered for obeying his state where its directions clashed with a provision of the federal Constitution may set the point in a clear light. A statute of California had committed to the

---

[14] This was the first assertion by arms of the supreme authority of the Union, and produced an enormous effect upon opinion.

[15] President Tyler ordered the militia of Connecticut and Massachusetts to be prepared (in case a requisition came from the R.I. executive) to guard the frontier of Rhode Island against insurgents attempting to enter, and himself took steps for sending in (in case of need) U.S. regular troops, but the Rhode Island militia proved equal to the occasion and succeeded in suppressing Dorr.

city and county authority of San Francisco the power of making regulations for the management of gaols. This authority had in 1876 passed an ordinance directing that every male imprisoned in the county gaol should "immediately on his arrival have his hair clipped to a uniform length of one inch from the scalp." The sheriff having, under this ordinance, cut off the queue of a Chinese prisoner, Ho Ah Kow, was sued for damages by the prisoner, and the court, holding that the ordinance had been passed with a special view to the injury of the Chinese, who consider the preservation of their queue a matter of honour, and that it operated unequally and oppressively upon them, in contravention of the Fourteenth Amendment to the Constitution of the United States, declared the ordinance invalid, and gave judgment against the sheriff.[16] Similar subsequent attempts against the Chinese, made under cover of the Constitution of California of 1879 and divers statutes passed thereunder, have been defeated by the courts.

The safe rule for the private citizen may be thus expressed: "Ascertain whether the federal law is constitutional (i.e., such as Congress has power to pass). If it is, conform your conduct to it at all hazards. If it is not, disregard it, and obey the law of your state." This may seem hard on the private citizen. How shall he settle for himself such a delicate point of law as whether Congress had power to pass a particular statute, seeing that the question may be doubtful and not have come before the courts? But in practice little inconvenience arises, for Congress and the state legislatures have learnt to keep within their respective spheres, and the questions that arise between them are seldom such as need disturb an ordinary man.

The same remarks apply to conflicts between the commands of executive officers of the national government on the one hand, and those of state officials on the other. If the national officer is acting within his constitutional powers, he is entitled to be obeyed in preference to a state official, and conversely, if the state official is within his powers, and the national officer acting in excess of those which the federal Constitution confers, the state official is to be obeyed.

The limits of judicial power are more difficult of definition. Every citizen can sue and be sued or indicted both in the courts of his state and in the federal courts, but in some classes of cases the former, in others the latter, is the proper tribunal, while in many it is left to the choice of the parties before which tribunal they will proceed. Sometimes a plaintiff who has brought his action in a state court finds when the case has gone a certain

---

[16] Case of *Ho Ah Kow* v. *Matthew Nunan* (July 1879), 5 Sawyer, *Circuit Court Reports*, p. 552. A similar ordinance had been some years before courageously vetoed by Mr. Alvord, then mayor of San Francisco.

length that a point of federal law turns up which entitles either himself or the defendant to transfer it to a federal court, or to appeal to such a court should the decision have gone against the applicability of the federal law. Suits are thus constantly transferred from state courts to federal courts, but you can never reverse the process and carry a suit from a federal court to a state court. Within its proper sphere of pure state law—and of course the great bulk of the cases turn on pure state law—there is no appeal from a state court to a federal court; and though the point of law on which the case turns may be one which has arisen and been decided in the Supreme Court of the Union, a state judge, in a state case, is not bound to regard that decision. It has only a moral weight, such as might be given to the decision of an English court, and where the question is one of state law, whether common law or statute law, in which state courts have decided one way and a federal court the other way, the state judge ought to follow his own courts. So far does this go, that a federal court in administering state law, ought to reverse its own previous decision rather than depart from the view which the highest state court has taken.[17] All this seems extremely complex. I can only say that it is less troublesome in practice than could have been expected, because American lawyers are accustomed to the intricacies of their system.

When a plaintiff has the choice of proceeding in a state court or in a federal court, he is sometimes, especially if he has a strong case, inclined to select the latter, because the federal judges are more independent than those of most of the states, and less likely to be influenced by any bias. So, too, if he thinks that local prejudice may tell against him, he will prefer a federal court, because the jurors are summoned from a wider area, and because the judges are accustomed to exert a larger authority in guiding and controlling the jury. But it is usually more convenient to sue in a state court, seeing that there is such a court in every county, whereas federal courts are comparatively few; in many states there is but one.[18]

The federal authority, be it executive or judicial, acts upon the citizens of a state directly by means of its own officers, who are quite distinct from and independent of the state officials. Federal indirect taxes, for instance,

---

[17] This is especially the rule in cases involving the title to land. But though the theory is as stated in the text, the federal courts not unfrequently (especially in commercial cases) act upon their own view of the state law, and have sometimes been accused of going so far as to create a sort of federal common law.

[18] Of course a plaintiff who thinks local prejudice will befriend him will choose the state court, but the defendant may have the cause removed to a federal court if he be a citizen of another state or an alien, or if the question at issue is such as to give federal jurisdiction.

are levied all along the coast and over the country by federal customhouse collectors and excisemen, acting under the orders of the Treasury Department at Washington. The judgments of federal courts are carried out by United States marshals, likewise dispersed over the country and supplied with a staff of assistants. This is a provision of the utmost importance, for it enables the central national government to keep its finger upon the people everywhere, and make its laws and the commands of its duly constituted authorities respected whether the state within whose territory it acts be heartily loyal or not, and whether the law which is being enforced be popular or obnoxious. The machinery of the national government ramifies over the whole Union as the nerves do over the human body, placing every point in direct connection with the central executive. The same is, of course, true of the army; but the army is so small and stationed in but few spots, mostly in the Far West where Indian raids used to be feared, and where there are federal reservations to protect, it scarcely comes into a view of the ordinary working of the system.

What happens if the authority of the national government is opposed, if, for instance, an execution levied in pursuance of a judgment of a federal court is resisted, or federal excisemen are impeded in the seizure of an illicit distillery?

Should the United States marshal or other federal officers be unable to overcome the physical force opposed to him, he may summon all good citizens to assist him, just as the sheriff may summon the *posse comitatus*. If this appeal proves insufficient, he must call upon the president, who may either order national troops to his aid or may require the militia of the state in which resistance is offered to overcome that resistance. Inferior federal officers are not entitled to make requisitions for state force. The common law principle that all citizens are bound to assist the ministers of the law holds in America as in England, but it is as true in the one country as in the other, that what is everybody's business is nobody's business. Practically, the federal authorities are not resisted in the more orderly states and more civilized districts. In such regions, however, as the mountains of Tennessee, Eastern Kentucky, and North Carolina the inland revenue officials find it very hard to enforce the excise laws, because the country is wild, concealment is easy among the woods and rocks, and the population sides with the smugglers. And in some of the Western states an injunction granted by a court, whether a federal or a state court, is occasionally disregarded.[19]

[19] Attacks upon the Chinese, Japanese, and Hindus have taken place from time to time in Pacific coast states and have not always been repressed with sufficient firmness by the local authorities.

Things were, of course, much worse before the War of Secession had established the authority of the central government on an immovable basis. Federal law did not prove an unquestioned protection either to persons who became in some districts unpopular from preaching abolitionism, or to those Southern slave-catchers, who endeavoured, under the Fugitive Slave laws, to recapture in the Northern states slaves who had escaped from their masters.[20] Passion ran high, and great as is the respect for law, passion in America, as everywhere else in the world, will have its way.

If the duly constituted authorities of a state resist the laws and orders of the national government, a more difficult question arises. This has several times happened.

In November 1798 the legislature of Kentucky adopted resolutions declaring that the Constitution was not a submission of the states to a general government, but a compact whereby they formed such a government for special purposes and delegated to it certain definite powers; that when the general government assumed undelegated powers, its acts were unauthoritative and void; and that it had not been made the exclusive or final judge of the extent of the powers delegated to it. Five weeks later the Virginia legislature passed similar but more guarded resolutions, omitting, *inter alia*, the last of the above-mentioned deliverances of Kentucky. Both states went on to declare that the Sedition and Alien Acts recently pased by Congress were unconstitutional, and asked the other states to join in this pronouncement and to cooperate in securing the repeal of the statutes.[21] Seven states answered, all in an adverse sense.

In 1808 the legislatures of some of the New England states passed resolutions condemning the embargo which the national government had laid upon shipping by an act of that year. The state judges, emboldened by these resolutions, took an attitude consistently hostile to the embargo,

---

[20] It was held that a state could not authorize its courts to enforce the Fugitive Slave laws. Being federal statutes, their enforcement belonged to the national government only. See *Prigg* v. *Pennsylvania*, 16 Pet. 539.

[21] There have been endless discussions in America as to the true meaning and intent of these famous resolutions, a lucid account of which may be found in the article (by Mr. Alex. Johnston) "Kentucky Resolutions," in the *American Cyclopædia of Political Science*. The Kentucky resolutions were drafted by Jefferson, who however did not acknowledge his authorship till 1821, the Virginia resolutions by the more cautious Madison. Those who defend Jefferson's action argue, and probably rightly, that what he aimed at was not forcible resistance, but the amendment of the Constitution so as to negative the construction that was being put upon it by the Federalists.

Judge Cooley observes to me, "The most authoritative exponents of the States' Rights creed would probably have said that 'the nullification by the States of all unauthorized acts done under cover of the Constitution' intended by the Resolutions, was a nullification by constitutional means."

holding it to be unconstitutional; popular resistance broke out in some of the coast towns; and the federal courts in New England seldom succeeded in finding juries which would convict even for the most flagrant violation of its provisions. At the outbreak of the war of 1812 the governors of Massachusetts and Connecticut refused to allow the state militia to leave their state in pursuance to a requisition made by the president under the authority of an act of Congress, alleging the requisition to be unconstitutional; and in October 1814 the legislatures of these two states and of Rhode Island, states in which the New England feeling against the war had risen high, sent delegates to a convention at Hartford, which, after three weeks of secret session, issued a report declaring that "it is as much the duty of the State authorities to watch over the rights reserved as of the United States to exercise the powers delegated," laying down doctrines substantially similar to those of the Kentucky resolutions, and advising certain amendments to the federal Constitution, with a menace as to further action in case these should be rejected. Massachusetts and Connecticut adopted the report; but before their commissioners reached Washington, peace with Great Britain had been concluded. In 1828–30 Georgia refused to obey an act of Congress regarding the Cherokee Indians, and to respect the treaties which the United States had made with that tribe and the Creeks. The Georgian legislature passed and enforced acts in contempt of federal authority, and disregarded the orders of the Supreme Court, President Jackson, who had an old frontiersman's hatred to the Indians, declining to interfere.

Finally, in 1832, South Carolina, first in a state convention and then by her legislature, amplified while professing to repeat the claim of the Kentucky resolutions of 1798, declared the tariff imposed by Congress to be null and void as regarded herself, and proceeded to prepare for secession and war. In none of these cases was the dispute fought out either in the courts or in the field;[22] and the questions as to the right of a state to resist federal authority, and as to the means whereby she could be coerced, were left over for future settlement. Settled they finally were by the Civil War of 1861–65, since which time the following doctrines may be deemed established:

---

[22] The acts complained of by Kentucky and Virginia provoked a reaction which led to the overthrow of the Federalist party which had passed them. Of the most important among them, one was repealed and the other, the Sedition Act, expired in 1801 by effluxion of time. Jefferson, when he became president in that year, showed his disapproval of it by pardoning persons convicted under it. The Embargo was raised by Congress in consequence of the strong opposition of New England. In these cases, therefore, it may be thought that the victory substantially remained with the protesting states, while the resistance of South Carolina to the tariff was settled by a compromise.

No state has a right to declare an act of the federal government invalid.[23]

No state has a right to secede from the Union.

The only authority competent to decide finally on the constitutionality of an act of Congress or of the national executive is the federal judiciary.[24]

Any act of a state legislature or state executive conflicting with the Constitution, or with an act of the national government done under the Constitution, is really an act not of the state government, which cannot legally act against the Constitution, but of persons falsely assuming to act as such government, and is therefore *ipso jure* void.[25] Those who disobey federal authority on the ground of the commands of a state authority are therefore insurgents against the Union who must be coerced by its power. The coercion of such insurgents is directed not against the state but against them as individual though combined wrongdoers. A state cannot secede and cannot rebel. Similarly, it cannot be coerced.

This view of the matter, which seems on the whole to be that taken by the Supreme Court in the cases that arose after the Civil War, disposes, as has been well observed by Judge Hare,[26] of the difficulty which President Buchanan felt (see his message of December 3, 1860) as to the coercion of a state by the Union. He argued that because the Constitution did not provide for such coercion, a proposal in the Convention of 1787 to authorize it having been ultimately dropped, it was legally impossible. The best answer to this contention is that such a provision would have been superfluous, because a state cannot legally act against the Constitution. All that is needed is the power, unquestionably contained in the Constitution (art. III, § 3), to subdue and punish individuals guilty of treason against the Union.[27]

---

[23] Of course, as already observed, a state officer or a private citizen may disregard an act of the federal government if he holds it unconstitutional. But he does so at his peril.

[24] Any court, state or federal, may decide on such a question in the first instance. But if the question be a purely political one, it may be incapable of being decided by any court whatever (see Chapter 24), and in such cases the decision of the political departments (Congress or the president, as the case may be) of the federal government is necessarily final, though, of course, liable to be reversed by a subsequent Congress or president. The cases which arose on the Reconstruction Acts, after the War of Secession, afford an illustration. The attempts made to bring these before the courts failed, and the acts were enforced. See *Georgia* v. *Stanton*, 6 Wall. p. 57.

[25] It may, however, happen that a state law is unconstitutional in part only, perhaps in some trifling details, and in such cases that part only will be invalid, and the rest of the law will be upheld. For instance, a criminal statute might be framed so as to apply retrospectively as well as prospectively. So far as retrospective it would be bad, but good for all future cases. (See Constit., art. I, § 10, par. 1.)

[26] *American Constitutional Law*, p. 61.

[27] Swiss practice allows the federal government to coerce a disobedient canton. This is commonly done by quartering federal troops in it at its expense till its government yields—a form of coercion which Swiss frugality dislikes—or by withholding its share of federal grants.

Except in the cases hereinbefore specified, the national government has no right whatever of interfering either with a state as a commonwealth or with the individual citizens thereof, and may be lawfully resisted should it attempt to do so.

"What then?" the European reader may ask. "Is the national government without the power and the duty of correcting the social and political evils which it may find to exist in a particular state, and which a vast majority of the nation may condemn? Suppose widespread brigandage to exist in one of the states, endangering life and property. Suppose contracts to be habitually broken, and no redress to be obtainable in the state courts. Suppose the police to be in league with the assassins. Suppose the most mischievous laws to be enacted, laws, for instance, which recognize polygamy, leave homicide unpunished, drive away capital by imposing upon it an intolerable load of taxation. Is the nation obliged to stand by with folded arms while it sees a meritorious minority oppressed, the prosperity of the state ruined, a pernicious example set to other states? Is it to be debarred from using its supreme authority to rectify these mischiefs?"

The answer is, yes. Unless the legislation or administration of such a state transgresses some provision of the federal Constitution (such as that forbidding *ex post facto* laws, or laws impairing the obligation of a contract), the national government not only ought not to interfere but cannot interfere. The state must go its own way, with whatever injury to private rights and common interests its folly or perversity may cause.

Such a case is not imaginary. In the slave states before the war, although the Negroes were not, as a rule, harshly treated, many shocking laws were passed, and society was going from bad to worse. Even now it sometimes happens that in one or two Western states the roads and even the railways are infested by robbers, there are parts of the country where justice is uncertain and may be unattainable when popular sentiment does not support the law, so that homicide often goes unpunished by the courts, though sometimes punished by Judge Lynch. There are districts where armed bands occasionally appear, perpetrating nocturnal outrages which no state police has been provided to check. So, too, in a few of these states statutes opposed to sound principles of legislation have been passed, and have brought manifold evils in their train. But the federal government looks on unperturbed, with no remorse for neglected duty.

The obvious explanation of this phenomenon is that the large measure of independence left to the states under the federal system makes it necessary to tolerate their misdoings in some directions. As a distinguished authority[28]

[28] Judge Cooley.

observes to me, "The Federal Constitution provided for the protection of contracts, and against those oppressions most likely to result from popular passion and demoralization; and if it had been proposed to go further and give to the Federal authority a power to intervene in still more extreme cases, the answer would probably have been that such cases were far less likely to arise than was the Federal power to intervene improperly under the pressure of party passion or policy, if its intervention were permitted. To have authorized such intervention would have been to run counter to the whole spirit of the Constitution, which kept steadily in view as the wisest policy local government for local affairs, general government for general affairs only. Evils would unquestionably arise. But the Philadelphia Convention believed that they would be kept at a minimum and most quickly cured by strict adherence to this policy. The scope for Federal interference was considerably enlarged after the Civil War, but the general division of authority between the States and the nation was not disturbed."

So far from lamenting as a fault, though an unavoidable fault, of their federal system, the state independence I have described, the Americans are inclined to praise it as a merit. They argue, not merely that the best way on the whole is to leave a state to itself, but that this is the only way in which a permanent cure of its diseases will be effected. They are consistent not only in their federal principles but in their democratic principles. "As *laissez aller*," they say, "is the necessary course in a federal government, so it is the right course in all free governments. Law will never be strong or respected unless it has the sentiment of the people behind it. If the people of a state make bad laws, they will suffer for it. They will be the first to suffer. Let them suffer. Suffering, and nothing else, will implant that sense of responsibility which is the first step to reform. Therefore let them stew in their own juice: let them make their bed and lie upon it. If they drive capital away, there will be less work for the artisans; if they do not enforce contracts, trade will decline, and the evil will work out its remedy sooner or later. Perhaps it will be later rather than sooner; if so, the experience will be all the more conclusive. Is it said that the minority of wise and peaceable citizens may suffer? Let them exert themselves to bring their fellows round to a better mind. Reason and experience will be on their side. We cannot be democrats by halves; and where self-government is given, the majority of the community must rule. Its rule will in the end be better than that of any external power." No doctrine more completely pervades the American people, the instructed as well as the uninstructed. Philosophers will tell you that it is the method by which Nature governs, in whose economy error is followed by pain and suffering, whose laws carry their own sanction with them. Divines will tell you that it is the method by which God governs: God is a righteous Judge and God is provoked every day, yet He makes His sun to rise on the evil and the good, and sends His rain upon the just and the unjust. He does not directly intervene to punish faults, but leaves sin to bring its own appointed penalty. Statesmen will point to the troubles which followed the attempt to govern the reconquered seceding states, first, by military force and then by keeping a great part of their population disfranchised, and will declare that such evils as still exist in the South are far less grave than those which the denial of ordinary self-government involved. "So," they pursue, "Texas and California will in time unlearn their bad habits and come out right if we leave them alone: Federal interference, even had we the machinery needed for prosecuting it, would check the natural process by which the better elements in these raw communities are purging away the maladies of youth, and reaching the settled health of manhood."

A European may say that there is a dangerous side to this application of democratic faith in local majorities and in *laissez aller*. Doubtless there is; yet those who have learnt to know the Americans will answer that no nation so well understands its own business.

Criticism of the Federal System

All Americans have long been agreed that the only possible form of government for their country is a federal one. All have perceived that a centralized system would be inexpedient, if not unworkable, over so large an area, and have still more strongly felt that to cut up the continent into absolutely independent states would not only involve risks of war but injure commerce and retard in a thousand ways the material development of every part of the country. But regarding the nature of the federal tie that ought to exist there have been keen and frequent controversies, dormant at present, but which might break out afresh should there arise a new question of social or economic change capable of bringing the powers of Congress into collision with the wishes of any state or group of states. The general suitability to the country of a federal system is therefore accepted, and need not be discussed. I pass to consider the strong and weak points of that which exists.

The faults generally charged on federations as compared with unified governments are the following:

    I. Weakness in the conduct of foreign affairs
   II. Weakness in home government, that is to say, deficient authority over the component states and the individual citizens
  III. Liability to dissolution by the secession or rebellion of states
  IV. Liability to division into groups and factions by the formation of separate combinations of the component states
   V. Absence of the power of legislating on certain subjects wherein legislation uniform over the whole Union is needed
  VI. Want of uniformity among the states in legislation and administration
 VII. Trouble, expense, and delay due to the complexity of a double system of legislation and administration

The first four of these are all due to the same cause, viz., the existence within one government, which ought to be able to speak and act in the name and with the united strength of the nation, of distinct centres of force, organized political bodies into which part of the nation's strength has flowed, and whose resistance to the will of the majority of the whole nation is likely to be more effective than could be the resistance of individuals, because such bodies have each of them a government, a revenue, a militia, a local patriotism to unite them, whereas individual recalcitrants, however numerous, would be unorganized, and less likely to find a legal standing ground for opposition. The gravity of the first two of the four alleged faults has been exaggerated by most writers, who have assumed, on insufficient grounds, that federal governments are necessarily weak. Let us, however, see how far America has experienced such troubles from these features of a federal system.

I. In its early years, the Union was not successful in the management of its foreign relations. Few popular governments are, because a successful foreign policy needs in a world such as ours conditions which popular governments seldom enjoy. In the days of Adams, Jefferson, and Madison, the Union put up with a great deal of ill-treatment from France as well as from England. It drifted rather than steered into the war of 1812. The conduct of that war was hampered by the opposition of the New England states. The Mexican war of 1846 was due to the slaveholders; but the combination among the Southern leaders which entrapped the nation into that conflict might have been equally successful in a unified country; the blame need not be laid at the door of federalism. The principle of abstention from Old World complications has been so heartily and consistently adhered to that the capacities of the federal system for the conduct of foreign affairs have been seldom seriously tried, so far as concerned European powers; and the likelihood of any danger from abroad is so slender that it may be practically ignored. But when a question of external policy arises which interests only one part of the Union (such, for instance, as the immigration of Asiatic labourers), the existence of states feeling themselves specially affected may have a strong and probably an unfortunate influence. Only in this way can the American government be deemed likely to suffer in its foreign relations from its federal character.

II. For the purposes of domestic government the federal authority is now, in ordinary times, sufficiently strong. However, as was remarked in the last chapter, there have been occasions when the resistance of even a single state disclosed its weakness. Had a man less vigorous than Jackson occupied the presidential chair in 1832, South Carolina would probably have prevailed against the Union. In the Kansas troubles of 1855–56 the national executive played a sorry part; and even in the resolute hands of President Grant it was hampered in the reestablishment of order in the reconquered Southern states by the rights which the federal Constitution secured to those states. The only general conclusion on this point which can be drawn from history is that while the central government is likely to find less and less difficulty in enforcing its will against a state or disobedient subjects, because the prestige of its success in the Civil War has strengthened it, and the facilities of communication make the raising and moving of troops more easy, nevertheless recalcitrant states, or groups of states, still enjoy certain advantages for resistance, advantages due partly to their legal position, partly to their local sentiment, which rebels might not have in unified countries like England, France, or Italy.

III. Everybody knows that it was the federal system and the doctrine of state sovereignty grounded thereon, and not excluded, though not recognized, by the Constitution, which led to the secession of 1861, and which gave European powers a plausible ground for recognizing the insurgent minority as belligerents. Nothing seems now less probable than another secession, not merely because the supposed legal basis for it has been abandoned, and because the advantages of continued union are more obvious than ever before, but because the precedent of the victory won by the North will discourage like attempts in the future.[1] This is so strongly felt that it has not even been thought worth while to add to the Constitution an amendment negativing the right to secede. The doctrine of the legal indestructibility of the Union is now well established. To establish it, however, cost thousands of millions of dollars and the lives of a million of men.

IV. The combination of states into groups was a familiar feature of politics before the war. South Carolina and the Gulf states constituted one such, and the most energetic, group; the New England states frequently acted as another, especially during the war of 1812. At present, though there are several sets of states whose common interests lead their representatives in Congress to act together, it is no longer the fashion for states to combine in an official way through their state organizations, and their doing so would excite reprehension. It is easier, safer, and more effective to act through the great national parties. Any considerable state interest (such as that of the

---

[1] The Roman Catholic cantons of Switzerland (or rather the majority of them) formed a separate league (the so-called Sonderbund) which it needed the war of 1847 to put down. And the effect of that war was, as in the parallel case of America, to tighten the federal bond for the future.

silver miners or cattlemen, or protectionist manufacturers) can generally compel a party to conciliate it by threatening to forsake the party if neglected. Political action runs less in state channels than it did formerly, and the only really threatening form which the combined action of states could take, that of using for a common disloyal purpose state revenues and the machinery of state governments, has become, since the failure of secession, most improbable.

It has been a singular piece of good fortune that lines of religious difference have never happened to coincide with state lines; nor has any particular creed ever dominated any group of states. The religious forces which in some countries and times have given rise to grave civil discord, have in America never weakened the federal fabric.

V. Towards the close of the nineteenth century two significant phenomena began to be seen. One was the increasing power of incorporated companies and combinations of capitalists. It began to be felt that there ought to be a power of regulating corporations, and that such regulation cannot be effective unless it proceeds from federal authority and applies all over the Union. At present the power of Congress is deemed to be limited to the operations of interstate commerce, so that the rest of the work done by corporations, with the law governing their creation and management, belongs to the several states. The other phenomenon was the growing demand for various social reforms, some of which (such as the regulation of child labour) are deemed to be neglected by the more backward states, while others cannot be fully carried out except by laws of general application. The difficulty of meeting this demand under existing conditions has led to many complaints, and while some call for the amendment of the Constitution, others have gone so far as to suggest that the courts ought now to construe the Constitution as conferring powers it has not hitherto been deemed to include.

VI. The want of uniformity in private law and methods of administration is an evil which different minds will judge by different standards. Some may think it a positive benefit to secure a variety which is interesting in itself and makes possible the trying of experiments from which the whole country may profit. Is variety within a country more a gain or a loss? Diversity in coinage, in weights and measures, in the rules regarding bills and cheques and banking and commerce generally, is obviously inconvenient. Diversity in dress, in food, in the habits and usages of society, is almost as obviously a thing to rejoice over, because it diminishes the terrible monotony of life. Diversity in religious opinion and worship excited horror in the Middle Ages, but now passes unnoticed, except where governments are intolerant. In the United States the possible diversity of laws is immense. Subject to a few prohibitions contained in the Constitution, each state can play whatever tricks it pleases with the law of family relations, of inheritance, of contracts, of torts, of crimes. But the actual diversity is not great, for all the states, save Louisiana, have taken the English common and statute law of 1776 as their point of departure, and have adhered to its main principles. A more complete uniformity as regards marriage and divorce is desirable, for it is particularly awkward not to know whether you are married or not, nor whether you have been or can be divorced or not; and several states have tried bold experiments in divorce laws.[2] But, on the whole, far less inconvenience than could have been expected seems to be caused by the varying laws of different states, partly because commercial law is the department in which the diversity is smallest, partly because American practitioners and judges have become expert in applying the rules for determining which law, where those of different states are in question, ought to be deemed to govern a given case.[3] However, some states have taken steps to reduce this diversity by appointing commissions, instructed to meet and confer as to the best means of securing uniform state legislation on some important subjects, and progress in this direction has been made.

VII. He who is conducted over an ironclad warship, and sees the infinite intricacy of the machinery and mechanical appliances which it contains and by which its engines, its guns, its turrets, its torpedoes, its apparatus for anchoring and making sail, are worked, is apt to think that it must break down in the rough practice of war. He is told, however, that the more is done by machinery, the more safely and easily does everything go on, because the machinery can be relied on to work accurately, and the performance by it of the heavier work leaves the crew free to attend to the

---

[2] There is, however, little substantial diversity in the laws of marriage in different states, the rule everywhere prevailing that no special ceremony is requisite, and the statutory forms not being deemed imperative. The divergences in divorce law are greater, and the laxity of the law and of procedure in some states altogether lamentable; yet even as regards divorce more trouble arises from frauds practised on the laws as well as from the abuse of allowing divorces to be granted on a fictitious domicil without due notice to the other party, than from divergent provisions in the laws themselves.

There was a recent case in which it seems to have been held that a marriage might be still valid in one state though terminated by divorce in another.

[3] Although the law of Scotland still differs in many material points from that of England and Ireland, having had a different origin, British subjects and courts do not find the practical inconveniences arising from the diversities to be serious except as respects marriage and the succession to property. The mercantile law of the two countries tends to become practically the same.

general management of the vessel and her armament. So in studying the elaborate devices with which the federal system of the United States has been equipped, one fancies that with so many authorities and bodies whose functions are intricately interlaced, and some of which may collide with others, there must be a great risk of breakdowns and deadlocks, not to speak of an expense much exceeding that which is incident to a simple centralized government. In America, however, smoothness of working is secured by elaboration of device; and complex as the mechanism of the government may appear, the citizens have grown so familiar with it that its play is smooth and easy, attended with less trouble, and certainly with less suspicion on the part of the people, than would belong to a scheme which vested all powers in one administration and one legislature. The expense is admitted, but is considered no grave defect when compared with the waste which arises from untrustworthy officials and legislators whose depredations would, it is thought, be greater were their sphere of action wider, and the checks upon them fewer. He who examines a system of government from without is generally disposed to overrate the difficulties in working which its complexity causes. Few things, for instance, are harder than to explain to a person who has not been a student in one of the two ancient English universities the nature of their highly complex constitution and the relation of the colleges to the university. If he does apprehend it he pronounces it too intricate for the purposes it has to serve. To those who have grown up under it, nothing is simpler and more obvious.

There is a blemish characteristic of the American federation which Americans seldom notice because it seems to them unavoidable. This is the practice in selecting candidates for federal office of regarding not so much the merits of the candidate as the effect which his nomination will have upon the vote of the state to which he belongs. Second-rate men are run for first-rate posts, not because the party which runs them overrates their capacity, but because it expects to carry their state either by their local influence or through the pleasure which the state feels in the prospect of seeing one of its own citizens in high office. This of course works in favour of the politicians who come from a large state. No doubt the leading men of a large state are prima facie more likely to be men of high ability than those of a small state, because the field of choice is wider and the competition keener. One is reminded of the story of the leading citizen in the isle of Seriphus who observed to Themistocles, "You would not have been famous had you been born in Seriphus," to which Themistocles replied, "Neither would you had you been born in Athens." The two great states of Virginia and Massachusetts reared one half of the men who won distinction in the first fifty years of the history of the Republic. Nevertheless it often happens that a small state produces a first-rate man, whom the country ought to have in its highest places, but who is passed over because the federal system gives great weight to the voice of a state, and because state sentiment is so strong that the voters of a state which has a large and perhaps a doubtful vote to cast in national elections, prefer an inferior man in whom they are directly interested to a superior one who is a stranger. It is also unfortunate that the president's liberty of choice in forming his cabinet should be restricted by the doctrine that he must not have in it, if possible, two persons from the same state.

I have left to the last the gravest reproach which Europeans have been wont to bring against federalism in America. They attributed to it the origin, or at least the virulence, of the great struggle over slavery which tried the Constitution so severely. That struggle created parties which, though they had adherents everywhere, no doubt tended more and more to become identified with states, controlling the state organizations and bending the state governments to their service. It gave tremendous importance to legal questions arising out of the differences between the law of the slave states and the free states, questions which the Constitution had either evaded or not foreseen. It shook the credit of the Supreme Court by making the judicial decision of those questions appear due to partiality to the slave states. It disposed the extreme men on both sides to hate the federal Union which bound them in the same body with their antagonists. It laid hold of the doctrine of states' rights and state sovereignty as entitling a commonwealth which deemed itself aggrieved to shake off allegiance to the national government. Thus at last it brought about secession and the great civil war. Even when the war was over, the dregs of the poison continued to haunt and vex the system, and bred fresh disorders in it. The constitutional duty of reestablishing the state governments of the conquered states on the one hand, and on the other hand the practical danger of doing so while their people remained disaffected, produced the military governments, the "carpet bag" governments, the Ku Klux Klan outrages, the gift of suffrage to a Negro population unfit for such a privilege, yet apparently capable of being protected in no other way. All these mischiefs, it has often been argued, are the results of the federal structure of the government, which carried in its bosom the seeds of its own destruction, seeds sure to ripen so soon as there arose a question that stirred men deeply.

It may be answered not merely that the national government has survived this struggle and emerged from it stronger than before, but also that federalism did not produce the struggle, but only gave to it the particular form of a series of legal controversies over the federal pact followed by a war of states against the Union. Where such vast economic interests were involved, and such hot passions roused, there must anyhow have been a conflict, and it may well be that a conflict raging within the vitals of a centralized government would have proved no less terrible and would have left as many noxious *sequelae* behind.

In blaming either the conduct of a person or the plan and scheme of a government for evils which have actually followed, one is apt to overlook those other evils, perhaps as great, which might have flowed from different conduct or some other plan. All that can fairly be concluded from the history of the American Union is that federalism is obliged by the law of its nature to leave in the hands of states powers whose exercise may give to political controversy a peculiarly dangerous form, may impede the assertion of national authority, may even, when long-continued exasperation has suspended or destroyed the feeling of a common patriotism, threaten national unity itself. Against this danger is to be set the fact that the looser structure of a federal government and the scope it gives for diversities of legislation in different parts of a country may avert sources of discord, or prevent local discord from growing into a contest of national magnitude.

Merits of the Federal System

I do not propose to discuss in this chapter the advantages of federalism in general, for to do this we should have to wander off to other times and countries, to talk of Achaia and the Hanseatic League and the Swiss Confederation. I shall comment on those merits only which the experience of the American Union illustrates.

There are two distinct lines of argument by which their federal system was recommended to the framers of the Constitution, and upon which it is still held forth for imitation to other countries. These lines have been so generally confounded that it is well to present them in a precise form.

The first set of arguments point to federalism proper, and are the following:

1. That federalism furnishes the means of uniting commonwealths into one nation under one national government without extinguishing their separate administrations, legislatures, and local patriotisms. As the Americans of 1787 would probably have preferred complete state independence to the fusion of their states into a unified government, federalism was the only resource. So when the new Germanic Empire, which is really a federation, was established in 1871, Bavaria and Würtemberg could not have been brought under a national government save by a federal scheme. Similar suggestions, as everyone knows, have been made for resettling the relations of Ireland to Great Britain, and of the self-governing British colonies to the United Kingdom. There are causes and conditions which dispose nations living under loosely compacted governments, to form a closer union in a federal form. There are other causes and conditions which dispose the subjects of one government, or sections of these subjects, to desire to make their governmental union less close by substituting a federal for a unitary system. In both sets of cases, the centripetal or centrifugal forces spring from the local position, the history, the sentiments, the economic needs of

those among whom the problem arises; and that which is good for one people or political body is not necessarily good for another. Federalism is an equally legitimate resource where it is adopted for the sake of tightening or for the sake of loosening a preexisting bond.[1]

2. That federalism supplies the best means of developing a new and vast country. It permits an expansion whose extent, and whose rate and manner of progress, cannot be foreseen to proceed with more variety of methods, more adaptation of laws and administration to the circumstances of each part of the territory, and altogether in a more truly natural and spontaneous way, than can be expected under a centralized government, which is disposed to apply its settled system through all its dominions. Thus the special needs of a new region are met by the inhabitants in the way they find best: its laws can be adapted to the economic conditions which from time to time present themselves; its special evils are cured by special remedies, perhaps more drastic than an old country demands, perhaps more lax than an old country would tolerate; while at the same time the spirit of self-reliance among those who build up these new communities is stimulated and respected.

3. That federalism prevents the rise of a despotic central government, absorbing other powers, and menacing the private liberties of the citizen. This may now seem to have been an idle fear, so far as America was concerned. It was, however, a very real fear among the ancestors of the present Americans, and nearly led to the rejection even of so undespotic an instrument as the federal Constitution of 1789. Congress (or the president, as the case may be) is still sometimes described as a tyrant by the party which does not control it, simply because it is a central government; and the states are represented as bulwarks against its encroachments.

The second set of arguments relate to and recommend not so much federalism as local self-government. I state them briefly because they are familiar.

4. Self-government stimulates the interest of people in the affairs of their neighbourhood, sustains local political life, educates the citizen in his daily round of civic duty, teaches him that perpetual vigilance and the sacrifice of his own time and labour are the price that must be paid for individual liberty and collective prosperity.

5. Self-government secures the good administration of local affairs by

---

[1] I have treated of this subject in an essay on the centripetal and centrifugal forces in constitutional law in a book entitled *Studies in History and Jurisprudence*.

giving the inhabitants of each locality due means of overseeing the conduct of their business.

That these two sets of grounds are distinct appears from the fact that the sort of local interest which local self-government evokes is quite a different thing from the interest men feel in the affairs of a large body like an American state. So, too, the control over its own affairs of a township, or even a small county, where everybody can know what is going on, is quite different from the control exercisable over the affairs of a commonwealth with a million of people. Local self-government may exist in a unified country like England, and may be wanting in a federal country like Germany. And in America itself, while some states, like those of New England, possessed an admirably complete system of local government, others, such as Virginia, the old champion of state sovereignty, were imperfectly provided with it. Nevertheless, through both sets of arguments there runs the general principle, applicable in every part and branch of government, that, where other things are equal, the more power is given to the units which compose the nation, be they large or small, and the less to the nation as a whole and to its central authority, so much the fuller will be the liberties and so much greater the energy of the individuals who compose the people. This principle, though it had not been then formulated in the way men formulate it now, was heartily embraced by the Americans. Perhaps it was because they agreed in taking it as an axiom that they seldom referred to it in the subsequent controversies regarding state rights. These controversies proceeded on the basis of the Constitution as a law rather than on considerations of general political theory. A European reader of the history of the first seventy years of the United States is surprised how little is said, through the interminable discussions regarding the relation of the federal government to the states, on the respective advantages of centralization or localization of powers as a matter of historical experience and general expediency.

Three further benefits to be expected from a federal system may be mentioned, benefits which seem to have been unnoticed or little regarded by those who established it in America.

6. Federalism enables a people to try experiments in legislation and administration which could not be safely tried in a large centralized country. A comparatively small commonwealth like an American state easily makes and unmakes its laws; mistakes are not serious, for they are soon corrected; other states profit by the experience of a law or a method which has worked well or ill in the state that has tried it.

7. Federalism, if it diminishes the collective force of a nation, diminishes

also the risks to which its size and the diversities of its parts expose it. A nation so divided is like a ship built with watertight compartments. When a leak is sprung in one compartment, the cargo stowed there may be damaged, but the other compartments remain dry and keep the ship afloat. So if social discord or an economic crisis has produced disorders or foolish legislation in one member of the federal body, the mischief may stop at the state frontier instead of spreading through and tainting the nation at large.

8. Federalism, by creating many local legislatures with wide powers, relieves the national legislature of a part of that large mass of functions which might otherwise prove too heavy for it. Thus business is more promptly despatched, and the great central council of the nation has time to deliberate on those questions which most nearly touch the whole country.

All of these arguments recommending federalism have proved valid in American experience.

To create a nation while preserving the states was the main reason for the grant of powers which the national government received; an all-sufficient reason, and one which holds good today. The several states have changed greatly since 1789, but they are still commonwealths whose wide authority and jurisdiction practical men are agreed in desiring to maintain.

Not much was said in the Convention of 1787 regarding the best methods of extending government over the unsettled territories lying beyond the Allegheny mountains.[2] It was, however, assumed that they would develop as the older colonies had developed, and in point of fact each district, when it became sufficiently populous, was formed into a self-governing state, the less populous divisions still remaining in the status of semi-self-governing Territories. Although many blunders have been committed in the process of development, especially in the reckless contraction of debt and the wasteful disposal of the public lands, greater evils might have resulted had the creation of local institutions and the control of new communities been left to the central government.[3] Congress would have been not less improvident

---

[2] In 1787, however, the great ordinance regulating the Northwest Territory was enacted by the Congress of the Confederation.

[3] The United States is proprietor of the public domain in the Territories, and when a new state is organized the ownership is not changed. The United States, however, makes grants of wild lands to the new state as follows: (1) Of every section numbered 16 (being one thirty-sixth of all) for the support of common schools; (2) of lands to endow a university; (3) of the lands noted in the surveys as swamp lands, and which often are valuable. (4) It has usually made further grants to aid in the construction of railroads, and for an agricultural college. The grants commonly leave the United States a much larger landowner within the state than is the state itself, and when all the dealings of the national government with its lands are considered, it is more justly chargeable with squandering the public domain than the states are.

than the state governments, for it would have been even less closely watched. The opportunities for jobbery would have been irresistible, the growth of order and civilization probably slower. It deserves to be noticed that, in granting self-government to all those of her colonies whose population is of English race, England has practically adopted the same plan as the United States have done with their Western territory. The results have been generally satisfactory, although England, like America, has found that her colonists are disposed to treat the aboriginal inhabitants, whose lands they covet and whose persons they hate, with a harshness and injustice which the mother country would gladly check.

The arguments which set forth the advantages of local self-government were far more applicable to the states of 1787 than to those of 1907. Virginia, then the largest state, had only half a million free inhabitants, less than the present population of Baltimore. Massachusetts had 450,000, Pennsylvania 400,000, New York 300,000; while Georgia, Rhode Island, and Delaware had (even counting slaves) less than 200,000 between them.[4] These were communities to which the expression "local self-government" might be applied, for, although the population was scattered, the numbers were small enough for the citizens to have a personal knowledge of their leading men, and a personal interest (especially as a large proportion were landowners) in the economy and prudence with which common affairs were managed. Now, however, when of the nearly fifty states twenty-nine have more than a million inhabitants, and six have more than three millions, the newer states, being, moreover, larger in area than most of the older ones, the stake of each citizen is relatively smaller, and generally too small to sustain his activity in politics, and the party chiefs of the state are known to him only by the newspapers or by their occasional visits on a stumping tour.[5]

All that can be claimed for the federal system under this head of the argument is that it provides the machinery for a better control of the taxes raised and expended in a given region of the country, and a better oversight

---

[4] I give the round numbers, reduced a little from the numbers which appear in the census of 1790.
[5] To have secured the real benefits of local self-government the states ought to have been kept at a figure not much above that of their original population, their territory being cut up into new states as the population increased. Had this been done—no doubt at the cost of some obvious disadvantages, such as the diminution of state historical feeling, the undue enlargement of the Senate, and the predominance of a single large city in a state—there would now be more than two hundred states. Of course in one sense the states are no larger than they were in the early days, because communication from one part to another is in all of them far easier, quicker, and cheaper than it then was.

of the public works undertaken there than would be possible were everything left to the central government.[6] As regards the educative effect of numerous and frequent elections, a European observer is apt to think that elections in America are too many and come too frequently. Overtaxing the attention of the citizen and frittering away his interest, they leave him at the mercy of knots of selfish adventurers.

The utility of the state system in localizing disorders or discontents, and the opportunities it affords for trying easily and safely experiments which ought to be tried in legislation and administration, constitute benefits to be set off against the risk, referred to in the last preceding chapters, that evils may continue in a district, may work injustice to a minority and invite imitation by other states, which the wholesome stringency of the central government might have suppressed.

A more unqualified approval may be given to the division of legislative powers. The existence of the state legislatures relieves Congress of a burden too heavy for its shoulders; for although it has far less foreign policy to discuss than the parliaments of England, France, or Italy, and although the separation of the executive from the legislative department gives it less responsibility for the ordinary conduct of the administration than devolves on those chambers, it could not possibly, were its competence as large as theirs, deal with the multiform and increasing demands of the different parts of the Union. There is great diversity in the material conditions of different parts of the country, and at present the people, particularly in the West, are eager to have their difficulties handled, their economic and social needs satisfied, by the state and the law. It would be extremely difficult for any central legislature to pass measures suited to these dissimilar and varying conditions. How little Congress could satisfy them appears by the very imperfect success with which it cultivates the field of legislation to which it is now limited.

These merits of the federal system of government which I have enumerated are the counterpart and consequences of that limitation of the central authority whose dangers were indicated in the last chapter. They are, if one may reverse the French phrase, the qualities of federalism's defects. The problem which all federalized nations have to solve is how to secure an efficient central government and preserve national unity, while allowing free scope for the diversities, and free play to the authorities, of the members of the

---

[6] It must be remembered that in most parts of the Union the local self-government of cities, counties, townships, and school districts exists in a more complete form than in any of the great countries of Europe.—See Chapters 48–52 *post.*

federation. It is, to adopt that favourite astronomical metaphor which no American panegyrist of the Constitution omits, to keep the centrifugal and centripetal forces in equilibrium, so that neither the planet states shall fly off into space, nor the sun of the central government draw them into its consuming fires. The characteristic merit of the American Constitution lies in the method by which it has solved this problem. It has given the national government a direct authority over all citizens, irrespective of the state governments, and has therefore been able safely to leave wide powers in the hands of those governments. And by placing the Constitution above both the national and the state governments, it has referred the arbitrament of disputes between them to an independent body, charged with the interpretation of the Constitution, a body which is to be deemed not so much a third authority in the government as the living voice of the Constitution, the unfolder of the mind of the people whose will stands expressed in that supreme instrument.

The application of these two principles, unknown to or at any rate little used by, any previous federation,[7] has contributed more than anything else to the stability of the American system, and to the reverence which its citizens feel for it, a reverence which is the best security for its permanence. Yet even these devices would not have succeeded but for the presence of a mass of moral and material influences stronger than any political devices, which have maintained the equilibrium of centrifugal and centripetal forces. On the one hand there has been the love of local independence and self-government; on the other, the sense of community in blood, in language, in habits and ideas, a common pride in the national history and the national flag.

Quid leges sine moribus? The student of institutions, as well as the lawyer, is apt to overrate the effect of mechanical contrivances in politics. I admit that in America they have had one excellent result; they have formed a legal habit in the mind of the nation. But the true value of a political contrivance resides not in its ingenuity but in its adaptation to the temper and circumstances of the people for whom it is designed, in its power of using, fostering, and giving a legal form to those forces of sentiment and interest which it finds in being. So it has been with the American system. Just as the passions which the question of slavery evoked strained the federal fabric, disclosing unforeseen weaknesses, so the love of the Union, the

---

[7] The central government in the Achæan League had apparently a direct authority over the citizens of the several cities, but it was so ill defined and so little employed that we can hardly cite that instance as a precedent.

sense of the material and social benefits involved in its preservation, appeared in unexpected strength, and manned with zealous defenders the ramparts of the sovereign Constitution. It is this need of determining the suitability of the machinery for the workmen and its probable influence upon them, as well as the capacity of the workmen for using and their willingness to use the machinery, which makes it so difficult to predict the operation of a political contrivance, or, when it has succeeded in one country, to advise its imitation in another. The growing strength of the national government in the United States is largely due to sentimental forces that were weak a century ago, and to a development of internal communications which was then undreamt of. And the devices which we admire in the Constitution might prove unworkable among a people less patriotic and self-reliant, less law-loving and law-abiding, than are the English of America.

Supplementary Note to Edition of 1910

Though I have made such corrections in the foregoing chapters as are needed to bring the statements made in them up to the present time, it is proper to note here in a concise way certain general tendencies which have affected, and may hereafter more largely affect, the working of the federal system.

The growth of population, the extension of communications and their larger use both for commerce and for the goings to and fro of the inhabitants, as well as the emergence of new ideas and new needs, have brought about many changes. Three deserve to be singled out as of special importance. (1) The importance of the things which the national government does, has tended to increase as compared with the things which the states do. (2) Uniformity of regulation over the country has become more needful. (3) In the matters which are regulated partly by the national government and partly by the states, the inconvenience arising from a division and intermingling of powers has become more evident and more serious.

(1) The army and navy are larger and more costly than they were; and excite more attention. Questions of tariff more and more affect industry and trade. There is more interest, though perhaps not yet as much as there ought to be, in the conservation of natural resources, including the development of internal waterways, and the control and distribution of water power.

(2) The evils arising from the backwardness of some states, and the boldness or levity of some others, in legislating upon such subjects as child labour, sanitation, divorce, the prevention of accidents in mining and other industries, seem more evident, not because things are any worse than they were, for they are in most respects better, but because the spirit of reform and the humanitarian sympathy which seeks to amend the ills of life have become more active. For instance it is

now held regrettable that temptations should be offered to capitalists to establish factories in states where the law gives deficient protection to children or makes the requirements of health and safety less stringent. In those fields of action wherein neither Congress nor the states enjoy complete authority, the want of a power to deal with the whole of a subject makes legislation halting and imperfect.

(3) The regulation of railroads, as respects both their methods of operation and their rates, by one law and one administrative authority seems needed not only in the interest of traders and passengers but in that of the employees, and indeed of the railroad owners themselves, who are harassed by the varying (and sometimes vexatious) legislation of different states superadded to the legislation of Congress controlling interstate commerce. Whether all railroads should be subjected to federal legislation, or whether such legislation should be extended only to cover the whole working of railroads doing extrastate business or operating in more than one state, is a further question as to which opinion is divided. There has grown up strong demand for the suppression of all monopolies by general measures. There is a desire to see more control and a uniform control exerted by national law over large industrial and trading corporations. All these convergent wishes and demands represent a tendency which has not as yet found in federal law and federal administration a concrete expression proportionate to its strength. The mind of the nation is now awake to these needs and desires, but it is reluctant to depart from the existing boundaries of federal action and state action. Thus it continues to wrestle with the problem, the difficulties of which lie not merely in the solution to be attained but in the manner of attaining the solution, because there are objections to both the courses which might have to be taken, the course of amending the Constitution and the course of encouraging the federal courts to effect by interpretation alterations so large as are desired. No one desire to weaken confidence in the fundamental instrument.

Whatever changes may come, and whether they come sooner or later, it is clear that the nation feels itself more than ever before to be one for all commercial and social purposes, every part of it more interlaced with and dependent on all the other parts than at any previous epoch of its history. This feeling, due to influences which have been steadily gaining ground, cannot but have its effect upon political institutions. It does not necessarily portend any menace to the states. Everyone feels that they are necessary and must be maintained. But it presages some further extensions of federal authority.

One new fact which was expected to exalt the majesty and strengthen the power of the national government has so far made little if any difference—I mean the acquisition of transmarine possessions and particularly of the Philippine Islands, which are immediately dependent upon that government, and bring it into relation with new foreign problems. These conquests are too relatively small and too distant to occupy the thoughts of the people. The lustre of the national government has not been visibly enhanced by its control of the new possessions, and still less has its character as a constitutional government suffered from the fact that it exercises a larger sway than is permitted to it at home. It is not through the so-called "imperial position" which the government of the United States now holds, nor through the place it has assumed as a world power, but rather through the internal causes above referred to, that the forces which make for the unification of the country seem to be working. Yet in one respect the war with Spain did contribute to the strengthening of a sentiment of unity, for it obliterated the relics of sectional antagonism which had lingered on from the days of the Civil War. Soldiers from the North and soldiers from the South fought side by side in Cuba under one flag.

Growth and Development
of the Constitution

There is another point of view from which we have still to consider the Constitution. It is not only a fundamental law, but an unchangeable law, unchangeable, that is to say, by the national legislature, and changeable even by the people only through a slow and difficult process. How can a country whose very name suggests to us movement and progress be governed by a system and under an instrument which remains the same from year to year and from century to century?

By the "constitution" of a state or a nation we mean those of its rules or laws which determine the form of its government, and the respective rights and duties of the government towards the citizens and of the citizens towards the government. These rules, or the most important among them, may be contained in one document, such as the Swiss or Belgian Constitution, or may be scattered through a multitude of statutes and reports of judicial decisions, as is the case with regard to what men call the English Constitution. This is a distinction of practical consequence. But a still more important difference exists in the fact that in some countries the rules or laws which make up the constitution can be made and changed by the ordinary legislature just like any other laws, while in other countries such rules are placed above and out of the reach of the legislature, having been enacted and being changeable only by some superior authority. In countries of the former class the so-called constitution is nothing more than the aggregate of those laws— including of course customs and judicial decisions—which have a political character; and this description is too vague to be scientifically useful, for no three jurists would agree as to which laws ought to be deemed political. In such countries there is nothing either in the form of what are commonly called constitutional laws, or in the source from which they emanate, or in the degree of their authority, to mark them off from other laws. The Constitution of England is constantly changing, for as the legislature, in the ordinary exercise of its powers, frequently passes enactments which affect the methods of government and the political rights of the citizens, there is no certainty that what is called the Constitution will stand the same at the end of a given session of Parliament as it stood at the beginning.[1] A constitution of this kind, capable at any moment of being bent or turned, expanded or contracted, may properly be called a flexible constitution.

In countries of the other class the laws and rules which prescribe the nature, powers, and functions of the government are contained in a document or documents emanating from an authority superior to that of the legislature. This authority may be a monarch who has *octroyé* a charter alterable by himself only. Or it may be the whole people voting at the polls; or it may be a special assembly, or combination of assemblies, appointed ad hoc. In any case we find in such countries a law or group of laws distinguished from other laws not merely by the character of their contents, but by the source whence they spring and by the force they exert, a force which overrides and breaks all enactments passed by the ordinary legislature. Where the constitution consists of such a law or laws, I propose to call it a rigid constitution, i.e., one which cannot be bent or twisted by the action of the legislature, but stands stiff and solid, opposing a stubborn resistance to the attacks of any majority who may desire to trangress or evade its provisions. As the English Constitution is the best modern instance of the flexible type, so is the American of the rigid type.

It will at once be asked, How can any constitution be truly rigid? Growth and decay are the necessary conditions of the life of institutions as well as of individual organisms. One constitution may be altered less frequently or

---

[1] The first statesman who remarked this seems to have been James Wilson, who said in 1788, "The idea of a constitution limiting and superintending the operations of legislative authority, seems not to have been accurately understood in Britain. There are at least no traces of practice conformable to such a principle. The British Constitution is just what the British Parliament pleases. When the Parliament transferred legislative authority to Henry VIII, the act transferring could not, in the strict acceptation of the term, be called unconstitutional. To control the powers and conduct of the legislature by an overruling constitution was an improvement in the science and practice of government reserved to the American States."—Elliot's *Debates*, vol. ii, 432. Paley had made the observation relating to England in his *Moral Philosophy*, published just before 1787. Read and consider Oliver Cromwell's Instrument, called "The Government of the Commonwealth of England, Scotland, and Ireland," printed in the *Parliamentary History*, vol. iii, p. 1417. It was provided by this instrument that statutes passed in Parliament should take effect, even if not assented to by the Lord Protector, but only if they were agreeable to the articles of the instrument, which would therefore appear to have been a genuine rigid constitution within the terms of the definition given in the text. Some of the provisions of the articles are so minute that they can hardly have been intended to be placed above change by Parliament; but Cromwell seems from the remarkable speech which he delivered on December 16, 1653, in promulgating the Instrument, to have conceived that what he called the fundamentals should be unchangeable.

easily than another, but an absolutely unchangeable constitution is an impossibility.[2]

The question is pertinent; the suggestion is true. No constitution can be made to stand unsusceptible of change, because if it were, it would cease to be suitable to the conditions amid which it has to work, that is, to the actual forces which sway politics. And being unsuitable, it would be weak, not rooted in the nature of the state and in the respect of the citizens for whom it exists; and being weak, it would presently be overthrown. If therefore we find a rigid constitution tenacious of life, if we find it enjoying, as Virgil says of the gods, a fresh and green old age, we may be sure that it has not stood wholly changeless, but has been so modified as to have adapted itself to the always altering circumstances that have grown up round it. Most of all must this be true of a new country where men and circumstances change faster than in Europe, and where, owing to the equality of conditions, the leaven of new ideas works more thoroughly upon the whole lump.

We must therefore be prepared to expect that the American Constitution will, when its present condition is compared with its fire-new condition in 1789, prove to have felt the hand of time and change.

Historical inquiry verifies this expectation. The Constitution of the United States, rigid though it be, has changed, has developed. It has developed in three ways to which I devote the three following chapters.

It has been changed by amendment. Certain provisions have been struck out of the original document of 1787–88; certain other, and more numerous, provisions have been added. This method needs little explanation, because it is open and direct. It resembles the method in which laws are changed in England, the difference being that whereas in England statutes are changed by the legislature alone, here in the United States the fundamental law is changed in a more complex fashion by the joint action of Congress and the states.

---

[2] The constitutions of the ancient world were all or nearly all flexible, because the ancient republics were governed by primary assemblies, all whose laws were of equal validity. By far the most interesting and instructive example is the Constitution of Rome. It presents some striking resemblances to the Constitution of England—both left many points undetermined, both relied largely upon semi-legal usages and understandings. (As to the characteristics of rigid and flexible constitutions, remarks may be found in my book entitled *Studies in History and Jurisprudence*, already referred to.)

However, one finds here and there in Greek constitutions provisions intended to secure certain laws from change. At Athens, for instance, there was a distinction between laws (νόμοι) which required the approval of a committee called the nomothetae, and decrees (ψηφίσματα), passed by the assembly alone, and any person proposing a decree inconsistent with a law was liable to an action (γραφὴ παρανόμων) for having, so to speak, led the people into illegality. His conviction in his action carried with it a declaration of the invalidity of the decree.

It has been developed by interpretation, that is, by the unfolding of the meaning implicitly contained in its necessarily brief terms; or by the extension of its provisions to cases which they do not directly contemplate, but which their general spirit may be deemed to cover.

It has been developed by usage, that is, by the establishment of rules not inconsistent with its express provisions, but giving them a character, effect, and direction which they would not have if they stood alone, and by which their working is materially modified. These rules are sometimes embodied in statutes passed by Congress and repealable by Congress. Sometimes they remain in the stage of a mere convention or understanding which has no legal authority, but which everybody knows and accepts. Whatever their form, they must not conflict with the letter of the Constitution, for if they do conflict with it, they will be deemed invalid whenever a question involving them comes before a court of law.

It may be observed that of these three modes of change, the first is the most obvious, direct, and effective, but also the most difficult to apply, because it needs an agreement of many independent bodies which is rarely attainable. The second mode is less potent in its working, because an interpretation put on a provision may be recalled or modified by the same authority, viz., the courts of law (and especially the Supreme Federal Court), which has delivered it. But while a particular interpretation stands, it is as strong as the Constitution itself, being indeed incorporated therewith, and therefore stronger than anything which does not issue from the same ultimate source of power, the will of the people. The weakest, though the easiest and most frequent method, is the third. For, legislation and custom are altogether subordinate to the Constitution, and can take effect only where the letter of the Constitution is silent, and where no authorized interpretation has extended the letter to an unspecified case. But they work readily, quickly, freely; and the developments to be ascribed to them are therefore as much larger in quantity than those due to the two other methods as they are inferior in weight and permanence.

We shall perceive after examining these three sources of change not only that the Constitution as it now stands owes much to them, but that they are likely to modify it still further as time goes on. We shall find that, rigid as it is, it suffers constant qualification and deflection, and that while its words continue in the main the same, it has come to mean something different to the men of 1910 from what it meant to those of 1810, when it had been at work for more than twenty years, or even to those of 1860, when the fires of protracted controversy might be thought to have thrown a glare of light into every corner of its darkest chambers.

The Amendment of the Constitution

The men who sat in the Convention of 1787 were not sanguine enough, like some of the legislating sages of antiquity, or like such imperial codifiers as the emperor Justinian, to suppose that their work could stand unaltered for all time to come. They provided (art. V) that "Congress, whenever two-thirds of both houses shall deem it necessary, shall propose amendments to this Constitution, or on the application of the legislatures of two-thirds of the several States, shall call a convention for proposing amendments, which, in either case, shall be valid to all intents and purposes as part of this Constitution when ratified by the legislatures of three-fourths of the several States, or by conventions in three-fourths thereof, as the one or the other mode may be prescribed by Congress."

There are therefore two methods of framing and proposing amendments.

(A) Congress may itself, by a two-thirds vote in each house, prepare and propose amendments.

(B) The legislatures of two-thirds of the states may require Congress to summon a Constitutional Convention. Congress shall thereupon do so, having no option to refuse; and the convention when called shall draft and submit amendments. No provision is made as to the election and composition of the convention, matters which would therefore appear to be left to the discretion of Congress.

There are also two methods of enacting amendments framed and proposed in either of the foregoing ways. It is left to Congress to prescribe one or other method as Congress may think fit.

(X) The legislatures of three-fourths of the states may ratify any amendments submitted to them.

(Y) Conventions may be called in the several states, and three-fourths of these conventions may ratify.[1]

---

[1] No time is fixed within which the ratification must take place, a somewhat inconvenient omission.

On all the occasions on which the amending power has been exercised, method A has been employed for proposing and method X for ratifying, i.e., no drafting conventions of the whole Union or ratifying conventions in the several states have ever been summoned. The preference of the action of Congress and the state legislatures may be ascribed to the fact that it has never been desired to remodel the whole Constitution, but only to make changes or additions on special points. Moreover, the procedure by national and state conventions might be slower, and would involve controversy over the method of electing those bodies. The consent of the president is not required to a constitutional amendment.[2] A two-thirds majority in Congress can override his veto of a bill, and at least that majority is needed to bring a constitutional amendment before the people.

There is only one provision of the Constitution which cannot be changed by this process. It is that which secures to each and every state equal representation in one branch of the legislature. "No State without its consent shall be deprived of its equal suffrage in the Senate" (art. V). It will be observed that this provision does not require unanimity on the part of the states to a change diminishing or extinguishing state representation in the Senate, but merely gives any particular state proposed to be affected an absolute veto on the proposal. If a state were to consent to surrender its rights, and three-fourths of the whole number to concur, the resistance of the remaining fourth would not prevent the amendment from taking effect.

Following President Lincoln, the Americans speak of the Union as indestructible; and the expression, "An indestructible Union of indestructible States," has been used by the Supreme Court in a famous case.[3] But looking at the Constitution simply as a legal document, one finds nothing in it to prevent the adoption of an amendment providing a method for dissolving the existing federal tie, whereupon such method would be applied so as to form new unions, or permit each state to become an absolutely sovereign and independent commonwealth. The power of the people of the United States appears competent to effect this, should it ever be desired, in a perfectly legal way, just as the British Parliament is legally competent to redivide Great Britain into the sixteen or eighteen independent kingdoms which existed within the island in the eighth century.

The amendments made by the above process (A + X) to the Constitution have been in all seventeen in number. These have been made on five

---

[2] The point was decided by the Supreme Court in 1794 in the case of *Hollingsworth* v. *State of Vermont* (3 Dall. 378); and the Senate came to the same conclusion in 1865. See Jameson on *Constitutional Conventions*, § 560.

[3] *Texas* v. *White*, see *ante*, p. 285.

occasions, and fall into five groups, two of which consist of one amendment each. The first group, including ten amendments made immediately after the adoption of the Constitution, ought to be regarded as a supplement or postscript to it, rather than as changing it. They constitute what the Americans, following the English precedent, call a Bill of Rights, securing the individual citizen and the states against the encroachments of federal power.[4] The second and third groups, if a single amendment can be properly called a group (viz., amendments XI and XII), are corrections of minor defects which had disclosed themselves in the working of the Constitution.[5] The fourth group marked a political crisis and registered a political victory. It comprises three amendments (XIII, XIV, XV) which forbid slavery, define citizenship, secure the suffrage of citizens against attempts by states to discriminate to the injury of particular classes, and extend federal protection to those citizens who may suffer from the operation of certain kinds of unjust state laws. These three amendments are the outcome of the War of Secession, and were needed in order to confirm and secure for the future its results. The requisite majority of states was obtained under conditions altogether abnormal, some of the lately conquered states ratifying while actually controlled by the Northern armies, others as the price which they were obliged to pay for the readmission to Congress of their senators and representatives.[6] The details belong to history. All we need here note

---

[4] These ten amendments were proposed by the First Congress, having been framed by it out of 103 amendments suggested by various states, and were ratified by all the states but three. They took effect in December 1791.

[5] The Eleventh Amendment negatived a construction which the Supreme Court had put upon its own judicial powers (see above, p. 210); the twelfth corrected a fault in the method of choosing the president.

[6] The Thirteenth Amendment was proposed by Congress in February 1865, ratified and declared in force December 1865; the fourteenth was proposed by Congress June 1866, ratified and declared in force July 1868; the fifteenth was proposed by Congress February 1869, ratified and declared in force March 1870. The Fourteenth Amendment had given the states a strong motive for enfranchising the Negroes by cutting down the representation in Congress of any state which excluded male inhabitants (being citizens of the United States) from the suffrage; the fifteenth went further and forbade "race, colour, or previous condition of servitude," to be made a ground of exclusion.

The effect of these three amendments was fully considered by the Supreme Court (in 1872) in the so-called Slaughterhouse Cases (16 Wall. 82), the effect of which is thus stated by Mr. Justice Miller: "With the exception of the specific provisions in the three amendments for the protection of the personal rights of the citizens and people of the United States, and the necessary restrictions upon the power of the States for that purpose, with the additions to the power of the general government to enforce those provisions, no substantial change has been made in the relations of the State governments to the Federal government."—Address delivered before the University of Michigan, June 1887.

The provision of the Fourteenth Amendment which enables the representation of a state to be

is that these deep-reaching, but under the circumstances perhaps unavoidable, changes were carried through not by the free will of the peoples of three-fourths of the states, but under the pressure of a majority which had triumphed in a great war, and used its command of the national government and military strength of the Union to effect purposes deemed indispensable to the reconstruction of the federal system.[7]

The two amendments of 1913 may be called a fifth group, for though they relate to quite different matters, both are the products of what may be described as the "radical tendencies" which had grown powerful in the early years of the present century. One of these amendments extended and defined the power of Congress to impose an income tax. The other took the election of senators away from the state legislatures to vest it in the peoples of the states, a concession to the principle of direct popular sovereignty as well as an expression of distrust in legislative bodies. The former of these two met with considerable opposition in the older states of the East, where capitalistic influences have power; the latter was readily accepted in every state.

Many amendments to the Constitution have been at various times suggested to Congress by presidents, or brought forward in Congress by members, but very few of these have ever obtained the requisite two-thirds vote of both houses. In 1789, however, and again in 1807, amendments were passed by Congress and submitted to the states for which the requisite majority of three-fourths of the states was not obtained; and in February and March 1861 an amendment forbidding the Constitution to be ever so amended as to authorize Congress to interfere with the "domestic institutions," including slavery, of any state, was passed in both houses, but never submitted to the states, because war broke out immediately afterwards. It would doubtless, had peace been preserved, have failed to obtain the acceptance of three-fourths of the states, and its effect could only have been to require those who might thereafter propose to amend the Constitution so as to deal with slavery, to propose also the repeal of this particular amendment itself.[8]

---

reduced has not so far been applied. As to the practical results of the Fifteenth Amendment and the present state of the suffrage in the former slave states, see Chapters 93 to 95 *post*.

[7] But though military coercion influenced the adoption of the Thirteenth Amendment, while political coercion bore a large part in securing the adoption of the others, it must be remembered that some changes in the Constitution were an absolutely necessary corollary to the war which had just ended.

[8] The Greek republics of antiquity sometimes placed some particular law under a special sanction by denouncing the penalty of death on anyone who should propose to repeal it. In such cases, the man who intended to repeal the law so sanctioned of course began by proposing the repeal of the law which imposed the penalty. So it would have been in this case; so it must always be. No sovereign body can limit its own powers. The British Parliament seems to have attempted to bind itself by providing in the Act of Union with Ireland (39 and 40 George III, c. 67) that the

The moral of these facts is not far to seek. Although it has long been the habit of the Americans to talk of their Constitution with almost superstitious reverence, there have often been times when leading statesmen, perhaps even political parties, would have materially altered it if they could have done so. There have, moreover, been some alterations suggested in it, which the impartial good sense of the wise would have approved, but which have never been submitted to the states, because it was known they could not be carried by the requisite majority.[9] If, therefore, comparatively little use has been made of the provisions for amendment, this has been due, not solely to the excellence of the original instrument, but also the difficulties which surround the process of change. Alterations, though seldom large alterations, have been needed, to cure admitted faults or to supply dangerous omissions, but the process has been so difficult that it has been successfully applied only in three kinds of cases: (*a*) matters of minor consequence involving no party interests (amendments XI, XII, and XVI), (*b*) in the course of a revolutionary movement which had dislocated the Union itself (amendments XIII, XIV, XV), and (*c*) matters in which there existed a general sentiment common to both parties desiring alteration (amendments I to X and amendment XVII).

The passing of the two amendments of 1913 may suggest that the Constitution is more likely to undergo change in the near future than had

---

maintenance of the Protestant Episcopal Church as an Established Church in Ireland should be "deemed an essential and fundamental part of the Union." That church was, however, disestablished in 1869 with as much ease as though this provision had never existed.

[9] In the Forty-ninth Congress (1884–86) no fewer than forty-seven propositions were introduced for the amendment of the Constitution, some of them of a sweeping, several of a rather complex, nature. (Some of these covered the same ground, so the total number of alterations proposed was less than forty-seven.) None seems to have been voted on by Congress; and only five or six even deserved serious consideration. One at least, that enabling the president to veto items in an appropriation bill, would have effected a great improvement. I find among them the following proposals: To prohibit the sale of alcoholic liquors, to forbid polygamy, to confer the suffrage on women, to vest the election of the president directly in the people, to elect representatives for three instead of two years, to choose senators by popular election, to empower Congress to limit the hours of labour, to empower Congress to pass uniform laws regarding marriage and divorce, to enable the people to elect certain federal officers, to forbid Congress to pass any local, private, or special enactment, to forbid Congress to direct the payment of claims legally barred by lapse of time, to forbid the states to hire out the labour of prisoners.

In the Sixtieth Congress thirty-six such propositions were introduced, including proposals for the election of judges, for the election of postmasters, for uniform laws regarding divorce, for the repeal of the Fourteenth and of the Fifteenth Amendments to the Constitution, for altering the term of the presidential office, for altering the succession to that office, for an initiative and referendum, for acknowledging the Deity in the federal Constitution, for altering the method of electing United States senators.

seemed probable twenty years ago. Still it is worth while to enquire why the regular procedure for amendment had therefore proved in practice so hard to apply.

Partly, of course, owing to the inherent disputatiousness and perversity (what the Americans call "cussedness") of bodies of men. It is difficult to get two-thirds of two assemblies (the houses of Congress) and three-fourths of forty-eight commonwealths, each of which acts by two assemblies, for the state legislatures are all double-chambered, to agree to the same practical proposition. Except under the pressure of urgent troubles, such as were those which procured the acceptance of the Constitution itself in 1788, few persons or bodies will consent to forego objections of detail, perhaps in themselves reasonable, for the mere sake of agreeing to what others have accepted. They want to have what seems to themselves the very best, instead of a second best suggested by someone else. Now, bodies enjoying so much legal independence as do the legislatures of the states, far from being disposed to defer to Congress or to one another, are more jealous, more suspicious, more vain and opinionated, than so many individuals. Rarely will anything but an active party spirit, seeking either a common party object or individual gain to flow from party success, make them work together.

If an amendment comes to the legislatures recommended by the general voice of their party, they will be quick to adopt it. But in that case it will encounter the hostility of the opposite party, and parties are in many states pretty evenly balanced. It is seldom that a two-thirds majority in either house of Congress can be secured on a party issue; and of course such majorities in both houses, and a three-fourths majority of state legislatures on a party issue, are still less probable. Now, in a country pervaded by the spirit of party, most questions either are at starting, or soon become, controversial.[10] A change in the Constitution, however useful its ultimate consequences, is likely to be for the moment deemed more advantageous to one party than to the other, and this is enough to make the other party oppose it. Indeed, the mere fact that a proposal comes from one side, rouses the suspicion of the other. There is always that dilemma of which England has so often felt the evil consequences. If a measure of reform is immediately pressing, it becomes matter of party contention, it excites temper and passion. If it is not pressing, neither party, having other and nearer aims,

---

[10] Nevertheless neither the Sixteenth nor the Seventeenth Amendment had a party character, though the former was more generally acceptable to one party than to the other.

cares to take it up and push it through. In America, a party amendment to the Constitution can very seldom be carried. Most nonparty amendments fall into the category of those things which, because they are everybody's business, are the business of nobody.

It is evident when one considers the nature of a rigid or supreme constitution, that some method of altering it so as to make it conform to altered facts and ideas is indispensable. A European critic may remark that the American method has failed to answer the expectations formed of it. The belief, he will say, of its authors was that while nothing less than a pretty general agreement would justify alteration, that agreement would exist when obvious omissions preventing its smooth working were discovered. But this has not come to pass. There have been long and fierce controversies over the construction of several points in the Constitution, over the right of Congress to spend money on internal improvements, to charter a national bank, to impose a protective tariff, above all, over the treatment of slavery in the Territories. But the method of amendment was not applied to any of these questions, because no general agreement could be reached upon them, or indeed upon any but secondary matters. So the struggle over the interpretation of a document which it was found impossible to amend, passed from the law courts to the battlefield. Americans reply to such criticisms by observing that the power of amending the Constitution is one which cannot prudently be employed to conclude current political controversies, that if it were so used no constitution could be either rigid or reasonably permanent, that some latitude of construction is desirable, and that in the above-mentioned cases amendments excluding absolutely one or other of the constructions contended for would either have tied down the legislature too tightly or have hastened a probably inevitable conflict. And they now (1914) add that the ease and speed with which the Seventeenth Amendment was passed that when there exists a widespread popular wish for any particular change, it can be promptly gratified.

Ought the process of change to be made easier, say by requiring only a bare majority in Congress, and a two-thirds majority of states? American statesmen think not. A swift and easy method would not only weaken the sense of security which the rigid Constitution now gives, but would increase the troubles of current politics by stimulating a majority in Congress to frequently submit amendments to the states. The habit of mending would turn into the habit of tinkering. There would be too little distinction between changes in the ordinary statute law, which require the agreement of majorities in the two houses and the president, and changes in the more solemnly enacted fundamental law. And the rights of the states, upon which congressional legislation cannot now directly encroach, would be endangered. The French scheme, under which an absolute majority of the two chambers, sitting together, can amend the constitution; or even the Swiss scheme, under which a bare majority of the voting citizens, coupled with a majority of the cantons, can ratify constitutional changes drafted by the chambers, in pursuance of a previous popular vote for the revision of the constitution,[11] is considered by the Americans dangerously lax. The idea reigns that solidity and security are the most vital attributes of a fundamental law.

From this there has followed another interesting result. Since modifications or developments are often needed, and since they can rarely be made by amendment, some other way of making them must be found. The ingenuity of lawyers has discovered one method in interpretation, while the dexterity of politicians has invented a variety of devices whereby legislation may extend, or usage may modify, the express provisions of the apparently immovable and inflexible instrument.

[11] See the Swiss Federal Constitution, arts. 118–21.

CHAPTER 3 3

The Interpretation of the Constitution

The Constitution of England is contained in hundreds of volumes of statutes and reported cases; the Constitution of the United States (including the amendments) may be read through aloud in twenty-three minutes. It is about half as long as St. Paul's first Epistle to the Corinthians, and only one-fortieth part as long as the Irish Land Act of 1881. History knows few instruments which in so few words lay down equally momentous rules on a vast range of matters of the highest importance and complexity. The Convention of 1787 were well advised in making their draft short, because it was essential that the people should comprehend it, because fresh differences of view would have emerged the further they had gone into details, and because the more one specifies, the more one has to specify and to attempt the impossible task of providing beforehand for all contingencies. These sages were therefore content to lay down a few general rules and principles, leaving some details to be filled in by congressional legislation, and foreseeing that for others it would be necessary to trust to interpretation.

It is plain that the shorter a law is, the more general must its language be, and the greater therefore the need for interpretation. So too the greater the range of a law, and the more numerous and serious the cases which it governs, the more frequently will its meaning be canvassed. There have been statutes dealing with private law, such as the Lex Aquilia at Rome and the Statute of Frauds in England, on which many volumes of commentaries have been written, and thousands of juristic and judicial constructions placed. Much more then must we expect to find great public and constitutional enactments subjected to the closest scrutiny in order to discover every shade of meaning which their words can be made to bear. Probably no writing except the New Testament, the Koran, the Pentateuch, and the Digest of the emperor Justinian has employed so much ingenuity and labour as the American Constitution, in sifting, weighing, comparing, illustrating, twisting, and torturing its text. It resembles theological writings in this, that both, while taken to be immutable guides, have to be adapted to a constantly changing world, the one to political conditions which vary from year to year and never return to their former state, the other to new phases of thought and emotion, new beliefs in the realms of physical and ethical philosophy. There must, therefore, be a development in constitutional formulas, just as there is in theological. It will come, it cannot be averted, for it comes in virtue of a law of nature: all that men can do is to shut their eyes to it, and conceal the reality of change under the continued use of time-honoured phrases, trying to persuade themselves that these phrases mean the same thing to their minds today as they meant generations or centuries ago. As a great living theologian says, "In a higher world it is otherwise; but here below to live is to change, and to be perfect is to have changed often."[1]

The Constitution of the United States is so concise and so general in its terms, that even had America been as slowly moving a country as China, many questions must have risen on the interpretation of the fundamental law which would have modified its aspect. But America has been the most swiftly expanding of all countries. Hence the questions that have presented themselves have often related to matters which the framers of the Constitution could not have contemplated. Wiser than Justinian before them or Napoleon after them, they foresaw that their work would need to be elucidated by judicial commentary. But they were far from conjecturing the enormous strain to which some of their expressions would be subjected in the effort to apply them to new facts.

I must not venture on any general account of the interpretation of the Constitution, nor attempt to set forth the rules of construction laid down by judges and commentators, for this is a vast matter and a matter for law books. All that this chapter has to do is to indicate, very generally, in what way and with what results the Constitution has been expanded, developed, modified, by interpretation; and with that view there are three points that chiefly need discussion: (1) the authorities entitled to interpret the Constitution, (2) the main principles followed in determining whether or not the Constitution has granted certain powers, (3) the checks on possible abuses of the interpreting power.

---

[1] Newman, *Essay on Development*, p. 39.

I. To whom does it belong to interpret the Constitution? Any question arising in a legal proceeding as to the meaning and application of this fundamental law will evidently be settled by the courts of law. Every court is equally bound to pronounce and competent to pronounce on such questions, a state court no less than a federal court;[2] but as all the more important questions are carried by appeal to the Supreme Federal Court, it is practically that court whose opinion determines them.

Where the federal courts have declared the meaning of a law, everyone ought to accept and guide himself by their deliverance. But there are always questions of construction which have not been settled by the courts, some because they have not happened to arise in a lawsuit, others because they are such as cannot arise in a lawsuit. As regards such points, every authority, federal or state, as well as every citizen, must be guided by the best view he or they can form of the true intent and meaning of the Constitution, taking, of course, the risk that this view may turn out to be wrong.

There are also points of construction on which every court, following a well-established practice, will refuse to decide, because they are deemed to be of "a purely political nature," a vague description, but one which could be made more specific only by an enumeration of the cases which have settled the practice. These points are accordingly left to the discretion of the executive and legislative powers, each of which forms its view as to the matters falling within its sphere, and in acting in that view is entitled to the obedience of the citizens and of the states also.

It is therefore an error to suppose that the judiciary is the only interpreter of the Constitution, for a large field is left open to the other authorities of the government, whose views need not coincide, so that a dispute between those authorities, although turning on the meaning of the Constitution, may be incapable of being settled by any legal proceeding. This causes no great confusion, because the decision, whether of the political or the judicial authority, is conclusive so far as regards the particular controversy or matter passed upon.

The above is the doctrine now generally accepted in America. But at one time the presidents claimed the much wider right of being, except in questions of pure private law, generally and prima facie entitled to interpret the Constitution for themselves, and to act on their own interpretation, even when it ran counter to that delivered by the Supreme Court. Thus Jefferson denounced the doctrine laid down in the famous judgment of Chief Justice

[2] See Chapter 24 *ante*.

Marshall in the case of *Marbury* v. *Madison;*[3] thus Jackson insisted that the Supreme Court was mistaken in holding that Congress had power to charter the United States Bank, and that he, knowing better than the court did what the Constitution meant to permit, was entitled to attack the bank as an illegal institution, and to veto a bill proposing to recharter it.[4] Majorities in Congress have more than once claimed for themselves the same independence. But of late years both the executive and the legislature have practically receded from the position which the language formerly used seemed to assert; while, on the other hand, the judiciary, by their tendency during the whole course of their history to support every exercise of power which they did not deem plainly unconstitutional, have left a wide field to those authorities. If the latter have not used this freedom to stretch the Constitution even more than they have done, it is not solely the courts of law, but also public opinion and their own professional associations (most presidents, ministers, and congressional leaders having been lawyers) that have checked them.

II. The Constitution has been expanded by construction in two ways. Powers have been exercised, sometimes by the president, more often by the legislature in passing statutes, and the question has arisen whether the powers so exercised were rightfully exercised, i.e., were really contained in the Constitution. When the question was resolved in the affirmative by the court, the power has been henceforth recognized as a part of the Constitution, although, of course, liable to be subsequently denied by a reversal of the decision which established it. This is one way. The other is where some piece of state legislation alleged to contravene the Constitution has been judicially decided to contravene it, and to be therefore invalid. The decision, in narrowing the limits of state authority, tends to widen the prohibitive authority of the Constitution, and confirms it in a range and scope of action which was previously doubtful.

Questions of the above kinds sometimes arise as questions of interpretation

---

[3] As the court dismissed upon another point in the case the proceedings against Mr. Secretary Madison, the question whether Marshall was right did not arise in a practical form.

[4] There was, however, nothing unconstitutional in the course which Jackson actually took in withdrawing the deposits from the United States Bank and in vetoing the bill for a recharter. It is still generally admitted that a president has the right in considering a measure coming to him from Congress to form his own judgment, not only as to its expediency but as to its conformability to the Constitution. Judge Cooley observes to me: "If Jackson sincerely believed that the Constitution had been violated in the first and second charter, he was certainly not bound, when a third was proposed, to surrender his opinion in obedience to precedent. The question of approving a new charter was political; and he was entirely within the line of duty in refusing it for any reasons which, to his own mind, seemed sufficient."

in the strict sense of the term, i.e., as questions of the meaning of a term or phrase which is so far ambiguous that it might be taken either to cover or not to cover a case apparently contemplated by the people when they enacted the Constitution. Sometimes they are rather questions to which we may apply the name of construction, i.e., the case that has arisen is one apparently not contemplated by the enacters of the Constitution, or one which, though possibly contemplated, has for brevity's sake been omitted; but the Constitution has nevertheless to be applied to its solution. In the former case the enacting power has said something which bears, or is supposed to bear, on the matter, and the point to be determined is, What do the words mean? In the latter it has not directly referred to the matter, and the question is, Can anything be gathered from its language which covers the point that has arisen, which establishes a principle large enough to reach and include an unmentioned case, indicating what the enacting authority would have said had the matter been present to its mind, or had it thought fit to enter on an enumeration of specific instances?[5] As the Constitution is not only a well-drafted instrument with few ambiguities but also a short instrument which speaks in very general terms, mere interpretation has been far less difficult than construction.[6] It is through the latter chiefly that the Constitution has been, and still continues to be, developed and expanded. The nature of these expansions will appear from the nature of the federal government. It is a government of delegated and specified

[5] For example, the question whether an agreement carried out between a state and an individual by a legislative act of a state is a "contract" within the meaning of the prohibition against impairing the obligation of a contract, is a question of interpretation proper, for it turns on the determination of the meaning of the term "contract." The question whether Congress had power to pass an act emancipating the slaves of persons aiding in a rebellion was a question of construction, because the case did not directly arise under any provision of the Constitution, and was apparently not contemplated by the framers thereof. It was a question which had to be solved by considering what the war powers contained in the Constitution might be taken to imply. The question whether the national government has power to issue treasury notes is also a question of construction, because, although this is a case which may possibly have been contemplated when the Constitution was enacted, it is to be determined by ascertaining whether the power "to borrow money" covers this particular method of borrowing. There is no ambiguity about the word "borrow"; the difficulty is to pronounce which out of various methods of borrowing, some of which probably were contemplated, can be properly deemed, on a review of the whole financial attributes and functions of the national government, to be included within the borrowing power.

As to the provision restraining states from passing laws impairing the obligation of a contract, see note at the end of this volume on the case of *Dartmouth College* v. *Woodward*.

[6] As the Constitution is deemed to proceed from the people who enacted it, not from the Convention who drafted it, it is regarded for the purposes of interpretation as being the work not of a group of lawyers but of the people themselves. For a useful summary of some of the general rules of constitutional interpretation, see Patterson's *Federal Restraints on State Action*, pp. 215–17.

powers. The people have entrusted to it, not the plenitude of their own authority but certain enumerated functions, and its lawful action is limited to these functions. Hence, when the federal executive does an act, or the federal legislature passes a law, the question arises, Is the power to do this act or pass this law one of the powers which the people have by the Constitution delegated to their agents? The power may never have been exerted before. It may not be found expressed, in so many words, in the Constitution. Nevertheless it may, upon the true construction of that instrument, taking one clause with another, be held to be therein contained.

Now the doctrines laid down by Chief Justice Marshall, and on which the courts have constantly since proceeded, may be summed up in two propositions.

1. Every power alleged to be vested in the national government, or any organ thereof, must be affirmatively shown to have been granted. There is no presumption in favour of the existence of a power; on the contrary, the burden of proof lies on those who assert its existence, to point out something in the Constitution which, either expressly or by necessary implication, confers it. Just as an agent, claiming to act on behalf of his principal, must make out by positive evidence that his principal gave him the authority he relies on; so Congress, or those who rely on one of its statutes, are bound to show that the people have authorized the legislature to pass the statute. The search for the power will be conducted in a spirit of strict exactitude, and if there be found in the Constitution nothing which directly or impliedly conveys it, then whatever the executive or legislature of the national government, or both of them together, may have done in the persuasion of its existence, must be deemed null and void, like the act of any other unauthorized agent.[7]

2. When once the grant of a power by the people to the national government has been established, that power will be construed broadly. The strictness applied in determining its existence gives place to liberality in supporting its application. The people—so Marshall and his successors have argued—when they confer a power, must be deemed to confer a wide discretion as to the means whereby it is to be used in their service. For their

---

[7] For instance, several years ago a person summoned as a witness before a committee of the House of Representatives was imprisoned by order of the House for refusing to answer certain questions put to him. He sued the sergeant-at-arms for false imprisonment, and recovered damages, the Supreme Court holding that as the Constitution could not be shown to have conferred on either house of Congress any power to punish for contempt, that power (though frequently theretofore exercised) did not exist, and the order of the House therefore constituted no defence for the sergeant's act (*Kilbourn* v. *Thompson*, 103 United States, 168).

main object is that it should be used vigorously and wisely, which it cannot be if the choice of methods is narrowly restricted; and while the people may well be chary in delegating powers to their agents, they must be presumed, when they do grant these powers, to grant them with confidence in the agents' judgment, allowing all that freedom in using one means or another to attain the desired end which is needed to ensure success.[8] This, which would in any case be the common-sense view, is fortified by the language of the Constitution, which authorizes Congress "to make all laws which shall be necessary and proper for carrying into execution the foregoing powers, and all other powers vested by this Constitution in the Government of the United States, or in any department or office thereof." The sovereignty of the national government, therefore, "though limited to specified objects, is plenary as to those objects"[9] and supreme in its sphere. Congress, which cannot go one step beyond the circle of action which the Constitution has traced for it, may within that circle choose any means which it deems apt for executing its powers, and is in its choice of means subject to no review by the courts in their function of interpreters, because the people have made their representatives the sole and absolute judges of the mode in which the granted powers shall be employed. This doctrine of implied powers, and the interpretation of the words "necessary and proper," were for many years a theme of bitter and incessant controversy among American lawyers and publicists.[10] The history of the United States is in a large measure a history

---

[8] For instance, Congress having power to declare war, has power to prosecute it by all means necessary for success, and to acquire territory either by conquest or treaty. Having power to borrow money, Congress may, if it thinks fit, issue treasury notes, and may make them legal tender.

[9] See *Gibbons* v. *Ogden*, 9 Wheat. 1 *sqq.*, judgment of Marshall, C. J.

[10] "The powers of the government are limited, and its limits are not to be transcended. But the sound construction of the Constitution must allow to the national legislature that discretion with respect to the means by which the powers it confers are to be carried into execution, which will enable that body to perform the high duties assigned to it in the manner most beneficial to the people. Let the end be legitimate, let it be within the scope of the Constitution, and all means which are appropriate, which are plainly adapted to that end, which are not prohibited but consistent with the letter and spirit of the Constitution, are constitutional."—Marshall, C. J., in *M'Culloch* v. *Maryland* (4 Wheat. 316). This is really a working-out of one of the points of Hamilton's famous argument in favour of the constitutionality of a United States bank: "Every power vested in a government is in its nature sovereign, and includes by force of the term a right to employ all the means requisite and fairly applicable to the attainment of the ends of such power, and which are not precluded by restrictions and exceptions specified in the Constitution." —*Works* (Lodge's ed.), vol. iii, p. 181.

Judge Hare sums up the matter by saying, "Congress is sovereign as regards the objects and within the limits of the Constitution. It may use all proper and suitable means for carrying the powers conferred by the Constitution into effect. The means best suited at one time may be inadequate at another; hence the need for vesting a large discretion in Congress. . . . 'Necessary

of the arguments which sought to enlarge or restrict its import. One school of statesmen urged that a lax construction would practically leave the states at the mercy of the national government, and remove those checks on the latter which the Constitution was designed to create; while the very fact that some powers were specifically granted must be taken to import that those not specified were withheld, according to the old maxim *expressio unius exclusio alterius*, which Lord Bacon concisely explains by saying, "as exception strengthens the force of a law in cases not excepted, so enumeration weakens it in cases not enumerated." It was replied by the opposite school that to limit the powers of the government to those expressly set forth in the Constitution would render that instrument unfit to serve the purposes of a growing and changing nation, and would, by leaving men no legal means of attaining necessary but originally uncontemplated aims, provoke revolution and work the destruction of the Constitution itself.[11]

This latter contention derived much support from the fact that there were certain powers that had not been mentioned in the Constitution, but which were so obviously incident to a national government that they must be deemed to be raised by implication.[12] For instance, the only offences which Congress is expressly empowered to punish are treason, the counterfeiting of the coin or securities of the government, and piracies and other offences against the law of nations. But it was very early held that the power to declare other acts to be offences against the United States, and punish them as such, existed as a necessary appendage to various general powers. So the power to regulate commerce covered the power to punish offences obstructing commerce; the power to manage the post office included the right to fix penalties on the theft of letters; and, in fact, a whole mass of criminal law grew up as a sanction to the civil laws which Congress had been directed to pass.

The three lines along which this development of the implied powers of the government has chiefly progressed, have been those marked out by the three express powers of taxing and borrowing money, of regulating

---

and proper' are therefore, as regards legislation, nearly if not quite synonymous, that being 'necessary' which is suited to the object and calculated to attain the end in view."—*American Constitutional Law*, p. 107.

[11] See the philosophical remarks of Story, J., in *Martin* v. *Hunter's Lessee* (1 Wheat. p. 304 *sqq.*)

[12] Stress was also laid on the fact that whereas the Articles of Confederation of 1781 contained (art. II) the expression, "Each State retains every power and jurisdiction and right not expressly delegated to the United States in Congress assembled," the Constitution merely says (amend. X), "The powers not granted to the United States are reserved to the States respectively or to the people," omitting the word "expressly." See the text of the Articles in the Appendix to this volume.

commerce, and of carrying on war. Each has produced a progeny of subsidiary powers, some of which have in their turn been surrounded by an unexpected offspring. Thus from the taxing and borrowing powers there sprang the powers to charter a national bank and exempt its branches and its notes from taxation by a state (a serious restriction on state authority), to create a system of customhouses and revenue cutters, to establish a tariff for the protection of native industry. Thus the regulation of commerce has been construed to include legislation regarding every kind of transportation of goods and passengers, whether from abroad or from one state to another, regarding navigation, maritime and internal pilotage, maritime contracts, etc., together with the control of all navigable waters not situate wholly within the limits of one state, the construction of all public works helpful to commerce between states or with foreign countries, the power to prohibit immigration, and finally a power to establish a railway commission and control all interstate traffic.[13] The war power proved itself even more elastic. The executive and the majority in Congress found themselves during the War of Secession obliged to stretch this power to cover many acts trenching on the ordinary rights of the states and of individuals, till there ensued something approaching a suspension of constitutional guarantees in favour of the federal government.

The courts have occasionally gone even further afield, and have professed to deduce certain powers of the legislature from the sovereignty inherent in the national government. In its last decision on the legal tender question, a majority of the Supreme Court seems to have placed upon this ground, though with special reference to the section enabling Congress to borrow money, its affirmance of that competence of Congress to declare paper money a legal tender for debts, which the earlier decision of 1871 had referred to the war power. This position evoked a controversy of wide scope, for the question what sovereignty involves belongs as much to

---

[13] The case of *Gibbons* v. *Ogden* supplies an interesting illustration of the way in which this doctrine of implied powers works itself out. The state of New York had, in order to reward Fulton and Livingston for their services in introducing steamboats, passed a statute giving them an exclusive right of navigating the Hudson River with steamers. A case having arisen in which this statute was invoked, it was alleged that the statute was invalid, because inconsistent with an act passed by Congress. The question followed, Was Congress entitled to pass an act dealing with the navigation of the Hudson? And it was held that the power to regulate commerce granted to Congress by the Constitution implied a power to legislate for navigation on such rivers as the Hudson, and that Congress having exercised that power, the action of the states on the subject was necessarily excluded. By this decision a vast field of legislation was secured to Congress and closed to the states.

political as to legal science, and may be pushed to great lengths upon considerations with which law proper has little to do.

The above-mentioned instances of development have been worked out by the courts of law. But others are due to the action of the executive, or of the executive and Congress conjointly. Thus, in 1803, President Jefferson negotiated and completed the purchase of Louisiana, the whole vast possessions of France beyond the Mississippi. He believed himself to be exceeding any powers which the Constitution conferred; and desired to have an amendment to it passed, in order to validate his act. But Congress and the people did not share his scruples, and the approval of the legislature was deemed sufficient ratification for a step of transcendent importance, which no provision of the Constitution bore upon. In 1807 and 1808 Congress laid, by two statutes, an embargo on all shipping in United States ports, thereby practically destroying the lucrative carrying trade of the New England states. Some of these states declared the act unconstitutional, arguing that a power to regulate commerce was not a power to annihilate it, and their courts held it to be void. Congress, however, persisted for a year, and the act, on which the Supreme Court never formally pronounced, has been generally deemed within the Constitution, though Justice Story (who had warmly opposed it when he sat in Congress) remarks that it went to the extreme verge. More startling, and more far-reaching in their consequences, were the assumptions of federal authority made during the War of Secession by the executive and confirmed, some expressly, some tacitly, by Congress and the people.[14] It was only a few of these that came before the courts, and the courts, in some instances, disapproved them. But the executive continued to exert this extraordinary authority. Appeals made to the letter of the Constitution by the minority were discredited by the fact that they were made by persons sympathizing with the Secessionists who were seeking to destroy it. So many extreme things were done under the

---

[14] See Judge Cooley's *History of Michigan*, p. 353. The same eminent authority observes to me: "The President suspended the writ of *habeas corpus*. The courts held this action unconstitutional (it was subsequently confirmed by Congress), but he did not at once deem it safe to obey their judgment. Military commissioners, with the approval of the War Department and the President, condemned men to punishment for treason, but the courts released them, holding that the guaranties of liberty in the Constitution were as obligatory in war as in peace, and should be obeyed by all citizens, and all departments, and officers of government (*Milligan's case*, 4 Wall. 1). The courts held closely to the Constitution, but as happens in every civil war, a great many wrongs were done in the exercise of the war power for which no redress, or none that was adequate, could possibly be had." *Inter arma silent leges* must be always to some extent true, even under a Constitution like that of the United States.

pressure of necessity that something less than these extreme things came to be accepted as a reasonable and moderate compromise.[15]

The best way to give an adequate notion of the extent to which the outlines of the Constitution have been filled up by interpretation and construction, would be to take some of its more important sections and enumerate the decisions upon them and the doctrines established by those decisions. This process would, however, be irksome to any but a legal reader, and the legal reader may do it more agreeably for himself by consulting one of the annotated editions of the Constitution. He will there find that upon some provisions such as art. I, § 8 (powers of Congress), art. I, § 10 (powers denied to the states), art. III, § 2 (extent of judicial power), there has sprung up a perfect forest of judicial constructions, working out the meaning and application of the few and apparently simple words of the original document into a variety of unforeseen results. The same thing has more or less befallen nearly every section of the Constitution and of the seventeen amendments. The process shows no signs of stopping; nor can it, for the new conditions of economics and politics bring up new problems for solution. But the most important work was that done during the first half century, and especially by Chief Justice Marshall during his long tenure of the presidency of the Supreme Court (1801–35). It is scarcely an exaggeration to call him, as an eminent American jurist has done, a second maker of the Constitution. I will not borrow the phrase which said of Augustus that he found Rome of brick and left it of marble, because Marshall's function was not to change but to develop. The Constitution was, except of course as regards the political scheme of national government, which was already well established, rather a ground plan than a city. It was, if I may pursue the metaphor, much what the site of Washington was at the beginning of this century, a symmetrical ground plan for a great city, but with only some tall edifices standing here and there among fields and woods. Marshall left it what Washington has now become, a splendid and commodious capital within whose ample bounds there are still some vacant spaces and some mean dwellings, but which, built up and beautified as it has been by the taste and wealth of its rapidly growing population, is worthy to be the centre of a mighty nation. Marshall was, of course, only one among seven judges, but his majestic intellect and the elevation of his character gave him such an ascendency, that he found himself only once in

---

[15] Such as the suspension of the writ of habeas corpus, the emancipation of the slaves of persons aiding in rebellion, the suspension of the statute of limitations, the practical extinction of state banks by increased taxation laid on them under the general taxing power.

a minority on any constitutional question.[16] His work of building up and working out the Constitution was accomplished not so much by the decisions he gave as by the judgments in which he expounded the principles of these decisions, judgments which for their philosophical breadth, the luminous exactness of their reasoning, and the fine political sense which pervades them, have never been surpassed and rarely equalled by the most famous jurists of modern Europe or of ancient Rome. Marshall did not forget the duty of a judge to decide nothing more than the suit before him requires, but he was wont to set forth the grounds of his decision in such a way as to show how they would fall to be applied in cases that had not yet arisen. He grasped with extraordinary force and clearness the cardinal idea that the creation of a national government implies the grant of all such subsidiary powers as are requisite to the effectuation of its main powers and purposes, but he developed and applied this idea with so much prudence and sobriety, never treading on purely political ground, never indulging the temptation to theorize, but content to follow out as a lawyer the consequences of legal principles, that the Constitution seemed not so much to rise under his hands to its full stature, as to be gradually unveiled by him till it stood revealed in the harmonious perfection of the form which its framers had designed. That admirable flexibility and capacity for growth which characterize it beyond all other rigid or supreme constitutions, is largely due to him, yet not more to his courage than to his caution.[17]

III. We now come to the third question: How is the interpreting authority restrained? If the American Constitution is capable of being so developed by this expansive interpretation, what security do its written terms offer to the people and to the states? What becomes of the special value claimed for rigid constitutions that they preserve the frame of government unimpaired in its essential merits, that they restrain the excesses of a transient majority, and (in federations) the aggressions of a central authority?

The answer is twofold. In the first place, the interpreting authority is, in questions not distinctly political, different from the legislature and from the executive, amenable to neither, and composed of lawyers imbued with

---

[16] In that one case (*Ogden* v. *Sanders*) there was a bare majority against him, and professional opinion now approves the view which he took. When Marshall became chief justice only two decisions on constitutional law had been pronounced by the court. Between that time and his death fifty-one were given.

[17] Had the Supreme Court been in those days possessed by the same spirit of strictness and literality which the Judicial Committee of the British Privy Council has recently applied to the construction of the British North America Act of 1867 (the act which creates the constitution of the Canadian Federation), the United States Constitution would never have grown to be what it now is.

professional habits. There is therefore a probability that it will disagree with either of them when they attempt to transgress the Constitution, and will decline to stretch the law so as to sanction encroachments those authorities may have attempted. In point of fact, there have been few cases, and those chiefly cases of urgency during the war, in which the judiciary has been even accused of lending itself to the designs of the other organs of government. The period when extensive interpretation was most active (1800–1835) was also the period when the party opposed to a strong central government commanded Congress and the executive, and so far from approving the course the court took, the dominant party then often complained of it.

In the second place, there stands above and behind the legislature, the executive, and the judiciary, another power, that of public opinion. The president, Congress, and the courts are all, the two former directly, the latter practically, amenable to the people, and anxious to be in harmony with the general current of its sentiment. If the people approve the way in which these authorities are interpreting and using the Constitution, they go on; if the people disapprove, they pause, or at least slacken their pace. Generally the people have approved of such action by the president or Congress as has seemed justified by the needs of the time, even though it may have gone beyond the letter of the Constitution. Generally they have approved the conduct of the courts whose legal interpretation has upheld such legislative or executive action. Public opinion sanctioned the purchase of Louisiana, and the still bolder action of the executive in the Secession War. It approved the Missouri Compromise of 1820, which the Supreme Court thirty-seven years afterwards declared to have been in excess of the powers of Congress. But it disapproved the Alien and Sedition laws of 1798, and although these statutes were never pronounced unconstitutional by the courts, this popular censure has prevented any similar legislation since that time.[18] The people have, of course, much less exact notions of the Constitution than the legal profession or the courts. But while they generally desire to see the powers of the government so far expanded as to enable it to meet the exigencies of the moment, they are sufficiently attached to its general doctrines, they sufficiently prize the protection it affords them against their own impulses, to censure any interpretation which palpably departs from the old lines. And their censure is, of course, still more severe if the court seems to be acting at the bidding of a party.

[18] So it disapproved strongly, in the Northern states, of the judgments delivered by the majority of the Supreme Court in the Dred Scott case.

A singular result of the importance of constitutional interpretation in the American government may be here referred to. It is this, that the United States legislature has been very largely—though less in recent years than formerly—occupied in purely legal discussions. When it is proposed to legislate on a subject which has been heretofore little dealt with, the opponents of a measure have two lines of defence. They may, as Englishmen would in a like case, argue that the measure is inexpedient. But they may also, which Englishmen cannot, argue that it is unconstitutional, i.e., illegal, because transcending the powers of Congress. This is a question fit to be raised in Congress, not only as regards matters with which, as being purely political, the courts of law will refuse to interfere, but as regards all other matters also, because since a decision on the constitutionality of a statute can never be obtained from the judges by anticipation, the legislature ought to consider whether they are acting within their competence. And it is a question on which a stronger case can often be made, and made with less exertion, than on the issue whether the measure be substantially expedient. Hence it was usually put in the forefront of the battle, and argued with great vigour and acumen by leaders who might be more ingenious as lawyers than farsighted as statesmen.

A further consequence of this habit is pointed out by one of the most thoughtful among American constitutional writers. Legal issues are apt to dwarf and obscure the more substantially important issues of principle and policy, distracting from these latter the attention of the nation as well as the skill of congressional debaters.

"The English legislature," says Judge Hare, "is free to follow any course that will promote the welfare of the State, and the inquiry is not, 'Has Parliament power to pass the Act?' but, 'Is it consistent with principle, and such as the circumstances demand?' These are the material points, and if the public mind is satisfied as to them there is no further controversy. In the United States, on the other hand, the question primarily is one of power, and in the refined and subtle discussion which ensues, right is too often lost sight of or treated as if it were synonymous with might. It is taken for granted that what the Constitution permits it also approves, and that measures which are legal cannot be contrary to morals."

The interpretation of the Constitution has at times become so momentous as to furnish a basis for the formation of political parties; and the existence of parties divided upon such questions has of course stimulated the interest with which points of legal interpretation have been watched and canvassed. Soon after the formation of the national government in 1789 two parties grew up, one advocating a strong central authority, the other championing the rights of the states. Of these parties the former naturally came to insist on a liberal, an expansive, perhaps a lax construction of the words of the Constitution, because the more wide is the meaning placed upon its grant of powers, so much the wider are those powers themselves. The latter party, on the other hand, was acting in protection both of the states and of the individual citizen against the central government, when it limited by a strict and narrow interpretation of the fundamental instrument the powers which that instrument conveyed. The distinction which began in those early days has never since vanished. There has always been a party professing itself disposed to favour the central government, and therefore a party of broad construction. There has always been a party claiming that it aimed at protecting the rights of the states, and therefore a party of strict construction. Some writers have gone so far as to deem these different views of interpretation to be the foundation of all the political parties that have divided America. This view, however, inverts the facts. It is not because men have differed in their reading of the Constitution that they have advocated or opposed an extension of federal powers; it is their attitude on this substantial issue that has determined their attitude on the verbal one. Moreover, the two great parties have several times changed sides on the very question of interpretation. The purchase of Louisiana and the Embargo acts were the work of the strict constructionists, while it was the loose constructionist party which protested against the latter measure, and which, at the Hartford Convention of 1814, advanced doctrines of state rights almost amounting to those subsequently asserted by South Carolina in 1832 and by the Secessionists of 1861. Parties in America, as in most countries, have followed their temporary interest; and if that interest happened to differ from some traditional party doctrine, they have explained the latter away. Whenever there has been a serious party conflict, it has been in reality a conflict over some living and practical issue, and only in form a debate upon canons of legal interpretation. What is remarkable, though natural enough in a country governed by a written instrument, is that every controversy has gotten involved with questions of constitutional construction. When it was proposed to exert some power of Congress, as for instance to charter a national bank, to grant money for internal improvements, to enact a protective tariff, the opponents of these schemes could plausibly argue, and therefore of course did argue, that they were unconstitutional. So any suggested interference with slavery in states or territories was immediately declared to violate the states' rights which the Constitution guaranteed. Thus every serious question came to be fought as a constitutional question. But as regards most questions, and certainly as regards the great majority of the party combatants, men did not attack or defend a proposal because they held it legally unsound or sound on the true construction of the Constitution, but alleged it to be constitutionally wrong or right because they thought the welfare of the country, or at least their party interests, to be involved. Constitutional interpretation was a pretext rather than a cause, a matter of form rather than of substance.

The results were both good and evil. They were good in so far as they made both parties profess themselves defenders of the Constitution, zealous only that it should be interpreted aright; as they familiarized the people with its provisions, and made them vigilant critics of every legislative or executive act which could affect its working. They were evil in distracting public attention from real problems to the legal aspect of those problems, and in cultivating a habit of casuistry which threatened the integrity of the Constitution itself.

Since the Civil War there has been much less of this casuistry because there have been fewer occasions for it, the broad construction view of the Constitution having practically prevailed—prevailed so far that the Supreme Court now holds that the power of Congress to make paper money legal tender is incident to the sovereignty of the national government, and that a Democratic House of Representatives passes a bill giving a federal commission vast powers over all the railways which pass through more than one state. There is still a party inclined to strict construction, but the strictness which it upholds would have been deemed lax by the broad constructionists of the days before the Civil War. The interpretation which has thus stretched the Constitution to cover powers once undreamt of, may be deemed a dangerous resource. But it must be remembered that even the constitutions we call rigid must make their choice between being bent or being broken. The Americans have more than once bent their Constitution in order that they might not be forced to break it.

The Development of the Constitution by Usage

Tₕere is yet another way in which the Constitution has been developed. This is by laying down rules on matters which are within its general scope, but have not been dealt with by its words, by the creation of machinery which it has not provided for the attainment of objects it contemplates, or, to vary the metaphor, by ploughing or planting ground which though included within the boundaries of the Constitution, was left waste and untilled by those who drew up the original instrument.

Although the Constitution is curiously minute upon some comparatively small points, such as the qualifications of members of Congress and the official record of their votes, it passes over in silence many branches of political action, many details essential to every government. Some may have been forgotten, but some were purposely omitted, because the Convention could not agree upon them, or because they would have provoked opposition in the ratifying conventions, or because they were thought unsuited to a document which it was desirable to draft concisely and to preserve as far as possible unaltered. This was wise and indeed necessary, but it threw a great responsibility upon those who had to work the government which the Constitution created. They found nothing within the four corners of the instrument to guide them on points whose gravity was perceived as soon as they had to be settled in practice. Many of such points could not be dealt with by interpretation or construction, however liberally extensive it might be, because there was nothing in the words of the Constitution from which such construction could start, and because they were in some instances matters which, though important, could not be based upon principle, but must be settled by an arbitrary determination.

Their settlement, which began with the First Congress, has been effected in two ways, by congressional legislation and by usage.

Congress was empowered by the Constitution to pass statutes on certain prescribed topics. On many other topics not specially named, but within its general powers, statutes were evidently needed. For instance, the whole subject of federal taxation, direct and indirect, the establishment of federal courts, inferior to the Supreme Court, and the assignment of particular kinds and degrees of jurisdiction to each class of courts, the organization of the civil, military, and naval services of the country, the administration of Indian affairs and of the Territories, the rules to be observed in the elections of presidents and senators, these and many other matters of high import are regulated by statutes, statutes which Congress can of course change but which, in their main features, have been not greatly changed since their first enactment. Although such statutes cannot be called parts of the Constitution in the same sense as the interpretations and constructions judicially placed upon it, for these latter have (subject to the possibility of their reversal) become practically incorporated with its original text, still they have given to its working a character and direction which must be borne in mind in discussing it, and which have, in some instances, produced results opposed to the ideas of its framers. To take a recent instance, the passing of the Interstate Commerce Act, which regulates all the greater railways over the whole United States, is an assertion of federal authority over numerous and powerful corporations chartered by and serving the various states, which gives a new aspect and significance to the clause in the Constitution empowering Congress to regulate commerce. Legal interpretation held that clause to be sufficiently wide to enable Congress to legislate on interstate railways; but when Congress actually exerted its power in enacting this statute a further step, and a long one, was taken towards bringing the organs of transportation under national control.[1] Legislation, therefore, though it cannot in strictness enlarge the frontiers fixed by the Constitution, can give to certain provinces lying within those frontiers far greater importance than they formerly possessed, and by so doing, can substantially change the character of the government. It cannot engender a new power, but it can turn an old one in a new direction, and call a dormant one into momentous activity.

Next as to usage. Custom, which is a law-producing agency in every department, is specially busy in matters which pertain to the practical

---

[1] The recognition that the Contitition empowers Congress to deal with a given subject does not imply that every detail of the act dealing therewith is above objection. Although prima facie Congress, when competent to legislate on a subject, is free to choose its means, still it remains open to anyone to challenge the constitutionality of any particular provisions in a statute.

conduct of government. Understandings and conventions are in modern practice no less essential to the smooth working of the English Constitution, than are the principles enunciated in the Bill of Rights. Now understandings are merely long-established usages, sanctioned by no statute, often too vague to admit of precise statement,[2] yet in some instances deemed so binding that a breach of them would damage the character of a statesman or a ministry just as much as the transgression of a statute. In the United States there are fewer such understandings than in England, because under a Constitution drawn out in one fundamental document everybody is more apt to stand upon his strict legal rights, and the spirit of institutions departs less widely from their formal character. Nevertheless some of those features of American government to which its character is chiefly due, and which recur most frequently in its daily working, rest neither upon the Constitution nor upon any statute, but upon usage alone. Here are some instances.

The presidential electors have by usage and by usage only lost the right the Constitution gave them of exercising their discretion in the choice of a chief magistrate.

No president has been elected to more than two continuous terms, though the Constitution in no way restricts reeligibility.[3]

The president uses his veto more freely than he did at first, and for a wider range of purposes.

The Senate now never exercises its undoubted power of refusing to confirm the appointments made by the president to cabinet offices.

The president is permitted to remove, without asking the consent of the Senate, officials to whose appointment the consent of the Senate is necessary. This was for a time regulated by statute, but the statute having been repealed the old usage has revived. (See Chapter 6.)

Both the House and the Senate conduct their legislation by means of standing committees. This vital peculiarity of the American system of government has no firmer basis than the standing orders of each house, which can be repealed at any moment, but have been maintained for many years.

The Speaker of the House was for a long time entrusted with the

---

[2] For instance, it is difficult to state precisely the practical (as distinguished from the legal) rights of the House of Lords to reject bills passed by the House of Commons, or the duty of the Crown when a Cabinet makes some very unusual request; although it is admitted that as a rule the Lords ought to yield to the Commons and the Crown to be guided by the advice of its ministers.

[3] See *ante*, Chapter 5. The *Federalist* (No. 68) says that the president will be and ought to be reelected as often as the people think him worthy of their confidence.

nomination of all the House committees. That function now belongs to the Committee of Ways and Means.

The chairmen of the chief committees of both houses, which control the great departments of state (e.g., foreign affairs, navy, justice, finance), have practically become an additional set of ministers for those departments.

The custom of going into caucus, by which the parties in each of the two houses of Congress determine their action, and the obligation on individual members to obey the decision of the caucus meeting, are mere habits or understandings, without legal sanction. So is the right claimed by the senators from a state to control the federal patronage of that state. So is the usage that appropriation bills shall be first presented to the House.

The rule that a member of Congress must be chosen from the district, as well as from the state, in which he resides, rests on no federal enactment; indeed, neither Congress nor any state legislature would be entitled thus to narrow the liberty of choice which the words of the Constitution imply.

Jackson introduced, and succeeding presidents continued the practice of dismissing federal officials belonging to the opposite party, and appointing none but adherents of their own party to the vacant places. This is the so-called Spoils System, which, having been applied also to state and municipal offices, became and long continued to be the cornerstone of "practical politics" in America. The Constitution was nowise answerable for it, and legislation only partially.

Neither in English law nor in American is there anything regarding the reeligibility of a member of the popular chamber; nor can it be said that usage has established in either country any broad general rule on the subject. But whereas the English tendency has been to reelect a member unless there is some positive reason for getting rid of him, in many parts of America men are disposed the other way, and refuse to reelect him just because he has had his turn already. Anyone can understand what a difference this makes in the character of the chamber.

We see, then, that several salient features of the present American government, such as the popular election of the president, the restriction of eligibility to Congress to persons resident in the district to be represented, the influence of senators and congressmen over patronage, the immense power of the Speaker, the Spoils System, are due to usages which have sprung up round the Constitution and profoundly affected its working, but which are not parts of the Constitution, nor necessarily attributable to any specific provision which it contains. The most remarkable instance of all, the working of the system of government by highly organized parties, including the choice of presidential candidates by the great parties assembled in their national conventions, will be fully considered in later chapters.

One of the changes which began about twenty years after the adoption of the Constitution deserves special mention. The Constitution contains no provision regarding the electoral franchise in Congressional elections save the three following:

> That the franchise shall in every state be the same as that by which the members of the "most numerous branch of the State legislature" are chosen (art. I, § 2);
>
> That when any male citizens over twenty-one years of age are excluded by any state from the franchise (except for crime) the basis of representation in Congress of that state shall be proportionately reduced (amend. XIV, 1868);
>
> That "the right of citizens of the United States to vote shall not be denied or abridged on account of race, colour, or previous condition of servitude" (amend. XV, 1870).

Subject to these conditions every state may regulate the electoral franchise as it pleases.

In the first days of the Constitution the suffrage was in nearly all states limited by various conditions (e.g., property qualification, length of residence, etc.) which excluded, or might have excluded, though in some states the proportion of very poor people was small, a considerable number of the free inhabitants. At present the suffrage is in every state practically universal. It had become so in the free states[4] even before the war. Here is an advance towards pure democracy effected without the action of the national legislature, but solely by the legislation of the several states, a legislation which, as it may be changed at any moment, is, so far as the national government is concerned, mere custom. And of this great step, modifying profoundly the colour and character of the government, there is no trace in the words of the Constitution other than the provisions of the Fourteenth and Fifteenth Amendments introduced for the benefit of the liberated Negroes.

It is natural, it is indeed inevitable, that there should be in every country such a parasitic growth of usages and conventions round the solid legal framework of government. But must not the result of such a growth be different where a rigid constitution exists from what it is in countries where

---

[4] Save that in many of them persons of colour were placed at a disadvantage.

the constitution is flexible? In England usages of the kind described become inwoven with the law of the country as settled by statutes and decisions, and modify that law. Cases come before a court in which a usage is recognized and thereby obtains a sort of legal sanction. Statutes are passed in which an existing usage is taken for granted, and which therefore harmonize with it. Thus the always changing Constitution becomes interpenetrated by custom. Custom is in fact the first stage through which a rule passes before it is embodied in binding law. But in America, where the fundamental law cannot readily be, and is in fact very rarely altered, may we not expect a conflict, or at least a want of harmony, between law and custom, due to the constant growth of the one and the immutability of the other?

In examining this point one must distinguish between subjects on which the Constitution is silent and subjects on which it speaks. As regards the former there is little difficulty. Usage and legislation may expand the Constitution in what way they please, subject only to the control of public opinion. The courts of law will not interfere, because no provision of the Constitution is violated; and even where it may be thought that an act of Congress or of the executive is opposed to the spirit of the Constitution, still if it falls within the range of the discretion which these authorities have received, it will not be questioned by the judges.[5]

If, on the other hand, either Congressional legislation or usage begins to trench on ground which the Constitution expressly covers, the question at once arises whether such legislation is valid, or whether an act done in conformity with such usage is legal. Questions of this kind do not always come before the courts, and if they do not, the presumption is in favour of whatever act has been done by Congress or by any legally constituted authority. When, however, such a question is susceptible of judicial

---

[5] "It is an axiom in our jurisprudence that an Act of Congress is not to be pronounced unconstitutional unless the defect of power to pass it is so clear as to admit of no doubt. Every doubt is to be resolved in favour of the validity of the law."—Swayne, J., *U.S.* v. *Rhodes,* 1 Abb. U.S. 49.

An interesting illustration of the application of legislative power in uncontemplated ways is supplied by a case which arose in the efforts made to check the evils arising from lotteries. Congress, being unable to strike at a lottery established in Louisiana, passed a statute forbidding the post office to carry newspapers containing lottery advertisements (since it was by these that mischief was done over the rest of the Union), and imposing a penalty on anyone posting lottery advertisements in breach of the statute. A newspaper proprietor arrested for such breach carried his case to the Supreme Court, alleging the statute to be unconstitutional because inconsistent with the First Amendment to the Constitution. The court however unanimously held (1892) that that amendment did not apply, and supported the right of Congress to use the control of the post office as a means of dealing with the harm done by lotteries; and public opinion heartily welcomed this decision.

determination and is actually brought before a tribunal, the tribunal is disposed rather to support than to treat as null the act done. Applying that expansive interpretation which has prevailed since the war as it prevailed in the days of Chief Justice Marshall, the Supreme Court is apt to find grounds for moving in the direction which it perceives public opinion to have taken, and for putting on the words of the Constitution a sense which legalizes what Congress has enacted or custom approved. When this takes place things proceed smoothly. The change which circumstances call for is made gently, and is controlled, perhaps modified, in its operation.

But sometimes the courts feel bound to declare some statute, or executive act done in pursuance of usage, contrary to the Constitution. What happens? In theory the judicial determination is conclusive, and ought to check any further progress in the path which has been pronounced unconstitutional. But whether this result follows will in practice depend on the circumstances of the moment. If the case is not urgent, if there is no strong popular impulse behind Congress or the president, no paramount need for the usage which had sprung up and is now disapproved, the decision of the courts will be acquiesced in; and whatever tendency towards change exists will seek some other channel where no constitutional obstacle bars its course. But if the needs of the time be pressing, courts and Constitution may have to give way. *Salus populi lex suprema.* Above the written law, however sacred, stands the safety of the commonwealth, which will be secured, if possible in conformity with the Constitution; but if that be not possible, then by evading, or even by overriding the Constitution.[6] This is what happened in the Civil War, when men said that they would break the Constitution in order to preserve it.

Attempts to disobey the Constitution have been rare, because the fear of clashing with it has arrested many mischievous proposals in their earlier stages, while the influence of public opinion has averted possible collisions by leading the courts to lend their ultimate sanction to measures or usages

---

[6] In a remarkable letter written to Mr. Hodges (April 4, 1864), President Lincoln said: "My oath to preserve the Constitution imposed on me the duty of preserving by every indispensable means that government, that nation, of which the Constitution was the organic law. Was it possible to lose the nation and yet preserve the Constitution? By general law life and limb must be protected, yet often a limb must be amputated to save a life, but a life is never wisely given to save a limb. I felt that measures, otherwise unconstitutional, might become lawful by becoming indispensable to the preservation of the Constitution through the preservation of the nation. Right or wrong I assumed this ground, and now avow it. I could not feel that to the best of my ability I had even tried to preserve the Constitution, if, to save slavery, or any minor matter, I should permit the wreck of government, country, and Constitution altogether."

which, had they come under review at their first appearance, might have been pronounced unconstitutional.[7] That collisions have been rare is good evidence of the political wisdom of American statesmen and lawyers. But politicians in other countries will err if they suppose that the existence of a rigid or supreme constitution is enough to avert collisions, or to secure the victory of the fundamental instrument. A rigid constitution resembles, not some cliff of Norwegian gneiss which bears for centuries unchanged the lash of Atlantic billows, but rather a seawall, such as guards the seaside promenade of an English town, whose smooth surface resists the ordinary waves and currents of the Channel but may be breached or washed away by some tremendous tempest. The American Constitution has stood unbroken, because America has never seen, as some European countries have seen, angry multitudes or military tyrants bent on destroying the institutions which barred the course of their passions or ambition. And it has also stood because it has submitted to a process of constant, though sometimes scarcely perceptible, change which has adapted it to the conditions of a new age.

The solemn determination of a people enacting a fundamental law by which they and their descendants shall be governed cannot prevent that law, however great the reverence they continue to profess for it, from being worn away in one part, enlarged in another, modified in a third, by the ceaseless action of influences playing upon the individuals who compose the people. Thus the American Constitution has necessarily changed as the nation has changed, has changed in the spirit with which men regard it, and therefore in its own spirit. To use the words of the eminent constitutional lawyer whom I have more than once quoted: "We may think," says Judge Cooley, "that we have the Constitution all before us; but for practical purposes the Constitution is that which the government, in its several departments, and the people in the performance of their duties as citizens, recognize and respect as such; and nothing else is. . . . Cervantes says: Every one is the son of his own works. This is more emphatically true of an instrument of government than it can possibly be of a natural person. What it takes to itself, though at first unwarrantable, helps to make it over into a new instrument of government, and it represents at last the acts done under it."

---

[7] Such as the expenditure of vast sums on "internal improvements" and the assumption of wide powers over internal communications.

The Results of Constitutional Development

We have seen that the American Constitution has changed, is changing, and by the law of its existence must continue to change, in its substance and practical working even when its words remain the same. "Time and habit," said Washington, "are at least as necessary to fix the true character of governments as of other human institutions:"[1] and while habit fixes some things, time remoulds others.

It remains to ask what has been the general result of the changes it has suffered, and what light an examination of its history, in this respect, throws upon the probable future of the instrument and on the worth of rigid or supreme constitutions in general.

The Constitution was avowedly created as an instrument of checks and balances. Each branch of the national government was to restrain the others, and maintain the equipoise of the whole. The legislature was to balance the executive, and the judiciary both. The two houses of the legislature were to balance one another. The national government, taking all its branches together, was balanced against the state governments. As this equilibrium was placed under the protection of a document, unchangeable save by the people themselves, no one of the branches of the national government has been able to absorb or override the others, as the House of Commons and the cabinet, itself a child of the House of Commons, have in England overridden and subjected the Crown and the House of Lords. Each branch maintains its independence, and can, within certain limits, defy the others.

But there is among political bodies and offices (i.e., the persons who from time to time fill the same office) of necessity a constant strife, a struggle for existence similar to that which Mr. Darwin has shown to exist

---

[1] Farewell Address, September 17, 1796.

among plants and animals; and as in the case of plants and animals so also in the political sphere this struggle stimulates each body or office to exert its utmost force for its own preservation, and to develop its aptitudes in any direction wherein development is possible. Each branch of the American government has striven to extend its range and its powers; each has advanced in certain directions, but in others has been restrained by the equal or stronger pressure of other branches. I shall attempt to state the chief differences perceptible between the ideas which men entertained regarding the various bodies and offices of the government when they first entered life, and the aspect they now wear to the nation.

The president has developed a capacity for becoming, in moments of national peril, something like a Roman dictator. He is in quiet times no stronger than he was at first. Now and then he has seemed weaker. Congress has occasionally encroached on him, but at other times the country has given its confidence to the man as against the assembly. With a succession of strong and popular presidents this might tend to become a habit. Needless to say that history has shown how the office may in the hands of a trusted leader and at the call of a sudden necessity, rise to a tremendous height.

The ministers of the president have not become more important either singly or collectively as a cabinet. Cut off from the legislature on one side, and from the people on the other, they have been a mere appendage to the president.

The Senate has come to press heavily on the executive, and at the same time has developed legislative functions which, though contemplated in the Constitution, were comparatively rudimentary in the older days. It has, in the judgment of American publicists, grown relatively stronger than it then was, but it is not more trusted by the people.

The vice-president of the United States has become even more insignificant than the Constitution seemed to make him.

On the other hand, the Speaker of the House of Representatives, whom the Constitution mentions only once, and on whom it bestows no powers, has now secured one of the leading parts in the piece, and could for many years prior to 1910 affect the course of legislation more than any other single person.

An oligarchy of chairmen of the leading committees has sprung up in both houses as a consequence of the increasing demands on its time as well as of the working of the committee system.

The judiciary was deemed to be making large strides during the first forty years, because it established its claim to powers which, though doubtless really granted, had been but faintly apprehended in 1789. After 1830 the development of those powers advanced more slowly. But the position which the Supreme Court has taken in the scheme of government, if it be not greater than the framers of the Constitution would have wished, is yet greater than they foresaw.

Although some of these changes are considerable, they are far smaller than those which England has seen pass over her government since 1789. So far, therefore, the rigid Constitution has maintained a sort of equilibrium between the various powers, whereas that which was then supposed to exist in England between the king, the peers, the House of Commons, and the people (i.e., the electors) has vanished irrecoverably.

In the other struggle that has gone on in America, that between the national government and the states, the results have been still more considerable, though the process of change has sometimes been interrupted. During the first few decades after 1789 the states, in spite of a steady and often angry resistance, sometimes backed by threats of secession, found themselves more and more entangled in the network of federal powers which sometimes Congress, sometimes the president, sometimes the judiciary, as the expounder of the Constitution, flung over them. Provisions of the Constitution whose bearing had been inadequately realized in the first instance were put in force against a state, and when once put in force became precedents for the future. It is instructive to observe that this was done by both of the great national parties, by those who defended states' rights and preached state sovereignty as well as by the advocates of a strong central government. For the former, when they saw the opportunity of effecting by means of the central legislative or executive power an object of immediate party importance, did not hesitate to put in force that central power, forgetful or heedless of the example they were setting.

It is for this reason that the process by which the national government has grown may be called a natural one. A political force has, like a heated gas, a natural tendency to expansion, a tendency which works even apart from the knowledge and intentions of those through whom it works. In the process of expansion such a force may meet, and may be checked or driven back by, a stronger force. The expansive force of the national government proved ultimately stronger than the force of the states, so the centralizing tendency prevailed. And it prevailed not so much by the conscious purpose of the party disposed to favour it, as through the inherent elements of strength which it possessed, and the favouring conditions amid which it acted, elements and conditions largely irrespective of either political party, and operative under the supremacy of the one as well as of the other. Now and then the centralizing process was checked. Georgia defied the Supreme Court in 1830–32, and was not made to bend because the executive sided with her. South Carolina defied Congress and the president in 1832, and the issue was settled by a compromise. Acute foreign observers then and often during the period that followed predicted the dissolution of the Union. For some years before the outbreak of the Civil War the tie of obedience to the national government was palpably loosened over a large part of the country. But during and after the war the former tendency resumed its action, swifter and more potent than before.

A critic may object to the view here presented by remarking that the struggle between the national government and the states has not, as in the case of the struggles between different branches of the national government, proceeded merely by the natural development of the Constitution, but has been accelerated by specific changes in the Constitution, viz., those made by the three last amendments.

This is true. But the dominance of the centralizing tendencies is not wholly or even mainly due to those amendments. It had begun before them. It would have come about, though less completely, without them. It has been due not only to these amendments but also:

To the extensive interpretation by the judiciary of the powers which the Constitution vests in the national government;

To the passing by Congress of statutes on topics not exclusively reserved to the states, statutes which have sensibly narrowed the field of state action;

To exertions of executive power which, having been approved by the people, and not condemned by the courts, have passed into precedents.

These have been the modes in which the centralizing tendency has shown itself and prevailed. What have been the underlying causes?

They belong to history. They are partly economical, partly moral. Steam and electricity have knit the various parts of the country closely together, have made each state and group of states more dependent on its neighbours, have added to the matters in which the whole country benefits by joint action and uniform legislation. The power of the national government to stimulate or depress commerce and industries by legislation, whether in matters of currency and finance, or on the tariff, or on the means of transportation, has given it a wide control over the material prosperity of the Union, till "the people, and especially the trading and manufacturing classes, came to look more and more to the national capital for what enlists their interests, and less and less to the capital of their own State. . . . It is the nation and not the State that is present to the imagination of the citizens as sovereign, even in the States of Jefferson and Calhoun. . . . The Constitution as it is, and the Union as it was, can no longer be the party watchword. There is a new Union, with new grand features, but with new engrafted evils."[2] There has grown up a pride in the national flag, and in the national government as representing national unity. In the North there is gratitude to that government as the power that saved the Union in the Civil War; in the South a sense of the strength which Congress and the president then exerted; in both a recollection of the immense scope which the war powers took and might take again. All over the country there is a great army of federal officeholders who look to Washington as the centre of their hopes and fears. As the modes in and by which these and other similar causes can work are evidently not exhausted, it is clear that the development of the Constitution as between the nation and the states has not yet stopped, and present appearances suggest that the centralizing tendency will continue to prevail.

How does the inquiry we have been conducting affect the judgment to be passed upon the worth of rigid constitutions, i.e., of written instruments of government emanating from an authority superior to that of the ordinary legislature? The question is a grave one for European countries, which seem to be passing from the older or flexible to the newer or rigid type of constitutions.

A European reader who has followed the facts stated in the last foregoing chapters may be inclined to dismiss the question summarily. "Rigid constitutions," he will say, "are on your own showing a delusion and a sham. The American Constitution has been changed, is being changed, will continue to be changed, by interpretation and usage. It is not what it was even thirty years ago; who can tell what it will be thirty years hence? If its transformations are less swift than those of the English Constitution, this is only because England has not even yet so completely democratized herself as had America nearly a century ago, and therefore there has been more room for change in England. If the existence of the fundamental Constitution did not prevent violent stretches of executive power during the war, and of legislative power after as well as during the war, will not its paper guarantees be trodden under foot more recklessly the next time a crisis arrives? It was

[2] Cooley, *History of Michigan*.

intended to protect not only the states against the central government, not only each branch of the government against the other branches, but the people against themselves, that is to say, the people as a whole against the impulses of a transient majority. What becomes of this protection when you admit that even the Supreme Court is influenced by public opinion, which is only another name for the reigning sentiment of the moment? If every one of the checks and safeguards contained in the document may be overset, if all taken together may be overset, where are the boasted guarantees of the fundamental laws? Evidently it stands only because it is not at present assailed. It is like the walls of Jericho, tall and stately, but ready to fall at the blast of the trumpet. It is worse than a delusion: it is a snare; for it lulls the nation into a fancied security, seeming to promise a stability for the institutions of government, and a respect for the rights of the individual, which are in fact baseless. A flexible constitution like that of England is really safe, because it practises no similar deceit, but by warning good citizens that the welfare of the commonwealth depends always on themselves and themselves only, stimulates them to constant efforts for the maintenance of their own rights and the deepest interests of society."

This statement of the case errs as much in one direction by undervaluing, as common opinion errs by overvaluing, the stability of rigid constitutions. They do not perform all that the solemnity of their wording promises. But they are not therefore useless.

To expect any form of words, however weightily conceived, with whatever sanctions enacted, permanently to restrain the passions and interests of men is to expect the impossible. Beyond a certain point, you cannot protect the people against themselves any more than you can, to use a familiar American expression, lift yourself from the ground by your own bootstraps. Laws sanctioned by the overwhelming physical power of a despot, laws sanctioned by supernatural terrors whose reality no one doubted, have failed to restrain those passions in ages of slavery and superstition. The world is not so much advanced that in this age laws, even the best and most venerable laws, will of themselves command obedience. Constitutions which in quiet times change gradually, peacefully, almost imperceptibly, must in times of revolution be changed more boldly, some provisions being sacrificed for the sake of the rest, as mariners throw overboard part of the cargo in a storm in order to save the other part with the ship herself. To cling to the letter of a constitution when the welfare of the country for whose sake the constitution exists is at stake, would be to seek to preserve life at the cost of all that makes life worth having—*propter vitam vivendi perdere causas.*

Nevertheless the rigid Constitution of the United States has rendered, and renders now, inestimable services. It opposes obstacles to rash and hasty change. It secures time for deliberation. It forces the people to think seriously before they alter it or pardon a transgression of it. It makes legislatures and statesmen slow to overpass their legal powers, slow even to propose measures which the Constitution seems to disapprove. It tends to render the inevitable process of modification gradual and tentative, the result of admitted and growing necessities rather than of restless impatience. It altogether prevents some changes which a temporary majority may clamour for, but which will have ceased to be demanded before the barriers interposed by the Constitution have been overcome.

It does still more than this. It forms the mind and temper of the people. It strengthens their conservative instincts, their sense of the value of stability and permanence in political arrangements. It trains them to habits of legality as the law of the Twelve Tables trained the minds of the educated Romans. It makes them feel that to comprehend their supreme instrument of government is a personal duty, incumbent on each one of them. It familiarizes them with, it attaches them by ties of pride and reverence to, those fundamental truths on which the Constitution is based.

These are enormous services to render to any free country, but above all to one which, more than any other, is governed not by the men of rank or wealth or special wisdom, but by public opinion, that is to say, by the ideas and feelings of the people at large. In no country were swift political changes so much to be apprehended, because nowhere has material growth been so rapid and immigration so enormous. In none might the political character of the people have seemed more likely to be bold and prone to innovation, because their national existence began with a revolution, which even now lies only a century and a half behind. That none has ripened into a more prudently conservative temper may be largely ascribed to the influence of the famous instrument of 1789, which, enacted in and for a new republic, summed up so much of what was best in the laws and customs of an ancient monarchy.

PART II

THE STATE GOVERNMENTS

C H A P T E R   3 6

Nature of the American State

From the study of the national government, we may go on to examine
that of the several states which make up the Union. This is the part of the
American political system which has received least attention both from
foreign and from native writers. Finding in the federal president, cabinet,
and Congress a government superficially resembling those of their own
countries, and seeing the federal authority alone active in international
relations, Europeans have forgotten and practically ignored the state governments to which their own experience supplies few parallels, and on whose
workings the intelligence published on their side of the ocean seldom throws
light. Even the European traveller who makes the six or seven days' run
across the American continent, from New York or Philadelphia via Chicago
to San Francisco, though he passes in his journey of three thousand miles
over the territories of eleven self-governing commonwealths, hardly notices
the fact. He uses one coinage and one post office; he is stopped by no
customhouses; he sees no officials in a state livery; he thinks no more of
the difference of jurisdictions than the passenger from London to Liverpool
does of the counties traversed by the line of the Northwestern Railway. So,
too, our best informed English writers on the science of politics, while
discussing copiously the relation of the American states to the central
authority, have failed to draw on the fund of instruction which lies in the
study of state governments themselves. Mill in his *Representative Government*
scarcely refers to them. Mr. Freeman in his learned essays, Sir H. Maine
in his ingenious book on popular government, pass by phenomena which
would have admirably illustrated some of their reasonings.

American publicists, on the other hand, have been too much absorbed in
the study of the federal system to bestow much thought on the state
governments. The latter seem to them the most simple and obvious things

in the world, while the former, which has been the battleground of their political parties for a century, excites the keenest interest, and is indeed regarded as a sort of mystery, on which all the resources of their metaphysical subtlety and legal knowledge may well be expended. Thus while the dogmas of state sovereignty and states' rights, made practical by the great struggle over slavery, were discussed with extraordinary zeal and acumen by three generations of men, the character, power, and working of the states as separate self-governing bodies have received little attention or illustration. Yet they are full of interest; and he who would understand the changes that have passed on the American democracy will find far more instruction in a study of the state governments than of the federal Constitution. The materials for this study are unfortunately, at least to a European, either inaccessible or unmanageable. They consist of constitutions, statutes, the records of the debates and proceedings of constitutional conventions and legislatures, the reports of officials and commissioners, together with that continuous transcript and picture of current public opinion which the files of newspapers supply. Of these sources only one, the constitutions, is practically available to an European writer. To be able to use the rest one must go to the state and devote one's self there to these original authorities, correcting them, where possible, by the recollections of living men. It might have been expected that in most of the states, or at least of the older states, persons would have been found to write political, and not merely antiquarian or genealogical, state histories, describing the political career of their respective communities, and discussing the questions on which political contests have turned. But this was not (except in a very few cases) attempted till near the end of the nineteenth century, so that the European enquirer found a scanty measure of the assistance which he would naturally have expected from previous labourers in this field. I call it a field: it was till lately rather a primeval forest, where the vegetation is rank, and through which even now but few trails have been cut. The new historical school which is growing up at the leading American universities, and has already investigated the colonial period with so much thoroughness, and has now begun to grapple with this task;[1] in the meantime, the difficulties I have stated must be my excuse for treating this branch of my subject with a brevity out of proportion to its real interest and importance. It is better to endeavour to bring into relief a few leading features than to attempt a detailed account which would run to inordinate length.

---

[1] Since this book was first published (in 1888) much excellent work has been done on state history all over the country, and state constitutions have received much study.

The American state is a peculiar organism, unlike anything in modern Europe, or in the ancient world. The only parallel is to be found in the cantons of Switzerland, the Switzerland of our own day, for until 1815, if one ought not rather to say until 1848, Switzerland was not so much a nation or a state as a league of neighbour commonwealths. But Europe so persistently ignores the history of Switzerland, that most instructive patent museum of politics, apparently only because she is a small country, and because people go there to see lakes and to climb mountains, that I should perplex instead of enlightening the reader by attempting to illustrate American from Swiss phenomena.

Let me attempt to sketch the American states as separate political entities, forgetting for the moment that they are also parts of a federation.

The admission, under a statute of 1910, of two new states[2] brought the number of states in the American Union up to forty-eight, varying in size from Texas, with an area of 265,780 square miles, to Rhode Island, with an area of 1,250 square miles; and in population from New York, with over 9,000,000 inhabitants, to Nevada, with 81,000. That is to say, the largest state is much larger than either France or the Germanic Empire; the most populous much more populous than Sweden, or Portugal, or Denmark, while the smallest is smaller than Warwickshire or Corsica, and the least populous less populous than the city of York, or the town of Reading in Berks. Considering not only these differences of size, but the differences in the density of population (which in Nevada is .7 and in Wyoming 1.5 to the square mile, while in Rhode Island it is 508.5 and in Massachusetts 418.8 to the square mile); in its character[3] (in South Carolina the blacks are 835,843 against 679,161 whites, in Mississippi 1,009,487 against 786,111 whites); in its birthplace (in North Carolina the foreign-born persons are less than $\frac{1}{400}$ of the population, in California, nearly one-third, in North Dakota more than one-half); in the occupations of the people, in the amount of accumulated wealth, in the proportion of educated persons to the rest of the community—it is plain that immense differences might be looked for between the aspects of politics and conduct of government in one state and in another.

Be it also remembered that the older colonies had different historical origins. Virginia and North Carolina were unlike Massachusetts and Connecticut; New York, Pennsylvania, and Maryland different from both; while in

[2] Arizona and New Mexico.
[3] Census of 1900.

recent times the stream of European immigration has filled some states with Irishmen, others with Germans or Italians, others with Scandinavians or Poles, and has left most of the Southern states wholly untouched.

Nevertheless, the form of government is in its main outlines, and to a large extent even in its actual working, the same in all these forty-eight republics, and the differences, instructive as they are, relate to the points of secondary consequence.

The states fall naturally into five groups:

The New England states—Massachusetts, Connecticut, Rhode Island, New Hampshire, Vermont, Maine

The Middle states—New York, New Jersey, Pennsylvania, Delaware,[4] Maryland, Ohio, Indiana[5]

The Southern, or old slave states—Virginia, West Virginia (separated from Virginia during the war), North Carolina, South Carolina, Georgia, Alabama, Florida, Kentucky, Tennessee, Mississippi, Louisiana, Arkansas, Missouri, Texas, Oklahoma, New Mexico (these two last, however, formed long after the extinction of slavery)

The Northwestern states—Michigan, Illinois, Wisconsin, Minnesota, Iowa, Nebraska, Kansas, Colorado, North Dakota, South Dakota, Wyoming, Montana, Idaho

The Pacific states—California, Nevada, Arizona, Utah, Oregon, Washington

Each of these groups has something distinctive in the character of its inhabitants, which is reflected, though more faintly now than formerly, in the character of its government and politics.

New England is the old home of Puritanism, the traces whereof, though waning under the influence of Irish and French Canadian immigration, are not yet extinct. The Southern states will long retain the imprint of slavery, not merely in the presence of a host of Negroes, but in the backwardness of the poor white population, and in certain attributes, laudable as well as regrettable, of the upper class. The Northwest is the land of hopefulness, and consequently of bold experiments in legislation: its rural inhabitants

---

[4] Delaware and Maryland were slave states, but did not secede, and are in some respects to be classed rather with the Middle than with the Southern group, as indeed are West Virginia, Missouri, and Oklahoma (this last really Western in character), perhaps even Tennessee and Kentucky.

[5] Ohio has become, and Indiana is becoming, rather Middle than Western, and the former at least cannot now be classed among Western states.

have the honesty and somewhat limited horizon of agriculturists. The Pacific West, or rather California and Nevada, for Oregon and Washington belong in point of character quite as much to the Northwestern group, tinges the energy and sanguine good nature of the Westerners with a speculative recklessness natural to mining communities, where great fortunes have rapidly grown and vanished, and into which elements have been suddenly swept together from every part of the world, as a Rocky Mountain rainstorm fills the bottom of a valley with sand and pebbles from all the surrounding heights.

As the dissimilarity of population and of external conditions seems to make for a diversity of constitutional and political arrangements between the states, so also does the large measure of legal independence which each of them enjoys under the federal Constitution. No state can, as a commonwealth, politically deal with or act upon any other state.[6] No diplomatic relations can exist nor treaties be made between states,[7] no coercion can be exercised by one upon another. And although the government of the Union can act on a state, it rarely does act, and then only in certain strictly limited directions, which do not touch the inner political life of the commonwealth.

Let us pass on to consider the circumstances which work for uniformity among the states, and work more powerfully as time goes on.

He who looks at a map of the Union will be struck by the fact that so many of the boundary lines of the states are straight lines. Those lines tell the same tale as the geometrical plans of cities like St. Petersburg or Washington, where every street runs at the same angle to every other. The states are not areas set off by nature. Their boundaries are for the most part not natural boundaries fixed by mountain ranges, nor even historical boundaries due to a series of events, but boundaries, purely artificial, determined by an authority which carved the national territory into strips of convenient size, as a building company lays out its suburban lots. Of the states subsequent to the original thirteen, California is the only one with a genuine natural frontier, finding it in the chain of the Sierra Nevada on the east and the Pacific Ocean on the west. No one of these later states can be regarded as a naturally developed political organism. They are trees planted by the forester, not self-sown with the help of the seed-scattering wind. This absence of physical lines of demarcation has tended and must tend to

---

[6] Except with consent of Congress.
[7] Ibid.

prevent the growth of local distinctions. Nature herself seems to have designed the Mississippi basin, as she has designed the unbroken levels of Russia, to be the dwelling place of one people.

Each state makes its own constitution; that is, the people agree on their form of government for themselves, with no interference from the other states or from the Union. This form is subject to one condition only: it must be republican.[8] But in each state the people who make the constitution have lately come from other states, where they have lived under and worked constitutions which are to their eyes the natural and almost necessary model for their new state to follow; and in the absence of an inventive spirit among the citizens, it was the obvious course for the newer states to copy the organizations of the older states, especially as these agreed with certain familiar features of the federal Constitution. Hence the outlines, and even the phrases of the elder constitutions reappear in those of the more recently formed states. The precedents set by Virginia, for instance, had much influence on Tennessee, Alabama, Mississippi, and Florida, when they were engaged in making or amending their constitutions during the early part of this century.

Nowhere is population in such constant movement as in America. In some states more than one-fourth of the inhabitants are foreign-born. Many of the townsfolk, not a few even of the farmers, have been till lately citizens of some other state, and will, perhaps, soon move on farther west. The Western states are like a chain of lakes through which there flows a stream which mingles the waters of the higher with those of the lower. In such a constant flux of population local peculiarities are not readily developed, or if they have grown up when the district was still isolated, they disappear as the country becomes filled. Each state takes from its neighbours and gives to its neighbours, so that the process of assimilation is always going on over the whole wide area.

Still more important is the influence of railway communication, of newspapers, of the telegraph. A Greek city like Samos or Mitylene, holding her own island, preserved a distinctive character in spite of commercial intercourse and the sway of Athens. A Swiss canton like Uri or Appenzell, entrenched behind its mountain ramparts, remains, even now under the strengthened central government of the Swiss nation, unlike its neighbours

---

[8] The case of Kansas immediately before the War of Secession, and the cases of the rebel states, which were not readmitted after the war till they had accepted the constitutional amendments forbidding slavery and protecting the freedmen, are quite exceptional cases.

As to any special conditions imposed by Congress, see Chapter 37 *post*.

of the lower country. But an American state traversed by great trunk lines of railway, and depending on the markets of the Atlantic cities and of Europe for the sale of its grain, cattle, bacon, and minerals, is attached by a hundred always tightening ties to other states, and touched by their weal or woe as nearly as by what befalls within its own limits. The leading newspapers are read over a vast area. The inhabitants of each state know every morning the events of yesterday over the whole Union.

Finally the political parties are the same in all the states. The tenets (if any) of each party are (with some slight exceptions) the same everywhere, their methods the same, their leaders the same, although of course a prominent man enjoys especial influence in his own state. Hence, state politics are largely swayed by forces and motives external to the particular state, and common to the whole country, or to great sections of it; and the growth of local parties, the emergence of local issues and development of local political schemes, are correspondingly restrained.

These considerations explain why the states, notwithstanding the original diversities between some of them, and the wide scope for political divergence which they all enjoy under the federal Constitution, are so much less dissimilar and less peculiar than might have been expected. European statesmen have of late years been accustomed to think of federalism and local autonomy as convenient methods either for recognizing and giving free scope to the sentiment of nationality which may exist in any part of an empire, or for meeting the need for local institutions and distinct legislation which may arise from differences between such a part and the rest of the empire. It is one or other or both of these reasons that have moved statesmen in such cases as those of Finland in her relations to Russia, Hungary in her relations to the Austro-Hungarian monarchy, Iceland in her relations to Denmark, Bulgaria in her relations to the Turkish sultan, Ireland in her relations to Great Britain. But the final causes, so to speak, of the recognition of the states of the American Union as autonomous commonwealths, have been different. Their self-government is not the consequence of differences which can be made harmless to the whole body politic only by being allowed free course. It has been due primarily to the historical fact that they existed as commonwealths before the Union came into being; secondarily, to the belief that localized government is the best guarantee for civic freedom, and to a sense of the difficulty of administering a vast territory and population from one centre and by one government.

I return to indicate the points in which the legal independence and right of self-government of the several states appears. Each has its own:

Constitution (whereof more anon)

Executive, consisting of a governor, and various other officials

Legislature of two houses

System of local government in counties, cities, townships, and school districts

System of state and local taxation

Debts, which it may (and sometimes does) repudiate at its own pleasure

Body of private law, including the whole law of real and personal property, of contracts, of torts, and of family relations

System of procedure, civil and criminal

Courts, from which no appeal lies (except in cases touching federal legislation or the federal Constitution) to any federal court

Citizenship, which may admit persons (e.g., recent immigrants) to certain privileges of citizens at times, or on conditions, wholly different from those prescribed by other states

Three points deserve to be noted as illustrating what these attributes include.

I. A man gains active citizenship of the United States (i.e., a share in the government of the Union) only by becoming a citizen of some particular state. Being such, he is forthwith entitled to the national franchise. That is to say, voting power in the state carries voting power in federal elections, and however lax a state may be in its grant of such power, e.g., to foreigners just landed or to persons convicted of crime, these state voters will have the right of voting in congressional and presidential elections.[9] The only restriction on the states in this matter is that of the Fourteenth and Fifteenth Constitutional Amendments, which have already been discussed. They were intended to secure equal treatment to the Negroes, and incidentally they declare the protection given to all citizens of the United States.[10] Whether

---

[9] Congress has power to pass a uniform rule of naturalization (Constitution, art. I, § 8).

Under the present naturalization laws a foreigner must have resided in the United States for five years, and for one year in the state or Territory where he seeks admission to United States citizenship, and must declare two years before he is admitted that he renounces allegiance to any foreign prince or state. Before being admitted he must have taken an oath of renunciation. Naturalization makes him a citizen not only of the United States, but of the state or Territory where he is admitted, but does not necessarily confer the electoral franchise, for that depends on state laws.

In more than a third of the states the electoral franchise is now enjoyed by persons not naturalized as United States citizens.

[10] "The line of distinction between the privileges and immunities of citizens of the United States, and those of citizens of the several States, must be traced along the boundary of their respective spheres of action, and the two classes must be as different in their nature as are the functions of

they really enlarge it, that is to say, whether it did not exist by implication before, is a legal question not needing to be discussed here.

II. The power of a state over all communities within its limits is absolute. It may grant or refuse local government as it pleases. The population of the city of Providence is nearly one-half of that of the state of Rhode Island, and that of New York City about one-half of that of the state of New York. But the state might in either case extinguish the municipality, and govern the city by a single state commissioner appointed for the purpose, or leave it without any government whatever. The city would have no right of complaint to the federal president or Congress against such a measure. Massachusetts remodelled the city government of Boston just as the British Parliament might remodel that of Birmingham and once superseded the city government of Chelsea by appointing a sort of temorary dictator to administer it for a time. Let an Englishman imagine a county council for Warwickshire suppressing the municipality of Birmingham, or a Frenchman imagine the department of the Rhone extinguishing the municipality of Lyons, with no possibility of intervention by the central authority, and he will measure the difference between the American states and the local governments of Western Europe.

III. A state commands the allegiance of its citizens, and may punish them for treason against it. The power has rarely been exercised, but its undoubted legal existence had much to do with inducing the citizens of the Southern states to follow their governments into secession in 1861. They conceived themselves to owe allegiance to the state as well as to the Union, and when

---

their respective governments. A citizen of the United States as such has a right to participate in foreign and inter-state commerce, to have the benefit of the postal laws, to make use in common with others of the navigable waters of the United States, and to pass from State to State, and into foreign countries, because over all these subjects the jurisdiction of the United States extends, and they are covered by its laws. The privileges suggest the immunities. Wherever it is the duty of the United States to give protection to a citizen against any harm, inconvenience, or deprivation, the citizen is entitled to an immunity which pertains to Federal citizenship. One very plain immunity is exemption from any tax, burden, or imposition under State laws as a condition to the enjoyment of any right or privilege under the laws of the United States. . . . Whatever one may claim as of right under the Constitution and laws of the United States by virtue of his citizenship, is a privilege of a citizen of the United States. Whatever the Constitution and laws of the United States entitle him to exemption from, he may claim an exemption in respect to. And such a right or privilege is abridged whenever the State law interferes with any legitimate operation of Federal authority which concerns his interest, whether it be an authority actively exerted, or resting only in the express or implied command or assurance of the Federal Constitution or law. But the United States can neither grant nor secure to its citizens rights or privileges which are not expressly or by reasonable implication placed under its jurisdiction, and all not so placed are left to the exclusive protection of the States."—Cooley, *Principles*, pp. 245–47.

it became impossible to preserve both, because the state had declared its secession from the Union, they might hold the earlier and nearer authority to be paramount. Allegiance to the state must now, since the war, be taken to be subordinate to allegiance to the Union. But allegiance to the state still exists; treason against the state is still possible. One cannot think of treason against Warwickshire or the department of the Rhone.

These are illustrations of the doctrine which Europeans often fail to grasp, that the American states were originally in a certain sense, and still for certain purposes remain, sovereign states. Each of the original thirteen became sovereign (so far as its domestic affairs were concerned, though not as respects international relations) when it revolted from the mother country in 1776. By entering the Confederation of 1781–88 it parted with one or two of the attributes of sovereignty; by accepting the federal Constitution in 1788–91 it subjected itself for certain specified purposes to a central government, but claimed to retain its sovereignty for all other purposes. That is to say, the authority of a state is an inherent, not a delegated, authority. It has all the powers which any independent government can have, except such as it can be affirmatively shown to have stripped itself of, while the federal government has only such powers as it can be affirmatively shown to have received. To use the legal expression, the presumption is always for a state, and the burden of proof lies upon anyone who denies its authority in a particular matter.[11]

What state sovereignty means and includes is a question which incessantly engaged the most active legal and political minds of the nation, from 1789 down to 1870. Some thought it paramount to the rights of the Union. Some considered it as held in suspense by the Constitution, but capable of reviving as soon as a state should desire to separate from the Union. Some maintained that each state had in accepting the Constitution finally renounced its sovereignty, which thereafter existed only in the sense of such an undefined domestic legislative and administrative authority as had not been conferred upon Congress. The conflict of these views, which became acute in 1830

[11] As the colonies had associated themselves into a league, at the very time at which they revolted from the British Crown, and as their foreign relations were always managed by the authority and organs of this league, no one of them ever acted in international affairs as a free and independent sovereign state. Abraham Lincoln was in this sense justified in saying that the Union was older than the states, and had created them as states. But what are we to say of North Carolina and Rhode Island, after the acceptance of the Constitution of 1787–89 by the other eleven states? They were out of the old Confederation, for it had expired. They were not in the new Union, for they refused during many months to enter it. What else can they have been during those months except sovereign commonwealths?

when South Carolina claimed the right of nullification, produced secession and the war of 1861–65. Since the defeat of the Secessionists, the last of these views may be deemed to have been established, and the term "state sovereignty" is now but seldom heard. Even "states' rights" have a different meaning from that which they had before the War of Secession.[12]

A European who now looks calmly back on this tremendous controversy of tongue, pen, and sword, will be apt to express his ideas of it in the following way. He will remark that much of the obscurity and perplexity arose from confounding the sovereignty of the American nation with the sovereignty of the federal government. The federal government clearly was sovereign only for certain purposes, i.e., only in so far as it had received specified powers from the Constitution. These powers did not, and in a strict legal construction do not now, abrogate the supremacy of the states. A state still possesses one important attribute of sovereignty—immunity from being sued except by another state. But the American nation which had made the Constitution, had done so in respect of its own sovereignty, and might well be deemed to retain that sovereignty as paramount to any rights of the states. The feeling of this ultimate supremacy of the nation was what swayed the minds of those who resisted secession, just as the equally well-grounded persuasion of the limited character of the central federal government satisfied the conscience of the seceding South.

The Constitution of 1789 was a compromise, and a compromise arrived at by allowing contradictory propositions to be represented as both true. It has been compared to the declarations made with so much energy and precision of language in the ancient hymn *Quicunque Vult*, where, however, the apparent contradiction has always been held to seem a contradiction only because the human intellect is unequal to the comprehension of such profound mysteries. To everyone who urged that there were thirteen states, and therefore thirteen governments, it was answered, and truly, that there was one government, because the people were one. To everyone who declared that there was one government, it was answered with no less truth that there were thirteen. Thus counsel was darkened by words without knowledge; the question went off into metaphysics, and found no end, in wandering mazes lost.

There was, in fact, a divergence between the technical and the practical

---

[12] States' rights was a watchword in the South for many years. In 1851 there was a student at Harvard College from South Carolina who bore the name of States Rights Gist, baptized, so to speak, into Calhounism. He rose to be a brigadier general in the Confederate army, and fell in the Civil War.

aspects of the question. Technically, the seceding states had an arguable case; and if the point had been one to be decided on the construction of the Constitution as a court decides on the construction of a commercial contract, they were possibly entitled to judgment. Practically, the defenders of the Union stood on firmer ground, because circumstances had changed since 1789 so as to make the nation more completely one nation than it then was, and had so involved the fortunes of the majority which held to the Union with those of the minority seeking to depart that the majority might feel justified in forbidding their departure. Stripped of legal technicalities, the dispute resolved itself into the problem often proposed but capable of no general solution: When is a majority entitled to use force for the sake of retaining a minority in the same political body with itself? To this question, when it appears in a concrete shape, as to the similar question when an insurrection is justifiable, an answer can seldom be given beforehand. The result decides. When treason prospers, none dare call it treason.

The Constitution, which had rendered many services to the American people, did them an inevitable disservice when it fixed their minds on the legal aspects of the question. Law was meant to be the servant of politics, and must not be suffered to become the master. A case had arisen which its formulæ were unfit to deal with, a case which had to be settled on large moral and historical grounds. It was not merely the superior physical force of the North that prevailed; it was the moral forces which rule the world, forces which had long worked against slavery, and were ordained to save North America from the curse of hostile nations established side by side.

The word "sovereignty," which has in many ways clouded the domain of public law and jurisprudence, confused men's minds by making them assume that there must in every country exist, and be discoverable by legal inquiry, either one body invested legally with supreme power over all minor bodies, or several bodies which, though they had consented to form part of a larger body, were each in the last resort independent of it, and responsible to none but themselves.[13] They forgot that a constitution may not have determined

---

[13] A further confusion arises from the fact that men are apt in talking of sovereignty to mix up (as the Benthamite school did unfortunately) legal supremacy with practical predominance, sovereignty *de jure* with sovereignty *de facto*. They ought to go together, and law seeks to make them go together. But it may happen that the person or body in whom law vests supreme authority is unable to enforce that authority: so the legal sovereign and the actual sovereign—that is to say, the force which will prevail in physical conflict—are different. There is always a strongest force; but the force recognized by law may not be really the strongest; and of several forces it may be impossible to tell, till they have come into actual physical conflict, which is the strongest. This subject has been discussed in an essay on sovereignty in the author's *Studies in History and Jurisprudence*.

where legal supremacy shall dwell. Where the Constitution of the United States placed it was at any rate doubtful, so doubtful that it would have been better to drop technicalities, and recognize the broad fact that the legal claims of the states had become incompatible with the historical as well as legal claims of the nation. In the uncertainty as to where legal right resided, it would have been prudent to consider where physical force resided. The South, however, thought herself able to resist any physical force which the rest of the nation might bring against her. Thus encouraged, she took her stand on the doctrine of states' rights; and then followed a pouring out of blood and treasure such as was never spent on determining a point of law before, not even when Edward III and his successors waged war for a hundred years to establish the claim of females to inherit the crown of France.

What, then, do the rights of a state now include? Every right or power of a government except:

The right of secession (not abrogated in terms, but admitted since the war to be no longer claimable. It is expressly negatived in the recent constitutions of several Southern states.);

Powers which the Constitution withholds from the states (including that of intercourse with foreign governments);

Powers which the Constitution expressly confers on the federal government.

As respects some powers of the last class, however, the states may act concurrently with, or in default of action by, the federal government. It is only from contravention of its action that they must abstain. And where contravention is alleged to exist, whether legislative or executive, it is by a court of law, and, in case the decision is in the first instance favourable to the pretensions of the state, ultimately by a federal court, that the question falls to be decided.[14]

A reference to the preceding list of what each state may create in the way of distinct institutions will show that these rights practically cover nearly all the ordinary relations of citizens to one another and to their government, nearly all the questions which have been most agitated in England and France of recent years. An American may, through a long life, never be reminded of the federal government, except when he votes at presidential and congressional elections, buys a package of tobacco bearing the government stamp, lodges a complaint against the post office, and opens his trunks

[14] See Chapter 22 *ante*.

for a customhouse officer on the pier at New York when he returns from a tour in Europe. His direct taxes are paid to officials acting under state laws. The state, or a local authority constituted by state statutes, registers his birth, appoints his guardian, pays for his schooling, gives him a share in the estate of his father deceased, licenses him when he enters a trade (if it be one needing a licence), marries him, divorces him, entertains civil actions against him, fines him for overspeeding his automobile, declares him a bankrupt, hangs him for murder. The police that guard his house, the local boards which look after the poor, control highways, impose water rates, manage schools—all these derive their legal powers from his state alone. Looking at this immense compass of state functions, Jefferson would seem to have been not far wrong when he said that the federal government was nothing more than the American department of foreign affairs. But although the national government touches the direct interests of the citizen less than does the state government, it touches his sentiment more. Hence the strength of his attachment to the former and his interest in it must not be measured by the frequency of his dealings with it. In the partitionment of governmental functions between nation and state, the state gets the most but the nation the highest, so the balance between the two is preserved.

Thus every American citizen lives in a duality of which Europeans, always excepting the Swiss, and to some extent the Germans, have no experience. He lives under two governments and two sets of laws; he is animated by two patriotisms and owes two allegiances. That these should both be strong and rarely be in conflict is most fortunate. It is the result of skilful adjustment and long habit, of the fact that those whose votes control the two sets of governments are the same persons, but above all of that harmony of each set of institutions with the other set, a harmony due to the identity of the principles whereon both are founded, which makes each appear necessary to the stability of the other, the states to the nation as its basis, the national government to the states as their protector.

State Constitutions

The government of each state is determined by and set forth in its constitution, a comprehensive fundamental law, or rather group of laws included in one instrument, which has been directly enacted by the people of the state, and is capable of being repealed or altered, not by their representatives, but by themselves alone. As the Constitution of the United States stands above Congress and out of its reach, so the constitution of each state stands above the legislature of that state, cannot be varied in any particular by the state legislature, and involves the invalidity of any statute passed by the legislature which is found to be inconsistent with it.

The state constitutions are the oldest things in the political history of America, for they are the continuations and representatives of the royal colonial charters, whereby the earliest English settlements in America were created, and under which their several local governments were established, subject to the authority of the English Crown and ultimately of the British Parliament. But, like most of the institutions under which English-speaking peoples now live, they have a pedigree which goes back to a time anterior to the discovery of America itself. It begins with the English trade guild of the Middle Ages, itself the child of still more ancient corporations, dating back to the days of imperial Rome, and formed under her imperishable law. Charters were granted to merchant guilds in England as far back as the days of King Henry I. In 1463, Edward IV gave an elaborate one to the merchant adventurers trading with Flanders. In it we may already discern the arrangements which are more fully set forth in two later charters of greater historical interest, the charter of Queen Elizabeth to the East India Company in 1599, and the charter of Charles I to the "Governor and Company of the Mattachusetts Bay in Newe-England" in 1628. Both these instruments establish and incorporate trading companies, with power to implead and be impleaded, to use a common seal, to possess and acquire lands, tenements and hereditaments, with provisions for the making of ordinances for the welfare of the company. The Massachusetts Charter creates a frame of government consisting of a governor, deputy-governor, and eighteen assistants (the term still in use in many of the London city guilds), and directs them to hold four times a year a general meeting of the company, to be called the "greate and generall Court," in which general court "the Governor or deputie Governor, and such of the assistants and Freemen of the Company as shall be present, shall have full power and authority to choose other persons to be free of the Company, and to elect and constitute such officers as they shall thinke fitt for managing the affaires of the said Governor and Company, and to make Lawes and Ordinances for the Good and Welfare of the saide Company, and for the Government and Ordering of the saide Landes and Plantasion, and the People inhabiting and to inhabite the same, soe as such Lawes and Ordinances be not contrary or repugnant to the Lawes and Statuts of this our realme of England." In 1691, the charter of 1628 having been declared forfeited in 1684, a new one was granted by King William and Queen Mary, and this instrument, while it retains much of the language and some of the character of the trade guild charter, is really a political frame of government for a colony. The assistants receive the additional title of councillors; their number is raised to twenty-eight; they are to be chosen by the general court, and the general court itself is to consist, together with the governor and assistants, of freeholders elected by towns or places within the colony, the electors being persons with a forty shilling freehold or other property worth £40. The governor is directed to appoint judges, commissioners of oyer and terminer, etc.; the general court receives power to establish judicatories and courts of record, to pass laws (being not repugnant to the laws of England), and to provide for all necessary civil offices. An appeal from the courts shall always be to the King in his privy council. This is a true political constitution.[1] Under it the colony was

---

[1] The oldest truly political constitution in America is the instrument called the Fundamental Orders of Connecticut, framed by the inhabitants of Windsor, Hartford, and Wethersfield in 1638, memorable year, when the ecclesiastical revolt of Scotland saved the liberties of England. The government of Connecticut was afterwards regularized by Charles II's charter of 1662 to "the Governor and Company of the English colony of Connecticut." The agreement drawn up in the cabin of the Mayflower may perhaps claim to have in it the germs of a government.

I am here tracing only the formal and legal growth of state constitutions. Their democratic spirit and contents are largely due to the ideas with which the theology of the Reformers, and especially of Calvin, had filled the minds of the Puritan emigrants; and the ecclesiastical arrangements the latter set up powerfully influenced those of the nascent political communities.

governed, and in the main well and wisely governed, till 1780. Much of it, not merely its terms, such as the name general court, but its solid framework, was transferred bodily to the Massachusetts Constitution of 1780, which is now in force, and which profoundly influenced the Convention that prepared the federal Constitution in 1787. Yet the charter of 1691 is nothing but an extension and development of the trading charter of 1628, in which there already appears, as there had appeared in Edward IV's charter of 1463, and in the East India Company's charter of 1599, the provision that the power of lawgiving, otherwise unlimited, should be restricted by the terms of the charter itself, which required that every law for the colony should be agreeable to the laws of England. We have therefore in the three charters which I have named, those of 1463, 1599, and 1628, as well as in that of 1691, the essential and capital characteristic of a rigid or supreme constitution—viz., a frame of government established by a superior authority, creating a subordinate lawmaking body, which can do everything except violate the terms and transcend the powers of the instrument to which it owes its own existence. So long as the colony remained under the British Crown, the superior authority, which could amend or remake the frame of government, was the British Crown or Parliament. When the connection with Britain was severed, that authority passed over, not to the state legislature, which remained limited, as it always had been, but to the people of the now independent commonwealth, whose will speaks through what is now the state constitution, just as the will of the Crown or of Parliament had spoken through the charters of 1628 and 1691.

I have taken the case of Massachusetts as the best example of the way in which the trading company grows into a colony, and the colony into a state. But some of the other colonies furnish illustrations scarcely less apposite. The oldest of them all, the acorn whence the oak of English dominion in America has sprung, the colony of Virginia, was, by the second charter, of 1609, established under the title of "The Treasurer and Company of Adventurers and Planters of the City of London for the first colony in Virginia."[2]

Within the period of ten years, under the last of the Tudors and the first of the Stuarts, two trading charters were issued to two companies of English adventurers. One of these charters is the root of English title to the East and the other to the West. One of these companies has grown into the

---

[2] The phrase first colony distinguishes what afterwards became the state of Virginia from the more northerly parts of Virginia, afterwards called New England. The second colony was to be Plymouth, one of the two settlements which became Massachusetts.

Empire of India; the other into the United States of North America. If England had done nothing else in history, she might trust for her fame to the work which these charters began. And the foundations of both dominions were laid in the age which was adorned by the greatest of all her creative minds, and gave birth to the men who set on a solid basis a frame of representative government which all the free nations of the modern world have copied.

When, in 1776, the thirteen colonies threw off their allegiance to King George III, and declared themselves independent states, the colonial charter naturally became the state constitution.[3] In most cases it was remodelled, with large alterations, by the revolting colony. But in three states it was maintained unchanged (except, of course, so far as Crown authority was concerned), viz., in Massachusetts till 1780, in Connecticut till 1818, and in Rhode Island till 1842.[4] The other thirty-five states admitted to the Union in addition to the original thirteen, have all entered it as organized self-governing communities, with their constitutions already made by their respective peoples. Each act of Congress which admits a new state admits it as a subsisting commonwealth, sometimes empowering its people to meet and enact a constitution for themselves (subject to conditions mentioned in the act), sometimes accepting and confirming a constitution already made

---

[3] Even in declaring herself independent, New Jersey clung to the hope that the mother country would return to wiser counsels, and avert the departure of her children. She added at the end of her constitution of July 2, 1776, the following proviso: "Provided always, and it is the true intent and meaning of this Congress, that if a reconciliation between Great Britain and these colonies should take place, and the latter be taken again under the protection and government of the Crown of Britain, this charter shall be null and void, otherwise remain firm and inviolable." The truth is that the colonists, till alienated by the behaviour of England, had far more kindly feelings towards her than she had towards them. To them she was the old home, to her they were simply customers. Some interesting illustrations of the views then entertained as to the use of colonies may be found in the famous discussion in the fourth book of Adam Smith's *Wealth of Nations*, which appeared in 1776.

[4] Rhode Island simply passed a statute by her legislature in May 1776, substituting allegiance to the colony for allegiance to the King. Connecticut passed the following statute: "Be it enacted by the Governor and Council and House of Representatives, in general court assembled, that the ancient form of civil government contained in the charter from Charles II, King of England, and adopted by the people of this State, shall be and remain the civil Constitution of this State, under the sole authority of the people thereof, independent of any king or prince whatever; and that this republic is, and shall for ever be and remain, a free, sovereign, and independent State, by the name of the State of Connecticut." (Three paragraphs follow containing a short "Bill of Rights," and securing to the inhabitants of any other of the United States the same law and justice as natives of the state enjoyed.) This is all that Connecticut thought necessary. She had possessed, as did Rhode Island also, the right of appointing her own governor, and therefore did not need to substitute any new authority for a royal governor.

by the people.[5] Congress may impose conditions which the state constitution must fulfil; and in admitting the eight newest states has affected to retain the power of maintaining these conditions in force. But the authority of the state constitutions does not flow from Congress, but from acceptance by the citizens of the states for which they are made. Of these instruments, therefore, no less than of the constitutions of the thirteen original states, we may say that although subsequent in date to the federal Constitution, they are, so far as each state is concerned, *de jure* prior to it. Their authority over their own citizens is nowise derived from it.[6] Nor is this a mere piece of technical law. The antiquity of the older states as separate commonwealths, running back into the heroic ages of the first colonization of America and the days of the Revolutionary War, is a potent source of the local patriotism of their inhabitants, and gives these states a sense of historic growth and indwelling corporate life which they could not have possessed had they been the mere creatures of the federal government.

The state constitutions of America well deserve to be compared with those of the self-governing British colonies. But one remarkable difference must be noted here. The constitutions of British colonies have all proceeded from the Imperial Parliament of the United Kingdom,[7] which retains its full legal power of legislating for every part of the British dominions. In many cases a colonial constitution provides that it may be itself altered by the colonial legislature, of course with the assent of the Crown; but inasmuch as in its origin it is a statutory constitution, not self-grown, but planted as

---

[5] In the Act of 1889 for the admission of North Dakota, South Dakota, Montana, and Washington, and in the Act of 1894 for the admission of Utah, and that of 1906 for the admission of Oklahoma, the former course, in the admission of Idaho and Wyoming in 1890, and of New Mexico and Arizona in 1910, the latter course, was followed.

[6] In practice Congress can influence the character of a state constitution, because a state whose constitution contains provisions which Congress disapproves may be refused admission. But since the extinction of slavery and completion of the process of reconstruction, occasions for the serious exercise of such a power rarely arise. It was used to compel the seceding states to modify their constitutions so as to get rid of all taint of slavery before their senators and representatives were readmitted to Congress after the war. Of course Congress is not bound to admit a community desiring to be recognized as a state. Utah was kept knocking at the door of the Union for many years, because the nation wished to retain for the purpose of preventing polygamy that full control which can be exercised over a Territory but not over a state. Her admission was accompanied by a prohibition of polygamy. Sometimes a dominant party postpones the admission of a state likely to strengthen by its vote the opposite party; and sometimes, as happened in the cases of Wyoming, Montana, Idaho, and New Mexico, communities whose fitness for statehood was doubtful were admitted for partisan reasons.

[7] However, though the constitutions of the Canadian and Australian Dominions and of United South Africa were enacted by British statutes of 1867, 1900, and 1909 respectively, all three had been drafted by the colonists.

a shoot by the Imperial Parliament at home, Parliament may always alter or abolish it. Congress, on the other hand, has no power to alter a state constitution. And whatever power of alteration has been granted to a British colony is exercisable by the legislature of the colony, not, as in America, by the citizens at large.

The original constitutions of the states, whether of the old thirteen or of those subsequently admitted, have been in nearly every case (except those of the twelve newest states) subsequently recast, in some instances, five, six, or even seven times, as well as amended in particular points. Thus constitutions of all dates are now in force in different states, from that of Massachusetts, enacted in 1780, but largely amended since, to that of Arizona enacted in 1912.

The constitutions of the revolutionary period were in a few instances enacted by the state legislature, acting as a body with plenary powers, but more usually by the people acting through a convention, i.e., a body specially chosen by the voters at large for the purpose, and invested with full powers, not only of drafting, but of adopting the instrument of government.[8] Since 1835, when Michigan framed her constitution, the invariable practice in the Northern states has been for the convention, elected by the voters, to submit in accordance with the precedents set by Massachusetts in 1780, and by Maine in 1820, the draft constitution framed by it to the citizens of the state at large, who vote upon it yes or no. They usually vote on it as a whole, and adopt or reject it *en bloc*, but sometimes provision is made for voting separately on some particular point or points. In the Southern states the practice has varied. In 1890, Mississippi enacted a new constitution by a convention alone; and in Kentucky (in 1891), after the draft constitution which the convention had prepared had been submitted to and accepted by a popular vote (as provided by the statute which summoned the convention), the convention met again and made some alterations on which, strange to say, the people have not been since consulted.[9] Alabama in 1901 submitted her new constitution to the people. But South Carolina in 1895 and Louisiana in 1898 allowed conventions to

[8] In Rhode Island and Connecticut the legislature continued the colonial constitution. In South Carolina a body calling itself the "Provincial Congress" claimed to be the "General Assembly," or legislature of the colony, and as such enacted the constitution. In the other revolting colonies, except Massachusetts, conventions or congresses enacted the constitution not submitting it to the voters for ratification. In Massachusetts the convention submitted its draft to the voters in 1780, and the voters adopted it, a previous draft tendered by the legislature in 1778 having been rejected.

[9] Proceedings were taken before the Court of Appeals of Kentucky to determine the validity of these alterations, and the court by a majority upheld them, on the ground, it would seem, that the legislature and executive had treated them as operative. *Sed quære.*

adopt constitutions, and Virginia in 1902 followed their example, although the statute under which the constitutional convention was acting had directed that the revised constitution should be "submitted to the qualified voters."

The people of a state retain forever in their hands, altogether independent of the national government, the power of altering their constitution. When a new constitution is to be prepared, or the existing one amended, the initiative usually comes from the legislature, which (either by a simple majority, or by a two-thirds majority, or by a majority in two successive legislatures, as the constitution may in each instance provide) submits the matter to the voters in one of two ways. It may either propose to the people certain specific amendments,[10] or it may ask the people to decide by a direct popular vote on the propriety of calling a constitutional convention to revise the whole existing constitution. In the former case the amendments suggested by the legislature are directly voted on by the citizens; in the latter the legislature, so soon as the citizens have voted for the holding of a convention, provides for the election by the people of this convention. When elected, the convention meets, sets to work, goes through the old constitution, and prepares a new one, which is then presented to the people for ratification or rejection at the polls. Only in the little state of Delaware is the function of amending the constitution still left to the legislature without the subsequent ratification of a popular vote, subject, however, to the provision that changes must be passed by two successive legislatures, by a two-thirds majority of the members elected to each house, and must have been put before the people at the election of members for the second.[11] Some states provide for the submission to the people at fixed intervals, of seven, ten, sixteen, or twenty years, of the propriety of calling a convention to revise the constitution, and a few allow a prescribed percentage of the voters to propose amendments by their own initiative. Be it observed, however, that whereas the federal Constitution can be amended only by a vote of three-fourths of the states, a constitution can in nearly every state be changed by a bare majority of the citizens voting at the polls.[12] Hence we may expect to find,

---

[10] In New Hampshire the legislature has no power to propose amendments, so the local authorities take the sense of the people every seven years as to the need for a revising convention. In some states the legislature can do so only after stated intervals, e.g., of five years.

[11] Constitution of 1897, which however also provides that the legislature may, by a like majority, submit to popular vote the question of summoning a convention to revise the constitution.

[12] Sometimes, however, an absolute majority of all the qualified voters is required. In Rhode Island (where the voting is in town and ward meetings) a three-fifths majority is needed, and in South Carolina the ratification of the next elected legislature by a two-thirds majority in each house is necessary. In Delaware the proposal to call a convention must be approved by a majority of all the voters, in Kentucky by at least one-fourth of the total number who voted at the last preceding general election. Delaware having during several years failed in the attempt to amend her

and shall find, that these instruments are altered more frequently and materially than the federal Constitution has been. Between 1889 and 1908 only two states, Tennessee and Wyoming, abstained from altering their constitutions (Wyoming's was enacted in 1889) and in those twenty years California altered hers forty-two times. Between 1892 and 1908 she adopted forty-seven amendments.

The tendency of late years has been to make the process of alteration quicker, for recent constitutions generally provide that one legislature, not two successive legislatures, may propose an amendment, which shall at once take effect if accepted by the people,[13] and also to make it easier, for some of the Western states now allow the people to start the process.

A state constitution is not only independent of the central national government (save in certain points already specified), it is also the fundamental organic law of the state itself. The state exists as a commonwealth by virtue of its constitution, and all state authorities, legislative, executive, and judicial, are the creatures of, and subject to, the state constitution.[14] Just as the president and Congress are placed beneath the federal Constitution, so the governor and houses of a state are subject to its constitution, and any act of theirs done either in contravention of its provisions, or in excess of the powers it confers on them, is absolutely void. All that has been said in preceding chapters regarding the functions of the courts of law where an act of Congress is alleged to be inconsistent with the federal Constitution,

---

constitution (of 1831) by the legislature, fell back, in 1887, on the proposal to hold a constitutional convention, and at last gave herself a new constitution in 1897.

[13] In the more recent constitutions more than a bare majority of members of each of the two houses of the legislature must agree to propose an amendment, the amendment being in every case ultimately submitted to the people.

[14] Some details as to the provisions of state constitutions may be found in Mr. F. J. Stimson's *American Statute Law*, and in the same author's *Federal and State Constitutions of the United States* (1908). The subject of state constitutions has also been very well treated by Professor J. Q. Dealey in his book *Our State Constitutions*. The great authority was the collection of the state constitutions, embracing (together with the colonial charters) all that have been duly enacted since 1776, in the two thick quarto volumes entitled *Federal and State Constitutions*, published under the authority of Congress by Ben. Perley Poore, Washington, 1878. In 1909 a new collection was under the authority of Congress published in seven volumes entitled *The Federal and State Constitutions, Colonial Charters and other Organic Laws of the States, Territories, and Colonies now or heretofore forming the United States of America*, edited by Francis Newton Thorpe, Ph.D. LL.D. It is much to be wished that an annual, or a biennial or even quinquennial supplement to this new collection should be officially published, containing all the new consitutions and constitutional amendments. At present it is very difficult, even for residents in the United States, to ascertain exactly how the constitution of each state stands at a given moment; and I have not found it possible to keep abreast of the changes made since the aforesaid new collection went to press.

applies equally where a statute passed by a state legislature is alleged to transgress the constitution of the state, and of course such validity may be contested in any court, whether a state court or a federal court, because the question is an ordinary question of law, and is to be solved by determining whether or no a law of inferior authority is inconsistent with a law of superior authority. Whenever in any legal proceeding before any tribunal, either party relies on a state statute, and the other party alleges that this statute is *ultra vires* of the state legislature, and therefore void, the tribunal must determine the question just as it would determine whether a bye-law made by a municipal council or a railway company was in excess of the lawmaking power which the municipality or the company had received from the higher authority which incorporated it and gave it such legislative power as it possesses. But although federal courts are fully competent to entertain a question arising on the construction of a state constitution, their practice is to follow the precedents set by any decision of a court of the state in question, just as they would follow the decision of a French court in determining a point of law. Each state must be assumed to know its own law better than a stranger can; but also that the supreme court of a state is the authorized exponent of the mind of the people who enacted its constitution.

A state constitution is really nothing but a law made directly by the people voting at the polls upon a draft submitted to them. The people when they so vote act as a primary and constituent assembly, just as if they were all summoned to meet in one place like the folkmoots of our Teutonic forefathers. It is only their numbers that prevent them from so meeting in one place, and oblige the vote to be taken at a variety of polling places. Hence the enactment of a constitution is an exercise of direct popular sovereignty to which we find few parallels in modern Europe, though it was familiar enough to the republics of antiquity, and has lasted till now in some of the cantons of Switzerland.[15]

The importance of this character of a state constitution as a popularly-enacted law, overriding every minor state law, becomes all the greater when the contents of these constitutions are examined. Europeans conceive of a constitution as an instrument, usually a short instrument, which creates a frame of government, defines its departments and powers, and declares the "primordial rights" of the subject or citizen as against the rulers. An American state constitution does this, but does more; and in most cases,

---

[15] Nowadays, however, the Landesgemeinden (which survive only in Uri, Unterwalden, Glarus, and Appenzell, having been recently discontinued in Schwyz and Zug) do not act as constituent or constitution-enacting bodies, though they still directly legislate.

infinitely more. It deals with a variety of topics which in Europe would be left to the ordinary action of the legislature, or of administrative authorities; and it pursues these topics into a minute detail hardly to be looked for in a fundamental instrument. Some of these details will be mentioned presently. Meantime I will sketch in outline the frame and contents of the more recent constitutions, reserving for next chapter remarks on the differences of type between those of the older and those of the newer states.

A normal constitution consists of five parts:

I. The definition of the boundaries of the state. (This does not occur in the case of the older states.)

II. The so-called bill of rights—an enumeration (whereof more anon) of the citizens' primordial rights to liberty of person and security of property. This usually stands at the beginning of the constitution, but occasionally at the end.

III. The frame of government, i.e., the names, functions, and powers of the legislative bodies (including provisions anent the elective suffrage), the executive officers, and the courts of justice.

IV. Miscellaneous provisions relating to administration and law, including articles treating of education, of the militia, of taxation and revenue, of the public debts, of local government, of state prisons and hospitals, of agriculture, of labour, of corporations and railroads, of impeachment, and of the method of amending the constitution, besides other matters still less political in their character. The order in which these occur differs in different instruments, and there are some in which some of the above topics are not mentioned at all. The more recent constitutions and those of the newer states are much fuller on these points.

V. The schedule, which contains provisions relating to the method of submitting the constitution to the vote of the people, and arrangements for the transition from the previous constitution to the new one which is to be enacted by that vote. Being of a temporary nature, the schedule is not strictly a part of the constitution.

The bill of rights is historically the most interesting part of these constitutions, for it is the legitimate child and representative of Magna Charta, and of those other declarations and enactments, down to the Bill of Rights of the Act of 1 William and Mary, session 2, by which the liberties of Englishmen have been secured. Most of the thirteen colonies when they asserted their independence and framed their constitutions inserted a declaration of the fundamental rights of the people, and the example then set has been followed by the newer states, and, indeed, by the states generally in their most recent constitutions. Considering that all danger from the exercise of despotic power upon the people of the states by the executive has long since vanished, their executive authorities being the creatures of popular vote and nowadays rather too weak than too strong, it may excite surprise that these assertions of the rights and immunities of the individual citizen as against the government should continue to be repeated in the instruments of today. A reason may be found in the remarkable constitutional conservatism of the Americans, and in their fondness for the enunciation of the general maxims of political freedom. But it is also argued that these declarations of principle have a practical value, as asserting the rights of individuals and of minorities against arbitrary conduct by a majority in the legislature, which might, in the absence of such provisions, be tempted at moments of excitement to suspend the ordinary law and arm the magistrates with excessive powers. They are therefore, it is held, still safeguards against tyranny; and they serve the purpose of solemnly reminding a state legislature and its officers of those fundamental principles which they ought never to overstep.[16] Although such provisions certainly do restrain a state legislature in ways which the British Parliament would find inconvenient, few complaints of practical evils thence arising are heard.

A general notion of these bills of rights may be gathered from that enacted for itself in 1907 by the new state of Oklahoma, printed in the Appendix to this volume. I may mention, in addition, a few curious provisions which occur in some of them.

All provide for full freedom of religious opinion and worship, and for the equality before the law of all religious denominations and their members; and many forbid the establishment of any particular church or sect, and declare that no public money ought to be applied in aid of any religious body or sectarian institution.[17] But Delaware holds it to be "the duty of all

---

[16] Mr. F. J. Stimson (*Federal and State Constitutions*, p. 68) well observes that whereas the extreme democrats of the Revolutionary age desired to limit as much as possible the powers of the federal government, deeming it dangerous to liberty, they were glad to entrust very wide powers to the state legislatures which to them represented popular power. The propertied and educated classes on the other hand feared the state legislatures and sought to have restrictions placed upon them. The precedent of the Declaration of Independence, whose influence was great, helped them to secure the insertion of such restrictions in Bills of Rights. Of late years quite new reasons (to be presently referred to) have arisen for limiting legislative powers.

[17] Not till 1889, however, did New Hampshire strike out of her Constitution of 1792 a provision enabling the legislature to authorize towns to provide for the support of "public *Protestant* teachers of piety, religion, and morality."

men frequently to assemble for public worship"; and Vermont adds that "every sect or denomination of Christians ought to observe the Sabbath or Lord's Day." And thirteen states declare that the provisions for freedom of conscience are not to be taken to excuse acts of licentiousness, or justify practices inconsistent with the peace and safety of the state,[18] Mississippi adding (1890) that they shall not be construed to exclude the Bible from use in schools, and Idaho, Montana, and Utah (states familiar with Mormonism), denouncing bigamy and polygamy as crimes to be made punishable.

Louisiana (Constitution of 1898) declares that "all government of right originates with the people, is founded on their will alone, and is instituted solely for the good of the whole. Its only legitimate end is to secure justice to all, preserve peace, and promote the interest and happiness of the people."

A large majority of the states declare that "all men have a natural, inherent, and inalienable right to enjoy and defend life and liberty"; and all of these, except the melancholy Missouri, add, the "natural right to pursue happiness."

Most declare that all men have "a natural right to acquire, possess, and protect property," while Arkansas and Kentucky are so penetrated with the importance of this right that they declare it to be "before and higher than any constitutional sanction."

Mississippi and Louisiana (Constitutions of 1868) provided that "the right of all citizens to travel upon public conveyances shall not be infringed upon nor in any manner abridged." Both states have now dropped this injunction.[19]

Kentucky (Constitution of 1891) lays down that "absolute arbitrary power over the lives, liberty, and property of freemen exists nowhwere in a republic, not even in the largest majority. All men when they form a social compact are equal. All power is inherent in the people, and all free governments are founded on their authority, and instituted for their peace, safety, happiness, and security, and the protection of property. For the advancement of these ends they have at all times an inalienable and indefeasible right to alter, reform, or abolish their government in such manner as they may deem proper."[20]

---

[18] In Arkansas, Maryland, Mississippi, North Carolina, South Carolina, and Texas, a man is declared ineligible for office if he denies the existence of God; in Pennsylvania and Tennessee he is ineligible if he does not believe in God, and in the existence of future rewards and punishments. In Arkansas and Maryland such a person is also incompetent as a witness or juror.

[19] These provisions were inserted shortly after the Civil War in order to protect the Negroes.

[20] Until 1891, Kentucky added, "The right of property is before and higher than any constitutional sanction; and the right of the owner of a slave to such slave and its increase is the same and as

All in one form or another secure the freedom of writing and speaking opinions; and some add that the truth of a libel may be given in evidence.[21]

Nearly all secure the freedom of public meeting and petition. Considering that these are the last rights likely to be infringed by a state government, it is odd to find Florida in her Constitution of 1886 providing that "the people shall have the right to assemble together to consult for the common good, to instruct their representatives, and to petition the legislature for redress of grievances," and Kentucky in 1891 equally concerned to secure this right.

Many provide that no *ex post facto* law, nor law impairing the obligation of a contract, shall be passed by the state legislature; and that private property shall not be taken by the state without just compensation.

Many forbid the creation of any title of nobility.

Many declare that the right of citizens to bear arms shall never be denied, a provision which might be expected to prove inconvenient where it was desired to check the habit of carrying revolvers. Tennessee therefore (Constitution of 1870) prudently adds that "the legislature shall have power to regulate the wearing of arms, with a view to prevent crime." So also Texas, where such a provision is certainly not superfluous. And eight others[22] allow the legislature to forbid the carrying of concealed weapons.

Several forbid armed men to be brought into the state "for the suppression of domestic violence," in order to prevent employers from resorting to this means of protecting property in case of labour disputes accompanied by violence.

Some declare that the estates of suicides shall descend in the ordinary course of law.

Most provide that conviction for treason shall not work corruption of blood nor forfeiture of estate.

Eight forbid white and coloured children to be taught in the same public schools, while Wyoming provides that no distinction shall be made in the public schools on account of sex, race, or colour.

Many declare the right of trial by jury to be inviolate, even while permitting the parties to waive it. Several states empower a jury in civil

---

inviolable as the right of the owner of any property whatever," although this doctrine had been annulled, in effect, by the Thirteenth Amendment to the federal Constitution.

[21] A curious survival may be noted in the provisions enabling the jury to determine law as well as fact in libel cases; e.g., Mississippi (1890) and Kentucky (1891) in criminal, Wyoming (1889) also in civil cases.

[22] North Carolina, Mississippi, Missouri, Louisiana, Colorado, Kentucky, Oklahoma, and Montana, states in which daily experience shows that the measures taken have not hitherto proved successful.

cases to render a verdict by a three-fourths or two-thirds majority, and five states permit it to consist of less than twelve.

Some forbid imprisonment for debt, except in case of fraud, and secure the acceptance of reasonable bail, except for the gravest charges.[23]

Several declare that "perpetuities and monopolies are contrary to the genius of a free State, and ought not to be allowed."

Many forbid the granting of any hereditary honours, privileges, or emoluments.

North Carolina declares that "as political rights and privileges are not dependent upon or modified by property, therefore no property qualification ought to affect the right to vote or hold office"; and also, "secret political societies are dangerous to the liberties of a free people, and should not be tolerated."

Massachusetts sets forth, as befits a Puritan state, high moral views: "A frequent recurrence to the fundamental principles of the Constitution, and a constant adherence to those of piety, justice, moderation, temperance, industry, and frugality, are absolutely necessary to preserve the advantages of liberty and to maintain a free government. The people ought consequently to have a particular attention to all those principles in the choice of their officers and representatives, and they have a right to require of their law-givers and magistrates an exact and constant observance of them."

South Dakota and Wyoming provide that aliens shall have the same rights of property as citizens. Montana confers this benefit as respects mining property, while Washington prohibits the ownership of land by aliens, except for mining purposes. New York in her (now superseded) Constitution of 1846 declared, "All lands within the State are declared to be allodial."

North Dakota (1889) enacts: "Every citizen shall be free to obtain employment wherever possible, and any person, corporation, or agent thereof, maliciously interfering or hindering in any way any citizen from obtaining, or enjoying employment already obtained, from any other corporation or person, shall be deemed guilty of a misdemeanor."

Maryland (Constitution of 1867) declares that "a long continuance in the executive departments of power or trust is dangerous to liberty; a rotation, therefore, in those departments is one of the best securities of permanent

---

[23] Mississippi (Constitution of 1890) allows courts of justice to exclude, in some classes of prosecutions, persons not necessary for the conduct of the trial. Wyoming (1889) provides that no person detained as a witness be confined in any room where criminals are imprisoned, Oklahoma that if a verdict is rendered by less than the whole number of jurors, it shall be in writing and signed by each juror concurring therein.

freedom." She also pronounces all gifts for any religious purpose (except of a piece of land not exceeding five acres for a place of worship, parsonage, or burying-ground) to be void unless sanctioned by the legislature.

Montana and Idaho declare the use of lands for constructing reservoirs, watercourses, or ways for the purposes of mining or irrigation, to be a public use, subject to state regulation.

Oklahoma provides that "the right of the State to engage in any occupation or business for public purposes shall be be denied or prohibited" save that its agricultural enterprises are to be only "for scientific, educational or charitable purposes."

These instances, a few out of many, may suffice to show how remote from the common idea of a bill of rights, are some of the enactments which find a place under that heading. The constitution makers seem to have inserted here such doctrines or legal reforms as seemed to them matters of high import or of wide application, especially when they could find no suitable place for them elsewhere in the instrument.

Of the articles of each state constitution which contain the frame of state government it will be more convenient to speak in the chapters which describe the mechanism and character of the governments and administrative systems of the several states. I pass on therefore to what have been classed as the miscellaneous provisions. These are of great interest as revealing the spirit and tendencies of popular government in America, the economic and social condition of the country, the mischiefs that have arisen, the remedies applied to these mischiefs, the ideas and beliefs of the people in matters of legislation.

Among such provisions we find a great deal of matter which is in no distinctive sense constitutional law, but general law, e.g., administrative law, the law of judicial procedure, the ordinary private law of family, inheritance, contract, and so forth; matter therefore which seems out of place in a constitution because fit to be dealt with in ordinary statutes. We find minute provisions regarding the management and liabilities of banking companies, of railways, or of corporations generally; regulations as to the salaries of officials, the quorum of courts sitting in banco, the length of time for appealing, the method of changing the venue, the publication of judicial reports; detailed arrangements for school boards and school taxation (with rules regarding the separation of white and black children in schools), for a department of agriculture, a canal board, or a labour bureau; we find a prohibition of lotteries, of polygamy, of bribery, of lobbying, of the granting of liquor licenses, of usurious interest on money, an abolition of the distinction between sealed and unsealed instruments, a declaration of the extent of a mechanic's lien for work done. We even find the method prescribed in which stationery and coals for the use of the legislature shall be contracted for, and provisions for fixing the rates which may be charged for the storage of corn in warehouses. The framers of these more recent constitutions have in fact neither wished nor cared to draw a line of distinction between what is proper for a constitution and what ought to be left to be dealt with by the state legislature. And, in the case of three-fourths at least of the states, no such distinction now, in fact, exists.

How is this confusion to be explained? Four reasons may be suggested.

The Americans, like the English, have no love for scientific arrangement. Although the constitutions have been drafted by lawyers, and sometimes by the best lawyers of each state, logical classification and discrimination have not been sought after.

The people found the enactment of a new constitution a convenient opportunity for enunciating doctrines they valued and carrying through reforms they desired. It was a simpler and quicker method than waiting for legislative action, so, when there was a popular demand for the establishment of an institution, or for some legal change, this was shovelled into the new constitution and enacted accordingly.

The peoples of the states have come to distrust their respective legislatures. Hence they desire not only to do a thing forthwith and in their own way rather than leave it to the chance of legislative action, but to narrow as far as they conveniently can (and sometimes farther) the sphere of the legislature.

There is an unmistakable wish in the minds of the people to act directly rather than through their representatives in legislation. The same conscious relish for power which leads some democracies to make their representatives mere delegates, finds a further development in passing by the representatives, and setting the people itself to make and repeal laws.

Those who have read the chapters describing the growth and expansion of the federal Constitution, will naturally ask how far the remarks there made apply to the constitutions of the several states.

These instruments have less capacity for expansion, whether by interpretation or by usage, than the Constitution of the United States: first, because they are more easily, and therefore more frequently, amended or recast; secondly, because they are far longer, and go into much more minute detail. The federal Constitution is so brief and general that custom must fill up what it has left untouched, and judicial construction evolve the application of its terms to cases they do not expressly deal with. But the later state constitutions are so full and precise that they need little in the way of expansive construction, and leave comparatively little room for the action of custom.

The rules of interpretation are in the main the same as those applied to the federal Constitution. One important difference must, however, be noted, springing from the different character of the two governments. The national government is an artificial creation, with no powers except those conferred by the instrument which created it. A state government is a natural growth, which prima facie possesses all the powers incident to any government whatever. Hence, if the question arises whether a state legislature can pass a law on a given subject, the presumption is that it can do so: and positive grounds must be adduced to prove that it cannot. It may be restrained by some inhibition either in the federal Constitution, or in the constitution of its own state. But such inhibition must be affirmatively shown to have been imposed, or, to put the same point in other words, a state constitution is held to be, not a document conferring defined and specified powers on the legislature, but one regulating and limiting that general authority which the representatives of the people enjoy *ipso jure* by their organization into a legislative body.

"It has never been questioned that the American legislatures have the same unlimited power in regard to legislation which resides in the British Parliament, except where they are restrained by written Constitutions. That must be conceded to be a fundamental principle in the political organization of the American States. We cannot well comprehend how, upon principle, it could be otherwise. The people must, of course, possess all legislative power originally. They have committed this in the most general and unlimited manner to the several State legislatures, saving only such restrictions as are imposed by the Constitution of the United States or of the particular State in question."[24]

"The people, in framing the Constitution, committed to the legislature the whole law-making powers of the State which they did not expressly or impliedly withhold. Plenary power in the legislature, for all purposes of civil government, is the rule. A prohibition to exercise a particular power is an exception."[25]

It must not, however, be supposed from these dicta that even if the states were independent commonwealths, the federal government having

[24] Redfield, C.J., in 27 Vermont Reports, p. 142, quoted by Cooley, *Constit. Limit.*, p. 108.

[25] Denio, C.J., in 15 N.Y. Reports, p. 543, quoted *ibid.* p. 107.

disappeared, their legislatures would enjoy anything approaching the omnipotence of the British Parliament, "whose power and jurisdiction is," says Sir Edward Coke, "so transcendent and absolute that it cannot be confined, either for persons or causes, within any bounds." "All mischiefs and grievances," adds Blackstone, "operations and remedies that transcend the ordinary course of the laws are within the reach of this extraordinary tribunal." Parliament being absolutely sovereign, can command, or extinguish and swallow up the executive and the judiciary, appropriating to itself their functions. But in America, a legislature is a legislature and nothing more. The same instrument which creates it creates also the executive governor and the judges. They hold by a title as good as its own. If the legislature should pass a law depriving the governor of an executive function conferred by the constitution, that law would be void. If the legislature attempted to interfere with the jurisdiction of the courts, their action would be even more palpably illegal and ineffectual.[26]

The executive and legislative departments of a state government have of course the right and duty of acting in the first instance on their view of the meaning of the constitution. But the ultimate expounder of that meaning is the judiciary; and when the courts of a state have solemnly declared the true construction of any provision of the constitution, all persons are bound to regulate their conduct accordingly. As was observed in considering the functions of the federal judiciary (Chapter 23), this authority of the American courts is not in the nature of a political or discretionary power vested in them; it is a necessary consequence of the existence of a fundamental law superior to any statute which the legislature may enact, or to any right which a governor may conceive himself to possess.[27] To quote the words of an American decision:

"In exercising this high authority the judges claim no judicial supremacy; they are only the administrators of the public will. If an Act of the legislature is held void, it is not because the judges have any control over the legislative

---

[26] It has, for instance, been held that a state legislature cannot empower election boards to decide whether a person has by duelling forfeited his right to vote or hold office, this inquiry being judicial and proper only for the regular tribunals of the state.—Cooley, *Constit. Limit.*, p. 112. Acts passed by legislatures affecting some judicial decision already given, have repeatedly been held void by the courts.

[27] In Switzerland, however, the cantonal courts have not, except perhaps in Uri, the right to declare invalid a law made by a cantonal legislature, the legislature being apparently deemed the judge of its own powers. A cantonal law may, however, be quashed, in some cases, by the Federal Council, or pronounced invalid by the Federal Court. See an interesting discussion of the question in Dubs, *Das öffentliche Recht der Schweizerischen Eidgenossenschaft*, Part I, p. 113.

power, but because the Act is forbidden by the Constitution, and because the will of the people, which is therein declared, is paramount to that of their representatives expressed in any law."

It is a well-established rule that the judges will always lean in favour of the validity of a legislative act; that if there be a reasonable doubt as to the constitutionality of a statute they will solve that doubt in favour of the statute; that where the legislature has been left a discretion they will assume the discretion to have been wisely exercised; that where the construction of a statute is doubtful, they will adopt such construction as will harmonize with the constitution, and enable it to take effect. So it has been well observed that a man might with perfect consistency argue as a member of a legislature against a bill on the ground that it is unconstitutional, and after having been appointed a judge, might in his judicial capacity sustain its constitutionality. Judges must not inquire into the motives of the legislature, nor refuse to apply an act because they may suspect that it was obtained by fraud or corruption, still less because they hold it to be opposed to justice and sound policy. "A court cannot declare a statute unconstitutional and void solely on the ground of unjust and oppressive provisions, or because it is supposed to violate the natural, social, or political rights of the citizen, unless it can be shown that such injustice is prohibited, or such rights guaranteed or protected, by the Constitution.[28]. . . But when a statute is adjudged to be unconstitutional, it is as if it had never been. Rights cannot be built up under it; contracts which depend upon it for their consideration are void; it constitutes a protection to no one who has acted under it; and no one can be punished for having refused obedience to it before the decision was made. And what is true of an Act void *in toto*, is true also as to any

---

[28] This was not always admitted; just as in England it was at one time held that natural justice and equity were above acts of Parliament. So in the case of *Gardner* v. *The Village of Newburg* (Johnson's *Chancery Reports*, N. Y. 162), the New York legislature had authorized the village to supply itself with water from a stream, but had made no provision for indemnifying the owners of lands through which the stream flowed for the injury they must suffer from the diversion of the water. The Constitution of New York at that time contained no provision prohibiting the taking of private property for public use without compensation; notwithstanding this, Chancellor Kent restrained the village from proceeding upon the broad general principle which he found in Magna Charta, in a statutory Bill of Rights, which of course could not control the legislature, and in Grotius Puffendorf and Bynkershoek. (I owe that reference to the kindness of Mr. Theodore Bacon.)

  As the doctrine stated in the text has been doubted by some critics, I may refer for further confirmation of it to *Dash* v. *Van Kleech*, 7 Johns, 477 (words of Chancellor Kent), and *People* v. *Gillson*, 109 N. Y. 398. See further on this subject the late Professor Thayer's *Cases in Constitutional Law*, p. 48.

part of an Act which is found to be unconstitutional, and which consequently is to be regarded as having never at any time been possessed of legal force."[29]

It may be thought, and the impression will be confirmed when we consider as well the minuteness of the state constitutions as the profusion of state legislation and the inconsiderate haste with which it is passed, that as the risk of a conflict between the constitution and statutes is great, so the inconveniences of a system under which the citizens cannot tell whether their obedience is or is not due to a statute must be serious. How is a man to know whether he has really acquired a right under a statute? How is he to learn whether to conform his conduct to it or not? How is an investor to judge if he may safely lend money which a statute has empowered a community to borrow, when the statute may be itself subsequently overthrown?

To meet these difficulties some state constitutions[30] provide that the judges of the supreme court of the state may be called upon by the governor or either house of the legislature to deliver their opinions upon questions of law, without waiting for these questions to arise and be determined in an ordinary lawsuit.[31] This expedient seems a good one, for it procures a judicial and nonpartisan interpretation, and procures it at once before rights

---

[29] Cooley, *Constit. Limit.*, pp. 200, 227.

[30] Massachusetts, Maine, New Hampshire, Rhode Island, Colorado, Florida, and South Dakota. In Vermont a similar power is given by statute. In South Dakota the governor may require it "upon important questions of law involving the exercise of his executive powers and upon solemn occasions." In Florida it is only the governor to whom the power has been given, and whereas under the Constitution of 1868 he could obtain the opinion of the justices "upon any point of law," he can by the Constitution of 1886 require it only "upon any question affecting his executive powers and duties." A similar provision was inserted in the Constitution of Missouri of 1865, but omitted in the revised (and now operative) Constitution of 1875, apparently because the judges had so often refused to give their advice when asked for it by a house of the legislature, that there seemed little use in retaining the enactment. In the other states the judges have apparently always consented to answer, save on one or two occasions in Massachusetts. See on the whole subject an interesting pamphlet by the late Professor J. B. Thayer, of the Harvard Law School.

[31] The judges of the supreme court of Massachusetts suggest in their very learned and instructive opinion, delivered to the legislature, December 31, 1878, that this provision, which appears first in the Massachusetts Constitution of 1780, and was doubtless borrowed thence by the other States, "evidently had in view the usage of the English Constitution, by which the King as well as the House of Lords, whether acting in their judicial or in their legislative capacity, had the right to demand the opinion of the twelve judges of England." This is still sometimes done by the House of Lords; but the opinions of the judges so given are not necessarily followed by that House, and though always reported are not deemed to be binding pronouncements of law similar to the decisions of a court.

or interests have been created. But it is open to the objection that the opinions so pronounced by judges are given before cases have arisen which show how in fact a statute is working, and what points it may raise; and that in giving them the judges have not, as in contested lawsuits, the assistance of counsel arguing for their respective clients. And this is perhaps the reason why in most of the states where the provision exists, the judges have declared that they act under it in a purely advisory capacity, and that their deliverances are to be deemed merely expressions of opinion, not binding upon them should the point afterwards arise in a lawsuit involving the rights of parties.[32]

The highest court of a state may depart from a view it has previously laid down, even in a legal proceeding, regarding the construction of the constitution, that is to say, it has a legal right to do so if convinced that the former view was wrong. But it is reluctant to do so, because such a course unsettles the law and impairs the respect felt for the bench. And there is less occasion for it to do so than in the parallel case of the supreme federal court, because as the process of amending a state constitution is simpler and speedier than that of altering the federal Constitution, a remedy can be more easily applied to any mistake which the state judiciary has committed. This unwillingness to unsettle the law goes so far that state courts have sometimes refused to disturb a practice long acquiesced in by the legislature, which they have nevertheless declared they would have pronounced unconstitutional had it come before them while still new.

---

[32] Mr. Thayer shows, by an examination of the reported instances, that in Massachusetts, New Hampshire, and Rhode Island, as also in Missouri from 1865 to 1875, the courts held that their opinions rendered under these provisions of the state constitutions were not to be deemed judicial determinations, equal in authority to decisions given in actual litigation, but were rather prima facie impressions, which the judges ought not to hold themselves bound by, when subsequently required to determine the same point in an action or other legal proceeding. It is otherwise in Maine and Colorado.

CHAPTER 38

The Development of
State Constitutions

It was observed in the last chapter that the state constitutions furnish invaluable materials for history. Their interest is all the greater, because the succession of constitutions and amendments to constitutions from 1776 till today enables the annals of legislation and political sentiment to be read in these documents more easily and succinctly than in any similar series of laws in any other country. They are a mine of instruction for the natural history of democratic communities. Their fulness and minuteness make them, so to speak, more pictorial than the federal Constitution. They tell us more about the actual methods and conduct of the government than it does. If we had similar materials concerning the history of as many Greek republics during the ages of Themistocles and Pericles, we could rewrite the history of Greece. Some things, however, even these elaborately minute documents do not tell us. No one could gather from then what were the modes of doing business in the state legislatures, and how great a part the system of committees plays there. No one could learn what manner of men constitute those bodies and determine their character. No one would know that the whole machinery is worked by a restlessly active party organization. Nevertheless they are so instructive as records of past movements, and as an index to the present tendencies of American democracy, that I heartily regret that the space at my disposal permits me to make only a sparing use of the materials which I gathered during many months spent in studying the one hundred and thirteen constitutions enacted between 1776 and 1887, to which many more have since been added.[1]

[1] I venture again to commend the study of these constitutions to the philosophic inquirer into what may be called the science of comparative politics. Both among the pre-Revolutionary charters and the state constitutions he will find matter full of instruction. Among the former I may refer especially to the Frame of Government of Pennsylvania, 1682 and 1683, and to the Fundamental Constitutions of Carolina of 1669. These last were framed by John Locke, and revised by the first Lord Shaftesbury. They were found unsuitable, were only partially put in force, and were abrogated

Three periods may be distinguished in the development of state governments as set forth in the constitutions, each period marked by an increase in the length and minuteness of those instruments.

The first period covers about thirty years from 1776 downwards, and includes the earlier constitutions of the original thirteen states, as well as of Kentucky, Vermont, Tennessee, and Ohio.

Most of these constitutions were framed under the impressions of the Revolutionary War. They manifest a dread of executive power and of military power, together with a disposition to leave everything to the legislature, as being the authority directly springing from the people. The election of a state governor is in most states vested in the legislature. He is nominally assisted, but in reality checked, by a council not of his own choosing. He has not (except in Massachusetts) a veto on the acts of the legislature.[2] He has not, like the royal governors of colonial days, the right of adjourning or dissolving it. The idea of giving power to the people directly has scarcely appeared, because the legislature is conceived as the natural and necessary organ of popular government, much as the House of Commons is in England. And hence many of these early constitutions consist of little beyond an elaborate bill of rights and a comparatively simple outline of a frame of government, establishing a representative legislature,[3] with a few executive officers and courts of justice carefully separated therefrom.

The second period covers the first half of the present century down to the time when the intensity of the party struggles over slavery (1850–60) interrupted to some extent the natural processes of state development. It is a period of the democratization of all institutions, a democratization due not only to causes native to American soil, such as the rise in the West of new agricultural communities where all the settlers were practically equal, the supremacy in politics of the generation who had, as boys during the Revolutionary War, been permeated by the phrases of 1776, but also to the influence of French republican ideas, an influence which began to decline after 1805 and ended with 1851, since which time French examples and ideas have counted for little or nothing. Such provisions for the maintenance of religious institutions by the state as had continued to exist are now swept

by the proprietors in 1693, but they are scarcely less interesting to the student of history on that account.

[2] In New York a veto on acts of the legislature was by the first constitution vested in the governor and judges of the highest state court, acting together.

[3] The wide powers of these early legislatures are witnessed to by the fear which prudent statesmen entertained of their action. Madison said, in the Philadelphia Convention of 1787, "Experience proves a tendency in our governments to throw all power into the legislative vortex. The executives of the States are little more than ciphers; the legislatures are omnipotent."

away. The principle becomes established (in the North and West) that constitutions must be directly enacted by popular vote. The choice of a governor is taken from the legislature to be given to the people. Property qualifications are abolished,[4] and a suffrage practically universal, except that it often excludes free persons of colour, is introduced. Even the judges are not spared. Many constitutions shorten their term of office, and direct them to be chosen by popular vote. The state has emerged from the English conception of a community acting through a ruling legislature, for the legislature begins to be regarded as being only a body of agents exercising delegated and restricted powers, and obliged to recur to the sovereign people (by asking for a constitutional amendment) when it seeks to extend these powers in any particular direction. The increasing length of the constitutions during this half century shows how the range of the popular vote has extended, for these documents now contain a mass of ordinary law on matters which in the early days would have been left to the legislatures.

In the third period, which begins from about the time of the Civil War, a slight reaction may be discerned, not against popular sovereignty, which is stronger than ever, but in the tendency to strengthen the executive and judicial departments as against the legislative. The governor had begun to receive in the second period, and has now in every state but one, a veto on the acts of the legislature. His tenure of office has been generally lengthened; the restrictions on his reeligibility generally removed. In many states the judges have been granted larger salaries, and their terms of office lengthened. Some constitutions have even transferred judicial appointments from the vote of the people to the executive. But the most notable change of all has been the narrowing of the competence of the legislature, and the fettering its action by complicated restrictions. It may seem that to take powers away from the legislature is to give them to the people, and therefore another step towards pure democracy. But in America this is not so, because a legislature is apt to yield to any popular clamour, however transient, while direct legislation by the people involves delay. Such provisions may therefore prove to be conservative in their results, if not in their intention.

This process of development, which first exalted and then depressed the legislature, which extended the direct interference of the people, which changed the constitution itself from a short into a long, a simple into a highly complex document, has of course not yet ended. Forces are already at work which will make the constitutions of forty years hence different

---

[4] Though Massachusetts forgot till 1892 to abolish the property qualification for her governorship.

from those of today. To conjecture the nature of these forces we must examine a little further the existing constitutions of the states, especially the later among them; and more particularly that remarkable group enacted in 1889 by the six commonwealths which were admitted to the Union in 1889 and 1890, as well as the constitution which Oklahoma gave herself in 1907. We must also distinguish between different types of constitution corresponding to the different parts of the Union in which the states that have framed them are situate.

Three types were formerly distinguishable, the old colonial type, best seen in New England and the older Middle states, the Southern or slave state type (in which the influence of the first Constitution of Virginia was noticeable), and the new or Western type. At present these distinctions are less marked. All the Southern states have given themselves new constitutions since the war; and the differences between these and the new constitutions of the Northwestern and Pacific states are not salient. This is because the economic and social changes produced by the War of Secession and abolition of slavery broke to pieces the old social conditions, and made these Southern states virtually new communities like those of the West. There is still, however, a strong contrast between the New England states, to which for this purpose we may add New Jersey, whose present constitutions all date from the period between 1780 and 1844, and the Southern and Western states, nearly all of whose constitutions are subsequent to that year. In these older states the power of the executive is generally greater. The judges are frequently named by the governor, and not elected by the people. The electoral districts are not always equal. The constitutions are not so minute, and therefore the need of recurring to the people to change them arises less frequently.

Taking the newer, and especially the Western and Southern constitutions, and remembering that each is the work of an absolutely independent body, which (subject to the federal Constitution) can organize its government and shape its law in any way it pleases, so as to suit its peculiar conditions and reflect the character of its population, one is surprised to find how similar these newer instruments are. There is endless variety in details, but a singular agreement in essentials. The influences at work, the tendencies which the constitutions framed since 1865 reveal, are evidently the same over the whole Union. What are the chief of those tendencies? One is for the constitutions to grow longer. This is an absolutely universal rule. Virginia, for instance, put her first constitution, that of 1776, into four closely printed quarto pages, that is, into about three thousand two hundred words. In 1830, she needed seven pages; in 1870, twenty-two pages, or seventeen thousand words; her latest (1902) has thirty-five thousand words. Texas has doubled the length of her constitution from sixteen quarto pages in 1845 to thirty-four in 1876. Pennsylvania was content in 1776 with a document of eight pages, which for those times was a long one; she now requires twenty-three. The Constitution of Illinois filled ten pages in 1818; in 1870 it had swollen to twenty-five. These are fair examples, but the extremes are marked by the Constitution of New Hampshire of 1776, which was of about six hundred words (not reckoning the preamble), and the Constitution of Missouri of 1875 and of South Dakota of 1889, which have each more than twenty-six thousand words. Even these were surpassed by Oklahoma, whose Constitution of 1907 exceeded thirty-three thousand words, and by Louisiana, whose Constitution of 1898 has forty-five thousand. The new constitutions are longer, not only because new topics are taken up and dealt with, but because the old topics are handled in far greater detail. Such matters as education, ordinary private law, railroads, state and municipal indebtedness, were either untouched or lightly touched in the earlier instruments. The provisions regarding the judiciary and the legislature, particularly those restricting the power of the latter, have grown far more minute of late years, as abuses of power became more frequent, and the respect for legislative authority less. As the powers of a state legislature are prima facie unlimited, these bodies can be restrained only by enumerating the matters withdrawn from their competence, and the list grows always ampler. The time might almost seem to have come for prescribing that, like Congress, they should be entitled to legislate on certain enumerated subjects only, and be always required to establish affirmatively their competence to deal with any given topic.

I have already referred to the progress which the newer constitutions show towards more democratic arrangements. The suffrage is now in almost every state enjoyed by all adult males, and in ten by adult females also. Citizenship is quickly and easily accorded to immigrants. And, most significant of all, the superior judges, who were formerly named by the governor, or chosen by the legislature, and who held office during good behaviour, are now in most states elected by the people for fixed terms of years. I do not ignore the strongly marked democratic character of even the first set of constitutions, formed at and just after the Revolution; but that character manifested itself chiefly in negative provisions, i.e., in forbidding exercises of power by the executive, in securing full civil equality and the primordial rights of the citizen. The new democratic spirit is positive as well as negative. It refers everything to the direct arbitrament of the people. It calls their will into constant activity, sometimes by the enactment of laws on various subjects in the constitution, sometimes by prescribing to the legislature the purposes which legislation is to aim at. Even the tendency to support the executive against the legislature is evidence not so much of respect for authority as of the confidence of the people that the executive will be the servant of popular opinion, prepared at its bidding to restrain that other servant—the legislature—who is less trusted, because harder to fix with responsibility for misdoing. On the whole, therefore, there can be no doubt that the democratic spirit is now more energetic and pervasive than it was in the first generation. It is a different kind of spirit. It is more practical, more disposed to extend the sphere of governmental interference, less content to rely on general principles. One discovers in the wording of the most recent constitutions a decline of that touching faith in the efficacy of broad declarations of abstract human rights which marked the disciples of Jefferson. But if we compare the present with the second or Jacksonian age, it may be said that there has been in progress for some years past a certain reaction, not against democracy but towards a better scheme of democracy, a reaction as yet more discernible in feeling than in tangible results, fainter than the levelling movement of 1820–50, and not likely to restore the state of things that existed before that movement, yet noticeable as showing that the people do learn by experience, and are not indisposed to reverse their action and get clear of the results of past mistakes. The common saying that on the road to democracy there are *vestigia nulla retrorsum* is not universally true in America.

That there are strong conservative tendencies in the United States is a doctrine whose truth will be illustrated later on. Meantime it is worth while to ask how far the history of state constitutions confirms the current notion that democracies are fond of change. The answer is instructive, because it shows how flimsy are the generalizations which men often indulge in when discussing forms of government, as if all communities with similar forms of government behaved in the same way. All the states of the Union are democracies, and democracies of nearly the same type. Yet while some change their constitutions frequently, others scarcely change theirs at all. Let me recall the reader's mind to the distinction already drawn between the older or New England type and the newer type, which we find in the Southern as well as the Western states. It is among the latter that changes are frequent. Louisiana, for instance, whose state life began in 1812, has had seven complete new constitutions, without counting the so-called

Secession Constitution of 1861. Virginia, Georgia, and South Carolina (original states) have had six each. Kansas, which began in 1855, has had four. Among the Northern states, Pennsylvania (an original state) has had four; Illinois, dating from 1818, three; New York, five; Delaware, four; whereas Connecticut and Rhode Island (both original states), and Maine (dating from 1820), have had only one each, Vermont and New Hampshire, three each. Massachusetts still lives under her Constitution of 1780, which has indeed been amended at various dates, yet not to such an extent as to efface its original features. Of the causes of these differences I will now touch on two only. One is the attachment which in an old and historic, a civilized and well-educated community, binds the people to their accustomed usages and forms of government. It is the newer states, without a past to revere, with a population undisciplined or fluctuating, that are prone to change. In well-settled commonwealths the longer a constitution has stood untouched, the longer it is likely to stand, because the force of habit is on its side, because an intelligent people learns to value the stability of its institutions, and to love that which it is proud of having long ago created.

The other cause is the difference between the swiftness with which economic and social changes move in different parts of the country. They are the most constant sources of political change, and find their natural expression in alterations of the constitution. Such changes have been least swift and least sudden in the New England and Middle states, though in some of the latter the growth of great cities, such as New York and Philadelphia, has induced them, and induced therewith a tendency to amend the constitutions so as to meet new conditions and check new evils. They have been most marked in regions where population and wealth have grown with unexampled speed, and in those where the extinction of slavery has changed the industrial basis of society. Here lies the explanation of the otherwise singular fact that several of the original states, such as Virginia and Georgia, have run through many constitutions. These whilom slave states have not only changed greatly but changed suddenly. Society was dislocated by the Civil War, and has had to make more than one effort to set itself right.

The total number of distinct constitutions adopted in 1776 or enacted in the several states from that year down till 1909—the states being then 13 and in the latter 46 in number—is 127; and to these constitutions a vast number of amendments have been at different times adopted.[5] The period

---

[5] Owing to the absence of any general official record, it is hard to ascertain the exact number, but in the ten years between 1894 and 1904 it would appear that 381 were voted on, of which 217

since 1860 shows a somewhat greater frequency of change than the eighty-four years preceding; but that may be accounted for by the effects of the war on the Southern states. The average duration of a constitution has been estimated at thirty years, and there are now seven which have lasted more than sixty years. Both whole constitutions and particular amendments are frequently rejected by the people when submitted to them at the polls. This befel six draft constitutions and more than twenty-eight amendments between 1877 and 1887.

Putting all these facts together, and bearing in mind to how large an extent the constitutions now, whether wisely or foolishly, embody ordinary private and administrative law and therefore invite amendment, the American democracy seems less inclined to changefulness and inconstancy than either abstract considerations or the descriptions of previous writers, such as Tocqueville, would have led us to expect. The respect for these fundamental instruments would no doubt be greater if the changes in them were even fewer, and the changes would be fewer if the respect were greater; but I see little reason to think that the evil is increasing.

A few more observations on what the constitutions disclose are needed before I conclude this necessarily brief sketch of the most instructive sources for the history of popular government which the nineteenth century produced—documents whose clauses, while they attempt to solve the latest problems of democratic commonwealths, often recall the earliest efforts of our English forefathers to restrain the excesses of mediæval tyranny.

The constitutions witness to a singular distrust by the people of its own agents and officers, not only of the legislatures but also of local authorities, as well rural as urban, whose powers of borrowing or undertaking public works are strictly limited. Even the judges are in some states restrained in their authority to commit for contempt of court, and three recent constitutions contain severe provisions against abuse of his veto and appointing power by the governor, and against bribery offered to or by him.[6]

They witness also to a jealousy of the federal government. By most constitutions a federal official is made incapable, not only of state office, but of being a member of a state legislature. These prohibitions are almost the only references to the national government to be found in the state constitutions, which so far as their terms go might belong to independent

---

were adopted and 164 rejected (Dealey, *Our State Constitutions*, p. 13). Between 1892 and 1909 California adopted 47 amendments, Georgia and Minnesota 11 each, Florida, Oregon, and North Dakota 10 each, and some states none at all.

[6] Constitutions of North Dakota, South Dakota, and Wyoming, all of 1889.

communities. They usually talk of corporations belonging to other states as "foreign," and sometimes try to impose special burdens on them.

They show a wholesome anxiety to protect and safeguard private property in every way. The people's consciousness of sovereignty has not used the opportunity which the enactment of a constitution gives to override private rights; there is rather a desire to secure such rights from any encroachment by the legislature: witness the frequent provisions against the taking of property without due compensation, and against the passing of private or personal statutes which could unfairly affect individuals. The only exceptions to this rule are to be found in the case of anything approaching a monopoly, and in the case of wealthy corporations. But the "monopolist" is regarded as the enemy of the ordinary citizen, whom he oppresses; and the corporation—it is usually corporations that are monopolists—is deemed not a private person at all, but a sort of irresponsible tyrant whose resources enable him to overreach the law. Corporations are singled out for special taxation and are evidently the objects of growing suspicion and hostility, for the newer constitutions multiply provisions for holding them in check and keeping them under close supervision. Michigan and Mississippi limit their duration. Oklahoma denies them the rights of ordinary citizens before the courts; some states forbid trustees to invest in corporate securities. Labour laws are enacted to apply to them only. A remarkable instance of this dread of monopolies is to be found in the Constitution of Illinois of 1870, with its provisions anent grain elevators, warehouses, and railroads.[7] The newer constitutions of other Western states, such as California and Texas, are not less instructive in this respect. Nor is it surprising that efforts should be made in some of the more recent instruments to strike at the combinations called "trusts."

The extension of the sphere of state interference, with the corresponding departure from the doctrine of laissez faire is a question so large and so interesting as to require a chapter to itself in my second volume. Here it may suffice to remark, that some departments of governmental action, which on the continent of Europe have long been handled by the state, are in America still left to private enterprise. For instance, the states neither own nor manage railways, or telegraphs, or mines, or forests, and they sell their public lands instead of working them. There is, nevertheless, visible in recent constitutions a strong tendency to extend the scope of public

---

[7] See the remarkable group of cases beginning with *Munn* v. *Illinois* (commonly called the Granger Cases) in 94 U.S. Reports, p. 113.

administrative activity. Most of the newer instruments establish not only railroad commissions, intended to control the roads in the interest of the public, but also bureaux of agriculture, labour offices, mining commissioners, land registration offices, dairy commissioners, insurance commissioners, and agricultural or mining colleges. And a reference to the statutes passed within the last few years in the Western states will show that more is being done in this direction by the legislatures, as exponents of popular sentiment, than could be gathered from the older among the Western constitutions.

A spirit of humanity and tenderness for suffering, very characteristic of the American people, appears in the directions which many constitutions contain for the establishment of charitable and reformatory institutions, and for legislation to protect children.[8] Sometimes the legislature is enjoined to provide that the prisons are made comfortable; or directions are given that homes or farms be provided as asylums for the aged and unfortunate.[9] On the other hand, this tenderness is qualified by the judicious severity which in most states debars persons convicted of crime from the electoral franchise. Lotteries are stringently prohibited by some of the recent constitutions.

In the older Northern constitutions, and in nearly all the more recent constitutions of all the states, ample provision is made for the creation and maintenance of schools. Even universities are the object of popular zeal, though a zeal not always according to knowledge. Most Western constitutions direct their establishment and support from public funds or land grants.[10] Some of the later constitutions contain significant provisions intended to propitiate labour. Thus Wyoming, California, Utah, and Idaho declare that eight hours shall be a lawful day's work on all state and municipal works, Wyoming adding "in all mines." Many prohibit the letting out of convict labour; and several prohibit contracts by which employers may attempt to escape from liability for accidents to their workpeople. Mississippi abolishes (1890), so far as concerns railroads, the established legal doctrine of an employer's nonliability for accidents caused to a workman by the fault of a fellow workman.

Although a constitution is the fundamental and supreme law of the state, one must not conclude that its provisions are any better observed and

---

[8] So Kentucky (Constitution of 1891, § 243) and North Dakota (Constitution of 1889, § 209) prohibit the labour of children under twelve. Wyoming forbids the employment of girls or women in mines.

[9] So Mississippi (Constitution of 1890, § 262).

[10] Mississippi seems to seek the political education of the legislator by requiring him to swear to read the constitution or have it read to him.

enforced than those of an ordinary statute. When an offence is thought worthy of being specially mentioned in a constitution, this happens because it is specially frequent, and because it is feared that the legislature may shrink from applying due severity to repress it, or the public prosecuting authorities may wink at it.[11] Certain it is that in many instances the penalties threatened by constitutions fail to attain their object. For instance, the constitutions of most of the Southern states have for many years past declared duellists, and even persons who abet a duel by carrying a challenge, incapable of office, or of sitting in the legislature. This may have checked the formal duel by challenge, which is now rarely heard of, but the practice of private warfare does not seem to have declined in Mississippi, Texas, or Arkansas, where these provisions exist. Virginia had such a provision in her Constitution of 1830. She repeated it in her Constitution of 1850, adding, however, that the disqualification should not attach to those who had offended previously—i.e., in violation of the Constitution of 1830.[12] Shooting at sight, not uncommon in some parts, is neither morally nor socially an improvement on duelling, though apparently exempt from these constitutional penalties.

New York has been so much exercised on the subject of bribery and corruption, as to declare (amendments of 1874), not only that every member of the legislature and every officer shall take an oath that he has given nothing as a consideration for any vote received for him, and that the legislature shall pass laws excluding from the suffrage all persons convicted of bribery or of any infamous crime but also that the giving or offering to or receiving by an officer of any bribe shall be a felony. These provisions are further strengthened in her Constituion of 1894. The recent constitutions

---

[11] This is said to have happened in some states as respects lotteries.

[12] "The General Assembly may provide that no person shall be capable of holding or being elected to any post of profit, trust, or emolument, civil or military, legislative, executive, or judicial, under the government of this commonwealth who shall hereafter fight a duel, or send or accept a challenge to fight a duel, the probable issue of which may be the death of the challenger or challenged, or who shall be second to either party, or shall in any manner aid or assist in such duel, or shall be knowingly the bearer of such challenge or acceptance; but no person shall be so disqualified by reason of his having heretofore fought such duel or sent or accepted such challenge, or been second in such duel, or bearer of such challenge or acceptance" (Constitution of 1830, art. III, § 12, repeated in Constitution of 1850, art. IV, § 17). In her Constitution of 1870 Virginia is not content with suggesting to the legislature to disqualify duellists, but does this directly by art. III, § 3. Many constitutions now declare duellists disqualified for office, and others add a disqualification for the franchise. Nearly all are Southern and West states. Kentucky (Constitution of 1891) requires all officers, members of the General Assembly, and persons being admitted to the bar to take an oath that they have not fought a duel since the adoption of the constitution, nor aided any person in so offending.

of North Dakota, Montana, and Wyoming declare logrolling to be bribery. South Dakota requires her legislators and officers to swear that they have not received and will not receive a free pass over a railroad for any vote or influence they may give, while Kentucky deprives of office (*ipso facto*) any legislative public officer or judge who accepts such a favour. And lobbying, which is openly practised in every building where a legislature meets, is declared by California to be a felony, and by Georgia to be a crime.

Direct Legislation by the People

The difficulties and defects inherent in the method of legislating by a constitution are obvious enough. Inasmuch as the people cannot be expected to distinguish carefully between what is and what is not proper for a fundamental instrument, there arises an inconvenient as well as unscientific mixture and confusion of private law and administrative regulation with the frame of government and the general doctrines of public law. This mixture, and the practice of placing in the constitution directions to the legislature to legislate in a certain sense, or for certain purposes, embarrass a legislature in its working by raising at every turn questions of its competence to legislate, and of the agreement between its acts and the directions contained in the constitution. And as the legislature is seldom either careful or well-advised, there follows in due course an abundant crop of questions as to the constitutionality of statutes, alleged by those whom they affect prejudicially in any particular instance to be either in substance inconsistent with the constitution, or such as the legislature was expressly forbidden by it to pass. These inconveniences are no doubt slighter in America than they would be in Europe, because the lawyers and the judges have had so much experience in dealing with questions of constitutional conflict and *ultra vires* legislation that they now handle them with amazing dexterity. Still, they are serious, and such as a well-ordered government ought to avoid. The habit of putting into the constitution matters proper for an ordinary statute has the further disadvantage that it heightens the difficulty of correcting a mistake or supplying an omission. The process of amending a constitution even in one specific point is a slow one, to which neither the legislature, as the proposing authority, nor the people, as the sanctioning authority, willingly resort. Hence blemishes remain and are tolerated, which a country possessing, like England, a sovereign legislature would correct in the next session of Parliament without trouble or delay.

It is sometimes difficult to induce the people to take a proper interest in the amendment of the constitution. In those states where a majority of all the qualified voters, and not merely of those voting, is required to affirm an amendment, it often happens that the requisite majority cannot be obtained owing to the small number who vote.[1] This has its good side, for it is a check on hasty or frequent change. But it adds greatly to the difficulty of working a rigid or supreme constitution, that you may find an admitted, even if not very grave evil, to be practically irremovable, because the mass of the people cannot be induced to care enough about the matter to come to the polls, and there deliver their judgment upon it.

These defects are so obvious that we are entitled to expect to find correspondingly strong grounds for the maintenance, and indeed the steady extension of the plan of legislating by and through a constitution. What are these grounds? Why does American practice tend more and more to remove legislation from the legislature and entrust it to the people?

One could quite well imagine the several state governments working without fundamental instruments to control them. In a federal government which rests on, or at least which began from, a compact between a number of originally separate communities, the advantages of having the relations of these communities to one another and to the central authority defined by an instrument placed beyond the reach of the ordinary legislature, and not susceptible of easy change, are clear and strong. Such an instrument is the guarantee for the rights of each member placed above the impulses of a chance majority. The case is quite different when we come to a single homogeneous community. Each American state might now, if it so pleased, conduct its own business, and govern its citizens as a commonwealth "at common law," with a sovereign legislature, whose statutes formed the highest expression of popular will. Nor need it do so upon the cabinet system of the British colonies. It might retain the separation from the legislature of the executive governor, elected by the people, and exercising his veto on their behalf, and yet dispense altogether with a rigid fundamental constitution, being content to vest in its representatives and governor the plenitude of its own powers. This, however, no American state does, or has ever done, or is likely to do. And the question why it does not suggests a point of interest for Europeans as well as for Americans.

In the republics of the ancient world, where representative assemblies were unknown, legislative power rested with the citizens meeting in what we should now call primary assemblies, such as the Ecclesia of Syracuse

---

[1] This has happened more than once of late years in Kentucky and Delaware.

or the Comitia of Rome. The same plan prevailed in the early Teutonic tribes, where the assembly of the freemen exercised all such powers as did not belong to the king. The laws of the kings of the Angles and Saxons, the capitularies of Charlemagne, were promulgated in assemblies of the nation, and may be said, though emanating from the prince, to have been enacted by the people. During the Middle Ages, these ancient assemblies died out, and the right of making laws passed either to the sovereign or to a representative assembly surrounding the sovereign, such as the English Parliament, the older scheme surviving only in such primitive communities as some of the Swiss cantons. The first reappearance in modern Europe of the scheme of direct legislation by the people is, so far as I know, the provision of the French Constitution framed by the National Convention in 1793, which directs that any law proposed by the legislative body shall be published and sent to all the communes of the Republic, whose primary assemblies shall be convoked to vote upon it, in case objections to it have been raised by one-tenth of these primary assemblies in a majority of the departments. In recent times the plan has become familiar by its introduction, not only into most of the cantons of Switzerland, but into the Swiss Federal Republic, which constantly applies it, under the name of referendum, by submitting to the vote of the people laws passed by the federal legislature.[2]

In Britain the influence of the same idea may be discovered in two phenomena of recent years. One is the proposal frequently made to refer to the direct vote of the inhabitants of a town or other local area the enactment of some ordinance affecting that district: as, for instance, one determining whether a rate shall be levied for a free library, or whether licences shall be granted for the sale, within the district, of intoxicating liquors. This method of deciding an issue, commonly known as local option, is a species of referendum. It differs from the Swiss form, not merely in being locally restricted, but rather in the fact that it is put to the people, not for the sake of confirming an act of the legislature, but of deciding whether a particular

---

[2] The Swiss Federal Constitution provides that any federal law and federal resolution of general application and not of an urgent character, must on the demand of eight cantons or of thirty thousand voters be submitted to popular vote for acceptance or rejection. This vote is frequently in the negative. See Swiss Federal Constitution, art. 89; and the remarks of ex-President Numa Droz in his *Instruction civique*, § 172. In nine cantons the submission of laws to popular vote was in 1907 compulsory and in eight *facultatif*. A referendum exists in every canton except Fribourg, Valais, and the four which retain a Langesgemeinde. See S. Deploige, *Le Referendum en Suisse*, Brussels, 1892. In 1891 the Federal Constitution was amended by introducing the provision called the initiative, which enables fifty thousand voters to demand the submission of a proposition to popular vote.

act shall be operative in a given area. But the principle is the same; it is a transference of legislative authority from a representative body, whether the parliament of the nation or the municipal council of the town (as the case may be), to the voters at the polls.

The other English illustration may seem far fetched, but on examination will be seen to involve the same idea. It is now beginning to be maintained as a constitutional doctrine, that when any large measure of change is carried through the House of Commons, the House of Lords has a right to reject it for the purpose of compelling a dissolution of Parliament, that is, an appeal to the voters. The doctrine is as warmly denied as it is asserted; but the material point is that many educated men contend that the House of Commons is not morally, though of course it is legally, entitled to pass a bill seriously changing the Constitution, which was not submitted to the electors at the preceding general election. A general election, although in form a choice of particular persons as members, has now practically become an expression of popular opinion on the two or three leading measures then propounded and discussed by the party leaders, as well as a vote of confidence or no confidence in the ministry of the day. It is in substance a vote upon those measures; although, of course, a vote only on their general principles, and not, like the Swiss referendum, upon the statute which the legislature has passed. Even therefore in a country which clings to and founds itself upon the absolute supremacy of its representative chamber, the notion of a direct appeal to the people has made progress.[3]

In the United States, which I need hardly say has in this matter been nowise affected by France or Switzerland or England, but has developed on its own lines, the conception that the people (i.e., the citizens at large) are and ought of right to be the supreme legislators, has taken the form of legislation by enacting or amending a constitution. Instead of, like the Swiss, submitting ordinary laws to the voters after they have passed the legislature, the Americans take subjects which belong to ordinary legislation out of the category of statutes, place them in the constitution, and then handle them as parts of this fundamental instrument. They are not called

---

[3] Much importance has come to be attached in England to casual parliamentary elections occurring when any important measure is before Parliament, because such an election is taken to indicate the attitude of the people generally towards the measure, and by consequence the judgment they would pronounce were a general election held. There have been instances in which a measure or part of a measure pending in Parliament has been dropped, because the result of the "bye-election" was taken to indicate that it displeased the people.

There are now those in England who advocate the introduction of a referendum as a method to be applied to certain classes of acts.

laws; but laws they are to all intents and purposes, differing from statutes only in being enacted by an authority which is not a constant but an occasional body, called into action only when a convention or a legislature lays propositions before it.

I have already explained the historical origin of this system, how it sprang from the fact that the constitutions of the colonies having been given to them by an external authority superior to the colonial legislature, the people of each state, seeing that they could no longer obtain changes in their constitution from Britain, assumed to themselves the right and duty of remodelling it; putting the collective citizendom of the state into the place of the British Crown as sovereign. The business of creating or remodelling an independent commonwealth was to their thinking too great a matter to be left to the ordinary organs of state life. This feeling, which had begun to grow from 1776 onwards, was much strengthened by the manner in which the federal Constitution was enacted in 1788 by state conventions. It seemed to have thus received a specially solemn ratification; and even the federal legislature, which henceforth was the centre of national politics, was placed far beneath the document which expressed the will of the people as a whole.

As the Republic went on working out both in theory and in practice those conceptions of democracy and popular sovereignty which had been only vaguely apprehended when enunciated at the Revolution, the faith of the average man in himself became stronger, his love of equality greater, his desire, not only to rule, but to rule directly in his own proper person, more constant. These sentiments would have told still further upon state governments had they not found large scope in local government. However, even in state affairs they made it (in the Northern states) an article of faith that no constitution could be enacted save by the direct vote of the citizens; and they inclined the citizens to seize such chances as occurred of making laws for themselves in their own way. Concurrently with the growth of these tendencies there had been a decline in the quality of the state legislatures, and of the legislation which they turned out. They were regarded with less respect; they inspired less confidence. Hence the people had the further excuse for superseding the legislature, that they might reasonably fear it would neglect or spoil the work they desired to see done.

Instead of being stimulated by this distrust to mend their ways and recover their former powers, the state legislatures fell in with the tendency, and promoted their own supersession. The chief interest of their members, as will be explained later, is in the passing of special or local acts, not of general public legislation. They are extremely timid, easily swayed by any active section of opinion, and afraid to stir when placed between the opposite fires of two such sections, as for instance, between the Prohibitionists and the liquor sellers. Hence they welcomed the direct intervention of the people as relieving them of embarrassing problems. They began to refer to the decision of a popular vote matters clearly within their own proper competence, such as the question of liquor traffic, or the creation of a system of gratuitous schools. This happened as far back as 1850–60. Presently they began to wash their hands by the same device of the troublesome and jealousy-provoking question where the capital of the state, or its leading public institutions, should be "located."[4] In New York, the legislature having been long distracted and perplexed by the question whether articles made by convicts in the state prisons should be allowed to be sold, and so to compete with articles made by private manufacturers, recently resolved to invite the opinion of the multitude, and accordingly passed an act under which the question was voted on over the whole state. They could not (except of course by proposing a constitutional amendment) enable the people to legislate on the point; for it has been often held by American courts that the legislature, having received a delegated power of lawmaking, cannot delegate that power to any other person or body.[5] But they could ask the people to advise them how they should legislate; and having obtained its view in this manner, could pass a statute in conformity with its wishes.

The methods by which legislative power is directly vested in the American

---

[4] This is now the general rule in new constitutions. Washington provides that though a bare majority may settle where the seat of state government shall be, a majority of two-thirds shall be required to change it.

[5] According to the maxim *Delegata potestas non delegatur*, a maxim which would not apply in England, because there Parliament has an original and not a delegated authority.

Judge Cooley says: "One of the settled maxims of constitutional law is that the power conferred upon the legislature to make laws cannot be delegated by that department to any other body or authority. Where the sovereign power of the State has located the authority, there it must remain; and by the constitutional authority alone the laws must be made until the Constitution itself is changed. The power to whose judgment, wisdom, and patriotism this high prerogative has been entrusted cannot relieve itself of the responsibility by choosing other agencies upon which the power shall be devolved" (*Constit. Limit.*, p. 141). He quotes from Locke (*Civil Government*, § 142) the remark that "The legislature neither must nor can transfer the power of making laws to anybody else, or place it anywhere but where the people have." This is one of Locke's "bounds set to the legislative power of every commonwealth in every form of government"; but it has not precluded the British Parliament from delegating large, and in many cases truly legislative, powers to particular persons or authorities, such as the Crown in Council, or the Council of Judges.

There has been much difference of opinion among American courts as to the extent to which a legislature may refer the operation of a general law to popular vote in a locality, but "the clear weight of authority is in support of legislation of the nature commonly known as local option laws."—Cooley, *ut supra*, p. 152; and see the cases collected in his notes.

voters are four. The first is the enactment or amendment by them of a constitution. Here the likeness to the Swiss referendum is close, because the particular provision to be enacted is first drafted and passed by the convention or legislature (as the case may be) and then submitted to the people. How wide the scope of this method is will be realized by one who has followed the account already given of the number and variety of the topics dealt with by state constitutions.

It is not uncommon for proposals submitted by the legislature in the form of constitutional amendments to be rejected by the people. Thus in Indiana, Nebraska, (twice in) Ohio, and Oregon, the legislature submitted amendments extending the suffrage to women, and the people in all four states refused the extension. So West Virginia by her Constitution of 1872, and South Dakota by hers of 1889, submitted proposals for proportional representation, which failed of acceptance.[6]

The second method is the submission to popular vote, pursuant to the provisions of the constitution, of a proposal or proposals therein specified. If such a proposal has been first passed by the legislature, we have here also a case resembling the Swiss referendum. If, however, the legislature have not given their decision on the proposal, but the popular vote at the polls takes place in obedience to a direction in that behalf contained in the constitution, this is not strictly a referendum, but a case of legislation by the people alone, as if the voters of the state were all gathered in one assembly. Examples of this method, in both its forms, abound in the more recent constitutions. So far back as 1848 we find Wisconsin referring it to the voters to decide whether or no banks shall be chartered.[7] Minnesota declares that a certain class of railway laws shall not take effect unless submitted to and ratified by a majority of the electors. And she provides, by a later amendment to her constitution, that "the moneys belonging to the internal improvement land fund shall never be appropriated for any purpose till the enactment for that purpose shall have been approved by a majority of the electors of the State, voting at the annual general election following the passage of the Act."[8] In this last instance the referendum goes the length of constituting the voters the ultimate financial authority for the state,

---

[6] Amendments to the constitution are now frequently made by the initiative in states which have adopted that institution.

[7] Constitution of 1848, art. XI, § 5.—This provision stood till 1902, when it was repealed by an amendment which gave the legislature power to regulate by general laws the creation and rules of banks. See also the constitutions of Iowa, Michigan, Illinois, Kansas, Ohio, and Missouri.

[8] Amendments of 1871 and 1874 to the Constitution of 1857.

withdrawing from the legislature what might seem the oldest and most essential of its functions. So in not a few states no debts beyond a certain specified amount may be contracted except in pursuance of a vote of the people, and in others the rate of taxation is limited by fixing it at a certain ratio to the total valuation of the state, subject to a power to increase the same by popular vote. And in California no law changing the seat of the state government is valid unless approved by the people.

The third and fourth methods are more recent than either of the preceding and mark a further long step in the extension of direct popular action. One is the true Swiss referendum, i.e., the submission to the people for their approval or rejection of ordinary laws passed by the state legislature; the other the Swiss initiative, i.e., a power for a certain proportion of voters to propose either ordinary laws or amendments to the state constitution. The state which has gone farthest in this path is Oklahoma, admitted to the Union in 1907. In her constitution (§ 52), "the people reserve to themselves the power to propose laws and amendments to the Constitution and to enact or reject the same at the polls independent of the Legislature, and also reserve power at their own option to approve or reject at the polls any act of the legislature (§ 53). The first power reserved by the people is the Initiative, and eight per centum of the legal voters shall have the right to propose any legislative measure and fifteen per centum of the legal voters shall have the right to propose amendments to the Constitution by petition. . . . The second power is the Referendum, and it may be ordered (except as to laws necessary for the immediate preservation of the public peace, health, or safety) either by petitions signed by five per centum of the legal voters or by the Legislature as other bills are enacted." The veto power of the governor is not to extend to measures voted on by the people. The referendum may be demanded against items or parts of a bill. Montana, Oregon, Nevada, South Dakota, and Utah have also referendum provisions generally similar.

In Oregon, the state which has made most use of these new methods, since the initiative and referendum were introduced in 1904, the people had down to the end of 1912 voted upon 76 initiative proposals, of which 33 were carried and 43 rejected; also upon 11 referendum proposals submitted either on demand of 5 per cent of the voters or referred to the voters by the legislature. Of these, 5 were carried and 6 rejected.[9] In Oregon the governor

---

[9] I take these figures from the very instructive book of President Lowell, *Pubic Opinion and Popular Government*.

has no veto on popular votes. Arguments prepared for and against proposals so submitted may be prepared and printed by the proposers and opponents, the cost of posting a copy to every voter being paid by the state.

The same principle of popular vote has been widely applied to local as well as to state government. Oklahoma applies it to every county and district, and to every municipality. Many recent constitutions provide that the approval of the people at the polls shall be needed in order to validate a decision of the city, or county, or school district, or township authority regarding borrowing, or taxing, or lending public funds to some enterprise it may be desired to assist. Licensing questions are usually left to popular determination alone, with no interference by the local representative authority: while as respects municipal government, California took the novel course of allowing cities of more than ten thousand inhabitants to make their own charters, by a drafting board of fifteen freeholders and a ratifying vote of the people, the state legislature having only a veto on the charter *en bloc*.[10] Other states have followed.

The application of the same principle to smaller areas has the advantage of defeating many jobs which local councils might desire to put through, but may impose on the average voter a heavier burden than his knowledge and capacity fit him to bear. For instance at a municipal election in the city of Portland, Oregon, in June 1909, the elector had to decide not only between twenty-five candidates for six offices, but also to vote on thirty-five distinct and separate legislative propositions, some of them relating to matters of small administrative detail.[11]

Thus the ancient scheme of vesting ordinary legislative power, as well as constitution-making power, in the whole body of citizens has been now (1913) adopted by seventeen states and seems likely to in other states also, for it finds favour as a legitimate development of the principle of popular sovereignty. It is advocated with special zeal by many of the leaders of the Labour party or those who promote such legislation as that party desires.

What are the practical advantages of this plan of direct legislation by the people in its various forms? Its demerits are obvious. Besides those I have already stated, it might be expected to lower the authority and sense of responsibility in the legislature; and it refers matters needing much elucidation

[10] Amendment of 1887 to the Constitution of California. Washington (Constitution of 1889, art. XI, § 12), in adopting a similar provision, restricts it to cities with a population of twenty thousand or over, but drops the requirement of approval by the state legislature. See, for specimens of popular vote provisions for local areas, Constitution of Oklahoma, § 415, *post*.

[11] I quote this from an interesting pamphlet by Professor Beard, entitled *The Ballot's Burden*.

by debate to the determination of those who cannot, on account of their numbers, meet together for discussion, and many of whom may have never thought about the matter. These considerations will to most Europeans appear decisive against it. The proper course, they will say, is to improve the legislatures. The less you trust them, the worse they will be. They may be ignorant; yet not so ignorant as the masses.

But the improvement of the legislatures is just what the Americans despair of, or, as they would prefer to say, have not time to attend to. Hence they fall back on the direct popular vote as the best course available under the circumstances of the case, and in such a world as the present. Though some claim that it has an educative effect on the people, this is not the argument chiefly employed to advocate it. The ground taken is rather this, that the mass of the people are equal in intelligence and character to the average state legislator, and are exposed to fewer temptations. The legislator can be "got at," the people cannot. The personal interest of the individual legislator in passing a measure for chartering banks or spending the internal improve-ment fund may be greater than his interest as one of the community in preventing bad laws. It will be otherwise with the bulk of the citizens. The legislator may be subjected by the advocates of women's suffrage or liquor prohibition to a pressure irresistible by ordinary mortals; but the citizens are too numerous to be all wheedled or threatened. Hence they can and do reject proposals which the legislature has assented to. Nor should it be forgotten that in a country where law depends for its force on the consent of the governed, it is eminently desirable that law should not outrun popular sentiment, but have the whole weight of the people's deliverance behind it.[12]

A brilliant, though severe, critic of Canadian institutions deplores the want of some similar arrangement in the several provinces of the dominion. Having remarked that the veto of the lieutenant-governor on the acts of a provincial legislature is in practice a nullity, and that the central government never vetoes such acts except where they are held to exceed the constitutional competence of the legislature, he urges that what is needed to cure the faults of provincial legislation is to borrow the American plan of submitting constitutional amendments (and, it may now be added, laws also) to popular

---

[12] In the case of local option there is the further argument that to commit the question of licences to a local representative is virtually to make the election of that authority turn upon this single question, and that there is an advantage in making a restricton on the freedom of the individual issue directly from the vote of the people, who may feel themselves doubly bound to enforce what they have directly enacted.

vote. "The people cannot be lobbied, wheedled, or bull-dozed; the people is not in fear of its re-election if it throws out something supported by the Irish, the Prohibitionist, the Catholic, or the Methodist vote."[13]

If the practice of recasting or amending state constitutions were to grow common, and if the initiative and referendum were to grow common, one of the advantages of direct legislation by the people would disappear, for the sense of permanence would be gone, and the same mutability which is now possible in ordinary statutes would become possible in the provisions of the fundamental law, the habit of passing ordinary laws under momentary impulse might prove mischievous. But this fault of small democracies,[14] especially when ruled by primary assemblies, is unlikely to recur in large democracies, such as most states have now become, nor does it seem to be on the increase among them. Reference to the people, therefore, acts as a conservative force; that is to say, there may be occasions when a measure which a legislature would pass, either at the bidding of a heated party majority or to gain the support of a group of persons holding the balance of voting power, or under the covert influence of those who seek some private advantage, will be rejected by the whole body of the citizens because their minds are cooler or their view of the general interest less biased by special predilections or interests.

In England, and indeed in most European countries, representative government has been hitherto an institution with markedly conservative elements, because the legislating representatives have generally belonged to the wealthy or well-born and educated classes, who, having something to lose by change, are disinclined to it, who have been looked up to by the masses, and who have been imperfectly responsive to popular impulses. American legislatures have none of these features. The men are not superior to the multitude, partly because the multitude is tolerably educated and tolerably well off. The multitude does not defer to them. They are horribly afraid of it, and indeed of any noisy section in it. They live in the breath of its favour; they hasten to fulfil its behests almost before they are uttered. Accordingly an impulse or passion dominant among the citizens may tell at once on the legislature, and find expression in a law, the only checks being, not the caution of that body and its willingness to debate at length, but the

---

[13] Mr. Goldwin Smith.

[14] So frequent a charge against the Greek republics and the Italian republics of the Middle Ages, as Dante says, apostrophizing Florence:

> "Ch' a mezzo Novembre,
> Non giunge quel che tu d'Ottobre fili."

power of some powerful group to stop a measure it dislikes, or possibly, the wisdom of a strong governor who may veto a bill which he thinks the people ought to have more time to consider. It may also happen that the legislature proves incapable of embodying in a practical form the wishes manifested by the people. Hence in the American states representative government has by no means that conservative quality which Europeans ascribe to it, whereas the direct vote of the people is the vote of men who are generally better instructed than the European masses, more experienced in politics, more sensible of their interest in the stability of the country. In its effect upon the state legislature, the referendum may therefore, in some states at least, be rather a bit and bridle than a spur. But in the new communities of the West it is more likely to be used as a means of effecting changes which they do not expect to get so speedily from the legislature in the drastic form and with the promptitude which they desire.

This method of legislation by means of a constitution or amendments thereto, arising from sentiments and under conditions in many respects similar to those which have produced the referendum in Switzerland, is an interesting illustration of the tendency of institutions, like streams, to wear their channels deeper. A historical accident, so to speak, suggested to the Americans the subjection of their legislatures to a fundamental law; and after a while the invention came to be used for other purposes far more extensively than its creators foresaw. It became, moreover, serviceable in a way which those who first used it did not contemplate, though they are well pleased with the result. It acts as a restraint not only on the vices and follies of legislators, but on the people themselves. Having solemnly bound themselves by their constitution to certain rules and principles, the people come to respect those principles. They have parted with powers which they might be tempted in a moment of excitement, or under the pressure of suffering, to abuse through their too pliant representatives; and although they can resume these powers by enacting a new constitution or amending the old one, the process of resumption requires time, and involves steps which secure care and deliberation, while allowing passion to cool, and the prospect of a natural relief from economic evils to appear. Thus the completeness and consistency with which the principle of the direct sover-eignty of the whole people is carried out in America has checked revolutionary tendencies, by pointing out a peaceful and legal method for the effecting of political or economical changes. So much may be said as to the states that have remained content with the process of legislation by amendments in constitutions. But now some of the more experimentally minded states have gone further. They have simplified the process of direct popular legislation by getting rid of the machinery of a convention and of legislatively drafted amendments, and they empower the people to vote directly on whatever proposal a percentage of the citizens may propose or whatever law an even smaller percentage may require to have submitted for the expression of the people's will. The initiative and referendum are natural developments of the process which began with the introduction into constitutions of what were really ordinary laws, and no one can tell how far the new movement may spread.

State constitutions, considered as laws drafted by a convention and enacted by the people at large, are better both in form and substance than laws made by the legislature, because they are the work of abler, or at any rate of honester, men, acting under a special commission which imposes special responsibilities on them. The appointment of a constitutional convention excites general interest in a state. Its functions are weighty, far transcending those of the regular legislature. Hence some of the best men in the state desire a seat in it, and, in particular, eminent lawyers become candidates, knowing how much it will affect the law they practise. It is therefore a body superior in composition to either the Senate or the House of a state. Its proceedings are followed with closer attention; and it is exempt from the temptations with which the power of disposing of public funds or public utilities bestrews the path of ordinary legislators; its debates are more instructive; its conclusions are more carefully weighed, because they cannot be readily reversed.[15] Or if the work of altering the constitution is carried out by a series of amendments, these are likely to be more fully considered by the legislature than ordinary statutes would be, and to be framed with more regard to clearness and precision.

In the interval between the settlement by the convention of its draft constitution, or by the legislature of its draft amendments, and the putting of the matter to the vote of the people, there is copious discussion in the press and at public meetings, so that the citizens often go well prepared to the polls. An all-pervading press does the work which speeches did in the ancient republics, and the fact that constitutions and amendments so submitted are frequently rejected, shows that the people, whether they act wisely or not, do not at any rate surrender themselves blindly to the judgment of a convention, or obediently adopt the proposals of a legislature.

---

[15] Where it is desired not to complicate the acceptance or rejection of a draft constitution with the enactment of some particular provision, that provision is separately submitted to the people; if they approve it, it is inserted in the constitution.

These merits are indeed not always claimable for conventions, or, in particular, for the more recent constitutions they have framed, much less for individual amendments. The Constitution of California of 1879 (whereof more in a later chapter) is an instance to the contrary; nor have the subsequent conventions even of such old states as Louisiana and Kentucky shown all the judgment that the problems before them required. But a general survey of this branch of our inquiry leads to the conclusion that the peoples of the several states, in the exercise of this their highest function, have not, on the whole, shown much of that haste, that recklessness, that love of change for the sake of change, with which European theorists, both ancient and modern, have been wont to credit democracy; and that the method of direct legislation by the citizens, liable as it doubtless is to abuse, causes, in the present condition of the states, fewer evils than it prevents.

It would doubtless be better, if good legislatures were attainable, to leave the enactment of what are really mere statutes to the legislature, instead of putting them in a constitution; and the initiative is a supersession of the legislature which tends even more to reduce its authority. But if good legislatures are unattainable, if it is impossible to raise the Senate and the House of each state above that low level at which (as we shall presently see) they now stand, then the system of direct popular action may be justified at least in some communities as a salutary effort of the forces which make for good government, opening for themselves a new channel.

In making the referendum and initiative parts of the regular machinery of government instead of applying the popular vote only to the amendment of constitutions, Oregon, Oklahoma, and the other Western states above referred to, have taken what may prove to be a momentous new departure, for the will of the sovereign people can through these methods express itself far more promptly and easily than heretofore. Some American publicists argue that to empower the people of a state to set aside their legislature when they are so disposed is virtually to abandon that "republican form of government" which was in 1787 supposed to be identical with a representative form. This contention ceases to be plausible when it is remembered that the oldest republics in the world, and many of the most famous, were ruled by primary, not by representative, assemblies. A more serious question has been raised by those who doubt the wisdom of arrangements that leave so much to the vote of a multitude which may act hastily, excited by the prospect of some benefit to be obtained, some grievance to be removed, through a sweeping and perhaps insufficiently debated change in the law.

The risk of careless and even reckless measures is undeniable. But they may, in some states, be just as likely to proceed from a legislature as from the people voting at the polls, for the average of knowledge and judgment is not substantially lower among the voters than among those who compose the legislatures; and the safeguards provided by the rules restraining legislative action cannot always be relied upon.

We must wait and watch for some time before venturing to pronounce a judgment upon the working of these new expedients; nor does the experience of Switzerland furnish much guidance, so dissimilar are the social conditions and the political habits of the two nations.[16]

---

[16] For a thoughtful judgment upon the new system see President Lowell's admirable book already referred to. Up to November 1913, initiative and referendum statewide in their operation had been adopted by South Dakota (which led the way in 1898), Utah, Oregon, Nevada, Montana, Oklahoma, Maine, Missouri, Arkansas, Colorado, Arizona, California, Nebraska, Washington, Idaho, Ohio, and Michigan.

So far as could be ascertained in 1913, the initiative, referendum, and recall exist in respect of municipal government either generally, or for such cities as may adopt them by popular vote, in all states except Virginia, New York, New Hampshire, Vermont, Delaware, and Indiana.

CHAPTER 40

State Governments: The Legislature

The similarity of the frame of government in the forty-eight republics which make up the United States, a similarity which appears the more remarkable when we remember that each of the republics is independent and self-determined as respects its frame of government, is due to the common source whence the governments flow. They are all copies, some immediate, some mediate, of ancient English institutions, viz., chartered self-governing corporations, which, under the influence of English habits, and with the precedent of the English parliamentary system before their eyes, developed into governments resembling that of England in the eighteenth century. Thirteen colonies had up to 1776 been regulated by a charter from the British Crown, which, according to the best and oldest of all English traditions, allowed each the practical management of its own affairs. The charter contained a sort of skeleton constitution, which usage had clothed with nerves, muscles, and sinews, till it became a complete and symmetrical working system of free government. There was in each a governor, in two colonies chosen by the people,[1] in the rest nominated by the Crown; there was a legislature; there were executive officers acting under the governor's commission and judges nominated by him; there were local self-governing communities. In none, however, did there exist what we call cabinet government, i.e., the rule of the legislature through a committee of its own members, coupled with the irresponsibility of the permanent nominal head of the executive. This separation of the executive from the legislature, which naturally arose from the fact that the governor

---

[1] However, in Rhode Island the governor was chosen, not as now by the people at large, but by the company assembled in general court, a body which passed into the legislature of the colony. See Charter of Rhode Island, 1663. In Connecticut the general court chose if the people failed to elect, or a sudden vacancy occurred.

427

was an officer directly responsible to another power than the colonial legislature, viz., the British Crown, his own master to whom he stood or fell,[2] distinguishes the old colonial governments of North America from those of the British colonies of the present day, in all of which cabinet government prevails.[3] The latter are copies of the present Constitution of England; the former resembled it as it existed in the first half of the eighteenth century before cabinet government had been fully developed.

When the thirteen colonies became sovereign states at the Revolution, they preserved this frame of government, substituting a governor chosen by the state for one appointed by the Crown. As the new states admitted to the Union after 1789 successively formed their constitutions prior to their admission to the Union, each adopted the same scheme, its people imitating, as was natural, the older commonwealths whence they came, and whose working they understood and admired.[4] They were the more inclined to do so because they found in the older constitutions that sharp separation of the executive, legislative, and judicial powers which the political philosophy of those days taught them to regard as essential to a free government, and they all take this separation as their point of departure.

I have observed in an earlier chapter that the influence on the framers of the federal Constitution of the examples of free government which they found in their several states, had been profound. We may sketch out a sort of genealogy of governments as follows:

First. The English incorporated company, a self-governing body, with its governor, deputy-governor, and assistants chosen by the freemen of the company, and meeting in what is called the general court or assembly.

Next. The colonial government, which out of this company evolves a governor or executive head and a legislature, consisting of representatives chosen by the citizens and meeting in one or two chambers.

Thirdly. The state government, which is nothing but the colonial govern-

---

[2] Even in Connecticut and Rhode Island the governor, though chosen by the colony, was in a sense responsible to the Crown. It was through him as executive head that the home government dealt with the colony.

[3] Of course in the British self-governing colonies the governor is still responsible to the Crown, but this responsibility is confined within narrow limits by the responsibility of his ministers to the colonial legislature and by the wide powers of that legislature.

[4] Massachusetts tried for several years the scheme of a small council as the executive power representing the former Crown governor, but in 1780 she came back to the plan of a single governor, while retaining, as she still retains, a council surrounding him.

ment developed and somewhat democratized, with a governor chosen originally by the legislature, now always by the people at large, and now in all cases with a legislature of two chambers. From the original thirteen states this form has spread over the Union and prevails in every state.

Lastly. The federal government, modelled after the state governments, with its president chosen, through electors, by the people, its two-chambered legislature, its judges named by the president.[5]

Out of such small beginnings have great things grown.

It would be endless to describe the minor differences in the systems of the several states. I will sketch the outlines only, which, as already observed, are in the main the same everywhere.

Every state has:

An executive elective head, the governor
A number of other administrative officers
A legislature of two houses
A system of courts of justice
Various subordinate local self-governing communities, counties, cities, townships, villages, school districts

The governor and the other chief officials are not now chosen by the legislature, as was the case under most of the older state constitutions, but by the people. They are as far as possible disjoined from the legislature. Neither the governor nor any other state official can sit in a state legislature.[6] He cannot lead it. It cannot, except of course by passing statutes, restrain him. There can therefore be no question of any government by ministers who link the executive to the legislature according to the system of the free countries of modern Europe and of the British colonies.

Of these several powers it is best to begin by describing the legislature, because it is by far the strongest and most prominent.

An American state legislature always consists of two houses, the smaller called the Senate, the larger usually called the House of Representatives,

---

[5] One might add another generation at the beginning of this genealogy by deriving the English corporate company from the Roman *collegia*, and a generation at the end by observing how much the constitution of modern Switzerland owes to that of the United States.

[6] In Rhode Island, however, the lieutenant-governor is a member of the Senate, the governor presiding, but with only a casting vote. When the governor is absent, the lieutenant-governor presides, and has a casting vote besides his own vote as senator. In some states the lieutenant-governor presides over the Senate.

though in six states it is entitled "the Assembly," and in three "the House of Delegates." The origin of this very interesting feature is to be sought rather in history than in theory. It is due partly to the fact that in some colonies there had existed a small governor's council in addition to the popular representative body, partly to a natural disposition to imitate the mother country with its Lords and Commons, a disposition which manifested itself both in colonial days and when the revolting states were giving themselves new constitutions, for up to 1776 some of the colonies had gone on with a legislature of one house only. Now, however, the need for two chambers has become an axiom of political science, being based on the belief that the innate tendency of an assembly to become hasty, tyrannical, and corrupt, needs to be checked by the coexistence of another house of equal authority. The Americans restrain their legislatures by dividing them, just as the Romans restrained their executive by substituting two consuls for one king. The only states that ever tried to do with a single house were Pennsylvania, Georgia, and Vermont, all of whom gave it up: the first after four years' experience, the second after twelve years, the last after fifty years.[7] It is with these trifling exceptions the *quod semper, quod ubique, quod ab omnibus* of American constitutional doctrine.[8]

Both houses are chosen by popular vote, generally[9] in equal electoral

---

[7] Upon this subject of the division of the legislature, see Kent's *Commentaries*, vol. i, 208–10; and Story's *Commentaries on the American Constitution*, §§ 548–70. It deserves to be remarked that the Pennsylvanian Constitution of 1786, the Georgian Constitution of 1777, and the Vermont Constitutions of 1786 and 1793, all of which constituted one house of legislature only, provided for a second body called the Executive Council, which in Georgia had the duty of examining bills sent to it by the House of Assembly, and of remonstrating against any provisions they disapproved, and in Vermont was empowered to submit to the Assembly amendments to bills sent up to them by the latter, and in case the Assembly did not accept such amendments, to suspend the passing of the bill till the next session of the legislature. In 1789, Georgia abolished her Council, and divided her legislature into two houses; Pennsylvania did the same in 1790; Vermont in 1836. Both Pennsylvania and Vermont had also a body called the Council of Censors, who may be compared with the Nomothetæ of Athens, elected every seven years, and charged with the duty of examining the laws of the State and their execution, and of suggesting amendments. This body was abolished in Pennsylvania in 1790, but lasted on in Vermont till 1870. All these experiments well deserve the study of constitutional historians.

[8] It ought to be noted as an illustration of the divergences between countries both highly democratic that in the Swiss cantons the legislatures consist of one chamber only. In most of these cantons there is, to be sure, a *referendum* and generally a small executive council. Another remarkable divergence is that whereas in America, and especially in the West, the tendency is towards "rotation" in office, in Switzerland an official and a member of a legislature is usually continued in his post from one term to another, in fact is seldom displaced except for some positive fault. At one time officials were steadily reelected in Connecticut.

[9] In Connecticut, by a provision of a constitutional amendment adopted in 1874, every town which then contained, or should thereafter contain, a population of 5,000, returns two members to the

districts, and by the same voters, although in a few states there are minor variations as to modes of choice.[10] Illinois by her Constitution of 1870 created a system of proportional representation by means of the cumulative vote; i.e., the elector may cast as many votes for any one candidate as there are representatives to be elected in the district, or may distribute his votes among the candidates. The plan was suggested to the people of Illinois, by the fact that the northern counties (called Canaan) had usually had a Republican, the southern (called Egypt) a Democratic, majority, so that there were special reasons for breaking the party solidity of each section. So far as I have been able to gather, experience has not commended the scheme, and it has not improved the quality of the legislature.

The following differences between the rules governing the two houses are general:

1. The senatorial electoral districts are always larger, usually twice or thrice as large as the house districts, and the number of senators is, of course, in the same proportion smaller than that of representatives.
2. A senator is usually chosen for a longer term than a representative. In twenty-nine states he sits for four years, in one (New Jersey) for three, in thirteen for two, in two (Massachusetts and Rhode Island) for one year only; the usual term of a representative being two years.
3. In most cases the Senate, instead of being elected all at once like the House, is only partially renewed, half its members going out when their two or four years have been completed, and a new half coming in. This gives it a sense of continuity which the House wants.
4. In some states the age at which a man is eligible for the Senate is

---

Assembly, and every other town retains the representation it had in that year. The Senate, however, is elected on a population basis. A great many small places have each two members. The state is virtually governed by the representatives of "rotten boroughs," and as they form the majority, they have hitherto refused to submit to the people a constitutional amendment for a redistribution of seats in the Assembly, on the basis of equal population. Some troubles that occurred in the state were partly due to this excessive difficulty in reforming an antiquated constitution. In some states there has been audacious gerrymandering. The supreme court of Wisconsin once declared inconsistent with the constitution a redistricting of the state which had neglected county boundaries and created very unqual districts.

[10] For instance, in Rhode Island every town or city, be it great or small, returns one senator; and thus it at one time befell that a population of 253,000 in 13 cities and towns had 13 senators, while 23 towns with 20,000 people sent 23 senators. In the House of 77 members each city or town had at least one member, and the city of Providence, with a population nearly half that of the state, only 12. An amendment to increase the House to 100 members and to give Providence 25 was carried in 1909. In Illinois, every district returns one senator and three representatives.

fixed higher than that for the House of Representatives.[11] Other
restrictions on eligibility, such as the exclusion of clergymen (which
still exists in a few states, and is of old standing), that of salaried
public officials (which exists everywhere), that of United States officials
and members of Congress, and that of persons not resident in the
electoral district (frequent by law and practically universal by custom),
apply to both houses. In some states this last restriction goes so far
that a member who ceases to reside in the district for which he was
elected loses his seat *ipso facto*.

I have dwelt in an earlier chapter (Chapter 14) on the strength of this
local feeling as regards congressional elections, and on the results, to a
European eye mostly unfortunate, which it produces. It is certainly no
weaker in state elections. Nobody dreams of offering himself as a candidate
for a place in which he does not reside, even in new states, where it might
be thought that there had not been time for local feeling to spring up. Hence
the educated and leisured residents of the greater cities have no chance of
entering the state legislature except for the city district wherein they dwell;
and as these city districts are those most likely to be in the hands of some
noxious and selfish ring of professional politicians, the prospect for such an
aspirant is a dark one. Nothing more contributes to make reform difficult
than the inveterate habit of choosing residents only as members. Suppose
an able and public-spirited man desiring to enter the Assembly or the Senate
of his state and shame the offenders who are degrading or plundering it. He
may be wholly unable to find a seat, because in his place of residence the
party opposed to his own may hold a permanent majority, and he will not
be even considered elsewhere. Suppose a group of earnest men who,
knowing how little one man can effect, desire to enter the legislature at the
same time and work together. Such a group can hardly arise except in or
near a great city. It cannot effect an entrance, because the city has at best
very few seats to be seized, and the city men cannot offer themselves in
any other part of the state. That the restriction often rests on custom, not
on law, makes the case more serious. A law can be repealed, but custom
has to be unlearned; the one may be done in a moment of happy impulse,
the other needs the teaching of long experience applied to receptive minds.

The fact is, that the Americans have ignored in all their legislative as in
many of their administrative arrangements, the differences of capacity

---

[11] In some states a senator must have attained thirty years of age, in some a representative must
have attained twenty-five.

between man and man. They underrate the difficulties of government and overrate the capacities of the man of common sense. Great are the blessings of equality; but what follies are committed in its name!

The unfortunate results of this local sentiment have been aggravated by the tendency to narrow the election areas, allotting one senator or representative to each district. Under the older Constitution of Connecticut, for instance, the twelve senators were elected out of the whole state by a popular vote. Now the thirty-five senators are chosen by districts, and the Senate is today an inferior body, because then the best men of the whole state might be chosen, now it is possible only to get the leading men of the districts. In Massachusetts, under the Constitution of 1780, the senators were chosen by districts, but a district might return as many as six senators: the assemblymen were chosen by towns,[12] each corporate town having at least one representative, and more in proportion to its population, the proportion being at the rate of one additional member for every 275 ratable polls. In 1836 the scale of population to representatives was raised, and a plan prescribed (too complicated to be here set forth) under which towns below the population entitling them to one representative, should have a representative during a certain number of years out of every ten years, the census being taken decennially. Thus a small town might send a member to the Assembly for five years out of every ten, choosing alternate years, or the first five, or the last five, as it pleased. Now, however (Amendments of 1857), the state has been divided into 40 senatorial districts, each of which returns one senator only, and into 175 assembly districts, returning one, two, or, in a few cases, three representatives each. The composition of the legislature has declined ever since this change was made. The area of choice being smaller, inferior men are chosen; and in the case of the assembly districts which return one member, but are composed of several small towns, the practice has grown up of giving each town its turn, so that not even the leading man of the district, but the leading man of the particular small community whose turn has come round, is chosen to sit in the Assembly.

Universal manhood suffrage, subject to certain disqualifications in respect of crime (including bribery and polygamy) and the receipt of poor-law relief, which prevail in many states—in nine states no pauper can vote—is the rule in nearly all the states. Ten states (Wyoming, Utah, Idaho, Colorado, Washington, Kansas, Arizona, California, Oregon, and Illinois) give the

---

[12] A town or township means in New England, and indeed generally in the United States, a small rural district, as opposed to a city. It is a community which has not received representative municipal government.—See Chapter 48 *post.*

suffrage to women. A property qualification was formerly required in many, and lasted till 1888 in Rhode Island, where the possession of real estate valued at $134, or the payment of a tax of at least $1 was required from all citizens not natives of the United States.[13] Ten other states require the voter to have paid some state or county tax (some call it a poll tax); but if he does not pay it, his party usually pay it for him, so the restriction is of little practical importance. Massachusetts also requires that he shall be able to read the state constitution in English, and to write his name (Amendment of 1857); Connecticut, that he shall be able to read any section of the constitution or of the statutes, and shall sustain a good moral character (Amendents of 1855 and 1845). This educational test is of no great consequence, partly, no doubt, because illiteracy is not high in either state; and the ballot laws have reduced the need for it. In Massachusetts it is now enforced, but for a while the party managers on both sides agreed not to trouble voters about it. Mississippi prescribes that the person applying to be registered "shall be able to read any section of the Constitution or be able to understand the same when read to him, or give a reasonable interpretation thereof" (Constitution of 1890).[14] Certain terms of residence within the United States, in the particular state, and in the voting districts, are also required. These vary greatly from state to state, but are usually short.

The suffrage is generally the same for other purposes as for that of elections to the legislature, and is in most states confined to male inhabitants. In many states women are permitted to vote at school district elections and on matters affecting libraries; and some confer a direct popular vote or referendum on women taxpayers where a question is submitted to the people. Nowhere is any disability imposed upon married women as such; nor has it been attempted, in the various constitutional amendments framed to give political suffrage to women, accepted in some states, and rejected by the

[13] Rhode Island, however, retains a qualification for the purposes of voting for members of city councils. A good many constitutions forbid the imposition of any property qualification.

[14] The "reasonable interpretation" of this remarkable provision seems to be that it is intended to furnish a peaceful method of excluding more or less illiterate Negroes and including illiterate whites, a result which has been in fact attained, and which, though it may appear at variance with the spirit of the Fifteenth Amendment to the federal Constitution, is under the circumstances of Mississippi possibly not the worst solution of a difficult problem. As to the provisions of recent Southern constitutions affecting the voting of Negroes, see Chapters 93 and 94 *post*.

The Constitution of Colorado, 1876, allowed the legislature to prescribe an educational qualification for electors, but no such law to take effect prior to 1890. Florida by its Constitution of 1868 directed its legislature to prescribe such qualifications, which, however, were not to apply till after 1880, nor to any person who might then be already a voter. (In the Constitution of 1886 I find no such provision.)

people in others, to draw such a distinction, which would indeed be abhorrent to the genius of American law.

It is important to remember that, by the Constitution of the United States, the right of suffrage in federal or national elections (i.e., for presidential electors and members of Congress) is in each state that which the state confers on those who vote at the election of its more numerous house. That the differences which might exist between one state and another in the width of the federal franchise thus granted, are at present (except in the South) insignificant is due, chiefly to the prevalence of democratic theories of equality over the whole Union, partly perhaps also to the provision of the Fourteenth Amendment to the federal Constitution, which provides that the representation of a state in the federal House of Representatives, and therewith also its weight in a presidential election, may be reduced in proportion to the number of adult male citizens disqualified in that state. As a state desires to have its full weight in national politics, it has a strong motive for the widest possible enlargement of its federal franchise, and this implies a corresponding width in its domestic franchise.

The number of members of the legislature varies greatly from state to state. Delaware, with seventeen senators, has the smallest Senate, Minnesota, with sixty-three, the largest. Delaware has also the smallest House of Representatives, consisting of thirty-five members; while New Hampshire, a very small state, has the largest with 389. The New York houses number 51 and 150 respectively, those of Pennsylvania 50 and 201, those of Massachusetts 40 and 240. In the Western and Southern states the number of representatives rarely exceeds 120.[15]

As there is a reason for everything in the world, if one could but find it out, so for this difference between the old New England states and those newer states which in many other points have followed their precedents. In the New England states local feeling was and is intensely strong, and every little town wanted to have its member. In the West and South, local divisions have had less natural life; in fact, they are artificial divisions rather than genuine communities that arose spontaneously. Hence the same reason did not exist in the West and South for having a large assembly; while the distrust of representatives, the desire to have as few of them as possible and pay them as little as possible, have been specially strong motives in the West and South, as also in New York and Pennsylvania, and have caused a restriction of numbers.

[15] North Dakota, however, provides that its Senate may have as many as 50, its House as many as 140, members.

There are about seven thousand state legislators in all in the United States.

In all states the members of both houses receive salaries, which in some cases are fixed at an annual sum of from $150 (Maine) to $1,500 (New York), the average being $500. More frequently, however, it is calculated at so much for every day during which the session lasts, varying from $1 (in Rhode Island) to $8 (in California and Nevada) per day ($5 seems to be the average), besides a small allowance, called mileage, for travelling expenses. These sums, although unremunerative to a man who leaves a prosperous profession or business to attend in the state capital, are an object of such desire to many of the representatives of the people, that the latter have thought it prudent to restrict the length of the legislative sessions, which now generally stand limited to a fixed number of days, varying from 40 days in Georgia, Nebraska, and Oregon, to 150 days in Pennsylvania. The states which pay by the day are also those which limit the session. Some states secure themselves against prolonged sessions by providing that the daily pay shall diminish, or shall absolutely cease and determine, at the expiry of a certain number of days, hoping thereby to expedite business and check inordinate zeal for legislation.[16]

It was formerly usual for the legislature to meet annually, but the experience of bad legislation and over legislation has led to fewer as well as shorter sittings; and sessions are now biennial in all states except two (Alabama and Mississippi)[17] where they are quadrennial, and in the six following: Massachusetts, Rhode Island, New York, New Jersey, South Carolina, Georgia, all of them old states. In these the sessions are annual, save in that odd little nook Rhode Island, which still convokes her legislature every May at Newport, and afterwards holds an adjourned session at Providence, the other chief city of the commonwealth. There is, however, in nearly all states a power reserved to the governor to summon the houses in extraordinary session should a pressing occasion arise, but the provisions for daily pay do not usually apply to these extra sessions.[18]

Bills may originate in either house, save that in most states money bills must originate in the House of Representatives, a rule for which, in the present condition of things, when both houses are equally directly representative of the people and chosen by the same electors, no sufficient ground appears. It is a curious instance of the wish which animated the

---

[16] These limitations on payment are sometimes, where statutory, repealed for the occasion. In the Swiss Federal Assembly a member receives pay (16s. per diem) only for those days on which he answers to his name on the roll call.

[17] Mississippi provides for a short special session for financial bills halfway through the term.

[18] Some of the biennially-meeting legislatures are apt to hold adjourned sessions in the off years.

framers of the first constitutions of the original thirteen states to reproduce the details of the English Constitution that had been deemed bulwarks of liberty. The newer states borrowed it from their elder sisters, and the existence of a similar provision in the federal Constitution has no doubt helped to perpetuate it in all the states. But there is a reason for it in Congress, the federal Senate not being directly representative of equal numbers of citizens, which is not found in the state legislatures; it is in these last a mere survival of no present functional value. Money bills may, however, be amended or rejected by the state Senates like any other bills, just as the federal Senate amends money bills brought up from the House.

In one point a state Senate enjoys a special power, obviously modelled on that of the English House of Lords and the federal Senate. It sits as a court under oath for the trial of state officials impeached by the House.[19] Like the federal Senate, it has in many states the power of confirming or rejecting appointments to office made by the governor. When it considers these it is said to "go into executive session." The power is an important one in those states which allow the governor to nominate the higher judges. In other respects the powers and procedure of the two houses of a state legislature are identical;[20] except that, whereas the lieutenant-governor of a state is generally *ex officio* president of the Senate, with a casting vote therein, the House always chooses its own Speaker. The legal quorum is usually fixed, by the constitution, at a majority of the whole number of members elected,[21] though a smaller number may adjourn and compel the attendance of absent members. Both houses do most of their work by committees, much after the fashion of Congress,[22] and the committees are in both usually chosen by the Speaker (in the Senate by the president of that body), though it is often provided that the House (or Senate) may on motion vary their composition.[23] Both houses sit with open doors, but in

---

[19] In New York impeachments are tried by the Senate and the judges of the Court of Appeal sitting together; in Nebraska by the judges of the supreme court.

[20] Here and there one finds slight differences, as, for instance, in Vermont the power decennially to propose amendments to the constitution belongs to the Senate, though the concurrence of the House is needed. However, I do not attempt in this summary to give every detail of every constitution, but only a fair general account of what commonly prevails, and is of most interest to the student of comparative politics.

[21] Four constitutions fix the quorum at two-thirds, and two specify a number.

[22] See, as to the committees of Congress, Chapter 15 *ante*. Many constitutions provide that no bill shall pass unless it has been previously referred to and considered by a committee.

[23] In Massachusetts there were in 1912 five standing committees of the Senate, seven of the House, and thirty joint standing committees of both houses. In North Dakota there were in 1891 thirty-three standing committees of the Senate, thirty-nine of the House, and six joint standing committees

most states the constitution empowers them to exclude strangers when the business requires secrecy.

The state governor has of course no right to dissolve the legislature, nor even to adjourn it unless the houses, while agreeing to adjourn, disagree as to the date. Such control as the legislature can exercise over the state officers by way of inquiry into their conduct is generally exercised by committees, and it is in committees that the form of bills is usually settled and their fate decided, just as in the federal Congress. The proceedings are rarely reported. Sometimes when a committee takes evidence on an important question reporters are present, and the proceedings more resemble a public meeting than a legislative session. In some states when a bill is referred to a committee any citizen of the state may appear and give evidence for or against it, so that ample security is taken for the ascertainment of public sentiment and for enabling all private interests affected to state their case. This liberty is largely used in Massachusetts, and with excellent results. It need scarcely be added that neither house separately, nor both houses acting together, can control an executive officer otherwise than either by passing a statute prescribing a certain course of action for him, which if it be in excess of their powers will be held unconstitutional and void, or by withholding the appropriations necessary to enable him to carry out the course of action he proposes to adopt. The latter method, where applicable, is the more effective, because it can be used by a bare majority of either house, whereas a bill passed by both houses may be vetoed by the governor, a point so important as to need a few words.

One state only, North Carolina, still vests legislative authority in the legislature alone. All the rest now require a bill to be submitted to the governor, and permit him to return it to the legislature with his objections. If he so returns it, it can only be again passed "over the veto" by something more than a bare majority. To so pass a bill over the veto there is required:

In one state (Connecticut) a majority in each house

In eight states a majority in each house of all the members elected to that house

In three states a majority of three-fifths in each house of all the members elected

In eight states a majority of two-thirds in each house of all the members present

---

of House and Senate. In New York there were in 1913 twenty-five standing committees of the Senate, thirty-one of the Assembly.

In twenty-seven states a majority of two-thirds of all the members elected

In one state (Massachusetts) two-thirds of the elected members of the house in which the bill originated, and two-thirds of the members present in the other house

In one state (Virginia) two-thirds of the members present and a majority of those elected in each house

Here, therefore, as in the federal Constitution, we find a useful safeguard against the unwisdom or misconduct of a legislature, and a method provided for escaping, in extreme cases, from those deadlocks which the system of checks and balances tends to occasion.

I have adverted in a preceding chapter to the restrictions imposed on the legislatures of the states by their respective constitutions. These restrictions, which are numerous, elaborate, and instructive, take two forms.

I. Exclusions of a subject from legislative competence, i.e., prohibitions to the legislature to pass any law on certain enumerated subjects. The most important classes of prohibited statutes are:

Statutes inconsistent with democratic principles, as, for example, granting titles of nobility, favouring one religious denomination, creating a property qualification for suffrage or office.

Statutes against public policy, e.g., tolerating lotteries, impairing the obligation of contracts, incorporating or permitting the incorporation of banks, or the holding by a state of bank stock.[24]

Statutes special or local in their application, a very large and increasing category, the fulness and minuteness of which in many constitutions show that the mischiefs arising from improvident or corrupt special legislation must have become alarming. The lists of prohibited subjects in the Constitutions of Missouri of 1875, Montana and North Dakota of 1889, Mississippi of 1890, and Oklahoma, 1907, are the most complete I have found.[25] Oklahoma enumerates twenty-eight topics, special legislation on which is forbidden.

Statutes increasing the state debt beyond a certain limited amount, or permitting a local authority to increase its debt beyond a prescribed

---

[24] See, for instance, Constitution of Texas of 1876.

[25] Similar lists occur in the constitutions of all the Western and Southern states as well as of some Eastern states (e.g., Pennsylvania and New York). Among them the prohibitions to grant divorces and to authorize the adoption or legitimation of children are frequent.

amount, the amount being usually fixed in proportion to the valuation of taxable property within the area administered by the local authority.[26]

II. Restrictions on the procedure of the legislature, i.e., directions as to the particular forms to be observed and times to be allowed in passing bills, sometimes all bills, sometimes bills of a certain specified nature. Among these restrictions will be found provisions:

As to the majorities necessary to pass certain bills, especially appropriation bills. Sometimes a majority of the whole number of members elected to each house is required, or a majority exceeding a bare majority of those present.

As to the method of taking the votes, e.g., by calling over the roll and recording the vote of each member.

As to allowing certain intervals to elapse between each reading of a measure, and for preventing the hurried passage of bills, especially appropriation bills, at the end of the session.

As to reading of bills publicly and at full length.

As to sending all bills to a committee, and prescribing the mode of its action.

Against secret sessions (Idaho).

As to preventing an act from taking effect until a certain time, e.g., ninety days after the adjournment of the session.

Against changing the purpose of a bill during its passage.

As to including in a bill only one subject, and expressing that subject in the title of the bill.

Against reenacting, or amending, or incorporating, any former act by reference to its title merely, without setting out its contents.[27]

The last two classes of provisions might be found wholesome in England, where much of the difficulty complained of by the judges in construing the law arises from the modern habit of incorporating parts of former statutes, and dealing with them by reference.[28]

---

[26] See also Chapter 43 on state finance. The local authorities had been usually forbidden by statute to borrow or tax beyond a certain amount, but as they had formed the habit of obtaining dispensations from the state legislatures, the check mentioned in the text has been imposed on the latter.

[27] Idaho, Indiana, and Oregon direct every act to be plainly worded, avoiding as far as possible technical terms, and Louisiana (Constitution of 1879, § 31) says: "The General Assembly shall never adopt any system or code of laws by general reference to such system or code of laws, but in all cases shall recite at length the several provisions of the laws it may enact."

[28] Not to add that the inclusion in one statute of wholly different matters may operate harshly on persons who have failed to note the minor contents of a bill whose principal purpose does not

Where statutes have been passed by a legislature upon a prohibited subject, or where the prescribed forms have been transgressed or omitted, the statute will be held void so far as inconsistent with the constitution.

Even these multiform restrictions on the state legislatures have not been found sufficient. Bitted and bridled as they are by the constitutions, they contrive, as will appear in a later chapter, to do plenty of mischief in the direction of private or special legislation.

Although state legislatures have of course no concern whatever with foreign affairs, this is not deemed a reason for abstaining from passing resolutions on that subject. The passion for resolutions is strong everywhere in America, and an expression of sympathy with an oppressed foreign nationality, or of displeasure at any unfriendly behaviour of a foreign power, is not only an obvious way of relieving the feelings of the legislators, but often an electioneering device, which appeals to some section of the state voters. Accordingly such resolutions are common, and, though of course quite irregular, quite innocuous.

Debates in these bodies are seldom well reported, and sometimes not reported at all. One result is that the conduct of members escapes the scrutiny of their constituents; a better one that speeches are generally short and practical, the motive for rhetorical displays being absent. If a man does not make a reputation for oratory, he may for quick good sense and business habits. However, so much of the real work is done in committees that talent for intrigue or "management" usually counts for more than debating power.

---

affect them. The commoners of the New Forest in Hampshire were once surprised to awake one morning and find that the Crown had smuggled through Parliament, in an act relating to foreshores in Scotland, a clause seriously prejudicial to their interests.

The State Executive

T he executive department in a state consists of a governor (in all the states), a lieutenant-governor (in thirty-five), and of various minor officials. The governor, who, under the earlier constitutions of most of the original thirteen states, was chosen by the legislature, is now always elected by the people, and by the same suffrage, practically universal, as the legislature. He is elected directly, not, as under the federal Constitution, by a college of electors. His term of office is, in twenty-three states, four years; in one state (New Jersey), three years; in twenty-two states, two years; and in two states (Massachusetts and Rhode Island), one year. His salary varies from $12,000 in New York and Pennsylvania to $2,500 in Vermont and one other state. Some states limit his reeligibility; but in those which do not there seems to exist no tradition forbidding a third term of office similar to that which has prevailed in the federal government.

The earlier constitutions of the original states (except South Carolina) associated with the governor an executive council[1] (called in Delaware the Privy Council), but these councils have long since disappeared, except in Massachusetts, Maine, and North Carolina, and the governor remains in solitary glory the official head and representative of the majesty of the state. His powers in the latter decades of the last century had come to be more specious than solid, but in the present century they have begun to revive.

---

[1] Another illustration of the tendency to reproduce England. Vermont was still under the influence of colonial precedents when it framed its Constitutions of 1786 and 1793. Maine was influenced by Massachusetts. None of the newer Western states has even tried the experiment of such a council.

New York had originally two councils, a "Council of Appointment," consisting of the governor and a senator from each of the (originally four) districts, and a "Council of Revision," consisting of the governor, the chancellor, and the judges of the supreme court, and possessing a veto on statutes. The governor has now, since the extinction of these two councils, obtained some of the patronage which belonged to the former as well as the veto which belonged to the latter.

One, that of veto, is recognized as of great practical value. He is charged with the duty of seeing that the laws of the state are faithfully administered by all officials and the judgments of the courts carried out. He has, in nearly all states, the power of reprieving the pardoning offenders, but in some this does not extend to treason or to conviction on impeachment (in Vermont he cannot pardon for murder), and in some, other authorities are associated with him in the exercise of this prerogative. Some recent constitutions impose restrictions which witness to a distrust of his action; nor can it be denied that the power has sometimes been used to release offenders (e.g., against the election laws) who deserved no sympathy. The governor is also commander in chief of the armed forces of the state, can embody the militia, repel invasion, suppress insurrection. The militia are now important chiefly as the force which may be used to suppress riots, latterly not unfrequent in connection with labour disputes. Massachusetts has also created a small state police force (called the District Police), placing it at the disposal of the governor for the maintenance of order, wherever disturbed, and for the enforcement of various administrative regulations. Pennsylvania, having frequently suffered from strikes accompanied by violence in the mining regions, has also a state police. Michigan has (and Massachusetts and Rhode Island formerly had) a state police for the enforcement of their anti-liquor legislation, and New York State has one for supervising elections in New York City. Delaware has two state detectives.

He appoints some few officials, but seldom to high posts, and in many states his nominations require the approval of the state Senate. Patronage, in which the president of the United States finds one of his most desired and most disagreeable functions, is in the case of a state governor of slight value, because the state offices are not numerous, and the more important and lucrative ones are filled by the direct election of the people. Nevertheless there has lately appeared a tendency to commit to him, as a person who can be held responsible, the selection of capable men for some of the posts recently created. He has the right of requiring information from the other executive officials, and is usually bound to communicate to the legislature his views regarding the condition of the commonwealth. He may also recommend measures, but is not expected to frame and present bills, though he may practically do this by having a measure introduced which embodies his recommendations. In a few states he is directed to present estimates. He has in all the states but one (North Carolina) a veto upon bills passed by the legislature.[2] This veto may be overridden in a manner already indicated

---

[2] It deserves to be remarked that neither the Constitution of the Swiss Confederation nor any cantonal constitution vests a veto in any officer. Switzerland seems in this respect more democratic

(see last preceding chapter), but generally kills the measure, because if the bill is a bad one, it calls the attention of the people to the fact and frightens the legislature, whereas if the bill be an unobjectionable one, the governor's motive for vetoing it is probably a party motive, and the requisite overriding majority can seldom be secured in favour of a bill which either party dislikes. The use of his veto is, in ordinary times, a governor's most serious duty, and chiefly by his discharge of it is he judged.

Although much less sought after and prized than in "the days of the Fathers," when a state governor sometimes refused to yield precedence to the president of the United States, the governorship is still, particularly in New England, and the greater states, a post of some dignity, and affords an opportunity for the display of character and talents. It was in his governorship of New York that Mr. Cleveland, for instance, commended himself to his party, and rose to be president of the United States. Similarly Mr. Hayes was put forward for the presidency in 1876 because he had been a good governor of Ohio. During the Civil War, when each governor was responsible for enrolling, equipping, officering, and sending forward troops from his state,[3] and when it rested with him to repress any attempts at disorder, much depended on his energy, popularity, and loyalty. In some states men still talk of the "war governors" of those days as heroes to whom the North owed deep gratitude. And since the Pennsylvanian riots of 1877 and those which have subsequently occurred in Cincinnati and Chicago have shown that tumults may suddenly grow to serious proportions, it has in many states become important to have a man of prompt decision and fearlessness in the office which issues orders to the state militia.[4]

---

than the American states, while in the amount of authority which the Swiss allow to the executive government over the citizen (as witness the case of the Salvation Army troubles in Canton Bern) they are less democratic.

[3] Commissions to officers up to the rank of colonel inclusive were usually issued by the governor of the state. The regiment, in fact, was a state product, though the regular federal army is of course raised and managed by the federal government directly.

[4] This is the place for noticing a remarkable novelty in the relations of the states and their respective executive heads to the nation and its head. In 1908 the president of the United States invited the governors of all the states to meet him and some persons of exceptional knowledge and experience in a conference at Washington for the purpose of considering a matter of high public consequence, namely the best method of conserving and turning to full account the natural resources of the country, such as forests, mines, and water power. The object was to enlist the interest of the states in the adoption of a national policy upon this great national matter, and if possible to induce them to legislate each for itself in accordance with some general principles which might also be recognized and carried out by the national government in its own sphere. The conference met in the winter of 1908 and again early in 1909. Not only did its deliberations command much attention

The decline already noted in the respect and confidence felt for and in the legislatures has latterly, in some states, tended to attach more influence to the office of governor, and has opened to a strong and upright man, the opportunity of making it a post of effective leadership. The people are coming to look upon the head of their commonwealth as the person responsible for giving them a firm and honest administration. When they are convinced of his rectitude, they regard him as the representative of their own best will and purpose, and have in some instances shown that they are prepared to support him against the legislature, and to require the latter to take the path he has pointed out.

The elective lieutenant-governor who, in most states, steps into the governor's place if it becomes vacant, is usually also *ex officio* president of the Senate,[5] as the vice-president of the United States is of the federal Senate. Otherwise he is an insignificant personage, though sometimes a member of some of the executive boards.[6]

The names and duties of the other officers vary from state to state. The most frequent are a secretary of state (in all states), a treasurer (in all), an attorney general, a comptroller, an auditor, a superintendent of public instruction. Now and then we find a state engineer, a surveyor, a superintendent of prisons. Some states have also various boards of commissioners, e.g., for railroads, for canals, for prisons, for the land office, for agriculture, for immigration, and (in a few states) for what are called "public utilities." Many of these officials are (in nearly all states) elected by the people at the general state election. Sometimes, however, they, or some of them, are either chosen by the legislature, or appointed by the governor, whose nomination usually requires the confirmation of the Senate. Their salaries, which of course vary with the importance of the office and the parsimony of the state, seldom exceed $5,000 per annum and are usually smaller. So, too, the length of the term of office varies. It is often the same as that of the governor, and never exceeds four years, except that in New Jersey, a

---

from the people, but the scheme of bringing the states through their governors into council with the national administration in a way not provided for by, but in nowise inconsistent with the federal Constitution, appeared to set a precedent capable of being used thereafter, as a means of arousing public opinion and concentrating it upon some common aim, which it might be found difficult to attain through the action of Congress. In 1910 arrangements were made for holding conferences of governors at stated times in the future.

[5] In Rhode Island the governor presides over the Senate, an interesting survival of European arrangements.

[6] Where there is no lieutenant-governor, the president of the state Senate or the secretary of state usually succeeds if the governor dies or becomes incapable of discharging his functions.

conservative state, the secretary and attorney general hold for five years; and in Tennessee the attorney general, who, oddly enough, is appointed by the supreme court of the state, holds for eight.

It has already been observed that the state officials are in no sense a ministry or cabinet to the governor. Holding independently of him, and responsible neither to him nor to the legislature, but to the people, they do not take generally his orders, and need not regard his advice.[7] Each has his own department to administer, and as there is little or nothing political in the work, a general agreement in policy, such as must exist between the federal president and his ministers, is not required. Policy rests with the legislature, whose statutes, prescribing minutely the action to be taken by the officials, leave little room for executive discretion. Europeans may realize the nature of the system by imagining a municipal government in which the mayor, town clerk, health officer, and city architect are all chosen directly by the people, instead of by the common council, and in which every one of these officials is for most purposes, independent not only of the mayor, but also of the common council, except in so far as the latter has the right of granting money, and as it can act by general ordinances— that is to say, act as a legislative and not as an administrative body.[8]

To give a clearer idea of the staff of a state government I will take the great state of Ohio, and give the functions of the officials by whom it is administered.

[7] Florida, by her Constitution of 1868, art. VI, 17, and art. VIII, created a "cabinet of administrative officers," consisting of eight officials, appointed by the governor, with the consent of the Senate, who are to hold office for the same time as the governor, and "assist the governor in the performance of his duties." However, in her Constitution of 1886 she simply provides that "the governor shall be assisted by administrative officers," viz., secretary of state, attorney general, comptroller, treasurer, superintendent of public instruction, and commissioner of agriculture, all elected by the people at the same time with the governor and for the same term. The council of North Carolina (Constitution of 1868) consists of five officials, who are to "advise the governor in the execution of his duty," but they are elected directly by the people. Their position may be compared with that of the Council of India under recent English statutes towards the secretary of state for India. Massachusetts has always had an "executive council" consisting of eight persons chosen annually by the people in districts. They "advise the governor in the executive part of the government" and have the right of rejecting nominations to office made by him. Here too we find a survival, which might seem to do more harm than good, because it lessens the governor's responsibility. However, a respected and successful recent governor told me that he found his council helpful, as its members frequently took up and dealt with particular questions on which he consulted them. They became to him almost a sort of cabinet of administrative heads.

[8] In the Swiss Confederation the Federal Council of Seven consists of persons belonging to different parties, who sometimes speak against one another in the chambers (where they have the right of speech), but this is not found to interfere with their harmonious working as an administrative body.

The executive officials of Ohio were in 1909:

A *Governor*, elected by the people for two years. His chief duties are to execute the laws, convene the legislature on extraordinary occasions, command the state forces, appoint staff officers and aides-de-camp, grant pardons and reprieves, issue commissions to state and county officers, make a variety of appointments, serve on certain boards, and remove, with the assent of the Senate, any official appointed by him and it. He is paid $10,000 a year.

A *Lieutenant-Governor*, elected for two years, salary $1,500 a year, with the duty of succeeding to the governor (in case of death or disability), and of presiding in the Senate.

A *Secretary of State*, elected for two years (along with the governor), salary $6,500 a year. His duties are to take charge of laws and documents of the state, gather and report statistics, distribute instructions to certain officers, and act as secretary to certain boards, to serve on the state printing and state library boards, to make an abstract of the votes for candidates at presidential and state elections.

A *State Auditor*, elected for four years, salary $6,500. Duties—to keep accounts of all moneys in the state treasury, and of all appropriations and warrants, to give warrants for all payments from or into the treasury, to conduct financial communications with county authorities, and direct the attorney general to prosecute revenue claims, to serve on various financial boards, and manage various kinds of financial business.

A *State Treasurer*, elected for two years, salary $6,500. Duties—to keep account of all drafts, paying the money into the treasury, and of auditor's warrants for drafts from it, and generally to assist and check the auditor in the supervision and disbursement of state revenues, publishing monthly statements of balances.

A *State Attorney General*, elected for two years, salary $6,500 a year. Duties—to appear for the state in civil and criminal cases, advise legally the governor and other state officers and the Assembly, proceed against offenders, enforce performance of charitable trusts, submit statistics of crime, sit upon various boards.

A *State Commissioner of Common Schools*, elected for three years, salary $4,000 a year. Duties—to visit and advise teachers' institutes, boards of education, and teachers, deliver lectures on educational topics, see that educational funds are legally distributed, prepare and submit annual reports on conditions of schools, appoint state board of examiners of teachers.

Three Members of Board of Public Works, elected for four years, salary $2,900 a year. Duties—to manage and repair the public works (including canals) of the state, appoint and supervise minor officials, let contracts, present annual detailed report to the governor.

A *State Dairy and Food Commissioner*, elected for two years, salary $4,000, and travelling expenses.

Besides these, the people of the state elect the judges and the clerk of the supreme court. Other officials are either elected by the people in districts, counties, or cities, or appointed by the governor or legislature.

Of the subordinate civil service of a state there is little to be said. Though it is not large, for the sphere of administrative action which remains to the state between the federal government on the one side, and the county, city, and township governments on the other, is not wide, it increases daily, owing to the eagerness of the people (especially in the West) to have state aid rendered to farmers, to miners, to stockkeepers, and generally in the material development of the country. Much is now done in the way of collecting statistics and issuing reports. These administrative bureaux are not always well manned, for state legislatures are not duly alive to the necessity of securing high competence, and some of them do little, by salaries or otherwise, to induce able men to enter their service: while the so-called "Spoils System," which has been hitherto applied to state no less than to federal offices, too often makes places the reward for electioneering and wire-pulling. Efforts are moreover being made, and have in some states already been successful (e.g., New York), to introduce reforms similar to those begun in the federal administration, whereby certain walks of the civil service shall be kept out of politics, at least so far as to secure competent men against dismissal on party grounds. Such reforms would in no case apply to the higher officials chosen by the people, for they are always elected for short terms and on party lines. In New York, however, recent legislation has created efficient administrative boards with suitable authority, such as the Public Service Commission, which has jurisdiction over railroads and over corporations providing gas, electric light and power, telegraph and telephone service.

Every state provides for the impeachment of executive officers for grave offences.[9] The state House of Representatives is the impeaching body,

[9] Oregon was long an exception, but now she too permits impeachment and used it in 1909 against two officials, one of whom resigned rather than face the trial, while the other escaped because the majority for conviction fell short of two-thirds.

except in Nebraska, where the impeachment is made by joint resolution of both houses; and in all but Nebraska the state Senate sits as the tribunal, a two-thirds majority being generally required for a conviction. Impeachments are rare in practice.

There has also been in many states a power of removing officials, sometimes by the vote of the legislature, sometimes by the governor on the address of both houses, or by the governor either alone, or with the concurrence of the Senate. Such removals must of course be made in respect of some offence, or for some other sufficient cause, not from caprice or party motives; and when the case does not seem to justify immediate removal, the governor is frequently empowered to suspend the officer, pending an investigation of his conduct.

A more promptly effective method of dealing with officials to whom objection is taken has been recently introduced in some states. This is the recall. A prescribed number of voting citizens may demand that a vote shall be taken on the question whether a certain official shall or shall not continue in office for the rest of his term. If such a popular vote when taken shows a majority against the official, he is thereby dismissed.

Up to the end of 1913 seven states had adopted this plan. They were Oregon, California, Arizona, Colorado, Nevada, Idaho, Washington.

C H A P T E R   4 2

The State Judiciary

The judiciary in every state includes three sets of courts: A supreme court or court of appeal; superior courts of record; local courts; but the particular names and relations of these several tribunals and the arrangements for criminal business vary greatly from state to state. We hear of courts of common pleas, probate courts,[1] surrogate courts, prerogative courts, courts of oyer and terminer, orphans' courts, court of general sessions of the peace and gaol delivery, quarter sessions, hustings' courts, county courts, etc., etc. All sorts of old English institutions have been transferred bodily, and sometimes look as odd in the midst of their new surroundings as the quaint gables of a seventeenth-century house among the terraces of a growing London suburb. As respects the distinction which Englishmen used to deem fundamental, that of courts of common law and courts of equity, there has been great diversity of practice. Most of the original thirteen colonies once possessed separate courts of chancery, and these were maintained for many years after the separation from England, and were imitated in a few of the earlier among the new states, such as Michigan, Arkansas, Missouri. In some of the old states, however, the hostility to equity jurisdiction, which marked the popular party in England in the seventeenth century, had transmitted itself to America. Chancery courts were regarded with suspicion, because thought to be less bound by fixed rules, and therefore more liable to be abused by an ambitious or capricious judiciary.[2] Massachusetts, for instance, would permit no such court, though she was eventually obliged to invest her ordinary judges with equitable powers, and to engraft a system

---

[1] Admiralty business is within the exclusive jurisdiction of the federal courts.

[2] Note that the grossest abuses of judicial power by American judges, such as the Erie Railroad injunctions of Judge Barnard of New York in 1869, were perpetrated in the exercise of equitable jurisdiction. Equity in granting discretion opens a door to indiscretion, or to something worse.

of equity on her common law, while still keeping the two systems distinct. Pennsylvania held out still longer, but she also now administers equity, as indeed every civilized state must do in substance, dispensing it, however, through the same judges as those who apply the common law, and having more or less worked it into the texture of the older system. Special chancery courts were abolished in New York, where they had flourished and enriched American jurisprudence by many admirable judgments, by the democratizing Constitution of 1846; and they now exist only in a few of the states, chiefly older Eastern or Southern states,[3] which, in judicial matters, have shown themselves more conservative than their sisters in the West. In seven states (Connecticut, New York, North Carolina, Georgia, Ohio, California, Idaho) there has been a complete fusion of law and equity, although there are several others which have provided that the legislature shall abolish the distinction between the two kinds of procedure. Many, especially of the newer states, provide for the establishment of tribunals of arbitration and conciliation.

The jurisdiction of the state courts, both civil and criminal, is absolutely unlimited, i.e., there is no appeal from them to the federal courts, except in certain cases specified by the federal Constitution, being cases in which some point of federal law arises. Certain classes of cases are, of course, reserved for the federal courts and in some the state courts enjoy a concurrent jurisdiction.[4] All crimes, except such as are punishable under some federal statute, are justiciable by a state court; and it is worth remembering that in all, or nearly all, states there exist much wider facilities for setting aside the verdict of a jury finding a prisoner guilty, by raising all sorts of points of law, than are permitted by the law and practice of any European country. Such facilities have been and are abused, to the great detriment of the community.

One or two other points relating to law and justice in the states require notice. Each state recognizes the judgments of the courts of a sister state, gives credit to its public acts and records, and delivers up to its justice any fugitive from its jurisdiction, permitting him, moreover, to be (if necessary) tried for some other offence than that in respect of which his extradition was obtained. Of course the courts of one state are not bound either by law or usage to follow the reported decisions of those of another state. They use such decisions merely for their own enlightenment, and as some evidence

---

[3] Delaware, New Jersey, Vermont, Tennessee, Michigan, Alabama, Mississippi.
[4] See Chapter 22 *ante.*

of the common law, just as they use the English law reports. Most of the states have within the last half century made sweeping changes, not only in their judicial system, but in the form of their law. They have revised and codified their statutes, a carefully corrected edition whereof is issued every few years. They have in many instances adopted codes of procedure, and in some cases have even enacted codes embodying the substance of the common law, and fusing it with the statutes. Such codes, however, have been condemned by the judgment of the abler and more learned part of the profession, as rendering the law more uncertain and less scientific.[5] But with the masses of the people the proposal is popular, for it holds out a prospect, unfortunately belied by the result in states which, like California, have tried the experiment, of a system whose simplicity will enable the layman to understand the law, and render justice cheaper and more speedy. A really good code might have these happy effects. But it may be doubted whether the codifying states have taken the steps requisite to secure the goodness of the codes they enact. And there is a grave objection to the codification of state law which does not exist in a country like England or France. So long as the law of a state remains common law, i.e., rests upon custom and decisions given by the judges, the law of each state tends to keep in tolerable harmony with that of other states, because each set of judges is enlightened by and disposed to be influenced by the decisions of the federal courts and of judges in other states. But when the whole law of a state has been enacted in the form of a code all existing divergences between one state and another are sharpened and perpetuated, while new divergences may probably be created. Hence codification increases the variations of the law between different states, and these variations tend to impede business and disturb the ordinary relations of life.

Important as are the functions of the American judiciary, the powers of a judge are limited by the state constitutions in a manner surprising to Europeans. He is not generally allowed to charge the jury on questions of fact,[6] but only to state the law. He is sometimes required to put his charge in writing. His power of committing for contempt of court is often restricted. Express rules forbid him to sit in causes wherein he can have any family or

---

[5] This is perhaps less true of Louisiana, where the civil law of Rome, which may be said to have been the common law of the state, offered a better basis for a code than the English common law does. The Louisiana code is based on the Code Napoleon.

[6] A frequent form is that in the Constitution of Tennessee of 1870 (art. VI, § 9)—"Judges shall not charge juries with respect to matters of fact, but may state the testimony and declare the law." Washington forbids even comments on the facts. Some constitutions are silent on the point.

pecuniary interest. In one constitution his punctual attendance is enforced by the provision that if he does not arrive in court within half an hour of the time fixed for the sitting, the attorneys of the parties may agree on some person to act as judge, and proceed forthwith to the trial of the cause. And in California he is not allowed to draw his salary till he has made an affidavit that no cause that has been submitted for decision for ninety days remains undecided in his court.[7]

I come now to three points, which are not only important in themselves, but instructive as illustrating the currents of opinion which have influenced the peoples of the states. These are:

The method of appointing the judges
Their tenure of office
Their salaries

The remarkable changes that have been made in the two former matters, and the strange practice which now prevails in the latter, are full of significance for the student of modern democracy, full of warning for Europe and the British colonies.

In colonial days the superior judges were appointed by the governors, except in Rhode Island and Connecticut, where the legislature elected them. When, in and after 1776, the states formed their first constitutions, four states,[8] besides the two just named, vested the appointment in the legislature, five[9] gave it to the governor with the consent of the council; Delaware gave it to the legislature and president (= governor) in joint ballot, while Georgia alone entrusted the election to the people.

In the period between 1812 and 1860, when the tide of democracy was running strong, the function of appointing was in several of the older states taken from the governor or the legislature to be given to the people voting at the polls; and this became the practice among the new states as they were successively admitted to the Union. Mississippi, in 1832, made all her judges elected by the people. The decisive nature of the change was marked by the great state of New York, which, in her highly democratic constitution of 1846, transferred all judicial appointments to the citizens at the polls.

At present we find that:

---

[7] The Californian judges are said to have contrived to evade this. Idaho has a similar provision, but gives the judge only thirty days. Montana provides that any judicial officer who absents himself more than sixty consecutive days from the state shall be deemed to have forfeited his office.

[8] Virginia, New Jersey, North Carolina, and South Carolina.

[9] Massachusetts, New Hampshire, Pennsylvania, Maryland, New York.

In four states[10] the judges are elected by the legislature;

In seven states[11] they are appointed by the governor, subject however to confirmation either by the council, or by the legislature, or by one house thereof;

In all the other states, the judges are elected by the people. These include nearly all the Western and Southwestern states, besides New York, Pennsylvania, and Ohio.

It will be observed that of the eleven states which do not appoint the judge by popular election all (except Maine and Mississippi) belong to the original thirteen colonies. It is these older commonwealths that have clung to the less democratic methods of choosing judicial officers; while the new democracies of the West, together with the most populous states of the East, New York and Pennsylvania, states thoroughly democratized by their great cities, have thrown this grave and delicate function into the rude hands of the masses, that is to say, of the wire-pullers.

Originally, the superior judges were, in most states, like those of England since the Revolution of 1688, appointed for life, and held office during good behaviour, i.e., were removable only when condemned on an impeachment, or when an address requesting their removal had been presented by both houses of the legislature.[12] A judge may now be removed upon such an address in nearly all states, a majority of two-thirds in each house being usually required. This salutary provision of the British Constitution against capricious removals has been faithfully adhered to. But the wave of democracy has in nearly all states swept away the old system of life tenure. Only three now retain it.[13] In the rest a judge is elected or appointed for a term, varying from two years in Vermont to twenty-one years in Pennsylvania. Eight to ten years is the average term prescribed; but a judge is always reeligible, and likely to be reelected if he be not too old, if he has given satisfaction to the bar, and if he has not offended the party which placed him on the bench.

The salaries paid to state judges of the higher courts range from $10,500

---

[10] Rhode Island, Vermont, Virginia, South Carolina.

[11] Massachusetts, Connecticut, New Hampshire, Delaware, Maine, Mississippi, New Jersey. In Maine and Connecticut probate judges are popularly elected. In Florida, though the three justices of the supreme court are now (Constitution of 1886) elected by the people, the seven circuit judges are appointed by the governor.

[12] The power of impeachment remains but is not often used.

[13] Massachusetts, Rhode Island, New Hampshire, all of them among the original thirteen. In Rhode Island the judges are in theory dismissible by the legislature.

(chief justice) in Pennsylvania, and $14,200 (chief justice) in New York (in one district $17,500), to $2,500 in Vermont. $5,000 to $6,000 (+ $500 to the chief judge) is the average, a sum which, especially in the greater states, fails to attract the best legal talent. To the rule that justices of the inferior courts receive salaries proportionately lower, there are exceptions in large cities, where judges of lower tribunals, being more "in politics" can sometimes secure salaries quite out of proportion to their status.[14] In general the new Western states are the worst paymasters, their population of farmers not perceiving the importance of securing high ability on the bench, and deeming $4,000 a larger sum than a quiet-living man can need. The lowness of the scale on which the salaries of federal judges are fixed confirms this tendency.

Any one of the three phenomena I have described—popular elections, short terms, and small salaries—would be sufficient to lower the character of the judiciary. Popular elections throw the choice into the hands of political parties, that is to say, of knots of wire-pullers inclined to use every office as a means of rewarding political services, and garrisoning with grateful partisans posts which may conceivably become of political importance. In some few states, judges have from time to time become accomplices in election frauds, tools in the hands of unscrupulous bosses. Injunctions granted by them were moves in the party game. Now, short terms, though they afford useful opportunities of getting rid of a man who has proved a failure, yet has done no act justifying an address for his removal, sap the conscience of the judge, for they oblige him to remember and keep on good terms with those who have made him what he is, and in whose hands his fortunes lie. They induce timidity, they discourage independence. And small salaries prevent able men from offering themselves for places whose income is perhaps only one-tenth of what a leading barrister can make by private practice. Putting the three sources of mischief together, no one will be surprised to hear that in many of the American states the state judges are men of moderate abilities and scanty learning, inferior, and sometimes vastly inferior, to the best of the advocates who practise before them. It is less easy to express a general opinion as to their character, and particularly as to what is called, even in America where fur capes are not worn, the "purity of the judicial ermine." Pecuniary corruption seems, so far as a stranger can ascertain, to be rare, in most states very rare, but there are

---

[14] E.g., the city magistrates of New York City and the circuit judges of Wayne County, Michigan, in which Detroit stands.

other ways in which sinister influences can play on a judge's mind, and impair that confidence in his impartiality which is almost as necessary as impartiality itself. And apart from all questions of dishonesty or unfairness, it is an evil that the bench should not be intellectually and socially at least on a level with the bar.

The mischief is serious. But it is in most states smaller than a European observer is prepared to expect. In most of the states where the elective system prevails the bench is respectable; and in some it is occasionally adorned by men of the highest eminence. Michigan, for instance, has during many years had a strong and respected judiciary. One of its more recent judges sat for thirty-two years, having been reelected six times in succession. Seldom are the results so lamentable as might have been predicted. New York City, under the dominion of the Tweed Ring, has afforded the only instance of flagrant judicial scandals; and even in those loathsome days, the Court of Appeals at Albany, the highest tribunal of the state, retained the respect of good citizens. Although judges are sometimes weak and sometimes subject to political influence, although juries are not always above suspicion, still justice in ordinary civil causes between man and man is fairly administered over the whole Union, and the frequent failures to convict criminals, or punish them when convicted, evils on which some eminent statesmen and lawyers have recently dwelt, are attributable not so much either to weakness or to partiality on a judge's part as to the tenderness of juries and the inordinate delays and complexity of criminal procedure.

Why then have sources of evil so grave failed to produce correspondingly grave results? Three reasons may be suggested.

One is the coexistence in every state of the federal tribunals, presided over by judges who are usually capable and always upright. Their presence helps to keep the state judges, however personally inferior, from losing the sense of responsibility and dignity which befits the judicial office, and makes even party wire-pullers ashamed of nominating as candidates men either tainted or notoriously incapable.

Another is the influence of a public opinion which not only recognizes the interest the community has in an honest administration of the law, but recoils from turpitude in a highly placed official. The people act as a check upon the party conventions that choose candidates, by making them feel that they damage themselves and their cause if they run a man of doubtful character, and the judge himself is made to dread public opinion in the criticisms of a very unreticent press. Democratic theory, which has done a mischief in introducing the elective system, partly cures it by subjecting the bench to a light of publicity which makes honesty the safest policy. Whatever passes in court is, or may be, reported. The judge must give his reasons for every judgment he delivers.

Lastly, there is the influence of the bar, a potent influence even in the present day, when its role is less brilliant than in former generations. The local party leaders who select the candidates and "run" the conventions are in some states mostly lawyers themselves, or at least in close relations with some leading lawyers of the state or district. Now lawyers have not only a professional dislike to the entrusting of law to incapable hands, the kind of dislike which a skilled bricklayer has to seeing walls badly laid, but they have a personal interest in getting fairly competent men before whom to plead. It is no pleasure to them to have a judge so ignorant or so weak that a good argument is thrown away upon him, or that you can feel no confidence that the opinion given to a client, or a point of law which you think clear, will be verified by the decision of the court. Hence the bar often contrives to make a party nomination for judicial office fall, not indeed on a leading counsel, because a leading counsel will not accept a place with $4,000 a year, when he can make $20,000 to $30,000 by private practice, but on as competent a member of the party as can be got to take the post. Having constantly inquired, in every state I visited wherein the system of popular elections to judgeships prevails, how it happened that the judges were not worse, I was usually told that the bar had interposed to prevent such and such a bad nomination, or had agreed to recommend such and such a person as a candidate, and that the party had yielded to the wishes of the bar. Occasionally, when the wire-pullers are on their good behaviour, or the bar is exceptionally public-spirited, a person will be brought forward who has no claims except those of character and learning. But it is perhaps more common for the lawyers to put pressure on one or other party in nominating its party candidates to select capable ones. Thus when a few years ago the Republicans of New York State were running bad candidates, some leading Republican lawyers persuaded the Democrats to nominate better men, and thereupon issued an appeal in favour of these latter, who were accordingly carried at the ensuing election.

These causes, and especially the last, go far to nullify the malign effects of popular election and short terms. But they cannot equally nullify the effect of small salaries. Accordingly, while corruption and partiality are uncommon, inferiority to the practising counsel is a conspicuous and frequent fault.

One is obliged to speak generally, because there are differences between the various states too numerous to be particularized. In some, especially in the Northwest, the tone of the party managers and of the bar is respectable, and the sense of common interest makes everybody wish to have as good men as the salaries will secure. In others there are traditions which even unscrupulous wire-pullers fear to violate. Pennsylvania, for instance, though her legislature and her city governments have been impure, still generally elects judges of sufficient learning. The scandals of Barnard and Cardozo[15] were due to the fact that the vast and ignorant population of New York was dominated by a gang of professional politicians who neither feared the good citizens nor regarded the bar.

As there are institutions which do not work as well as they theoretically ought, so there are happily others which work better. The sale of offices under the old monarchy of France, the sale of commissions in the English army till 1871, the bribery of electors which in England was once so rife, the sale of advowsons and next presentations to livings which still exists in the Anglican church establishment, were or are all of them indefensible in theory, all mischievous in practice. But none of them did so much harm as a philosophical observer would have predicted, because other causes were mitigating their evils.

As respects recent years, some changes have been for the better, some for the worse. Two states which had vested the appointment of judges in the legislature, like Connecticut, or in the people, like Mississippi, have by constitutional amendments or new constitutions, given it to the governor with the consent of the legislature or of one house thereof.[16] Others have raised the salaries, or lengthened the terms of the judges, or, like New York, have introduced both these reforms. But all the states admitted within that period have vested the choice of judges in the people. Even Kentucky in 1891 could not be induced, in spite of the decline of her bench from its ancient fame, to restore the system of appointment by the executive which had prevailed till 1850, while Georgia and Florida took appointments from legislature or governor to entrust them to popular vote. And Oklahoma, the state whose Constitution of 1907 is a fair indication of Western tendencies, made the judicial term of her highest court only six years. In this point, at least, the tide of democracy which went on rising for so many years, seems, if it has not risen further, yet not to have receded.

[15] The notorious Tweed Ring judges of 1869–71.

[16] In Connecticut the change was made at the instance of the Bar Association of the state, which had seen with regret that the dominant party in the state legislature was placing inferior men on the bench.

A significant evidence of the want of confidence in the state judiciary is afforded by the recent introduction into the Constitutions of Oregon, California, Arizona, Colorado, and Nevada of a provision for applying to the bench the system of recall mentioned in the last preceding chapter. The tendency of such a plan to reduce such independence as judges still retain is evident; and the only serious argument for it is to be found in the fact that in some states there are some few judges fit for nothing but to be recalled. One state, Colorado, also permits the people by a vote to reverse a particular decision, given by a state court, of which they disapprove.

When in a Western state where he finds that some of the judges command little respect, because known to be amenable to influences from powerful politicians, the traveller enquires why the people do not try to secure the independence of the bench by vesting appointments in the governor, or at least by choosing the judges for longer terms and paying them larger salaries, he is told that the masses consider the judges already too likely to be influenced by the corporations, already too liable to show insufficient sympathy for the people. That is no hopeful outlook, for it shows how deep the causes lie which have reduced the efficiency and the dignity of the judiciary. Nevertheless, even in such a state it may be hoped that the conditions which have worked so much evil will ultimately pass away. The American people, though sometimes overbold in their experiments, have a fund of good sense which makes them watchful of results, and will in time lead them to find the remedies which the case requires. It is to be regretted that the particualr remedy which some Western states are now applying does not seem to strike at the root of the disease.

State Finance

Ｔhe financial systems in force in the several states furnish one of the widest and most instructive fields of study that the whole range of American institutions presents to a practical statesman, as well as to a student of comparative politics. It is much to be wished that some person equipped with the necessary special knowledge could survey them with a philosophic eye, and present the results of his survey in a concise form. From such an attempt I am interdicted not only by the want of that special knowledge, but by the compass of the subject, and the difficulty of obtaining in Europe adequate materials. These materials must be sought not so much in the constitutions of the states as in their statutes, and in the reports presented by the various financial officials, and by the special commissions occasionally appointed to investigate the subject or some branch of it. All I can here attempt is to touch on a few of the more salient features of the topic, and to cull from the constitutions some illustrations of the dangers feared and the remedies desired by the people of the states. What I have to say falls under the heads following:

Purposes for which state revenue is required
Forms of taxation
Exemptions from taxation
Methods of collecting taxes
Limitations imposed on the power of taxing
State indebtedness
Restrictions imposed on the borrowing power

I. The budget of a state is seldom large, in proportion to the wealth of its inhabitants, because the chief burden of administration is borne not by the state, but by its subdivisions, the counties, and still more the cities and townships. The chief expenses which a state undertakes in its corporate capacity are (1) the salaries of its officials, executive and judicial, and the incidental expenses of judicial proceedings, such as payments to jurors and witnesses; (2) the state volunteer militia; (3) charitable and other public institutions, such as state lunatic asylums, state universities, agricultural colleges, etc.;[1] (4) grants to schools;[2] (5) state prisons, comparatively few, since the prison is usually supported by the county; (6) state buildings and public works, including, in a few cases, canals; (7) payment of interest on state debts. Of the whole revenue collected in each state under state taxing laws, a comparatively small part is taken by the state itself and applied to state purposes.[3] In 1882 only seven states raised for state purposes a revenue exceeding $2,000,000. In 1905–06 the gross revenue of New York State was $39,000,000 (pop. in 1905, 8,000,000); that of Massachusetts, $10,700,000. These are small sums when compared either with the population and wealth of these states, or with the revenue raised in them by local authorities for local purposes. They are also small in comparison with what is raised by indirect taxation for national purposes.

II. The national government raises its revenue by indirect taxation, and by duties of customs and excise,[4] though it has the power of imposing direct taxes, and used that power freely during the Civil War. In 1894 it imposed an income tax, exempting, however, smaller incomes, but the Supreme Court, by a majority, held this to be unconstitutional.[5] State revenue, on the other hand, arises almost wholly from direct taxation, since the federal

---

[1] The constitutions of Louisiana and Georgia allow state revenue to be applied to the supplying of wooden legs and arms to ex-Confederate soldiers; Mississippi directs pensions to be provided for them or their widows.

[2] All states have set apart for the support of schools, agricultural and mechanical colleges, and other educational or benevolent institutions, often including universities, a considerable fund derived from the sale of Western lands granted for the purpose by the federal government at various times, beginning from 1785, and derived in some cases also from lands appropriated originally by the state itself to these objects. Down to 1911, 96,428,833 acres had been granted by the United States government for educational purpose.

[3] In the state of Connecticut (population in 1910, about 1,114,756) the total revenue raised by taxation in 1908 was $15,324,873.25 which was collected by and for the following authorities and purposes:

The state	$3,622,002.87
Boroughs	738,422.32
Towns	4,798,213.91
Cities over 25,000 population	5,223,557.55
Smaller cities	942,676.60

[4] Stamp duties were also resorted to during the Civil War and the war with Spain, but at present none are levied by the national government.

[5] In 1913 an amendment to the Constitution (the sixteenth), authorizing Congress to levy an income tax, was passed, and a statute imposing an income tax was enacted.

Constitution forbids the levying of import or export duties by a state, except with the consent of Congress, and directs the produce of any such duties as Congress may permit to be paid into the federal treasury. The chief tax is in every state a property tax, based on a valuation of property, and generally of all property, real and personal, within the taxing jurisdiction.

The valuation is made by officials called appraisers or assessors, appointed by the local communities, though under general state laws.[6] It is their duty to put a value on all taxable property; that is, speaking generally, on all property of whatever nature which they can discover or trace within the area of their authority. As the contribution, to the revenues of the state or county, leviable within that area, is proportioned to the amount and value of taxable property situate within it, the local assessors have, equally with the property owners, an obvious motive for valuing on a low scale, for by doing so they relieve their community of part of its burden. The state accordingly strives in diverse ways to check and correct them, sometimes by creating what is called a board of equalization, which compares and revises the valuations made by the various local officers, with the aim of having taxable property in each locality equally and fairly valued, and made thereby to bear its due share of public burdens. Similarly a county has often an equalization board to supervise and adjust the valuations of the towns and cities within its limits. However, the existence of such boards does not overcome the difficulty of securing a really equal valuation, and the honest county or town which puts its property at a fair value suffers by paying more than its share. Valuations are generally made at a figure much below the true worth of property. In Connecticut, for instance, the law directs the market price to be the basis, but real estate is valued only at from one-third to two-thirds thereof.[7] Indeed one hears everywhere in America complaints of inequalities arising from the varying scales on which valuers proceed.[8]

[6] The account in the text does not, of course, claim to be true in all particulars for every state, but only to represent the general usage.

[7] The special commission on taxation in Connecticut, in their recent singularly clear and interesting report of 1887, observe: "One great defect in the practical execution of our tax laws consists in inequalities of assessment and valuation. This shows itself especially as between the different towns. . . . It is notorious that in few, if any, towns do the assessors value real estate at what they think it is fairly worth. On the contrary, they generally first make this appraisal of its actual value, and then put it in the list at a certain proportion of such appraisal, varying from 33⅓ to 75 per cent. Similar reductions are made in valuing personal property, though with less uniformity, and so perhaps with more injustice" (p. 8). "Household furniture above $500 in value constitutes an item of only $9,500 in one of our cities, while a neighbouring town of not more than half the population returns $12,900" (p. 16).

[8] In California much agitation arose in 1909 over the question whether the valuations made in and around Los Angeles in the southern part of the state had been unduly low as compared with those in the more northerly parts.

A still more serious evil is the fact that so large a part of taxable property escapes taxation. Lands and houses cannot be concealed; cattle and furniture can be discovered by a zealous tax officer. But a great part, often far the largest part of a rich man's wealth, consists in what the Americans call "intangible property," notes, bonds, book debts, and Western mortgages.[9] At this it is practically impossible to get, except through the declaration of the owner; and though the owner is required to present his declaration of taxable property upon oath, he is apt to omit this kind of property. The Connecticut commissioners report that

> the proportion of these intangible securities to other taxable property has steadily declined from year to year. In 1855 it was nearly 10 per cent of the whole, in 1865 about 7½ per cent, in 1875 a little over 5 per cent, and in 1885 about 3¾ per cent. Yet during the generation covered by these statistics the amount of State railroad and municipal bonds, and of Western mortgage loans has very greatly increased, and our citizens have, in every town in the State, invested large sums in them. Why then do so few get into the tax list? The terms of the law are plain, and the penalties for its infringement are probably as stringent as the people will bear. . . . The truth is that no system of tax laws can ever reach directly the great mass of intangible property. It is not to be seen, and its possession, if not voluntarily disclosed, can in most cases be only the subject of conjecture. The people also in a free government are accustomed to reason for themselves as to the justice and validity of the laws, and too apt to give themselves the benefit of the doubt when they have in any way the power to construe it for themselves. Such a power is practically given in the form of oath used in connection with our tax lists, since it refers only to such property of the parties giving them in as is taxable according to their best knowledge, remembrance, or belief. The man who does not believe that a western farm loan or foreign railroad bond (i.e., bond of a company outside the state) ought to be taxed, is too often ready to swear that to the best of his belief it is not liable to taxation. . . . As the law stands, it may be a burden on the conscience of many, but it is a burden on the property of few, not because there are few who ought to pay, but because there are few who can be made to pay. Bonds and notes held by an individual are for the most part concealed from the assessors, nor do they in most towns make much effort to ascertain their existence.[10] The result is that a few towns, a few

---

[9] The difficulty does not arise with stock or shares even when held in a company outside a state, because all states now tax corporations or companies within their jurisdiction, and the principle is generally (though not universally) adopted, that where stocks in a corporation outside the state have been so taxed, they shall not be again taxed in the hand of the holder of the stock, who may reside within the state. State laws and tax assessors can in each state succeed in reaching the property of the corporation itself.

[10] "A person, formerly assessor in one of our leading cities, reported that he had made efforts when in office to get this kind of property into the 'grand list,' and succeeded during his last two years in finding out and adding over $200,000 of it; but he adds, 'That may have had something to do

estates, and a few persons of a high sense of honesty, bear the entire weight of the tax. Such has been the universal result of similar laws elsewhere.

A comparison of the tax lists with the probate records convinced the commissioners that, whereas in 1884 more than a third of the whole personal property assessed in the state of Connecticut escaped taxes, the proportion not reached by taxation was in 1886 much greater; and induced them to recommend that "all the items of intangible property ought to be struck out of the tax list." The probate inventories of the estates of deceased persons, and the last returns made to the tax assessors by those persons, "show, to speak of it mildly, few points of contact." Connecticut is a commonwealth in most respects above the average. In every part of the country one hears exactly the same.[11] The tax returns sent in are rarely truthful; and not only does a very large percentage of property escape its lawful burdens, but "the demoralization of the public conscience by the frequent administration of oaths, so often taken only to be disregarded, is an evil of the greatest magnitude. Almost any change would seem to be an improvement."[12]

---

with my defeat when election came around.' " So in West Virginia when an assessor objecting to a merchant's declaration threatened to swear the merchant, the latter replied, "If you swear me, I'll vote against you next time."

[11] The West Virginian tax commission, in 1884, says, "At present all taxes from invisible property come from a few conspicuously conscientious citizens, from widows, executors, and from guardians of the insane and infants; in fact, it is a comparatively rare thing to find a shrewd trader who gives in any considerable amount of notes, stocks, or money. The truth is, things have come to such a condition in West Virginia that, as regards paying taxes on this kind of property, it is almost as voluntary and is considered pretty much in the same light as donations to the neighbourhood church or Sunday school." Reports of commissioners in several other states are to the same effect. See, especially, the Report of the Tax Commission of Baltimore, 1886; and the supplementary report of one member of the Maryland Tax Commission, Mr. Richard T. Ely, in which much instructive evidence as to the failure in various states of the efforts made to tax intangible property has been collected and set forth (Baltimore, 1888). A Boston commission reported, in 1891, in favour of taxing real estate only; arguing that under the laws of Massachusetts taxing personalty, much property was really twice taxed. Similarly a New York commission in 1906.

[12] Judge Foster, in the case of *Kirtland* v. *Hotchkiss*, 42 Conn. Rep., p. 449. So Mr. David A. Wells, in his report as Special Tax Commissioner to the New York legislature, says: "Oaths as a matter of restraint or as a guarantee of truth in respect to official statements have in great measure ceased to be effectual; or in other words, perjury, direct or constructive, has become so common as to almost cease to occasion notice. This is the all but unanimous testimony of officials who have of late had extensive experience in the administration of both the national and State revenue laws."

Professor E. R. A. Seligman, in a valuable article in the *Political Science Quarterly* for March 1890, sums up the case against a property tax as follows:

"The property tax of today, because of its attempt to tax intangible as well as tangible things, sins against the cardinal rules of uniformity, of equality, and of universality of taxation. It puts a premium on dishonesty and debauches the public conscience. It reduces deception to a system

There is probably not a state in the Union of which the same thing might not be said. In Ohio, for instance, the governor remarks in a special message of April 1887:

"The great majority of the personal property of this State is not returned, but entirely and fraudulently withheld from taxation. The idea seems largely to prevail that there is injustice and inequality in taxation, and that there is no harm in cheating the State, although to do so a false return must be made and perjury committed. This offence against the State and good morals is too frequently committed by men of wealth and reputed high character, and of corresponding position in society."

In New York there was a shrinkage in the valuation of personalty from 1871 to 1884 of $107,184,371, and in 1888 personalty paid only 10 per cent, realty 90 per cent, of the state taxation. In 1908 realty was valued at $8,553,298,187 and personalty at $620,268,058. Personalty paid only 6¾ per cent of the state taxation, realty 93½ per cent. In California personal property was assessed at $220,000,000 in 1872, and at $251,000,000 in 1902, while in the same thirty years real estate rose from $417,000,000 to $974,000,000.

I have dwelt upon these facts, not only because they illustrate the difficulties inherent in a property tax, difficulties of course greater where such independent taxing authorities as the several states are close together, but also because they help to explain the occasional bitterness of feeling among the American farmers as well as the masses against capitalists, much of whose accumulated wealth escapes taxation, while the farmer who owns his land, as well as the working man who puts his savings into the house he lives in, is assessed and taxed upon this visible property. We may, in fact, say of most states, that under the present system of taxation the larger is the city the smaller is the proportion of personalty reached by taxation (since concealment is easier in large communities), and the richer a man is the smaller in proportion to his property is the contribution he pays to the state.[13] Add to this that the rich man bears less, in proportion to his income, of the burden of indirect taxation, since the protective tariff raises the price not merely of luxuries but of all commodities, except some kinds of food.[14]

---

and makes a science of knavery. It presses hardest on those least able to pay. It imposes double taxation on one man and grants entire immunity to the next."

[13] In Iowa the state auditor reported that "the class of property that escapes taxation most is that which pays the largest dividend" and in Kentucky that "the property of the small owner is as a rule valued by a far higher standard than that of his wealthy neighbour."

[14] An experienced Massachusetts publicist writes to me apropos of the passage in the text: "If one State compels a man to make a full declaration of his personal property for taxation and another does not there will be a tendency for capital to flow from the former to the latter. In Vermont,

Besides the property tax, which is the main source of revenue, the states often levy taxes on particular trades or occupations,[15] sometimes in the form of a licence tax, taxes on franchises enjoyed by a corporation, taxes on railroad stock, or (in a few states) taxes on collateral inheritances. Comparatively little resort has hitherto been had to the so-called "death-duties," i.e., probate, legacy, and succession duties, nor is much use made of an income tax. Nine states, however, authorize it, and two (South Carolina and Oklahoma) allow it to be graduated. New York taxes stock exchange transactions. As regards poll taxes there is much variety of practice. A few state constitutions (e.g., Ohio) forbid such an impost, as "grievous and oppressive"; others direct it to be imposed, or allow the legislature to impose it, while about one-half do not mention it. Where it exists, there is sometimes a direction that it shall be applied to schools or some other specified useful purpose, such as poor relief, so as to give the poor, who perhaps pay no other direct tax, a sense of their duty to contribute

for instance, a law has been passed requiring every person under penalty to make sworn returns of his moveable property, and the result is that capital seems to be leaving the State.

"In New York the law taxes personal property, but if a person makes no return the assessors are instructed to 'doom' him according to the best of their knowledge and belief; and the amount becomes a matter of 'trade.' Returns are practically made only by trustees and corporations, not by capitalists. It is a case of bad law tempered by violation.

"In Massachusetts the practice in each town depends mainly upon the assessors. In Boston the chief office having resolved to let no one escape, has for twenty years gone on increasing the assessment each year till the victim makes a return. At first, men had some scruple about leaving the city before 1st May (the date of residence when taxes are assessed), but these were soon overcome, and now nearly all the capitalists have country places where they retire at a still inclement season, and are received with open arms by the local assessors, who accept just what they choose to pay, while their political influence, their taxes, and their public donations are lost to the city. Occasionally the assessors in a country town take it into their heads to apply the screw after the fashion of the city authority, and then there is a fine turmoil. As the rich men generally live in one quarter of the (country) town, the next step is to apply to the legislature to get the town divided, and the vicinity of Boston is thus being gradually cut up into small pieces."

[15] North Carolina empowers its legislature to tax all trades, professions, and franchises. Arkansas in 1868 (art. X, § 17) directed its general assembly to "tax all privileges, pursuits, and occupations that are of no real use to society," adding that all others shall be exempt. But having apparently found it hard to determine which occupations are useless, she dropped the direction in her Constitution of 1874, and now merely empowers the taxation of "hawkers, pedlers, ferries, exhibitions, and privileges."

The persons or things on whom licence taxes or occupation taxes may be imposed are the following, some being mentioned in one state constitution, some in another: Pedlers, hawkers, auctioneers, brokers, pawnbrokers, merchants, commission merchants, "persons selling by sample," showmen, jugglers, innkeepers, toll bridges, ferries, telegraphs, express agents (i.e., parcels' delivery), grocery keepers, liquor dealers, insurance, vendors of patents, persons or corporations using franchises or privileges, banks, railroads, destructive domestic animals, dealers in "options" or "futures."

to public objects, and especially to those in whose benefits they directly share. The amount of a poll tax is always small, $1 to $3—North Dakota allows $4. Sometimes (as in Tennessee) the payment of it is made a prerequisite to the exercise of the electoral franchise. It is scarcely ever imposed on women or minors.

In some states "foreign" corporations, i.e., those chartered by or domiciled in another state, are taxed more heavily than domestic corporations. The laws of the states differ widely in their provisions regarding the incorporation of companies.

Instances are beginning to appear of a progressive inheritance duty. Two states, Minnesota and Oklahoma, authorize it; and Oregon enacted (in 1909) such an impost which reaches 6 per cent for estates exceeding $50,000. California in her famous Constitution of 1879 attempted to tax the same property twice over.

There is always a desire to hit incorporated companies, especially banks and railroads.[16] The newer constitutions often direct the legislature to see that such undertakings are duly taxed, sometimes forbidding it ever to deprive itself of the power of taxing any corporation, doubtless from the fear that these powerful bodies may purchase from a pliant legislature exemption from civic burdens. The methods, however, of taxing corporations vary greatly from state to state, and are at present in a chaotic condition.

III. In most states, certain descriptions of property are exempted from taxation, as for instance, the buildings or other property of the state, or of any local community, burying grounds, schools and universities, educational, charitable, scientific, literary, or agricultural institutions or societies, public libraries, churches and other buildings or property used for religious purposes, cemeteries, household furniture, farming implements, deposits in savings banks. Often too it is provided that the owner of personal property below a certain figure shall not pay taxes on it, and occasionally ministers of religion are allowed a certain sum (as for instance in New York, $1,500) free from taxation.

No state can tax any bonds, debt certificates, or other securities issued by, or under the authority of, the federal government, including the circulating notes commonly called "greenbacks." This has been held to be the law on the construction of the federal Constitution, and has been so declared in a statute of Congress. Many intricate questions have arisen on

---

[16] As to banks, which were an object of as much popular dislike in the middle of last century, as railroads subsequently became, see Ohio Constitution of 1851, art. XII, § 3.

this doctrine; which, moreover, introduces an element of difficulty into state taxation, because persons desiring to escape taxation are apt to turn their property into these exempted forms just before they make their tax returns.

IV. Some of the state taxes, such, for instance, as licence taxes, or a tax on corporations, are directly levied by and paid to the state officials. But others, and particularly the property tax, which forms so large a source of revenue, are collected by the local authorities. The state having determined what income it needs, apportions this sum among the counties, or in New England, sometimes directly among the towns, in proportion to their paying capacity, that is, to the value of the property situate within them.[17] So similarly the counties apportion not only what they have to pay to the state, but also the sum they have to raise for county purposes, among the cities and townships within their area, in proportion to the value of their taxable property. Thus, when the township or city authorities assess and collect taxes from the individual citizen, they collect at one and the same time three distinct sets of taxes, the state tax, the county tax, and the city or township tax. Retaining the latter for local purposes,[18] they hand on the two former to the county authorities, who in turn retain the county tax, handing on to the state what it requires. Thus trouble and expense are saved in the process of collecting, and the citizen sees in one tax paper all he has to pay.

V. Some states, taught by their sad experience of reckless legislatures, limit by their constitutions the amount of taxation which may be raised for state purposes in any one year. Thus Texas in 1876 forbade the state property tax to exceed one-half per cent on the valuation (exclusive of the sum needed to pay interest on the state debt), and has since reduced the percentage to .35. North Dakota (1889) fixed .4, Montana .3, as the percentage. A similar provision exists in Missouri, and in some other Southern or Western states. We shall see presently that this method of restriction has been more extensively applied to cities and other subordinate communities. Sometimes we find directions that no greater revenue shall be raised than the current needs of the state require, a rule which Congress would have done well to observe, seeing that a surplus revenue invites reckless expenditure and gives opportunity for legislative jobbery.[19]

It may be thought that the self-interest of the people is sufficient to secure

---

[17] As ascertained by the assessors and board of equalization.

[18] Sometimes, however, the town or township in its corporate capacity pays the state its share of the state tax, instead of collecting it specifically from individual citizens.

[19] Sir T. More in his *Utopia* mentions with approval a law of the Macarians forbidding the king to have ever more than £1,000 in the public treasury.

economy and limit taxation. But, apart from the danger of a corrupt legislature, if is often remarked that as in many states a large proportion of the voters do not pay state taxes, the power of imposing burdens lies largely in the hands of persons who have no direct interest, and suppose themselves to have no interest at all, in keeping down taxes which they do not pay. So far, however, as state finance is concerned, this has been no serious source of mischief, and more must be attributed to the absence of efficient control over expenditure,[20] and to the fact that (as in Congress) the committee which reports on appropriations of the revenue is distinct from that which deals with the raising of revenue by taxation.

Another illustration of the tendency to restrict the improvidence of representatives is furnished by the prohibitions in many constitutions to pass bills appropriating moneys to any private individual or corporation, or to authorize the payment of claims against the state arising under any contract not strictly and legally binding, or to release the claims which the state may have against railroads or other corporations. One feels, in reading these multiform provisions, as if the legislature was a rabbit seeking to issue from its burrow to ravage the crops wherever it could, and the people of the state were obliged to close every exit, because they could not otherwise restrain its inveterate propensity to mischief.

VI. Nothing in the financial system of the states better deserves attention than the history of the state debts, their portentous growth, and the efforts made, when the people had taken fright, to reduce their amount, and to set limits to them in the future.

In the first decades of the nineteenth century when those rich and ample Western lands which now form the states of Ohio, Indiana, Illinois, Michigan, and Missouri were being opened up and settled, and again, some time later, when the railway system was in the first freshness of its marvellous extension, and was filling up the lands along the Mississippi at an increasingly rapid rate, everyone was full of hope; and states, counties, and cities, not less than individual men, threw themselves eagerly into the work of developing the resources which lay around them. The states, as well as these minor communities, set to work to make roads and canals and railways; they promoted or took stock in trading companies, they started or subsidized banks, they embarked in, or pledged their credit for, a hundred enterprises which they were ill-fitted to conduct or supervise. Some undertakings failed

---

[20] Virginia in her Constitution of 1902 creates a standing Committee of Audit composed of five members of the Assembly, who have the duty of inspecting all the financial officers of the state and are to report to the governor.

lamentably, while in others the profits were grasped by private speculators, and the burden left with the public body. State indebtedness, which in 1825 (when there were twenty-four states) stood at an aggregate over the whole Union of $12,790,728 (£2,500,000), had in 1842 reached $203,777,916,[21] in 1870 $352,866,898.

A part of the increase in the years between 1842 and 1870 was due to loans contracted for the raising and equipping of troops by many Northern states to serve in the Civil War, the intention being to obtain ultimate reimbursement from the national treasury. There was also a good deal, in the way of executed works, to show for the money borrowed and expended, and the states (in 1870 thirty-seven in number) had grown vastly in taxable property. Nevertheless the huge and increasing total startled the people, and, as everybody knows, some states repudiated their debts. The diminution in the total indebtedness of 1880, which stood at $290,326,643, and was the indebtedness of thirty-eight states and three Territories, is partly due to this repudiation. In 1890 the total (then of forty-four states and two Territories) stood at $223,107,883, and in 1902 it was (for the then forty-five states, omitting minor civil divisions) $235,000,000. Even after the growth of state debts had been checked (in the way to be presently mentioned), minor communities, towns, counties, but above all, cities trod in the same path, the old temptations recurring, and the risks seeming smaller because a municipality had a more direct and close interest than a state in seeing that its money or credit was well applied. Municipal indebtedness has advanced, especially in the larger cities, at a dangerously swift rate. Of the state and county debt much the largest part had been incurred for, or in connection with, so-called "internal improvements"; but of the city debt, though a part was due to the bounties given to volunteers in the Civil War, much must be set down to extremely lax and wasteful administration, and much more to mere stealing, practised by methods to be hereafter explained, but facilitated by the habit of subsidizing, or taking shares in, corporate enterprises which had excited the hopes of the citizens.

VII. The disease spread till it terrified the patient, and a remedy was found in the insertion in the constitutions of provisions limiting the borrowing powers of state legislatures. Fortunately the evil had been perceived in time to enable the newest states to profit by the experience of their predecessors. For the last half century, whenever a state has enacted a constitution, it has

---

[21] In 1838 it was estimated that of the total debt of the states, then calculated at $170,800,000, $60,200,000 had been incurred for canals, $42,800,000 for railroads, and $52,600,000 for banking.

inserted sections restricting the borrowing powers of states and local bodies, and often also providing for the discharge of existing liabilities. Not only the passing of bills for raising a state loan has been surrounded with special safeguards, such as the requirement of a two-thirds majority in each house of the legislature; not only have there been prohibitions ever to borrow money for, or even to undertake, internal improvements (a fertile source of jobbery and waste, as the experience of Congress shows); and not only also almost invariably a provision that whenever a debt is contracted the same act shall create a sinking fund for paying it off within a few years, but in most constitutions the total amount of the debt was limited, and limited to a sum beautifully small in proportion to the population and resources of the state.[22] Thus Wisconsin fixes its maximum at $200,000 (£40,000); Minnesota and Iowa at $250,000, Ohio at $750,000; Wyoming at one and Idaho at one and one-half per cent of the assessed value of taxable property; Nebraska and Montana at $10,000; prudent Oregon at $50,000; and the great and wealthy state of Pennsylvania, with a population now exceeding 5,300,000 (Constitution of 1873, art. IX, § 4), at $1,000,000.[23]

In four-fifths of the states, including all those with recent constitutions, the legislature is forbidden to "give or lend the credit of the State in aid of any person, association, or corporation, whether municipal or other, or to pledge the credit of the State in any manner whatsoever for the payment of the liabilities present or prospective of any individual association, municipal, or other corporation,"[24] as also to take stock in a corporation, or otherwise embark in any gainful enterprise. Many constitutions also forbid the assumption by the state of the debts of any individual or municipal corporation.

The care of the people for their financial freedom and safety extends even to local bodies. Many of the recent constitutions limit, or direct the legislature to limit, the borrowing powers of counties, cities, or towns, sometimes even of incorporated school districts, to a sum not exceeding a certain percentage

[22] Debts incurred for the purpose of suppressing insurrection or repelling invasion are excepted from these limitations.

[23] New York (Constitution of 1846, art. VII, §§ 10–12) also names a million of dollars as the maximum, but permits laws to be passed raising loans for "some single work or object," provided that a tax is at the same time enacted sufficient to pay off this debt in eighteen years; and that any such law has been directly submitted to the people and approved by them at an election. Similar provisions permitting increase by special popular vote are frequent in recent constitutions.

[24] Constitution of Missouri of 1875 (art. IV, § 45), a constitution whose provisions on financial matters and restrictions on the legislature are copious and instructive. Similar words occur in nearly all Western and Southern, as well as in some of the more recent Eastern, constitutions.

on the assessed value of the taxable property within the area in question. This percentage is usually 5 per cent; sometimes, however, 7 per cent; or even (New York, Amendment of 1884) 10 per cent. Sometimes also the amount of the tax leviable by a local authority in any year is restricted to a definite sum—for instance, to one-half per cent on the valuation.[25] And in nearly all the states, cities, counties, or other local incorporated authorities are forbidden to pledge their credit for, or undertake the liabilities of, or take stock in, or otherwise give aid to, any undertaking or company. Sometimes this prohibition is absolute; sometimes it is made subject to certain conditions, and may be avoided by their observance. For instance, there are states in which the people of a city can, by special vote, carried by a two-thirds majority, or a three-fifths majority, or (in Colorado) by a bare majority of the taxpayers, authorize the contracting of a debt which the municipality could not incur by its ordinary organs of government. Sometimes there is a direction that any municipality creating a debt must at the same time provide for its extinction by a sinking fund. Sometimes the restrictions imposed apply only to a particular class of undertakings—e.g., banks or railroads. The differences between state and state are endless; but everywhere the tendency is to make the protection against local indebtedness and municipal extravagance more and more strict; nor will anyone who knows these local authorities, and the temptations, both good and bad, to which they are exposed, complain of the strictness.[26]

Cases, of course, occur in which a restriction on the taxing power or borrowing power of a municipality is found inconvenient, because a costly public improvement is rendered more costly if it has to be done piecemeal. The corporation of Brooklyn was thus prevented from making all at once a great street which would have been a boon to the city, and more money had to be spent in buying up the land for it bit by bit. But the evils which have followed in America from the immixture both of states and of cities in enterprises of a public nature, and the abuses incident to an unlimited power of undertaking improvements, have been so great as to make people willing to bear with the occasional inconveniences which are inseparable from restriction.

"A catalogue of these evils would include the squandering of the public domain; the enrichment of schemers whose policy it has been first to obtain all they can

---

[25] See the elaborate provisions of the Constitution of Missouri of 1875 (art. X, § 11), and the Constitution of Montana, 1889 (art. XII, § 9).

[26] A specimen of the provisions restricting borrowing powers will be found in the extracts from the Constitution of Oklahoma in the Appendix.

by fair promises, and then avoid, as far and as long as possible, the fulfilment of the promises; the corruption of legislation; the loss of State credit; great public debts recklessly contracted for; moneys often recklessly expended; public discontent, because the enterprises fostered from the public treasury, and on the pretence of public benefit, are not believed to be managed in the public interest; and finally, great financial panic, collapse, and disaster."[27]

The provisions above described have had the effect of steadily reducing the amount of state and county debts, although the wealth of the country makes rapid strides. This reduction was between 1870 and 1880, about 25 per cent in the case of state debts, and in that of county, town, and school district debts about 8 per cent. In the decade ending with 1890 the reduction in state debts was $67,218,760 (nearly half of this, however, due to scaling down of debts of Southern states); but county debts rose from $124,105,027 to $145,048,045, and the school district debts from $17,580,682 to $36,701,948. In cities there was within the decade 1870–80, not only no reduction, but an increase of over 100 per cent, possibly as much as 130 per cent. In 1890 the total debt, less sinking fund, of municipalities exceeding 4,000 inhabitants was returned at $646,507,644 against $623,784,262 in 1880, but owing to the growth of population the amount per capita which was $45.06 in 1880, had fallen in 1890 to $31.69. In 1902, while the total state debt was, as above mentioned, $235,000,000, that of counties and minor civil divisions was $1,630,000,000.

This striking difference between the cities and the states may be explained in several ways. One is that cities cannot repudiate, while sovereign states can and do.[28] Another may be found in the later introduction into state constitutions of restrictions on the borrowing powers of municipalities. But the chief cause is to be found in the conditions of the government of great cities, where the wealth of the community is largest, and is also most at the disposal of a multitude of ignorant voters. Several of the greatest cities lie in states which did not till recently, or have not even now, imposed adequate restrictions on the borrowing power of city councils. Now city councils, as we shall see presently, are not only incapable administrators, but are prone to such public improvements as present opportunities for speculation, for jobbery, and possibly even for wholesale embezzlement.

---

[27] Cooley, *Constit. Limit.*, p. 266.

[28] In some parts of New England the city, town, or other municipal debt is also the personal debt of every inhabitant, and is therefore an excellent security.

The Working of State Governments

The difficulty I have already remarked of explaining to Europeans the nature of an American state, viz., that there is in Europe nothing similar to it, recurs when we come to inquire how the organs of government which have been described play into one another in practice. To say that a state is something lower than the nation but greater than a municipality, is to say what is obvious, but not instructive; for the peculiarity of the state is that it combines some of the features which are to Europeans characteristic of a nation and a nation only, with others that belong to a municipality.

The state seems great or small according to the point of view from which one regards it. It is vast if one regards the sphere of its action and the completeness of its control in that sphere, which includes the maintenance of law and order, nearly the whole field of civil and criminal jurisprudence, the supervision of all local governments, an unlimited power of taxation. But if we ask, Who are the persons that manage this great machine of government; how much interest do the citizens take in it; how much reverence do they feel for it? the ample proportions we had admired begin to dwindle, for the persons turn out to be insignificant, and the interest of the people to have steadily declined. The powers of state authorities are powers like those of a European parliament; but they are wielded by men most of whom are less distinguished and less respected by their fellows than are those who fill the city councils of Manchester or Cologne. Several states exceed in area and population some ancient European monarchies. But their annals may not have been illumined by a single striking event or brilliant personality.

A further difficulty in describing how a state government works arises from the endless differences of detail between the several states. The organic frame of government is similar in all; but its functional activities vary according to the temper and habits, the ideas, education, and traditions of the inhabitants of the state. A European naturally says, "Select a typical state, and describe that to us." But there is no such thing as a typical state. Massachusetts or Connecticut is a fair sample of New England, Minnesota or Iowa of the Northwest; Georgia or Alabama shows the evils, accompanied no doubt by great recuperative power, that still vex the South; New York and Illinois the contrast between the tendencies of an ignorant city mob and the steady-going farmers of the rural counties. But to take any one of these states as a type, asking the reader to assume what is said of it to apply equally to the other forty-seven commonwealths, would land us in inextricable confusions. I must therefore be content to speak quite generally, emphasizing those points in which the colour and tendencies of state governments are much the same over the whole Union, and begging the European reader to remember that illustrations drawn, as they must be drawn, from some particular state, will not necessarily be true of every other state government, because its life may go on under different conditions.

The state governments, as has been observed already, bear a family likeness to the national or federal government, a likeness due not only to the fact that the latter was largely modelled after the systems of the old thirteen states, but also to the influence which the federal Constitution has exerted ever since 1789 on those who have been drafting or amending state constitutions. Thus the federal Constitution has been both child and parent. Where the state constitutions differ from the federal, they invariably differ in being more democratic. It still expresses the doctrines of 1787. They express the views of later days, when democratic ideas have been more rampant, and men less cautious than the sages of the Philadelphia Convention have given legal form to popular beliefs. This difference, which appears not only in the mode of appointing judges, but in the shorter terms which the states allow to their officials and senators, comes out most clearly in the relations established between the legislative and the executive powers. The national executive, though disjoined from the legislature in a way strange to Europeans, is nevertheless all of a piece. The president is supreme; his ministers are his subordinates, chosen by him from among his political associates. They act under his orders; he is responsible for their conduct. But in the states there is nothing even distantly resembling a cabinet. The chief executive officials are directly elected by the people. They hold by a title independent of the state governor. They are not, except so far as some special statute may provide, subject to his directions, and he is not responsible for their conduct, since he cannot control it. As the governor need not belong to the party for the time being dominant in the legislature, so the other state officials need not be of the same party as the governor.[1] They may even have been elected at a different time, or for a longer period.

A European, who studies the mechanism of state government—very few Europeans so far having studied it—is at first puzzled by a system which contradicts his preconceived notions. "How," he asks, "can such machinery work? One can understand the scheme under which a legislature rules through officers whom it has, whether legally or practically, chosen and keeps in power. One can even understand a scheme in which the executive, while independent of the legislature, consists of persons acting in unison, under a head directly responsible to the people. But will not a scheme, in which the executive officers are all independent of one another, yet not subject to the legislature, want every condition needed for harmonious and efficient action? They obey nobody. They are responsible to nobody, except a people which only exists in concrete activity for one election day every two years, when it is dropping papers into the ballot box. Such a system seems the negation of a system, and more akin to chaos."

In his attempts to penetrate this mystery, our European receives little help from his usually helpful American friends, simply because they do not understand his difficulty. Light dawns on him when he perceives that the executive business of a state is such as not to need any policy, in the European sense, and therefore no harmony of view or purpose among those who manage it. Everything in the nature of state policy belongs to the legislature, and to the legislature alone.

Compare the federal president with the state governor. The former has foreign policy to deal with, the latter has none. The former has a vast patronage, the latter has scarcely any. The former has the command of the army and navy, the latter has only that of the militia, insignificant in ordinary times. The former has a post office, but there is no state postal service. Little remains to the governor except his veto, which is not so much an executive as a legislative function; the duty of maintaining order, which becomes important only when insurrection or riot breaks out; and the almost mechanical duty of representing the state for various matters of routine, such as demanding from other states the extradition of offenders, issuing writs for the election of congressmen or of the state legislature, receiving the reports of the various state officials. These officials, even the highest of

---

[1] Thus Massachusetts sometimes elects a Democratic governor, but her other state officials usually come from the Republican party, and she has for a very long time returned a Republican majority to the legislature. So in 1908, Ohio elected a Democratic governor while remaining otherwise Republican.

them who correspond to the cabinet ministers in the national government, are either mere clerks, performing work, such as that of receiving and paying out state moneys, strictly defined by statute, and usually checked by other officials, or else are in the nature of commissioners of inquiry, who may inspect and report, but can take no independent action of importance. Policy does not lie within their province; even in executive details their discretion is confined within narrow limits. They have, no doubt, from the governor downwards, opportunities for jobbing and malversation; but even the less scrupulous are restrained from using these opportunities by the fear of some investigating committee of the legislature, with possible impeachment or criminal prosecution as a consequence of its report. Holding for terms which seldom exceed two or three years, they feel the insecurity of their position; but the desire to earn reelection by the able and conscientious discharge of their functions, is a less effective motive than it would be if the practice of reelecting competent men were more frequent. Unfortunately here, as in Congress, the tradition of many states is, that when a man has enjoyed an office, however well he may have served the public, someone else ought to have the next turn.

The reason, therefore, why the system I have sketched rubs along in the several states is, that the executive has little to do, and comparatively small sums to handle. The further reason why it has so little to do is twofold. Local government is so fully developed that many functions, which in Europe would devolve on a central authority, are in all American states left to the county, or the city, or the township, or the school district. These minor divisions narrow the province of the state, just as the state narrows the province of the central government. And the other reason is, that legislation has in the several states pushed itself to the farthest limits, and so encroached on subjects which European legislatures would leave to the executive, that executive discretion is extinct, and the officers are the mere hands of the legislative brain, which directs them by statutes drawn with extreme minuteness, carefully specifies the purposes to which each money grant is to be applied, and supervises them by inquisitorial committees.

It is a natural consequence of these arrangements that state office carries little either of dignity or of power. A place is valued chiefly for its salary, or for such opportunities of obliging friends or securing commissions on contracts as it may present, though in the greatest states the post of attorney general or comptroller is often sought by able men. A state governor, however, has never been a nonentity and (as already observed) his post seems latterly to have been gaining importance. In more than one state a sort of perfume from the old days lingers round the office, as in Massachusetts, where the traditions of last century were renewed by the eminent man who occupied the chair of the commonwealth during the War of Secession and did much to stimulate and direct the patriotism of its citizens. Though no one would nowadays, like Mr. Jay in 1795, exchange the chief justiceship of the United States for the governorship of his state, a cabinet minister has been known to quit his place in order to obtain the governorship of a great state like New York. In all states, the governor, as the highest official and the depositary of state authority, may at any moment become the pivot on whose action public order turns. In the Pennsylvania riots of 1877 it was the accidental absence of the governor on a tour in the West which enabled the forces of sedition to gather strength. During the more recent disturbances which large strikes, especially among railway employees, have caused in the West, the prompt action of a governor has preserved or restored tranquillity in more than one state; while the indecision of the governor of an adjoining one has emboldened strikers to stop traffic, or to molest workmen who had been hired to replace them. So in a commercial crisis, like that which swept over the Union in 1837, when the citizens are panic-stricken and the legislature hesitates, much may depend on the initiative of the governor, to whom the eyes of the people naturally turn. His right of suggesting legislative remedies, usually neglected, then becomes significant, and may abridge or increase the difficulties of the community.

It is not, however, as an executive magistrate that a state governor usually makes or mars a reputation, but in his quasi-legislative capacity of agreeing to or vetoing bills passed by the legislature. The merit of a governor is usually tested by the number and the boldness of his vetoes; and a European enjoys, as I did in the state of New York in 1870, the odd spectacle of a governor appealing to the people for reelection on the ground that he had defeated in many and important instances the will of their representatives solemnly expressed in the votes of both houses. That such appeals should be made, and often made successfully, is due not only to the distrust which the people entertain of their legislatures, but also, to their honour be it said, to the respect of the people for courage. They like above all things a strong man; just as English constituencies prefer a candidate who refuses to swallow pledges or be dictated to by cliques.

This view of the governor as a check on the legislature explains why the Americans think it rather a gain than an injury to the state that he should belong to the party which is for the time being in a minority in the legislature. How the phenomenon occurs may be seen by noting the different methods of choice employed. The governor is chosen by a mass vote of all citizens over the state. The representatives are chosen by the same voters, but in districts. Thus one party may have a majority on a gross poll of the whole state, but may find itself in a minority in the larger number of electoral districts. In New York State at one time the mass vote shows a Democratic majority, because the Democrats are overwhelmingly strong in New York City, and some other great centres of population. But in the rural districts and most of the smaller towns the Republican party commands a majority sufficient to enable them to carry most districts. Hence, while the governor is usually a Democrat, the legislature is usually Republican. Little trouble need be feared from the opposition of the two powers, because such issues as divide the parties have scarce any bearing on state affairs. Some good may be hoped, because a governor of the other party is more likely to check or show up the misdeeds of a hostile Senate or Assembly than one who, belonging to the group of men which guides the legislature, has a motive for working with them, and might expect to share any gains they can amass.[2]

Thus we are led back to the legislature, which is normally the strongest force in the states, though sometimes a strong governor can by his influence with the people bend it to his will. Let us see how it gets on without that guidance which an executive ministry supplies to the chambers of every free European country.

As the frame of a state government generally resembles the national government, so a state legislature resembles Congress. In most states, it exaggerates the characteristic defects of Congress. It has fewer able and high-minded men among its members. It has less of recognized leadership. It is surrounded by temptations relatively greater. It is guarded by a less watchful and less interested public opinion. But before we inquire what sort of men fill the legislative halls, let us ask what kinds of business draw them there.

The matter of state legislation may be classified under three heads:

   I. Ordinary private law, i.e., contracts, torts, inheritance, family relations, offences, civil and criminal procedure;

  II. Administrative law, including the regulation of municipal and rural local government, public works, education, the liquor traffic, vaccination, adulteration, charitable and penal establishments, the inspection

---

[2] Sometimes, however, inconvenience arises from the hostility of the state Senate and the governor. On one occasion the Senate of New York persistently refused to confirm the nominations made to certain offices by the governor, with the effect of securing the retention in office long beyond their legal term of several officials, these old officials holding on and drawing their salaries because no new men had been duly appointed to fill their places. The Senate was thought to have behaved ill; but the governor was not trusted and exerted nor deserved to exert any moral authority.

of mines or manufactories, together with the general law of corporations, of railroads, and of labour, together also with taxation, both
state and local, and the management of the public debt;

III. Measures of a local and special nature, such as are called in England
"private bills," i.e., bills for chartering and incorporating gas, water,
canal, tramway, telephone or railway companies, or for conferring
franchises in the nature of monopolies or privileges upon such bodies,
or for altering their constitutions, for incorporating cities and minor
communities and regulating their affairs.

Comparing these three classes of business, between the first and second
of which it is no doubt hard to draw a sharp line, we shall find that bills of
the second class are more numerous than those of the first, bills of the third
more numerous than those of the other two put together. Ordinary private
law, the law which guides or secures us in the everyday relations of life,
and upon which nine-tenths of the suits between man and man are founded,
is not greatly changed from year to year in the American states. Many
Western, and a few Eastern states have made bold experiments in the field
of divorce, others have added new crimes to the statute book and amended
their legal procedure. But commercial law, as well as the law of property
and civil rights in general, remains tolerably stable. People are satisfied
with things as they are, and the influence of the legal profession is exerted
against tinkering. In matters of the second class, which I have called
administrative, because they generally involve the action of the state or of
some of the communities which exist within it, there is more legislative
activity. Every session sees experiments tried in this field, generally with
the result of enlarging the province of government, both by interfering with
the individual citizen and by attempting to do things for him which apparently
he either does not do or does not do well for himself.[3] But the general or
"public" legislation is dwarfed by the "private bill" legislation which forms
the third of our classes. The bills that are merely local or special outnumber
general bills everywhere, and outnumber them enormously in those states
which do not require corporations to be formed under general laws.[4] Such

[3] See Chapter 98 on laissez faire, in Vol. II.

Many of these measures have been prepared by associations outside the legislature, who embody
their wishes in a bill, give it to a member or members, and get it passed, perhaps with scarcely
any debate. Thus not only the labour organizations, such as the Knights of Labour, and the
Grangers (farmers' clubs), but the Women's Christian Temperance Union, the medical profession,
the dentists, the dairymen, get their favourite schemes enacted.

[4] In 1901, of 1,132 acts passed by the legislature of Alabama, only 90 were general laws.

The restrictions imposed on special legislation by the more recent constitutions of Southern and
Western states seem to have done some good. Mr. Dealey (*Our State Constitutions*) observes: "In

special bills are condemned by thoughtful Americans, not only as confusing the general law, but because they furnish, unless closely watched, opportunities for perpetrating jobs, and for inflicting injustice on individuals or localities in the interest of some knot of speculators. They are one of the scandals of the country. But there is a further objection to their abundance in the state legislatures. They are a perennial fountain of corruption. Promoted for pecuniary ends by some incorporated company or group of men proposing to form a company, their passage is secured by intrigue, and by the free expenditure of money which finds its way in large sums to the few influential men who control a state Senate or Assembly, and in smaller sums to those among the rank and file of members who are accessible to these solid arguments, and careless of any others. It is the possibility of making profit in this way out of a seat in the legislature which draws to it not a few men in those states which, like New York, Pennsylvania, or Illinois, offer a promising field for large pecuniary enterprises. Where the carcase is there will the vultures be gathered together. The money power, which is most formidable in the shape of large corporations, chiefly attacks the legislatures of these great states. It is, however, felt in nearly all states.[5] And even where, as is the case in most states, only a small minority of members are open to bribes, the opportunity which these numerous local and special bills offer to a man of making himself important, of obliging his friends, of securing something for his locality, and thereby confirming his local influence, is sufficient to make a seat in the legislature desired chiefly in respect of such bills, and to obscure, in the eyes of most members, the higher functions of general legislation which these assemblies possess. One may apply to these commonwealths, though in a new sense, the famous dictum, *corruptissima republica plurimae leges*.

One form of this special legislation is peculiarly attractive and pernicious. It is the power of dealing by statute with the municipal constitution and actual management of cities. Cities grow so fast that all undertakings

---

all the States, in the years 1904 and 1905, 18,937 laws were passed, 8,362 of which were general. In the same years the (six) New England states whose legislatures are almost unrestricted, passed 3,877, of which 1,162 were general. Six states whose legislatures are fully restricted passed 1,558 laws, of which 1,127 were general. Thus in New England special legislation was 70 per cent of the whole, and in the six restricted States only 28 per cent of the whole."

[5] Efforts have of late years been made to remedy these evils. In the state of New York, for instance, the number of special bills has been reduced by compelling the application of general laws, and useful provisions introduced for bringing all bills to the notice of all members in final form before they come on for final passage (Amendment of 1894 to state constitution). Proposals for appropriations of money are now required to be filed a good while beforehand with the state comptroller and these, tabulated and commented on, are laid before the governor and the legislature.

connected with them are particularly tempting to speculators. City revenues are so large as to offer rich plunder to those who can seize the control of them. The vote which a city casts is so heavy as to throw great power into the hands of those who control it, and enable them to drive a good bargain with the wire-pullers of a legislative chamber. Hence the control exercised by the state legislature over city government is a most important branch of legislative business, a means of power to scheming politicians, of enrichment to greedy ones, and if not of praise to evil-doers, yet certainly of terror to them that do well.[6]

We are now in a position, having seen what the main business of a state legislature is, to inquire what is likely to be the quality of the persons who compose it. The conditions that determine their quality may be said to be the following:

    I. The system of selection by party conventions. As this will be described in subsequent chapters (Part III), I will here say no more than that it prevents the entrance of good men and favours that of bad ones.

   II. The habit of choosing none but a resident in any electoral district to represent that district, a habit which narrows the field of choice, and not only excludes competent men from other parts of the state, but deters able men generally from entering state politics, since he who loses his seat for his own district cannot find his way back to the legislature as member for any other.

  III. The fact that the capital of a state, i.e., the meeting place of the legislature and residence of the chief officials, is usually a small town, at a distance from the most populous city or cities of the state, and therefore a place neither attractive socially nor convenient for businessmen or lawyers, and which, it may be remarked in passing, is more shielded from a vigilant public opinion than is a great city, with its keen and curious press. Pennsylvanians who might be willing to serve in a legislature meeting at Philadelphia are less inclined to attend one at Harrisburg. An eminent citizen of Connecticut observed to me that, whereas everybody in that little state could reach Hartford in a few hours from its farthest corner, a member attending the legislature of Illinois or Wisconsin might often have to quit his home and live during the session at Springfield or Madison, because these capitals are remote from the outer parts of those large commonwealths.

---

[6] This is one reason why in some states the reformers have obtained permission for cities to make their own charters.

He thought this a factor in the comparative excellence of the Connecticut legislature.

IV. The nature of the business that comes before a state legislature. As already explained, by far the largest part of this business excites little popular interest and involves no large political issues.[7] Unimportant it is not. Nothing could well be more important than to repress special legislation, and deliver cities from the fangs of the spoiler. But its importance is not readily apprehended by ordinary people, the mischiefs that have to be checked being spread out over a multitude of bills, most of them individually insignificant, however ruinous in their cumulated potency. Hence, though a public-spirited or ambitious youth may enter a state legislature in order to become known there and work his way upward, a leading politician seldom troubles himself to seek a seat, while the men who combine high character with talent and energy are too much occupied in practising their profession or pushing their business to undertake the dreary task of wrangling over gas and railroad bills in committees, or exerting themselves to win some advantage for the locality that returns them.

I have not mentioned among these depressing conditions the payment of salaries to members, because it makes little difference. It is no doubt an attraction to some of the poorer men, to penurious farmers, or half-starved lawyers. But in attracting them it does not serve to keep out any better men. Probably the sense of public duty would be keener if legislative work was not paid at all. But, looking at the question practically, I doubt whether the discontinuance of salaries would improve the quality of American legislators. The drawbacks to the position which repel the best men, the advantages which attract inferior men, would remain the same as now; and there is nothing absurd in the view that the places of those who might cease to come if they did not get their five dollars a day would be taken by men who would manage to make as large an income in a less respectable way.

After this, it need scarcely be said that the state legislatures are not high-toned bodies. The best seem to be those of some of the New England states,

[7] Recently steps have been taken in some few states to improve the quality of legislation by providing legal aid for members in the drafting of bills and supplying them with information. Wisconsin in its state library department has set an excellent example in the West, and while the New York State library does admirable work in collecting data for legislation, lawyers are retained to do drafting for any member desiring it, and the skilled administrative departments give advice and criticism to those who need it, they are of course at the service of the governor. Commissions are pretty frequently appointed to investigate and report upon questions of special difficulty.

particularly Massachusetts, where the venerable traditions surrounding an ancient commonwealth do something to sustain the dignity of the body and induce good men to enter it. This legislature, called the General Court, is, according to the best authorities, substantially pure, and does its work passably well. Its composition is, however, said to be inferior to that of the General Courts of eighty years ago. Connecticut has a fair Senate, and a tolerable House of Representatives. It is also reported to be reasonably honest, though not free from demagogism. Vermont is pure; New Hampshire, a state where bossism throve and constituencies used to be reproached with bribery, is more open to censure.[8] Next come some of the Northwestern states, where the population, consisting almost entirely of farmers, who own as well as work their land, sends up members who fairly represent its average intelligence, and are little below the level of its average virtue. There are no traditions in such states, and there are already corporations rich enough to corrupt members and be themselves blackmailed. Hence one is prepared to find among the legislators professional politicians of the worst class. But the percentage of such men is small in states like Michigan, Iowa, Minnesota, Wisconsin, Oregon, probably not more than from 5 to 15 per cent, the other members being often ignorant and narrow, but honest and well-intentioned. In Ohio and Indiana the proportion of black sheep may be a little higher, and in some Western states, such as Missouri and Montana, there have now and then been grave scandals.

It is hard to present a general view of the Southern states, both because there are great differences among them, and because they are still in a state of transition, generally, it would seem, transition towards a better state of things. Roughly speaking, their legislatures stand below those of the Northwest, though in most a few men of exceptional ability and standing may be found. Kentucky and Georgia are among the better states, Mississippi and Arkansas are reported as among the less pure. Louisiana, infected by New Orleans, has been deemed the worst.

The lowest place belongs to the states which, posessing the largest cities, have received the largest influx of European immigrants, and have fallen most completely under the control of unscrupulous party managers. New York, Philadelphia, Baltimore, Chicago, Cincinnati, San Francisco, have done their best to poison the legislatures of the states in which they respectively lie by filling these bodies with members of a low type, as well

[8] A lively picture of boss methods as formerly practised in this state may be found in a story called "Coniston," by Mr. Winston Churchill.

as by being themselves the centres of enormous accumulations of capital. They have brought the strongest corrupting force into contact with the weakest and most corruptible material: and there has followed in Pennsylvania and New York such a Witches' Sabbath of jobbing, bribing, thieving, and prostitution of legislative power to private interest as the world has seldom seen. Of course even in these states the majority of the members are not bad men, for the majority come from the rural districts or smaller towns, where honesty and order reign as they do generally in Northern and Western America outside a few large cities. Many of them are farmers or small lawyers, who go up meaning to do right, but fall into the hands of schemers who abuse their inexperience and practise on their ignorance. One of the ablest and most vivacious of the younger generation of American politicians[9] says:

"Where a number of men, many of them poor, some of them unscrupulous, and others elected by constituents too ignorant to hold them to a proper accountability for their actions, are put into a position of great temporary power, where they are called to take action upon questions affecting the welfare of large corporations and wealthy private individuals, the chances for corruption are always great; and that there is much viciousness and political dishonesty, much moral cowardice, and a good deal of actual bribe-taking at Albany, no one who has had practical experience of legislation can doubt. At the same time, I think the good members outnumber the bad. . . . The representatives from the country districts are usually good men, well-to-do farmers, small lawyers, or prosperous store-keepers, and are shrewd, quiet, and honest. They are often narrow-minded, and slow to receive an idea; but they cling to it with the utmost tenacity. For the most part they are native Americans, and those who are not are men who have become completely Americanized in their ways and habits of thought. . . . The worst legislators come from the great cities. They are usually foreigners of little or no education, with exceedingly misty ideas as to morality, and possessed of an ignorance so profound that it could only be called comic were it not for the fact that it has at times such serious effects on our laws. It is their ignorance quite as much as actual viciousness which makes it so difficult to procure the passage of good laws, or to prevent the passage of bad ones; and it is the most irritating of the many elements with which we have to contend in the fight for good government."[10]

The same writer goes on to say that after sitting in three New York

---

[9] Mr. Theodore Roosevelt of New York, from whose instructive article in the *Century Magazine* for April 1885. [This passage was written in 1888.]

[10] Anyone with experience of legislative bodies will agree with the view that ignorance and stupidity cause more trouble than bad intentions, seeing that they are the materials on which men of bad intentions play.

legislatures he came to think that about one-third of the members were open to corrupt influences, but that although the characters of those men were known to their colleagues and to the "lobby," it was rarely possible to convict them. Many of this worst third had not gone into the legislature meaning to make gain out of the position, but had been corrupted by it. They found that no distinction was to be won there by legitimate methods, and when temptation came in their way they fell, having feeble consciences and no statesmanlike knowledge. Or they were anxious above all things to pass some local measure on which their constituents were set, and they found they could not win the support of other members except by becoming accomplices in the jobs or "steals" which these members were "putting through." Or they gained their seat by the help of some influential man or powerful company, and found themselves obliged to vote according to the commands of their "owner."[11]

The corrupt member has several methods of making gains. One, the most obvious, is to exact money or money's worth for his vote. A second is to secure by it the support of a group of his colleagues in some other measure in which he is personally interested, as for instance a measure which will add to the value of land near a particular city. This is "logrolling," and is the most difficult method to deal with, because its milder forms are scarcely distinguishable from that legitimate give and take which must go on in all legislative bodies. It is, however, deemed so mischievous, that several constitutions have expressly enacted that it shall be held to constitute the offence of solicitation or bribery, and be punishable accordingly.[12] A third is blackmailing. A member brings in a bill either specially directed against some particular great corporation, probably a railway, or proposing so to

---

[11] "There came before a committee (of the New York House) of which I happened to be a member, a perfectly proper bill in the interest of a certain corporation; the majority of the committee, six in number, were thoroughly bad men, who opposed with the hope of being paid to cease their opposition. When I consented to take charge of the bill, I stipulated that not a penny should be paid to ensure its passage. It therefore became necessary to see what pressure could be brought to bear on the recalcitrant members; and accordingly we had to find out who were the authors and sponsors of their political being. Three proved to be under the control of local statesmen of the same party as themselves, and of equally bad moral character; one was ruled by a politician of unsavoury reputation from a different city; the fifth, a Democrat, was owned by a Republican (!) Federal official, and the sixth by the president of a horsecar [street tramway] company. A couple of letters from these two magnates forced the last-mentioned members to change front on the bill with surprising alacrity."—Mr. Theodore Roosevelt, *ut supra*.

The New York legislature was thought to have begun to improve in the first years of the century, but this pleasing impression received a shock in 1910.

[12] E.g., North Dakota, Montana, Idaho, and Wyoming.

alter the general law as in fact to injure such a corporation, or a group of corporations. He intimates privately that he is willing to "see" the directors or the law-agents of the corporation, and is in many cases bought off by them, keeping his bill in the paper till the last moment so as to prevent some other member from repeating the trick. Even in the Northwestern states there is usually a group of such "scallawag" members, who, finding the $300 they receive insufficient, increase their legislative income by levying this form of taxation upon the companies of the state. Nor is the device (technically called a "strike") quite unknown in New England, where a ten hours' labour bill, for instance, has frequently been brought in to frighten the large corporations and other capitalists into inducing its author to drop it, the inducements being such as capitalists can best apply. Every considerable railway keeps an agent or agents continually on the spot while a state legislature is in session, watching the bills brought in and the committees that deal with them. Such an agent sometimes relies on the friends of the railway to defeat these bills, and uses the usual expedients for creating friends. But it is often cheaper and easier to square the assailant.[13] Of course the committees are the focus of intrigue, and the chairmanship of a committee the position which affords the greatest facilities for an unscrupulous man. Round the committees there buzzes that swarm of professional agents which Americans call "the lobby," soliciting the members, threatening them with trouble in their constituencies, plying them with all sorts of inducements, treating them to dinners, drinks, and cigars.[14]

In these demoralized states the state Senate is apt to be a worse body than the House, whereas in the better states the Senate is usually the superior body.[15] The reason is twofold. As the Senate is smaller—in New York it

---

[13] The president of a Western railroad, an upright as well as able man, told me that he was obliged to keep constant guard at the capital of the state in which the line lay, while the legislature was sitting, and to use every means to defeat bills aimed at the railway, because otherwise the shareholders would have been ruined. He deplored the necessity. It was a state of comparatively good tone, but there was such a prejudice against railroads among the farming population, that mischievous bills had a chance of success, and therefore desperate remedies were needed.

[14] "One senator, who was generally known as 'the wicked Gibbs,' spent two years at Albany, in which he pursued his 'business' so shamelessly that his constituents refused to send him there again; but he coolly came out a year later and begged for a return to the Assembly on the ground that he was financially embarrassed, and wished to go to the Assembly in order to retrieve his fortunes on the salary of an Assemblyman, which is $1500!"—Mr. J. B. Bishop of New York, in a paper entitled *Money in City Elections*, p. 6.

[15] Some of my informants would not admit this; and some fixed the percentage of corrupt men, even at Albany, much lower than Mr. Roosevelt does. Writers of the pessimistic school make it even higher. I give here and elsewhere what seem to me to be on the whole the best supported views, though, as Herodotus says of the rise of Cyrus, "knowing three other paths of story also."

consists of 51 members against 150 in the Assembly—the vote of each member is of more consequence, and fetches, when venal, a higher price. Other things being equal, a stronger temptation is more likely to overcome virtue, and other things practically are equal, because it is just as hard to fix responsibility on a senator as on an assemblyman, and the post is no more dignified. And the second reason is that the most adroit and practised intriguers work their way up into the Senate, where their power (which includes the confirmation of appointments) is greater and their vote more valuable. There is a survival of the fittest, but as fitness includes the absence of scruples, this comes in practice to mean the natural selection of the worst.

I escape from this Stygian pool to make some observations which seem applicable to state legislatures generally, and not merely to the most degraded.

The spirit of localism, surprisingly strong everywhere in America, completely rules them. A member is not a member for his state, chosen by a district but bound to think first of the general welfare of the commonwealth. He is a member for Brownsville, or Pompey, or the Seventh District, and so forth, as the case may be. His first and main duty is to get the most he can for his constituency out of the state treasury, or by means of state legislation. No appeal to the general interest would have weight with him against the interests of that spot. What is more, he is deemed by his colleagues of the same party to be the sole exponent of the wishes of the spot, and solely entitled to handle its affairs. If he approves a bill which affects the place and nothing but the place, that is conclusive. Nobody else has any business to interfere. This rule is the more readily accepted, because its application all round serves the private interest of every member alike, while members of more enlarged views, who ought to champion the interests of the state and sound general principles of legislation, are rare. When such is the accepted doctrine as well as invariable practice, logrolling becomes natural and almost legitimate. Each member being the judge of the measure which touches his own constituency, every other member supports that member in passing the measure, expecting in return the like support in a like cause. He who in the public interest opposes the bad bill of another, is certain to find that other opposing, and probably with success, his own bill, however good.

The defects noted (Chapters 14–17) as arising in Congress from the want of recognised leadership and of persons officially bound to represent and protect the interests of the people at large reappear in the state legislatures, on a smaller scale, no doubt, but in an aggravated form, because the level of ability is lower and the control of public opinion less. There is no one to withstand the petty localism already referred to; no one charged with the duty of resisting proposals which some noisy section may demand, but whose ultimate mischief, or pernicious effect as precedents, thoughtful men perceive. There are members for districts, but no members for the people of the state. Thus many needless bills and many bad bills are passed. And when some difficult question arises, it may happen that no member is found able to grapple with it. Sometimes the governor comes to the rescue by appointing a commission of eminent men to devise and suggest to the legislature a measure to deal with the question. Sometimes the constitution contains a provision that the judges shall report upon all defects in the judicial system in order that the needed reform may be thereupon carried.[16] Such are the roundabout ways in which efforts are made to supply the want of capacity in the legislators, and the absence of a proper system of cooperation between the executive and legislative departments.

A remarkable and important new departure was made in New York State in 1909 by the creation of a body called the Public Utilities Commission charged with the duty of dealing with the agencies of transportation and other public services. Its action is expected to remedy the evils which have arisen not only from the frequent exercise of improper influences by public service corporations, but also from the fragmentary and unsystematic way in which legislatures have treated these matters.

There is in state legislators, particularly in the West, a restlessness which, coupled with their limited range of knowledge and undue appreciation of material interests, makes them rather dangerous. Meeting for only a few weeks in the year, or perhaps in two years, they are alarmingly active during those weeks, and run measures through whose results are not apprehended till months afterwards. It is for this reason, no less than from the fear of jobbery, that the meeting of the legislature is looked forward to with anxiety by the "good citizens" in these communities, and its departure hailed as a deliverance. I once asked the governor of a far Western commonwealth how he got on with his legislature. "I won't say they are bad men," he answered, "but the pleasantest sight of the year to me is when at the end of the session I see their coat tails go round the street corner."

Both this restlessness and the general character of state legislation are

---

[16] In a Western state it recently happened that the most experienced judge had agreed upon certain much needed reforms in judicial procedure and caused a bill to be introduced into the legislature embodying them. There were, however, many lawyers of the meaner sort in that legislature who objected to these reforms because they would have lessened opportunities of gain; and by the efforts of these petty practitioners the bill was defeated. There was no one in the chamber able with official authority to insist that in the interests of the people at large the bill ought to pass.

illustrated by the enormous numbers of bills introduced in each session. Comparatively few pass, because the time is too short, or opposing influences can be brought to bear on the committees; yet those that do pass reach a high total.

The annual output of all the legislatures has been estimated at 15,000 statutes.[17] From 1899 to 1904, the number passed was 45,552. In 1909 there were passed in Maryland 741 acts, in California 729, in Pennsylvania 650, in New York 596, and in North Carolina 1,319. The large majority of these were local or special, intended to further the interests of particular persons or places.[18] In 1901 eight fairly typical states passed 7,032 statutes, of which 5,876 were local or special. Acts of incorporation, grants of inheritance, changes of names and releases from indebtedness, thus consume a large proportion of the time of the legislature at a great public expense, and often to the serious detriment of public interests, because it is through these bills that jobs are perpetrated. The expense to which the states are put by their legislatures, with results rather injurious than beneficial, is very great. Some years ago it was estimated that the cost of laws in the states varied from an average of about $1,000 per diem for every legislative session to over $4,000 per diem, making an aggregate, in the whole number of states, which could not be less than $10,000,000, not as an exceptional outlay, but as the price paid for current legislation.

Nothing is more remarkable about these state legislators than their timidity. No one seems to think of having an opinion of his own. In matters which touch the interests of his constituents, a member is, of course, their humble servant. In burning party questions—they are few, and mostly personal— he goes with his party. In questions of general public policy he looks to see how the cat jumps; and is ready to vote for anything which the people, or any active section of the people, cry out for, though of course he may be secretly unfriendly, and may therefore slyly try to spoil a measure. This want of independence has some good results. It enables a small minority of zealous men, backed by a few newspapers, to carry schemes of reform which the majority regard with indifference or hostility. Thus in bodies so depraved as the legislatures of New York and Pennsylvania, bills have lately

---

[17] By Professor Gilmore of the University of Wisconsin.

[18] Even among the acts which appear in the statute books of the states under the heading of general laws, there are many of a local or special character. Some states (e.g., Wyoming) now forbid the passing of any private act.

As remarked in an earlier chapter, the total number of bills of all kinds introduced in 1908 into the British Parliament, which is the sole legislative authority for a population of forty-three millions, was 482, of which 241 passed.

been passed greatly improving the charters of cities, creating a secret ballot, and even bettering the civil service and establishing an improved system of appointments to office. A few energetic reformers went to Albany and Harrisburg to strengthen the hands of the little knot of members who battle for good government there, and partly frightened, partly coaxed a majority of the Senate and House into adopting proposals opposed to the interests of professional politicians. About 1880, two or three high-minded and sagacious ladies obtained by their presence at Albany the introduction of valuable reforms into the charitable institutions of New York City. The ignorance and heedlessness of the "professionals," who do not always see the results of legislative changes, and do not look forward beyond the next few months, help to make such triumphs possible; and thus, as the Bible tells us that the wrath of man shall praise God, the faults of politicians are turned to work for righteousness.

In the recent legislation of many states, especially Western states, there is a singular mixture of philanthropy and humanitarianism with the folly and jobbery I have described, like threads of gold and silver woven across a warp of dirty sacking. Every year sees bills passed to restrict the sale of liquor, to prevent the sale of indecent or otherwise demoralizing literature, to protect women and children, to stamp out lotteries and gambling houses, to improve the care of the blind, the insane, and the poor, which testify to a warm and increasing interest in all good works. These measures are to be explained, not merely by that power which an active and compact minority enjoys of getting its own way against a crowd of men bent each on his own private gain, and therefore not working together for other purposes, but also by the real sympathy which many of the legislators, especially in the rural districts, feel for morality and for suffering. Even the corrupt politicians of Albany were moved by the appeals of the philanthropic ladies to whom I have referred; much more then would it be an error to think of the average legislator as a bad man, merely because he will join in a job, or try to blackmail a railroad. The moral standard of Western America is not quite the same as that of England, just as the standard of England differs from that of Germany or France. It is both higher and lower. Some sins excite more anger or disgust than they do in England; some are more lightly forgiven, or more quickly forgotten. Laxity in the discharge of a political trust belongs to the latter category. The newspapers accuse everybody; the ordinary citizen can seldom tell who is innocent and who is guilty. He makes a sort of compromise in his own mind by thinking nobody quite black, but everybody gray. And he goes on to think that what everybody does cannot be very sinful.

Note to the Edition of 1910

Reviewing the facts dealt with in this chapter, I find them to be still, broadly speaking, the same as they were in 1892; the factors working for good and for evil having not greatly changed. However, the tendency of recent years seems to be in most states towards better legislation, and especially towards a more active and vigilant control of legislative bodies by the public opinion. The legislature of New York, for instance, is probably no purer than formerly, and may do as many jobs at the instance of private interests as formerly, but its public acts are better, and it sometimes drops a job in deference to the opinion of good citizens. Moreover the legislature is now in some states curbed by the referendum. In some of the Western and Southern states plenty of crude measures and a few wild measures are still passed, and in most states private interests still have too much power in securing the legislation they want. But there has been enough progress to make the outlook hopeful. What seems now most needed is the separation of private (i.e., local and personal) bills from general public legislation, and the provision of some mode for dealing with them on general principles and, if possible, by quasi-judicial methods. The New York Public Utilities Commission is an experiment in this direction from which much may be hoped. But anyone who knows how useful the quasi-judicial methods applied in England to private legislation have proved cannot but wish that they were better known in the American states.

Note to the Edition of 1914

Upon the subject mentioned in the last preceding sentence I may refer to an address delivered by me to the New York State Bar Association published in a volume entitled *Addresses, University and Historical*, in 1913. The upward tendency referred to in the preceding note seems to be maintained.

Remedies for the Faults of State Governments

The defects in state governments, which our examination of their working has disclosed, are not those we should have expected. It might have been predicted, and it was at one time believed, that these authorities, consumed by jealousy and stimulated by ambition, would have been engaged in constant efforts to extend the sphere of their action and encroach on the national government. This does not happen, and seems most unlikely to happen. The people of each state are now not more attached to the government of their own commonwealth than to the federal government of the nation, whose growth has made even the greatest state seem insignificant beside it.

A study of the frame of state government, in which the executive department is absolutely severed from the legislative, might have suggested that the former would become too independent, misusing its powers for personal or party purposes, while public business would suffer from the want of concert between the two great authorities, that which makes and that which carries out the law.

This also has proved in practice to be no serious evil. The legislature might indeed conceivably work better if the governor, or some of his chief officials, could sit in it and exercise an influence on its deliberations. Such an approach to the European cabinet system has, however, never been thought of for American states; and the example of the provincial legislatures of Canada, in each of which there is a responsible ministry sitting in the legislature, does not seem to recommend it for imitation. Those who founded the state governments did not desire to place any executive leaders in a representative assembly. Probably they were rather inclined to fear that the governor, not being accountable to the legislature, would retain too great an independence. The recent creation of various administrative officers or boards has gone some way to meet the difficulties which the incompetence of the legislatures causes, for these officers or boards frequently prepare bills which some member of the legislature introduces, and which are put through without opposition, perhaps even without notice, except from a handful of members. On the whole, the executive arrangements of the state work well, though they might, in the opinion of some judicious publicists, be improved by vesting the appointment of the chief officials in the governor, instead of leaving it to direct popular election. This would tend to give more unity of purpose and action to the administration. The collisions which occur in practice between the governor and the legislature relate chiefly to appointments, that is to say, to personal matters, not involving issues of state policy.

The real blemishes in the system of state government are all found in the composition or conduct of the legislatures. They are the following:

Inferiority in point of knowledge, of skill, and sometimes of conscience, of the bulk of the men who fill these bodies

Improvidence in matters of finance

Heedlessness in passing administrative bills

Want of proper methods for dealing with local and special bills

Failure of public opinion adequately to control legislation, and particularly local and special bills.

The practical result of these blemishes has been to create a large mass of state and local indebtedness which ought never to have been incurred, to allow foolish experiments in lawmaking to be tried, and to sanction a vast mass of private enterprises, in which public rights and public interests become the sport of speculators, or a source of gain to monopolists, with the incidental consequence of demoralizing the legislators themselves and creating an often unjust prejudice against all corporate undertakings.

What are the checks or remedies which have been provided to limit or suppress these evils? Anyone who has followed the account given of the men who compose the legislatures and the methods they follow will have felt that these checks must be considerable, else the results would have been worse than those we see. All remedies are directed against the legislative power, and may be arranged under four heads.

First, there is the division of the legislature into two houses. A job may have been smuggled through one house, but the money needed to push it through the other may be wanting. Some wild scheme, professing to benefit the farmers, or the cattlemen, or the railroad employees, may, during its passage through the Assembly, rouse enough attention from sensible people to enable them to stop it in the Senate. The mere tendency of two chambers to disagree with one another is deemed a benefit by those who hold, as the Americans do, that every new measure is prima facie likely to do more harm than good. Most bills are bad—ergo, kill as many as you can. Each house, moreover, has, even in such demoralized state legislatures as those of New York or Pennsylvania, a satisfaction, if not an interest, in unveiling the tricks of the other.

Secondly, there is the veto of the governor. How much the Americans value this appears from the fact that, whereas in 1789 there was only one state, Massachusetts, which vested this power in the chief magistrate, all of the now existing states except one give it to him. Some constitutions (including all the new ones) contain the salutary provision that the governor may reject one or more items of an appropriation bill (sometimes even of any bill) while approving the bill as a whole; and this has been found to strengthen his hands immensely in checking the waste of public money on bad enterprises. This veto power, the great standby of the people of the states, illustrates admirably the merits of concentrated responsibility. The citizens, in choosing the governor to represent the collective authority of the whole state, lay on him the duty of examining every bill on its merits. He cannot shelter himself behind the will of the representatives of the people, because he is appointed to watch and check those representatives as a policeman watches a suspect. He is bound to reject the bill, not only if it seems to him to infringe the constitution of the state, but also if he thinks it in any wise injurious to the public, on pain of being himself suspected of carelessness, or of complicity in some corrupt design. The legislature may, of course, pass the bill over his veto by a two-thirds vote; but although there may exist a two-thirds majority in favour of the measure, they may fear, after the veto has turned the lamp of public opinion upon it, to take so strong a step. There are, of course, great differences between one governor and another, as well as between one state and another, as regards the honesty with which the power is exercised, for it may be, and sometimes is, used by a "Ring" governor to defeat measures of reform. But it is a real and effective power everywhere; and in the greatest states, where the importance of the office often secures the election of an able and courageous man, it has done inestimable services.[1]

---

[1] Although the existence of this ultimate remedy tends to make good members relax their opposition to bad bills, because they know that the veto will kill them, this is a less evil than the disuse of the veto would be.

Thirdly, there are limitations imposed on the competence of the legislature. I have already mentioned some of these limitations, the most numerous, and at present the most important of which relate to special and local (or what would be called in England "private") bills. These bills, while they destroy the harmony and simplicity of the law, and consume the time of the legislature, are also so fertile a source of jobbery[2] that to expunge them or restrict them to cases where a special statute was really needed, would be a great benefit. The constitutional prohibitions described effect this to some extent. Illinois, for instance, has by such prohibitions reduced her sessional statutes to about three hundred pages, and Iowa averages only two hundred to two hundred and fifty pages, whereas the Wisconsin statutes of 1885 reached two thousand pages, there being in that state far less effective restrictions. But the powers of evil do not yield without a battle. All sorts of evasions are tried, and some succeed. Suppose, for instance, that there is a prohibition in the Constitution of New York to pass any but general laws relating to the government of cities. An act is passed which is expressed to apply to cities with a population exceeding one hundred thousand but less than two hundred thousand. There happens to be then only one such city in the state, viz., Buffalo, but as there might be more, the law was deemed general, and escaped the prohibition. So the Constitution of Ohio expressly provides that the legislature "shall pass no special act conferring

---

[2] "In twelve States the legislature is forbidden to create any corporation whatever, municipalities included, except by general law, and in thirteen others to create by special Act any except municipal corporations, or those to which no other law is applicable. In some States corporations can be created by special Act only for municipal, charitable, or reformatory purposes. Such provisions are not intended to discourage the formation of private corporations. On the contrary, in all these States general laws exist under which they can be formed with great facility. Indeed the defects in some of these statutes, and their failure to provide safeguards against some at least of the very evils which they were intended to meet, might well suggest to legislators the question whether in avoiding the Scylla of special legislation they have not been drawn into the Charybdis of franchises indiscriminately bestowed. Perhaps the time will come when recommendations such as those urged by the New York railroad commission will be acted on, and the promoters of a new railroad will be obliged to furnish some better reason for its existence, and for their exercising the sovereign power of eminent domain, than the chance of forcing a company already established to buy them out—or, failing that, the alternative of being sold out under foreclosure, pending a receivership."—Hitchcock, *State Constitutions*, p. 36. Prohibitions have become more stringent since the above was written.

"A great field for favouritism and jobbery exists, when special Acts of incorporation are required for each case in which special favours and special privileges may be given away by a legislation that may be corruptly influenced, without imposing any reciprocal obligation on the corporation. Fully two-thirds of the lobbyism, jobbery, and log-rolling, the fraud and trickery that are common to our State legislatures, is due to this power of creating private corporations."—Ford, *Citizens' Manual*, vol. ii, p. 68.

corporate powers." But in 1890 nearly fifty such acts were passed, the provision being evaded by the use of general enacting words which can in fact apply only to one place. One act, for instance, authorized villages with a population of not less than 1,903 nor more than 1,912 to issue bonds for natural gas developments; another empowered any city having a population of 15,435, by the census of 1890, to levy a library tax.[3]

Provisions against special legislation are evaded in another way, viz., by passing acts which, because they purport to amend general acts, are themselves deemed general. Here is a recent instance. The Constitution of New York prohibits the legislature from passing any private or local act incorporating villages, or providing for building bridges. A general act was passed in 1885 for the incorporation of villages, with general provisions as to bridges. Next year the following act was passed, which I give verbatim. It amends the act of 1885, by taking out of it all the counties in the state except Westchester, and then excludes application of the act to two towns in Westchester. It is thus doubly a "private or local act," but the prohibition of the constitution was got round.[4]

CHAP. 556.

AN ACT to amend chapter two hundred and ninety-one of the laws of eighteen hundred and seventy, entitled "An Act for the Incorporation of Villages."

Passed June 4, 1886; three-fifths being present. The People of the State of New York, represented in Senate and Assembly, do enact as follows:

Village Incorporation Act of 1885, as to bridges, to apply only to parts of Westchester County.

Section I. Section two of chapter four hundred and fifty of the laws of eighteen hundred and eighty-five, is hereby amended so as to read as follows:

Section 2. All of the counties in this State are hereby exempted from the provisions of this Act except the county of Westchester, but nothing in this Act contained shall be construed so as to apply to the towns of Greenburgh and Mount Pleasant in said county of Westchester.

Section 3. This Act shall take effect immediately.

Where evasions of this kind become frequent the confusion of the statute

---

[3] Mr. Hitchcock (from whose address I take the Ohio instance) adds that the Supreme Court of Ohio has held such evasions unconstitutional, but that they continue notwithstanding, the legislature, and the villages or cities, taking their chance.

[4] The Constitution of North Dakota (§ 70) expressly prohibits this evasion.

book is worse than ever, because you cannot tell without examination whether an act is general or special.

The reader will have noticed in the heading of the act just quoted the words "three-fifths being present." This is one of the numerous safeguards imposed on the procedure of the state legislatures. Others have been specified in Chapter 40. Their abundance in the newest constitutions shows how these efforts to deal with the symptoms have failed to eradicate the endless evasions they seek to anticipate.[5]

The inventive genius of American legislators finds or makes many holes in the net which the people have tried to throw over them by the constitution. Yet, though there be none of the restrictions and regulations mentioned which is not sometimes violated or evaded, they have, on the whole, worked well. The enemy is held at bay, and a great deal of bad legislation is prevented. Some bills have to be dropped, because too plainly repugnant to the constitution to be worth carrying farther. The more ignorant members do not always apprehend where the difficulty lies. They can barely read the constitution, and the nature of its legal operation is as far beyond them as the cause of thunder is beyond cats. A friend of mine who sat for some years in the New York Assembly was once importuned by an Irish member to support that particular member's little bill. He answered that he could not, because the bill was against the constitution. "Och, Mr. Robert," was the reply, "shure the Constitootion should niver be allowed to come between friends."

Some bills again the governor can scarcely help vetoing, because they violate a constitutional restriction; while of those that pass him unscathed, a fair number fall victims to the courts of law. It may be added that the

---

[5] For instance, it is sometimes provided that no bill shall be introduced within a certain period after the beginning or before the end of the session, so as to prevent bills from being smuggled through in the last days. This provision is evaded "by introducing a new bill after the time has expired when it may constitutionally be done, as an amendment to some pending bill, the whole of which, except the enacting clause, is struck out to make way for it. Thus, the member who thinks he may have occasion for the introduction of a new bill after the constitutional period has expired, takes care to introduce sham bills in due season, which he can use as stocks to graft upon, and which he uses irrespective of their character or contents. The sham bill is perhaps a bill to incorporate the city of Siam. One of the member's constituents applies to him for legislative permission to construct a dam across the Wild Cat River. Forthwith, by amendment, the bill, entitled a bill to incorporate the city of Siam, has all after the enacting clause stricken out, and it is made to provide, as its sole object, that John Doe may construct a dam across the Wild Cat. With this title, and in this form it is passed; but the house then considerably amends the title to correspond with the purpose of the bill, and the law is passed, and the Constitution at the same time saved!"—Cooley, *Constit. Limit.*, p. 169 note.

enforcement of the limitations imposed by a state constitution necessarily rests with the judges, since it is they who pronounce, if and when the point is brought up in a suit between parties, whether or no a statute has transgressed the bounds which the fundamental instrument sets, or whether a constitutional amendment has been duly carried.[6]

Someone may remark that there are two material differences between the position of these state judges and that of the federal judges. The latter are not appointed by a state, and are therefore in a more independent position when any question of conflict between state laws or constitutions and the federal Constitution or statutes comes before them. Moreover they hold office for life, whereas the state judge usually holds for a term of years, and has his reelection to think of. Can the state judge then be expected to show himself equally bold in declaring a state statute to be unconstitutional? Will he not offend the legislature, and the party managers who control it, by flying in their faces?

The answer is that although the judge may displease the legislature if he decides against the validity of an unconstitutional statute, he may displease the people if he decides for it; and it is safer to please the people than the legislature. The people at large may know little about the matter, but the legal profession know, and are sure to express their opinion. The profession look to the courts to save them and their clients from the heedlessness or improbity of the legislature, and will condemn a judge who fails in this duty. Accordingly, the judges seldom fail. They knock about state statutes most unceremoniously, and they seldom suffer for doing so. In one case only is their position a dangerous one. When the people, possessed by some strong desire or sentiment, have either by the provisions of a new constitution, or by the force of clamour, driven the legislature to enact some measure meant to cure a pressing ill, they may turn angrily upon the judge who

---

[6] A remarkable instance of the technical literalism with which the courts sometimes enforce constitutional restrictions is afforded by the fate of a recent liquor prohibition amendment to the Constitution of Iowa. This amendment had been passed by both houses of the state legislature in two successive legislatures, had been submitted to the people and enacted by a large majority, had been proclaimed by the governor and gone into force. It was subsequently discovered that one house of the first legislature had, through the carelessness of a clerk, neglected to "spread the Amendment, in full on its journal," as prescribed by the constitution. The point being brought before the Supreme Court of Iowa, it was held that the amendment, owing to this informality, had not been duly passed, and was wholly void.

An illustration of the range which the action of courts may take in enforcing constitutional safeguards was well given by the Supreme Court of Wisconsin, when it held invalid a [gerrymandering] redistricting of the state (for elections to the state legislature), as being inconsistent with the provision of the constitution that districts should be reasonably equal.

holds that measure to have been unconstitutional. This has several times happened, and is always liable to happen where elective judges hold office for short terms, with the unfortunate result of weakening the fortitude of the judges. In 1786 the Supreme Court of Rhode Island decided that an act passed by the legislature was invalid, because contravening the provisions of the colonial charter (which was then still the constitution of the state), securing to every accused person the benefit of trial by jury.[7]

The legislature were furious, and summoned the judges to appear before them and explain the grounds of their decision. The attempt to dismiss them failed, but the judges were not reelected by the legislature when their term of office expired at the end of the year. In Ohio, the legislature passed in 1805 an act which Judge Pease, in a case arising under it, held to be repugnant to the Constitution of Ohio, as well as to the federal Constitution, and accordingly declined to enforce. In 1808, he and another judge of the supreme court of the state who had concurred with him, were impeached by the House before the Senate of Ohio, but were acquitted. In 1823, the Supreme Court of Kentucky held invalid a debtors' relief act passed by the legislature on the ground that it violated the obligation of contracts clause of the federal Constitution by making paper issued by a state bank legal tender. The judges were impeached, but a two-thirds majority for conviction could not be obtained, so the angry legislature extinguished the court itself and created a new court of appeals, to which the governor appointed new men as judges. The old court, however, held its ground, insisting that the new court was unconstitutional, and after a passionate struggle, a new legislature repealed in 1825 the act creating the new court. So justice and reason prevailed. In 1871, the legislature of Illinois passed a law, intending to carry out a provision of the Constitution of 1870, which was held unconstitutional by Judge Lawrence, greatly to the disappointment of the farmers, who had expected valuable results from it. He was not impeached, but when shortly afterwards he sought reelection, he was defeated solely on the ground of this decision.[8] These instances show that the courts have had

---

[7] See p. 222 *ante*. The act was one for forcing state paper money into circulation by imposing a penalty, recoverable on summary conviction without a jury, on whoever should refuse to receive on the same terms as specie the bills of a state-chartered bank. No question of the United States Constitution could arise, because it did not yet exist. To these Rhode Island judges belongs the credit not only of having resisted a reckless multitude, but of having set one of the first examples in American history of the exercise of a salutary function. Their decision was that they had no jurisdiction.

[8] I quote from Mr. Hadley's book on railroad transportation (through Dr. Hitchcock's essay already referred to) the following account of the circumstances: "The Constitutional Convention of Illinois in 1870 made an important declaration concerning State control of railway rates, on the basis of

to fight for their freedom in the discharge of the duty which the constitutions throw on them. But the paucity of such conflicts shows that this freedom is now generally recognized, and may be deemed, at least for the present, to be placed above the storms of popular passion.[9]

It will be seen from what has been said that the judges are an essential part of the machinery of state government. But they are so simply as judges, and not as invested with political powers or duties. They have not received, any more than the federal judges, a special commission to restrain the legislature or pronounce on the validity of its acts. There is not a word in the state constitutions, any more than in the federal Constitution, conferring any such right upon the courts, or indeed conferring any other right than all courts of law must necessarily enjoy. When they declare a statute unconstitutional they do so merely in their ordinary function of expounding the law of the state, its fundamental law as well as its laws of inferior authority, just as an English judge might hold an order made by the king in council to be invalid, because in excess of the powers granted by the act of Parliament under which it was made. It would be as clearly the duty of an English county court judge so to hold as of the highest court of appeal. So it is the duty of the humblest American state judge to decide on the constitutionality of a statute.

So far we have been considering restrictions imposed on the competence of the legislature, or on the methods of its procedure. We now come to the

---

which a law was passed in 1871 establishing a system of maxima. This law was pronounced unconstitutional by Judge Lawrence. The result was that he immediately afterwards failed of re-election, solely on this ground. The defeat of Judge Lawrence showed the true significance of the farmers movement [the so-called Granger movement]. They were concerned in securing what they felt to be their rights, and were unwilling that any constitutional barrier should be made to defeat the popular will. They had reached the point where they regarded many of the forms of law as mere technicalities. They were dangerously near the point where revolutions begin. But they did not pass the point. The law of 1873 avoided the issue raised by Judge Lawrence against that of 1871. Instead of directly fixing maxima, it provided that rates must be reasonable, and then provided for a commission to fix reasonable rates." The courage of Judge Lawrence was therefore not thrown away; it cost him his place, but it served the people and vindicated the law.

In 1890, the executive committee of the Minnesota Farmers' Alliance in passing resolutions demanding the abolition of the federal Supreme Court, which had recently held that the state legislature had no power to fix railroad freight rates, relieved their feelings by saying. "We call attention to the fact that the citizens of England, from whom we have largely derived our form of government, would not permit for one instant a bench of judges to nullify an Act of Parliament. There the people are properly omnipotent. . . . In our anxiety to protect the rights of property we have created a machine that threatens to destroy the rights of man."

[9] There have of course been other instances in which judges have been impeached or removed; but I am here dealing only with those in which the ground of complaint was the declaring a legislative act to be invalid.

fourth and last of the checks which the prudence of American states imposes. It is a very simple, not to say naïve, one. It consists in limiting the time during which the legislature may sit. Formerly these bodies sat, like the English Parliament, so long as they had business to do. The business seldom took long. When it was done, the farmers and lawyers naturally wished to go home, and home they went. But when the class of professional politicians grew up, these wholesome tendencies lost their power over a section of the members. Politics was their business, and they had none other to call them back to the domestic hearth.[10] They had even a motive for prolonging the session, because they prolonged their legislative salary, which was usually paid by the day. Thus it became the interest of the taxpayer to shorten the session; and he had already a still stronger interest in cutting short the jobs and improvident bestowal of moneys and franchises in which he found his representatives employed. Accordingly most states have fixed a number of days beyond which the legislature may not sit. Many of these fix it absolutely; but a few prefer the method of cutting off the pay of their legislators after the prescribed number of days has expired, so that if they do continue to devote themselves still longer to the work of lawmaking, their virtue shall be its own reward.[11] Experience has, however, disclosed a danger in these absolutely limited sessions. It is that of haste and recklessness in rushing bills through without due discussion. Sometimes it happens that a bill introduced in response to a vehement popular demand is carried with a rush (so to speak), because the time for considering it cannot be extended, whereas longer consideration would have disclosed its dangers. An ill-framed railway bill was thus defeated in the Iowa legislature because full discussion (there being no time limit) brought out its weak points. Hence some states have largely extended their sessions. Thus California in 1907 abolished the provision which limited payment to a regular session of sixty days, substituting a general limit of $1,000 to each member whatever the length of the session; and Colorado in 1885 extended the maximum of her session from forty to ninety days, also raising legislative pay from $4 to $7 per diem.

[10] The English Parliament found the tendency of members to slip away so strong that in the sixteenth century it enacted "that no knight of the shire or burgess do depart before the end of Parliament," and inflicted on the member leaving without the permission of Mr. Speaker, the penalty of losing "all those sums of money which he should or ought to have had for his wages."

[11] Thus the Constitution of Oregon, for instance, gives its members for forty days only. Texas is a little more liberal, for her constitution was content to reduce the pay after sixty days from $5 to $3 (now $2) per day, at which reduced rate members might apparently go on as long as they please. Nearly all the states which fix a limit of time are Southern or Western. The forty days' session of Georgia may be extended by a two-thirds vote of an absolute majority of each house.

Many recent constitutions have tried another and probably a better expedient. They have made sessions less frequent. At one time every legislature met once a year. Now in all the states but six it is permitted to meet only once in two years or (in Alabama and Mississippi) once in four years.[12] It does not appear that the interests of the commonwealths suffer by this suspension of the action of their chief organ of government.[13] On the contrary, they get on so much better without a legislature that certain bold spirits ask whether the principle might not with advantage be pushed farther. As Mr. Butler said in 1886—and the statement remains substantially true—

> For a people claiming pre-eminence in the sphere of popular government, it seems hardly creditable that in their seeming despair of a cure for the chronic evils of legislation, they should be able to mitigate them only by making them intermittent. Under the biennial system the relief enjoyed in what are called the "off-years" seems to have reconciled the body politic of the several States which have adopted it to the risk of an aggravation of the malady when the legislative year comes round and the old symptoms recur.
>
> The secretaries of State (of the several States) with whom I have communicated concur in certifying that no public inconvenience is caused by the biennial system; and one of them, of the State of Nebraska, in answer to my query if biennial sessions occasion any public inconvenience, writes "None whatever. The public interests would be better subserved by having legislative sessions held only once in four years."

The Americans seem to reason thus: "Since a legislature is very far gone from righteousness, and of its own nature inclined to do evil, the less chance it has of doing evil the better. If it meets, it will pass bad laws. Let us therefore prevent it from meeting."

They are no doubt right as practical men. They are consistent, as sons of the Puritans, in their application of the doctrine of original sin. But this is a rather pitiful result for self-governing democracy to have arrived at.

"Is there not," someone may ask, "a simpler remedy? Why all these efforts to deal with the symptoms of the malady, instead of striking at the root of the malady itself? Why not reform the legislatures by inducing good

---

[12] The six are Massachusetts, New Jersey, New York, Rhode Island, South Carolina, Georgia—all original states. Where the meetings are biennial or quadrennial, the legislature by adjourning sometimes gives itself a second session.

[13] The members, however, being usually new to the work, are rawer and positively more dangerous when their term includes only one session than they are during the second session in those states which allow two.

men to enter them, and keeping a more constantly vigilant public opinion fixed upon them?"

The answer to this very pertinent question will be found in the chapters of Part III which follow. I will only so far anticipate what is there stated as to observe that the better citizens have found it so difficult and troublesome to reform the legislatures that they have concluded to be content with curing such and so many symptoms as they can find medicines for, and waiting to see in what new direction the virus will work. "After all," they say, "the disease, though it is painful and vexing, does not endanger the life of the patient, does not even diminish his strength. The worst that the legislatures can do is to waste some money, and try some foolish experiments from which the good sense of the people will presently withdraw. Everyone has his crosses to bear, and ours are comparatively light." All which is true enough, but ignores two important features in the situation, one, that the constitutional organs of government become constantly more discredited, the other that the tremendous influence exerted by wealth and the misuse of public rights permitted to capitalists, and especially to companies, have created among the masses of the people ideas which may break out in demands for legislation of a new and dangerous kind.

The survey of the state governments which we have now completed suggests several reflections.

One of these is that the political importance of the states is no longer what it was in the early days of the Republic. Although the states have grown enormously in wealth and population, they have declined relatively to the central government. The excellence of state laws and the merits of a state administration make a great difference to the inhabitants, but the more thorough consolidation of the country and the fact that some of the most important questions, such as those relating to trusts and to railroads, are questions in which the hand of the national government is felt, dispose people to look rather to the latter. The matters which the state deals with, largely as they influence the welfare of the citizen, do not touch his imagination like those which Congress handles, because the latter determine the relations of the Republic to the rest of the world, and affect all the area that lies between the two oceans. The state set out as an isolated and self-sufficing commonwealth. It is now merely a part of a far grander whole, which seems to be slowly absorbing its functions and stunting its growth, as the great tree stunts the shrubs over which its spreading boughs have begun to cast their shade.

I do not mean to say that the people have ceased to care for their states;

far from it. They are proud of their states, even where there may be little to be proud of. That passionate love of competition which possesses English-speaking men, makes them eager that their state should surpass the neighbouring states in the number of the clocks it makes, the hogs it kills, the pumpkins it rears, that their particular star should shine at least as brightly as the other forty-seven in the national flag. But if these commonwealths meant to their citizens what they did in the days of the Revolution, if they commanded an equal measure of their loyalty, and influenced as largely their individual welfare, the state legislatures would not be left to professionals or third-rate men. The truth is that the state has shrivelled up. It retains its old legal powers over the citizens, its old legal rights as against the central government. It still displays its peculiar patriotism at every public celebration, and recalls its historic heroes. In Virginia and Massachusetts, for instance, in Vermont and Kentucky, and again in such a great Western state as California, there is plenty of state pride. But it does not interest its citizens as it once did. Men do not now say, like Ames in 1782, that their state is their country.[14] And as the central government overshadows it in one direction, so the great cities have encroached upon it in another. The population of a single city is sometimes a fourth or a fifth part of the whole population of the state; and city questions interest this population more than state questions do; city officials have begun to rival or even to dwarf state officials.

Observe, however, that while the growth of the Union has relatively dwarfed the state, the absolute increase of the state in population has changed the character of the state itself. In 1790 seven of the thirteen original states had each of them less than 300,000, only one more than 500,000 inhabitants. Now thirty-one have more than 1,000,000 each, twenty have more than 2,000,000, and ten of these have more than 2,500,000. Hence, in spite of railroads and telegraphs, the individual citizens know less of one another, have less personal acquaintance with their leading men, and less personal interest in the affairs of the community than in the old days when the state was no more populous than an English county like Bedford or Somerset. Thus the special advantages of local government have to a large extent vanished from the American states of today. They are local bodies in the sense of having no great imperial interests to fire men's minds. They are not local in the sense of giving their members a familiar knowledge and a

---

[14] So even in 1811 Josiah Quincy said in Congress: "Sir, I confess it, the first public love of my heart is the Commonwealth of Massachusetts. There is my fireside: there are the tombs of my ancestors."

lively interest in the management of their affairs. Hamilton may have been right in thinking that the large states ought to be subdivided.[15] At any rate it is to this want of direct local interest on the part of the people, that some of the faults of their legislatures may be ascribed.

The chief lesson which a study of the more vicious among the state legislatures teaches, is that power does not necessarily bring responsibility in its train. I should be ashamed to write down so bald a platitude, were it not that it is one of those platitudes which are constantly forgotten or ignored. People who know well enough that, in private life, wealth or rank or any other kind of power is as likely to mar a man as to make him, to lower as to raise his sense of duty, have nevertheless contracted the habit of talking as if human nature changed when it entered public life, as if the mere possession of public functions, whether of voting or of legislating, tended of itself to secure their proper exercise. We know that power does not purify men in despotic governments, but we talk as if it did so in free governments. Everyone would of course admit, if the point were put flatly to him, that power alone is not enough, but that there must be added to power, in the case of the voter, a direct interest in the choice of good men; in the case of the legislator, responsibility to the voters; in the case of both, a measure of enlightenment and honour. What the legislatures of the worst states show is not merely the need for the existence of a sound public opinion, for such a public opinion exists, but the need for methods by which it can be brought into efficient action upon representatives, who, if they are left to themselves, and are not individually persons with a sense of honour and a character to lose, will be at least as bad in public life as they could be in private. The greatness of the scale on which they act, and of the material interests they control, will do little to inspire them. New York and Pennsylvania are by far the largest and wealthiest states in the Union. Their legislatures are confessedly among the worst.

---

[15] It is however, also argued that there are some large states in which the mischievous action of the multitude of a great city is held in check by the steadier rural voters. If such states had been subdivided, the subdivision which happened to contain the great city would lie at the mercy of this multitude. The question has not taken practical shape, for no state has asked to be divided, though there was once a movement to divide Kansas into two states by a N. and S. line, and some Southern Californians have talked of seceding.

Texas is the only state which possesses (under the statute admitting her) a right to divide herself into several states without obtaining permission from Congress. She is big enough for four or five.

Hamilton's reason seems to have been a fear that the states would be too strong for the national government.

CHAPTER 46

State Politics

In the last preceding chapters I have attempted to describe first the structure of the machinery of state governments, and then this machinery in motion as well as at rest, that is to say, the actual working of the various departments in their relations to one another. We may now ask, What is the motive power which sets and keeps these wheels and pistons going? Where is the steam that drives the machine?

The steam is supplied by the political parties. In speaking of the parties I must, to some slight extent, anticipate what will be more fully explained in Part III; but it seems worth while to incur this inconvenience for the sake of bringing together all that refers specifically to the states, and of completing the picture of their political life.[1]

The states evidently present some singular conditions for the development of a party system. They are self-governing communities with large legislative and administrative powers, existing inside a much greater community of which they are for many purposes independent. They must have parties, and this community, the federal Union, has also parties. What is the relation of the one set of parties to the other?

There are three kinds of relations possible, viz.:

Each state might have a party of its own, entirely unconnected with the national parties, but created by state issues, i.e., advocating or opposing measures which fall within the exclusive competence of the state.

Each state might have parties which, while based upon state issues, were influenced by the national parties, and in some sort of affiliation with the latter.

---

[1] Many readers may find it better to skip this chapter until they have read those which follow (Chapters 53–56) upon the history, tenets, and present condition of the great national parties.

507

The parties in each state might be merely local subdivisions of the national parties, the national issues and organizations swallowing up, or rather pushing aside, the state issues and the organizations formed to deal with them.

The nature of the state governments would lead us to expect to find the first of these relations existing. The sphere of the state is different, some few topics of concurrent jurisdiction excepted, from that of the national government. What the state can deal with, the national government cannot touch. What the national government can deal with lies beyond the province of the state.[2] The state governor and legislature are elected without relation to the president and Congress, and when elected have nothing to do with those authorities. Hence a question fit to be debated and voted upon in Congress can seldom be a question fit to be also debated and voted upon in a state legislature, and the party formed for advocating its passage through Congress will have no scope for similar action within a state, while on the other hand a state party, seeking to carry some state law, will have no motive for approaching Congress, which can neither help it nor hurt it. The great questions which have divided the Union since its foundation, and on which national parties have been based, have been questions of foreign policy, of the creation of a national bank, of a protective tariff, of the extension of slavery, of the reconstruction of the South after the war. With none of these had a state legislature any title to deal; all lay within the federal sphere. So the questions of currency and tariff reform, which towards the close of the nineteenth century came to be among the most important questions before the country, were outside the province of the state governments. We might therefore expect that the state parties would be as distinct from the national parties as are the state governments from the federal.

The contrary has happened. The national parties have engulfed the state parties. The latter have disappeared absolutely as independent bodies, and survive merely as branches of the national parties, working each in its own state for the tenets and purposes which a national party professes and seeks to attain. So much is this the case that one may say that a state party has rarely (save to some extent in the South) any marked local colour, that it is seldom, and then but slightly, the result of a compromise between state

---

[2] Some topics, such as legislation relating to railways and to corporations generally, lie partly in one sphere, partly in the other, and much inconvenience has thence resulted. See Chapter 29 *supra*.

issues and national issues, such as I have indicated in suggesting the second form of possible relation. The national issues have thrown matters of state competence entirely into the shade, and have done so almost from the foundation of the Republic. The local parties which existed in 1789 in most or all of the states were soon absorbed into the Federalists and Democratic Republicans who sprang into life after the adoption of the federal Constitution.

The results of this phenomenon have been so important that we may stop to examine its causes.

Within four years from their origin, the strife of the two great national parties became intense over the whole Union. From 1793 till 1815 grave issues of foreign policy, complicated with issues of domestic policy, stirred men to fierce passion and strenuous effort. State business, being more commonplace, exciting less feeling, awakening no interest outside state boundaries, fell into the background. The leaders who won fame and followers were national leaders; and a leader came to care for his influence within his state chiefly as a means of gaining strength in the wider national field. Even so restlessly active and versatile a people as the Americans cannot feel warmly about two sets of diverse interests at the same time, cannot create and work simultaneously two distinct and unconnected party organizations. The state, therefore, had, to use the transatlantic phrase, "to take the back seat." Before 1815 the process was complete; the dividing lines between parties in every state were those drawn by national questions. And from 1827 down to the end of the century the renewed keenness of party warfare kept these parties constantly on the stretch, and forced them to use all the support they could win in a state for the purposes of the national struggle.

There was one way in which predominance in a state could be so directly used. The federal senators are chosen by the state legislatures. The party therefore which gains a majority in the state legislature gains two seats in the smaller and more powerful branch of Congress. As parties in Congress are generally pretty equally balanced, this advantage is well worth fighting for and is a constant spur to the efforts of national politicians to carry the state elections in a particular state. Besides, in America, above all countries, nothing succeeds like success; and in each state the party which carries the state elections is held likely to carry the elections for the national House of Representatives, and for the president also.

Moreover, there are the offices. The federal offices in each state are very numerous. They are in the gift of whichever national party happens to be in power, i.e., counts among its members the president for the time being.

He bestows them upon those who in each state have worked hardest for the national party there. Thus the influence of Washington and its presiding deities is everywhere felt, and even the party which is in a minority in a particular state, and therefore loses its share of the state offices, may be cheered and fed by morsels of patronage from the national table. The national parties are in fact all-pervasive, and leave little room for the growth of any other groupings or organizations. A purely state party, indifferent to national issues, would, if it were started now, have no support from outside, would have few posts to bestow, because the state offices are neither numerous nor well paid, could have no pledge of permanence such as the vast mechanism of the national parties provides, would offer little prospect of aiding its leaders to win wealth or fame in the wider theatre of Congress.

Accordingly the national parties have complete possession of the field. In every state from Maine to Texas all state elections for the governorship and other offices are fought on their lines; all state legislatures are divided into members belonging to one or other of them. Every trial of strength in a state election is assumed to presage a similar result in a national election. Every state office is deemed as fitting a reward for services to the national party as for services in state contests. In fact the whole machinery is worked exactly as if the state were merely a subdivision of the Union for electoral purposes. Yet nearly all the questions which come before state legislatures have nothing whatever to do with the tenets of the national parties, while votes of state legislatures, except in respect of the choice of senators, can neither advance nor retard the progress of any cause which lies within the competence of Congress.

How has this system affected the working of the state governments, and especially of their legislatures?

It has prevented the growth within a state of state parties addressing themselves to the questions which belong to its legislature, and really affect its welfare.

The natural source of a party is a common belief, a common aim and purpose. For this men league themselves together, and agree to act in concert. A state party ought therefore to be formed out of persons who desire the state to do something, or not to do it; to pass such and such a law, to grant money to such and such an object. It is, however, formed with reference to no such aim or purpose, but to matters which the state cannot influence. Hence a singular unreality in the state parties. In the legislatures as well as through the electoral districts they cohere very closely. But this cohesion is of no service or significance for nine-tenths of the questions that come before the legislature for its decision, seeing that such questions are not touched by the platform of either party. Party, therefore, does not fulfil its legitimate ends. It does not produce the cooperation of leaders in preparing, of followers in supporting, a measure or line of policy. It does not secure the keen criticism by either side of the measures or policy advocated by the other. It is an artificial aggregation of persons linked together for purposes unconnected with the work they have to do.

This state of things may seem to possess the advantage of permitting questions to be considered on their merits, apart from that spirit of faction which in England, for instance, disposes the men on one side to reject a proposal of the other side on the score, not of its demerits, but of the quarter it proceeds from. Such an advantage would certainly exist if members were elected to the state legislatures irrespective of party, if the practice was to look out for good men who would manage state business prudently and pass useful laws. This, however, is not the practice. The strength of the national parties prevents it. Every member is elected as a party man; and the experiment of legislatures working without parties has as little chance of being tried in the several states as in Congress itself. There is yet another benefit which the plan seems to promise. The state legislatures may seem a narrow sphere for an enterprising genius, and their work uninteresting to a superior mind. But if they lead into the larger field of national politics, if distinction in them opens the door to a fame and power extending over the country, able men will seek to enter and to shine in the legislatures of the states. This is the same argument as is used by those who defend the practice, now general in England, of fighting municipal and other local elections on party lines. Better men, it is said, are glad to enter the town councils than could otherwise be induced to do so, because in doing so they serve the party, and establish a claim on it; they commend themselves to their fellow citizens as fit candidates for Parliament. The possible loss of not getting a good set of town councillors irrespective of party lines is thought to be more than compensated by the certain gain of men whose ambition would overlook a town council, were it not thus made a stage in their political career. This case is the more like that of America because these English municipal bodies have rarely anything to do with the issues which divide the two great English parties. Men are elected to them as Tories or Liberals whose Toryism or Liberalism is utterly indifferent so far as the business of the council goes.

Whether or no this reasoning be sound as regards England, I doubt if the American legislatures gain in efficiency by having only party men in them, and whether the elections would be any worse cared for if party was a secondary idea in the voters' minds. Already these elections are entirely in the hands of party managers, to whom intellect and knowledge do not commend an aspirant, any more than does character. Experience in a state legislature certainly gives a politician good chances of seeing behind the scenes, and makes him familiar with the methods employed by professionals. But it affords few opportunities for distinction in the higher walks of public life, and it is as likely to lower as to raise his aptitude for them. However, a good many men find their way into Congress through the state legislatures—though it is no longer the rule that persons chosen federal senators by those bodies must have served in them—and perhaps the average capacity of members is kept up by the presence of persons who seek to use the state legislature as a stepping-stone to something further. The question is purely speculative. Party has dominated and will dominate all state elections. Under existing conditions the thing cannot be otherwise.

It is, however, obviously impossible to treat as party matters many of the questions that come before the legislatures. Local and personal bills, which, it will be remembered, occupy by far the larger part of the time and labours of these bodies, do not fall within party lines at all. The only difference the party system makes to them is that a party leader who takes up such a bill has exceptional facilities for putting it through, and that a district which returns a member belonging to the majority has some advantage when trying to secure a benefit for itself. It is the same with appropriations of state funds to any local purpose. Members use their party influence and party affiliations; but the advocacy of such schemes and opposition to them have comparatively little to do with party divisions, and it constantly happens that men of both parties are found combining to carry some project by which they or their constituents will gain. Of course the less reputable a member is, the more apt will he be to enter into "rings" which have nothing to do with politics in their proper sense, the more ready to scheme with any trickster, to whichever party he adheres. Of measures belonging to what may be called genuine legislation, i.e., measures for improving the general law and administration of the state, some are so remote from any party issue, and so unlikely to enure to the credit of either party, that they are considered on their merits. A bill, for instance, for improving the state lunatic asylums, or forbidding lotteries, or restricting the freedom of divorce, would have nothing either to hope or to fear from party action. It would be introduced by some member who desired reform for its own sake, and would be passed if this member, having convinced the more enlightened among his colleagues that it would do good, or his colleagues generally that the people wished it, could overcome the difficulties which the pressure of a crowd of competing bills is sure to place in its way. Other public measures, however, may excite popular feeling, may be demanded by one class or section of opinion and resisted by another. Bills dealing with the sale of intoxicants, or regulating the hours of labour, or attacking railway companies, or prohibiting the sale of oleomargarine as butter, are matters of such keen interest to some one section of the population, that a party will gain support from many citizens by espousing them, and may possibly estrange others. Hence, though such bills have rarely any connection with the tenets of either party, it is worth the while of a party to win votes by throwing its weight for or against them, according as it judges that there is more to gain by taking the one course or the other. In the case of oleomargarine, for instance, there was clearly more to be gained by supporting than by opposing, because the farmers, especially in the agricultural Northwest, constitute a much stronger vote than any persons who could suffer by restricting the sale of the substance. We should accordingly expect to find, and observers did in fact find, both parties competing for the honour of passing such a bill. There was a race between a number of members, anxious to gain credit for themselves and their friends. Intoxicants open up a more difficult problem. Strong as the Prohibitionists and local option men are in all the Northern and Western, and, recently, in the Southern states also, the Germans, not to speak of the Irish and the liquor dealers, are in many states also so strong, and so fond of their beer, that it is a hazardous thing for a party to hoist the anti-liquor flag. Accordingly both parties are apt to fence with this question. Speaking broadly, therefore, these questions of general state legislation are not party questions, though liable at any moment to become so, if one or other party takes them up.

Is there then no such thing as a real state party, agitating or working solely within state limits, and inscribing on its banner a principle or project which state legislation can advance?

Such a party does sometimes arise. In California, for instance, there has long been a strong feeling against the Chinese, and a desire to exclude them. Both Republicans and Democrats were affected by the feeling, and fell in with it. But there sprang up a little later a third party, which claimed to be specially "anti-Mongolian," while also attacking capitalists and railways; and it lasted for some time, confusing the politics of the state. Questions affecting the canals of the state became at one time a powerful factor in the parties of New York. In Virginia the question of repudiating the state debt gave birth some time after the Civil War to a party which called itself the "Readjusters," and by the help of Negro votes carried the state at several elections. In some of the Northwestern states the farmers associated themselves in societies called "Granges," purporting to be formed for the promotion of agriculture, and created a Granger party, which secured drastic legislation against the railroad companies and other so-called monopolists. The same forces acting over a still wider area produced more recently the so-called Farmers' Alliance, which figured so prominently in the congressional elections of 1890, and under the name of the People's Party, in those of 1892. And in most states there now exists an active Prohibitionist party, which agitates for the strengthening and better enforcement of laws restricting or forbidding the sale of intoxicants. It deems itself also a national party, since it has an organization which covers a great part of the Union. But its operations are far more active in the states, because the liquor traffic belongs to state legislation, although the victories recently won for the anti-liquor cause have not usually been won by its own direct party action, but by the acceptance of the doctrine by one other of the regular parties.[3] Since, however, it can rarely secure many members in a state legislature, it acts chiefly by influencing the existing parties, and frightening them into pretending to meet its wishes.

All these groups or factions were or are associated on the basis of some doctrine or practical proposal which they put forward. But it sometimes also happens that, without any such basis, a party is formed in a state inside one of the regular national parties; or, in other words, that the national party in the state splits up into two factions, probably more embittered against each other than against the other regular party. Such state factions, for they hardly deserve to be called parties, generally arise from, or soon become coloured by, the rivalries of leaders, each of whom draws a certain number of politicians with him. New York is the state that has seen most of them; and in it they have tended of late years to grow more distinctly personal. The Hunkers and Barnburners who divided the Democratic party many years ago, and subsequently passed into the "Hards" and the "Softs," began in genuine differences of opinion about canal management and other state questions.[4] The "Stalwart" and "Half-breed" sections of the Republican party in the same state, whose bitter feuds amused the country a few years

---

[3] Congress has of course power to impose, and has imposed, an excise upon liquor, but this is far from meeting the demands of the temperance party.

[4] The names of these factions, the changes they pass through, and the way in which they immediately get involved with the ambitions and antipathies of particular leaders, recall the factions in the

ago, were mere factions, each attached to a leader, or group of leaders, but without distinctive principles. Still more purely personal were the factions of "Regular" and "Union" Republicans in Delaware, due to the efforts of a single politician to secure a seat in the United States Senate.

It will be seen from this fact, as well as from others given in the preceding chapter, that the dignity and magnitude of state politics have declined. They have become more pacific in methods, but less serious and more personal in their aims. In old days the state had real political struggles, in which men sometimes took up arms. There was a rebellion in Massachusetts in 1786–87, which it needed some smart fighting to put down, and another in Rhode Island in 1842, due to the discontent of the masses with the then existing constitution.[5] The battles of later generations have been fought at the polling booths, though sometimes won in the rooms where the votes are counted by partisan officials. That heads are counted instead of being broken is no doubt an improvement. But these struggles do not always stir the blood of the people as those of the old time did: they seem to evoke less patriotic interest in the state, less public spirit for securing her good government.

This change does not necessarily indicate a feebler sense of political duty. It is due to that shrivelling up of the state to which I referred in the last chapter. A century ago the state was a commonwealth comparable to an Italian republic like Bologna or Siena, or one of the German free imperial cities of the Middle Ages, to Lübeck, for instance, or to Nürnberg, which, though it formed part of the Empire, had a genuine and vigorous political life of its own, in which the faiths, hopes, passions of the citizens were involved. Nowadays the facilities of communication, the movements of trade, the unprecedented diffusion of literature, and, perhaps not least, the dominance of the great national parties, whose full tide swells all the creeks and inlets of a state no less than the mid channel of national politics at Washington, have drawn the minds of the masses as well as of the more

---

Italian cities of the thirteenth and fourteenth centuries, such as the White and Black Guelfs of Florence in the time of Dante.

[5] In these miniature civil wars there was a tendency for the city folk to be on one side and the agriculturists on the other, a phenomenon which was observed long ago in Greece, where the aristocratic party lived in the city and the poor in the fields. In the sixth century B.C. the oligarchic poet Theognis mourned over the degradation of political life which had followed the intrusion of the country churls. The hostility of the urban and rural population sometimes recurs in Switzerland. The country people of the canton of Basel fought a bloody battle some years ago with the people of the city, and the little commonwealth had to be subdivided into two, Basel City and Basel Country.

enlightened citizens away from the state legislatures, whose functions have come to seem trivial and their strifes petty.[6]

In saying this I do not mean to withdraw or modify what was said, in an earlier chapter, of the greatness of an American state, and the attachment of its inhabitants to it. Those propositions are, I believe, true of a state as compared to any local division of any European country, the cantons of Switzerland excepted. I am here speaking of a state as compared with the nation, and of men's feelings towards their state today as compared with the feelings of a century ago. I am, moreover, speaking not so much of sentimental loyalty to the state, considered as a whole, for this is still strong, but of the practical interest taken in its government. Even in Great Britain many a man is proud of his city, of Edinburgh say, or of Manchester, who takes only the slenderest interest in the management of its current business.

There is indeed some resemblance between the attitude of the inhabitants of a great English town towards their municipal government and that of the people of a state to their state government. The proceedings of English town councils are little followed or regarded either by the wealthier or the poorer residents. The humble voter does not know or care who is mayor. The head of a great mercantile house never thinks of offering himself for such a post. In London the Metropolitan Board of Works raised and spent a vast revenue; but its discussions were seldom commented on in the newspapers and very few persons of good social standing were to be found among it members. Even the London County Council attracts less attention than the magnitude of its operations deserves. Allowing for the contrast between the English bodies, with their strictly limited powers, and the immense competence of an American state legislature, this English phenomenon is sufficiently like those of America to be worth taking as an illustration.

We may accordingly say that the average American voter, belonging to the labouring or farming or shopkeeping class, troubles himself little about the conduct of state business. He votes the party ticket at elections as a good party man, and is pleased when his party wins. When a question comes up which interests him, like that of canal management, or the regulation of railway rates, or a limitation of the hours of labour, he is eager to use his vote, and watches what passes in the legislature. He is sometimes excited over a contest for the governorship, and if the candidate of the other

---

[6] Similar feelings made the three last surviving Hanseatic free cities willingly resign their independence to become members of the new German Empire, because the sentiment of pan-Germanic patriotism had so overborne the old fondness for local independence, that no regret was felt in resigning part of the latter in order to secure a share in the fuller national life of the great German state.

party is a stronger and more honest man, may possibly desert his party on that one issue. But in ordinary times he follows the proceedings of the legislature so little that an American humourist, describing the initial stages of dotage, observes that the poor old man took to filing the reports of the debates in his state legislature. The politics which the voter reads by preference are national politics; and especially whatever touches the next presidential election. In state contests that which chiefly fixes his attention is the influence of a state victory on an approaching national contest.

The more educated and thoughtful citizen, especially in great states, like New York and Pennsylvania, is apt to be disgusted by the sordidness of many state politicians and the pettiness of most. He regards Albany and Harrisburg much as he regards a wasps' nest in one of the trees of his suburban garden. The insects eat his fruit, and may sting his children; but it is too much trouble to set up a ladder and try to reach them. Some public-spirited young men have, however, occasionally thrown themselves into the muddy whirlpool of the New York legislature, chiefly for the sake of carrying acts for the better government of cities. When the tenacity of such men proves equal to their courage, they gain in time the active support of those who have hitherto stood aloof, regarding state politics as a squabble over offices and jobs. With the help of the press they were able to carry measures such as an improved Ballot Act, or Civil Service Act, or an act for checking expenditure at elections, reforms not only valuable in their own state but setting an example which other states are apt to follow. But the prevalence of the rule that a man can be elected only in the district where he lives, renders it difficult permanently to maintain a reforming party in a legislature, so those who, instead of shrugging their shoulders, put them to the wheel, generally prefer to carry their energies into the field of national politics, thinking that larger and swifter results are to be obtained there, because victories achieved in and through the national government have an immediate moral influence upon the country at large.

A European observer, sympathetic with the aims of the reformers, is inclined to think that the battle for honest government ought to be fought everywhere, in state legislatures and city councils as well as in the national elections and in the press, and is at first surprised that so much effort should be needed to secure what all good citizens, to whichever party they belong, might be expected to work for. But he would be indeed a self-confident European who should fancy he had discovered anything which had not already occurred to his shrewd American friends; and the longer such an observer studies the problem, the better does he learn to appreciate the difficulties which the system of party organization, which I must presently proceed to describe, throws in the way of all reforming efforts.

Note to the Edition of 1910

RECENT TENDENCIES IN STATE POLITICS

Upon a review of the last twenty years, I am led to believe that state legislatures, which had in most parts of the country lost some of the respect formerly entertained for them, have not declined any further in intellectual quality, and are on the whole less open to moral censure than they were in 1888. In some states, especially in the West, they are believed to have improved. Nevertheless the disposition of the people to distrust them continues. This appears not only in the restriction of their powers and the shortening of their sessions but also in two other noteworthy forms.

One is the tendency to turn from the legislature to the governor and encourage him to take the initiative and assert himself as a motive power leading the legislature and appealing directly to the people for their support. The difficulty of fixing responsibility upon large representative bodies seems both in states and in cities to be inducing the people to invest the executive head of the state or city with a discretion wider than would have formerly been allowed to him or than is allowed to executive officials in Great Britain. This is now visible not so much in the widening of his legal functions (although his power of appointing to posts has been in some states extended), as in the kind of authority which the governor is able, when personally capable, firm and upright, to exert.

The other form is the introduction of those highly democratic institutions, the referendum and the initiative. These, though as yet established in only a few of the Western states, give evidence of the desire which is spreading in the West for the people to take power out of the hands of the legislature and wield it themselves. The source of this desire probably lies not so much in the eagerness of the masses to carry further the principle of popular sovereignty, as in a certain impatience with the representative assemblies, which are supposed to be too largely the creatures of the party organizations and to be liable to yield to the influences which powerful financial interests can bring to bear. Such impatience is not always justified, for the masses sometimes expect from legislation benefits which no legislation can give and blame their representatives when the fault lies not in the latter but in the nature of things. But the people will in trying to do themselves the work they desire to have done doubtless come to learn in time how much harder that work is than they had believed, and how much more skill it needs than either they or their legislators have yet acquired.

The Territories

The national government has ever since its establishment possessed a vast area of land outside the limits of the several states, the larger part of which long remained wild, inhabited only by Indian tribes. When, with the westward advance of the whites, any particular region became sufficiently settled to require a regular government and be capable of some form of self-government, its boundaries were set, and it was erected into what is called a Territory. Most of the states admitted subsequently to the original thirteen were for a time Territories, and became states when they reached a certain population. The process went on till all the continental area of the United States was thus, after passing through the Territorial stage, distributed into states, and there now remains in that area only one region still called a Territory. This is Alaska. Outside the continent there is another Territory, viz., the Hawaiian Islands, of which I shall speak in a later chapter. Besides these two regions there is one part of the country which is not a state and has no self-governing institutions. The District of Columbia is a piece of land set apart to contain the city of Washington, which is the seat of the federal government. It is governed by three commissioners appointed by the president, and has no local legislature nor municipal government, the only legislative authority being Congress, in which it is not represented. Being well administered, it is held up by unfriendly critics of democracy as a model of the happy results of an enlightened despotism.

Alaska (area 590,884 square miles, population in 1910, 64,356, of whom half were Indians[1]) was under the direct authority of officers appointed by the president and of laws passed by Congress, until 1912, when Congress

---

[1] The total number of Indians in the United States (excluding Alaska) was returned in 1890 at 248,253, and in 1912 at 327,348.

provided for a local legislature. Its population has grown with the discovery of valuable minerals, but it is hardly likely for a long time to come to receive complete self-governing institutions.

Although the Territorial form of government has now ceased on the North American continent, it seems to deserve some description, not only because it still exists in Hawaii, and may possibly be applied elsewhere in the dominions of the United States, but also because it was so long in force over a vast area that some knowledge of it is needed to understand the phases through which the country passed.

Until 1889, the Organized Territories, eight in number, formed a broad belt extending from Canada on the north to Mexico on the south, and separating the states of the Mississippi Valley from those of the Pacific slope. In that year Congress passed acts under which three of them, Dakota (which divided itself into North Dakota and South Dakota), Montana, and Washington became entitled to be admitted as states; while in 1890 two others (Idaho and Wyoming) were similarly permitted to become states. Then the Territory of Utah was admitted and became a state (1894). Finally in 1910 an act was passed providing for the admission of Arizona and New Mexico so soon as they should give themselves proper constitutions. The Territory of Oklahoma and the region called Indian Territory, united to form the state of Oklahoma, were admitted in 1907. The Territorial form of government had some interesting features, for it differed from that which exists in the several states, and was in some points more akin to that of the self-governing colonies of Great Britain. This form was in each Territory created by federal statutes, beginning with the great Ordinance for the Government of the Territory of the United States northwest of the River Ohio, passed by the Congress of the Confederation in 1787. Since that year different statutes, not always similar in their provisions, were enacted for creating particular Territories, under the general power conferred upon Congress by the federal Constitution (art. IV, § 3).

The fundamental law of every Territory, as of every state, is the federal Constitution; but whereas every state has also its own popularly enacted state constitution, the Territories are not regulated by any similar instruments, which for them are replaced by the federal statutes establishing their government and prescribing its form.

In a Territory, as in every state, the executive, legislative, and judicial departments were kept distinct. At first local legislative power was vested in the governor and the judges; it was afterwards conferred on an elective legislature. In the later form, the executive consisted of a governor appointed for four years by the president of the United States, with the consent of the Senate, and removable by the president, together with a secretary, treasurer, auditor, and usually also a superintendent of public instruction and a librarian. The governor commanded the militia, and had a veto upon the acts of the legislature, which, however, was (in most Territories) capable of being overriden by a two-thirds majority in each house. He was responsible to the federal government, and reported yearly to the president on the condition of the Territory, often making his report a sort of prospectus in which the advantages which his dominions offered to intending immigrants were fondly set forth. He also sent a message to the legislature at the beginning of each session. Important as was the post of governor, it was often bestowed as a mere piece of party patronage, with no great regard to the fitness of the appointee.

The Territorial legislature was composed of two houses, a council of twelve persons, and a house of representatives of twenty-four persons, elected by districts. The session was limited (by federal statutes) to sixty days, and the salary of a member fixed at $4 per day. The houses worked much like those in the states, doing the bulk of their business by standing committees, and frequently suspending their rules to run measures through with little or no debate. The electoral franchise was left to be fixed by Territorial statute, but federal statutes prescribed that every member should be resident in the district he represented. The sphere of legislation allowed to the legislature was wide, indeed practically as wide as that enjoyed by the legislature of a state, but subject to certain federal restrictions.[2] It was subject also to the still more important right of Congress to annul or modify by its own statutes any Territorial act. In some Territories every act was directed to be submitted to Congress for its approval, and, if disapproved, to be of no effect; in others submission was not required. But in all Congress could exercise without stint its power to override the statutes passed by a Territorial legislature, as the British Parliament may override those of a self-governing colony. This power was not largely or often exercised. The

---

[2] Revised Statutes of U.S. of 1878, § 1854: "The legislative power of every Territory shall extend to all rightful subjects of legislation not inconsistent with the Constitution and laws of the United States. But no law shall be passed interfering with the primary disposal of the soil; no tax shall be imposed on the property of the United States, nor shall the lands or other property of non-residents be taxed higher than the lands or other property of residents."

§ 1889: "The legislative assemblies of the several Territories shall not grant private charters or especial privileges, but they may, by general incorporation acts, permit persons to associate themselves together" for various industrial and benevolent purposes specified. Other restrictions have been imposed by subsequent statutes.

most remarkable instance was furnished by Utah, where congressional legislation has had a hard fight in breaking down polygamy, finding it necessary even to impose a test oath upon voters.

The judiciary consisted of three or more judges of a supreme court, appointed for four years by the president, with the consent of the Senate, together with a U.S. district attorney and a U.S. marshal. The law administered was partly federal, all federal statutes being construed to take effect, where properly applicable, in the Territories, partly local, created in each Territory by its own statutes; and appeals, where the sum in dispute was above a certain value, went to the Supreme Federal Court. Although these courts were created by Congress in pursuance of its general sovereignty—they did not fall within the provisions of the Constitution for a federal judiciary— the Territorial legislature regulated their practice and procedure. The expenses of Territorial governments are borne by the federal treasury.

The Territories sent neither senators nor representatives to Congress, nor did they take part in presidential elections. The House of Representatives, under a statute, admitted a delegate from each of them to sit and speak, but of course not to vote, because the right of voting in Congress depends on the federal Constitution. The position of a citizen in a Territory therefore was, and is, a peculiar one.[3] What may be called his private or passive citizenship is complete: he has all the immunities and benefits which any other American citizen enjoys. But the public or active side is wanting, so far as the national government is concerned, although complete for local purposes.[4] He is in the position of an Australian subject of the British Crown, who has full British citizenship as respects private civil rights, and a share in the government of his own colony, but does not participate in the government of the British Empire at large, although personally eligible for any political office in the United Kingdom or any other part of the empire. It may seem inconsistent with principle that citizens should be taxed by a government in whose legislature they were not represented; but the practical objections to giving the full rights of states to these comparatively rude communities outweigh any such theoretical difficulties. It must moreover

---

[3] This applies to persons resident in Alaska and Hawaii.

[4] The Romans drew a somewhat similar distinction between the private rights of citizenship and the public rights, which included the suffrage and eligibility to office, but with them the distinction attached to the person; in the United States and the British Empire it is an affair of residence, and affects the suffrage only, not competence to fill an office. In the British general election of 1892 a distinguished Canadian statesman and a Parsi gentleman from Bombay were elected to the House of Commons, the former by an Irish and the latter by a London constituency, and other Canadians have sat in subsequent Parliaments.

be remembered that a Territory, which may be called an inchoate or rudimentary state, looks forward to becoming a complete state. When its population reached that of an average congressional district, its claim to be admitted as a state was strong, and in the absence of specific objections was granted. Congress, however, having absolute discretion in the matter, often used its discretion under the influence of partisan motives. Nevada was admitted to be a state when its population was only about 20,000, mainly for the sake of getting its vote for the Thirteenth Constitutional Amendment. After it rose to 62,266 it declined in 1890 to 45,000 but by 1910 had risen again to 81,875. Utah was long refused admission, because deemed, on account of the strength and peculiar institutions of the Mormon Church, not fit for that emancipation from the tutelage of Congress which its erection into a state would confer. When Congress resolved to turn a Territory into a state, it either (as happened in the cases of Idaho and Wyoming) passed an act accepting and ratifying a constitution already made for themselves by the people, and forthwith admitting the community as a state, or else passed what is called an Enabling Act, under which the inhabitants elected a constitutional convention, empowered to frame a draft constitution. When this constitution had been submitted to and accepted by the voters of the Territory, the act of Congress took effect; the Territory was transformed into a state, and proceeded to send its senators and representatives to Congress in the usual way. The enabling act might prescribe conditions to be fulfilled by the state constitution, but did not usually attempt to narrow the right to be enjoyed by the citizens of the newly-formed state of subsequently modifying that instrument in any way not inconsistent with the provisions of the federal Constitution. However, in the case of the Dakotas, Montana, Washington, Idaho, and Wyoming, the enabling act required the conventions to make "by ordinance irrevocable without the consent of the United States and the people of the said States" certain provisions, including one for perfect religious toleration and another for the maintenance of public schools free from sectarian control. This the six states did accordingly. But whether this requirement of the consent of Congress would be held binding if the people of the state should hereafter repeal the ordinance, *quaere*.

The arrangements above described worked well. Self-government was practically enjoyed by the Territories, despite the supreme authority of Congress, just as it is enjoyed by Canada, Australia, New Zealand, and South Africa despite the legal right of the British Parliament to legislate for every part of the king's dominions. The want of a voice in Congress and presidential elections, and the fact that the governor was set over them by an external power, were not felt to be practical grievances, partly of course because these young communities were too small and too much absorbed in the work of developing the country to be keenly interested in national politics. Their local political life resembled that of the newer Western states. Both Democrats and Republicans had their regular party organizations, but the business of a Territorial legislature gave little opportunity for any real political controversies, though abundant opportunities for local jobbing.

Before we pass away from the Territories, it may be proper to say a few words regarding the character and probable future of those which have passed into states since 1889.

The largest, the most populous, and in every way the most advanced was Dakota (now the two states of North Dakota and South Dakota) which lies west of Minnesota, and south of the Canadian province of Manitoba. Its area is 147,700 square miles, greater than that of Prussia, and much greater than that of the United Kingdom (120,500 square miles). Its eastern and southern parts are becoming filled, though less rapidly now than was the case some years back, by an intelligent farming population, largely Scandinavian in blood. Possessing a vast area of undulating prairie land, well fitted for wheat crops, and at least the eastern part of which receives enough rain to make tillage easy without irrigation, the two Dakotas may be ultimately destined to stand among the wealthiest and most powerful commonwealths in the Union.

Montana has an enormus area (145,310 square miles), but much of it consists of bare mountains or thin and scarcely profitable forest. There are, however, so many rich valleys and such an abundance of ranching land, together with some fine woodland, not to speak of the valuable mines, that the still scanty population will soon be large in some districts. In others, however, it must long remain sparse. But here, as in the western parts of Dakota, the introduction of irrigation, and of the dry farming methods, promises to increase largely the area of cultivable soil.

Washington, situated on the shores of the Pacific between Oregon and British Columbia, had a stronger claim than Montana, and was fully fit for the rank of a self-governing state. That part of it which lies west of the Cascade Range has a moist and equable climate, resembling the climate of western England, though somewhat less variable. Many of the familiar genera and even species of British plants reappear on its hillsides. The forests are by far the finest which the United States possess, and will, though they are being sadly squandered, remain a source of wealth for a century or more to come. I have travelled through many miles of woodland where nearly every tree was over 250 feet high. The eastern half of the state, lying on the inland side of the mountains, is very much drier, and with greater extremes of heat and cold; but it is in parts extremely fertile. Washington, which had in 1870 a population of only 23,955, had, in 1890, 349,390 inhabitants, and in 1910, 1,141,990.

The states of Wyoming and Idaho, which lie to the south and southwest of Montana and are traversed by a number of lofty ranges belonging to the Rocky Mountain system, have comparatively little argicultural land, and even their wide pastoral tracts suffer somewhat from the dryness of the climate. There are, however, rich mineral deposits, especially in Idaho; there are in some places extensive forests, though of trees inferior in size to those of the Pacific coast. The population of these states will therefore continue to increase rapidly, especially when the fertile lands of Dakota have been filled up. But that population seemed likely to remain for some time to come less dense, and less stable in its character, than the Dakotan; so it was doubted whether their admission, which was mainly due to party political motives, was a prudent act at a time when Wyoming had only 60,589 inhabitants (census of 1890) and Idaho only 84,229.

Utah was, before the arrival of the Mormons in 1848, a desert, and indeed an arid desert, whose lower grounds were convered with that growth of alkaline plants which the Americans call sagebrush.[5] The patient labour of the Saints, directed, at least during the pontificate of Brigham Young, by an able and vigilant autocracy, has transformed the tracts lying along the banks of streams into fertile grain, vegetable, and fruit farms. The water which descends from the mountains is turned over the level ground; the alkaline substances are soon washed out of the soil, and nothing more than irrigation is needed to produce excellent crops. After this process had advanced some way the discovery of rich silver mines drew in a swarm of Gentile colonists, and the non-Mormon population of some districts is now considerable. As Utah had, in 1890, 207,000 inhabitants, it would long before 1894 have been admitted as a state but for the desire of Congress to retain complete legislative control, and thereby to stamp out polygamy. That object seemed, however, at last likely to be attained, as at the latest Territorial election before 1894 the Gentiles proved to be in a majority. Although much of its surface is likely to remain barren and uninhabited,

---

[5] The so-called sagebrush plants are not species of what in England is called sage (*Salvia*) but mostly belong to the order *Compositae*, which is unusually strong in America. Something like a third of the total phaenogamous genera of the United States have been estimated to belong to it.

enough is fit for tillage and for dairy farming to give it a prospect of supporting a large settled population, and of late years many tracts have been rendered productive by irrigation.

Oklahoma (Indian: "beautiful lands") was the name of the Territory which a statute of 1890 created out of the central and almost unoccupied parts of the Indian Territory, which lay west of Arkansas and south of Kansas. The rest of that Indian Territory was united with it to form the new state of Oklahoma admitted in 1907. It is a rolling prairie country, diversified by ranges of picturesque hills, the eastern and central parts of it fit for agriculture without irrigation, and producing cotton and tobacco as well as wheat and maize. The soil, though sandy in parts, is generally fertile. Besides coal, zinc, and other minerals, there are oil-bearing tracts of great value. The population, which in 1890 was 61,834, and had in 1910 reached 1,657,155,[6] consists of recent immigrants, the northern counties having been occupied by men from Kansas, the southern by Texans and Arkansans, both of whom flooded it in a sudden wave, seeking to seize the land when it was thrown open to settlement. There are about 68,433 Indians, nearly all settled as landholding citizens, and each has a land allotment from the United States varying from forty acres to several thousand, according to value. The five civilized Indian nations (Cherokees, Creeks, Seminoles, Choctaws, and Chickasaws) have retained a certain measure of local organization and self-government, but they are also qualified voters. Most of them speak English, and most have settled down to agriculture or other industrial pursuits. All the Cherokees can read and write. There are also other Indian tribes, of whom the most numerous are the Osages. Of the 111,969 persons of colour some are descended from Negroes who before the Civil War were slaves of the Indians.

New Mexico, with an area larger than the United Kingdom (population in 1910, 327,301), is still largely peopled by Indo-Spanish Mexicans, who speak Spanish, and was, until 1910, deemed to be scarcely qualified for the self-government which organization as a state implies.[7] Over a large part of the country water is still too scarce and the soil too hilly to make tillage possible. The same remark applies to Arizona, in the southern part of which

---

[6] A part of this large increase is of course due to the union of Oklahoma and Indian Territories in 1907.

[7] There were, in 1900, 13,000 and in 1910, 20,000 Indians, some of them settled and comparatively civilized. Of these, many inhabit the so-called "pueblos," villages built on or excavated in rocks. They have preserved more traces of the primitive American culture than any other Indians in the United States.

the sides of the splendid mountain groups are barren, and the plains support only a scanty vegetation. There are however fine forests in the more northerly tracts, and in some places irrigation enables the soil to be cultivated. Both Territories are rich in minerals, but a mining population is not only apt to be disorderly, but is fluctuating, moving from camp to camp as richer deposits are discovered or old veins worked out. Ranching and mining are pursuits which do not draw in many permanent settlers. Still the time must come when the increase of population in the region immediately to the east of the Rocky Mountains will turn a fuller stream of immigration into these less promising regions, and bring under irrigation culture large tracts which are now not worth working. No one can yet say when that time will arrive. Many, including not a few of the more sober minded residents, thought that it was for the benefit of these two Territories themselves that they should remain content with that limited and qualified form of self-government which they had been enjoying. Congress has, however, thought otherwise; and now that statehood has been conferred upon them there remain no more Territories of the organized type on the American continent.

Europeans may ask why the theory of American democracy, which deems all citizens entitled to a voice in the national government, was not allowed to prevail at least so far as to give the inhabitants of the Territories the right of suffrage in congressional and presidential elections.

The question is a fair one. Were it possible under the federal Constitution to admit Territorial residents to active federal citizenship—i.e., to federal suffrage—admitted they would be. But the Union is a union of states. It knows no representatives in Congress, no electors for the presidency, except those chosen in states by state voters. The only means of granting federal suffrage to citizens in a Territory would be to turn the Territory into a state. To do this is to confer a power of self-government, guaranteed by the federal Constitution, for which the Territory may be still unfit, and therewith entitle this possibly small and rude community to send two senators to the federal Senate who have there as much weight as the two senators from New York with its nine millions of people. And a practical illustration of the evils to be feared has been afforded by the case of Nevada, a state whose inhabitants number only about 81,000, and which is really a group of mining camps, some of them already abandoned. Its population is obviously unworthy of the privilege of sending two men to the Senate, and did in fact allow itself to sink forthwith, for political purposes, into a sort of rotten borough which could be controlled or purchased by the leaders of a Silver Ring. It would evidently have been better to allow Nevada to remain in the condition of a

Territory till a large settled and orderly community had occupied her surface, which is at present a parched and dismal desert, where the streams that descend from the eastern slope of the Sierra Nevada soon lose themselves in lakes or marshes.

On a review of the whole matter it may safely be said that the American scheme of Territorial government, though it suffered from the occasional incompetence of the governor, and is inconsistent with democratic theory, worked well in practice, and gave little ground for discontent to the inhabitants of the Territories themselves.

Local Government

This is the place for an account of local government in the United States, because it is a matter regulated not by federal law but by the several states and Territories, each of which establishes such local authorities, rural and urban, as the people of the state or Territory desire, and invests them with the requisite powers. But this very fact indicates the immensity of the subject. Each state has its own system of local areas and authorities, created and worked under its own laws; and though these systems agree in many points, they differ in so many others, that a whole volume would be needed to give even a summary view of their peculiarities. All I can here attempt is to distinguish the leading types of local government to be found in the United States, to describe the prominent features of each type, and to explain the influence which the large scope and popular character of local administration exercise upon the general life and well-being of the American people.

Three types of rural local government are discernible in America. The first is characterized by its unit, the town or township, and exists in the six New England states. The second is characterized by a much larger unit, the county, and prevails in the Southern states. The third combines some features of the first with some of the second, and may be called the mixed system. It is found, under a considerable variety of forms, in the middle and Northwestern states. The differences of these three types are interesting, not only because of the practical instruction they afford, but also because they spring from original differences in the character of the colonists who settled along the American coast, and in the conditions under which the communities there founded were developed.

The first New England settlers were Puritans in religion, and sometimes inclined to republicanism in politics. They were largely townsfolk, accus-

tomed to municipal life and to vestry meetings. They planted their tiny
communities along the seashore and the banks of rivers, enclosing them
with stockades for protection against the warlike Indians. Each was obliged
to be self-sufficing, because divided by rocks and woods from the others.
Each had its common pasture on which the inhabitants turned out their
cattle, and which officers were elected to manage. Each was a religious as
well as a civil body politic, gathered round the church as its centre; and the
equality which prevailed in the congregation prevailed also in civil affairs,
the whole community meeting under a president or moderator to discuss
affairs of common interest. Each such settlement was called a town, or
township, and was in fact a miniature commonwealth, exercising a practical
sovereignty over the property and persons of its members—for there was as
yet no state, and the distant home government scarcely cared to interfere—
but exercising it on thoroughly democratic principles. Its centre was a group
of dwellings, often surrounded by a fence or wall, but it included a rural
area of several square miles, over which farmhouses and clusters of houses
began to spring up when the Indians retired. The name "town" covered the
whole of this area, which was never too large for all the inhabitants to come
together to a central place of meeting. This town organization remained
strong and close, the colonists being men of narrow means, and held together
in each settlement by the needs of defence. And though presently the towns
became aggregated into counties, and the legislature and governor, first of
the whole colony, and, after 1776, of the state, began to exert their superior
authority, the towns (which, be it remembered, remained rural communities,
making up the whole area of the state) held their ground, and are to this
day the true units of political life in New England, the solid foundation of
that well-compacted structure of self-government which European philosophers have admired and the new states of the West have sought to reproduce.
Till 1821[1] the towns were the only political corporate bodies in Massachusetts,
and till 1857 they formed, as they still form in Connecticut, the basis of
representation in her Assembly, each town, however small, returning at
least one member. Not a little of that robust, if somewhat narrow, localism
which characterizes the representative system of America is due to this

---

[1] Boston continued to be a town governed by a primary assembly of all citizens till 1822; and even
then the town meeting was not quite abolished, for a provision was introduced, intended to satisfy
conservative democratic feeling, into the city charter granted by statute in that year, empowering
the mayor and aldermen to call general meetings of the citizens qualified to vote in city affairs
"to consult upon the common good, to give instructions to their representatives, and to take all
lawful means to obtain a redress of any grievances." Such primary assemblies are, however, never
now convoked.

originally distinct and self-sufficing corporate life of the seventeenth-century towns. Nor is it without interest to observe that although they owed much to the conditions which surrounded the early colonists, forcing them to develop a civic patriotism resembling that of the republics of ancient Greece and Italy, they owed something also to those Teutonic traditions of semi-independent local communities, owning common property, and governing themselves by a primary assembly of all free inhabitants, which the English had brought with them from the Elbe and the Weser, and which, though already decaying, had been perpetuated in the practice of many parts of England, down till the days of the Stuart kings.

Very different were the circumstances of the Southern colonies. The men who went to Virginia and the Carolinas were not Puritans, nor did they mostly go in families and groups of families from the same neighbourhood. Many were casual adventurers, often belonging to the upper class, Episcopalians in religion, and with no such experience of, or attachment to, local self-government as the men of Massachusetts or Connecticut. They settled in a region where the Indian tribes were comparatively peaceable, and where therefore there was little need of concentration for the purposes of defence. The climate along the coast was somewhat too hot for European labour, so slaves were imported to cultivate the land. Population was thinly scattered; estates were large; the soil was fertile and soon enriched its owners. Thus a semi-feudal society grew up, in which authority naturally fell to the landowners, each of whom was the centre of a group of free dependants as well as the master of an increasing crowd of slaves. There were, therefore, comparatively few urban communities, and the life of the colony took a rural type. The houses of the planters lay miles apart from one another; and when local divisions had to be created, these were made large enough to include a considerable area of territory and number of landowning gentlemen. They were therefore rural divisions, counties framed on the model of English counties. Smaller circumscriptions there were, such as hundreds and parishes, but the hundred died out,[2] the parish ultimately became a purely ecclesiastical division, and the parish vestry was restricted to ecclesiastical functions, while the county remained the practically important unit of local administration, the

---

[2] In Maryland hundreds, which still exist in Delaware, were for a long time the chief administrative divisions. We hear there also of "baronies" and "town lands," as in Ireland; and Maryland is usually called a "province," while the other settlements are colonies. Among its judicial establishments there were courts of pypowdry (*piè poudré*) and "hustings."

The hundred is a division of small consequence in southern England, but in Lancashire it has some important duties. It repairs the bridges; it is liable for damage done in a riot; and it had its high constable.

unit to which the various functions of government were aggregated, and which, itself controlling minor authorities, was controlled by the state government alone. The affairs of the county were usually managed by a board of elective commissioners, and not, like those of the New England towns, by a primary assembly; and in an aristocratic society the leading planters had of course a predominating influence. Hence this form of local government was not only less democratic, but less stimulating and educative than that which prevailed in the New England states. Nor was the Virginian county, though so much larger than the New England town, ever as important an organism over against the state. It may almost be said, that while a New England state is a combination of towns, a Southern state is from the first an administrative as well as political whole, whose subdivisions, the counties, had never any truly independent life, but were and are mere subdivisions for the convenient dispatch of judicial and financial business.

In the Middle states of the Union, Pennsylvania, New Jersey, and New York, settled or conquered by Englishmen sometime later than New England, the town and town meeting did not as a rule exist, and the county was the original basis of organization. But as there grew up no planting aristocracy like that of Virginia or the Carolinas, the course of events took in the Middle states a different direction. As trade and manufactures grew, population became denser than in the South. New England influenced them, and influenced still more the newer commonwealths which arose in the Northwest, such as Ohio and Michigan, into which the surplus population of the East poured. And the result of this influence is seen in the growth through the Middle and Western states of a mixed system, which presents a sort of compromise between the county system of the South and the town system of the Northeast. There are great differences between the arrangements in one or other of these Middle and Western states. But it may be said, speaking generally, that in them the county is relatively less important than in the Southern states, the township less important than in New England. The county is perhaps to be regarded, at least in New York, Pennsylvania, and Ohio, as the true unit, and the townships (for so they are usually called) as its subdivisions. But the townships are vigorous organisms, which largely restrict the functions of the county authority, and give to local government, especially in the Northwest, a character generally similar to that which it wears in New England.

So much for the history of the subject; a history far more interesting in its details than will be supposed from the rough sketch to which limits of space restrict me. Let us now look at the actual constitution and working of the organs of local government in the three several regions mentioned, beginning with New England and the town system.[3] I will first set forth the dry but necessary outline, reserving comments for the following chapter.

The town is in rural districts the smallest local circumscription. English readers must be reminded that it is a rural, not an urban community, and that the largest group of houses it contains may be only what would be called in England a hamlet or small village. Its area seldom exceeds five square miles; its population is usually small, averaging less than 3,000, but occasionally ranges up to 13,000 and sometimes falls below 200.[4] It is governed by an assembly of all qualified voters resident within its limits, which meets at least once a year, in the spring (a reminiscence of the Easter vestry of England), and from time to time as summoned. There are usually three or four meetings each year. Notice is required to be given at least ten days previously, not only of the hour and place of meeting, but of the business to be brought forward. This assembly has, like the Roman Comitia and the Landesgemeinde in three of the older Swiss Cantons, the power both of electing officials and of legislating. It chooses the selectmen, school committee, and executive officers for the coming year; it enacts bye-laws and ordinances for the regulation of all local affairs; it receives the reports of the selectmen and the several committees, passes their accounts, hears what sums they propose to raise for the expenses of next year, and votes the necessary taxation accordingly, appropriating to the various local purposes—schools, aid to the poor, the repair of highways, and so forth— the sums directed to be levied. Its powers cover the management of the town lands and other property, and all local matters whatsoever, including police and sanitation. Every resident has the right to make, and to support by speech, any proposal. The meeting, which is presided over by a chairman called the moderator—a name recalling the ecclesiastical assemblies of the English Commonwealth[5]—is held in the town hall, if the town possesses

---

[3] The word Town, which I write with a capital when using it in the American sense, is the Icelandic *tún*, Anglo-Saxon *tûn*, German *Zaun*, and seems originally to have meant a hedge, then a hedged or fenced plot or enclosure. In Scotland (where it is pronounced "toon") it still denotes the farmhouse and buildings; in Iceland the manured grass plot, enclosed within a low green bank or raised dyke, which surrounds the baer or farmhouse. In parts of eastern England the chief cluster of houses in a parish is still often called "the town." In the North of England, where the parishes are more frequently larger than they are in the South, the civil divisions of a parish are called townships.

[4] I find in Massachusetts (census of 1910) one town (New Ashford) with only 92 inhabitants, and one (Brookline, a suburb of Boston) with 27,792, while Revere has 18,219. But both in this and other New England states most towns have a population of from 1,200 to 2,500.

[5] The presiding officer in the synods and assemblies of the Scottish Presbyterian Churches is still called the moderator. This is also the president's title in the synods of the American Presbyterian churches, and in the councils of the Congregationalist and associations of the Baptist churches.

one, or in the principal church or schoolhouse, but sometimes in the open air. The attendance is usually good; the debates sensible and practical. Much of course depends on the character and size of the population. Where it is of native American stock, and the number of voting citizens is not too great for thorough and calm discussion, no better school of politics can be imagined, nor any method of managing local affairs more certain to prevent jobbery and waste, to stimulate vigilance and breed contentment.[6] When, however, the town meeting has grown to exceed seven or eight hundred persons, where the element of farmers has been replaced by that of factory operatives, and still more when any considerable section are strangers, such as the Irish or French Canadians who have latterly poured into New England, the institution no longer works well, because the multitude is too large for debate, factions are likely to spring up, and the new immigrants, untrained in self-government, become the prey of wire-pullers or petty demagogues. The social conditions of today in New England are less favorable than those which gave birth to it; and there are now in the populous manufacturing states of Massachusetts, Rhode Island, and Connecticut comparatively few purely rural towns, such as those which suggested the famous eulogium of Jefferson, who eighty years ago desired to see the system transplanted to his own Virginia:

"Those wards called townships in New England are the vital principle of their governments, and have proved themselves the wisest invention ever devised by the wit of man for the perfect exercise of self-government, and for its preservation. . . . As Cato then concluded every speech with the words 'Carthago delenda est,' so do I every opinion with the injunction 'Divide the counties into wards.' "

The executive of a town consists of the selectmen, from three to nine in number, usually either three, five, or seven. They are elected annually, and manage all the ordinary business, of course under the directions given them by the last preceding meeting. There is also a town clerk, who keeps the records, and minutes the proceedings of the meeting, and is generally also registrar of births and deaths; a treasurer; assessors, who make a valuation of property within the town for the purposes of taxation; the collector, who gathers the taxes, and diverse minor officers, such as hogreeves[7] (now

---

[6] See an interesting account of the town meeting sixty years ago in Mr. J. K. Hosmer's *Life of Samuel Adams*, chap. xxiii. An instructive description of a typical New England town may be found in a pamphlet entitled *The Town of Groton*, by Dr. S. Green, late mayor of Boston.

[7] Mr. R. W. Emerson served in this capacity in his town, fulfilling the duty understood to devolve on every citizen of accepting an office to which the town appoints him.

usually called field drivers), cemetery trustees, library trustees, and so forth, according to local needs. There is always a school committee, with sometimes subcommittees for minor school districts if the town be a large one. Some of these officers and committees are paid (the selectmen usually), some unpaid, though allowed to charge their expenses actually incurred in town work; and there has generally been no difficulty in getting respectable and competent men to undertake the duties. Town elections are not professedly political, i.e., they are not usually fought on party lines, though occasionally party spirit affects them, and a man prominent in his party is more likely to obtain support.[8]

Next above the town stands the county. Its area and population vary a good deal. Massachusetts with an area of 8,040 square miles has fourteen counties; Rhode Island with 1,053 square miles has five; the more thinly peopled Maine, with 29,985 square miles, has sixteen, giving an average of about 1,100 square miles to each county on these three states, though in Rhode Island the average is only 211 square miles. The populations of the counties run from 3,000 upwards; the average population being, where there

---

[8] When a town reaches a certain population it is usually transformed by law into a city; but occasionally, while the city is created as a municipal corporation within the limits of a town, the town continues to exist as a distinct organization. A remarkable instance is furnished by the Town and City of New Haven, in Connecticut. New Haven was incorporated as a city in 1784. But it continued to be and is still a town also. Three-fourths of the area of the town and seventeen-eighteenths of its population are within the limits of the city. But the two governments remain completely distinct. The city has its mayor, aldermen, and common council, and its large executive staff. The town meeting elects its selectmen and other officers, 152 in all, receives their reports, orders and appropriates taxes, and so forth. Practically, however, it is so much dwarfed by the city as to attract little attention. Says Mr. Levermore: "This most venerable institution appears to-day in the guise of a gathering of a few citizens, who do the work of as many thousands. The few individuals who are or have been officially interested in the government of the town, meet together, talk over matters in a friendly way, decide what the rate of taxation for the coming year shall be, and adjourn. If others are present, it is generally as spectators rather than as participants. Even if Demos should be present in greater force, he would almost inevitably obey the voice of some well informed and influential member of th town government of his own party. But citizens of all parties and of all shades of respectability ignore the town meeting and school meeting alike. Not one-seventieth part of the citizens of the town has attended an annual town meeting; they hardly know when it is held. The newspapers give its transactions a scant notice, which some of their subscribers probably read. The actual governing force of the town is therefore an oligarchy in the bosom of a slumbering democracy. But the town is well governed. Its government carries too little spoil to attract those unreliable politicians who infest the city council. If the ruling junto should venture on too lavish a use of the town's money, an irresistible check would appear at once. Any twenty citizens could force the selectmen to summon the town together, and the apparent oligarchy would doubtless go down before the awakened people."—"The Town and City Government of New Haven," in *Johns Hopkins University Studies*, Fourth Series.

The student of Roman history will find in this quaint survival of an ancient assembly some resemblance to the *comitia curiata* of Rome under the later Republic.

are no large cities, from 30,000 to 50,000.[9] The county was originally an aggregation of towns for judicial purposes, and is still in the main a judicial district in and for which civil and criminal courts are held, some by county judges, some by state judges, and in and for which certain judicial officers are elected by the people at the polls, who also choose a sheriff and a clerk. Police belongs to the towns and cities, not to the county within which they lie. The chief administrative officers are the county commissioners, of whom there are three in Massachusetts (elected for three years, one in each year), and county treasurer.[10] They are salaried officers, and have the management of county buildings, such as courthouses and prisons, with power to lay out new highways from town to town, to grant licences, estimate the amount of taxation needed to defray county charges,[11] and apportion the county tax among the towns and cities by whom it is to be levied. But except in this last-mentioned respect the county authority has no power over the towns, and it will be perceived that while the county commissioners are controlled by the legislature, being limited by statute to certain well-defined administrative functions, there exists nothing in the nature of a county board or other assembly with legislative functions. The functions of the county are in fact of small consequence: it is a judicial district and a highway district and little more.

This New England system resembles that of Old England as the latter stood during the centuries that elapsed between the practical disappearance of the old county court or shire moot and the creation by comparatively recent statutes of such intermediate bodies and authorities as poor-law unions, highway districts and boards, local sanitary authorities. If we compare the New England scheme with that of the England of today, we are struck not only by the greater simplicity of the former, but also by the fact that it is the smaller organisms, the towns, that are most powerful and most highly vitalized. Nearly everything belongs to them, only those duties devolving on the counties which a small organism obviously cannot undertake. The system of self-governing towns no doubt works under the

---

[9] The average population of a Massachusetts county if 240,450, the two smallest counties having only 4,504 and 2,962 respectively, the largest 669,915.

[10] In Connecticut the commissioners are appointed by the state legislature and have no taxing power. In Rhode Island there are none but judicial officers for the counties. In Vermont I find besides judges, a state attorney, high bailiff, and county clerk. In Massachusetts all judges are appointed by the governor.

[11] The chief items of county expenditure are those for judicial purposes, including the maintenance of buildings, and for roads and bridges. But in some states roads, except the few state roads, are maintained by the town.

supervision of a body, the state legislature, which can give far closer attention to local affairs than the English Parliament can give to English local business. But in point of fact the state legislature interferes but little (less, I think, than the Local Government Board interferes in England) with the conduct of rural local business, though often required to deal with the applications which towns make to be divided or have their boundaries altered, and which are frequently resisted by a part of the inhabitants.

The town meeting system has, in the opinion of American publicists, begun to decline in New England. Many of the rural areas have become too populous for it, and the new immigrants that have flocked in—French-speaking Canadians, Irish, and people from Central or Southern Europe—are less fit to work such a system than were the pure English stock of a century ago.

The system which prevails in the Southern states need not long detain us, for it is less instructive and has proved less successful. Here the unit is the county, except in Louisiana, where the equivalent division is called a parish. The county was originally a judicial division, established for the purposes of local courts, and a financial one, for the collection of state taxes. It has now, however, generally received some other functions, such as the superintendence of public schools, the care of the poor, and the management of roads. In the South counties are larger than in New England, but not more populous, for the country is thinly peopled.[12] The county officers, whose titles and powers vary somewhat in different states, are usually the board or court of county commissioners, an assessor (who prepares the valuation), a collector (who gathers the taxes[13]), a treasurer, a superintendent of education, an overseer of roads—all of course salaried, and now, as a rule, elected by the people, mostly for one or two years.[14] These county officers have, besides the functions indicated by their names, the charge of the police and the poor, and of the construction of public works, such as bridges and prisons. The county judges and the sheriff, and frequently the coroner, are also chosen by the people. The sheriff is everywhere in America neither an ornamental person, as he has become in England, nor a judge,

[12] Georgia, with 59,475 square miles, has 137 counties; Alabama, with 52,250 square miles, has 66. Speaking generally, the newer states have the larger counties, just as in England the smallest parishes are in the first settled parts of England, or rather in those parts where population was comparatively dense at the time when parishes sprang up.

[13] Sometimes, as in Louisiana, the sheriff is also tax collector.

[14] In some states some of these officials are nominated by the governor. In Florida the governor appoints even the board of five county commissioners. The other county officers, viz., clerk of circuit court, sheriff, constables, assessor of taxes, tax collector, treasurer, superintendent of public instruction, and surveyor, are elected by the people for two or four years.

with certain executive functions, as in Scotland, but the chief executive officer of the judicial machinery of the county.

In these Southern states there exist various local divisions smaller than the counties.[15] Their names and their attributions vary from state to state, but they have no legislative authority like that of the town meeting of New England, and their officers have very limited powers, being for most purposes controlled by the county authorities. The most important local body is the school committee for each school district. In several states, such as Virginia and North Carolina, we now find townships, and the present tendency seems in these states to be towards the development of something resembling the New England town. It is a tendency which grows with the growth of population, with the progress of manufactures and of the middle and industrious working class occupied therein, and especially with the increased desire for education. The school, someone truly says, is becoming the nucleus of local self-government in the South now, as the church was in New England two centuries ago.[16] Nowhere, however, has there appeared either a primary assembly; while the representative local assembly is still in its infancy. Local authorities in the South, and in the states which, like Nevada and Oregon, may be said to have adopted the county system, are generally executive officers and nothing more.

The third type is less easy to characterize than either of the two preceding, and the forms under which it appears in the Middle and Northwestern states are even more various than those referable to the second type. Two features mark it. One is the importance and power of the county, which in the history of most of these states appears before any smaller division; the other is the activity of the township,[17] which has more independence and a larger range of competence than under the system of the South. Now of these two features the former is the more conspicuous in one group of states— Pennsylvania, New Jersey, New York, Ohio, Indiana, Iowa; the latter in another group—Michigan, Illinois, Wisconsin, Minnesota, the two Dakotas, the reason being that the New Englanders, who were often the largest and always the most intelligent and energetic element among the settlers in the more northern of these two state groups, carried with them their attachment to the town system and their sense of its value, and succeeded, though

---

[15] In South Carolina the parish was originally a pretty strong local unit, but it withered away as the county grew under the influence of the plantation system. The word "parish" is in America now practically equivalent to "congregation," and does not denote a local area.

[16] Virginia has moved in this direction. See Mr. Gerge E. Howard's treatise, *Local Constitutional History of the United States,* and Mr. Fairlie's recent book on *Local Government in Counties, Towns, and Villages.*

[17] "Township" is the term most frequently used outside New England, "town" in New England.

sometimes not without a struggle, in establishing it in the six great and prosperous commonwealths which form that group. On the other hand, while Pennsylvania, New Jersey, and New York had not (from the causes already stated) started with the town system, they never adopted it completely; while in Ohio and Indiana the influx of settlers from the slave states, as well as from New York and Pennsylvania, gave to the county an early preponderance, which it has since retained. The conflict of the New England element with the Southern element is best seen in Illinois, the northern half of which state was settled by men of New England blood, the southern half by pioneers from Kentucky and Tennessee. The latter, coming first, established the county system, but the New Englanders fought against it, and in the constitutional convention of 1848 carried a provision, embodied in the constitution of that year, and repeated in the present constitution of 1870, whereby any county may adopt a system of township organization "whenever the majority of the legal voters of the county voting at any general election shall so determine."[18] Under this power four-fifths of the 102 counties have now adopted the township system.[19]

Illinois furnishes so good a sample of that system in its newer form that I cannot do better than extract, from a clear and trustworthy writer, the following account of the whole scheme of local self-government in that state, which is fairly typical of the Northwest:

> When the people of a county have voted to adopt the township system, the commissioners proceed to divide the county into towns, making them conform with the congressional or school townships, except in special cases. Every town is invested with corporate capacity to be a party in legal suits, to own and control property, and to make contracts. The annual town-meeting of the whole voting population, held on the first Tuesday in April, for the election of town officers and the transaction of miscellaneous business, is the central fact in the town government. The people assembled in town-meeting may make any orders concerning the acquisition, use, or sale of town property; direct officers in the exercise of their duties; vote taxes for roads and bridges, and for other lawful purposes; vote to institute or defend suits at law; legislate on the subject of noxious weeds, and offer rewards to encourage the extermination of noxious plants and vermin; regulate the running at large of cattle and other animals; establish pounds, and provide for the impounding and sale of stray and trespassing

[18] See Constitution of 1870, art. x, § 5, where a provision is added that any county desiring to forsake township organization may do so by a vote of the electors in the county, in which case it comes under the county system prescribed in the following sections of that article.

[19] Illinois has 102 counties, with an average population, in 1910, of 55,000; Iowa 99 counties, with an average population in 1910 of 22,675. The average population of the 40 counties of England (excluding Wales) was (in 1901) 548,000.

animals; provide public wells and watering-places; enact bye-laws and rules to carry their powers into effect; impose fines and penalties, and apply such fines in any manner conducive to the interests of the town.[20]

The town officers are a supervisor, who is *ex officio* overseer of the poor, a clerk, an assessor, and a collector, all of whom are chosen annually; three commissioners of highways elected for three years, one retiring every year; and two justices of the peace and two constables, who hold office for four years.

Every male citizen of the United States who is twenty-one years old, who has resided in the State a year, in the county ninety days, and in the township thirty days, is entitled to vote at town meeting; but a year's residence in the town is required for eligibility to office.

The supervisor is both a town and a county officer. He is general manager of town business, and is also a member of the county board, which is composed of the supervisors of the several towns, and which has general control of the county business. He also acts as overseer of the poor. The law leaves it to be determined by the people of a county whether the separate towns or the county at large shall assume the care of paupers. When the town has the matter in charge, the overseer generally provides for the indigent by a system of out-door relief. If the county supports the poor, the county board is authorized to establish a poorhouse and farm for the permanent care of the destitute, and temporary relief is afforded by the overseers in their respective towns, at the county's expense. The supervsor, assessor, and clerk constitute a Board of Health.

Town officers are compensated according to a schedule of fixed fees for specific services, or else receive certain *per diem* wages for time actually employed in official duties. The tax collector's emolument is a percentage.

For school purposes, the township is a separate and distinct corporation, with the legal style, "Trustees of Schools of Township ———, Range ———," according to the number by which the township is designated in the Congressional Survey. The school trustees, three in number, are usually elected with the officers of the civil township at town meetings, and hold office for three years. They can divide the township into school districts. It must be remembered that the township is exactly six miles square. It is the custom to divide it into nine districts, two miles square, and to erect a schoolhouse near the centre of each. As the county roads are, in most instances, constructed on the section lines—and therefore run north and south, east and west, at intervals of a mile—the traveller expects to find a schoolhouse at every alternate crossing. The people who live in these sub-districts elect three school directors, who control the school in their neighbourhood. They are obliged to maintain a free school for not less than five nor more than nine months in every year, are empowered to build and furnish schoolhouses,

---

[20] There are English analogies to all these powers, but in England some of them are or were exercised in the manor court and not in the vestry.

hire teachers and fix their salaries, and determine what studies shall be taught. They may levy taxes on all the taxable property in their district, but are forbidden to exceed a rate of two per cent for educational or three per cent for building purposes.

The township funds for the support of schools arise from three sources. (1) The proceeds of the school lands given by the United States Government, the interest from which alone may be expended. (2) The State annually levies on all property a tax of one-fifth of one per cent, which constitutes a State school fund, and is divided among the counties in the ratio of their school population, and is further distributed among the townships in the same ratio. (3) Any amount needed in addition to these sums is raised by taxation in the districts under authority of the directors. All persons between the ages of six and twenty-one years are entitled to free school privileges. Women are eligible to every school office in the State, and are frequently chosen directors.

The average Illinois county contains sixteen townships. The county government is established at some place designated by the voters, and called the "county seat." The corporate powers of the county are exercised by the county board, which, in counties under township organization, is composed of the several town supervisors, while in other counties it consists of three commissioners elected by the people of the whole country. The board manage all county property, funds, and business; erect a court-house, jail, poorhouse, and any necessary buildings; levy county taxes, audit all accounts and claims against the county, and, in counties not under township organization, have general oversight of highways and paupers. Even in counties which have given the care of highways to the townships, the county board may appropriate funds to aid in constructing the more important roads and expensive bridges. The treasurer, sheriff,[21] coroner, and surveyor are county functionaries.[22]

The county superintendent of schools has oversight of all educational matters, advises town trustees and district directors, and collects complete school statistics, which he reports to the county board, and transmits to the State superintendent of public instruction.

Every county elects a judge, who has full probate jurisdiction, and appoints administrators and guardians. He also has jurisdiction in civil suits at law, involving not more than $1,000, in such minor criminal cases as are cognizable by a justice of the peace, and may entertain appeals from justices or police courts. The State is divided into thirteen judicial districts, in each of which the people elect three judges, who constitute a circuit court. The tribunal holds two or more sessions annually in each county within the circuit, and is attended at every term

---

[21] The sheriff is the executive officer of the higher courts, with responsibility for the peace of the county. In case of riot he may call out the county militia.

[22] Ordinary police work, other than judicial, is not a county matter, but left to the township with its constables.

by a grand or petit jury. It has a general original jurisdiction, and hears appeals from the county judge and from justices' courts.

To complete the judicial system of the State there are four appellate courts and one supreme court of last resort. Taxes whether for State, county, or town purposes are computed on the basis of the assessment made by the town assessor, and are collected by the town collector. The assessor views and values all real estate, and requires from all persons a true list of their personal property. The assessor, clerk, and supervisor, constitute a town equalizing board, to hear complaints and to adjust and correct the assessment.

The assessors' books from all the towns then go before the county board, who make such corrections as cause valuations in one town to bear just relation to valuations in the others. The county clerk transmits an abstract of the corrected assessment to the auditor of the State, who places it in the hands of a State board of equalization.

This board adjust valuations between counties. All taxes are estimated and collected on this finally corrected assessment. The State authorities, the county board, the town supervisors, the highway commissioners, the township school trustees, and the proper officers of incorporated cities and villages, all certify to the county clerk a statement of the amount they require for their several purposes. The clerk prepares a collection-book for each town explaining therein the sum to be raised for each purpose. Having collected the total amount the collector disburses to each proper authority its respective quota. In all elections, whether for President of the United States, representatives in Congress, State officers or county officers, the township constitutes an election precinct, and the supervisor, assessor, and collector sit as the election judges.

The words "town" and "township" signify a territorial division of the county, incorporated for purposes of local government. There remains to be mentioned a very numerous class of municipal corporations known in Illinois statutes as "villages" and "cities." A minimum population of three hundred, occupying not more than two square miles in extent, may by popular vote become incorporated as a "village," under provisions of the general law. Six village trustees are chosen, and they make one of their number president, thereby conferring on him the general duties of a mayor. At their discretion the trustees appoint a clerk, a treasurer, a street commissioner, a village constable, and other officers as they deem necessary. The people may elect a police magistrate whose jurisdiction is equal to that of a justice of the peace.[23]

A similar picture of the town meeting in Michigan is given by another recent authority:

---

[23] "Local Government in Illinois," by Albert Shaw, LL.D., in *Johns Hopkins University Studies*, Baltimore, 1883.

The first Monday in April of each year every citizen of the United States twenty-one years of age and upwards who has resided in the State six months, and in the township the ten days preceding, has the right of attending and participating in the meeting. The supervisor, the chief executive officer of the township, presides. After the choice of officers for the ensuing year the electors proceed to the discussion of town business. Complaint is perhaps made that the cattle in a certain part of the township are doing damage by running at large, a bye-law is passed forbidding the same under penalty not exceeding ten dollars.

A bridge may be wanted in another part of the township, but the inhabitants of that road district cannot bear the expense; the town-meeting votes the necessary amount not exceeding the limits of law, for the laws restricting the amount of taxation and indebtedness are very particular in their provisions.

The voters may regulate the keeping and sale of gunpowder, the licensing of dogs and the maintenance of hospitals, and may order the vaccination of all inhabitants. They can also decide how much of the one-mil tax on every dollar of the valuation shall be applied to the purchase of books for the township library, the residue going to schools.

The annual reports of the various township officers charged with the disbursement of public moneys are also submitted at this time. In short, whatever is local in character and affecting the township only is subject to the control of the people assembled in town-meeting.

Yet we may notice some minor differences between the New England town meeting and its sister in Michigan. In the latter the bye-laws and regulations are less varied in character.

This is due to the fact that in the West that part of the township where the inhabitants are most numerous, the village, and for whose regulation many laws are necessary, is set off as an incorporated village, just as in nearly all the Central and Western States. These villages have the privilege, either directly in village meeting or more often through a council of five or more trustees, of managing their own local affairs, their police, fire department, streets and waterworks. In some States, however, they are considered parts of the township, and as such vote in town meeting on all questions touching township roads, bridges, the poor and schools.[24]

The conspicuous feature of this system is the reappearance of the New England town meeting, though in a somewhat less primitive and at the same time less perfect form, because the township of the West is a more artificial organism than the rural town of Massachusetts or Rhode Island, where, until after the middle of the nineteenth century, nearly everybody was of English blood, everybody knew everybody else, everybody was educated,

---

[24] *Local Government in Michigan*, by E. W. Bemis, in *Johns Hopkins University Studies*, Baltimore, 1883.

not only in book learning, but in the traditions of self-government. However, such as it is, the Illinois and Michigan system has spread and seems likely to spread further. It exists in Wisconsin and Minnesota. Recent legislation permits its adoption in California, Nebraska, and in the two Dakotas, though in the western parts of these two last-named states few townships have been as yet established.[25]

A high authority writes to me:

"Attendance and interest in the town-meetings of the Northwest are much below those in the New England towns.[26] The importance of township government in these States is also diminished by the separate organization of villages and small cities and by the greater development of county functions."

In the proportion to the extent in which a state has adopted the township system the county has tended to decline in importance. It is nevertheless of more consequence in the West than in New England. It has frequently an educational official who inspects the schools, and it raises a tax for aiding schools in the poorer townships. It has duties, which are naturally more important in a new than in an old state, of laying out main roads and erecting bridges and other public works. And sometimes it has the oversight of township expenditure.[27] The board of county commissioners consists in Michigan and Illinois of the supervisors of all the townships within the county; in Wisconsin and Minnesota the commissioners are directly chosen at a county election.

---

[25] In Switzerland the rural Gemeinde or Commune is the basis of the whole republican system of the canton. It has charge of the police, the poor, and schools, and owns land. It has a primary assembly, meeting several times a year, which discusses communal business and elects an administrative council. It resembles in these respects an American town or township, but is subject for some purposes to the jurisdiction of an official called the Statthalter, appointed by the canton for a district comprising a number of communes.

[26] "In townships of 500 to 600 voters an attendance of 10 to 20 is often reported, while in many cases the business is transacted by members of the township board. Under these conditions there can be little of the active popular debate, which makes the New England meeting an interesting object of study." Fairlie, *Local Government in Counties, Towns, and Villages*, p. 170.

[27] Mr. Bemis says: "Inasmuch as many of the thousand or more townships of a State lack the political education and conservatism necessary for perfect self-control, since also many through lack of means cannot raise sufficient money for roads, bridges, schools, and the poor, a higher authority is needed, with the power of equalizing the valuation of several contiguous towns, of taxing the whole number for the benefit of the poorer, and of exercising a general oversight over township expenses. . . . All educators earnestly advocate county and State control of schools, that there may be uniformity of methods, and that the country districts, the nurseries of our great men in the past, may not degenerate. But two influences oppose: the fear of centralization on the part of the small towns which need it most, and the dislike of the rich cities to tax themselves for the country districts."—*Local Government in Michigan, ut supra*, p. 18.

The authority to whom I have already referred observes:

The County is of much more consequence throughout the Middle and North-West than in New England. In addition to judicial administration, county expenditures for charities, roads and bridges, and educational purpose are of considerable importance. County poorhouses are maintained; and poor relief is largely a county function. Main roads and bridges and sometimes drainage ditches and other public works are built by the county, though county expenditure for these purposes is less in States like Illinois and Michigan, where the town-meeting exists, than in Ohio and Indiana. The per capita county expenditure in the States of the Middle West is in fact larger than in any other group of States except the Mountain and Pacific States; while in addition to county expenditures, county officials collect an important part of the State revenues, and sometimes have the oversight of township expenditure.

In Michigan, in most counties in Illinois, and in Wisconsin, county administration and finances are in charge of a board of supervisors elected by townships and cities, as in New York. In some Illinois counties and in Minnesota, the Dakotas, and Nebraska, there are small county boards of three to seven members, usually elected by districts. The larger boards of supervisors are more representative, but seem to be less efficient administrative authorities; and in a number of the larger counties of Michigan some of the powers of these boards have been transferred to small boards of auditors. As a rule, these county boards have no important legislative power; but in Michigan, by an act of 1909, the boards of supervisors were given a general grant of local legislative power, to meet the conditions brought about by the restriction on special acts by the legislature in the new constitution of that state.

Other elective county officers in these states are the prosecuting attorney, sheriff, coroner, county clerk, county treasurer, auditor or assessor, and surveyor.

The political importance of the county is indicated by the position occupied by the county committee in the party organizations, and by the centring of campaign activity within this district.

I pass to the mixed or compromise system as it appears in the other group of states, of which Pennsylvania, Ohio, Indiana, and Iowa may be taken as samples. In these states we find no town meeting. Their township may have greater or less power, but its members do not come together in a primary assembly; it elects its local officers, and acts only through and by them. In Ohio there are three township trustees with the entire charge of local affairs, a clerk, and a treasurer. In Pennsylvania the township is governed by two or three supervisors, elected for three years, one each year, together with an assessor (for valuation purposes), a town clerk, three auditors, six school directors, elected for three years, two each year; and (where the poor are a township charge) two overseers of the poor. The supervisors may lay a rate on the township not exceeding one per cent on the valuation of the property within its limits for the repair of roads, highways, and bridges, and the overseers of the poor may, with the consent of two justices,[28] levy a similar tax for the poor. But as the poor are usually a county charge, and as any ratepayer may work out his road tax in labour, township rates amount to very little. "In Iowa," says Mr. Macy,

the civil township, which is usually six miles square, is a local government for holding elections, repairing roads, testing property, giving relief to the poor, and other business of local interest. Its officers are three trustees, one clerk, a road supervisor for each road district, one assessor, two or more justices of the peace, and two or more constables. The justices and constables are in a sense county officers. Yet they are elected by townships, and if they remove from the township in which they are chosen, they cease to be officers. The trustees are chosen for three years, but their terms of office are so arranged that one is chosen each year. The other officers are chosen for two years. If there is within the limits of the township an incorporated town or city, the law requires that at least one of the justices shall live within the town or city. The voters within the town or city choose a separate assessor. The voters of the city are not allowed to vote for road supervisors nor for the township assessor; they vote for all other township officers. . . .

The trustees of the township have various duties in the administration of the poor laws. An able-bodied person applying for aid may be required to work upon the streets or highways. If a person who has acquired a legal settlement in the county, and who has no near relatives able to support him, applies to the trustees for aid, it is their duty to look into the case and furnish or refuse relief. If they decide to furnish it, they may do so by sending the person to the county poorhouse, or by giving him what they think needful in food, clothing, medical attendance, or money. If they refuse aid, the applicant may go to the county supervisors, and they may order the trustees to furnish aid; or if the supervisors think the trustees are giving aid unwisely, they may order them to withhold it. In all cases where aid is furnished directly by the trustees to the applicant they are required to send a statement of the expense incurred to the auditor of the county, who presents the bills to the board of supervisors. All bills for the relief of the poor are paid by the county, and the supervisors if they choose may take the entire business out of the hands of the trustees. But in counties where no poorhouse is provided,

---

[28] Justices are elected by the people for five years, and commissioned by the governor of the state.

and where the supervisors make no provision for the poor, the trustees are required to take entire charge of the business. Yet in any case the county must meet the expenses. The trustees are the health officers of the township. They may require persons to be vaccinated; they may require the removal of filth injurious to health; they may adopt bye-laws for preserving the health of the community and enforce them by fine and imprisonment.[29]

In most of these states the county overshadows the township. Taking Pennsylvania as an example, we find each county governed by a board of three commissioners, elected for three years, upon a minority vote system, the elector being allowed to vote for two candidates only. Besides these there are officers, also chosen by popular vote for three years, viz., a sheriff, coroner, prothonotary, registrar of wills, recorder of deeds, treasurer, surveyor, three auditors, clerk of the court, district attorney. Some of these officers are paid by fees, except in counties whose population exceeds 50,000, where salaries are usually provided. A county with at least 40,000 inhabitants is a judicial district, and elects its judge for a term of ten years. No new county is to contain less than 400 square miles or 20,000 inhabitants.[30] The county, besides its judicial business and the management of the prisons incident thereto, besides its duties as respects highways and bridges, has educational and usually also poor-law functions; and it levies its county tax and the state taxes through a collector for each township whom it and not the township appoints. It audits the accounts of townships, and has other rights of control over these minor communities exceeding those allowed by Michigan or Illinois. I must not omit to remark that where any local area is not governed by a primary assembly of all its citizens, as in those states where there is no town meeting, and in all states in respect to counties, a method is frequently provided for taking the judgment of the citizens of the local area, be it township or county, by popular vote at the polls upon a specific question, usually the borrowing of money or the levying of a rate beyond the regular amount. This is an extension to local divisions of the so-called "plebiscitary" or *referendum* method, whose application to state legislation has been discussed in a preceding chapter. It seems to work well, for by providing an exceptional method of meeting exceptional cases, it enables the ordinary powers of executive officials, whether in township or county, to be kept within narrow limits.

[29] *Our Government Text-Book for Iowa Schools*, pp. 21–23.
[30] See Constitution of Pennsylvania of 1873, arts. XIV, XIII, and V.
  The average population of a county in Pennsylvania was, in 1910, 114, 405. There are sixty-seven.

Want of space has compelled me to omit from this sketch many details which might interest European students of local government, nor can I attempt to indicate the relations of the rural areas, townships, and counties, to the incorporated villages and cities which lie within their compass further than by observing that cities, even the smaller ones, are usually separated from the townships, that is to say, the township government is superseded by the city government, while cities of all grades remain members of the counties, bear their share in county taxation, and join in county elections. Often, however, the constitution of a state contains special provisions to meet the case of a city so large as practically to overshadow or absorb the county, as Chicago does the county of Cook, and Cincinnati the county of Hamilton, and sometimes the city is made a county by itself.

Observations on Local Government

It may serve to clear up a necessarily intricate description if I add here a few general remarks applicable to all, or nearly all, of the various systems of local government that prevail in the several states of the Union.

I. Following American authorities, I have treated the New England type of system as a distinct one, and referred the Northwestern states to the mixed type. But the European reader may perhaps figure the three systems most vividly to his mind if he will divide the Union into three zones—Northern, Middle, and Southern. In the Northern, which, beginning at the the Bay of Fundy, stretches west to Puget Sound, he will find a primary assembly, the town or township meeting, in preponderant activity as the unit of local government. In the Middle zone, stretching from New York to California, inclusive, along the fortieth parallel of latitude, he will find the township dividing with the county the interests and energy of the people. In some states of this zone the county is the more important organism and dwarfs the township; in some the township seems to be gaining on the county; but all are alike in this, that you cannot lose sight for a moment of either the smaller or the larger area, and that both areas are governed by elected executive officers. The third zone includes all the Southern states, in which the county is the predominant organism, though here and there school districts and even townships are growing in significance.

II. Both county and township are, like nearly everything else in America, English institutions which have suffered a sea change. "The Southern county is an attenuated English shire with the towns left out."[1] The Northern township is an English seventeenth-century parish, in which age the English

---

[1] Professor Macy, *Our Government*, an admirable elementary sketch, for school use, of the structure and functions of the federal and states governments.

parish was still in full working order as a civil no less than an ecclesiastical organization, holding common property, and often coextensive with a town. The town meeting is partly perhaps the manor court, partly the English vestry; the selectmen correspond in a way to the churchwardens, or select vestrymen, called back by the conditions of colonial life into an activity fuller than they exerted in England even in the seventeenth century, and far fuller than they retained in the nineteenth.[2] In England local self-government, except as regards the poor law, tended to decay in the smaller (i.e., parish or township) areas; the greater part of such administration as these latter needed, fell either to the justices in petty sessions or to officials appointed by the county or by the central government, until the legislation of the present century began to create new districts, especially poor law and sanitary districts, for local administration.[3] In the wider English area, the county, true self-government died out with the ancient shire moot, and fell into the hands of persons (the justices assembled in Quarter Sessions) nominated by the Crown, on the recommendation of the lord-lieutenant. It was only in 1888 that a system of elective county councils was created by statute, only in 1894 that primary parish meetings were created in the less populous local areas, parish councils in those somewhat larger. In the American colonies the governor filled the place which the Crown held in England; but even in colonial days there was a tendency to substitute popular election for gubernatorial nomination; and county government, obeying the universal impulse, is now everywhere democratic in form; though in the South, while slavery and the plantation system lasted, it was practically aristocratic in its spirit and working.

III. In England the control of the central government—that is, of Parliament—is now maintained not only by statutes defining the duties and

---

[2] Few things in English history are better worth studying, or have exercised a more pervading influence on the progress of events, than the practical disappearance from rural England of that commune or Gemeinde which has remained so potent a factor in the economic and social as well as the political life of France and Italy, of Germany (including Austrian Germany) and of Switzerland. If Englishmen were half as active in the study of their own local institutions as Americans have begun to be in that of theirs, we should have had a copious literature upon this interesting subject.

In England the primary meeting died out in the form of the parish vestry, but in 1894 a system of parish meetings and councils was created by statute and the primary meeting thereby restored in a new form to meet the now more democratic conditions of the country. See Chapter 39 *ante*.

[3] However, the parish constables and way-wardens in some places continue to be elected by popular vote; and the manor courts and courts leet (still surviving in places) were semi-popular institutions.

In counties the coroner continued to be elected by the freeholders, but in 1888 the appointment was transferred by statute to the newly created county councils.

limiting the powers of the various local bodies, but also by the powers vested in sundry departments of the executive, the Local Government Board, Home Office, and Treasury, of disallowing certain acts of these bodies, and especially of supervising their expenditure and checking their borrowing. In American states the executive departments have no similar functions. The local authorities are restrained partly by the state legislature, whose statutes of course bind them, but still more effectively, because legislatures are not always to be trusted, by the state constitutions. These instruments usually— the more recent ones I think invariably—contain provisions limiting the amount which a county, township, village, school district, or other local area may borrow, and often also the amount of tax it may levy, by reference to the valuation of the property contained within its limits. They have been found valuable in checking the growth of local indebtedness, which had become, even in rural districts, a serious danger.[4] The total local debt was in 1902:

Counties	$196,564,619
School Districts	46,188,015
Total	$242,752,634

This sum bears a comparatively small proportion to the total debt of the several states and of the cities, which was then:

States	$ 234,908,837
Cities, villages, townships, precincts, etc.	1,387,316,976

County and school district debts declined 8 per cent between 1870 and 1880, whereas city indebtedness was then rapidly increasing. Since 1880 all three have risen, though slowly, except the school district debt, which grew fast. The aggregate debt of counties and minor civil divisions (including cities) was in 1902 $1,630,069,610, being $20.74 per capita, a large rise from 1890, when it was $14.79 per capita.

IV. County and township or school district taxes are direct taxes, there being no octroi in America, and are collected along with state taxes in the

---

[4] See also Chapter 43 on state finance. These provisions are of course applied to cities also, which need them even more. They vary very much in their details, and in some cases a special popular vote is allowed to extend the limit.

In New York State, for instance, no county or city can incur a debt bringing its total indebtedness up to more than 10 per cent of the assessed valuation of its real estate, and its taxation, beyond what is required to pay interest on the debt, shall not exceed 2 per cent of the assessed valuation of its real and personal estate.

smallest tax-gathering area, i.e., the township, where townships exist.[5] Local rates are not, however, as in England, levied on immovable property only, but also on personal property, or rather so much of it as the assessors can reach. Lands and houses are often assessed far below their true value, because the township assessors have an interest in diminishing the share of the county tax which will fall upon their township similar to the interest of the county assessors in diminishing the share of the state tax to be borne by their county.[6] Real property is taxed in the place where it is situate; personalty only in the place where the owner resides.[7] But the suffrage, in local as well as in state and national elections, is irrespective of property. It goes with residence, and no citizen can vote in more than one place. A man may have a dozen houses or farms in as many cities, counties, or townships; he will vote, even for local purposes, only in the spot where he is held to reside.

The great bulk of local expenditure is borne by local taxes. But in some states a portion of the county taxes is allotted to the aid of school districts, so as to make the wealthier districts relieve the burden of the poorer, and often a similar subvention is made from state revenues. The public schools, which are everywhere and in all grades gratuitous, absorb a very large part of the whole revenue locally raised,[8] and in addition to what taxation provides they receive a large revenue from the lands which, under federal or state legislation, have been set apart for educational purposes.[9] On the whole, the burden of taxation in rural districts is not heavy, nor is the expenditure often wasteful, because the inhabitants, especially under the town-meeting system, look closely after it.[10]

V. It is noteworthy that the Americans, who are supposed to be especially

---

[5] Sometimes, however, they are paid at the county seat.

[6] As to this and the Boards of Equalization see Chapter 43 ante.

[7] Of course what is really the same property may be taxed in more than one place, e.g., a mining company may be taxed as a company in Montana, and the shares held by individual proprietors be possibly also taxed in the several states in which these shareholders reside.

[8] The total expenditure on public schools in the United States is stated by the U.S. Commissioner of Education in his annual report for 1910 as being, in 1909, $401,397,747.

[9] Students of economic science will hear without surprise that in some of the states which have the largest permanent school fund the effect on the efficiency of the schools, and on the interest of the people in them, has been pernicious. In education, as well as in eleemosynary and ecclesiastical matters, endowments would seem to be a very doubtful benefit.

[10] Expenditure has, however, greatly risen. In the Massachusetts town of Quincy, for instance, the average annual levy of taxation between 1792 and 1800 was $1,000, about $1 to each inhabitant taxpayer; it was in 1892, $12.57. In 1792 the education of each child in the public school cost $3 per annum: in 1892 it cost $16 (*The Centennial Milestone*, by Charles F. Adams).

fond of representative assemblies, have made very little use of representation in their local government. The township is usually governed either by a primary assembly of all citizens or else, as in such states as Ohio and Iowa, by a very small board, not exceeding three, with, in both sets of cases, several purely executive officers.[11] In the county there is seldom or never a county board possessing legislative functions (though New York has begun to tend that way), usually only three commissioners or supervisors with some few executive or judicial officers. Local legislation (except in so far as it appears in the bye-laws of the town meeting or selectmen) is discouraged. The people seem jealous of their county officials, electing them for short terms, and restricting each to a special range of duties. This is perhaps only another way of saying that the county, even in the South, has continued to be an artificial entity, and has drawn to itself no great part of the interest and affections of the citizens. Over five-sixths of the Union each county presents a square figure on the map, with nothing distinctive about it, nothing "natural" about it, in the sense in which such English counties as Kent or Cornwall are natural entities. It is too large for the personal interest of the citizens: that goes to the township. It is too small to have traditions which command the respect or touch the affections of its inhabitants: these belong to the state.[12]

VI. The chief functions local government has to discharge in the United States may be summarized in a few paragraphs:

Making and repairing roads and bridges. These prime necessities of rural life are provided for by the township, county, or state, according to the class to which a road or bridge belongs. That the roads of America are proverbially ill-built and ill-kept is due partly to the climate, with its alternations of severe frost, occasional torrential rains (in the Middle and Southern states), and long droughts; partly to the hasty habits of the people, who are too busy with other things, and too eager to use their capital in private enterprises to be willing to spend freely on highways; partly also to the thinness of population, which is, except in a few manufacturing districts, much less dense than in Western Europe. In many districts railways have come before roads, so roads have been the less used and cared for.[13]

---

[11] In a few Western states the town board has (like the New England selectmen) a limited taxing power, as well as administrative duties.

[12] In Virginia there used to be a county feeling resembling that of England, but this vanished in the social revolution that has transformed the South.

[13] In some parts of New England and New York, and conspicuously in New Jersey, there has been of late years a great improvement in the roads, and several states have constructed state roads equal to those of France.

The administration of justice was one of the first needs which caused the formation of the county, and matters connected with it still form a large part of county business. The voters elect a judge or judges, and the local prosecuting officer, called the district attorney, and the chief executive officer, the sheriff.[14] Prisons are a matter of county concern. Police is always locally regulated, but in the Northern states more usually by the township than by the county. However, this branch of government, so momentous in continental Europe, is in America comparatively unimportant outside the cities. The rural districts get on nearly everywhere with no guardians of the peace, beyond the township constable;[15] nor does the state government, except, of course, through statutes, exercise any control over local police administration.[16] In the rural parts of the Eastern and Middle states property is as safe as anywhere in the world. In such parts of the West as are disturbed by dacoits, or by solitary highwaymen, travellers defend themselves, and, if the sheriff is distant or slack, lynch law may usefully be invoked. The care of the poor is thrown almost everywhere upon local and not upon state authorities,[17] and defrayed out of local funds, sometimes by the county, sometimes by the township. The poor laws of the several states differ in so many particulars that it is impossible to give even an outline of them here. Little outdoor relief is given, though in most states the relieving authority may, at his or their discretion, bestow it; and pauperism is not, and has never been, a serious malady, except in some few of the greater cities, where it is vigorously combated by volunteer organizations largely composed of ladies. The total number of persons returned as alms-house-paupers in the whole Union was, in 1880, 73,045, and in 1910, 84,419. There are no trustworthy statistics regarding the number of persons receiving outdoor relief over the country as a whole, but it is extremely small, being 1.014 per thousand to the estimated population.

Sanitation, which has become so important a department of English local administration, plays a small part in the rural districts of America, because their population is so much more thinly spread over the surface that the need for drainage and the removal of nuisances is less pressing; moreover, as the humbler classes are better off, unhealthy dwellings are far less

[14] The American sheriff remains something like what the English sheriff was before his wings were clipped by legislation early in the nineteenth century. Even then he mostly acted by deputy. The justices and the county police have since that legislation largely superseded his action.

[15] Or, in states where there are no townships, some corresponding officer.

[16] As to recent experiments, see p. 443 *ante*, state police.

[17] In some states there are poor-law superintendents, and usually state institutions for particular classes of paupers, e.g., pauper lunatics.

common. Public health officers and sanitary inspectors would, over the larger part of the county, have little occupation.[18]

To education, I can refer only in passing, because the differences between the arrangements of the several states are too numerous to be described here. It has hitherto been not only a more distinctively local matter, but one relatively far more important than in England, France, or Italy. And there is usually a special administrative body, often a special administrative area, created for its purposes—the school committee and the school district.[19] The vast sum expended on public instruction has been already mentioned. Though primarily dealt with by the smallest local circumscription, there is a growing tendency for both the county and the state to interest themselves in the work of instruction by way of inspection, and to some extent of pecuniary subventions. Not only does the county often appoint a county superintendent, but there are in some states county high schools and (in most) county boards of education, besides a State Board of Commissioners.[20] I need hardly add that the schools of all grades are more numerous and efficient in the Northern and Western than in the Southern states, which are still comparatively poor, where the population is seldom dense, and where it is deemed needful to separate white and coloured children. In old colonial days, when the English Commissioners for Foreign Plantations asked for information on the subject of education from the governors of Virginia and Connecticut, the former replied, "I thank God there are no free schools or printing presses, and I hope we shall not have any these hundred years";[21] and the latter, "One-fourth of the annual revenue of the colony is laid out in maintaining free schools for the education of our children." The disparity was prolonged and intensified in the South by the existence of slavery. Now that slavery has gone, the South makes rapid advances; but the proportion of illiteracy, especially of course among the Negroes, is still high.[22]

[18] Sanitation, however, has received much attention in the cities, and the death rate has in many been greatly reduced.

[19] Though the school district frequently coincides with the township, it has generally (outside of New England) distinct administrative officers, and when it coincides it is often subdivided into lesser districts.

[20] In some states provision is made for the combination of several school districts to maintain a superior school at a central spot.

[21] Governor Sir William Berkeley, however, was among the Virginians who in 1660 subscribed for the erection in Virginia of a "a colledge of students of the liberal arts and sciences." As to elementary instruction he said that Virginia pursued "the same course that is taken in England out of towns, every man according to his ability instructing his children. We have forty-eight parishes, and our ministry are well paid, and, by consent, should be better if they would pray oftener and preach less."—*The College of William and Mary*, by Dr. H. B. Adams.

[22] The percentage of illiterate persons at least 10 years of age to the whole population of continental United States was, in 1900, 10.7, and in 1910, 7.7 (of white population, 5.0 of Negroes, 30.4);

It will be observed that of the general functions of local government above described, three, viz., police, sanitation, and poor relief, are simpler and less costly than in England, and indeed in most parts of western and central Europe. It has therefore proved easier to vest the management of all in the same local authority, and to get on with a smaller number of special executive officers. Education is indeed almost the only matter which has been deemed to demand a special body to handle it. Nevertheless, even in America the increasing complexity of civilization, and the growing tendency to invoke governmental aid for the satisfaction of wants which were not previously felt, or if felt, were met by voluntary action, tend to enlarge the sphere and multiply the functions of local government.

VII. How far has the spirit of political party permeated rural local government? I have myself asked this question a hundred times in travelling through America, yet I find it hard to give any general answer, because there are great diversities in this regard not only between different states, but between different parts of the same state, diversities due sometimes to the character of the population, sometimes to the varying intensity of party feeling, sometimes to the greater or less degree in which the areas of local government coincide with the election districts in which state senators or representatives are chosen. On the whole it would seem that county officials are apt to be chosen on political lines, not so much because any political questions come before them, or because they can exert much influence on state or federal elections, as because these paid offices afford a means of rewarding political services and securing political adhesions. Each of the great parties usually holds its county convention and runs its "county ticket," with the unfortunate result of intruding national politics into matters with which they have nothing to do, and of making it more difficult for good citizens outside the class of professional politicians to find their way into county administration. However, the party candidates are seldom bad men, and the ordinary voter is less apt to vote blindly for the party nominee than he would be in federal or state elections. In the township and rural school district party spirit is much less active. The offices are often unpaid, and the personal merits of the candidates are better known to the voters than are

---

it was highest in Louisiana, 29.0, and South Carolina, 25.7; lowest in Iowa, 1.7; and Nebraska and Oregon, each 1.9.

It has recently been proposed in Congress to reduce the surplus in the U.S. treasury by distributing sums among the states in aid of education, in proportion to the need which exists for schools, i.e., to their illiteracy. The objections on the score of economic policy, as well as of constitutional law, are so obvious as to have stimulated a warm resistance to the bill.

those of the politicians who seek for county office.[23] Rings and bosses (of whom more anon) are not unknown even in rural New England. School committee elections are often influenced by party affiliations. But on the whole, the township and its government keep themselves pretty generally out of the political whirlpool. Their posts are filled by honest and reasonably competent men.

VIII. The apparent complexity of the system of local government sketched in the last preceding chapter is due entirely to the variations between the several states. In each state it is, as compared with that of rural England, eminently simple. There are few local divisions, few authorities; the divisions and authorities rarely overlap. No third local area and local authority intermediate between township and county, and similar to the English Rural District with its Council has been found necessary. Especially simple is the method of levying taxes. In most states a citizen pays at the same time, to the same officer, upon the same paper of demand, all his local taxes, and not only these, but also his state tax; in fact, all the direct taxes which he is required to pay. The state is spared the expense of maintaining a separate collecting staff, for it leans upon and uses the local officials who do the purely local work. The taxpayer has not the worry of repeated calls upon his cheque book.[24] Nor is this simplicity and activity of local administration due to its undertaking fewer duties, as compared with the state, than is the case in Europe. On the contrary, the sphere of local government is in America unusually wide,[25] and widest in what may be called the most characteristically American and democratic regions, New England and the Northwest. Americans often reply to the criticisms which Europeans pass on the faults of their state legislatures and the shortcomings of Congress by pointing to the healthy efficiency of their rural administration, which enables them to bear with composure the defects of the higher organs of government, defects which would be less tolerable in a centralized country, where the national government deals directly with local affairs, or where local authorities await an initiative from above.

Of the three or four types or systems of local government which I have described, that of the town or township with its popular primary assembly has been the best. It is the cheapest and the most efficient; it is the most

---

[23] Sometimes the party "ticket" leaves a blank space for the voter to insert the name of the candidates for whom he votes for township offices.

[24] City taxes, however, and the local school tax, are sometimes paid separately. Some states give the option of paying half-yearly or quarterly; and many allow discount upon payment in advance.

[25] The functions are not perhaps so numerous as in England, but this is because fewer functions are needed. The practical competence of local authorities for undertaking any new functions that may become needed, and which the state may entrust to them, is deemed sufficient.

educative to the citizens who bear a part in it. The town meeting has been not only the source but the school of democracy.[26] The action of so small a unit needs, however, to be supplemented, perhaps also in some points supervised, by that of the county, and in this respect the mixed system of the Middle states is deemed to have borne its part in the creation of a more perfect type. For some time past an assimilative process has been going on over the United States tending to the evolution of such a type.[27] In adopting the township system of New England, the Northwestern states have borrowed some of the attributes of the Middle states' county system. The Middle states have developed the township into a higher vitality than it formerly possessed there. Some of the Southern states are introducing the township, and others are likely to follow as they advance in population and education. It is possible that by the middle or end of the twentieth century there will prevail one system, uniform in its outlines, over the whole country, with the township for its basis, and the county as the organ called to deal with those matters which, while they are too large for township management, it seems inexpedient to remit to the unhealthy atmosphere of a state capital.

[26] In Rhode Island it was the towns that made the state.

[27] This tendency is visible not least as regards the systems of educational administration. The National Teachers' Association of the United States not long since prepared an elaborate report on the various existing systems, and the more progressive states are on the alert to profit by one another's experience.

The Government of Cities

The growth of great cities has been among the most significant and least fortunate changes in the character of the population of the United States during the century that has passed since 1787. The census of 1790 showed only five cities with more than 8,000, and only one with more than 33,000 inhabitants. In 1880 there were 286 exceeding 8,000, forty-five exceeding 40,000, nineteen exceeding 100,000; while the census of 1910 showed 774 exceeding 8,000, 228 exceeding 25,000, 50 exceeding 100,000. The ratio of persons living in cities exceeding 8,000 inhabitants to the total population was, in 1790, 3.35 per cent, in 1840, 8.52, in 1880, 22.57, in 1890, 29.12, in 1910, 38.74 per cent. And this change has gone on with accelerated speed notwithstanding the enormous extension of settlement over the vast regions of the West. Needless to say that a still larger and increasing proportion of the wealth of the country is gathered into the larger cities. Their government is therefore a matter of high concern to America, and one which cannot be omitted from a discussion of transatlantic politics. Such a discussion is, however, exposed to two difficulties. One is that the actual working of municipal government in the United States is so inextricably involved with the party system that it is hard to understand or judge it without a comprehension of that system, an account of which I am, nevertheless, forced to reserve for subsequent chapters. The other is that the laws which regulate municipal government are even more diverse from one another than those whence I have drawn the account already given of state governments and rural local government. For not only has each state its own system of laws for the government of cities, but within a state there is, as regards the cities, little uniformity in municipal arrangements. Larger cities are often governed differently from the smaller ones; and one large city is differently organized from another. So far as the legal arrangements go, no general description, such as might be given of English municipal governments under the Municipal Corporation Acts, is possible in America. I am therefore obliged to confine myself to a few features common to most city governments, occasionally taking illustrations from the constitution or history of some one or other of the leading municipalities.

The history of American cities, though striking and instructive, has been short. Of the ten greatest cities of today only three—Baltimore, New York, and Philadelphia—were municipal corporations in 1820.[1] Every city has received its form of government from the state in which it stands, and this form has been repeatedly modified. Formerly each city obtained a special charter; now in nearly all states there are general laws under which a population of a certain size and density may be incorporated. Yet, as observed above, special legislation for particular cities, especially the greater ones, continues to be very frequent.

Although American city governments have a general resemblance to those English municipalities which were their first model,[2] their present structure shows them to have been much influenced by that of the state governments. We find in most of the larger cities:[3]

A mayor, head of the executive, and elected directly by the voters within the city

Certain executive officers or boards, some directly elected by the city voters, others nominated by the mayor or chosen by the city legislature

A legislature, consisting usually of two, but sometimes of one chamber, directly elected by the city voters

Judges, usually elected by the city voters, but sometimes appointed by the state, or (as to some judges) by the mayor

What is this but the frame of a state government applied to the smaller area of a city? The mayor corresponds to the governor, the officers or boards to the various state officials and boards (described in Chapter 41) elected, in most cases, by the people; the aldermen and common council (as they

---

[1] The term "city" denotes in America what is called in England a municipal borough, and has nothing to do with either size or antiquity. The constitution or frame of government of a city is called its charter and is given by a state statute, general or special, or else is enacted by the city itself under powers given to it by the state.

[2] American municipalities have, of course, never been, since the Revolution, close corporations like most English boroughs before the Act of 1835.

[3] This statement would have been universally true before the recent adoption in a constantly increasing number of cities of the plan of government by a small board of commissioners.

are generally called) to the state Senate and Assembly; the city elective judiciary to the state elective judiciary.[4]

A few words on each of these municipal authorities. The mayor is by far the most conspicuous figure in city governments, much more important than the mayor of an English or Irish borough, or the provost of a Scotch one. He holds office, sometimes for one year, but now more frequently for two, three, or four years. The general tendency is toward a four-year term, as in New York, Baltimore, Chicago, Philadelphia, Boston, and St. Louis. In some cities he is not reeligible. He is directly elected by the people of the whole city, and is usually not a member of the city legislature.[5] He has, almost everywhere, a veto on all ordinances passed by that legislature, which, however, can be overriden by a two-thirds majority. In many cities he appoints some among the heads of departments and administrative boards, though usually the approval of the legislature or of one branch of it[6] is required. Quite recently some city charters have gone so far as to make him generally responsible for all the departments (subject to the control of supply by the legislative body), and therewith, liable to impeachment for misfeasance.[7] He receives a considerable salary, varying with the size of the city, and in New York City reaching $15,000. It rests with him, as the chief executive officer, to provide for the public peace, to quell riots, and, if necessary, to call out the militia. He often exerts, in practice, some discretion as to the enforcement of the law; he may, for instance, put in force Sunday Closing Acts or regulations, or omit to do so.

The practical work of administration is carried on by a number of departments, sometimes under one head, sometimes constituted as boards or commissions. The most important of these are directly elected by the people, for a term of one, two, or four years. Some, however, are chosen by the city legislature, some by the mayor with the approval of the legislature or its upper chamber. In most cities the chief executive officers have been disconnected from one another, owing no common allegiance, except that

---

[4] American municipal governments are of course subject to three general rules: that they have no powers other than those conferred on them by the state, that they cannot delegate their powers, and that their legislation and action generally is subject to the Constitution of the United States as well as to the constitution and statutes of the state to which they belong.

[5] In Chicago and San Francisco the mayor sits in the legislature.

[6] In New York and Boston the mayor appoints and removes heads of departments, and the tendency is generally toward an increase of his powers.

[7] Much complexity has arisen from the practice of giving special charters to particular cities, or passing special bills relating to them, and there is now a tendency to empower cities to make their own charters.

which their financial dependence on the city legislature involves, and communicating less with the city legislature as a whole than with its committees, each charged with some one branch of administration, and each apt to job it.

Education has been generally treated as a distinct matter, with which neither the mayor nor the legislature has been suffered to meddle. It is committed to a Board of Education, whose members are separately elected by the people, or, as in Brooklyn, appointed by the mayor, levy (though they do not themselves collect) a separate tax, and have an executive staff of their own at their disposal.[8]

The city legislature usually consists in small cities of one chamber, in large ones of two, the upper of which generally bears the name of the board of aldermen, the lower that of the common council.[9] All are elected by the citizens, generally in wards, but the upper house occasionally by districts or on what is called a "general ticket," i.e., a vote over the whole city.[10] Usually the common council is elected for one year, or at most for two years, the upper chamber frequently for a longer period.[11] Both are usually unpaid in the smaller cities, sometimes paid in the larger. All city legislation, that is to say, ordinances, bye-laws, and votes of money from the city treasury, are passed by the council or councils, subject in many cases to the mayor's veto. Except in a few cities governed by very recent charters, the councils have some control over at least the minor officials. Such control is exercised by committees, a method borrowed from the state and national legislatures, and suggested by the same reasons of convenience which have established it there, but proved by experience to have the evils of secrecy

---

[8] There are some points of resemblance in this system to the government of English cities, and especially of London. The English common councils elect certain officials and manage their business by committees. In the ancient City of London the sheriffs and chamberlain are elected by the liverymen. Note, however, that in no English borough or city do we find a two-chambered legislature, nor (except as last aforesaid in London) officials elected by popular vote, nor a veto on legislation vested in the mayor. London (outside the ancient city which retains a separate government) is now governed by an elected assembly called the county council, and by the elected councils of the boroughs into which it is divided.

[9] Some large cities, however (e.g., Greater New York, Chicago with its thirty-six aldermen, San Francisco with its twelve supervisors), have only one chamber.

[10] In some few cities, among which is Chicago and (as respects police magistrates and school directors) Philadelphia, the plan of minority representation has been to some extent adopted by allowing the voter to cast his vote for two candidates only when there are three places to be filled. It was tried in New York, but the State Court of Appeals held it unconstitutional. So far as I can ascertain, this method has in Philadelphia proved rather favourable than otherwise to the "machine politicians," who can rely on their masses of drilled voters, obedient to orders.

[11] Sometimes the councilman is required by statute to be a resident in the ward he represents.

and irresponsibility as well as that of disconnecting the departments from one another.

The city judges are only in so far a part of the municipal government that in most of the larger cities they are elected by the citizens, like the other chief officers. There are usually several superior judges, chosen for terms of five years and upwards, and a larger number of "police judges" or "city magistrates,"[12] generally for shorter terms. Occasionally, however, the state has prudently reserved to itself the appointment of judges. Thus in New Haven, Connecticut (population in 1910, 133,605):

> Constables, justices of the peace, and a sheriff, are elected by the citizens, but the city courts derive existence directly from the State legislature. . . . The mode of selecting judges is this: the New Haven county delegation to the dominant party in the legislature assembles in caucus and nominates two of the same political faith to be respectively judge and assistant judge of the New Haven city court. Their choice is adopted by their party, and the nominations are duly ratified, often by a strict party vote. Inasmuch as the legislature is usually Republican, and the city of New Haven is unfailingly Democratic, these usages amount to a reservation of judicial offices from the "hungry and thirsty" local majority, and the maintenance of a certain control by the Republican country towns over the Democratic city.[13]

It need hardly be said that all the above officers, from the mayor and judges downwards, are, like state officers, elected by manhood suffrage. Their election is usually made to coincide with that of state officers, perhaps also of federal congressmen. This saves expense and trouble. But as it not only bewilders the voter in his choice of men by distracting his attention between a large number of candidates and places, but also confirms the tendency, already strong, to vote for city officers on party lines, there has

---

[12] Sometimes the police justices are nominated by the mayor.

[13] "During the session of the legislature in March 1885 this argument was put forward in answer to a Democratic plea for representation upon the city court bench. 'The Democrats possess all the other offices in New Haven. It's only fair that the Republicans should have the city court.' Each party accepted the statement as a conclusive reason for political action. It would be gratifying to find the subject discussed upon a higher plane, and the incumbents of the offices who had done well continued from term to term without regard to party affiliations. But in the present condition of political morals, the existing arrangements are probably the most practicable that could be made. It goes without saying that country districts are, as a rule, more deserving of political power than are cities. If the city judges were locally elected upon the general party ticket, the successful candidates would often be under obligations to elements in the community which are the chief source and nurse of the criminal class—an unseemly position for a judge."—Mr. Charles H. Levermore in his interesting sketch of the *Town and City Government of New Haven*, p. 77.

of late years been a movement in some few spots to have the municipal elections fixed for a different date from that of state or federal elections, so that the undistracted and nonpartisan thought of the citizens may be given to the former.[14]

At present the disposition to run and vote for candidates according to party is practically universal, although the duty of party loyalty is deemed less binding than in state or federal elections. When both the great parties put forward questionable men, a nonpartisan list, or so-called "citizens' ticket," may be run by a combination of respectable men of both parties. Sometimes this attempt succeeds. However, though the tenets of Republicans and Democrats have absolutely nothing to do with the conduct of city affairs, though the sole object of the election, say of a city comptroller or auditor, may be to find an honest man of good business habits, four-fifths of the electors in nearly all cities give little thought to the personal qualifications of the candidates, and vote the "straight ticket."

Early in the present century a new form of municipal government began to spread through the country. The city of Galveston in Texas had been struck by a tidal wave, which did frightful damage, and the people in order to deal with the emergency appointed three commissioners to handle city business *ad interim*. The plan succeeded so well that it was permanently adopted, and the Galveston charter of 1901 provides a body of five commissioners, elected by the voters at large for two years, one being mayor, president of the board, and each of the others having a special department of city business allotted to him. The commission as a whole passes ordinances, votes the annual budget, gives out contracts, and makes the principal appointments, upon the nomination of the commissioner in whose department the appointment lies. Under this form of government marked improvements have been effected in every branch of municipal work, and the whole floating debt has been paid off. The city owns its waterworks, sewer plant, and electric light plant. The large city of Des Moines in Iowa subsequently, under a general state law permitting cities to frame for themselves their schemes of government, enacted generally a similar plan in which the four commissioners who serve with the mayor have (1) accounts and finance, (2) public safety, (3) streets and public improvements, (4) parks and public property, as their several provinces. One-fourth of the voters can demand a recall vote, and all grants of

---

[14] On the other hand, there are cities which hope to draw out a larger vote, and therefore obtain a better choice, by putting their municipal elections at the same time as the state elections.

franchises, as well as ordinances not of an urgent character, have to be submitted to a referendum vote. The example of these two cities has been so largely followed that in 1913 there were 371 cities, including some in the Eastern states, in which the plan was in operation, while several states have passed statutes permitting their cities to adopt it. So far, it seems to be working well, though the elections "at large" in which party has been to a considerable extent eliminated, sometimes give odd results.[15]

The functions of city governments may be distributed into three groups: (*a*) those which are delegated by the state out of its general coercive and administrative powers, including the police power, the granting of licences, the execution of laws relating to adulteration and explosives; (*b*) those which though done under general laws are properly matters of local charge and subject to local regulation, such as education and the care of the poor; and (*c*) those which are not so much of a political as of a purely business order, such as the paving and cleansing of streets, the maintenance of proper drains, the provision of water and light. In respect of the first, and to some extent of the second of these groups, the city may be properly deemed a political entity; in respect of the third it is rather to be compared to a business corporation or company, in which the taxpayers and shareholders, doing, through the agency of the city officers, things which each might do for himself, though with more cost and trouble. All three sets of functions are dealt with by American legislation in the same way, and are alike given to officials and (where the commission plan has not been adopted) a legislature elected by persons of whom a large part pay no direct taxes. Education, however, is usually detached from the general city government and entrusted to a separate authority,[16] while in some cities the control of the police has been withheld or withdrawn from that government, and entrusted to the hands of a separate board.[17] The most remarkable instance is that of Boston in which city a Massachusetts statute of 1885 entrusts the police department and the power to license, regulate, and restrain the sale of intoxicating liquors, to a special board of three persons, to be appointed for five years by the state governor and council. Both political parties are directed by the statute to be represented on the board. (This is a frequent

---

[15] There are many varieties of the plan, the number of commissioners being sometimes larger than four. In some cities one commissioner is elected annually, so that the whole board never goes out of office together.

[16] Though sometimes, as in Baltimore, the city legislature appoints a Board of Education. Unhappily, in some cities education is "within politics," and, as may be supposed, with results unfavourable to the independence and even to the quality of the teachers.

[17] So in Baltimore and St. Louis.

provision in recent charters.) The city pays on the board's requisition all the expenses of the police department. In New York the police commissioners were for a time appointed by the mayor, but in order to "take the department out of politics" an unwritten understanding was established that he, though himself always a partisan, should appoint two Democratic and two Republican commissioners.[18] The post of policeman has been "spoils" of the humbler order, but spoils sometimes equally divided between the parties.

Taxes in cities, as in rural districts, are levied upon personal as well as real property; and the city tax is collected along with the county tax and state tax by the same collectors. There are, of course, endless varieties in the practice of different states and cities as to methods of assessment and to the minor imposts subsidiary to the property tax. Both real and personal property are usually assessed far below their true value, the latter because owners are reticent, the former because the city assessors are anxious to take as little as possible of the state and county burden on the shoulders of their own community, though in this patriotic effort they are checked by the county and state boards of equalization. Taxes are usually so much higher in the larger cities than in the country districts or smaller municipalities, that there is a strong tendency for rich men to migrate from the city to its suburbs in order to escape the city collector. Perhaps the city overtakes them, extending its limits and incorporating its suburbs; perhaps they fly farther afield by the railway and make the prosperity of country towns twenty or thirty miles away. The unfortunate consequence follows, not only that the taxes are heavier for those who remain in the city, but that the philanthropic and political work of the city loses the participation of those who ought to have shared in it. For a man votes in one place only, the place where he resides and pays taxes on his personalty; and where he has no vote, his is neither eligible for local office nor deemed entitled to take a part in local political agitation.

Among the great cities, one of those which have recently given themselves a new frame of government is Boston (population in 1910, 670,585). The main features of that scheme, which came into force in 1909, are as follows:

The government of the city is now in the hands of a mayor elected by the voters for a term of four years, and a single council of nine members similarly elected for a three-year term. Three councillors retire annually.

The Mayor. Nominations to the office of mayor may be made only by

---

[18] Now under the new charter of Greater New York there is one commissioner appointed by the mayor.

petitions signed by at least 5,000 qualified voters of the city, these signatures to be obtained upon official forms and verified by affidavit. No voter may sign more than one petition. The petitions must be filed with the election commissioners (who are appointed by the mayor) at least twenty-five days prior to the date of the municipal election. The signatures are then scrutinized by these election commissioners and not less than sixteen days before the date of the election the commissioners announce the names of those candidates whom they have found to have been validly nominated. Such names are then placed upon an official ballet, without party designation, and in an order of names determined by lot. The municipal election takes place on the Tuesday after the second Monday in January, and the city's fiscal year begins on the first Monday in February.

Although the mayor is elected for a four-year term, provision is made for his recall (i.e., dismissal) at the end of two years. The regular state election is used to provide the machinery for this recall; but in order to be effective the recall must secure, at this election, a majority of the total enrolled votes, not merely a majority of the polled votes. This means in practice that about two-thirds of the polled votes are necessary in order to recall a mayor, and it ought to be emphasized that this recall may be put into operation only at one stage in the mayor's term, namely, at the point where half his term has been served. The salary of the mayor is $10,000 per annum.

The mayor appoints all heads of city departments whose appointments are not otherwise provided for; and appointments made by the mayor are not subject to confirmation by the municipal council. But appointments made by him are not valid unless a certificate is obtained from the state Civil Service Commission "that the appointee is in its opinion qualified by education, training, and experience for the said office." Any official appointed by the mayor may be removed by him at any time, but he must state "in detail the specific reasons for such removal."

All recommendations for the expenditure of money must originate with the mayor, and while the council may omit or reduce any item of expenditure he recommends, it is not empowered to insert or increase any such item. Any resolution or vote of the council may be vetoed by the mayor and such veto is final.

The Council. The city council consists of nine members elected not by wards but from the city at large. Candidates are placed in nomination only by petitions signed by at least 5,000 registered voters, the regulations relating to the filing and verification of these petitions being in all respects similar to those prescribed in connection with nominations for the mayoralty. The names of candidates for election to the council are placed upon an official ballot in an order determined by lot and without any party designation. There is no provision for the recall of councillors before their three-year terms have expired; but three of the nine councillors go out of office each year. Councillors are paid $1,500 per annum.

The powers of the council include the making of city ordinances, the approving of appropriations including the annual budget, the authorization of loans, and the sanctioning of certain contracts extending over more than one year. All these powers are exercised, however, subject to the mayor's veto power. Authority to grant privileges in the streets, and franchises, permits, and locations, is vested in a board of three street commissioners appointed by the mayor, but the city council, with the mayor's approval, may fix the general terms upon which such privileges may be granted.

An interesting feature of Boston government is the Finance Commission, a body of five members appointed by the governor of the state. These commissioners are appointed for a five-year term, and one member retires annually. The chairman of the commission, designated by the governor, is paid $5,000 per annum; the other members are paid $3,000 each. The Finance Commission is given no mandatory or executive powers in any branch of city government; but it is empowered to investigate "any and all matters relating to appropriations, loans, expenditures, accounts, and methods of administration," reporting the results of its investigations to the mayor, the city council, the governor, and the state legislature. The commission is authorized to employ experts to assist in its investigations, and in this connection may spend not more than $25,000 per year. It has power to compel the attendance of witnesses and the production of papers.

Administrative Departments. The administration of Boston is immediately conducted by some thirty different departments. Most of these have a single commissioner in charge; but some have boards of three men. Most of the heads of departments are paid; a few of the boards are unpaid. None are elected by popular vote, and none are appointed by the council. Nearly all are appointed by the mayor, the only important exceptions being the police commissioner, and the board of excise commissioners who are appointed by the governor, and the Trustees of the Franklin Fund who are appointed by the supreme court of the state. All judges, including municipal justices, are in Massachusetts appointed by the state governor with the confirmation of his council.

Metropolitan Commissions. Boston is the centre of a metropolitan district comprising over thirty municipalities with a total population of about a million and a quarter. In order that certain services throughout this area should be somewhat coordinated, a number of metropolitan commissions have been established, the members of these commissions being appointed by the governor of the state. The Metropolitan Water and Sewerage Board has charge of the main water supply and trunk sewers throughout the greater part of the metropolitan district; and the Metropolitan Parks Commission has created and maintains an extensive system of parks and boulevards. For carrying through various undertakings which concern two or more municipalities (including Boston) various *ad hoc* commissions have been established, such as the Charles River Basin Commission (composed of three members appointed by the governor); and the Boston Transit Commission (composed of five members appointed, three by the governor and two by the mayor of Boston).

School Administration. Quite distinct from the regular city administration is the Boston School Committee, composed of five members elected for three years with provision for one or two members retiring each year. These are elected by popular vote from the city at large, the rules relating to their nomination and election being in all respects similar to those applying in the case of municipal councillors.

As respect school administration, a branch of city work whose importance is more and more recognized, and which suffers, perhaps more than any other, from the application of machine and spoils methods, reference may be made to a change recently introduced into the government of the great city of St. Louis. Under a state statute of 1897 the board of education consists of twelve members chosen by the voters at large for six years, four members retiring every second year. Every member swears that he will consider merit and fitness only in making appointments. The functions of the board, which is by common consent divided equally between the two parties, are chiefly those of supervision, executive work being left to the superintendent of schools and other officials. By this method education is said to have been "taken out of politics," and the efficiency of the schools has been raised.

St. Louis (population in 1910, 687,029), though it has latterly had upright mayors, and often a fair upper house of its city legislature, has suffered from deficient purity in its lower house; and in 1910 tried to use the power entrusted to it of giving itself a new charter. The draft was rejected by the people.

The Working of City Governments

wo tests of practical efficiency may be applied to the government of a city: What does it provide for the people, and what does it cost the people? Space fails me to apply in detail the former of these tests, by showing what each city does or omits to do for its inhabitants; so I must be content with observing that in the United States generally constant complaints are directed against the bad paving and cleansing of the streets, the nonenforcement of the laws forbidding gambling and illicit drinking, and in some places against the sanitary arrangements and management of public buildings and parks. It would appear that in the greatest cities there is far more dissatisfaction than exists with the municipal administration in such cities as Glasgow, Manchester, Dublin, Hamburg, Lyons.

The following indictment of the government of Philadelphia is somewhat exceptional in its severity, and however well founded as to that city, must not be taken to be typical. A memorial presented to the Pennsylvania legislature some time ago by a number of the leading citizens of the Quaker City contained these words:

> The affairs of the city of Philadelphia have fallen into a most deplorable condition. The amounts required annually for the payment of interest upon the funded debt and current expenses render it necessary to impose a rate of taxation which is as heavy as can be borne.
>
> In the meantime the streets of the city have been allowed to fall into such a state as to be a reproach and a disgrace. Philadelphia is now recognized as the worst-paved and worst-cleaned city in the civilized world.
>
> The water supply is so bad that during many weeks of the last winter it was not only distasteful and unwholesome for drinking, but offensive for bathing purposes.
>
> The effort to clean the streets was abandoned for months, and no attempt was

made to that end until some public-spirited citizens, at their own expense, cleaned a number of the principal thoroughfares.

The system of sewerage and the physical condition of the sewers is notoriously bad—so much so as to be dangerous to the health and most offensive to the comfort of our people.

Public work has been done so badly that structures have had to be renewed almost as soon as finished. Others have been in part constructed at enormous expense, and then permitted to fall to decay without completion.

Inefficiency, waste, badly-paved and filthy streets, unwholesome and offensive water, and slovenly and costly management, have been the rule for years past throughout the city government.[1]

In most of the points comprised in the above statement, Philadelphia was probably—and though she has been several times reformed since then, is still—among the least fortunate of American cities. He, however, who should interrogate one of the "good citizens" of Pittsburgh, Cincinnati, New Orleans, New York, Chicago, San Francisco, would have heard then, and would hear now, similar complaints, some relating more to the external condition of the city, some to its police administration, but all showing that the objects for which municipal government exists have been very imperfectly attained.

The other test, that of expense, is easily applied. Both the debt and the taxation of American cities have risen with unprecedented rapidity, and now stand at an alarming figure.

A table of the increase of population, valuation, taxation, and debt, in fifteen of the largest cities of the United States, from 1880 to 1905, shows the following result:

Increase in population .   .   .   .   88.0 per cent.
Increase in taxable valuation . . 221.6 per cent
Increase in debt .   .   .   .   .   . 186.0 per cent
Increase in taxation .   .   .   .   . 165.5 per cent

Looking at some individual cases, we find that the debt rose as follows:

Philadelphia .   .   . $54,223,850   to $69,950,640
Boston 28,244,018   "   99,191,856
Cleveland 6,467,046   "   27,685,874

(continued)

---

[1] *Municipal Development of Philadelphia*, by Messrs. Allinson and Penrose, p. 275.

Milwaukee. . . .   2,160,289   "   8,575,813
New York . . . . 149,721,614[2]   " 647,806,295[3]

Much of this debt is doubtless represented by permanent improvements, yet for another large, and in some cities far larger, part there is nothing to show; it is due to simple waste or to malversation on the part of the municipal authorities.

As respects current expenditure, New York in 1884 spent on current city purposes, exclusive of payments on account of interest on debt, sinking fund, and maintenance of judiciary, the sum of $20,232,786—equal to $16.76 for each inhabitant (census of 1880). In Boston, in the same year, the city expenditure was $9,909,019—equal to $27.30 for each inhabitant (census of 1880). In 1908 the total ordinary expenditure of New York was $156,545,148 (being $32.30 for each inhabitant); that of Boston, $17,464,573 (being $28.75 for each inhabitant).[4]

There is no denying that the government of cities is the one conspicuous failure of the United States. The deficiencies of the national government tell but little for evil on the welfare of the people. The faults of the state governments are insignificant compared with the extravagance, corruption, and mismanagement which mark the administrations of most of the great cities. For these evils are not confined to one or two cities. The commonest mistake of Europeans who talk about America is to assume that the political vices of New York are found everywhere. The next most common is to suppose that they are found nowhere else. In New York they have revealed themselves on the largest scale. They are "gross as a mountain, open, palpable." But there is not a city with a population exceeding 200,000 where the poison germs have not sprung into a vigorous life; and in some of the smaller ones, down to 50,000, it needs no microscope to note the results of their growth. Even in cities of the third rank similar phenomena may occasionally be discerned, though there, as someone has said, the jet black of New York or San Francisco dies away into a harmless gray.

For evils which appear wherever a large population is densely aggregated,

[2] Including the figures for the territory which by 1905 had been incorporated into Greater New York.

[3] The cost of opening or improving highways and of placing sewers in streets is of course not included in the aggregate of moneys annually levied and debt rolled up, because the cost of those improvements is levied directly upon the land by way of assessments.

In New York the total net funded debt was in December 1908, $735,782,594.

[4] These totals of 1908 (census report of 1905 brought up to 1908 from city records) include all the ordinary expenditures, but not sums paid for investment securities or redemption of municipal debt.

there must be some general and widespread causes. What are these causes? Adequately to explain them would be to anticipate the account of the party system to be given in the second volume of this work, for it is that party system which has, not perhaps created, but certainly enormously aggravated them, and impressed on them their specific type.[5] I must therefore restrict myself for the present to a brief enumeration of the chief sources of the malady, and the chief remedies that have been suggested for or applied to it. No political subject has been so copiously discussed of late years in America by able and experienced publicists, nor can I do better than present the salient facts in the words which some of these men, speaking in a responsible position, have employed.

The New York commissioners of 1876 appointed "to devise a plan for the government of cities in the State of New York," sum up the mischief as follows:[6]

> 1. The accumulation of permanent municipal debt: In New York it was, in 1840, $10,000,000; in 1850, $12,000,000; in 1860, $18,000,000; in 1870, $73,000,000; in 1876, $113,000,000.[7]
>
> 2. The excessive increase of the annual expenditure for ordinary purposes: In 1816 the amount raised by taxation was less than $\frac{1}{2}$ per cent on the taxable property; in 1850, 1.13 per cent; in 1860, 1.69 per cent; in 1870, 2.17 per cent; in 1876, 2.67 per cent. . . . The increase in the annual expenditure since 1850, as compared with the increase of population, is more than 400 per cent, and as compared with the increase of taxable property, more than 200 per cent.

[5] See Part III and especially Chapters 62 and 63. See also the chapters in Vol. II on the Tammany Ring in New York City, and the Gas Ring in Philadelphia. The full account given in those chapters of the phenomena of municipal misgovernment in the two largest cities in the United States seems to dispense me from the duty of here describing those phenomena in general.

[6] The commission, of which Mr. W. M. Evarts (now senator from New York) was chairman, included some of the ablest men in the state, and its report, presented 6th March 1877, may be said to have become classical. Much of it is as applicable now to great cities as it was in 1876; and I quote it not only in respect of its historical value, but also because no abler presentment of the facts has since appeared.

[7] The New York commissioners say: "The magnitude and rapid increase of this debt are not less remarkable than the poverty of the results exhibited as the return for so prodigious an expenditure. It was abundantly sufficient for the construction of all the public works of a great metropolis for a century to come, and to have adorned it besides with the splendours of architecture and art. Instead of this, the wharves and piers are for the most part temporary and perishable structures; the streets are poorly paved; the sewers in great measure imperfect, insufficient, and in bad order; the public buildings shabby and inadequate; and there is little which the citizen can regard with satisfaction, save the aqueduct and its appurtenances and the public park. Even these should not be said to be the product of the public debt; for the expense occasioned by them is, or should have been, for the most part already extinguished. In truth, the larger part of the city debt represents a vast aggregate of moneys wasted, embezzled, or misapplied."

They suggest the following as the causes:
1. Incompetent and unfaithful governing boards and officers.

A large number of important offices have come to be filled by men possessing little, if any, fitness for the important duties they are called upon to discharge. . . . These unworthy holders of public trusts gain their places by their own exertions. The voluntary suffrage of their fellow-citizens would never have lifted them into office. Animated by the expectation of unlawful emoluments, they expend large sums to secure their places, and make promises beforehand to supporters and retainers to furnish patronage or place. The corrupt promises must be redeemed. Anticipated gains must be realized. Hence old and educated subordinates must be dismissed and new places created to satisfy the crowd of friends and retainers. Profitable contracts must be awarded, and needless public works undertaken. The amounts required to satisfy these illegitimate objects enter into the estimates on which taxation is eventually based, in fact, they constitute in many instances a superior lien upon the moneys appropriated for government, and not until they are in some manner satisfied do the real wants of the public receive attention. It is speedily found that these unlawful demands, together with the necessities of the public, call for a sum which, if taken at once by taxation, would produce dissatisfaction and alarm in the community, and bring public indignation upon the authors of such burdens. For the purpose of averting such consequences divers pretences are put forward suggesting the propriety of raising means for alleged exceptional purposes by loans of money, and in the end the taxes are reduced to a figure not calculated to arouse the public to action, and any failure thus to raise a sufficient sum is supplied by an issue of bonds. . . . Yet this picture fails altogether to convey an adequate notion of the elaborate systems of depredation which, under the name of city governments, have from time to time afflicted our principal cities; and it is moreover a just indication of tendencies in operation in all our cities, and which are certain, unless arrested, to gather increased force. It would clearly be within bounds to say that more than one-half of all the present city debts are the direct results of the species of intentional and corrupt misrule above described.

2. The introduction of state and national politics into municipal affairs.

The formation of general political parties upon differences as to general principles or methods of State policy is useful, or at all events inevitable. But it is rare indeed that any such questions, or indeed any upon which good men ought to differ, arise in connection with the conduct of municipal affairs. Good men cannot and do not differ as to whether municipal debt ought to be restricted, extravagance checked, and municipal affairs lodged in the hands of competent and faithful officers. There is no more reason why the control of the public works of a great city should be lodged in the hands of a Democrat or a Republican than there is why an adherent of one or the other of the great parties should be made the superintendent of a business corporation. Good citizens interested in honest municipal government can secure that object only by acting together. Political divisions separate them at the start, and render it impossible to secure the object desired equally by both. . . . This obstacle to the union of good citizens paralyses all ordinary efforts for good municipal government. . . . The great prizes in the shape of place and power which are offered on the broad fields of national and State politics offer the strongest incentives to ambition. Personal advancement is in these fields naturally associated with the achievement of great public objects, and neither end can be secured except through the success of a political party to which they are attached. The strife thus engendered develops into a general battle in which each side feels that it cannot allow any odds to the other. If one seeks to turn to its advantage the patronage of municipal office, the other must carry the contest into the same sphere. It is certain that the temptation will be withstood by neither. It then becomes the direct interest of the foremost men of the nation to constantly keep their forces in hostile array, and these must be led by, among other ways, the patronage to be secured by the control of local affairs. . . . Next to this small number of leading men there is a large class who, though not dishonest or devoid of public spirit, are led by habit and temperament to take a wholly partisan view of city affairs. Their enjoyment of party struggles, their devotion to those who share with them the triumphs and defeats of the political game, are so intense that they gradually lose sight of the object for which parties exist or ought to exist, and considerable proportions of them in their devotion to politics suffer themselves to be driven from the walks of regular industry, and at last become dependent for their livelihood on the patronage in the hands of their chiefs. Mingled with them is nearly as large a number to whom politics is simply a mode of making a livelihood or a fortune, and who take part in political contests without enthusiasm, and often without the pretence of an interest in the public welfare, and devote themselves openly to the organization of the vicious elements of society in combinations strong enough to hold the balance in a closely-contested election, overcome the political leaders, and secure a fair share of the municipal patronage, or else extort immunity from the officers of the law. . . . The rest of the community, embracing the large majority of the more thrifty classes, averse to engaging in what they deem the 'low business' of politics, or hopeless of accomplishing any substantial good in the face of such powerful opposing interests, for the most part content themselves with acting in accordance with their respective parties. . . . It is through the agency of the great political parties, organized and operating as above described, that our municipal officers are and have long been selected. It can scarcely be matter of wonder then that the present condition of municipal affairs should present an aspect so desperate.

3. The assumption by the state legislature of the direct control of local affairs.

This legislative intervention has necessarily involved a disregard of one of the most fundamental principles of republican government (the self-government of municipalities). . . . The representatives elected to the central (State) legislature have not the requisite time to direct the local affairs of the municipalities. . . . They have not the requisite knowledge of details. . . . When a local bill is under consideration in the legislature, its care and explanation are left exclusively to the representatives of the locality to which it is applicable; and sometimes by express, more often by a tacit understanding, local bills are 'log-rolled' through the houses. Thus legislative duty is delegated to the local representatives, who, acting frequently in combination with the sinister elements of their constituency, shift the responsibility for wrongdoing from themselves to the legislature. But what is even more important, the general representatives have not that sense of personal interest and personal responsibility to their constituents which are indispensable to the intelligent administration of local affairs. And yet the judgment of the local governing bodies in various parts of the State, and the wishes of their constituents, are liable to be overruled by the votes of legislators living at a distance of a hundred miles. . . . To appreciate the extent of the mischief done by the occupation of the central legislative body with the consideration of a multitude of special measures relating to local affairs, some good, probably the larger part bad, one has only to take up the session laws of any year at random and notice the subjects to which they relate. Of the 808 acts passed in 1870, for instance, 212 are acts relating to cities and villages, 94 of which relate to cities, and 36 to the city of New York alone. A still larger number have reference to the city of Brooklyn. These 212 acts occupy more than three-fourths of the 2000 pages of the laws of that year. . . . The multiplicity of laws relating to the same subjects thus brought into existence is itself an evil of great magnitude. What the law is concerning some of the most important interests of our principal cities can be ascertained only by the exercise of the patient research of professional lawyers. In many instances even professional skill is baffled. Says Chief-Justice Church: 'It is scarcely safe for any one to speak confidently on the exact condition of the law in respect to public improvements in the cities of New York and Brooklyn. The enactments referring thereto have been modified, superseded, and repealed so often and to such an extent that it is difficult to ascertain just what statutes are in force at any particular time.

"The uncertainties arising from such multiplied and conflicting legislation lead to incessant litigation with its expensive burdens, public and private." . . . But this is not all nor the worst. It may be true that the first attempts to secure legislative intervention in the local affairs of our principal cities were made by good citizens in the supposed interest of reform and good government, and to counteract the schemes of corrupt officials. The notion that legislative control was the proper remedy was a serious mistake. The corrupt cliques and rings thus sought to be baffled were quick to perceive that in the business of procuring special laws concerning local affairs they could easily outmatch the fitful and clumsy labours of disinterested citizens. The transfer of the control of the municipal resources from the localities to the (State) capitol had no other effect than to cause a like transfer of the methods and arts of corruption, and to make the fortunes of our principal cities the traffic of the lobbies. Municipal corruption, previously confined within territorial limits, thenceforth escaped all bounds and spread to every quarter of the State. Cities were compelled by legislation to buy lands for parks and places because the owners wished to sell them; compelled to grade, pave, and sewer streets without inhabitants, and for no other purpose than to award corrupt contracts for the work. Cities were compelled to purchase, at the public expense, and at extravagant prices, the property necessary for streets and avenues, useless for any other purpose than to make a market for the adjoining property thus improved. Laws were enacted abolishing one office and creating another with the same duties in order to transfer official emoluments from one man to another, and laws to change the functions of officers with a view only to a new distribution of patronage, and to lengthen the terms of offices for no other pupose than to retain in place officers who could not otherwise be elected or appointed.

This last-mentioned cause of evil is no doubt a departure from the principle of local popular control and responsibility on which state governments and rural local governments have been based. It is a dereliction which has brought its punishment with it. But the resulting mischiefs have been immensely aggravated by the vices of the legislatures in a few of the states, such as New York and Pennsylvania. As regards the two former causes, they are largely due to what is called the Spoils System, whereby office becomes the reward of party service, and the whole machinery of party government made to serve, as its main object, the getting and keeping of places. Now the Spoils System, with the party machinery which it keeps oiled and greased and always working at high pressure, is far more potent and pernicious in great cities than in country districts. For in great cities we find an ignorant multitude, largely composed of recent immigrants, untrained in self-government; we find a great proportion of the voters paying no direct taxes, and therefore feeling no interest in moderate taxation and economical administration; we find able citizens absorbed in their private businesses, cultivated citizens unusually sensitive to the vulgarities of practical politics, and both sets therefore specially unwilling to sacrifice their time and tastes and comfort in the struggle with sordid wire-pullers and noisy demagogues. In great cities the forces that attack and pervert democratic government are exceptionally numerous, the defensive forces that protect it exceptionally ill-placed for resistance. Satan has turned his heaviest batteries on the weakest part of the ramparts.

Besides these three causes on which the commissioners dwell, and the effects of which are felt in the great cities of other states as well as of New York, there are what may be called mechanical defects in the structure of municipal governments, whose nature may be gathered from the account given in last chapter. There is a want of methods for fixing public responsibility on the governing persons and bodies. When the mayor jobs his patronage he can indeed no longer, under the new charters, such as that of New York, throw part of the blame on the aldermen or other confirming council, alleging that he would have selected better men could he have hoped that the aldermen would approve his selection. But if he has failed to keep the departments up to their work, he may argue that the city legislature hampered him and would not pass the requisite ordinances. Each house of a two-chambered legislature can excuse itself by pointing to the action of the other, or of its own committees, and among the numerous members of the chambers—or even of one chamber if there be but one— responsibility is so divided as to cease to come forcibly home to anyone. The various boards and officials have generally had little intercommunication;[8] and the fact that some were directly elected by the people made these feel themselves independent both of the mayor and the city legislature. The mere multiplication of elective posts distracts the attention of the people, and deprives the voting at the polls of its efficiency as a means of reproof or commendation.[9]

To trace municipal misgovernment to its sources was comparatively easy. To show how these sources might be dried up was more difficult, though as to some obvious remedies all reformers were agreed. What seemed all but impracticable was to induce the men who had produced these evils, who used them and profited by them, who were so accustomed to them that even the honester sort did not feel their turpitude, to consent to the measures needed for extinguishing their own abused power and illicit gains. It was from the gangs of city politicians and their allies in the state legislatures that reforms had to be sought, and the enactment of their own abolition obtained. In vain would the net be spread in the sight of such birds.

---

[8] In Philadelphia someone has observed that there were four distinct and independent authorities with power to tear up the streets, and that there was no authority upon whom the duty was specifically laid to put them in repair again.

[9] Mr. Seth Low has well remarked in an address on municipal government: "Greatly to multiply important elective officers is not to increase popular control, but to lessen it. The expression of the popular will at the ballot-box is like a great blow struck by an engine of enormous force. It can deliver a blow competent to overthrow any officer, however powerful. But, as in mechanics, great power has to be subdivided in order to do fine work, so in giving expression to the popular will the necessity of choosing amid a multitude of unimportant officers involves inevitably a loss of power to the people."

The remedies proposed by the New York commission need not be enumerated, for the birds saw the net and refused to allow the amendments required to be submitted, so nothing was done at the time. Yet the reformers ultimately prevailed, for nearly all of their suggestions have by degrees been in substance adopted. The city was enlarged in 1902 by the inclusion of the great city of Brooklyn and the districts called Queen's and the Bronx, and Staten Island, so Greater New York now consists of the five boroughs of Manhattan (the island on which New York City proper stands), Brooklyn, Queen's, Richmond, and Bronx. Each of these boroughts has its own president and local administrative authorities, all being under the general authority of the mayor of the Greater City. Legislative power is divided between the aldermen and the Board of Estimate and Apportionment which consists of the mayor, the comptroller, the president of the board of aldermen, and the presidents of the five boroughs. It is the chief financial authority. The state constitution has been so amended as to limit the legislature's power of passing special acts relating to cities. State and city elections have been separated. The city's borrowing powers have been restricted and the functions of the mayor in appointing and removing officials extended. Thus though the new charter is far from perfect, it is admittedly much better than that of 1876.[10]

The most novel of the proposals made by the commissioners of 1876 and the one which excited most hostile criticism, that of creating a council elected by voters having a tax-paying (or rent-paying) qualification, has never been tried in any great city. It is deemed undemocratic; practical men say there is no use submitting it to a popular vote.[11] Nevertheless, there are still some who advocate it, appealing to the example of Australia, where it is said to have worked well.

[10] The Municipal Reform Movement continues active in certain directions. Important economics have been effected in New York, and an organization called the Bureau of Municipal Research works energetically for reducing the cost and increasing the efficiency of city administration.

See further as to New York municipal government the observations of Mr. Seth Low, ex-mayor of Greater New York, in Chapter 52.

[11] Though, as the commission pointed out (Report, p. 33), the principle that no one should vote upon any proposition to raise a tax or appropriate its proceeds unless himself liable to be assessed for such tax, was one generally applied in the village charters of the state of New York, and even in the charters of some of the smaller cities. The report repels the charge that this proposal is inconsistent with the general recognition of the value of universal suffrage by saying, "No surer method could be devised to bring the principle of universal suffrage into discredit and prepare the way for its overthrow than to pervert it to a use for which it was never intended, and subject it to a service which it is incapable of performing. . . . To expect frugality and economy in financial concerns from its operation in great cities, where perhaps half of the inhabitants feel no interest in these objects, is to subject the principle to a strain which it cannot bear. All the friends of the system should unite in rescuing it from such perils."—Page 40.

Among the other reforms in city government which I find canvassed in America are the following:

(*a*) Civil service reform, i.e., the establishment of examinations as a test for admission to posts under the city, and the bestowal of these posts for a fixed term of years, or generally during good behaviour, instead of leaving the civil servant at the mercy of a partisan chief, who may displace him to make room for a party adherent or personal friend.

(*b*) The lengthening of the terms of service of the mayor and the heads of departments, so as to give them a more assured position and diminish the frequency of elections.—This has been done to some extent in recent charters.

(*c*) The vesting of almost autocratic executive power in the mayor and restriction of the city legislature to purely legislative work and the voting of supplies.—This also now finds place in some charters, notably in the new one of New York, and has worked, on the whole, well. It is, of course, a remedy of the "cure or kill" order. If the people are thoroughly roused to choose an able and honest man, the more power he has the better; it is safer in his hands than in those of city councils. If the voters are apathetic and let a bad man slip in, all may be lost till the next election. I do not say "all is lost," for there have been remarkable instances of men who have been sobered and elevated by power and responsibility. The Greek proverb "office will show the man" was generally taken in an unfavourable sense. The proverb of the steadier headed Germans, "office gives understanding" (*Amt gibt Verstand*), represents a more hopeful view of human nature, and one not seldom justified in American experience.

(*d*) The election of a city legislature, or one branch of it, or of a school committee, on a general ticket instead of by wards.—When aldermen or councilmen are chosen by the voters of a small local area, it is assumed, in the United States, that they must be residents within it; thus the field of choice among good citizens generally is limited. It follows also that their first duty is deemed to be to get the most they can for their own ward; they care little for the general interests of the city, and carry on a game of barter in contracts and public improvements with the representatives of other wards. Hence the general ticket system is preferable.

(*e*) The limitation of taxing powers and borrowing powers by reference to the assessed value of the taxable property within the city.—Restrictions of this nature have been largely applied to cities as well as to counties and other local authorities. The results have been usually good, yet not uniformly so, for evasions may be practised. The New York commission say: "The apparent prohibition, both as to taxation and the percentage of debt, could be readily evaded by raising the assessment. Such restrictions do not attempt to prevent the wastefulness or embezzlement of the public funds otherwise than by limiting the amount of the funds subject to depredation. The effect of such measures would simply be to leave the public necessities without adequate provision."[12] And Messrs. Allinson and Penrose observe:

> By the Constitution of 1874 it is provided that the debt of a county, city, borough, township, or school district shall never exceed 7 per cent on the assessed value of the taxable property therein. This provision was intended to prevent the encumbering of the property of any citizen for public purposes to a greater extent than 7 per cent. In its workings it has been an absolute failure. In every city of the State, except Philadelphia, the city is part of the county government. The county has power to borrow to the extent of 7 per cent: so has the city: so has the general school district: so has the ward school district—making 28 per cent in all, which can be lawfully imposed, and has been authorized by the Act of 1874. But there is still another cause of failure to which Philadelphia is more peculiarly liable. In order to evade the provision of the Constitution limiting the power to contract debts to 7 per cent, the assessed value of property in nearly every city of the State was largely increased—in some instances, incredible as it may seem, to the extent of 1000 per cent. It is therefore clear that no sufficient protection against an undue increase of municipal debt can be found in constitutional and legislative provisions of this kind.—*Philadelphia, a History of Municipal Development* (1887), p. 276.

Nevertheless, such restrictions are now often found embodied in State constitutions, and have, so far as I could ascertain, generally diminished the evil they are aimed at.

(*f*) The introduction of methods for referring questions to the direct vote of the citizens in the three forms of initiative, where a prescribed percentage of the voters submit an ordinance for enactment by the citizens, referendum, where the city council is required, on the petition of a prescribed percentage of voters, to refer to the citizens at the polls an ordinance it has passed, and recall, whereby a prescribed percentage can demand the election of a successor to the holder of any elective office whom they seek to remove. —The holder is permitted to be a candidate at such election, and if he obtains the largest number of votes is therewith reelected. By these methods it is hoped to prevent the jobbing of contracts by city legislatures and to secure the good conduct of officials. They are drastic remedies, and their working is being watched with lively interest.[13]

---

[12] Another disadvantage is that such restriction may sometimes compel a public improvement to be executed piecemeal which could be executed more cheaply if done all at once. See Chapter 43.

[13] For a good example of these provisions see the charter of the city of Los Angeles, as revised and amended up to 1909.

(g) The supersession of the usual frame of government by a mayor and council by the creation of a small Board of Commissioners elected by 'a general ticket' vote over the whole city.—This so-called Galveston or Des Moines Plan has been already mentioned (*supra*, page 564). It is now (1910) spreading fast over the Union in various forms. It is expected, in its most advanced form, to reduce the power of the machine by nominations through open primaries (see note to Chapter 60 *post*) and by making the election on 'general ticket' instead of by wards, to secure due responsibility by concentrating power in very few hands, to keep officials up to the mark by the threat of a recall vote, to prevent jobs and corruption by letting the people as a whole vote upon the grant of franchises and to secure effective popular control by a referendum on city ordinances. It is the most sweeping of all the schemes of reform hitherto propounded or applied, but has not been long enough in operation for its possible defects to have yet fully revealed themselves.

I must not attempt to discuss the interesting question of the results of

---

In 1909 a demand for a recall vote for the office of mayor was submitted in Los Angeles, whereupon the existing incumbent of that office disappeared and a successor was elected.

A warm advocate of the recall, who has had wide experience of municipal misrule, has stated the case for that remedy as follows:

"From twenty-five to forty per cent of the income of most of our large cities is dissipated by extravagance, mismanagement and corruption, and (what is worse) the moral tone of the citizenship lowered thereby.

"This condition results from the rule of political machines.

"These machines are created and maintained by public utility corporations, liquor interests, gamblers and other disreputable elements of society aided by some eminently respectable business men who receive special privileges through reason of the existence of corrupt government, and by a large number of honest voters who, unfortunately, are narrow partisans always voting the straight ticket. All these, however, constitute a minority of the entire electorate, but owing to a complicated system of nominations, perfect organization, and enormous corruption funds supplied principally by public utility corporations, the machine is kept in power despite the fact that the majority of the electorate is honest and desires good government.

"Various panaceæ—increased power of mayors, civil service reform, election of councilmen at large, etc.—are of little avail, for with the Machine in full control these measures give it increased power. Even the election of good men to office (when through herculean efforts this is spasmodically achieved) frequently fails to produce any marked effect, because these men often cease to be good.

"This condition then confronts us: a minority controlling corruptly, while a majority of the electorate is honest. The remedy is plain and very simple. If it is desired to have a true representative and an efficient and honest government, give to the honest majority of the electorate the power to initiate legislation which their legislative bodies may refuse: this is the Initiative. Give to the honest majority the power to veto the undesired acts of their legislators; this is the Referendum, and give to the same honest majority the power to discharge from office at any time any inefficient or incompetent officer: this is the Recall."

entrusting to city governments the supply of water, gas, and electricity, perhaps also street railways, because American cities are accumulating such a mass of experience on the subject that it could not be dealt with save at considerable length, while the wise still differ as to the general conclusions to be formed.[14] The objections to placing this function in the hands of such men as rule most municipalities are obvious. One group of these objections will be found illustrated in a later chapter, describing the Gas Ring in Philadelphia. There are, however, some reformers sanguine enough to believe that when city councils obtain functions whose exercise has a strong and obvious interest for the citizens, the latter are roused to a more active and watchful control, and may be counted on to eject corrupt politicians from power. Nor must we forget that the plan of leaving the function to private corporate companies is open to evils scarcely less patent than those which flow from dishonest public management, because these companies when they prosper and grow large bring their wealth to bear upon the municipal authorities, and have even been known to scatter bribes widely among the voters for the sake of retaining or extending their monopoly. Each plan has its dangers. It is not the least among the many mischiefs entailed by the pollution of city governments that citizens who resent the high prices charged and poor supply given by private companies often prefer to bear these hardships and to wink at the impure methods which some companies employ rather than face the risk of throwing to the rings that control the larger municipalities the additional mass of patronage and additional material for jobbery which the business of water and gas supply carries with it.

The question of city government is that which chiefly occupies practical publicists in America, because they have long deemed it the weakest point of the country. That adaptability of the institutions to the people and their conditions, which judicious strangers have been wont to admire in the United States, and that consequent satisfaction of the people with their institutions, which contrasts so agreeably with the discontent of European nations, is wholly absent as regards municipal administration. Wherever there is a large city there are loud complaints, and Americans who deem themselves in other respects a model for the Old World are in this respect anxious to study Old World models, those particularly which the cities of

---

[14] Of about 160 cities with a population exceeding 20,000, water supply is in 59 left to private corporations, and in 101 belongs to the municipality.

See upon this subject the Report (1907) of the Civic Federation Committees on municipal ownership.

Great Britain present. The best proof of dissatisfaction is to be found in the frequent changes of system and method. What Dante said of his own city may be said of the cities of America: they are like the sick man who finds no rest upon his bed, but seeks to ease his pain by turning from side to side. Every now and then the patient finds some relief in a drastic remedy, such as the enactment of a new charter and the expulsion at an election of a gang of knaves. Presently, however, the weak points of the charter are discovered, the state legislature again begins to interfere by special acts, or a "public service corporation" begins to seduce the virtue of officials; civic zeal grows cold and allows bad men to creep back into the chief posts; Federal issues are allowed to supersede at municipal elections that which ought to be always deemed the real issue, the character and capacity of the candidates for office. All this is discouraging. Yet no one who studies the municipal history of the last decades will doubt that things are better than they were twenty-five years ago. The newer frames of government are an improvement upon the older. Rogues are less audacious. Good citizens are more active. Party spirit is still permitted to dominate and pervert municipal politics, yet the mischief it does is more clearly discerned and the number of those who resist it daily increases. In the increase of that number and the growth of a stronger sense of civic duty rather than in any changes of mechanism, lies the ultimate hope for the reform of city governments.

CHAPTER 52

An American View of Municipal Government in the United States

By the Hon. SETH LOW, formerly mayor of New York City

In England there are said to be three kinds of cities: cities by prescription, like London and Exeter, which have been cities from time immemorial; cities that are such because they have been the seat of a bishop; and cities organized under the modern Municipal Corporations Act. In the United States, twenty municipal corporations received charters as cities during the Colonial period. These charters, in order to be valid, had to be confirmed after the Revolution by the legislature of the state in which the city was located. In other words, a city in the United States is the creature of the legislature of the state in which it is. The legislature's power over the city's form of government is substantially absolute, except as the legislative power may be limited by the state constitution. As there are forty-eight states in the Union, and as there were, according to the census of 1910, seven hundred and seventy-four cities in the United States with a population of eight thousand or more, it will be readily understood why there is no uniform type of city charter even for the more modern cities. The city of Washington, in the District of Columbia, which belongs to the nation, is subject to the direct legislation of Congress. In this respect it is unique. Its inhabitants enjoy no vote even as to local affairs. It is administered by a Commission of Three, appointed by the president of the United States, subject to confirmation by the Senate, and is probably the only city in the United States without a mayor.

Any European student of politics who wishes to understand the problem of government in the United States, whether of city government or any other form of it, must first of all transfer himself, if he can, to a point of view precisely the opposite of that which is natural to him. This is scarcely, if at all, less true of the English than of the Continental student. In England as upon the Continent, from time immemorial, government has descended from the top down. Until recently, society in Europe has accepted the idea, almost without protest, that there must be governing classes, and that the great majority of men must be governed. The French Revolution doubtless modified this idea everywhere, and especially in France, but even in France public sentiment on this point is a resultant of a conflict of views. In the United States, however, that idea does not obtain at all, and, what is of no less importance, it never has obtained. No distinction is recognized between governing and governed classes, and the problem of government is, in effect, an effort on the part of society as a whole to learn and apply to itself the art of government. Bearing this in mind, it becomes apparent that the immense tide of immigration into the United States is a continually disturbing factor. The immigrants come from many countries, a very large proportion of them being of the classes which, in their old homes, from time out of mind, have been governed. Arriving in America, they shortly become citizens in a society which undertakes to govern itself. However well disposed they may be as a rule, they have not had experience in self-government, nor do they always share the ideas which have expressed themselves in the Constitution of the United States. This foreign element settles largely in the cities of the country. It is estimated that the population of New York City contains approximately eighty per cent of people who either are foreign-born, or are the children of foreign-born parents. Consequently, in a city like New York, the problem of learning the art of government is handed over to a population that begins, in point of experience, very low down. In many of the cities of the United States, indeed in almost all of them, the population not only is thus largely untrained in the art of self-government, but it is not even homogeneous. So that an American city is confronted not only with the necessity of instructing large and rapidly growing bodies of people in the art of government, but it is compelled at the same time to assimilate strangely different component parts into an American community. It will be apparent to the student that either one of these functions by itself would be difficult enough. When both are found side by side the problem is increasingly difficult as to each. Together they represent a problem such as confronts no city in the United Kingdom, or in Europe.

The American city has had problems to deal with also of a material character, quite different from those which have confronted the cities of the

Old World. With the exception of Boston, Philadelphia, Baltimore, New Orleans, and New York, there is no American city of great consequence whose roots go back into the distant past even of America. American cities as a rule have grown with a rapidity to which the Old World presents few parallels. London, in the extent of its growth, but not in the proportions of it; Berlin since 1870, and Rome in the last few years, are perhaps the only places in Europe which have been compelled to deal with this element of rapid growth in anything like a corresponding degree. All of these cities, London, Berlin, and Rome, are the seats of the national government, and receive from that source more or less help and guidance in their development. In all of them an immense nucleus of wealth existed before this great and rapid growth began. The problem in America has been to make a great city in a few years out of nothing. There has been no nucleus of wealth upon which to found the structure which every succeeding year has enlarged. Recourse has been had of necessity, under these conditions, to the freest use of the public credit.

The city of Chicago, for example, with its population of two millions of people, was a small frontier trading post eighty years ago. Within that period everything has been created out of the fields. The houses in which the people live, the waterworks, the paved streets, the sewers, everything which makes up the permanent plant of a city, all have been produced while the city has been growing from year to year at a fabulous rate. Besides these things are to be reckoned the public schools, the public parks, and many municipal monuments of every kind. American cities as a rule have a more abundant supply of water than European cities, and they are usually more enterprising in furnishing themselves with things which in Europe may be called the luxuries of city life, but which, in America, are so common as to be regarded as necessities. Especially is this true of every convenience involving the use of electricity. There are more than half as many telephones, for example, in the city of New York alone, as there are in the whole of the United Kingdom.

The necessity of doing so much so quickly, has worked to the disadvantage of the American city in two ways. First, it has compelled very lavish expenditure under great pressure for quick results. This is precisely the condition under which the best trained businessmen make their greatest mistakes, and are in danger of running into extravagance and wastefulness. Few candid Americans will deny that American cities have suffered much, not alone from extravagance and wastefulness, but also from dishonesty; but in estimating the extent of the reproach, it is proper to take into consideration these general conditions under which the cities have been compelled to work. The second disadvantage under which American cities have laboured arising from this state of things has been a very general inability to provide adequately for current needs, while discounting the future so freely in order to provide their permanent plant. When the great American cities have paid for the permanent plant which they have been accumulating during the last half century, so that the duty which lies before them is chiefly that of caring adequately for the current life of their population, a vast improvement in all these particulars may reasonably be expected. The standard of city paving and of street cleaning in American cties, as a whole, is much higher now than it was when the first edition of this book appeared in 1888. In other words, time is a necessary element in making a great city, as it is in every other great and enduring work. American cities are judged by their size, rather than by the time which has entered into their growth. It cannot be denied that larger results could have been produced with the money expended, if it had always been used with complete honesty and good judgment. But to make an intelligent criticism upon the American city, in its failures upon the material side, these elements of difficulty must be taken into consideration.

Looked at in this light, the marvel would seem to be, not so much that the American cities are justly criticisable for many defects, but rather that results so great have been achieved in so short a time. New York City, for example, is just finishing the last of three suspension bridges, every one of which, in size and capacity, exceeds all other suspension bridges in the world. The city has also built a fourth bridge of the cantilever type, which, in capacity, much exceeds the great Forth Bridge, though the span is less long. New York has also developed in its corporate capacity, in cooperation with and under the direction of organizations of private citizens, a natural history museum that is second to no other, an art museum that is fairly counted among the greatest of art museums, a botanical garden that is rapidly forging towards the first rank, a zoological garden that in size and equipment excels any other, and an aquarium that is also worthy of leading rank. Each of these institutions is free. They are visited annually by millions of people; are all related to the public school system of the city, and stand as high for scientific usefulness as for public service. The city of Boston is steadily carrying towards completion one of the most remarkable systems of municipal parks and boulevards to be found in any country; and that is a poor American city, indeed, that does not tax itself freely to provide pleasure grounds for its people. Probably Berlin alone, among the great cities of Europe, is as well lighted as New York; and some of the cities of the Middle and Far West are proportionately better lighted than New York.

The city of St. Louis, a city of 687,000 people, conducted successfully, a few years ago, a World's Fair on a scale as great as has ever been attempted. These are but illustrations of what American cities have accomplished in many important fields.

One particular in which the American city may be thought to have come short of what might have been expected, may be described in general terms as a lack of foresight. It would have been comparatively easy to have preserved in all of them small open parks, and generally to have made them more beautiful, if there had been a greater appreciation of the need for these things and of their future growth. The Western cities probably have erred in this regard less than those upon the Atlantic coast. But while it is greatly to be regretted that this large foresight has not been displayed, it is, after all, only repeating in America what has taken place in Europe. The improvement of cities seems everywhere to be made by tearing down and replacing at great cost, rather than by a far-sighted provision for the demands and opportunities of the future. This unfortunate result in America has flowed, in part from the frequent tendency of population to grow in precisely the direction which was not anticipated. An interesting illustration of this last factor is to be found in the city of Washington. The Capitol was made to face towards the east, under the impression that population would settle in that direction. As matter of fact, the city has grown towards the west, so that the Capitol stands with its back to the city and faces a district that is scarcely built upon at all.

All the troubles which have marked the development of cities in the United States, however, are not due to these causes. Cities in the United States, as forms of government, are of comparatively recent origin. The city of Boston, for example, in the state of Massachusetts, although the settlement was founded more than two hundred and fifty years ago, received its charter as a city so recently as 1822. The city of Brooklyn received its charter from the state of New York in 1835. In other words, the transition from village and town government into government by cities, has simply followed the transition of small places into large communities. This suggests another distinction between the cities of the United States and those of Great Britain. The great cities of England and of Europe, with few exceptions, have their roots in the distant past. Many of their privileges and chartered rights were wrested from the Crown in feudal times. Some of these privileges have been retained, and contribute still to the income, the pride, and the influence of the municipality. The charter of an American city represents no element of prestige or inspiration. It is only the legal instrument which gives the community authority to act as a corporation, and which defines the duties of its officers. The motive for passing from town government to city government, in general, has been the same everywhere—to acquire a certain readiness of action, and to make more available the credit of the community in order to provide adequately for its own growth. The town meeting, in which every citizen takes part, serves its purpose admirably in communities up to a certain size, or for the conducting of public work on not too large a scale. But the necessity for the easy use of the public credit in providing for the needs of growth has compelled rapidly growing communities, in all the states, to seek the powers of a corporation as administered through a city government.

It will be perceived that the great growth of cities in the United States has thus resulted in the rapid transformation of a rural population into a population largely dwelling in cities; and this rapidly transformed urban population has been called upon, without any qualifying experience, to solve the difficult problem of city government. For many years, Americans applied to cities the theories which they had successfully embodied in the government of their states. It is only as some of these theories have broken down, when applied to cities, that Americans have begun to realize that they have on their hands a problem, new for them, which must be solved, so to speak, by rules of its own. Superficial observers may think that they have said all that needs to be said, when they have asked, "How can anyone expect to get good city government with manhood suffrage?" Manhood suffrage is an element in the problem, certainly; and the problem must be solved with manhood suffrage as a factor. But manhood suffrage, even in cities, is by no means a source of difficulty only. Every European city, comparable in size to any one of a half dozen American cities, swarms with soldiers. Outside of London this is less true of England than of the Continent. The population of American cities is much more heterogeneous than the population of these European cities; yet the American cities are free from soldiers, and although they have a smaller police force than corresponding European cities, public order is just as well preserved. The fact is that in American cities the people keep themselves in order, because they feel that the city is theirs. Manhood suffrage in American cities, as everywhere else in the United States, wakes the people up and develops a population of great average capacity.

Why is it, then, that Americans are less proud of their institutions, as illustrated in city government, than anywhere else?

In other words, why is it that American cities, despite their good points, have so much difficulty in securing a city government that needs no apology?

Some of the reasons, at least, may be indicated. Growing, as they have done, out of villages and towns, and compelled to go to the legislature of the state for their charters, American cities have seldom received in the first instance such adequate grants of power over their local affairs as to enable them to grow without constant resort to the legislature for additional powers. The states, also, have used the city for many purposes as the agent of the state. Out of these two circumstances has grown the habit, in almost every state, of interfering through the legislature with the details of city expenditure and city administration. The story of municipal reform in the United States is everywhere a story of the effort, by constitutional amendment, to limit the power of the state legislature to interfere with the details of city government.

The Constitution of the United States gives to the president great administrative power, including great power of appointment. The constitutions of the states, on the other hand—certainly of all the original states—looked to division of power as a source of safety; so that, instead of electing a governor with power to appoint the administrative officers of the state, as the president does for the United States, the principal administrative officers of the state, as well as the governor, are all elected by the people. Unhappily, this latter policy was almost uniformly followed in the organization of cities. Elective officers were made numerous, and the terms of office short. As a result, efficiency was impossible, and anything like effective responsibility to the voters could not be secured. It is taken, and will still take, a long time for Americans to realize that responsibility to the people is best maintained when elective officers are few in number, but have ample authority; and that efficiency is greatest when elected officials have adequate power to do right, even if they sometimes do wrong. The progress making in the direction of reducing the number of elected city officials is well illustrated by Boston's new charter, granted in 1909. This charter reduces the number of elected officials, in Boston, from ninety-seven to ten.

City inefficiency was greatly increased, also, by the demoralizing maxim, which came into the political life of the country in 1834, "To the Victors belong the Spoils." Under the influence of that battle cry, which was adopted by all political parties, even the subordinate civil service of the cities became as unstable as the sea.

In the matter of preventing interference by the state in the local affairs of the city, one state after another has passed constitutional amendments aimed at that evil. In the state of New York, no law affecting a city can be passed until it has first been submitted to the local authorities: in the larger cities to the mayor, and in the smaller cties to the mayor and common council. Public hearings are given in every city before action can be taken by the local authorities, and the bill is then returned, with or without the approval of the city, to the branch of the legislature in which the bill originated. The legislature has the authority to repass the bill, notwithstanding the protest of the city. The bill, if accepted by the city, or if passed by the legislature a second time, then goes to the governor for approval or disapproval, as in the case of any other state law. If a bill is passed for the first time by the legislature, so near the end of its session that the time given to the city for its consideration does not admit of its repassage by the legislature in the event of its nonacceptance by the city, then the nonacceptance by the city is fatal to the bill. In other words, by reason of this amendment to the constitution of the state of New York, adopted in 1894, no action can be taken by the legislature of the state without notice to the city. In almost every case the attitude of the city is final. It is only in matters of the first consequence that the judgment of the city is ever overruled by the legislature.

When this chapter was revised in 1906, the states of Missouri, California, Washington, Minnesota, and Colorado had adopted constitutions granting to the cities of those states, with various restrictions, the authority to make their own charters, which, when made, are not easily amendable by the legislature. City-made charters in California must be confirmed by the legislature; but the legislature, thus far, has always confirmed the city's action. Since 1906, the states of Oregon, Oklahoma, and Michigan have followed in the same path. In other words, the movement to prevent the interference by legislatures in the local affairs of cities throughout the states of the Union has already acquired great momentum, and it is not likely to be many years before this obstacle to good city administration has been overcome throughout the Union.

In the matter of securing more efficient administration of cities, it is evident that permanency of tenure of the subordinate administrative officials is a great factor in the situation. The definite adoption of the policy of civil service reform by the United States, in 1883, has been followed very generally by the states of the Union in relation to the civil service not only of the states, but also of the cities of the states. In the state of New York this policy has been embodied in the constitution of the state, and applies not only to the state administration, but to the administration of all the cities and local subdivisions of the state. Much remains to be done to bring about an ideal condition throughout the Union, but the right path has been entered upon, and it is likely to be followed to the end.

Responsibility to the people for administration in cities has been sought by two main methods. In the cities of New York and Philadelphia, and now in Boston, by its new charter, the mayor of the city is given the absolute power of appointment and removal of the heads of the administrative departments. The recent charter of the city of Boston provides a new limitation upon the power of appointment, from which, theoretically, much is to be hoped. It will be interesting to observe how it works in practice. The charter requires that the mayor, in filling responsible offices, shall appoint "recognized experts in such work as may devolve upon the incumbents of said offices, or persons specially fitted by education, training, and experience to perform the same." These officers are to be "appointed without regard to party affiliation or residence at the time of appointment"; and the mayor's appointment does not become operative, unless at least a majority of the state Civil Service Commission certify, within thirty days, that a careful inquiry into the qualifications of the appointee satisfies them that the appointee "is qualified by education, training, and experience" for the office to which he has been appointed. It will be observed that this provision gives to the state a certain administrative control over the appointments of the mayor of Boston; but administrative control by the state is far less objectionable than legislative control; for administrative control by the state is likely to be used, as it is in England, to help and not to embarrass the city. It is, evidently, clearly within the right of the state to insist, as a matter of uniform policy, that all appointments to office, within the state, shall involve the element of fitness as determined by a standard fixed by the state itself. It is a commentary on city administration, as it has been illustrated in Boston, that the state of Massachusetts should find it necessary to pass upon the special fitness for the work to be done, of an appointed city official. But no one familiar with the government of large cities throughout the United States imagines for a moment that Boston has been a sinner in this particular above all other cities. The special importance of this charter provision lies, on the contrary, in the fact that it is an intelligent effort to find a remedy for a widespread evil. The working of this clause, therefore, will be of immense interest, not only to the city of Boston but to all the cities of the Union.

The conclusions of the Boston Finance Commission, which was appointed originally by the mayor, and subsequently given special authority by the state of Massachusetts, and which proposed the new charter, are of interest as indicating the trend of modern American opinion. The Commission says:

The legislative measures which the commission regards as essential to enable the people of Boston to redeem their government may be summarized as follows:

1. A simplified ballot, with as few names thereon as possible.
2. The abolition of party nominations.
3. A city council consisting of a single small body elected at large.
4. The concentration of executive power and responsibility in the mayor.
5. The administration of the departments by trained experts, or persons with special qualifications for the office.
6. Full publicity secured through a permanent finance commission.

The permanent Finance Commission referred to is a body of five, to be appointed by the governor of the state, with power "to investigate, publish, and advise." This, also, is a new departure in American practice, and one that is likely to be widely followed, if it works well.

The other direction in which greater efficiency in city administration has been sought, is that which is known as the "Commission" or "Galveston" plan. In 1900 the city of Galveston, in Texas, was visited by a great tidal wave. The damage done to the city was so great as almost to threaten it with obliteration. In the presence of this emergency, the people of Galveston besought the legislature to amend the city charter, so as to give the city power to deal with the situation. The governing body of the city was reduced to a board of five members, presided over by an official known as mayor-president. This board has full legislative and administrative power for the city. It creates the city departments to be administered, and, by a majority vote, divides the administration of the departments among the members of the board, including the mayor. The mayor, in general, has no greater authority than any of his associates, although he is, in a sense, the general manager. The men first chosen in Galveston to administer this new system were thoroughly competent and upright men. They not only redeemed Galveston from its disaster, but set the city upon a plane which it had never reached before. The result has been that this system of city government has been widely adopted not only in Texas, but in other states of the Union. Massachusetts and Idaho, by special charter, have granted this form of government to certain of their cities, and the states of Iowa, Kansas, North Dakota, South Dakota, and Mississippi have passed laws enabling their cities, if they choose, to have charters embodying the general features of this plan. In cities of a moderate size the plan has worked sufficiently well, where it has been tried, to encourage its adoption by a continually increasing number of cities. The Report of the Secretary of the National Municipal League, made at the annual meeting of the League in 1909, calls attention to the fact that, within the previous two years, 138 cities in the Union have been seriously considering the question of charter making and charter revision. This statement shows how keenly alive the people of the United

States are to the importance of having for cities charters which give promise of efficiency. But the fact is noteworthy that the largest cities have chosen to seek administrative responsibility by centring the power to appoint and remove administrative officials in the hands of the mayor, while it is only the cities of moderate size, say, of 100,000 or fewer, inhabitants, that have chosen the Galveston type. Galveston itself has about 37,000 inhabitants. The power of political machinery increases with the size of the population. The largest cities have chosen to concentrate power in the hands of the mayor, because, in such cities, the leader of the dominant political party, usually called a "boss," becomes so strong as often to dominate even the mayor of the city, who may belong to his party. The "boss," as such, exerts power without responsibility; and the only way to dislodge him from control of the city, through the machinery of an election, is to give to the mayor, by law, the power which the "boss" exercises without legal authority, so that by dislodging a mayor who is subservient to a "boss," the people can take the city government, on its administrative side, out of the hands of the "boss." This system was first tried in the city of Brooklyn, New York, which was then an independent city, in 1882. Brooklyn is now a borough of the city of New York, and the Brooklyn system, in this respect, has been accepted by the larger city. It has been substantially adopted by Philadelphia; and, again, by the city of Boston, in the newest charter granted to any of the large cities of the country.

This discussion raises the question, how it is, that, in the United States, anyone not legally related to the government of a city can acquire such power as is exercised in all the large American cities by the so-called "boss" of the dominant party. The answer to this question is partly historical and partly philosophical. It is historical in the sense that the American people are strong partisans, and vote with their party, ordinarily, on local issues, no less than on national issues. In the state of New York, as early as 1815, when the local officials, including the mayor of New York, were appointed by a state Board of Appointment, so important a man as DeWitt Clinton, a man who had been senator of the United States, and who, later, as governor of the state of New York, constructed the Erie Canal, was removed from the office of mayor of New York by a state Board of Appointment that differed from him on national politics, in the execution of a party programme. This illustrates the pregnant fact that, even at that early day, when neither manhood suffrage nor immigration entered into the problem at all, the habit existed, in New York State at any rate, on the part of those controlling the national parties, of using the cities as pawns in the game of national politics. It is important to notice that this habit was not created by the extension of the suffrage, nor by the growth of immigration. On the contrary, the curious and interesting fact is that the habit has survived the extension of the suffrage. The same attitude of mind on the part of the national political parties towards the cities continues largely unchecked to the present day. It is the strong partisanship of the American people which has made this possible; and it is only within the last thirty years, since the consciousness of the city problem, as a problem by itself, has been pressed home on the American mind and conscience, that any pause has been given to this sort of thing. Now, the demand for home rule by the cities is so intelligent and so insistent that the political parties find it good judgment, very often, to recognize this sentiment. The habit persists, nevertheless, with the great majority of Americans, of voting with their national party, even in local elections. This is the historical condition which creates the "boss."

The philosophical explanation of the "boss" is to be found in the fact, that, where the voting population is large, it requires efficient organization to get out the vote. In the city of New York, for example, more than 600,000 people voted in the election of 1909. Simply to send one letter to all of the voters would cost more than $12,000. To acquaint the voters with the issues of the campaign, to interest them to go to the polls, and to see that their vote is cast, involves organization of a high order, and this is costly; and, in order to be efficient, the organization must also be manned by men thoroughly competent. This means that the organization needed for the service of a party not infrequently becomes so strong as to dominate the party; so that the organization, instead of being the servant of the party, becomes its master. The organization itself, to be most efficient, must be under permanent and capable control. The result is, first, the development of the professional politican who lives by politics; and, second, in cities, the leadership of this band by some one man who often becomes in the end its autocratic ruler.

This tendency is felt everywhere throughout the United States, and for the same reasons. It is probably true, that, in every state organization, the political machinery is subject to the same tendencies as have revealed themselves in cities. But the political "boss" of the city is more frequently an arbitrary potentate than the political "boss" of a state; because, in a state, the population is not so much concentrated, and there is a wider range of interests to be considered. Proportionately, moreover, the city budget is much greater than the state budget. The budget of the city of New York, for example, in 1908, was $143,000,000. The budget of the state of New York in the same year was $34,000,000. In addition to the budget, the city of New York issued, for municipal purposes, in the year 1908, $82,000,000 of bonds; the state of New York $15,000,000 of bonds. It is apparent, therefore, that the pecuniary motive for desiring to control city expenditure, which appeals to the professional politician, operates more strongly in cities than in the states. All of these considerations tend to make the political organization of the dominant party, in a city, more and more of a machine; so that the problem in cities, where the political majority is one-sided, is how to get good government despite the machine of the dominant party, rather than how to get it through that party. The same tendencies, of course, work in the minority party as well as in the majority party; but the habit of Americans of voting on local questions on the lines of national party makes the majority party, for the most part, the one to be dreaded. The danger from the minority party machine, in a city, comes when its leaders make terms with the leaders of the majority party for mutual advantage. The idea of "a community of interest" is not confined to the railroads of the United States, but finds its place in politics as well, and especially in municipal politics, for the reasons that have been given.

Of course this difficulty has been recognized ever since Americans began to have experience with large cities; and the effort has been constant to minimize it. There has grown up in the cities of the country a very considerable body of voters who will not vote any longer on local issues simply on national lines. They vote gladly with their national party, if they think that their national party is right on the local question at issue; but this body of independents does not hesitate to vote against the nominee of their party if they think the other party better deserves their support. This spirit of local independence in voting is the spirit which ultimately will secure good government for the American cities. The changes of charter which have been advocated have their principal value in the encouragement which they give to this spirit of independent voting, by making success at an election more fruitful of good results. It is evidently idle to set up machinery that is well calculated to give home rule, if the people of the city itself are determined to follow the old habit of permitting the city to be used as a pawn in the game of national politics. Deep-seated as this habit is in the American people, it has yielded and will yield to an effective opportunity, once gained, by the people of a city to control their own local affairs.

In the last ten years, in many of the smaller cities of the country, the effort has been made to weaken the power of the municipal machine by the system of direct primaries, and to increase the power of the people of the city over their own affairs by the adoption of "the initiative," "the referendum," and "the recall." The system of "direct primaries," so called, has been applied in a number of states, not only in cities, but as of universal application to all nominations made in the state. Ordinarily, in American communities, nominations are made by party conventions, and the delegates who form these conventions are chosen from political divisions of various kinds. It is believed by many Americans that political leaders get their abnormal power by the control of this party machinery, as a result of which they can generally control party nominations. The direct primary plan is an effort to compel such leaders to get the popular endorsement of the voters of their party before nominations can be known as party nominations. Under the direct primary system the people of the same party vote at the primaries directly for the persons to be chosen as the candidates of the party, the primary thus becoming a sort of preliminary election. It is too soon to say positively whether this system, in its general application, will lead to a betterment of conditions at large; but there is some reason to hope that it may do so in small districts. The difficulty is that the system of direct nominations itself involves a great deal of machinery; and it is not at all clear that the professional political element will not learn how to dominate this machinery as well as that which now exists. Possibly, in cities, nomination by petition may take the place of both the convention and the direct primary systems. It is indicative of popular opinion, at the moment, that the question was submitted to the people of Boston in November 1909, whether nominations for mayor and other local officers should be made by the convention system or by petition. By a majority of 3,000, out of a vote of 74,000, the people of Boston voted in favour of nomination of local officers by petition, without the use of any party machinery whatever. It will be exceedingly interesting to observe the outcome of this experiment in a city like Boston; for it is not only one of the larger cities of the country, but it is also an old city. If the plan succeeds in Boston, it is likely to be adopted widely in other cties. If it should not work well there, it is likely to put a check to further developments in this direction on the part of the large cties of the country. The writer is inclined to think, that, in order to work well, the plan of nominating in cities by petition must be supplemented by two other provisions: first, a majority vote must be required for election; and, second, in the event of a second ballot being necessary, the candidates to be voted for the second time should be the two who receive the highest and the next to the highest number of votes at the first voting. When an election is possible by a plurality vote, it is too easy for the machine to divide its enemies to their destruction.

In the smaller cities there appears to be no reason why the direct primary system should not work well. The difficulties of the system appear when the vote to be got out becomes so large that extensive machinery is required to get the vote out for the primary election, precisely as such machinery is required to get the vote out for the official election. On the other hand, it is certainly true, that, owing to the habit of the American people of voting with their national party, the nomination by the dominant party in probably nine-tenths of the constituencies of the United States, whether you speak of a state, or of a city, or of a district within any state or city, is equivalent to an election. There appears to be every reason, therefore, why the people should be permitted to make their wishes effectually known at the time when the nomination is made. The practical question is, whether the method of direct nomination will do this any more effectively than the method of nomination by convention. It will not be surprising if the line comes to be drawn, between the two methods, somewhat by the size of the vote to be cast.

In some cities of California, the largest of which to adopt the plan is Los Angeles, with a population of over 300,000, the system of "recall" has been adopted; which signifies, ordinarily, that upon the filing of a petition, asking for the recall of any official before the expiration of his term, a special election shall be held to determine whether or not the official shall be permitted to serve out his term. At such special election the official concerned may be a candidate for reelection or not, at his pleasure. The most important instance in which a recall has been resorted to was in the city of Los Angeles, where a mayor whose administration was unsatisfactory, was subjected to the "recall." The mayor declined to appeal to the verdict of the people; and accordingly another man was elected to serve out the remainder of his term. A modification of this system is embodied in the new charter of Boston. The mayor is elected for four years; but at the regular stated election during his second year, the question is submitted to the voters of the city, "Shall there be an election for mayor at the next municipal election?" If a majority of the voters vote in the affirmative, a new election ensues. On the other hand, a mayor has the right, if he wishes, to withdraw from the office, at his own pleasure, at the end of the second year. All of these movements are interesting, because they show how steadily the people of the cities of the United States are striving, first, to acquire the necessary power for complete local self-government; and, next, to make that local government completely responsive to the popular will.

The "initiative" and the "referendum," in their relation to the cities of the United States, are not different in substance from the "initiative" and the "referendum" as practised in Switzerland. It has been claimed that, in the matter of franchises, for example, the "referendum" would be a great protection against the abuse of power to grant franchises. In many places it doubtless is; but there is at least one case upon record, according to Judge Lindsey, of Denver, Colorado, in which the submission of a franchise to the vote of the people of Denver resulted in debauching the electorate of a whole city on a scale never known before. Private persons who were interested in securing the franchise were entirely ready to pay money to get it, even in such a way as that. On the other hand, Kansas City, through the "referendum," has recently defeated a franchise which was recommended by its Common Council.

This leads to the consideration of the control of franchises in the public interest, and of their relation to city governments. Only so recently as when this chapter was revised, in 1906, the tendency to adopt both municipal ownership and operation of franchises, as a cure for the unregulated granting of franchises to private corporations, seemed likely to be very widely adopted. The tendency towards municipal ownership has happily strengthened in the interval; but the indications today are that the tendency towards municipal operation of franchises is less strong now than then. This is largely due to the effect of the Report upon Municipal Ownership and Operation, prepared in 1907, under the auspices of the National Civic Federation. The commission which prepared this report was thoroughly representative, not only of those who believed in municipal ownership and operation, but also of those who were opposed to this plan. It was equally representative, both of capitalists and of organized labour. The tendency of organized labour to favour municipal operation as well as municipal ownership, has been greatly weakened by that report. Many of the leaders of organized labour in the United States feel that they can obtain better terms from private corporations operating such franchises than they can from the government. The American does not enjoy government service, per se, as much as he enjoys the independence of a private occupation; and organized labour recognizes that the conditions affecting governmental action are less friendly to its ambitions than those which apply to private corporations. The salaries of government employees, for example, are fixed by law, and only so much money is available for the payment of salaries. Many of the leaders of organized labour feel that, in the long run, labour can get a larger share of the earnings, under private control, than under governmental control. This is one of the reasons affecting the change in public sentiment; but, whether this explanation of the fact be complete or not, the change in sentiment is very real. In the meanwhile, in the state of New York, a method has been instituted for controlling the operations of public service corporations which thus far has worked exceedingly well.

Two public service commissioners have been created by the legislature, with large powers, one for New York City, and one for the rest of the state. Such corporations are brought under official supervision in ways that protect the public interests very much more completely than the public interests were ever protected before in the state of New York. This development, also, has weakened the tendency towards municipal operation of public franchises, because it decreases the abuses under which the public used to suffer through private administration of public franchises. The feeling is becoming very general throughout the cities of the United States that local franchises should not be given in perpetuity; and that the public, as well as the grantees, should profit from the grant. By constitutional restrictions upon the right to grant franchises, by such methods as have been described as prevailing in the state of New York, and by the referendum, the cities of the country are endeavouring to secure a larger share of the benefit than formerly accrued to the community from the operation of franchises in rapidly growing centres. It is not too much to say that the old era in this respect is at an end. Some improper grants may yet be made here and there; but the conviction is widespread that franchises are a public asset, and the public is determined to secure its share of the profits accruing from their use.

In the last revision of this chapter, it was said that the only organic problem in connection with the charters of cities which apparently remains as far from solution as ever, is that which concerns the legislative branch of the city government. That statement is not quite so true today as it was then. The difficulty never has been in devising a local legislature that theoretically would be satisfactory. The difficulty always has been to secure the election of suitable persons to the city legislature. The cities which have chosen the Galveston or commission plan of goverment claim to have made great advances in this particular by reducing the number of persons to be elected to a small body elected from the city at large, and by giving to them executive as well as legislative powers, such as are enjoyed by a board of directors in a business corporation. This, it is claimed, has enabled them to secure a better type of men in the city government. As was pointed out in this chapter, when last revised, the only large city in the United States which has importantly improved the character of its aldermen as a whole is the city of Chicago. This fact remains true to the present time. Mr. Horace E. Deming, in his valuable book on "The Government of American Cities," published in 1909, to which the writer is indebted for many of the details which have enabled him to bring his information down to date, makes the interesting suggestion, that the reason why Chicago has succeeded in doing this, when no other large city in the country has done it, is because, in the case of Chicago, the people had to do it, in order to get anything done at all. Mr. Deming points out that a constitutional amendment had deprived the legislature of Illinois of all power of legislating for the city of Chicago. The people of Chicago, therefore, realized, that, in order to get things done in the city of Chicago, they must get them done by their local legislature. Mr. Deming's claim is, that, when the people of the city of Chicago found that they had no other alternative, they devoted themselves intelligently and successfully to the problem of improving the personnel of their local legislature. He claims that the same result would follow in any American city under corresponding conditions. There is much to be said for this point of view.

The movement in favour of requiring uniform accounting from cities, alluded to in the last edition, continues to make progress. Three years ago, Ohio was the only state which had adopted this requirement. Since then, the states of Massachusetts, New York, Indiana, West Virginia, Colorado, and Wyoming have moved in this direction, wholly or in part, and at least three other states have it under consideration.

This outline sufficiently emphasizes present marked tendencies in municipal government, which show their effect in legislation. It may truthfully be said that the general standard of local administration is higher today, in most cities, than it was twenty years ago. This is undoubtedly so in the city of New York; and, so far as the observation of one man can go, it is generally true elsewhere. But there has been, within the last twenty years, a change in the form which municipal corruption has taken that amounts almost to a revolution. In the earlier days, officials who were dishonest stole openly from the public treasury; but, beginning with the overthrow of Tweed in the city of New York in 1871, that was seen to be a method so hazardous as to have fewer and fewer followers. The more modern method was never more succinctly stated than by a leader of Tammany Hall in the heyday of his power in the city of New York, when he publicly avowed before a legislative committee, that "he was in politics for his own pocket all the time." By this he meant that, indirectly, he made his political power a source of personal advantage to himself all the time. Those who wanted franchises, for example, must make their peace with "the boss" before they could have them. Those who wanted contracts must do the same thing. Those who wanted appointments or nominations must do likewise. The system of "graft," as it is now popularly called, has permeated the whole political organism. Only recently, a book has been written about another prominent member of Tammany Hall, in which that member argues openly, that there is such a thing as "honest graft"; that is to say, that it is entirely legitimate for men, having political power, to use it for their personal advantage, provided they do it in such a way as not to expose themselves to the criminal law. This seems to have been the idea of not a few men until recently connected with the large life insurance companies of the United States; and it is hard to say whether it has spread from such bodies as Tammany Hall into private business, or the reverse. The writer inclines to the former view; for it is manifestly impossible for a city to sustain, year after year, an organization like Tammany Hall, which avows such principles, without degrading the moral sense of the citizens in all walks of life. In both cases, it is caused in part, without doubt, by the unexampled prosperity through which the country has been passing during the last few years. No demoralizing influence which unchecked prosperity can exert was lacking in the United States from 1898 until 1907. The encouraging fact is, that when this sort of dishonesty is compelled to face the light of day, whether in public or in private life, it is openly and unhesitatingly condemned by the public conscience. Tammany Hall has been defeated twice, not to say three times, within the last fifteen years; a fate that befell it substantially only once in the previous sixty years.

In a country so large as the United States, it is impossible to generalize as to all the cities in the country; and yet it is doubtless true, that, in the city of New York, tendencies that exist everywhere are to be found in their most extreme development. It may happily be said today, as was said when this chapter was first written, that those who are students of the problems of city government in the United States are by no means discouraged. They find, indeed, in the interval under review, much more ground for encouragement than for loss of courage. It is true today, as it was true then, that the cities of the United States are the least successful parts of American administration; but it is still truer today than it was twenty years ago, that, under conditions of unexampled difficulty, such as are outlined in this chapter, they have not only made important progress, but they have also shown a capacity constantly to improve.

The shortcomings of the American city have been admitted, and the effort has been made to show the peculiar difficulties with which such a city has to deal. It is much to be able to say that, despite all of these difficulties, the average American city is not going from bad to worse. Life and property are more secure in almost all of them than they used to be. Certainly there has been no decrease of security such as might reasonably have been expected to result from increased size, and from an increasing diversity of population. Forty years ago it was impossible to have a fair election in New York or Brooklyn. Today, under the present system of registry laws, every election is held with substantial fairness, though the most recent election has shown the necessity for a change in the form of the ballot. The health of our cities does not deteriorate, but on the average improves. So that in large and fundamental matters, the progress, if slow, is steady in the direction of better things. It is not strange that a people at first almost wholly rural, conducting an experiment in city government for which there is absolutely no precedent, under conditions of exceptional difficulty, should have to stumble towards correct and successful methods through experiences that are both costly and distressing. There is no other road towards improvement in the coming time. But it is probable that in another decade Americans will look back on some of the scandals of the present epoch in city government, with as much surprise as they now regard the effort to control fires by the volunteer fire department, which was insisted upon, even in the city of New York, until within fifty years. As American cities grow in stability and provide themselves with the necessary working plant, they approximate more and more in physical conditions to those which prevail in most European cities.

It may justly be said, therefore, that the American city, if open to serious blame, is also deserving of much praise. Everyone understands that universal suffrage has its drawbacks, and in cities these defects become especially evident. It would be uncandid to deny that many of the problems of American cities spring from this factor, especially because the voting population is continually swollen by foreign immigrants whom time alone can educate into an intelligent harmony with the American system. In this Americanizing of the large immigration into the United States, the American cities, through their public-school systems, are doing their full share and are doing it rapidly and well. Zangwill likens the United States to a melting pot. But because there is scum upon the surface of a boiling liquid, it does not follow that the material, nor the process to which it is subjected, is itself bad. Universal suffrage, as it exists in the United States, is not only a great element of safety in the present day and generation, but is perhaps the mightiest educational force to which the masses of men ever have been exposed. In a country where wealth has no hereditary sense of obligation to its neighbours, it is hard to conceive what would be the condition of society if universal suffrage did not compel everyone having property to consider, to some extent at least, the well-being of the whole community.

It is probable that no other system of government would have been able to cope any more successfully, on the whole, with the actual conditions that American cities have been compelled to face. It may be claimed for American institutions even in cities, that they lend themselves with wonderfully little friction to growth and development and to the peaceful assimilation of new and strange populations. Whatever defects have marked the progress of such cities, no one acquainted with their history will deny that since their problem assumed its present aspect, progress has been made, and substantial progress, from decade to decade. The problem will never be anything but a most difficult one, but with all its difficulties there is every reason to be hopeful.

A P P E N D I X

Note to Chapter 3

ON CONSTITUTIONAL CONVENTIONS

In America it is always by a convention (i.e., a representative body called together for some occasional or temporary purpose) that a constitution is framed. It was thus that the first constitutions for the thirteen revolting colonies were drawn up and enacted in 1776 and the years following; and as early as 1780 the same plan had suggested itself as the right one for framing a constitution for the whole United States.[1] Recognized in the federal Constitution (art. V.) and in the successive constitutions of the several states as the proper method to be employed when a new constitution is to be prepared, or an existing constitution revised throughout, it has now become a regular and familiar part of the machinery of American government, almost a necessary part, because all American legislatures are limited by a fundamental law, and therefore when a fundamental law is to be repealed or largely recast, it is desirable to provide for the purpose a body distinct from the ordinary legislature. Where it is sought only to change the existing fundamental law in a few specified points, the function of proposing these changes to the people for their acceptance may safely be left, and generally is left, to the legislature. Originally a convention was conceived of as a sovereign body, wherein the full powers of the people were vested by popular election. It is now, however, merely an advisory body, which prepares a draft of a new constitution and submits it to the people for their acceptance or rejection.[2] And it is not deemed to be sovereign in the sense of possessing the plenary authority of the people, for its powers may be, indeed now invariably are, limited by the statute under which the people elect it.[3]

Questions relating to the powers of a constitutional convention have several times come before the courts, so that there exists a small body of

---

[1] It is found in a private letter of Alexander Hamilton (then only twenty-three years of age) of that year.

[2] As to Kentucky, see p. 384.

[3] The state conventions which carried, or rather affected to carry, the seceding slave states out of the Union, acted as sovereign bodies. Their proceedings, however, though clothed with legal forms, were practically revolutionary.

law as well as a large body of custom and practice regarding the rights and powers of such assemblies. Into this law and practice I do not propose to enter. But it is worth while to indicate certain advantages which have been found to attach to the method of entrusting the preparation of a fundamental instrument of government to a body of men specially chosen for the purpose instead of to the ordinary legislature. The topic suggests interesting comparisons with the experience of France and other European countries in which constitutions have been drafted and enacted by the legislative, which has been sometimes also practically the executive, authority. Nor is it wholly without bearing on problems which have recently arisen in England, where Parliament has found itself, and may find itself again, invited to enact what would be in substance a new constitution for a part of the United Kingdom.

An American constitutional convention, being chosen for the sole purpose of drafting a constitution, and having nothing to do with the ordinary administration of government, no influence or patronage, no power to raise or appropriate revenue, no opportunity of doing jobs for individuals or corporations, is not necessarily elected on party lines or in obedience to party considerations.[4] Hence men comparatively indifferent to party are sometimes elected; while those who seek to enter a legislature for the sake of party advancement or the promotion of some gainful object do not generally care to serve in a convention.

When the convention meets, it is not, like a legislature, a body strictly organized by party. A sense of individual independence and freedom may prevail unknown in legislatures. Proposals have therefore a chance of being considered on their merits. A scheme does not necessarily command the support of one set of men nor encounter the hostility of another set because it proceeds from a particular leader or group. And as the ordinary party questions do not come up for decision while its deliberations are going on, men are not thrown back on their usual party affiliations, nor are their passions roused by exciting political issues.

Having no work but constitution-making to consider, a convention is free to bend its whole mind to that work. Debate has less tendency to stray off to irrelevant matters. Business advances because there are no such interruptions as a legislature charged with the ordinary business of government must expect.

Since a convention assembles for one purpose only, and that a purpose specially interesting to thoughtful and public-spirited citizens, and since its

---

[4] The questions of practical importance to the states with which a state convention would deal are very often not in issue between the two state parties, seeing that the latter are formed on national lines.

duration is short, men who would not care to enter a legislature, men pressed by professional labours, or averse to the "rough and tumble" of politics, a class large in America and increasing in Europe, are glad to serve on it, while mere jobbers or office-seekers find little to attract them in its functions.[5] Thus the level of honesty, even more than of ability, is higher in conventions than in legislatures.

The fact that the constitution when drafted has to be submitted to the people, by whose authority it will (if accepted) be enacted, gives to the convention a somewhat larger freedom for proposing what they think best than a legislature, courting or fearing its constituents, commonly allows itself. As the convention vanishes altogether when its work is accomplished, the ordinary motives for popularity hunting are less potent. As it does not legislate but merely proposes, it need not fear to ask the people to enact what may offend certain persons or classes, for the odium, if any, of harassing these classes will rest with the people. And as the people must accept or reject the draft *en bloc* (unless in the rare case where provision is made for voting on particular points separately), more care is taken in preparing the draft, in seeing that it is free from errors and repugnances, than a legislature capable of repealing or altering in its next session what it now provides, is likely to bestow on the details of its measures.

Those who are familiar with European parliaments may conceive that as a set-off to these advantages there will be a difficulty in getting a number of men not organized by parties to work promptly and efficiently, that a convention will be, so to speak, an amorphous body, that if it has no leaders nor party allegiance it will divide one way today and another way tomorrow, that the abundance of able men will mean an abundance of doctrinaire proposals and a reluctance to subordinate individual prepossessions to practical success. Admitting that such difficulties do sometimes arise, it may be observed that in America men quickly organize themselves for any and every purpose, and that doctrinairism is there so uncommon a fault as to be almost a merit. When a complete new constitution is to be prepared, the balance of convenience is decidedly in favour of giving the work to a convention, for although conventions are sometimes unwise, they are usually composed of far abler men than those who fill the legislatures, and discharge their function with more wisdom as well as with more virtue. But where it

[5] Many of the men conspicuous in the public life of Massachusetts during the succeeding thirty years first made their mark in the Constitutional Convention of 1853. The draft framed by that convention was, however, rejected by the people. The new constitution for New York, framed by the Convention of 1867, was also lost at the polls. That convention was remarkable as being (according to Judge Jameson) the only one in which the requirement that a delegate must be resident in the district electing him was dispensed with (*Constit. Conventions,* § 267).

is not desired to revise the whole frame of government, the simpler and better plan is to proceed by submitting to the people specific amendments, limited to particular provisions of the existing constitution. This has been latterly the method most generally employed in improving state constitutions. Recently, however, a prescribed number of the citizens have been in six Western states empowered by their constitutions to propose by means of the initiative amendments of the constitution, which are thereupon submitted to popular vote without the intervention either of the legislature or of a convention. (See page 652, Extracts from the Constitution [1907] of Oklahoma.)

The above remarks are of course chiefly based on the history of state conventions, because no national constitutional convention has sat since 1787. But they apply in principle to any constitution-making body.

Note to Chapter 4

WHAT THE FEDERAL CONSTITUTION OWES TO THE CONSTITUTIONS OF THE SEVERAL STATES

The following statement of the provisions of the federal Constitution which have been taken from or modelled upon state constitutions, is extracted from a valuable article by Mr. Alexander Johnston in the *New Princeton Review* for September 1887:

"That part of the Constitution, which has attracted most notice abroad, is probably its division of Congress into a Senate and a House of Representatives, with the resulting scheme of the Senate as based on the equal representation of the States. It is probably inevitable that the upper or hereditary House in foreign legislative bodies shall disappear in time. And it is not easy to hit on any available substitute; and English writers for example, judging from the difficulty of finding a substitute for the House of Lords, have rated too high the political skill of the Convention in hitting upon so brilliant a success as the Senate. But the success of the Convention was due to the antecedent experience of the States. Excepting Pennsylvania and Vermont, which then gave all legislative powers to one House, and executive powers to a governor and council, all the States had bicameral systems in 1787.[1]

[1] Georgia, however, had not till 1789 a true second chamber, her constitution of 1777 having merely created an executive council elected by the assembly from among its own members.

Vermont was not one of the thirteen original states, but was a semi-independent commonwealth,

"The name 'Senate' was used for the Upper House in Maryland, Massachusetts, New York, North Carolina, New Hampshire, and South Carolina and Virginia; and the name 'House of Representatives,' for the Lower House, was in use in Massachusetts, New Hampshire, and South Carolina, as well as in Pennsylvania and Vermont.

"The rotation, by which one-third of the Senate goes out every two years, was taken from Delaware, where one-third went out each year, New York (one-fourth each year), Pennsylvania (one-third of the council each year), and Virginia (one-fourth each year). The provisions of the whole fifth section of Art. i., the administration of the two Houses, their power to decide the election of their members, make rules and punish their violation, keep a journal, and adjourn from day to day, are in so many state constitutions that no specification is needed for them.

"The provision that money-bills shall originate in the House of Representatives is taken almost word for word from the Constitutions of Massachusetts and New Hampshire, as is the provision, which has never been needed, that the President may adjourn the two Houses when they cannot agree on a time of adjournment. The provision for a message is from the Constitution of New York. All the details of the process of impeachment as adopted by the Convention may be found in the Constitutions of Delaware, Massachusetts, New Hampshire, New York, Pennsylvania, South Carolina, Vermont, Virginia, even to the provision in the South Carolina system that conviction should follow the vote of two-thirds of the members present. (It should be said, however, that the limitation of sentence in case of conviction to removal from office and disqualification for further office-holding is a new feature.) Even the much-praised process of the veto is taken *en bloc* from the Massachusetts Constitution of 1780, and the slight changes are so evidently introduced as improvements on the language alone as to show that the substance was copied.

"The adoption of different bases for the two Houses—the House of Representatives representing the States according to population, while the Senate represented them equally—was one of the most important pieces of work which the Convention accomplished as well as the one which it reached most unwillingly. All the States had been experimenting to find different bases for their two Houses. Virginia had come nearest to the appearance of the final result in having her Senate chosen by districts and her representatives by counties; and, as the Union already had its 'districts'

---

not a member of the Confederation of 1781, not represented in the Convention of 1787, and not admitted to the Union till 1791.

formed (in the States), one might think that the Convention merely followed
Virginia's experience. But the real process was far different and more
circuitous. There were eleven States represented in the Convention, New
Hampshire taking New York's place when the latter withdrew, and Rhode
Island sending no delegates. Roughly speaking, five States wanted the
'Virginia plan' above stated; five wanted one House as in the Confederation
with State equality in it; and one (Connecticut) had a plan of its own to
which the other ten States finally acceded. The Connecticut system since
1699, when its legislature was divided into two Houses, had maintained the
equality of the towns in the Lower House, while choosing the members of
the Upper House from the whole people. In like manner its delegates now
proposed that the States should be equally represented in the Senate, while
the House of Representatives, chosen from the States in proportion to
population, should represent the people numerically. The proposition was
renewed again and again for nearly a month until the two main divisions of
the Convention, unable to agree, accepted the 'Connecticut compromise,'
as Bancroft calls it, and the peculiar constitution of the Senate was adopted.

"The President's office was simply a development of that of the governors
of the States. The name itself had been familiar; Delaware, New Hampshire,
Pennsylvania, and South Carolina, had used the title of President instead of
that of Governor. In all the States the governor was commander-in-chief,
except that in Rhode Island he was to have the advice of six assistants, and
the major part of the freemen, before entering upon his duties. The President's
pardoning power was drawn from the example of the States; they had
granted it to the governors (in some cases with the advice of a council) in
all the States except Connecticut, Rhode Island, and Georgia, where it was
retained to the legislature, and in South Carolina, where it seems to have
been forgotten in the Constitution of 1778, but was given to the governor
in 1790. The governor was elected directly by the people in Connecticut,
Massachusetts, New York, and Rhode Island, and indirectly by the two
Houses in the other eight States; and in this nearly equal division we may,
perhaps, find a reason for the Convention's hesitation to adopt either system,
and for its futile attempt to introduce an electoral system, as a compromise.
The power given to the Senate of ratifying or rejecting the President's
appointments seems to have been an echo of New York's council of
appointment; the most strenuous and persistent efforts were made to provide
a council to share in appointments with the President; the admission of the
Senate as a substitute was the furthest concession which the majority would
make; and hardly any failure of details caused more heart-burnings than the
rejection of this proposed council for appointments.

"The President's power of filling vacancies, by commissions to expire at the end of the next session of the Senate, is taken in terms from the Constitution of North Carolina.

"Almost every State prescribed a form of oath for its officers; the simple and impressive oath of the President seems to have been taken from that of Pennsylvania, with a suggestion, much improved in language, from the oath of allegiance of the same State. The office of vice-president was evidently suggested by that of the deputy, or lieutenant-governor (in four States the vice-president) of the States. The exact prototype of the office of vice-president is to be found in that of the lieutenant governor of New York. He was to preside in the Senate, without a vote, except in case of a tie, was to succeed the governor, when succession was necessary, and was to be succeeded by the President *pro tempore* of the Senate.

"The provisions for the recognition of inter-State citizenship, and for the rendition of fugitive slaves and criminals, were a necessity in any such form of government as was contemplated, but were not at all new. They had formed a part of the eighth article of the New England Confederation of 1643. Finally the first ten amendments, which were tacitly taken as a part of the original instrument, are merely a selection from the substance or the spirit of the Bills of Rights which preceded so many of the State constitutions.

"The most solid and excellent work done by the Convention was its statement of the powers of Congress (in § 8 of Art. i.) and its definition of the sphere of the Federal judiciary (in Art. iii.). The results in both of these cases were due, like the powers denied to the States and to the United States (in §§ 9 and 10 of Art. i.), to the previous experience of government by the States alone. For eleven years or more (to say nothing of the antecedent colonial experience) the people had been engaged in their State governments in an exhaustive analysis of the powers of government. The failures in regard to some, the successes in regard to others, were all before the Convention for its consideration and guidance.

"Not creative genius, but wise and discreet selection was the proper work of the Convention; and its success was due to the clear perception of the antecedent failures and successes, and to the self-restraint of its members.

"The (presidential) electoral system was almost the only feature of the Constitution not suggested by State experience,[2] almost the only feature

---

[2] But it is well observed by Mr. J. H. Robinson (*Original and Derived Features of the United States Constitution*, p. 29) that this system may have been suggested by the Constitution of Maryland (1776), which provided for a choice of the state senators by a body of electors chosen every five years by the people for this purpose. Mr. Robinson rightly disapproves Sir H. Maine's comparison of the electoral system of the Romano-Germanic Empire.

which was purely artificial, not a natural growth; it was the one which met with least criticism from contemporary opponents of the Constitution and most unreserved praise from the *Federalist;* and democracy has ridden right over it."

Note to Chapter 10

EXTRACTS FROM THE RULES OF THE SENATE

A quorum shall consist of a majority of the senators, duly chosen and sworn.

The legislative, the executive, the confidential legislative proceedings, and the proceedings when sitting as a Court of Impeachment, shall each be recorded in a separate book.

When the yeas and nays are ordered, the names of senators shall be called alphabetically; and each senator shall, without debate, declare his assent or dissent to the question, unless excused by the Senate; and no senator shall be permitted to vote after the decision shall have been announced by the presiding officer, but may for sufficient reasons, with unanimous consent, change or withdraw his vote.

When a senator declines to vote on call of his name, he shall be required to assign his reasons therefor, and on his having assigned them, the presiding officer shall submit the question to the Senate, "Shall the senator for the reasons assigned by him, be excused from voting?" which shall be decided without debate.

In the appointment of the standing committees, the Senate, unless otherwise ordered, shall proceed by ballot to appoint severally the chairman of each committee, and then, by one ballot, the other members necessary to complete the same. A majority of the whole number of votes given shall be necessary to the choice of a chairman of a standing committee, but a plurality of votes shall elect the other members thereof. All other committees shall be appointed by ballot, unless otherwise ordered, and a plurality of votes shall appoint.

At the second or any subsequent session of a Congress, the legislative business which remained undetermined at the close of the next preceding session of that Congress shall be resumed and proceeded with in the same manner as if no adjournment of the Senate had taken place.

On a motion made and seconded to close the doors of the Senate, on the discussion of any business which may, in the opinion of a senator, require secrecy, the presiding officer shall direct the galleries to be cleared; and during the discussion of such motion the doors shall remain closed.

When the President of the United States shall meet the Senate in the Senate chamber for the consideration of executive business, he shall have a seat on the right of the presiding officer. When the Senate shall be convened by the President of the United States to any other place, the presiding officer of the Senate and the senators shall attend at the place appointed, with the necessary officers of the Senate.

When acting upon confidential or executive business the Senate chamber shall be cleared of all persons except the secretary, the chief clerk, the principal legislative clerk, the executive clerk, the minute and journal clerk, the sergeant-at-arms, the assistant doorkeeper, and such other officers as the presiding officer shall think necessary, and all such officers shall be sworn to secrecy.

All confidential communications made by the President of the United States to the Senate shall be by the senators and the officers of the Senate kept secret; and all treaties which may be laid before the Senate, and all remarks, votes, and proceedings thereon, shall also be kept secret until the Senate shall, by their resolution, take off the injunction of secrecy, or unless the same shall be considered in open executive session.

Any senator or officer of the Senate who shall disclose the secret or confidential business or proceedings of the Senate shall be liable, if a senator, to suffer expulsion from the body; and if an officer, to dismissal from the service of the Senate, and to punishment for contempt.

On the final question to advise and consent to the ratification of a treaty in the form agreed to, the concurrence of two-thirds of the senators present shall be necessary to determine it in the affirmative; but all other motions and questions upon a treaty shall be decided by a majority vote, except a motion to postpone indefinitely, which shall be decided by a vote of two-thirds.

When nominations shall be made by the President of the United States to the Senate, they shall, unless otherwise ordered, be referred to appropriate committees; and the final question on every nomination shall be, "Will the Senate advise and consent to this nomination?" Which question shall not be put on the same day on which the nomination is received, nor on the day on which it may be reported by a committee, unless by unanimous consent.

All information communicated or remarks made by a senator, when acting upon nominations, concerning the character or qualifications of the person nominated, also all votes upon any nomination, shall be kept secret. If, however, charges shall be made against a person nominated, the committee may, in its discretion, notify such nominee thereof, but the name of the person making such charges shall not be disclosed. The fact that a nomination has been made, or that it has been confirmed or rejected, shall not be regarded as a secret.

Note (A) to to Chapter 16

PRIVATE BILLS

In England a broad distinction is drawn between public bills and local or private bills. The former class includes measures of general application, altering or adding to the general law of the land. The latter includes measures intended to apply only to some particular place or person, as for instance, bills incorporating railway or gas or water companies or extending the powers of such bodies, bills authorizing municipalities to execute public improvements, as well as estate bills, bills relating to charitable foundations, and (for Ireland) divorce bills.[1] Bills of the local and personal class have for many years past been treated differently from public bills. They are brought in, as it is expressed, on petition, and not on motion. Notice is required to be given of such a bill by advertisement nearly three months before the usual date of the meeting of Parliament and copies must be deposited some weeks before the opening of the session. The second reading is usually granted as a matter of course; and after second reading, instead of being, like a public bill, considered in Committee of the Whole House, it goes (if opposed) to a private bill committee consisting (usually) of four members, who take evidence regarding it from the promoters and opponents, and hear counsel argue for and against its preamble and its clauses. In fact, the proceedings on private bills are to some extent of a judicial nature, although of course the committee must have regard to considerations of policy.

Pecuniary claims against the government are in England not raised by way of private bill. They are presented in the courts by a proceeding called

---

[1] The official distinction in the yearly editions of the statutes is into Public General Acts, Public Acts of a local character (which include Provisional Order Acts and Local Acts), and Private Acts. But in ordinary speech, those measures which are brought in at the instance of particular persons for a local purpose are called private.

a petition of right, the Crown allowing itself to be sued by one of its subjects.

In America no such difference of treatment as the above exists between public and private bills; all are dealt with in substantially the same way by the usual legislative methods. A bill of purely local or personal nature gets its second reading as a matter of course, like a bill of general application, is similarly referred to the appropriate committee (which may hear evidence regarding it, but does not hear counsel), is considered and if necessary amended by the committee, is, if time permits, reported back to the House, and there takes its chance among the jostling crowd of other bills, Fridays, however, being specially set apart for the consideration of private business. There is a calendar of private bills, and those which get a place early upon it have a chance of passing. A great many are unopposed, and can be hurried through "by unanimous consent."

Private bills are in Congress even more multifarious in their contents, as well as incomparably more numerous, than in England, although they do not include the vast mass of bills for the creation or regulation of various public undertakings within a particular state, since these would fall within the province of the state legislature. They include three classes practically unknown in England, pension bills, which propose to grant a pension to some person (usually a soldier or his widow), bills for satisfying some claim of an individual against the federal government—these, however, have been largely reduced by the creation of the Court of Claims—and bills for dispensing in particular cases with a variety of administrative statutes. Matters which in England would be naturally left to be dealt with at the discretion of the executive are thus assumed by the legislature, which is (for reasons that will appear in later chapters) more anxious to narrow the sphere of the executive than are the ruling legislatures of European countries. I subjoin some instances showing how wide is the range of congressional interference.

IN THE HOUSE OF REPRESENTATIVES

Read twice, referred to the Committee on Invalid Pensions, and ordered to be printed.

Mr. Murch introduced the following bill:

A BILL

For the relief of James E. Gott

Be it enacted,

1 *By the Senate and House of Representatives of the*
2 *United States of America in Congress Assembled.*
3 That the Secretary of the Interior be, and he is hereby,
4 Authorized and directed to increase the pension of James E.
5 Gott, late a member of Company A, Fourteenth Regiment,
6 Maine Volunteers, to twenty-four dollars per month.

––––––––

Read twice, referred to the Committee on War Claims, and ordered to be printed.

A BILL

For the relief of the heirs of George W. Hayes

Be it enacted,

That the proper accounting officer of the Treasury be, and he is hereby, directed to pay to the heirs of George W. Hayes, of North Carolina, the sum of four hundred and fifty dollars, for three mules furnished the United States Army in eighteen hundred and sixty-four, for which they hold proper vouchers.

––––––––

Read twice, referred to the Committee on Commerce, and ordered to be printed.

A BILL

For the relief of Thomas G. Corbin

Be it enacted, etc.

That the President of the United States be, and is hereby, authorized to restore Thomas G. Corbin, now a captain on the retired list of the Navy, to the active list, and to take rank next after Commodore J. W. A. Nicholson, with restitution, from December twelfth, eighteen hundred and seventy-three, of the difference of pay between that of a commodore on the active list, on "waiting orders" pay, and that of a captain retired on half-pay, to be paid out of any money in the Treasury not otherwise appropriated.

––––––––

Read twice, referred to the Committee on Ways and Means, and ordered to be printed.

Mr. Robinson introduced the following joint resolution:

JOINT RESOLUTION

Authorizing the remission or refunding of duty on a painted-glass window from London, England, for All Souls' Church, in Washington, District of Columbia.

Resolved by the Senate and House of Representatives of the United States of America in Congress Assembled.

That the Secretary of the Treasury be, and he is hereby, authorized and directed to remit or refund, as the case may be, the duties paid or accruing upon a painted-glass window from London, England, for All Souls' Church, in Wasington, District of Columbia, imported, or to be imported into Baltimore, Maryland, or other port.

Note (B) to Chapter 16

THE LOBBY

"The lobby" is the name given in America to persons, not being members of a legislature, who undertake to influence its members, and thereby to secure the passing of bills. The term includes both those who, since they hang about the chamber, and make a regular profession of working upon members, are called "lobbyists," and those persons who on any particular occasion may come up to advocate, by argument or solicitation, any particular measure in which they happen to be interested. The name, therefore, does not necessarily impute any improper motive or conduct, though it is commonly used in what Bentham calls a dyslogistic sense.

The causes which have produced lobbying are easily explained. Every legislative body has wide powers of affecting the interests and fortunes of private individuals, both for good and for evil. It entertains in every session some public bills, and of course many more private (i.e., local or personal) bills, which individuals are interested in supporting or resisting. Such, for instance, are public bills imposing customs duties or regulating the manufacture or sale of particular articles (e.g., intoxicants, explosives), and private bills establishing railroad or other companies, or granting public franchises, or (in state legislatures) altering the areas of local government, or varying the taxing or borrowing powers of municipalities. When such bills are before a legislature, the promoters and the opponents naturally seek to represent their respective views, and to enforce them upon the members with whom the decision rests. So far there is nothing wrong, for advocacy of this kind is needed in order to bring the facts fairly before the legislature.

Now both in America and in England it has been found necessary, owing to the multitude of bills and the difficulty of discussing them in a large body, to refer private bills to committees for investigation; and the legislature has in both countries formed the habit of accepting generally, though not invariably, the decisions of a committee upon the bills it has dealt with. America has, however, gone farther than England, for Congress refers all public bills as well as private bills to committees. And whereas in England private bills are dealt with by a semi-judicial procedure, the promoters and opponents appearing by professional agents and barristers, in America no such procedure has been created, either in Congress or in the state legislatures, and private bills are handled much like public ones. Moreover, the range of private bills is wider in America than in England, in respect that they are used to obtain the satisfaction of claims by private persons against the government, (although there exists a federal Court of Claims, and in some states the state permits itself to be sued) whereas in England such claims would either be brought before a law court in the form of a Petition of Right, or, though this rarely happens, be urged upon the executive by a motion made in Parliament.

We see, therefore, that in the United States:

All business goes before committees, not only private bills but public bills, often involving great pecuniary interests;

To give a bill a fair chance of passing, the committee must be induced to report in favour of it;

The committees have no quasi-judicial rules of procedure, but inquire into and amend bills in their uncontrolled discretion, upon such evidence or other statements as they choose to admit or use;

Bills are advocated before committees by persons not belonging to any recognized and legally regulated body;

The committees, both in the state legislatures and in the federal House of Representatives, are largely composed of new men, unused to the exercise of the powers entrusted to them, though in the House of Representatives the chairman is a person of some experience.

It results from the foregoing state of facts that the efforts of the promoters and opponents of a bill will be concentrated upon the committee to which the bill has been referred; and that when the interests affected are large it will be worth while to employ every possible engine of influence. Such influence can be better applied by those who have skill and a tact matured by experience; for it is no easy matter to know how to handle a committee collectively and its members individually. Accordingly, a class of persons springs up whose profession it is to influence committees for or against bills. There is nothing necessarily illegimate in doing so. As Mr. Spofford remarks:

"What is known as lobbying by no means implies in all cases the use of money to affect legislation. This corruption is frequently wholly absent in cases where the lobby is most industrious, numerous, persistent, and successful. A measure which it is desired to pass into law, for the benefit of certain interests represented, may be urged upon members of the legislative body in every form of influence except the pecuniary one. By casual interviews, by informal conversation, by formal presentation of facts and arguments, by printed appeals in pamphlet form, by newspaper communications and leading articles, by personal introductions from or through men of supposed influence, by dinners, receptions, and other entertainments, by the arts of social life and the charms of feminine attraction, the public man is beset to look favourably upon the measure which interested parties seek to have enacted. It continually happens that new measures or modifications of old ones are agitated in which vast pecuniary interests are involved. The power of the law, which when faithfully administered is supreme, may make or unmake the fortunes of innumerable corporations, business firms, or individuals. Changes in the tariff duties, in the internal revenue taxes, in the banking system, in the mining statutes, in the land laws, in the extension of patents, in the increase of pensions, in the regulation of mail contracts, in the currency of the country, or proposed appropriations for steamship subsidies, for railway legislation, for war damages, and for experiments in multitudes of other fields of legislation equally or more important, come before Congress. It is inevitable that each class of interests liable to be affected should seek its own advantage in the result. When this is done legitimately, by presentation and proof of facts, by testimony, by arguments, by printed or personal appeals to the reason and sense of justice of members, there can be no objection to it."[1]

Just as a plaintiff in a lawsuit may properly employ an attorney and barrister, so a promoter may properly employ a lobbyist. But there is plainly a risk of abuse. In legal proceedings, the judge and jury are bound to take

[1] Mr. A. R. Spofford (formerly Librarian of Congress) in *American Cyclopædia of Political Science*, Article "Lobby."

nothing into account except the law and the facts proved in evidence. It would be an obvious breach of duty should a judge decide in favour of a plaintiff because he had dined with or been importuned by him (as in the parable), or received £50 from him. The judge is surrounded by the safeguards, not only of habit but of opinion, which would condemn his conduct and cut short his career were he to yield to any private motive. The attorney and barrister are each of them also members of a recognized profession, and would forfeit its privileges were they to be detected in the attempt to employ underhand influence. No such safeguards surround either the member of a committee or the lobbyist. The former usually comes out of obscurity, and returns to it; the latter does not belong to any disciplined profession. Moreover, the questions which the committee has to decide are not questions of law, nor always questions of fact, but largely questions of policy, on which reasonable men need not agree, and as to which it is often impossible to say that there is a palpably right view or wrong view, because the determining considerations will be estimated differently by different minds.

These dangers in the system of private bill legislation made themselves so manifest in England, especially during the great era of railway construction between 1835 and 1850, as to have led to the adoption of the quasi-judicial procedure described in the Note on Private Bills, and to the erection of parliamentary agents into a regularly constituted profession, bound by professional rules. Public opinion has fortunately established the doctrine that each member of a private bill committee is to be considered as a quasi-judicial person, whose vote neither a brother member nor any outsider may attempt to influence, but who is bound to decide, as far as he can, in a judicial spirit on the footing of the evidence tendered. Of course practice is not up to the level of theory in Parliament any more than elsewhere; still there is little solicitation to members of committees, and an almost complete absence of even the suspicion of corruption.

"In the United States," says an experienced American publicist, whose opinion I have inquired, "though lobbying is perfectly legitimate in theory, yet the secrecy and want of personal responsibility, the confusion and want of system in the committees, make it rapidly degenerate into a process of intrigue, and fall into the hands of the worst men. It is so disagreeable and humiliating that all men shrink from it, unless those who are stimulated by direct personal interest; and these soon throw away all scruples. The most dangerous men are ex-members, who know how things are to be managed."

That this unfavourable view is the prevailing one, appears not merely from what one hears in society or reads in the newspapers, though in America one must discount a great deal of what rumour asserts regarding illicit influence, but from the constitutions and statutes of some states, which endeavour to repress it.

What has been said above applies equally to Congress and to the state legislatures, and to some extent also to the municipal councils of the great cities. All legislative bodies which control important pecuniary interests are as sure to have a lobby as an army to have its camp followers. Where the body is, there will the vultures be gathered together. Great and wealthy states, like New York and Pennsylvania, support the largest and most active lobbies. It must, however, be remembered that although no man of good position would like to be called a lobbyist, still such men are often obliged to do the work of lobbying—i.e., they must dance attendance on a committee, and endeavour to influence its members for the sake of getting their measure through. They may have to do this in the interests of the good government of a city, or the reform of a charity, no less than for some private end.

The permanent professional staff of lobbyists at Washington is of course from time to time recruited by persons interested in some particular enterprise, who combine with one, two, or more professionals in trying to push it through. Thus there are at Washington, says Mr. Spofford, "pension lobbyists, tariff lobbyists, steamship subsidy lobbyists, railway lobbyists, Indian ring lobbyists, patent lobbyists, river and harbour lobbyists, mining lobbyists, bank lobbyists, mail-contract lobbyists, war damages lobbyists, back-pay and bounty lobbyists, Isthmus canal lobbyists, public building lobbyists, state claim lobbyists, cotton-tax lobbyists, and French spoliations lobbyists. Of the office-seeking lobbyists at Washington it may be said that their name is legion. There are even artist lobbyists, bent upon wheedling Congress into buying bad paintings and worse sculptures; and too frequently with success. At times in our history there has been a British lobby, with the most genteel accompaniments, devoted to watching legislation affecting the great importing and shipping interests."

A committee whose action can affect the tariff is of course surrounded by a strong lobby.[2] I remember to have heard an anecdote of a quinine manufacturer, who had kept a lawyer as his agent to "take care of" a committee during a whole session, and prevent them from touching the duty on that drug. On the last day of sitting the agent went home, thinking the danger past. As soon as he had gone, the committee suddenly recommended

[2] The phrase one often hears "there was a strong lobby" (i.e., for or against such and such a bill) denotes that the interests and influences represented were numerous and powerful.

an alteration of the duty, on the impulse of someone who had been watching all the time for his opportunity.

Women were at one time among the most active and successful lobbyists at Washington. Very few are now seen.

Efforts have been made to check the practice of lobbying, both in Congress and in state legislatures. Statutes have been passed severely punishing any person who offers any money or value to any member with a view to influence his vote.[3] It has been repeatedly held by the courts that "contracts which have for their object to influence legislation in any other manner than by such open and public presentation of facts, arguments, and appeals to reason, as are recognized as proper and legitimate with all public bodies, must be held void."[4] It has also been suggested that a regular body of attorneys, authorized to act as agents before committees of Congress, should be created. A bill for this purpose was laid before the Senate in January 1875.

Note (A) to Chapter 30

CONSTITUTION OF THE CONFEDERATE STATES, 1861–65

The constitution adopted 11th March 1861 by the slave states which seceded from the Union and formed the short-lived Southern Confederacy, was a reproduction of the federal Constitution of 1788–89, with certain variations,

---

[3] As to Congress, see § 5450 of Revised Statutes of the United States. The provisions of state statutes are too numerous to mention. See p. 410. Massachusetts endeavoured by statute to regulate her state lobby, by requiring every person promoting a bill to state whom he has employed for the purpose and what he has paid. New York, Missouri, and other states have also passed laws designed to regulate and check lobbying. Some good has been done, but the evils do not seem to have been extirpated.

[4] Cooley, *Constit. Limit.*, p. 166. He refers to the observations of Justice Chapman, in *Frost* v. *Belmont*, 6 Allen, 152:

"Though Committees properly dispense with many of the rules which regulate hearings before judicial tribunals, yet common fairness requires that neither party shall be permitted to have secret consultations and exercise secret influences that are kept from the knowledge of the other party. The business of 'lobby members' is not to go fairly and openly before the committees and present statements, proofs, and arguments, that the other side has an opportunity to meet and refute if they are wrong, but to go secretly to the members and ply them with statements and arguments that the other side cannot openly meet, however erroneous they may be, and to bring illegitimate influences to bear upon them. If the 'lobby member' is selected because of his political or personal influence, it aggravates the wrong. If his business is to unite various interests by means of projects that are called 'log-rolling,' it is still worse. The practice of procuring members of the legislature to act under the influence of what they have eaten and drunk at houses of entertainment tends to render those who yield to such influences wholly unfit to act in such cases."

interesting because they show the points in which the states' rights party thought the federal Constitution defective as inadequately safeguarding the rights of the several states, and because they embody certain other changes which have often been advocated as likely to improve the working of that instrument.

The most important of these variations are the following:

Art. I, § 2. A provision is inserted permitting the impeachment of a federal officer acting within the limits of any state by a vote of two-thirds of the legislature thereof.

Art. I, § 6. There is added: "Congress may by law grant to the principal officer in each of the executive departments, a seat upon the floor of either House, with the privilege of discussing any measure appertaining to his department."

Art. I, § 7. The president is permitted to veto any particular item or items in an appropriation bill.

Art. I, § 8. The imposition of protective duties and the granting of bounties on industry are forbidden, and the granting of money for internal improvements is strictly limited.

Art. I, § 9. Congress is forbidden to appropriate money from the Treasury, except by a vote of two-thirds of both houses, unless it be asked by the head of a department and submitted by the president, or be for the payment of its own expenses, or of claims against the Confederacy declared by a judicial tribunal to be just.

Art. II, § 1. The president and vice-president are to be elected for six years, and the president is not to be reeligible.

Art. II, § 2. The president is given power to remove the highest officials at his pleasure, and others for good cause, reporting the removals to the Senate.

Art. V. The process for amending the Constitution is to be by a convention of all the states, followed by the ratification of two-thirds of the states.

Of these changes, the third and fifth were obvious improvements; and much may be said in favour of the second, fourth, seventh, and eighth. The second was a very slight approximation towards the cabinet system of England.[1]

I omit the important changes relating to slavery, which was fully protected, because these have only a historical interest.

---

[1] A singular combination of the presidential with the cabinet system may be found in the present Constitution of the Hawaiian kingdom, promulgated 7th July 1887, which lasted till the islands were annexed to the United States in 1898. Framed under the influence of American traditions, it kept the cabinet, which consisted of four ministers, out of the legislature but having an irresponsible hereditary monarch, it was obliged to give the legislature the power of dismissing them by a vote of want of confidence. The legislature consisted of two sets of elective members, Nobles (unpaid), and Representatives (paid), who sat and voted together. Two successive legislatures could alter the constitution by certain prescribed majorities: the constitution was therefore a rigid one.

The working of the Constitution of the Confederate States cannot be fairly judged, because it was conducted under the exigencies of a war, which necessarily gave it a despotic turn. The executive practically got its way. Congress usually sat in secret and "did little beyond register laws prepared by the executive, and debate resolutions for the vigorous conduct of the war. Outside of the ordinary powers conferred by the legislature, the war powers openly or practically exercised by the executive were more sweeping and general than those assumed by President Lincoln."—(Alexander Johnston in *American Cyclopædia of Political Science*, Article "Confederate States.")

Note (B) to Chapter 30

THE FEDERAL CONSTITUTION OF CANADA

The federal Constitution of the Dominion of Canada is contained in the British North America Act 1867, a statute of the British Parliament (30 Vict. c. 3).[1] I note a few of the many points in which it deserves to be compared with that of the United States.

The federal or dominion government is conducted on the so-called "cabinet system" of England, i.e., the ministry sit in Parliament, and hold office at the pleasure of the House of Commons. The governor-general is in the position of an irresponsible and permanent executive similar to that of the Crown in Great Britain, acting on the advice of responsible ministers. He can dissolve Parliament. The Upper House or Senate is composed of 87 persons, nominated for life by the governor-general, i.e., the ministry. The House of Commons has at present 221 members, who are elected for five years. Both senators and members receive salaries. The Senate has little power or influence. The governor-general has a veto but rarely exercises it, and may reserve a bill for the Queen's pleasure. The judges, not only of the federal or dominion courts, but also of the provinces, are appointed by the Crown, i.e., by the dominion ministry, and hold for good behaviour.

Each of the provinces, at present nine in number, has a legislature of its own, which, however, consists in Ontario, British Columbia, Manitoba, and New Brunswick of one house only, and a Lieutenant-Governor, appointed by the dominion government, with a right of veto on the acts of the legislature, which he seldom exercises. Members of the dominion parliament cannot sit in a provincial legislature.

---

[1] See also 31 & 35 Vict. c. 28, and 49 & 50 Vict. c. 35.

The governor-general has a right of disallowing, on the advice of his ministers, acts of a provincial legislature, and sometimes (though rarely) exerts it, especially when a legislature is deemed to have exceeded its constitutional competence.

In each of the provinces there is a responsible ministry, working on the cabinet system of England, the lieutenant-governor representing the Crown and acting as a sort of constitutional sovereign.

The distribution of matters within the competence of the dominion parliament and of the provincial legislatures respectively, bears a general resemblance to that existing in the United States; but there is this remarkable distinction, that whereas in the United States, Congress has only the powers actually granted to it, the state legislatures retaining all such powers as have not been taken from them, the dominion Parliament has a general power of legislation, restricted only by the grant of certain specific and exclusive powers to the provincial legislatures (§§ 91–95). Criminal law is reserved for the dominion Parliament; and no province has the right to maintain a military force. Questions as to the constitutionality of a statute, whether of the dominion Parliament or of a provincial legislature, come before the courts in the ordinary way, and if appealed, before the Judicial Committee of the Privy Council in England.

The Constitution of the dominion was never submitted to popular vote, and can be altered only by the British Parliament, except as regards certain points left to its own legislature. It was drafted by a sort of convention in Canada, and enacted *en bloc* by the British Parliament. There exists no power of amending the provincial constitutions by popular vote similar to that which the peoples of the several states exercise in the United States.

As to the Constitution of the Commonwealth of Australia, drafted in Australia and enacted by the British Parliament in 1900, the reader may refer to the author's *Studies in History and Jurisprudence,* where it is described and commented on. The Constitution of the South African Union, enacted in 1909 by the British Parliament at the request of a convention held in South Africa, is more unitary in its character than are those of Canada and Australia.

Note to Chapter 33

THE DARTMOUTH COLLEGE CASE

The famous case of *Dartmouth College* v. *Woodward* (4 Wheat. 518), decided in 1818, has been so often brought up in English discussions, that it seems proper to give a short account of it, taken from an authoritative source, an address by Mr. Justice Miller (the senior justice, and one of the most eminent members, of the Supreme Court), delivered before the University of Michigan, June 1887.

"It may well be doubted whether any decision ever delivered by any court has had such a pervading operation and influence in controlling legislation as this. It is founded upon the clause of the Constitution (Art. i. § 10) which declares that no State shall make any law impairing the obligation of contracts.

"Dartmouth College existed as a corporation under a charter granted by the British Crown to its trustees in New Hampshire, in the year 1769. This charter conferred upon them the entire governing power of the college, and among other powers that of filling up all vacancies occurring in their own body, and of removing and appointing tutors. It also declared that the number of trustees should forever consist of twelve and no more.

"After the Revolution, the legislature of New Hampshire passed a law to amend the charter, to improve and enlarge the corporation. It increased the number of trustees to twenty-one, gave the appointment of the additional members to the executive of the State, and created a board of overseers to consist of twenty-five persons, of whom twenty-one were also to be appointed by the executive of New Hampshire. These overseers had power to inspect and control the most important acts of the trustees.

"The Supreme Court, reversing the decision of the Superior Court of New Hampshire, held that the original charter constituted a contract between the Crown, in whom the power was then vested and the trustees of the college, which was impaired by the act of the legislature above referred to. The opinion, to which there was but one dissent, establishes the doctrine that the act of a government, whether it be by a charter of the legislature or of the Crown, which creates a corporation, is a contract between the state and the corporation, and that all the essential franchises, powers, and benefits conferred upon the corporation by the charter become, when accepted by it, contracts within the meaning of the clause of the Constitution referred to.

"The opinion has been of late years much criticised, as including with the class of contracts whose foundation is in the legislative action of the States, many which were not properly intended to be so included by the framers of the Constitution, and it is undoubtedly true that the Supreme Court itself has been compelled of late years to insist in this class of cases upon the existence of an actual contract by the state with the corporation, when relief is sought against subsequent legislation.

"The main feature of the case, namely, that a State can make a contract by legislation, as well as in any other way, and that in no such case shall a subsequent act of the legislature interpose any effectual barrier to its enforcement, where it is enforceable in the ordinary courts of justice, has remained. The result of this principle has been to make void innumerable acts of State legislatures, intended in times of disastrous financial depression and suffering to protect the people from the hardships of a rigid and prompt enforcement of the law in regard to their contracts, and to prevent the States from repealing, abrogating, or avoiding by legislation contracts fairly entered into with other parties.

"This decision has stood from the day it was made to the present hour as a great bulwark against popular effort through State legislation to evade the payment of just debts, the performance of obligatory contracts, and the general repudiation of the rights of creditors."

As here intimated, the broad doctrine laid down in this case has been of late years considerably qualified and restricted. It has also become the practice for states making contracts by grants to which the principle of this decision could apply, to reserve power to vary or annul them, so as to leave the hands of the state free.

Articles of Confederation, 1781–88

Articles of Confederation and Perpetual Union between the States of New Hampshire, Massachusetts Bay, Rhode Island and Providence Plantations, Connecticut, New York, New Jersey, Pennsylvania, Delaware, Maryland, Virginia, North Carolina, South Carolina, and Georgia.

ARTICLE I. The style of this confederacy shall be, "The United States of America."

ART. II. Each State retains its sovereignty, freedom, and independence, and every power, jurisdiction, and right, which is not by this confederation expressly delegated to the United States in Congress assembled.

ART. III. The said States hereby severally enter into a firm league of friendship with each other, for their common defence, the security of their liberties, and their mutual and general welfare, binding themselves to assist each other against all force offered to, or attacks made upon them, or any of them, on account of religion, sovereignty, trade or any other pretence whatever.

ART IV. The better to secure and perpetuate mutual friendship and intercourse among the people of the different States in this Union, the free inhabitants of each of these States, paupers, vagabonds and fugitives from justice excepted, shall be entitled to all privileges and immunities of free citizens in the several States; and the people of each State shall have free ingress and regress to and from any other State, and shall enjoy therein all the privileges of trade and commerce, subject to the same duties, impositions, and restrictions, as the inhabitants thereof respectively; provided that such restrictions shall not extend so far as to prevent the removal of property imported into any State, to any other State of which the owner is an inhabitant; provided, also, that no imposition, duties, or restriction, shall be laid by any State on the property of the United States, or either of them.

If any person guilty of, or charged with, treason, felony, or other high misdemeanour in any State, shall flee from justice, and be found in any of the United States, he shall, upon demand of the governor or executive power of the State from which he fled, be delivered up, and removed to the State having jurisdiction of his offence.

Full faith and credit shall be given, in each of these States, to the records, acts, and judicial proceedings of the courts and magistrates of every other State.

ART. V. For the more convenient management of the general interests of the United States, delegates shall be annually appointed in such manner as the legislature of each State shall direct, to meet in Congress on the first Monday in November, in every year, with a power reserved to each State to recall its delegates, or any of them, at any time within the year, and to send others in their stead for the remainder of the year.

No State shall be represented in Congress by less than two, nor by more than seven members; and no person shall be capable of being a delegate for more than three years, in any term of six years; nor shall any person, being a delegate, be capable of holding any office under the United States, for which he, or another for his benefit, receives any salary, fees, or emolument of any kind.

Each State shall maintain its own delegates in any meeting of the States, and while they act as members of the committee of the States.

In determining questions in the United States, in Congress assembled, each State shall have one vote.

Freedom of speech and debate in Congress shall not be impeached or questioned in any court or place out of Congress; and the members of Congress shall be protected in their persons from arrests and imprisonments during the time of their going to and from, and attendance on Congress, except for treason, felony, or breach of the peace.

Art. VI. No State, without the consent of the United States, in Congress assembled, shall send any embassy to, or receive any embassy from, or enter into any conference, agreement, alliance, or treaty, with any king, prince, or state; nor shall any person holding any office of profit or trust under the United States, or any of them, accept of any present, emolument, office, or title of any kind whatever, from any king, prince, or foreign state; nor shall the United States, in Congress assembled, or any of them, grant any title of nobility.

No two or more States shall enter into any treaty, confederation, or alliance whatever between them, without the consent of the United States, in Congress assembled, specifying accurately the purposes for which the same is to be entered into, and how long it shall continue.

No States shall lay any imposts or duties which may interfere with any stipulations in treaties entered into by the United States, in Congress assembled, with any king, prince, or state, in pursuance of any treaties already proposed by Congress to the courts of France and Spain.

No vessels of war shall be kept up in time of peace by any State, except such number only as shall be deemed necessary by the United States, in Congress assembled, for the defence of such State or its trade; nor shall any body of forces be kept up by any State, in time of peace, except such number only as, in the judgment of the United States, in Congress assembled, shall be deemed requisite to garrison the forts necessary for the defence of such State; but every State shall always keep up a well-regulated and disciplined militia, sufficiently armed and accoutred, and shall provide and constantly have ready for use, in public stores, a due number of field-pieces and tents, and a proper quantity of arms, ammunition, and camp equipage.

No State shall engage in any war without the consent of the United States, in Congress assembled, unless such State be actually invaded by enemies, or shall have received certain advice of a resolution being formed by some nation of Indians to invade such State, and the danger is so imminent as not to admit of a delay till the United States, in Congress assembled, can be consulted; nor shall any State grant commissions to any ships or vessels of war, nor letters of marque or reprisal, except it be after a declaration of war by the United States, in Congress assembled, and then only against the kingdom or state, and the subjects thereof against which war has been so declared, and under such regulations as shall be established by the United States, in Congress assembled, unless such State be infested by pirates, in which case vessels of war may be fitted out for that occasion, and kept so long as the danger shall continue, or until the United States, in Congress assembled, shall determine otherwise.

ART. VII. When land forces are raised by any State for the common defence, all officers of or under the rank of colonel shall be appointed by the legislature of each State respectively by whom such forces shall be raised, or in such manner as such State shall direct, and all vacancies shall be filled up by the State which first made the appointment.

ART. VIII. All charges of war, and all other expenses that shall be incurred for the common defence or general welfare, and allowed by the United States, in Congress assembled, shall be defrayed out of a common treasury, which shall be supplied by the several States, in proportion to the value of all land within each State, granted to, or surveyed for, any person, as such land and the buildings and improvements thereon shall be estimated according to such mode as the United States, in Congress assembled, shall, from time to time, direct and appoint. The taxes for paying that proportion shall be laid and levied by the authority and direction of the legislatures of the several States, within the time agreed upon by the United States, in Congress assembled.

ART. IX. The United States, in Congress assembled, shall have the sole and exclusive right and power of determining on peace and war, except in the case mentioned in the sixth Article; of sending and receiving ambassadors; entering into treaties and alliances, provided that no treaty of commerce shall be made whereby the legislative power of the respective States shall be restrained from imposing such imposts and duties on foreigners, as their own people are subjected to, or from prohibiting the exportation or importation of any species of goods or commodities whatsoever; of establishing rules for deciding, in all cases, what captures on land or water shall be legal, and in what manner prizes taken by land or naval forces in the service of the United States shall be divided or appropriated; of granting letters of marque and reprisal in times of peace; appointing courts for the trial of piracies and felonies committed on the high seas; and establishing courts for receiving and determining finally appeals in all cases of captures; provided that no member of Congress shall be appointed as judge of any of the said courts.

The United States, in Congress assembled, shall also be the last resort on appeal, in all disputes and differences now subsisting, or that hereafter may arise between two or more States concerning boundary, jurisdiction, or any other cause whatever; which authority shall always be exercised in the manner following: Whenever the legislative or executive authority, or lawful agent of any State in controversy with another, shall present a petition to Congress, stating the matter in question, and praying for a hearing, notice thereof shall be given by order of Congress to the legislative or executive authority of the other State in controversy, and a day assigned for the appearance of the parties by their lawful agents, who shall then be directed to appoint, by joint consent, commissioners or judges to constitute a court for hearing and determining the matter in question; but if they cannot agree, Congress shall name three persons out of each of the United States, and from the list of such persons each party shall alternately strike out one, the petitioners beginning, until the number shall be reduced to thirteen; and from that number not less than seven nor more than nine names, as Congress shall direct, shall, in the presence of Congress, be drawn out by lot; and the persons whose names shall be so drawn, or any five of them, shall be commissioners or judges, to hear and finally determine the controversy, so always as a major part of the judges who shall hear the cause shall agree in the determination; and if either party shall neglect to attend at the day appointed, without showing reasons which Congress shall judge sufficient, or being present, shall refuse to strike, the Congress shall proceed to nominate three persons out of each State, and the secretary of Congress shall strike in behalf of such party absent or refusing; and the judgment and sentence of the court, to be appointed in the manner before prescribed, shall be final and conclusive; and if any of the parties shall refuse to submit to the authority of such court, or to appear or defend their claim or cause, the court shall nevertheless proceed to pronounce sentence or judgment, which shall in like manner be final and decisive; the judgment or sentence and other proceedings being in either case transmitted to Congress, and lodged among the acts of Congress for the security of the parties concerned; provided, that every commissioner, before he sits in judgment, shall take an oath, to be administered by one of the judges of the supreme or superior court of the State where the cause shall be tried, "well and truly to hear and determine the matter in question, according to the best of his judgment, without favour, affection, or hope of reward." Provided, also, that no State shall be deprived of territory for the benefit of the United States.

All controversies concerning the private right of soil claimed under different grants of two or more States, whose jurisdictions, as they may respect such lands, and the States which passed such grants, are adjusted, the said grants or either of them being at the same time claimed to have originated antecedent to such settlement of jurisdiction, shall, on the petition of either party to the Congress of the United States, be finally determined, as near as may be, in the same manner as is before prescribed for deciding disputes respecting territorial jurisdiction between different States.

The United States, in Congress assembled, shall also have the sole and exclusive right and power of regulating the alloy and value of coin struck by their own authority, or by that of the respective States; fixing the standard of weights and measures throughout the United States; regulating the trade and managing all affairs with the Indians not members of any of the States; provided that the legislative right of any State, within its own limits, be not infringed or violated; establishing and regulating post-offices from one State to another throughout all the United States, and exacting such postage on the papers passing through the same as may be requisite to defray the expenses of the said office; appointing all officers of the land forces in the service of the United States, excepting regimental officers; appointing all the officers of the naval forces, and commissioning all officers whatever in the service of the United States; making rules for the government and regulation of the said land and naval forces, and directing their operations.

The United States, in Congress assembled, shall have authority to appoint a committee, to sit in the recess of Congress, to be denominated "A Committee of the States," and to consist of one delegate from each State; and to appoint such other committees and civil officers as may be necessary for managing the general affairs of the United States under their direction; to appoint one of their number to preside, provided that no person be allowed to serve in the office of president more than one year in any term of three years; to ascertain the necessary sums of money to be raised for the service of the United States, and to appropriate and apply the same for defraying the public expenses; to borrow money or emit bills on the credit of the United States, transmitting every half year to the respective States an account of the sums of money so borrowed or emitted; to build and equip a navy; to agree upon the number of land forces, and to make requisitions from each State for its quota, in proportion to the number of white inhabitants in such State, which requisition shall be binding; and thereupon the legislature of each State shall appoint the regimental officers, raise the men, and clothe, arm, and equip them in a soldier-like manner at the expense of the United States; and the officers and men so clothed, armed, and equipped shall march to the place appointed, and within the time agreed on by the United States, in Congress assembled; but if the United States, in Congress assembled, shall, on consideration of circumstances, judge proper that any State should not raise men, or should raise a smaller number than its quota, and that any other State should raise a greater number of men than the quota thereof, such extra number shall be raised, officered, clothed, armed, and equipped in the same manner as the quota of such State, unless the legislature of such State shall judge that such extra number can not be safely spared out of the same, in which case they shall raise, officer, clothe, arm, and equip as many of such extra number as they judge can be safely spared, and the officers and men so clothed, armed, and equipped shall march to the place appointed, and within the time agreed on by the United States, in Congress assembled.

The United States, in Congress assembled, shall never engage in a war, nor grant letters of marque and reprisal in time of peace, nor enter into any treaties or alliances, nor coin money, nor regulate the value thereof, nor ascertain the sums and expenses necessary for the defence and welfare of the United States, or any of them, nor emit bills, nor borrow money on the credit of the United States, nor appropriate money, nor agree upon the number of vessels of war to be built or purchased, or the number of land or sea forces to be raised, nor appoint a commander-in-chief of the army or navy, unless nine States assent to the same, nor shall a question on any other point, except for adjourning from day to day, be determined, unless by the votes of a majority of the United States, in Congress assembled.

The Congress of the United States shall have power to adjourn to any time within the year, and to any place within the United States, so that no period of adjournment be for a longer duration than the space of six months, and shall publish the journal of their proceedings monthly, except such parts thereof relating to treaties, alliances, or military operations as in their judgment require secrecy; and the yeas and nays of the delegates of each State, on any question, shall be entered on the journal, when it is desired by any delegate; and the delegates of a State, or any of them, at his or their request, shall be furnished with transcript of the said journal, except such parts as are above excepted, to lay before the legislatures of the several States.

ART. X. The committee of the States, or any nine of them, shall be authorized to execute, in the recess of Congress, such of the powers of Congress as the United States, in Congress assembled, by the consent of nine States, shall, from time to time, think expedient to vest them with; provided that no power be delegated to the said committee, for the exercise of which, by the Articles of Confederation, the voice of nine States, in the Congress of the United States assembled, is requisite.

ART. XI. Canada acceding to this Confederation, and joining in the measures of the United States, shall be admitted into, and entitled to all the advantages of this Union; but no other colony shall be admitted into the same unless such admission be agreed to by nine States.

ART. XII. All bills of credit emitted, moneys borrowed, and debts contracted by or under the authority of Congress, before the assembling of the United States, in pursuance of the present Confederation, shall be deemed and considered as a charge against the United States, for payment and satisfaction whereof the said United States and the public faith are hereby solemnly pledged.

ART XIII. Every State shall abide by the determinations of the United States, in Congress assembled, on all questions which by this Confederation are submitted to them. And the Articles of this Confederation shall be inviolably observed by every State, and the Union shall be perpetual; nor shall any alteration at any time thereafter be made in any of them, unless such alteration be agreed to in a Congress of the United States, and be afterwards confirmed by the legislatures of every State.

And whereas it hath pleased the great Governor of the world to incline the hearts of the legislatures we respectively represent in Congress to approve of, and to authorize us to ratify the said Articles of Confederation and perpetual Union, Know ye, that we, the undersigned delegates, by virtue of the power and authority to us given for that purpose, do, by these presents, in the name and in behalf of our respective constituents, fully and entirely ratify and confirm each and every of the said Articles of Confederation and perpetual Union, and all and singular the matters and things therein contained. And we do further solemnly plight and engage the faith of our respective constituents, that they shall abide by the determinations of the United States, in Congress assembled, on all questions which by the said Confederation are submitted to them; and that the Articles thereof shall be inviolably observed by the States we respectively represent, and that the Union shall be perpetual. In witness whereof we have hereunto set our hands in Congress. Done at Philadelphia, in the State of Pennsylvania, the ninth day of July in the year of our Lord 1778, and in the third year of the Independence of America.

[These Articles were not ratified by all the states until 1st March 1781, when the delegates of Maryland, the latest in ratifying, signed for her.]

Constitution of the United States

We, the people of the United States, in order to form a more perfect union, establish justice, insure domestic tranquillity, provide for the common defence, promote the general welfare, and secure the blessings of liberty to ourselves and our posterity, do ordain and establish this Constitution for the United States of America.

ARTICLE I

SECTION 1. All legislative powers herein granted shall be vested in a Congress of the United States, which shall consist of a Senate and a House of Representatives.

SEC. 2. The House of Representatives shall be composed of members chosen every second year by the people of the several States, and the electors in each State shall have the qualifications requisite for electors of the most numerous branch of the State legislature.

No person shall be a Representative who shall not have attained the age of twenty-five years, and been seven years a citizen of the United States, and who shall not, when elected, be an inhabitant of that State in which he shall be chosen.

[Representatives and direct taxes shall be apportioned among the several States which may be included within this Union, according to their respective numbers, which shall be determined by adding to the whole number of free persons, including those bound to service for a term of years, and excluding Indians not taxed, three-fifths of all other persons.][1] The actual enumeration shall be made within three years after the first meeting of the Congress of the United States, and within every subsequent term of ten years, in such manner as they shall by law direct. The number of Representatives shall not exceed one for every thirty thousand, but each State shall have at least one Representative; and until such enumeration shall be made, the State of New Hampshire shall be entitled to choose three, Massachusetts eight, Rhode Island and Providence Plantations one, Connecticut five, New York six, New Jersey four, Pennsylvania eight, Delaware one, Maryland six, Virginia ten, North Carolina five, South Carolina five, and Georgia three.

When vacancies happen in the representation from any State, the executive authority thereof shall issue writs of election to fill such vacancies.

The House of Representatives shall choose their speaker and other officers; and shall have the sole power of impeachment.

SEC. 3. The Senate of the United States shall be composed of two Senators from each State, chosen by the legislature thereof, for six years; and each Senator shall have one vote.

Immediately after they shall be assembled in consequence of the first election, they shall be divided as equally as may be into three classes. The seats of the Senators of the first class shall be vacated at the expiration of the second year, of the second class at the expiration of the fourth year,

---

[1] The clause included in brackets is amended by the Fourteenth Amendment, 2d section.

and of the third class at the expiration of the sixth year, so that one-third may be chosen every second year; and if vacancies happen by resignation, or otherwise, during the recess of the legislature of any State, the executive thereof may make temporary appointments until the next meeting of the legislature, which shall then fill such vacancies.

No person shall be a Senator who shall not have attained to the age of thirty years, and been nine years a citizen of the United States, and who shall not, when elected, be an inhabitant of that State for which he shall be chosen.

The Vice-President of the United States shall be President of the Senate, but shall have no vote, unless they be equally divided.

The Senate shall choose their other officers, and also a President *pro tempore*, in the absence of the Vice-President, or when he shall exercise the office of President of the United States.

The Senate shall have sole power to try all impeachments. When sitting for that purpose, they shall be on oath or affirmation. When the President of the United States is tried, the Chief Justice shall preside; and no person shall be convicted without the concurrence of two-thirds of the members present.

Judgment in cases of impeachment shall not extend further than to removal from office, and disqualification to hold and enjoy any office of honour, trust, or profit under the United States; but the party convicted shall nevertheless be liable and subject to indictment, trial, judgment, and punishment, according to law.

SEC. 4. The times, places, and manner of holding elections for Senators and Representatives shall be prescribed in each State by the legislature thereof; but the Congress may at any time by law make or alter such regulations, except as to the places of choosing Senators.

The Congress shall assemble at least once in every year, and such meeting shall be on the first Monday in December, unless they shall by law appoint a different day.

SEC. 5. Each house shall be the judge of the elections, returns, and qualifications of its own members, and a majority of each shall constitute a quorum to do business; but a smaller number may adjourn from day to day, and may be authorized to compel the attendance of absent members, in such manner, and under such penalties as each house may provide.

Each house may determine the rules of its proceedings, punish its members for disorderly behaviour, and, with the concurrence of two-thirds, expel a member.

Each house shall keep a journal of its proceedings, and from time to time publish the same, excepting such parts as may in their judgment require secrecy; and the yeas and nays of the members of either house on any question shall, at the desire of one-fifth of those present, be entered on the journal.

Neither house, during the session of Congress, shall, without the consent of the other, adjourn for more than three days, nor to any other place than that in which the two houses shall be sitting.

SEC. 6. The Senators and Representatives shall receive a compensation for their services, to be ascertained by law, and paid out of the Treasury of the United States. They shall in all cases, except treason, felony, and breach of the peace, be privileged from arrest during their attendance at the session of their respective houses, and in going to and returning from the same; and for any speech or debate in either house they shall not be questioned in any other place.

No Senator or Representative shall, during the time for which he was elected, be appointed to any civil office under the authority of the United States, which shall have been created, or the emoluments whereof shall have been increased during such time; and no person holding any office under the United States shall be a member of either house during his continuance in office.

SEC. 7. All bills for raising revenue shall originate in the House of Representatives; but the Senate may propose or concur with amendments as on other bills.

Every bill which shall have passed the House of Representatives and the Senate shall, before it becomes a law, be presented to the President of the United States; if he approve he shall sign it, but if not he shall return it, with his objections, to that house in which it shall have originated, who shall enter the objections at large on their journal, and proceed to reconsider it. If after such reconsideration two-thirds of that house shall agree to pass the bill, it shall be sent, together with the objections, to the other house, by which it shall likewise be reconsidered, and if approved by two-thirds of that house, it shall become a law. But in all such cases the votes of both houses shall be determined by yeas and nays, and the names of the persons voting for and against the bill shall be entered on the journal of each house respectively. If any bill shall not be returned by the President within ten days (Sundays excepted) after it shall have been presented to him, the same shall be a law, in like manner as if he had signed it, unless the Congress by their adjournment prevents its return, in which case it shall not be a law.

Every order, resolution, or vote to which the concurrence of the Senate and the House of Representatives may be necessary (except on a question of adjournment) shall be presented to the President of the United States; and before the same shall take effect, shall be approved by him, or being disapproved by him, shall be repassed by two-thirds of the Senate and House of Representatives, according to the rules and limitations prescribed in the case of a bill.

SEC. 8. The Congress shall have power to lay and collect taxes, duties, imposts, and excises, to pay the debts and provide for the common defence and general welfare of the United States; but all duties, imposts, and excises shall be uniform throughout the United States;

To borrow money on the credit of the United States;

To regulate commerce with foreign nations, and among the several States, and with the Indian tribes;

To establish an uniform rule of naturalization, and uniform laws on the subject of bankruptcies throughout the United States;

To coin money, regulate the value thereof, and of foreign coin, and fix the standard of weights and measures;

To provide for the punishment of counterfeiting the securities and current coin of the United States;

To establish post-offices and post-roads;

To promote the progress of science and useful arts, by securing for limited times to authors and inventors the exclusive right to their respective writings and discoveries;

To constitute tribunals inferior to the Supreme Court;

To define and punish piracies and felonies commited on the high seas, and offences against the law of nations.

To declare war, grant letters of marque and reprisal, and make rules concerning captures on land and water;

To raise and support armies, but no appropriation of money to that use shall be for a longer term than two years;

To provide and maintain a navy;

To make rules for the government and regulation of the land and naval forces;

To provide for calling forth the militia to execute the laws of the Union, suppress insurrections, and repel invasions;

To provide for organizing, arming, and disciplining the militia, and for governing such part of them as may be employed in the service of the United States, reserving to the States respectively the appointment of the officers and the authority of training the militia according to the discipline prescribed by Congress;

To exercise exclusive legislation in all cases whatsoever, over such district (not exceeding ten miles square) as may, by cession of particular States, and the acceptance of Congress, become the seat of the Government of the United States, and to exercise like authority over all places purchased by the consent of the legislature of the State in which the same shall be, for the erection of forts, magazines, arsenals, dockyards, and other needful buildings; and

To make all laws which shall be necessary and proper for carrying into execution the foregoing powers, and all other powers vested by this Constitution in the Government of the United States, or in any department or officer thereof.

SEC. 9. The migration or importation of such persons as any of the States now existing shall think proper to admit, shall not be prohibited by the Congress prior to the year one thousand eight hundred and eight, but a tax or duty may be imposed on such importation, not exceeding ten dollars for each person.

The privilege of the writ of habeas corpus shall not be suspended, unless when in cases of rebellion or invasion the public safety may require it.

No bill of attainder or *ex post facto* law shall be passed.

No capitation, or other direct tax, shall be laid, unless in proportion to the census or enumeration hereinbefore directed to be taken.

No tax or duty shall be laid on articles exported from any State.

No preference shall be given by any regulation of commerce or revenue to the ports of one State over those of another; nor shall vessels bound to, or from, one State be obliged to enter, clear, or pay duties in another.

No money shall be drawn from the Treasury but in consequence of appropriations made by law; and a regular statement and account of the receipts and the expenditures of all public money shall be published from time to time.

No title of nobility shall be granted by the United States; and no person holding any office of profit or trust under them shall, without the consent of the Congress, accept of any present, emolument, office, or title, of any kind whatever, from any king, prince, or foreign state.

SEC. 10. No State shall enter into any treaty, alliance, or confederation; grant letters of marque or reprisal; coin money; emit bills of credit; make anything but gold and silver coin a tender in payment of debts; pass any bill of attainder, *ex post facto* law, or law impairing the obligation of contracts, or grant any title of nobility.

No State shall, without the consent of the Congress, lay any imposts or duties on imports or exports, except what may be absolutely necessary for executing its inspection laws; and the net produce of all duties and imposts, laid by any State on imports or exports, shall be for the use of the Treasury of the United States; and all such laws shall be subject to the revision and control of the Congress.

No State shall, without the consent of the Congress, lay any duty of tonnage, keep troops or ships of war in time of peace, enter into any agreement or compact with another State, or with a foreign power, or engage in war, unless actually invaded, or in such imminent danger as will not admit of delay.

ARTICLE II

SECTION 1. The executive power shall be vested in a President of the United States of America. He shall hold his office during the term of four years, and, together with the Vice-President, chosen for the same term, be elected as follows:

Each State shall appoint, in such manner as the legislature thereof may direct, a number of electors, equal to the whole number of Senators and Representatives to which the State may be entitled in the Congress; but no Senator or Representative, or person holding an office of trust or profit under the United States, shall be appointed an elector.

[The electors shall meet in their respective States, and vote by ballot for two persons, of whom one at least shall not be an inhabitant of the same State with themselves. And they shall make a list of all the persons voted for, and of the number of votes for each; which list they shall sign and certify, and transmit sealed to the seat of the Government of the United States directed to the President of the Senate. The President of the Senate shall, in the presence of the Senate and the House of Representatives, open all the certificates, and the votes shall then be counted. The person having the greatest number of votes shall be the President, if such number be a majority of the whole number of electors appointed; and if there be more than one who have such majority and have an equal number of votes, then the House of Representatives shall immediately choose by ballot one of them for President; and if no person have a majority, then from the five highest on the list the said House shall in like manner choose the President. But in choosing the President, the votes shall be taken by States, the representation from each State having one vote; a quorum for this purpose shall consist of a member or members from two-thirds of the States, and a majority of all the States shall be necessary to a choice. In every case, after the choice of the President, the person having the greatest number of votes of the electors shall be the Vice-President; but if there should remain two or more who have equal votes, the Senate shall choose from them, by ballot, the Vice-President.][2]

The Congress may determine the time of choosing the electors, and the day on which they shall give their votes; which day shall be the same throughout the United States.

No person except a natural-born citizen, or a citizen of the United States at the time of the adoption of this Constitution, shall be eligible to the office of President; neither shall any person be eligible to that office who shall not have attained the age of thirty-five years, and been fourteen years a resident within the United States.

In case of the removal of the President from office, or of his death, resignation, or inability to discharge the powers and duties of the said office, the same shall devolve on the Vice-President, and the Congress may by law provide for the case of removal, death, resignation, or inability, both of the President and Vice-President, declaring what officer shall then act as President, and such officer shall act accordingly until the disability be removed, or a President shall be elected.

The President shall, at stated times, receive for his services a compensation, which shall neither be increased nor diminished during the period for which he shall have been elected, and he shall not receive within that period any other emolument from the United States, or any of them.

Before he enter on the execution of his office, he shall take the following oath or affirmation:

"I do solemnly swear (or affirm) that I will faithfully execute the office of President of the United States, and will, to the best of my ability, preserve, protect, and defend the Constitution of the United States."

SEC. 2. The President shall be commander-in-chief of the army and navy of the United States, and of the militia of the several States, when called into the actual service of the United States; he may require the opinion, in writing, of the principal officer in each of the executive departments, upon any subject relating to the duties of their respective offices, and he shall have power to grant reprieves and pardons for offences against the United States, except in cases of impeachment.

He shall have power, by and with the advice and consent of the Senate, to make treaties, provided two-thirds of the Senators present concur; and he shall nominate, and by and with the advice and consent of the Senate, shall

---

[2] This clause in brackets has been superseded by the Twelfth Amendment.

appoint ambassadors, other public ministers and consuls, judges of the Supreme Court, and all other officers of the United States, whose appointments are not herein otherwise provided for, and which shall be established by law; but the Congress may by law vest the appointment of such inferior officers, as they think proper, in the President alone, in the courts of laws, or in the heads of departments.

The President shall have power to fill up all vacancies that may happen during the recess of the Senate, by granting commissions which shall expire at the end of their next session.

SEC. 3. He shall from time to time give to the Congress information of the state of the Union, and recommend to their consideration such measures as he shall judge necessary and expedient; he may, on extraordinary occasions, convene both houses, or either of them, and in case of disagreement between them, with respect to the time of adjournment, he may adjourn them to such time as he shall think proper; he shall receive ambassadors and other public ministers; he shall take care that the laws be faithfully executed, and shall commission all the officers of the United States.

SEC. 4. The President, Vice-President, and all civil officers of the United States, shall be removed from office on impeachment for, and conviction of, treason, bribery, or other high crimes and misdemeanours.

ARTICLE III

SECTION 1. The judicial power of the United States shall be vested in one Supreme Court, and in such inferior courts as the Congress may from time to time ordain and establish. The judges, both of the Supreme and inferior courts, shall hold their offices during good behaviour, and shall, at stated times, receive for their services a compensation, which shall not be diminished during their continuance in office.

SEC. 2. The judicial power shall extend to all cases, in law and equity, arising under this Constitution, the laws of the United States, and treaties made, or which shall be made, under their authority; to all cases affecting ambassadors, other public ministers, and consuls; to all cases of admiralty and maritime jurisdiction; to controversies to which the United States shall be a party; to controversies between two or more States; between a State and citizens of another State; between citizens of different States—between citizens of the same State claiming lands under grants of different States, and between a State, or the citizens thereof, and foreign states, citizens, or subjects.

In all cases affecting ambassadors, other public ministers and consuls, and those in which a State shall be a party, the Supreme Court shall have original jurisdiction. In all the other cases before mentioned, the Supreme Courts shall have appellate jurisdiction, both as to law and fact, with such exception, and under such regulations as the Congress shall make.

The trial of all crimes, except in cases of impeachment, shall be by jury; and such trial shall be held in the State where the said crimes shall have been committed; but when not committed within any State, the trial shall be at such place or places as the Congress may by law have directed.

SEC. 3. Treason against the United States shall consist only in levying war against them, or in adhering to their enemies, giving them aid and comfort. No person shall be convicted of treason unless on the testimony of two witnesses to the same overt act, or on confession in open court.

The Congress shall have power to declare the punishment of treason, but no attainder of treason shall work corruption of blood, or forfeiture except during the life of the person attainted.

ARTICLE IV

SECTION 1. Full faith and credit shall be given in each State to the public acts, records, and judicial proceedings of every other State. And the Congress may by general laws prescribe the manner in which such acts, records, and proceedings shall be proved, and the effect thereof.

SEC. 2. The citizens of each State shall be entitled to all privileges and immunities of citizens in the several States.

A person charged in any State with treason, felony, or other crime, who shall flee from justice and be found in another State, shall, on demand of the executive authority of the State from which he fled, be delivered up, to be removed to the State having jurisdiction of the crime.

No person held to service or labour in any State, under the laws thereof, escaping into another, shall, in consequence of any law or regulation therein, be discharged from such service or labour, but shall be delivered up on claim of the party to whom such service or labour may be due.

SEC. 3. New States may be admitted by the Congress into this Union; but no new State shall be formed or erected within the jurisdiction of any other State; nor any State be formed by the junction of two or more States, or parts of States, without the consent of the legislatures of the States concerned as well as of the Congress.

The Congress shall have power to dispose of and make all needful rules and regulations respecting the territory or other property belonging to the

United States; and nothing in this Constitution shall be so construed as to prejudice any claims of the United States, or of any particular State.

SEC. 4. The United States shall guarantee to every State in this Union a republican form of government, and shall protect each of them against invasion; and on application of the legislature, or of the executive (when the legislature cannot be convened), against domestic violence.

ARTICLE V

The Congress, whenever two-thirds of both houses shall deem it necessary, shall propose amendments to this Constitution, or on the application of the legislatures of two-thirds of the several States, shall call a convention for proposing amendments, which, in either case, shall be valid, to all intents and purposes, as part of this Constitution, when ratified by the legislatures of three-fourths of the several States, or by conventions in three-fourths thereof, as the one or the other mode of ratification may be proposed by the Congress; provided that no amendment which may be made prior to the year one thousand eight hundred and eight shall in any manner affect the first and fourth clauses in the ninth section of the first article; and that no State, without its consent, shall be deprived of its equal suffrage in the Senate.

ARTICLE VI

All debts contracted and engagements entered into, before the adoption of this Constitution, shall be as valid against the United States under this Constitution as under the Confederation.

This Constitution, and the laws of the United States which shall be made in pursuance thereof, and all treaties made, or which shall be made, under the authority of the United States, shall be the supreme law of the land; and the judges in every State shall be bound thereby, any thing in the constitution or laws of any State to the contrary notwithstanding.

The Senators and Representatives before mentioned, and the members of the several State legislatures, and all executive and judicial officers, both of the United States and of the several States, shall be bound by oath or affirmation to support this Constitution; but no religious test shall ever be required as a qualification to any office or public trust under the United States.

ARTICLE VII

The ratification of the conventions of nine States shall be sufficient for the establishment of this Constitution between the States so ratifying the same.

Done in Convention by the unanimous consent of the States present,[3] the Seventeenth day of September, in the year of our Lord 1787, and of the Independence of the United States of America the Twelfth.

IN WITNESS whereof we have hereunto subscribed our names.

G̤ WASHINGTON,
Presidt. and Deputy from Virginia.

New Hampshire—John Langdon, Nicholas Gilman. *Massachusetts*—Nathaniel Gorham, Rufus King. *Connecticut*—Wm. Saml. Johnson, Roger Sherman. *New York*—Alexander Hamilton. *New Jersey*—Wil. Livingston, Wm. Patterson, David Brearley, Jona. Dayton. *Pennsylvania*—B. Franklin, Thos. Fitzsimons, Thomas Mifflin, Jared Ingersoll, Robt. Morris, James Wilson, Geo. Clymer, Gouv. Morris. *Delaware*—Geo. Read, Richard Bassett, Gunning Bedford, Jun., Jaco. Broom, John Dickinson. *Maryland*—James M'Henry, Dan. Carroll, Dan. Jenifer, of St. Thomas. *Virginia*—John Blair, James Madison, Jun. *North Carolina*—Wm. Blount, Hugh Williamson, Rich'd. Dobbs Spaight. *South Carolina*—J. Rutledge, Charles Pinckney, Charles Cotesworth Pinckney, Pierce Butler. *Georgia*—William Few, Abr. Baldwin.

Attest: WILLIAM JACKSON, *Secretary.*

Articles in addition to, and amendment of, the Constitution of the United States of America, proposed by Congress, and ratified by the Legislatures of the several States, pursuant to the fifth Article of the original Constitution.

ARTICLE I[4]

Congress shall make no law respecting an establishment of religion, or prohibiting the free exercise thereof; or abridging the freedom of speech or

---

[3] Rhode Island was not represented. Several of the delegates had left the Convention before it concluded its labours, and some others who remained refused to sign. In all, 65 delegates had been appointed, 55 attended, 39 signed.

The first ratification was that of Delaware, Dec. 7, 1787; the ninth (bringing the Constitution into force) that of New Hampshire, June 21, 1788; the last, that of Rhode Island, May 29, 1790.

[4] Amendments I–X inclusive were proposed by Congress to the legislatures of the states, Sept. 25, 1789, and ratified 1789–91.

of the press; or the right of the people peaceably to assemble, and to petition the Government for a redress of grievances.

ARTICLE II

A well-regulated militia being necessary to the security of a free state, the right of the people to keep and bear arms shall not be infringed.

ARTICLE III

No soldier shall, in time of peace, be quartered in any house, without the consent of the owner, nor in the time of war, but in a manner to be prescribed by law.

ARTICLE IV

The right of the people to be secure in their persons, houses, papers, and effects, against unreasonable searches and seizures, shall not be violated, and no warrants shall issue, but upon probable cause, supported by oath or affirmation, and particularly describing the place to be searched, and the person or things to be seized.

ARTICLE V

No person shall be held to answer for a capital, or otherwise infamous crime, unless on a presentment or indictment of a grand jury, except in cases arising in the land or naval forces, or in the militia, when in actual service in time of war or public danger; nor shall any person be subject for the same offence to be twice put in jeopardy of life or limb; nor shall be compelled in any criminal case to be a witness against himself, nor be deprived of life, liberty, or property, without due process of law; nor shall private property be taken for public use, without just compensation.

ARTICLE VI

In all criminal prosecutions, the accused shall enjoy the right to a speedy and public trial, by an impartial jury of the State and district wherein the crime shall have been committed, which district shall have been previously ascertained by law, and to be informed of the nature and cause of the accusation; to be confronted with the witnesses against him; to have compulsory process for obtaining witnesses in his favour, and to have the assistance of counsel for his defence.

ARTICLE VII

In suits at common law, where the value in controversy shall exceed twenty dollars, the right of trial by jury shall be preserved, and no fact tried by a jury shall be otherwise re-examined in any court of the United States than according to the rules of the common law.

ARTICLE VIII

Excessive bail shall not be required, nor excessive fines imposed, nor cruel and unusual punishments inflicted.

ARTICLE IX

The enumeration of the Constitution, of certain rights, shall not be construed to deny or disparage others retained by the people.

ARTICLE X

The powers not delegated to the United States by the Constitution, nor prohibited by it to the States, are reserved to the States respectively, or to the people.

ARTICLE XI[5]

The judicial power of the United States shall not be construed to extend to any suit in law or equity, commenced or prosecuted against one of the United States by citizens of another State, or by citizens or subjects of any foreign State.

ARTICLE XII[6]

The electors shall meet in their respective States, and vote by ballot for President and Vice-President, one of whom at least shall not be an inhabitant

---

[5] Amendt. XI was proposed by Congress, Sept. 5, 1794, and declared to have been ratified by the legislatures of the three-fourths of the states, Jan. 8, 1798.

[6] Amendt. XII was proposed by Congress, Dec. 12, 1803, and declared to have been ratified, Sept. 25, 1804.

of the same State with themselves; they shall name in their ballots the person voted for as President, and in distinct ballots the person voted for as Vice-President, and they shall make distinct lists of all persons voted for as President, and of all persons voted for as Vice-President, and of the number of votes for each, which lists they shall sign and certify, and transmit sealed to the seat of the Government of the United States, directed to the President of the Senate;—The President of the Senate shall, in the presence of the Senate and the House of Representatives, open all the certificates, and the votes shall then be counted;—The person having the greatest number of votes for President shall be the President, if such number be a majority of the whole number of electors appointed; and if no person have such majority, then from the persons having the highest numbers not exceeding three on the list of those voted for as President, the House of Representatives shall choose immediately, by ballot, the President. But in choosing the President, the votes shall be taken by States, the representation from each State having one vote; a quorum for this purpose shall consist of a member or members from two-thirds of the States, and a majority of all the States shall be necessary to a choice. And if the House of Representatives shall not choose a President whenever the right of choice shall devolve upon them, before the fourth day of March next following, then the Vice-President shall act as President, as in the case of the death or other constitutional disability of the President.

The person having the greatest number of votes as Vice-President shall be the Vice-President, if such number be a majority of the whole number of electors appointed, and if no person have a majority, then from the two highest numbers on the list the Senate shall choose the Vice-President; a quorum for the purpose shall consist of two-thirds of the whole number of Senators, and a majority of the whole number shall be necessary to a choice. But no person constitutionally ineligible to the office of President shall be eligible to that of Vice-President of the United States.

ARTICLE XIII[7]

SECTION 1. Neither slavery nor involuntary servitude, except as a punishment for crime whereof the party shall have been duly convicted, shall exist within the United States, or any place subject to their jurisdiction.

SEC. 2. Congress shall have power to enforce this article by appropriate legislation.

[7] Amendt. XIII was proposed by Congress, Feb. 1, 1865, and declared to have been ratified by 27 of the 36 states, Dec. 18, 1865.

ARTICLE XIV[8]

SECTION 1. All persons born or naturalized in the United States, and subject to the jurisdiction thereof, are citizens of the United States and of the State wherein they reside. No State shall make or enforce any law which shall abridge the privileges or immunities of citizens of the United States; nor shall any State deprive any person of life, liberty, or property, without due process of law; nor deny to any person within its jurisdiction the equal protection of the laws.

SEC. 2. Representatives shall be apportioned among the several States according to their respective numbers, counting the whole number of persons in each State, excluding Indians not taxed. But when the right to vote at any election for the choice of electors for President and Vice-President of the United States, Representatives in Congress, the executive and judicial officers of the State, or the members of the legislature thereof, is denied to any of the male inhabitants of such State, being twenty-one years of age, and citizens of the United States, or in any way abridged, except for participation in rebellion, or other crime, the basis of representation therein shall be reduced in the proportion which the number of such male citizens shall bear to the whole number of male citizens twenty-one years of age in such State.

SEC. 3. No person shall be a Senator or Representative in Congress, or elector of President and Vice-President, or hold any office, civil or military, under the United States, or under any State, who, having previously taken an oath, as a member of the Congress, or as an officer of the United States, or as a member of any State legislature, or as an executive or judicial officer of any State, to support the Constitution of the United States, shall have engaged in insurrection or rebellion against the same, or given aid or comfort to the enemies thereof. But Congress may, by a vote of two-thirds of each House, remove such disability.

SEC. 4. The validity of the public debt of the United States, authorized by law, including debts incurred for payment of pensions and bounties for services in suppressing insurrection or rebellion, shall not be questioned. But neither the United States nor any State shall assume or pay any debt or obligation incurred in aid of insurrection or rebellion against the United States, or any claim for the loss or emancipation of any slave; but all such debts, obligations, and claims shall be held illegal and void.

SEC. 5. The Congress shall have power to enforce, by appropriate legislation, the provisions of this article.

[8] Amendt. XIV was proposed by Congress, June 16, 1866, and declared to have been ratified by 30 of the 36 states, July 28, 1868.

ARTICLE XV[9]

Section 1. The right of citizens of the United States to vote shall not be denied or abridged by the United States or any State on account of race, color, or previous condition of servitude.

SEC. 2. The Congress shall have power to enforce this article by appropriate legislation.

ARTICLE XVI[10]

The Congress shall have power to lay and collect taxes on incomes, from whatever source derived, without apportionment among the several States, and without regard to any census or enumeration.

ARTICLE XVII[11]

The Senate of the United States shall be composed of two senators from each State, elected by the people thereof, for six years; and each senator shall have one vote. The electors in each State shall have the qualifications requisite for electors of the most numerous branch of the State legislature.

When vacancies happen in the representation of any State in the Senate, the executive authority of such State shall issue writs of election to fill such vacancies: *Provided*, That the legislature of any State may empower the executive thereof to make temporary appointments until the people fill the vacancies by election as the legislature may direct.

This amendment shall not be so construed as to affect the election or term of any senator chosen before it becomes valid as part of the Constitution.

[9] Amendt. XV was proposed by Congress, Feb. 26, 1869, and declared to have been ratified by 29 of the 37 states, March 30, 1870.

[10] Passed July 1909; proclaimed February 25, 1913.

[11] Passed May 1912, in lieu of paragraph one, section 3, article I, of the Constitution and so much of paragraph two of the same Section as relates to the filling of vacancies; proclaimed May 31, 1913.

Extracts from the Constitution of the State of Oklahoma[1]

Adopted in Convention at the City of Guthrie in the Territory of Oklahoma on July 10th, 1907, and ratified by the People on Sept. 17th in the same year.

PREAMBLE

SECTION 1. — Invoking the guidance of Almighty God, in order to secure and perpetuate the blessing of liberty; to secure just and rightful government; to promote our mutual welfare and happiness, we, the people of the State of Oklahoma, do ordain and establish this Constitution.

SEC. 2. — *Constitution of the United States Supreme.* — Section 1. The State of Oklahoma is an inseparable part of the Federal Union, and the Constitution of the United States is the supreme law of the land.

SEC. 3. — *Toleration of Religious Sentiment.* — Perfect toleration of religious sentiment shall be secured, and no inhabitants of the State shall ever be molested in person or property on account of his or her mode of religious worship; and no religious test shall be required for the exercise of civil or political rights. Polygamous or plural marriages are forever prohibited.

SEC. 7. — *Public Schools.* — Provisions shall be made for the establishment and maintenance of a system of public schools, which shall be open to all the children of the State and free from sectarian control; and said schools shall always be conducted in English: Provided, That nothing herein shall preclude the teaching of other languages in said public schools: And Provided, Further, That this shall not be construed to prevent the establishment and maintenance of separate schools for white and colored children.

SEC. 8. — *Right of Suffrage; Abridgment of.* — The State shall never enact any law restricting or abridging the right of suffrage on account of race, color, or previous condition of servitude.

SEC. 9. — *Introduction and Sale of Liquor as Provided in Enabling Act.* — The manufacture, sale, barter, giving away, or otherwise furnishing, except as hereinafter provided, of intoxicating liquors within those parts of the State, heretofore known as the Indian Territory and the Osage Indian

[1] This constitution is the latest adopted by a new state up to 1910. Attention is specially called to the following provisions given in the extracts quoted, viz., Bill of Rights §§ 3, 8, 10–35, 38–42; Sale of intoxicants § 9; Primaries § 47; Initiative and Referendum §§ 51–62, 291–92, 415–19, 447–48; Limitations on the power of the legislature (35 restrictions specified) §§ 119–36; Corporations §§ 205–19, 231–42, 245, 251, 254–57, 260, 422–23; State Debts § 281, 289–93; Power to cities to make their own charters §§ 413–14; Homestead and Exemptions §§ 304–5; Making void contracts §§ 442–43.

Reservation, and within any other parts of the State which existed as Indian reservations on the first day of January, Nineteen Hundred and Six, is prohibited for a period of twenty-one years from the date of the admission of the State into the Union, and thereafter until the people of the State shall otherwise provide by amendment of this Constitution and proper State legislation. Any person, individual or corporate, who shall manufacture, sell, barter, give away, or otherwise furnish any intoxicating liquor of any kind, including beer, ale, and wine, contrary to the provisions of this section, or who shall, within the above described portions of the State, advertise for sale or solicit the purchase of any such liquors, or who shall ship or in any way convey such liquors from other parts of the State into the portions hereinbefore described, shall be punished, on conviction thereof, by fine not less than fifty dollars and by imprisonment not less than thirty days for each offense: Provided, That the Legislature may provide by law for one agency under supervision of the State in each incorporated town of not less than two thousand population in the portions of the State hereinbefore described; and if there be no incorporated town of two thousand population in any county in said portions of the State, such county shall be entitled to have one such agency, for the sale of such liquors for medicinal purposes; and for the sale, for industrial purposes, of alcohol which shall have been denaturized by some process approved by the United States Commissioner of Internal Revenue; and for the sale of alcohol for scientific purposes to such scientific institutions, universities, and colleges as are authorized to procure the same free of tax under the laws of the United States; and for the sale of such liquors to any apothecary who shall have executed an approved bond, in a sum not less than one thousand dollars, conditioned that none of such liquors shall be used or disposed of for any purpose other than in the compounding of precriptions or other medicines, the sale of which would not subject him to the payment of the special tax required of liquor dealers by the United States, and the payment of such special tax by any person within the parts of the State hereinabove defined shall constitute prima facie evidence of his intension to violate the provisions of this section. No sale shall be made except upon the sworn statement of the applicant in writing setting forth the purpose for which the liquor is to be used, and no sale shall be made for medicinal purposes except sales to apothecaries as hereinabove provided unless such statement shall be accompanied by a bona fide prescription signed by a regular practicing physician, which prescription shall not be filled more than once. Each sale shall be duly registered, and the register thereof, together with the affidavits and prescriptions pertaining thereto, shall be open to inspection by any officer or citizen of the State at all times during business hours. Any person who shall knowingly make a false affidavit for the purpose aforesaid shall be deemed guilty of perjury. Any physician who shall prescribe any such liquor, except for treatment of disease which, after his own personal diagnosis, he shall deem to require such treatment, shall, upon conviction thereof, by punished for each offense by fine of not less than two hundred dollars, or by imprisonment for not less than thirty days, or by both such fine and imprisonment; and any person connnected with any such agency, who shall be convicted of making any sale or other disposition of liquor contrary to these provisions, shall be punished by imprisonment for not less than one year and one day. Upon the admission of the State into the Union these provision shall be immediately enforcible in the courts of the State.

SEC. 10. — *All Political Power Inherent in People.* — Section 1. All political power is inherent in the people; and government is instituted for their protection, security, and benefit, and to promote their general welfare; and they have the right to alter or reform the same whenever the public good may require it: Provided, Such change be not repugnant to the Constitution of the United States.

SEC. 11. — *Right to Life, Liberty, etc.* — All persons have the inherent right to life, liberty, the pursuit of happiness, and the enjoyment of the gains of their own industry.

SEC. 12. — *Right of People to Peaceably Assemble.* — The people have the right peaceably to assemble for their own good, and to apply to those invested with the powers of government for redress of grievances by petition, address, or remonstrance.

SEC. 13. — *Restriction of Civil and Military Power.* — No power, civil or military, shall ever interfere to prevent the free exercise of the right of suffrage by those entitled to such right.

SEC. 14. — *Public Money; Cannot be Appropriated for Any Church, etc.* — No public money or property shall ever by appropriated, applied, donated, or used, directly or indirectly, for the use, benefit, or support of any sect, church, denomination, or system of religion, or for the use, benefit, or support of any priest, preacher, minister, or other religious teacher or dignitary, or sectarian institution as such.

SEC. 15. — *Courts of Justice Open; Speedy Remedy.* — The courts of justice of the State shall be open to every person, and speedy and certain remedy afforded for every wrong and for every injury to person, property, or reputation; and right and justice shall be administered without sale, denial, delay, or prejudice.

SEC. 16. — *Due Process of Law.* — No person shall be deprived of life, liberty, or property, without due process of law.

SEC. 17. — *All Offenses Bailable Except Capital.* — All persons shall be bailable by sufficient sureties, except for capital offenses when the proof of guilt is evident, or the presumption thereof is great.

SEC. 18. — *Excessive Bail.* — Excessive bail shall not be required, nor excessive fines imposed, nor cruel or unusual punishments inflicted.

SEC. 19. — *Writ of Habeas Corpus.* — The privilege of the writ of habeas corpus shall never be suspended by the authorities of this State.

SEC. 20. — *Officers; Personal Attention to Duties.* — Every person elected or appointed to any office or employment of trust or profit under the laws of the State, or under any ordinance of any municipality thereof, shall give personal attention to the duties of the office to which he is elected or appointed.

SEC. 21. — *Restriction on Right to Hold Office.* — No member of Congress from this State, or person holding any office of trust or profit under the laws of any other State, or of the United States, shall hold any office of trust or profit under the laws of this State.

SEC. 22. — *Imprisonment for Debt Prohibited.* — Imprisonment for debt is prohibited, except for the non-paytment of fines and penalties imposed for the violation of law.

SEC. 23. — *Military Subordinate to Civil Authority.* — The military shall be held in strict subordination to the civil authorities. No soldier shall be quartered in any house, in time of peace, without the consent of the owner, nor in time of war, except in a manner to be prescribed by law.

SEC. 24. — *Ex Post Facto Laws: Contracts.* — No bill of attainder, ex post facto law, nor any law impairing the obligation of contracts, shall ever be passed. No conviction shall work a corruption of blood or forfeiture of estate: Provided, That this provision shall not prohibit the imposition of pecuniary penalties.

SEC. 25. — *Treason.* — Treason against the State shall consist only in levying war against it or in adhering to its enemies, giving them aid and comfort. No person shall be convicted of treason, unless on the testimony of two witnesses to the same overt act, or on confession in open court.

SEC. 26. — *Indictment; Information; Examining Trial.* — No person shall be prosecuted criminally in courts of record for felony or misdemeanor otherwise than by presentment or indictment or by information. No person shall be prosecuted for a felony by information without having had a preliminary examination before an examining magistrate, or having waived such preliminary examination. Prosecutions may be instituted in courts not of record upon a duly verified complaint.

SEC. 27. — *Grand Jury.* — A grand jury shall be composed of twelve men, any nine of whom concurring may find an indictment or true bill. A grand jury shall be convened upon the order of a judge of a court having the power to try and determine felonies, upon his own motion; or such grand jury shall be ordered by such judge upon the filing of a petition therefor signed by one hundred resident taxpayers of the county; when so assembled such grand jury shall have power to investigate and return indictments for all character and grades of crime, and such other powers as the Legislature may prescribe: Provided, That the Legislature may make the calling of a grand jury compulsory.

SEC. 28. — *Petit Jury; Trial.* — The right of trial by jury shall be and remain inviolate, and a jury for the trial of civil and criminal cases in courts of record, other than county courts, shall consist of twelve men; but, in county courts and courts not of record, a jury shall consist of six men. This section shall not be so construed as to prevent limitations being fixed by law upon the right of appeal from judgments of courts not of record in civil cases concerning causes of action involving less than twenty dollars. In civil cases, and in criminal cases less than felonies, three-fourths of the whole number of jurors concurring shall have power to render a verdict. In all other cases the entire number of jurors must concur to render a verdict. In case a verdict is rendered by less than the whole number of jurors, the verdict shall be in writing and signed by each juror concurring therein.

SEC. 29. — *Criminal Prosecutions; Change of Venue; To be Confronted with Witnesses.* — In all criminal prosecutions the accused shall have the right to a speedy and public trial by an impartial jury of the county in which the crime shall have been committed: Provided, That the venue may be changed to some other county of the State, on the application of the accused, in such manner as may be prescribed by law. He shall be informed of the nature and cause of the accusation against him and have a copy thereof, and be confronted with the witnesses against him, and have compulsory process for obtaining witnesses in his behalf. He shall have the right to be heard by himself and counsel; and in capital cases, at least two days before the case is called for trail, he shall be furnished with a list of the witnesses that will be called in chief, to prove the allegations of the indictment or information, together with their postoffice addresses.

SEC. 30. — *Evidence Against Oneself; Jeopardy.* — No person shall be compelled to give evidence which will tend to incriminate him, except as in this Constitution specifically provided; nor shall any person, after having been once acquitted by a jury, be again put in jeoparty of life or liberty for that of which he has been acquitted. Nor shall any person be twice put in jeopardy of life or liberty for the same offense.

SEC. 31. — *Right of Free Speech; Libel.* — Every person may freely speak, write, or publish his sentiments on all subjects, being responsible for the abuse of that right; and no law shall be passed to restrain or abridge the liberty of speech or of the press. In all criminal prosecutions for libel, the truth of the matter alleged to be libelous may be given in evidence to the jury, and if it shall appear to the jury that the matter charged as libelous be true, and was written or published with good motives and for justifiable ends, the party shall be acquitted.

SEC. 32. — *Private Property Not to be Taken for Private Use.* — No private property shall be taken or damaged for private use, with or without compensation, unless by consent of the owner, except for private ways of necessity, or for drains and ditches across lands of others for agricultural, mining, or sanitary purposes, in such manner as may be prescribed by law.

SEC. 35. — *Right to Bear Arms: Weapons.* — The right of a citizen to keep and bear arms in defense of his home, person, or property, or in aid of the civil power, when thereunto legally summoned, shall never be prohibited; but nothing herein contained shall prevent the Legislature from regulating the carrying of weapons.

SEC. 36. — *Evidence; Compelled to Give; Immunity.* — Any person having knowledge or possession of facts that tend to establish the guilt of any other person or corporation charged with an offense against the laws of the State, shall not be excused from giving testimony or producing evidence, when legally called upon so to do, on the ground that it may tend to incriminate him under the laws of the State; but no person shall be prosecuted or subjected to any penalty or forfeiture for or on account of any transaction, matter, or thing concerning which he may so testify or produce evidence.

SEC. 37. — *Records of Corporations Open to Inspection.* — The records, books, and files of all corporations shall be, at all times, liable and subject to the full visitoral and inquisitorial powers of the State, notwithstanding the immunities and privileges in this Bill of Rights secured to the persons, inhabitants, and citizens thereof.

SEC. 38. — *No Person Transported Out of State; Due Process of Law.* — No person shall be transported out of the State for any offense committed within the State, nor shall any person be transported out of the State for any purpose, without his consent, except by due process of law; but nothing in this provision shall prevent the operation of extradition laws, or the transporting of persons sentenced for crime, to other states for the purpose of incarceration.

SEC. 39. — *Search Warrants and Seizures.* — The right of the people to be secure in their persons, houses, papers, and effects against unreasonable searches or seizures shall not be violated; and no warrant shall issue but upon probable cause supported by oath or affirmation, describing as particularly as may be the place to be searched and the person or thing to be seized.

SEC. 40. — *State May Engage in Business.* — The right of the State to engage in any occupation or business for public purposes shall not be denied nor prohibited, except that the State shall not engage in agriculture for any other than educational and scientific purposes and for the support of its penal, charitable, and educational institutions.

SEC. 41. — *Perpetuities and Monopolies Prohibited.* — Perpetuities and monopolies are contrary to the genius of a free government, and shall never be allowed, nor shall the law of primogeniture or entailments ever be in force in this State.

SEC. 42. — *Enumeration of Rights No Denial of Others.* — The enumeration in this Constitution of certain rights shall not be construed to deny, impair, or disparage others retained by the people.

SEC. 46. — *Election Board; Direct Vote for Senators.* — The Legislature shall enact laws creating an election board (not more than a majority of whose members shall be selected from the same political party), and shall provide the time and manner of holding and conducting all elections; and, at any time the Federal Constitution may permit the election of United States senators by direct vote of the people, the Legislature shall provide for their election as for the election of Governor and other elective officers.

SEC. 47. — *Mandatory Primary.* — The Legislature shall enact laws providing for a mandatory primary system, which shall provide for the nomination of all candidates in all elections for State, District, County, and municipal officers, for all political parties, including United States Senators: Provided, However, this provision shall not exclude the right of the people to place on the ballot by petition any non-partisan candidate.

SEC. 50. — *Legislative, Executive and Judicial.* — Section 1. The powers of the government of the State of Oklahoma shall be divided into three separate departments: The Legislative, Executive, and Judicial; and except as provided in this Constitution, the Legislative, Executive, and Judicial departments of government shall be separate and distinct, and neither shall exercise the powers properly belonging to either of the others.

SEC. 51. — *Reservation of Right of People.* — The Legislative authority of the State shall be vested in a Legislature, consisting of a Senate and a House of Representatives; but the people reserve to themselves the power to propose laws and amendments to the Constitution and to enact or reject the same at the polls independent of the Legislature, and also reserve power at their own option to approve or reject at the polls any act of the Legislature.

SEC. 52. — *Petition; Per Centum Required.* — The first power reserved by the people is the initiative, and eight per centum of the legal voters shall have the right to propose any legislative measure, and fifteen per centum of the legal voters shall have the right to propose amendments to the Constitution by petition, and every such petition shall include the full text of the measure so proposed. The second power is the referendum, and it may be ordered (except as to laws necessary for the immediate preservation of the public peace, health, or safety), either by petition signed by five per centum of the legal voters or by the Legislature as other bills are enacted. The ratio and per centum of legal voters hereinbefore stated shall be based upon the total number of votes cast at the last general election for the State office receiving the highest number of votes at such election.

SEC. 53. — *Referendum; Petition; Veto.* — Referendum petitions shall be filed with the Secretary of State not more than ninety days after the final adjournment of the session of the Legislature which passed the bill on which the referendum is demanded. The veto power of the Governor shall not extend to measures voted on by the people. All elections on measures referred to the people of the State shall be had at the next election held throughout the State, except when the Legislature or the Governor shall order a special election for the express purpose of making such reference. Any measure referred to the people by the initiative shall take effect and be in force when it shall have been approved by a majority of the votes cast in such election. Any measure referred to the people by the referendum shall take effect and be in force when it shall have been approved by a majority of the votes cast thereon and not otherwise.

SEC. 54. — *Style of Bills.* — The style of all bills shall be: "Be it Enacted By the People of the State of Oklahoma."

SEC. 55. — *Petitions to be Filed.* — Petitions and orders for the initiative and for the referendum shall be filed with the Secretary of State and addressed to the Governor of the State, who shall submit the same to the people. The Legislature shall make suitable provisions for carrying into effect the provisions of this article.

SEC. 56. — *Referendum Against One or More Items.* — The referendum may be demanded by the people against one or more items, sections, or parts of any act of the Legislature in the same manner in which such power may be exercised against a complete act. The filing of a referendum petition against one or more items, sections, or parts of an act shall not delay the remainder of such act from becoming operative.

SEC. 57. — *Reserved to County and District.* — The powers of the initiative and referendum reserved to the people by this Constitution for the State at large, are hereby further reserved to the legal voters of every county and district therein, as to all local legislation, or action, in the administration of county and district government in and for their respective counties and districts.

SEC. 58. — *Prescribed by General Laws; Power of County Commissioners in Local Matters.* — The manner of exercising said powers shall be prescribed by general laws, except that Boards of County Commissioners may provide for the time of exercising the initiative and referendum powers as to local legislation in their respective counties and districts.

SEC. 59. — *Number of Petitioners in County or District.* — The requisite number of petitioners for the invocation of the initiative and referendum in counties and districts shall bear twice, or double, the ratio to the whole number of legal voters in such county or district, as herein provided therefor in the State at large.

SEC. 60. — *Measures Rejected Cannot be Proposed for Three Years.* — Any measure rejected by the people, through the powers of the initiative and referendum, cannot be again proposed by the initiative within three years thereafter by less than twenty-five per centum of the legal voters.

SEC. 61. — *Right of Legislature to Pass or Repeal.* — The reservation of the powers of the initiative and referendum in this article shall not deprive the Legislature of the right to repeal any law, propose or pass any measure, which may be consistent with the Constitution of the State and the Constitution of the United States.

SEC. 62. — *Corruption in Initiative and Referendum.* — Laws shall be provided to prevent corruption in making, procuring, and submitting initiative and referendum petitions.

SEC. 119. — *Limitations upon Power of Legislature to Pass Local or Special Laws.* — The Legislature shall not, except as otherwise provided in this Constitution, pass any local or special law authorizing:

SEC. 119a. — The creation, extension, or impairing of liens;

SEC. 119b. — Regulating the affairs of counties, cities, towns, wards, or school districts;

SEC. 119c. — Changing the names of persons or places;

SEC. 119d. — Authorizing the laying out, opening, altering, or maintaining of roads, highways, streets, or alleys;

SEC. 119e. — Relating to ferries or bridges, or incorporating ferry or bridge companies, except for the erection of bridges crossing streams which form boundaries between this and any other State;

SEC. 119f. — Vacating roads, town plats, streets, or alleys;

SEC. 119g. — Relating to cemeteries, graveyards, or public grounds not owned by the State;

SEC. 119h. — Authorizing the adoption or legitimation of children;

SEC. 119i. — Locating or changing county seats;

SEC. 119j. — Incorporating cities, towns, or villages, or changing their charters;

SEC. 119k. — For the opening and conducting of elections, or fixing or changing the places of voting;

SEC. 119l. — Granting divorces;

SEC. 119m. — Creating offices, or prescribing the powers and duties of officers in counties, cities, towns, election or school districts;

SEC. 119n. — Changing the law of descent or succession;

SEC. 119o. — Regulating the practice or jurisdiction of, or changing the rules of evidence in judicial proceedings or inquiry before the courts, justices of the peace, sheriffs, commissioners, arbitrators, or other tribunals, or providing or changing the methods for the collection of debts, or the enforcement of judgments or prescribing the effect of judicial sales of real estate;

SEC. 119p. — Regulating the fees, or extending the powers and duties of aldermen, justices of the peace, or constables;

SEC. 119q. — Regulating the management of public schools, the building or repairing of school houses, and the raising of money for such purposes;

SEC. 119r. — Fixing the rate of interest;

SEC. 119s. — Affecting the estate of minors, or persons under disability;

SEC. 119t. — Remitting fines, penalties and forfeitures, and refunding moneys legally paid into the treasury;

SEC. 119u. — Exempting property from taxation;

SEC. 119v. — Declaring any named person of age;

SEC. 119w. — Extending the time for the assessment or collection of taxes, or otherwise relieving any assessor or collector of taxes from due performance of his official duties, or his securities from liability;

SEC. 119x. — Giving effect to informal or invalid wills or deeds;

SEC. 119y. — Summoning or impaneling grand or petit juries;

SEC. 119z. — For limitation of civil or criminal actions;

SEC. 119z1. — For incorporating railroads or other work of internal improvement;

SEC. 119z2. — Providing for change of venue in civil and criminal cases.

SEC. 120. — *No Officer to be Retired on Pay.* — The Legislature shall not retire any officer on pay or part pay, or make any grant to such retiring officer.

SEC. 121. — *Bureau of Immigration; No Money Appropriated For.* —

The Legislature shall have no power to appropriate any of the public money for the establishment and maintenance of a Bureau of Immigration in this State.

SEC. 122. — *Employees of Legislature; Number and Emolument.* — The legislature shall not increase the number or emolument of its employes, or the employes of either House, except by general law, which shall not take effect during the term at which such increase was made.

SEC. 123. — *No Property Exempt from Taxation.* — The legislature shall pass no law exempting any property withis [within] this State from taxation, except as otherwise provided in this Constitution.

SEC. 124. — *No Exclusive Rights Granted.* — The Legislature shall pass no law granting to any association, corporation, or individual any exclusive rights, privileges, or immunities within the State.

SEC. 125. — *No Power to Revive or Take Away Right of Action.* — The Legislature shall have no power to revive any right or remedy which may have become barred by lapse of time, or by any statute of this State. After suit has been commenced on any cause of action, the Legislature shall have no power to take away such cause of action, or destroy any existing defense to each suit.

SEC. 126. — *No Power to Release Indebtedness of Corporation or Individual.* — The Legislature shall have no power to release or extinguish, or to authorize the releasing or extinguishing, in whole or in part, the indebtedness, liabilities, or obligations of any corporation, or individual, to the State, or any county or other municipal corporation thereof.

SEC. 127. — *Repeal of Statute Does Not Affect Vested Rights.* — The repeal of a statute shall not revive a statute previously repealed by such statute, nor shall such repeal affect any accrued right, or penalty incurred, or proceedings begun by virtue of such repealed statute.

SEC. 130. — *Acts to Embrace One Subject; Amendments.* — Every act of the Legislature shall embrace but one subject, which shall be clearly expressed in its title, except general appropriation bills, general revenue bills, and bills adopting a code, digest, or revision of statutes; and no law shall be revised, amended, or the provisions thereof extended or conferred, by reference to its title only; but so much thereof as is revised, amended, extended, or conferred shall be re-enacted and published at length: Provided, That if any subject be embraced in any act contrary to the provisions of this section, such act shall be void only as to so much of the law as may not be expressed in the title thereof.

SEC. 131. — *Acts to Take Effect in Ninety Days; Franchises; Emergency.* — No act shall take effect until ninety days after the adjournment of the session at which it was passed, except enactments for carrying into effect provisions relating to the initiative and referendum, or a general appropriation bill, unless, in case of emergency, to be expressed in the act, the Legislature, by a vote of two-thirds of all members elected to each House, so directs. An emergency measure shall include only such measures as are immediately necessary for the preservation of the public peace, health, or safety, and shall not include the granting of franchises or license to a corporation or individual, to extend longer than one year, nor provision for the purchase or sale of real estate, nor the renting or encumbrance of real property for a longer term than one year. Emergency measures may be vetoed by the Governor, but such measures so vetoed may be passed by a three-fourths vote of each House, to be duly entered on the journal.

SEC. 132. — *General Laws to Have Uniform Operation.* — Laws of a general nature shall have a uniform operation throughout the State, and where a general law can be made applicable, no special law shall be enacted.

SEC. 133. — *System of Checks and Balances Between Officials.* — The Legislature shall provide by law for the establishment and maintenance of an efficient system of checks and balances between the officers of the Executive Department, and all commissioners and superintendents, and boards of control of State institutions, and all other officers entrusted with the collection, receipt, custody, or disbursement of the revenue or moneys of the State whatsoever.

ARTICLE VI

SEC. 134. — *Officials Constituting Executive Authority.* — The Executive authority of the State shall be vested in a Governor, Lieutenant Governor, Secretary of State, State Auditor, Attorney General, State Treasurer, Superintendent of Public Instruction, State Examiner and Inspector, Chief Mine Inspector, Commissioner of Labor, Commissioner of Charities and Corrections, Commissioner of Insurance, and other offices provided by law and this Constitution, each of whom shall keep his office and public records, books, and papers at the seat of government, and shall perform such duties as may be designated in this Constitution or prescribed by law.

SEC. 153. — *Term and Duties.* — A Department of Labor is hereby created to be under the control of a Commissioner of Labor who shall be elected by the people, whose term of office shall be four years, and whose duties shall be prescribed by law.

SEC. 154. — *Board of Arbitration and Conciliation.* — The Legislature shall create a Board of Arbitration and Conciliation in the Department of Labor and the Commissioner of Labor shall be ex-officio chairman.

SEC. 168. — *Seal of the State.* — In the center shall be a five pointed star, with one ray directed upward. The center of the star shall contain the central device of the seal of the Territory of Oklahoma, including the words, "Labor Omnia Vincit." The upper left hand ray shall contain the symbol of the ancient seal of the Cherokee Nation, namely: A seven pointed star partially surrounded by a wreath of oak leaves. The ray directed upwards shall contain the symbol of the ancient-seal of the Chickasaw Nation, namely: An Indian warrior standing upright with bow and shield. The lower left hand ray shall contain the symbol of the ancient seal of the Creek Nation, namely: A sheaf of wheat and a plow. The upper right hand ray shall contain the symbol of the ancient seal of the Choctaw Nation, namely: A tomahawk, bow, and three crossed arrows. The lower right and ray shall contain the symbol of the ancient seal of the Seminole Nation, namely: A village with houses and a factory beside a lake upon which an Indian is paddling a canoe. Surrounding the central star and grouped between its rays shall be forty-five small stars, divided into five clusters of nine stars each, representing the forty-five states of the Union, to which the forty-sixth is now added. In a circular band surrounding the whole device shall be inscribed, "Great Seal of the State of Oklahoma, 1907."

SEC. 193. — *Trial by Jury Waived.* — In all issues of fact joined in any court, all parties may waive the right to have the same determined by jury; in which case the finding of the judge, upon the facts, shall have the force and effect of a verdict by jury.

SEC. 194. — *Jury to Return General Verdict; Court May Direct Special Findings.* — In all jury trials, the jury shall return a general verdict, and no law in force, nor any law hereafter enacted, shall require the court to direct the jury to make findings on particular questions of fact; but the court may, in its discretion, direct such special findings.

ARTICLE IX

CORPORATIONS—DEFINITION

SEC. 205. — *Have All Powers not Possessed by Individuals.* — As used in this article, the term "corporation" or "company" shall include all associations and joint stock companies, having any power or privileges, not possessed by individuals, and exclude all municipal corporations and public institutions owned or controlled by the State; the term "charter" shall mean the charter of incorporation, by or under which any corporation is formed. The term "license" shall mean the authority under which all foreign corporations are permitted to transact business in this State.

SEC. 206. — *Common Carriers; Right to Construct and Operate Lines.* — Every railroad, oil pipe, car, express, telephone or telegraph corporation or association organized or authorized to do a transportation of transmission business under the laws of this State for such purpose, shall, each respectively, have the right to construct and operate its line between any points in this State, and as such to connect at the State line with like lines; and every such company shall have the right with its road or line, to intersect, connect with, or cross any railroad or such line.

SEC. 207. — *To transport Each Other's Cars and Passengers.* — Every railroad, car, or express company, shall each, respectively, receive and transport without delay or discrimination each other's cars, loaded or empty, tonnage, and passengers, under such rules and regulations as may be prescribed by law or any commission created by this Constitution or by act of the Legislature for that purpose.

SEC. 208. — *Oil Pipe Companies Subject to Control of Commission.* — All oil pipe companies shall be subject to the reasonable control and regulation of the Corporation Commission, and shall receive and transport each other's tonnage or oils, or commodities, under such rules and regulations as shall be prescribed by law, or such commission.

SEC. 209. — *Telephone and Telegraph Lines to Transmit Each Other's Messages.* — All telephone and telegraph lines, operated for hire, shall each, respectively, receive and transmit each other's messages without delay or discrimination, and make physical connections with each other's lines, under such rules and regulations as shall be prescribed by law, or by any commission created by this Constitution, or any act of the Legislature, for that purpose.

SEC. 210. — *Railroads Public Highways; Office in State; Meetings of Directors, etc.* — Railroads heretofore constructed, or which may hereafter be constructed in this State, are hereby declared public highways. Every railroad or other public service corporation organized or doing business in this State, under the laws or authority thereof, shall have and maintain a public office or place in this State, for the transaction of its business, where transfers of stock shall be made, and where shall be kept, for inspection by the stockholders of such corporation, books, in which shall be recorded the amount of capital stock subscribed, the names of the owners of stock, the amounts owned by them, respectively; the amount of stock paid, and by whom; the transfer of said stock, with the date of transfer; the amount of its assets and liabilities, and the names and places of residence of its officers, and such other matters required by law or by order of the Corporation Commission. The directors of every railroad company, or other public service corporation, shall hold at least one meeting annually in this State, public notice of which shall be given thirty days previously, and the president or superintendent of every railroad company and other public service corporation organized or doing business in this state under the laws of this State, or the authority thereof, shall report annually under oath, and make such other reports as may be required by law or order of the Corporation Commission, to said Commission, their acts and doings, which report shall include such matters relating to railroads and other public service corporations as may be prescribed by law. The Legislature shall pass all necessary laws enforcing, by suitable penalties, all the provisions in this section.

SEC. 211. — *Rolling Stock Considered Personal Property, Subject to Sale*. — The rolling stock and all other movable property belonging to any railroad, transportation, transmission, or other public corporation in this State, shall be considered personal property, and its real and personal property, or any part thereof, shall be liable to execution and sale in the same manner as the property of individuals; and the Legislature shall pass no laws exempting any such property from execution and sale.

SEC. 212. — *Must not Consolidate with Competing Lines*. — No public service corporation, or the lessees, purchasers, or managers thereof shall consolidate the stock, property, or franchises, of such corporation with, or lease or purchase the works of franchisers of, or in any way control, any other public service corporation owning or having under its control a parallel or competing line; except by enactment of the Legislature upon the recommendation of the Corporation Commission: Provided, however, That the Legislature shall never enact any law permitting any public service corporation, the lessees, purchasers, or managers thereof, when such public service corporation is organized under the laws of any other State or of the United States, to consolidate the stock, property, or franchise, of such corporation with, or lease, or purchase, the works of, franchises of, or in any way control, any other public service corporation, organized under the laws of any other State, or of the United States, owning or having under its control in this State, a parallel or competing line; nor shall any officer of such corporation act as an officer of any other corporation owning or controlling a parallel or competing line.

SEC. 213. — *Must not Consolidate with Company Organized in Another State.* — Neither shall any railroad company, transportation company, or transmission company, organized under the laws of this State, consolidate by private or judicial sale, or otherwise, with any railroad company, transportation company, or transmission company organized under the laws of any other State, or of the United States.

SEC. 214. — *Street Railroad; Consent of Local Authorities Required.* — No law shall be passed by the legislature granting the right to construct and operate a street railroad within any city, town, or village, or upon any public highway, without first acquiring the consent of the local authorities having control of the street or highway proposed to be occupied by such street railroad.

SEC. 215. — *Must Accept Provision of Constitution.* — No railroad, transportation, transmission, or other public service corporation in existence at the time of the adoption of this Constitution, shall have the benefit of any future legislation, except on condition of complete acceptance of all the provisions of this Constitution, applicable to railroads, transportation companies, transmission companies, and other public service corporations: Provided, That nothing herein shall be construed as validating any charter which may be invalid, or waiving any of the conditions contained in any charter.

SEC. 216. — *No Railroad to Transport Articles Manufactured by it.* — No railroad company shall transport, within this State, any article or commodity manufactured, mined, or produced by it, or under its authority, or which it may own, in whole or in part, or in which it may have any interest, direct or indirect, except such articles or commodities as may be necessary and intended for its use in the conduct of its business as a common carrier.

SEC. 217. — *No Free Transportation; Exceptions; Penalty for Viola- tion.* — No railroad corporation or transportation company, or transmission company shall, directly or indirectly, issue or give any free frank or free ticket, free pass or other free transportation, for any use, within this State, except to its employes and their families, its officers, agents, surgeons, physicians, and attorneys at law; to ministers of religion, traveling secretaries for railroad Young Men's Christian Associations, inmates of hospitals and charitable and eleemosynary institutions and persons exclusively engaged in charitable and eleemosynary work; to indigent, destitute, and homeless persons, and to such persons when transported by charitable societies or hospitals, and the necessary agents, employed in such transportations; to inmates of the National Homes, or State Homes for disabled Volunteer

Soldiers, and of Soldiers' and Sailors' Homes, including those about to enter and those returning home after discharge, and boards of managers of such Homes; to members of volunteer fire departments and their equipage while traveling as such; to necessary caretakers of live stock, poultry, and fruit; to employes of sleeping cars, of express cars, and to linemen of telegraph and telephone companies; to Railway Mail Service employes, postoffice inspectors, customs inspectors, and immigration inspectors; to newsboys on trains, baggage agents, witnesses attending any legal investigation in which the railroad company or transportation company is interested, persons injured in wrecks, and physicians and nurses attending such persons: Provided, That this provision shall not be construed to prohibit the interchange of passes for the officers, agents, and employes of common carriers and their families; nor prohibit any common carriers from carrying passengers free with the object of providing relief in cases of general epidemic, pestilence, or other calamitous visitation; nor to prevent them from transporting, free of charge, to their places of employment persons entering their service, and the interchange of passes to that end; and any railroad, transportation, or transmission company or any person, other than the persons excepted in this provision, who grants or uses any such free frank, free ticket, free pass, or free transportation within this State, shall be deemed guilty of a crime, and the Legislature shall provide proper penalties for the violation of any provision of this section by the railroad or transportation or transmission company, or by any individual: Provided, That nothing herein shall prevent the Legislature from extending these provisions so as to exclude such free transportations or franks from other persons.

SEC. 218. — *Railroads to Pass Through County Seats.* — No railroad hereafter constructed in this State shall pass within a distance of four miles of any county seat without passing through the same and establishing and maintaining a depot therein, unless prevented by natural obstacles such as streams, hills, or mountains: Provided, Such town, or its citizens, shall grant the right-of-way through its limits and sufficient ground for ordinary depot purposes.

SEC. 219. — *Election; Terms; Vacancy.* — A Corporation Commission is hereby created, to be composed of three persons, who shall be elected by the people at a general election for State officers, and their terms of office shall be six years: Provided, Corporation Commissioners first elected under this Constitution shall hold office as follows: One shall serve until the second Monday in January, nineteen hundred and nine; one until the second Monday in January, nineteen hundred and eleven; and one until the second Monday in January, nineteen hundred and thirteen; their terms to be decided by lot immediately after they shall have qualified: In case of a vacancy in said office, the Governor of the State shall fill such vacancy by appointment until the next general election, when a successor shall be elected to fill out any unexpired term.

SEC. 231. — *Appeals to Supreme Court; Acts of Commission Not to be Suspended Except by Supreme Court.* — From any action of the Commission prescribing rates, charges of classifications of traffic, or affecting the train schedule of any transportation company, or requiring additional facilities, conveniences, or public service of any transportation or transmission company, or refusing to approve a suspending bond, or requiring additional security thereon as hereinafter provided for, an appeal (subject to such reasonable limitations as to time, regulations as to procedure and provisions as to cost, as may be prescribed by law) may be taken by the corporation whose rates, charges, or classifications of traffic, schedule, facilities, conveniences, or service, are effected, or by any person deeming himself aggrieved by such action, or (if allowed by law) by the State. Until otherwise provided by law, such appeal shall be taken in the manner in which appeals may be taken to the Supreme Court from the District Courts, except that such an appeal shall be of right.

SEC. 242. — *Commission to Ascertain Cost, Indebtedness, Bonds, and Salaries; Annual Report of Information.* — The Commission shall ascertain, and enter of record, the same to be a public record, as early as practicable, the amount of money expended in construction and equipment per mile of every railroad and other public service corporation in Oklahoma, the amount of money expended to procure the right of way, and the amount of money it would require to reconstruct the roadbed, track, depots, and transportation facilities, and to replace all the physical properties belonging to the railroad or other public service corporation. It shall also ascertain the outstanding bonds, debentures, and indebtedness, and the amount, respectively thereof, when issued, and the rate of interest, when due, for what purposes issued, how used, to whom issued, to whom sold, and the price in cash, property, or labor, if any, received therefor, what became of the proceeds, by whom the indebtedness is held, the amount purporting to be due thereon, the floating indebtedness of the company, to whom due, and his address, the credits due on it, the property on hand belonging to the railroad company or other public service corporation, and the judicial or other sales of said road, its property or franchises, and the amounts purporting to have been paid, and in what manner paid therefor. The Commission shall also ascertain the amounts paid for salaries to the officers of the railroad, or other public service corporation, and the wages paid its employees.

SEC. 245. — *Duty of Commission to Investigate Rates; May Make Corrections and Notify Interstate Commerce Commission.* — The said Commission shall have power, and it is hereby made its duty, to investigate all through freight or passenger rates on railroads in this State, and when the same are, in the opinion of the Commission, excessive or levied or laid in violation of the Interstate Commerce Law, or the rules and regulations of the Interstate Commerce Commission, the proper officials of the railroads are to be notified of the facts and requested to reduce them or make the proper corrections, as the case may be. When the rates are not changed, or the proper corrections are not made according to the request of the Commission, it shall be the duty of the latter to notify the Interstate Commerce Commission and to make proper application to it for relief, and the Attorney General or such other persons as may be designated by law shall represent the Commission in all such matters.

SEC. 251. — *Two Cents Per Mile Rate.* — No person, company, or corporation, receiver, or other agency, operating a railroad, other than street railroad or electric railroad, in whole or in part, within this State, shall demand or receive for first-class transportation for each passenger, between points within this State on the portion of its road operated within this State, more than two cents per mile, until otherwise provided by law: Provided, However, The Corporation Commission shall have the power to exempt any railroad from the operation of this section upon satisfactory proof that it cannot earn a just compensation for the services rendered by it to the public, if not permitted to charge more than two cents per mile for the transportation of passengers within the State.

SEC. 254. — *Must Not Contribute to Elections.* — No corporation organized or doing business in this State shall be permitted to influence elections or official duty by contributions of money or anything of value.

SEC. 255. — *Shall Not Own Stock of Another Corporation.* — No corporation chartered or licensed to do business in this State shall own, hold, or control, in any manner whatever, the stock of any competitive corporation or corporations engaged in the same kind of business, in or out of the State, except such stock as may be pledged in good faith to secure bona fide indebtedness acquired upon foreclosure, execution, sale, or otherwise for the satisfaction of debt.

SEC. 256. — *Must Dispose of Stock in Twelve Months; Bank and Trust Company.* — In all cases where any corporation acquires stock in any other corporation, as herein provided, it shall be required to dispose of the same within twelve months from the date of acquisition; and during the period of its ownership of such stock it shall have no right to participate in the control of such corporation, except when permitted by order of the Corporation Commission. No trust company, or bank or banking company shall own, hold, or control, in any manner whatever, the stock of any other trust company, or bank or banking company, except such stock as may be pledged in good faith to secure bona fide indebtedness, acquired upon foreclosure, execution sale, or otherwise for the satisfaction of debt; and such stock shall be disposed of in the time and manner hereinbefore provided.

SEC. 257. — *Must Submit to Arbitration.* — Every license issued or charter granted to a mining or public service corporation, foreign or domestic, shall contain a stipulation that such corporation will submit any difference it may have with employes in reference to labor, to arbitration, as shall be provided by law.

SEC. 260. — *Monopoly; Must Not Discriminate.* — Until otherwise provided by law, no person, firm, association, or corporation engaged in the production, manufacture, distribution, or sale of any commodity of general use, shall, for the purpose of creating a monopoly or destroying competition in trade, discriminate between different persons, associations, or corporations, or different sections, communities, or cities of the State, by selling such commodity at a lower rate in one section, community, or city than in another, after making due allowance for the difference, if any, in the grade, quantity, or quality, and in the actual cost of transportation from the point of production or manufacture.

ARTICLE X

REVENUE AND TAXATION

SEC. 271. — *Exemptions; Manufacturing Establishments.* — The Legislature may authorize any incorporated city or town, by a majority vote of its electors voting thereon, to exempt manufacturing establishments and public utilities from municipal taxation, for a period not exceeding five years, as an inducement to their location.

SEC. 272. — *Assessments for Local Improvements.* — The Legislature may authorize county and municipal corporations to levy and collect assessments for local improvements upon property benefited thereby, homesteads included, without regard to a cash valuation.

SEC. 273. — *Property Assessed at Fair Cash Value; Penalty.* — All property which may be taxed ad valorem shall be assessed for taxation at its fair cash value, estimated at the price it would bring at a fair voluntary sale; and any officer, or other person authorized to assess values, or subjects, for taxation, who shall commit any wilful error in the performance of his duty, shall be deemed guilty of malfeasance, and upon conviction thereof shall forfeit his office, and be otherwise punished as may be provided by law.

SEC. 281. — *Credit of State Not Given.* — The credit of the State shall not be given, pledged, or loaned to any individual, company, corporation, or association, municipality, or political subdivision of the State; nor shall the State become an owner or stockholder in, nor make donation by gift, subscription to stock, by tax or otherwise, to any company, association, or corporation.

SEC. 289. — *State May Control Debts; Limitation.* — The State may, to meet casual deficits or failure in revenues, or for expenses not provided for, contract debts; but such debts, direct and contingent, singly or in the aggregate, shall not, at any time, exceed four hundred thousand dollars, and the moneys arising from the loans creating such debts shall be applied to the purpose for which they were obtained or to repay the debts so contracted, and to no other purpose whatever.

SEC. 290. — *May Contract Debts; to Repel Invasion.* — In addition to the above limited power to contract debts, the State may contract debts to repel invasion, suppress insurrection or to defend the State in war; but the money arising from the contracting of such debts shall be applied to the purpose for which it was raised, or to repay such debts, and to no other purpose whatever.

SEC. 291. — *Debts; Limitations; Submitted to People.* — Except the debts specified in sections twenty-three and twenty-four of this article, no debts shall hereafter be contracted by or on behalf of this State, unless such debt shall be authorized by law for some work or object, to be distinctly specified therein; and such law shall impose and provide for the collection of a direct annual tax to pay, and sufficient to pay, the interest on such debt as it falls due and also to pay and discharge the principal of such debt within twenty-five years from the time of the contracting thereof. No such law shall take effect until it shall, at a general election, have been submitted to the people and have received a majority of all the votes cast for and against it at such election. On the final passage of such bill in either House of the Legislature, the question shall be taken by yeas and nays, to be duly entered on the journals thereof, and shall be: "Shall this bill pass, and ought the same to receive the sanction of the people?"

SEC. 292. — *Limitation Upon Debts of City, County, etc.; Vote by People; Sinking Fund.* — No county, city, town, township, school district, or other political corporation, or subdivision of the State, shall be allowed to become indebted, in any manner, or for any purpose, to an amount exceeding, in any year, the income and revenue provided for such year, without the assent of three-fifths of the voters thereof, voting at an election, to be held for that purpose, nor in cases requiring such assent, shall any indebtedness be allowed to be incurred to an amount including existing indebtedness, in the aggregate exceeding five per centum of the valuation of the taxable property therein, to be ascertained from the last assessment for State and county purposes previous to the incurring of such indebtedness: Provided, That any county, city, town, township, school district, or other political corporation, or subdivision of the State, incurring any indebtedness, requiring the assent of the voters as aforesaid, shall, before or at the time of doing so, provide for the collection of an annual tax sufficient to pay the interest on such indebtedness as it falls due, and also to constitute a sinking fund for the payment of the principal thereof within twenty-five years from the time of contracting the same.

SEC. 293. — *Public Utilities; Indebtedness for; Sinking Fund.* — Any incorporated city or town in this State may, by a majority of the qualified property tax paying voters of such city or town, voting at an election to be held for that purpose, be allowed to become indebted in a larger amount than that specified in section twenty-six for the purpose of purchasing or constructing public utilities, or for repairing the same, to be owned exclusively by such city: Provided, That any such city or town incurring any such indebtedness requiring the assent of the voters as aforesaid, shall have the power to provide for, and, before or at the time of incurring such indebtedness, shall provide for the collection of an annual tax in addition to the other taxes provided for by this Constitution, sufficient to pay the interest on such indebtedness as it falls due, and also to constitute a sinking fund for the payment of the principal thereof within twenty-five years from the time of contracting the same.

ARTICLE XII

HOMESTEAD AND EXEMPTIONS

SEC. 304. — *What to Consist of.* — The homestead of any family in this State, not within any city, town, or village, shall consist of not more than one hundred and sixty acres of land, which may be in one or more parcels, to be selected by the owner. The homestead within any city, town, or village, owned and occupied as a residence only, shall consist of not exceeding one acre of land, to be selected by the owner: Provided, That the same shall not exceed in value the sum of five thousand dollars, and in no event shall the homestead be reduced to less than one-quarter of an acre, without regard to value: And Provided Further, That in case said homestead is used for both residence and business purposes, the homestead interest therein shall not exceed in value the sum of five thousand dollars: Provided, That nothing in the laws of the United States, or any treaties with the Indian Tribes in the State, shall deprive any Indian or other allottee of the benefit of the homestead and exemption laws of the State: And Provided Further, That any temporary renting of the homestead shall not change the character of the same when no other homestead has been acquired.

SEC. 305. — *Protected from Forced Sale; Consent of Wife.* — The homestead of the family shall be, and is hereby protected from forced sale, for the payment of debts, except for the purchase money therefor or a part of such purchase money, the taxes due thereon, or for work and material used in constructing improvements thereon; nor shall the owner, if married, sell the homestead without the consent of his or her spouse, given in such manner as may be prescribed by law: Provided, Nothing in this article shall prohibit any person from mortgaging his homestead, the spouse, if any, joining therein; nor prevent the sale thereof on foreclosure to satisfy any such mortgage.

SEC. 316. — *Legal Rate of Interest.* — The legal rate of interest shall not exceed six per centum per annum in the absence of any contract as to the rate of interest, and, by contract, parties may agree upon any rate not to exceed ten per centum per annum, and until reduced by the Legislature, said rates of six and ten per centum shall be, respectively, the legal and the maximum contract rates of interest.

ARTICLE XVIII

MUNICIPAL CORPORATIONS

SEC. 411. — *Legislature May Provide for Organization.* — Section 1. Municipal corporations shall not be created by special laws, but the Legislature, by general laws shall provide for the incorporation and organization of cities and towns and the classification of same in proportion to population, subject to the provisions of this article.

CHARTERS

SEC. 413. — *Procedure for Obtaining Special Charter; Election.* — Any city containing a population of more than two thousand inhabitants may frame a charter for its own government, consistent with and subject to the Constitution and laws of this State, by causing a board of freeholders, composed of two from each ward, who shall be qualified electors of said city, to be elected by the qualified electors of said city, at any general or special election, whose duty it shall be, within ninety days after such election, to prepare and propose a charter for such city, which shall be signed in duplicate by the members of such board or a majority of them, and returned, one copy of said charter to the chief executive officer of such city, and the other to the Register of Deeds to the county in which said city shall be situated. Such proposed charter shall then be published in one or more newspapers published and of general circulation within said city, for at least twenty-one days, if in a daily paper, or in three consecutive issues, if in a weekly paper, and the first publication shall be made within twenty days after the completion of the charter; and within thirty days, and not earlier than twenty days after such publication, it shall be submitted to the qualified electors of said city at a general or special election, and if a majority of such qualified electors voting thereon shall ratify the same, it shall thereafter be submitted to the Governor for his approval, and the Governor shall approve the same if it shall not be in conflict with the Constitution and laws of this State. Upon such approval it shall become the organic law of such city and supersede any existing charter and all amendments thereof and all ordinances inconsistent with it. A copy of such charter, certified by the chief executive officer, and authenticated by the seal of such city, setting forth the submission of such charter to the electors and its ratification by them shall after the approval of such charter by the Governor, be made in duplicate and deposited, one in the office of the Secretary of State, and the other, after being recorded in the office of said Register of Deeds, shall be deposited in the archives of the city; and thereafter all courts shall take judicial notice of said charter. The charter so ratified dmay be amended by proposals therefor, submitted by the legislative authority of the city to the qualified electors thereof (or by petition as hereinafter provided) at a general or special election, and ratified by a majority of the qualified electors voting thereion, and approved by the Governor as herein provided for the approval of the charter.

SEC. 414. — *Board of Freeholders to Draft Charter.* — An election of such board of freeholders may be called at any time by the legislative authority of any such city, and such election shall be called by the chief executive officer of any such city within ten days after there shall have been filed with him a petition demanding the same, signed by a number of qualified electors residing within such city, equal to twenty-five per centum of the totat number of votes cast at the next preceding general municipal election; and such election shall be held not later than thirty days after the call therefor. At such election a vote shall be taken upon the question of whether or not further proceedings toward adopting a charter shall be had in pursuance to the call, and unless a majority of the qualified electors voting thereon shall vote to proceed further, no further proceeding shall be had and all proceedings up to that time shall be of no effect.

INITIATIVE AND REFERENDUM

SEC. 415. — *Reserved to Every Municipality.* — The powers of the initiative and referendum, reserved by this Constitution to the people of the State and the respecvtive counties and districts therein, and hereby reserved to the people of every municipal corporation now existing or which shall hereafter be created within this State, with reference to all legislative authority which it may exercise, and amendments to charters for its own government in accordance with the provisions of this Constitution.

SEC. 416. — *Petition for; Requisite Number.* — Every petition for either the initiative or referendum in the goverment of a municipal corporation shall be signed by a number of qualified electors residing within the territorial limits of such municipal corporation, equal to twenty-five per centum of the total number of votes cast at the next preceding election, and every such petition shall be filed with the chief exective officer of such municipal corporation.

SEC. 417. — *Initiative; Enactment of Ordinance.* — When such petition demands the enactment of an ordinance or other legal act other than the grant, extension, or renewal of a franchise, the chief executive officer shall present the same to the legislative body of such corporation at its next meeting, and unless the said petition shall be granted more than thirty days before the next election at which any city officers are to be elected, the chief executive officer shall submit the said ordinance or act so petitioned for, to the qualified electors at said election; and if a majority of said electors voting thereon shall vote for the same, it shall thereupon become in full force and effect.

SEC. 418. — *Referendum on Ordinance.* — When such petition demands a referendum vote upon any ordinance or any other legal act other than the grant, extension, or renewal of a franchise, the chief executive offier shall submit said ordinance or act to the qualified electors of said corporation at the next succeeding general municipal election, and if, at said election, a majority of the electors voting thereon shall not vote for the same, it shall thereupon stand repealed.

SEC. 419. — *Amendment to Charter; How Made.* — When such petition demands an amendment to a charter, the chief executive officer shall submit such amendment to the qualified electors of said municipal corporation at the next election of any officer of said corporation, and if, at said election, a majority of said electors voting thereon shall vote for such amendment, the same shall thereupon become an amendment to and a part of said charter, when approved by the Governor and filed in the same manner and form as an original charter is required by the provisions of this article to be approved and filed.

FRANCHISES

SEC. 420. — *Vote by People; Election.* — No municipal corporation shall ever grant, extend, or renew a franchise, without the approval of a majority of the qualified electors residing within its corporate limits, who shall vote thereon at a general or special election; and the legislative body of any such corporation may submit any such matter for approval or disapproval to such electors at any general municipal election, or call a special election for such purpose at any time upon thirty days' notice; and no franchise shall be granted, extended, or renewed for a longer term than twenty-five years.

SEC. 421. — *Petition for Election.* — Whenever a petition signed by a number of qualified electors of any municipal corporation equal to twenty-five per centum of the total number of votes cast at the next preceding general municipal election, demanding that a franchise be granted, extended, or renewed, shall be filed with the chief executive officer of said corporation, the chief executive officer shall, within ten days thereafter, call a special election, at which he shall submit the question of whether or not such franchise shall be granted, extended, or renewed, and if, at said election, a majority of the said electors voting thereon shall vote for the grant, extension, or renewal of such franchise the same shall be granted by the proper authorities at the next succeeding regular meeting of the legislative body of the city.

SEC. 422. — *May Engage in Any Business.* — Every municipal corporation within this State shall have the right to engage in any business or enterprise which may be engaged in by a person, firm, or corporation by virtue of a franchise from said corporation.

SEC. 423. — *Reservation of Control Over Public Highways; Charges Regulated; Exclusive Franchises Prohibited.* — No grant, extension or renewal of any franchise or other use of the streets, alleys, or other public grounds or ways of any municipality, shall divest the State, or any of its subordinate subdivisions, of their control and regulation of such use and enjoyment.

Nor shall the power to regulate the charges for public services be surrendered; and no exclusive franchise shall ever be granted.

SEC. 435. — *Eight Hours.* — Eight hours shall constitute a day's work in all cases of employment by and on behalf of the State or any county or municipality.

CONVICT LABOR

SEC. 436. — *Contracting for.* — The contracting of convict labor is hereby prohibited.

CHILD LABOR

SEC. 437. — *Employment Prohibited.* — The employment of children, under the age of fifteen years, in any occupation, injurious to health or morals or especially hazardous to life or limb, is hereby prohibited.

SEC. 438. — *Underground Work Prohibited; Eight Hours a Day.* — Boys under the age of sixteen years, and women and girls, shall not be employed, underground, in the operation of mines; and, except in case of emergency, eight hours shall constitute a day's work underground in all mines in the State.

SEC. 439. — *Health and Safety of Employes.* — The Legislature shall pass laws to protect the health and safety of employes in factories, in mines, and on railroads.

CONTRIBUTORY NEGLIGENCE

SEC. 440. — *Defense of.* — The defense of contributory negligence or of assumption of risk shall, in all cases whatsoever, be a question of fact, and shall, at all times, be left to the jury.

PERSONAL INJURIES

SEC. 441. — *Rights of Action; Damages.* — The right of action to recover damages for injuries resulting in death and shall never be abrogated, and the amount recoverable shall not be subject to any statutory limitation.

SEC. 442. — *Contracts Void.* — Any provision of a contract, express or implied, made by any person, by which any of the benefits of this Constitution is sought to be waived, shall be null and void.

SEC. 443. — *Void Provisions in Contract.* — Any provision of any contract or agreement, express or implied, stipulating for notice or demand other than such as may be provided by law, as a condition precedent to estabish any claim, demand, or liability, shall be null and void.

DEFINITION OF RACES

SEC. 447. — *Convention; Referendum Vote.* — No convention shall be called by the Legislature to propose alterations, revisions, or amendments to this Constitution, or to propose a new Constitution, unless the law providing for such convention shall first be approved by the people on a referendum vote at a regular or special election, and any amendments, alterations, revisions, or new Constitution, proposed by such convention, shall be submitted to the electors of the State at a general or special election and be approved by a majority of the electors voting thereon, before the same shall become effective: Provided, That the question of such proposed convention shall be submitted to the people at least once in every twenty years.

SEC. 448. — *Initiative Petition.* — Sec. 3. This article shall not impair the right of the people to amend this Constitution by a vote upon an initiative petition therefor.

Extracts from the Constitution of the State of California

I subjoin some singular provisions from the Constitution of California adopted in 1879.

ARTICLE XIX

CHINESE

SECTION 1. The Legislature shall prescribe all necessary regulations for the protection of the State, and the counties, cities, and towns thereof from the burdens and evils arising from the presence of aliens who are or may become vagrants, paupers, mendicants, criminals, or invalids afflicted with contagious or infectious diseases, and from aliens otherwise dangerous or detrimental to the well-being or peace of the State, and to impose conditions upon which such persons may reside in the State, and provide the means and mode of their removal from the State, upon failure and refusal to comply with such conditions; *provided*, that nothing contained in this section shall be construed to impair or limit the power of the Legislature to pass such police laws or other regulations as it may deem necessary.

SEC. 2. No corporation now existing or hereafter formed under the laws of this State, shall, after the adoption of this Constitution, employ, directly or indirectly, in any capacity, any Chinese or Mongolian. The Legislature shall pass such laws as may be necessary to enforce this provision.

SEC. 3. No Chinese shall be employed on any State, county, municipal, or other public work, except in punishment for crime.

SEC. 4. The presence of foreigners ineligible to become citizens of the United States is declared to be dangerous to the well-being of the State, and the Legislature shall discourage their immigration by all the means within its power. Asiatic coolieism is a form of human slavery, and is for ever prohibited in this State, and all contracts for coolie labour shall be void. All companies or corporations, whether formed in this country or any foreign country, for the importation of such labour, shall be subject to such penalties as the Legislature may prescribe. The Legislature shall delegate all necessary power to the incorporated cities and towns of this State for the removal of Chinese without the limits of such cities and towns, or for the location within prescribed portions of those limits, and it shall also provide the necessary legislation to prohibit the introduction into this State of Chinese after the adoption of the Constitution. This section shall be enforced by appropriate legislation